IMAGES OF WOMEN

IN LITERATURE

IMAGES OF WOMEN

IN LITERATURE

THIRD EDITION

MARY ANNE FERGUSON

UNIVERSITY OF MASSACHUSETTS, BOSTON

HOUGHTON MIFFLIN COMPANY BOSTON

DALLAS GENEVA, ILLINOIS HOPEWELL, NEW JERSEY

PALO ALTO LONDON

Printed in the U.S.A.

Library of Congress Catalog Card Number: 80-82761

ISBN: 0-395-29113-5

Cover photo by Michael Malyszko. Clothing courtesy of The Mykonos Aegean Imports.

Art Credits

page 20   Frida Kahlo: *Portrait of Frida and Diego.* 1931. San Francisco Museum of Modern Art. Gift of Albert M. Bender.

page 64   Käthe Kollwitz: *Brot* (Bread). 1924. Philadelphia Museum of Art. Given by Mr. & Mrs. Carl Zigrosser.

page 157   Suzanne Valadon: *The Blue Room.* 1923. Musée National d'Art Moderne, Centre Georges Pompidou, Paris.

page 203   Harriet Hosmer: *Daphne.* 1853. Collection, Washington University, St. Louis.

page 255   Paula Modersohn-Becker: *Self-portrait.* 1906. Kunstmuseum Basel.

page 344   Mary Franke: Untitled (woman & landscape). Ca. 1970. Courtesy Zabriskie Gallery, New York.

page 406   Helen Frankenthaler: *Orange Shapes in Frame.* 1964. Collection of Mrs. Robert B. Mayer.

Photo credits: 25 United Press International; *31* Brown Brothers; *39* Carl Van Vechten; *49* Charles Scribner's Sons; *51* Charles Dixon; *52* Brown Brothers; *54* Frank Davis; *62* Harper & Row; *70* Harry Grier/Harper & Row; *87* Fran Ortiz/Delacorte Press; *111* Robert Gardner; *112* Marie Pelltier; *115* Levinson; *118* © 1980 by Jill Krementz; *124* self-portrait/Jayne Anne Phillips; *137* Sheila Munro; *160* United Press International; *167* A. E. Hotchner/Charles Scribner's Sons; *192* Florence Cohen; *207* U. of Rochester Library, Adelaide Crapsey Papers; *208* Marjorie Content Toomer; *212* National Portrait Gallery, London; *214* Picture courtesy of Open Court Publishing Company; *217, 229* Brown Brothers; *241* Photo by Dick Wilhelm; *253* Dennis A. Mahoney; *258* Culver Pictures; *263* Peter Powell/ Simon & Schuster, Inc.; *283* Copyright © 1973 Molly Malone Cook; *305* Jack Robinson/Fawcett; *314* St. Martin's Press, Inc.; *317* Isolde Ahlbaum/Simon & Schuster; *318* Jerry Bauer; *348* © 1980 by Jill Krementz; *352* George Cserna/Random House Inc.; *356* Culver Pictures; *366* Culver Pictures; *369* James Reber, Washington, D.C.; *393* John D. Schiff, courtesy of New Directions Publishing Co., *395* Missouri Historical Society; *415* Brown Brothers; *417* Ron Edwards/Delacorte Press/ Seymour Lawrence; *447* Photo by B. Karras; *448* Robert Shapiro; *450* Brown Brothers; *463* Harry Fong; *474* Stephen Hiller/Harcourt Brace Jovanovich; *480* Lydia Hammond; *481* Lynda Koolish; *484* Michael Commarota, courtesy of New Directions Publishing Corp.; *486* Joseph DeRoche; *489* © 1980 by Jill Krementz; *496* © Copyright 1980 Thomas Victor; *499* © Maxine Reizenstein; *501* Lotte Jacobi; *503* Ronald A. White; *505* Cynthia MacAdams ©1977; *550* Olive Pierce.

CONTENTS

Preface   ix

Introduction   1

PART ONE
TRADITIONAL IMAGES OF WOMEN

IMAGE ONE
THE SUBMISSIVE WIFE   21

IMAGE TWO
THE MOTHER: ANGEL OR "MOM"?   65

IMAGE THREE
THE DOMINATING WIFE: THE BITCH   157

CONTENTS

vi

P R E F A C E

The third edition of this anthology consists of sixty-three complete works —thirty-one short stories, three plays, and twenty-nine poems—that illustrate traditional images of women and also reflect the changes in those images brought about by the current women's movement and current serious scholarship about women. The images are organized in seven categories linked to women's various roles in society. Those in Part I, "Traditional Images," exemplify the major stereotypes of women associated with their biological roles: those of mother, wife, sex object, woman on a pedestal, and woman without a male partner. Both male and female authors show women characters caught in the traditional roles; yet each work is a critique of the limitations and costs that such role ascription imposes not only upon women but upon men. The images in Part II of this anthology, "Woman Becoming," illuminate the processes by which women seek to transcend the socially limiting stereotypes of their traditional roles. In this part women writers reveal that anger can be a liberating force, that women have suc- ceeded in the past in becoming independent individuals, that the search for individual identity, though often paid for with anguish, can bring joy.

One must read skillfully to perceive the critique of traditional roles re- vealed in Part I and to share in the liberating new images of Part II. Plot and characterization, tone and imagery, and the conventions of the genres must be carefully examined so that the complexity and depth of each literary image may be recognized. No image is merely a stereotype. This anthology can serve well not only various courses about women but also courses in critical thinking, in literature and literary criticism, and in writing (both ex- pository and creative). Its organization into categories invites study of classification, definition, and comparison. And the variety of genres repre- sented here allows comparative study of their strengths and boundaries.

Extensive introductions and an annotated bibliography provide ample criti- cal background for readers; they also invite research and the forming of inde- pendent judgments. Students and teachers alike will want not only to read published critiques of a work or an author but also to explore the entire *oeuvre* of an author as a basis for criticism. They might also study the lives of some of the authors and characters (for example, former slave Harriet Tubman or philosopher Simone Weil) in order to expand the context of the work.

To keep pace with the momentum of recent changes in women's roles and attitudes, this edition includes many new authors as well as some forgotten ones. It also offers new perceptions of images, especially those of mothers, daughters, and single women. Users of previous editions will miss some excellent works that had to be dropped in order to reflect the current reality about images of women. Most of the works eliminated are readily available elsewhere, and I hope their absence will not prove unduly inconvenient.

A number of people have contributed to the process of creating this edition. Published works, papers at meetings, and private conversations with friends and colleagues have all been valuable. Many heartening responses from users of the second edition yielded excellent suggestions for improving the third. My early debt to critics Nancy Reeves, Katharine Rogers, and Mary Ellman is now extended as well to Dorothy Dinnerstein, Nancy Chodorov, Sandra Gilbert, and Susan Gubar. I am grateful for the comments and suggestions of Andrea Green, Union College; Linda Pannill, University of Kentucky; and Virginia Pond, Catonsville Community College, who read the critical introductions in manuscript. Sarah Boslaugh and Kate White, graduate students at the University of Massachusetts/Boston, did most of the research and annotation for two sections of the Suggestions for Further Reading, Anthologies of Literary Criticism and Anthologies of Literature, respectively. Others who contributed concretely are Moira Ferguson, University of Nebraska—Lincoln; Annette Kolodny, University of New Hampshire; Kathy Loring and Libuse Reed, Ohio Wesleyan University; Phyllis Mael, Pasadena Community College; Karen Stein, University of Rhode Island; and Bonnie Zimmerman, San Diego State University. My greatest debts are to Tillie Olsen and my three daughters.

INTRODUCTION

The first two editions of this book (1973, 1977) opened with a riddle about the identity of the surgeon for a young man injured in an automobile accident in which his father was killed. The surgeon called to the scene looked at the patient and said, "I can't operate; this is my son." One would think that today everyone would know that the surgeon was the boy's mother. Yet recent trials of the riddle show that though some teenagers could get the answer immediately, their parents often could not.

The continuing capacity of this riddle to puzzle shows how hard it is to change our perceptions, even when they are contradicted by facts. Research by Professor Mary Roth Walsh for a recent book, *Doctors Wanted, No Women Need Apply: Sexual Barriers in the Medical Profession, 1835–1975*, indicates that the number of women medical students has increased by 700 percent since 1959. The presence of women doctors has alerted teenagers somewhat more to reality than it has their parents, whose view is still influenced by the comparative invisibility of women as doctors before 1959. The lag between experience and perception means that in this time of great change our images of women are confused and contradictory. Adjectives used by sociologists to describe real women and by literary critics to describe their reflections—or models—in literature include such baffling pairs of opposites as passive-aggressive, intuitive-logical, possessive–self-sacrificing, materialistic-spiritual, frigid-lustful. The only common factor among these contradictory descriptions is that they all use the same standard of measurement: the characteristics of men are the norm, those of women subsidiary.

Women are thought to be passive when compared to men, who assume the initiative in sex, in business, and in politics; passivity has a lower value because assertiveness is needed for success, and it is men who succeed. Aggressive women who succeed in male spheres are judged to be unfeminine and unnatural. When women are considered intelligent, their kind of intelligence, their mysterious intuition, is equated with flightiness and fuzzy thinking; male logicality is the norm few women achieve. The other opposing pairs of characteristics are extremes both of which are applicable

1

to women; the norm is a happy medium reached by men. Possessiveness in men is associated with protectiveness and responsibility, in women with narrowness and selfishness; self-sacrifice in men is marveled at, taken for granted in women. Women are seen paradoxically as highly materialistic and as devout and pious; but they carry these traits to undesirable extremes, whereas men exemplify admirable restraint by not allowing their religion to influence their business ethics. A woman may be less or more desirous of sex than a man; either frigidity or lust in a woman is a negative characteristic because the male appetite is the norm. Because of the conflicts among these images, women are bewildered about their identity: they feel damned if they do and damned if they don't.

Even for physical measurements the male is accepted as the standard: women are smaller, weaker, digitally more adept, and capable of longer periods of continuous effort than men. Smallness and weakness are signs of inferiority, even in situations where size and strength are irrelevant. Moreover, so universal is the association of masculinity with superiority that women's "good" qualities make them suitable for inferior positions: their skilled fingers and ability to withstand monotony fit them admirably for menial jobs in industry and business and for the unpaid job of housewife.

As Simone de Beauvoir has said, the image of women has been that of the second sex, the Other for man. This view has emphasized sexual differences instead of human similarities, to women's disadvantage. Even when exalted as a model of purity and generosity, woman has been considered strange and mysterious—superhuman or supermale. The adjectives used to describe woman make it apparent that she is not the equal of man: she may be supernatural, she may be childlike—she is both more and less than man. This sexist and reductive image of women has prevailed in myth and literature for so long that it seems inevitable and true in spite of the obvious logical impossibilities.

Illogical images resist change because of their basis in the emotions. A beautiful woman is despised, even feared, if she uses her "weapons" of tongue and sex to diminish a man's sense of worth. Though she may no longer be condemned to death as a witch because of her mysterious power, she may be ostracized by shame or ridicule. Yet a beautiful woman who uses her power benignly is worshipped as a goddess, exalted as the muse of poetry and music, propitiated as man's mediator and comfort. Such differing views may even be applied to the same woman or image; the difference in the image is in the eye of the beholder.

How have such images come to prevail both in life and in literature? If we try to understand what happens when a single individual forms an image of a particular woman, we begin to comprehend the process at work in history and in literature. Imagine that you are looking through a family album. You stop at a picture of your mother holding you in her arms the day she brought you home from the hospital. Is that slender girl in the too-short skirt really the same person as the matronly woman sitting beside you now? Which one do you *see* when you think the word *mother?*

Your image of your mother may be kaleidoscopic, a merging of past memories and present reality. You may see her primarily as she used to be, obscuring the present because the changes in her remind you of your own mortality. A deep need to think well of your mother in order to bolster your own self-esteem may transmute your image of an actually cold, selfish woman into a warm, loving one. Conversely, a need to avoid facing your own faults may reverse this process and turn your image of an ordinary, well-meaning person into a monster of greed and selfishness. Your vision of your mother is shaped by your own self-image and by your dreams for the future. If you are ambitious to become a doctor, say, you may credit your mother's tenderness with giving you the desire to serve humanity, but if you cannot stand the sight of blood and must change your goal, you will blame her squeamishness. Your sex too, according to Freud, influences your attitude toward your mother: if you are male, you may see your father as a rival; if you are female, you will see your mother as a threat to your relationship with your father. Our images of others may be a good deal more subjective than objective. Our pictures of the external world must fit our own pattern of memory, desire, and dream. When we look out, we look into a mirror.

Furthermore, to a degree we are only now realizing, each person's images of others are colored by the ideas of society as a whole, of family, peers, country, the age. In a time and place in which women are expected to stay home and care for children, the image of a mother who does not is tarnished. She herself is likely to feel guilty no matter how valid her reason for absenting herself and no matter how many other women do not fulfill society's expectations. In spite of the fact that 50 percent of all women in this country go out of their homes to work, the notion persists that most women are to "stay in their place," the home. Women's own deep agreement with this image, according to behavioral psychologists and sociobiologists, is based on biological conditioning as well as on cultural expectations. Regardless of their origin, such images are closely tied to emotions and thus are very subject to distortion, like images in the mirrors at carnivals. Trying to conform to such blurred images causes great emotional stress.

The rigidity of such images is reflected in the word used to describe them, *stereotypes,* a term taken by sociologists from printing, where it refers to metal plates used to make exact copies. Stereotypes of people differ in one major way from metal ones: they need not duplicate the pattern exactly. As long as some aspects of the stereotype are present, the observer supplies the others from previous experience. Such patterns are called *prejudices;* they provoke judgment before full knowledge is possible. To the pattern "beautiful and blonde," the observer adds "dumb," whether it applies to the specific person or not. A wife or mother, expected to be happy in putting others first, cannot have selfish goals. To win social approval, the beautiful blonde may use her intelligence to play dumb; women who assert their individuality may be laughed at or attacked unless they suppress it. Thus the stereotypes that shape our personalities are even more rigid than metal ones. The configuration of characteristics is held together by mental patterns harder to escape than factory-formed ones; the mind so quickly fills in the blanks that individual differences are not perceived. A person who deliberately departs from a socially approved stereotype by adopting a new role—developing a new life style—may pay a heavy cost in guilt, alienation, or psychosis; tendencies toward schizophrenia may be aggravated by the person's sense of divided self. Women's emotional disorders often stem from the stress of stereotypical thinking.

According to some psychologists, certain stereotypes are particularly strong because they are formed not by a single society but by the entire experience of humanity; they are the images of myths, stories told in every society to impose order upon and explain the inexplicable and chaotic aspects of experience. Jungian psychology teaches that our image of mother, for example, stems from deep within our minds in the realm of the Collective Unconscious, where images common to all people and perhaps also to animals are found. These images are too deeply embedded to be available to any individual's conscious mind, but they find expression through symbol and art. The figures in myths, which Jung called *archetypes,* are recognizable in art because they correspond to the images in the Collective Unconscious.

Sociologists who do not share Jung's theories about the genetic and universal structure of the psyche nonetheless testify that the archetypes, grounded in emotion, are strong; they represent our desires and fears about our nature and the structure of the world. A myth of creation must explain both our presence in the world (our beginning) and our knowledge of death (our ending). The images of good and evil embodied in the Great Mother, so widespread among primitive societies, reflect not only our love for the giver of life but also our fear of the inescapable death that the gift brings with it. Archetypes strongly resist modification by facts and logic and are often fortified by religion, which inevitably involves a large measure of myth.

One peculiarity of the images of women throughout history is that social stereotypes have been reinforced by archetypes. Another way of putting this would be to say that in every age woman has been seen primarily in her biological, primordial role as the mysterious source of life. Women have been viewed as mother, wife, mistress, sex object—their roles in relationship to men. Of course, men also are viewed in their biological roles, but not to the same degree as women; men are neither defined by nor limited to these roles. Cave drawings that show men casting spears or running after a boar also show women pregnant, their secondary sexual characteristics grossly exaggerated so that they seem all bosom, belly, and butt. Man has been defined by his relationship to the outside world—to nature, to society, indeed, to God—whereas woman has been defined in relationship to man. The word *defined* means "having a limit around," "fenced in." Women have been fenced into a small place in the world.

Because women's biological restriction is assumed to have existed forever, the tendency is to believe that it is part of the nature of things, that it is innate; because it has "always" been thus, it must ever be. It is upon this assumption that the dangers of departing from their biological roles have been impressed upon women. Perhaps more than anyone else, Sigmund Freud in our own century reinforced the idea that an unwillingness to accept fully her biological role was the cause of woman's hysteria, neurosis, and psychosis; if women are to be healthy, they should remain "natural." Though scholars have pointed out Freud's bias because of his place in history and though his theories have been modified by Karen Horney and others, Freud's analysis of women's assertiveness as based on "penis envy" has remained in the popular mind and underlies many literary images.

The Stereotypes in Literature

The study of literature does not proceed in a vacuum. Our understanding and evaluation of literary images must have a basis in what history, psychology, sociology, anthropology, and other disciplines—as well as our own experience—tell us about reality. Literary history and theory tell us something about the process by which literature is related to other interpretations of the world. Literature both reflects and helps create our views of reality; it puts us in touch with our deepest feelings, with our prerational knowledge of the world. It is through their preservation in works of art that we know what the stereotypes and archetypes have been and are; in turn, knowing the images influences not only our view of the world and ourselves but also our behavior. In Dante's *Inferno*, the famous lovers Paolo and Francesca are shown reading about those famous lovers Lancelot and Guenevere when they yield to the passion that leads to their damnation. It was largely from reading romances that Emma in Flaubert's *Madame Bovary* (1856) got the dreams that drove her to dissatisfaction, adultery, and suicide. Today serious literature is absorbed and adapted by the popular media so rapidly and effectively that the distinction between imaginary characters and real people has become blurred in the minds of many readers and viewers. Advertising images of impossibly slender women contribute not only to the huge diet industry but to *anorexia nervosa,* a psychological condition that causes young women to starve themselves to death. Stereotypical images are often destructive.

In literary criticism the word *stereotype* is usually a pejorative one; it has been traditionally felt that only fully developed, "round" characters are aesthetically valid. Yet there are legitimate uses of stereotypes in literature. A flat character may serve as a contrast or foil to a more rounded one; character types used in comedy and satire make readers who recognize them feel superior and hence in a position to laugh. Recent writers have deliberately created static characters to represent what they feel to be the inhumanity of our times. Furthermore, behind any rounded character must lie a recognizable human type with which readers may identify. Literature presents specific characters in concrete circumstances; we measure literary success by the individuality, complexity, and even ambiguity of characters. But readers must be able to extract from the specifics a generalization, an observation about human beings, which they see as relevant to other specific situations—especially their own. The problem with images of women in literature is that they are largely male representations. According to Tillie Olsen in *Silences,* of writers who have been recognized as significant even in our time, only one out of twelve has been a woman. It is not surprising, then, that female characters have been most often presented as stereotypes, serving as foils, motivators, barriers, rewards, and comforters to males who actively pursue adventure and their own identities. From a male perspective, the central and most desirable characteristic of female characters has been their passivity.

Traditional Stereotypes

The Mother   Images of women in literature have always been ambivalent; for every biological role there has been both a negative and a positive view. In the Biblical creation myth, Eve, the mother of us all, is the temptress who brought sin and death into the world. But the Virgin Mary, passively acted on by the Holy Ghost, pondering in her heart the experience of her Son, is the Queen of Heaven, the Mother of God and, through Him, of us all. Eve could be tolerated as a necessary evil; Mary was worshipped as a model for all womankind. In Greek mythology, Pandora, sent to earth by the gods to marry and establish the human race, brings with her a magic box or vial; opening it, she releases not only all evil but the greatest gift humankind can have—hope. Both Eve and Pandora act in defiance of divine law. If they had passively obeyed (experienced the world vicariously, as Mary did), humanity would have been spared the particular kind of life known as human. In both myths, except for the action of a woman humans would have been godlike. Because of woman, we are condemned to be mortal; we must die. Yet all of us in our early years see our mothers as bringers of life, nurturers, sources of pleasure and comfort. We soon learn that she also takes away pleasure; she says no, and we blame her for denying satisfaction, no matter what her reasons may be. The role of mother is ambiguous. Myths about woman's dual nature are attempts to explain primordial reactions to her double role as the giver of life and death, of pleasure and pain.

The Wife   Both in myth and in life the roles of mother and wife overlap; the difficulty even a husband has in separating the roles in his mind is reflected in the common American custom of a man's referring to his wife as "Mother." A wife performs many of the functions of the mother; both her children and her husband require her attentions as cook and nurse. But when she extends to her husband her motherly role of disciplinarian, scolding, nagging, or withholding her services, her husband reacts as negatively as a child. For him the very qualities desirable in a good mother— firmness, decisiveness, ability to organize time—seem undesirable in a wife. A submissive wife, happy to be supportive and to "stay in her place," is the ideal; a dominating wife is ridiculed or hated.

Woman on a Pedestal   Outside of marriage, a beautiful woman may be exalted; her beauty makes her seem superhuman and exonerates men who fall victim to her power. Frequently the effect of the seductress is disastrous. In the *Iliad,* Helen of Troy's decision to run away with Alexandros (Paris) brought death to thousands of men, the destruction of Troy, and the enslavement of the Trojan women. Though objectively Alexandros's weakness and disregard of the mores might seem to have been equally at fault, it was Helen's face "that launched a thousand ships and burnt the topless towers of Ilium" in Marlowe's *Dr. Faustus* (1588). Similarly, Guenevere, married to King Arthur, caused her lover Lancelot to betray his king and start a civil war. Both Malory (fifteenth century) and Tennyson (nineteenth century) put the blame squarely on Guenevere for seducing the noble Lancelot.

   Yet other beautiful women are seen as ennobling to men who loved them: Dante is led through Purgatory by the vision and guidance of Beatrice; Petrarch worships Laura even though he can never possess her. Perhaps it is significant that Beatrice and Laura, in life both apparently happy as the wives of other men, are exalted by the poets more after death than before; inconvenient facts must not interfere with mythical roles. The lack of children among the goddesslike heroines of romance can be ascribed only to literary convenience, the fictitiousness of their roles. Yet it is this unrealistic image that most powerfully shapes images of women today. Not only in courtship but within marriage the obligation to be beautiful and to use one's powers beneficiently is woman's heritage from the view first established in the fantasies of twelfth-century courtly love romances.

The Sex-Object and Sexual Politics   In another biological role the woman is the opposite of the all-powerful woman on a pedestal: the sex object is man's prey, the fulfiller of man's sexual needs, a receptacle for his passions. Once she fulfills this role and becomes a fallen woman, she may be callously discarded; even the sexual revolution has not overcome adherence to a double standard in sexual mores.

It is impossible to consider women as sex objects without discussing what Kate Millett has called "sexual politics," the system by which men have kept women subordinate. It is their usefulness to men that has determined women's value in society. Virgins have been valued not only because of youth, possible beauty, and freedom from venereal disease, but also because they could become wives and mothers, the legitimacy of whose children would not be questioned; through their offspring, property could be lawfully transferred. Virgins have been exalted not only because of myths about their special powers over beasts like the unicorn, but also because of their value as commodities. As late as the eighteenth century Dr. Samuel Johnson remarked about chastity: "Upon that all the property in the world depends." The primitive practice of the bride-price, the careful negotiation of dowry, and the vesting of all property rights in the husband are aspects of the economics of marriage. Until the late nineteenth century and in many parts of the world even today, economic and social considerations have been the primary basis of marriage. For both men and women marriage has been a way of obtaining comfort and status as well as sexual service. But this avenue was closed to women who lost their virtue; their disgrace meant living somehow on the fringes of society as servant or governess, seamstress or washerwoman, "kept woman" or prostitute—or it could result in being stoned to death. Sexual politics have kept women (whether married or not) as men's dependents, often literally their chattel, properly to be kept locked into a chastity belt—as rigid as any stereotype can be.

Woman Alone The roles we have considered so far—those of mother, wife, mistress, and sex object—have received more literary treatment than any others, though women as daughters, sisters, grandmothers, and aunts have appeared frequently in drama, fiction, and poetry. An examination of their images would show just as much ambivalence as in women's major roles (those more explicitly connected with sex). Yet throughout history many women have not been wives or mothers or sex objects; many have been single. Unlike the other stereotypes, the image of the single woman has not been at all ambivalent; with very few exceptions the old maid—a single woman beyond the marriageable age of, say, thirty—has been either pitied or ridiculed in literature. The exception is the nun, admired for giving herself to a supernatural cause as bride of the church. But a single woman who remains in society is seen as queer, frequently thin and emaciated to symbolize withdrawal from life, prim, highly conventional, excessively curious, and quarrelsome. Seldom does she function as a main character; normally she acts in a subordinate role reflecting her marginal position in society. Earlier centuries used to give single women the title of "mistress" or "madame" after they had passed the age of consent; the title "miss" is an ironically apt reflection of the opinion that they have missed out on living. The term "old maid" is always pejorative in our society.

Other single women historically have been viewed as marginal in society. Widows and divorcées, assumed to be on the lookout for new mates, are often viewed fearfully as predators both by men and by wives. The children of such women undergo emotional turmoil if their fathers are usurped, yet experience guilt if they themselves do not fill their mothers' emotional needs. In the past widowhood represented freedom from the eternal cycle of child-bearing; yet the need for a male "protector" usually led to a new marriage, and the widow's freedom was as short as the interlude between marriage and the first child. Our modern knowledge of contraception and the possibility of abortion allow a new freedom: the decision to marry or remain single may be based on personal desires instead of on social necessity.

So far we have considered stereotypes closely related to woman's biological role as man's mate; she has been defined according to her assumption or nonassumption of this role. But there are other stereotypes less closely related to biology.

The Young Girl Though the young unmarried girl experiences the major biological events of a woman's life—the onset of menstruation and the development of secondary sex characteristics—she has traditionally been viewed as asexual, as a pure symbol exalted like the woman on a pedestal. A young girl is viewed as silly, flirtatious, concerned with the externals of sexual attractiveness such as cosmetics and clothes, but without any serious sexual desires. Her years of development are seen as if she were asleep; like the Sleeping Beauty of the fairy tale, only identification with a male will make her a real person. Though the fairy story uses a kiss as the means of awakening, it is rape that serves as a girl's rite of passage into adulthood in archetypal myths like that of Persephone. All the other elements of a human being's maturation are ignored—the establishment of metabolic rates that make one a morning or night person, the determination of body size and shape, decisions about religion and philosophy of life, intellectual interests. Indeed, in Freudian terms women are viewed as cases of arrested development; because they do not fully separate from their mothers, their characters as adult individuals are considered inferior to men's. Recent research indicates a pattern of development different from and later than men's; the continued closeness to their mothers that extends into early middle age probably accounts for women's traditional skills in and concern for interpersonal relationships. Expectation of a need to reject their mothers because of the prevalence of Freudian attitudes may be the cause of the much-publicized tension between mothers and daughters, a tension that often is absent. Persephone continued to love her mother Demeter; both were sad that they had to be separated but both accepted their adult roles. The Persephone myth reflects the reality that adulthood involves loss as well as gain. The Greek myth of Psyche, who was the beloved of Cupid, shows a young woman establishing her individuality; her name, Psyche, means "soul" or "spirit." Women do have an inner development that makes them fully human.

The Educated Woman Whether married or single, young or old, a learned woman has usually been suspect and the butt of ridicule in literature. Particularly mocking is the picture Byron gives in *Don Juan* (1819) of Donna Inez, who flaunts her little Latin and even less Greek and henpecks her husband. One does not know whether Byron despises her more for her learning or her domination, but he sees them as part of the same pattern. Even now the stereotype of a highly educated woman is of an unattractive female in sturdy oxfords and tailored suit. When Germaine Greer, a professor at Warwick University in England and author of *The Female Eunuch* (1971), appeared in television interviews in this country, reviewers invariably expressed amazement at her attractiveness. Beginning in puberty, American girls become afraid of success in school, hiding their learning as much as possible or deliberately failing. Though they make better grades than men, their success is usually dismissed as superficial, not goal-directed, or insignificant because it is not in important areas such as math and science. Even women do not expect high intellectual achievement from other women. Asked to "grade" the performance of scholars, a group of college women rated as inferior articles ostensibly by women and rated the same articles as superior when men's names were attached to them. Perhaps this tendency accounts for the fact that many successful women downgrade women in general; these women see themselves as successful *and* feminine but use the stereotype when they view other women.

The Lady Another stereotype, dependent more on social class than biology, is that of the *grande dame* or lady. Special rules for her behavior were prescribed by rigid social systems including that of the antebellum South in this country. A gentlewoman truly gentle, such as Melanie in *Gone with the Wind* (1936), has been a part of the romantic exaltation of women; but D. H. Lawrence's view in *Lady Chatterley's Lover* (1926) that *gentilesse* diverts women from their true role as sexual creatures has prevailed in modern literature. Lady Chatterley realized that her place in life was not presiding at a tea table but being serviced by her gardener;

since the sexual liberation of the 1920s, ladies have removed themselves from their pedestals. But popular images of clubwomen, idle rich women playing at social work, pampered wives who "entertain" but do not work, show that the stereotype is still alive.

Images in This Anthology

Part I of this anthology includes examples of the six images of women most closely related to their biological roles: the submissive wife, the mother, the dominating wife, woman on a pedestal, the sex object, and woman without man. Although a stereotype underlies all the examples of each image, not a single work stops with merely describing the stereotype; all go beyond to show the complexity of the role both for the woman and for those associated with her. Authors—both male and female—expose the wastefulness of stereotypical thinking and its cost to individuals and society through irony and satire, through description of women's self-perception, through overt expression of anger. Some works reveal the mythic base that reinforces the stereotype; others use stark realism to explode the myth. But cumulatively the selections document the tenacity of the stereotypes in spite of a variety of perspectives. The effect of reading these works, especially for women, is likely to be anger and depression.

Writers, especially since the beginning of the current Women's Movement, have been trying to find ways not only to counter these universal stereotypes and the negative emotions they evoke but to create new images. Part II of this anthology, "Woman Becoming," shows women in the process of changing, of breaking out of the old rigid patterns. Women writers are finding support for their deepest perceptions in the work of women scholars; readers recognize themselves in the new images. A more detailed introduction to Part II will discuss the new images; here a review of feminist scholarship will help us understand how such a significant change has come about.

The nature of the change is symbolized by the existence of Professor Walsh's book on women doctors, published by a prestigious university press. Like the Women's Movement as Betty Friedan perceived it in 1980, Women's Studies in the late 1970s reached a "second stage." Perceptions about women have moved from the realm of cocktail party jokes into that of serious scholarship. Today several extensive bibliographies document the explosion in research about women; they also reveal the interdisciplinary nature of Women's Studies and the difficulty of mastering the field. In order to survive in the academic world, feminist scholars must usually establish themselves within a traditional discipline. They must investigate, even attack, the principles of the discipline they choose to enter before the feminist perspective can begin to affect the mainstream research and teaching within that discipline; at the same time they must acquire insights and methodological strategies from feminist colleagues in other disciplines. They must also be in touch with new information about women's lives now being collected from oral histories, diaries, letters, and autobiographies. A literary critic needs knowledge from psychologists and sociologists to evaluate a woman writer's description of adolescent trauma or mother-daughter interaction; women writers learn from literary historians that they have a female tradition of imagery, attitudes, style. Professor Walsh, for example, though writing about history and medicine, is a psychologist. Without the work of social historians and without her understanding of women's desires and motives, she would not have had the fresh insight to ask the right questions about previous medical historians' assumption that there have been no women physicians to speak of.

The need for exchange of information caused by the interdisciplinary nature of Women's Studies resulted in the formation in 1978 of the National Women's Studies Association, which publishes a national newsletter and holds national conventions annually. The organization recognizes the need for communication among women working for feminist education and social change on all levels; its members are trying to create a structure to achieve egalitarian goals by egalitarian means. Such structure has few models in our society where hierarchy and credentials are the framework for institutions, academic and otherwise. Feminist educators find that the learning style of the Women's Movement and of the early days of Women's Studies—group interaction of peers—leads to trustworthy knowledge. They have found that such devices as admitting their ignorance, sharing their insights and questions with peers, involving students actively in real research, passing around syllabi and bibliographies, and team-teaching lead to the demystification of research as a prerogative of the initiated, to the use of the language of everyday life to communicate new knowledge, to a critique of established disciplines.

In every field feminist scholars are showing the inadequacy of previous research, which has failed to ask appropriate questions about women because of the predominantly male frame of reference. For example, Dr. Mary Jane Sherfey shows that scientists have done more research on male hormones than on female hormones largely because they have assumed that hormonal imbalance is "normal" for women. Dr. Sherfey also puts into perspective a fact long known to biologists: that the human fetus is initially female; this fact should preclude the attitude that male development must be the basis for comparison. In anthropology recent studies of extant hunter-gatherer societies have contradicted the earlier conclusion that in primitive societies hunting by males was the main source of food. Archaeology had discovered only the stone tools used by hunters; observation of extant societies reveals that probably two-thirds of the food consumed in such societies is gathered by women using sticks and leather pouches, which perish with the society. To rediscover women who lived during historical times has required new techniques also. After raising the question of why half the human race has rarely been mentioned in history books, feminist historians have turned to methods found useful in the study of other groups previously considered insignificant. They are re-examining archives with new questions in mind, using demographic techniques to deduce individual and group history from statistics, focusing on social units such as the family instead of on political and military figures, and using biography and personal records as a resource to recreate the past. A new encyclopedia, *Notable American Women,* documents the lives of women active in politics, business, religion, the abolitionist movement, and the fight for women's rights, and of women writers, artists, philosophers—all deserving fame in their own right. Discovering that we as women have "foremothers" who achieved in the public sphere gives us a basis for countering the argument that women *should* function only in their biological roles because they always have. Knowledge of their achievements gives us a sense of continuity and a basis for perceiving women as agents, as actors in history, rather than as an undifferentiated passive mass.

Recovering their history and finding role models of women who have been achievers is an important step for women in overcoming their characteristic low self-esteem, an attitude that causes them to undervalue other women as well as themselves. Important psychological research about women's views of their own incompetence has led scholars Rosalind Barnett and Grace Baruch not only to reinterpret previous research but to suggest ways of changing the socialization of women and men so that their perceptions will accord with the facts of women's competence. In *Beyond Sugar and Spice: How Women Learn to Grow, Learn, and Thrive* (1979), Barnett and Baruch make practical suggestions for helping children perceive women as autonomous beings. They suggest that seeing parents work both at home and away on an equal basis can begin to change perceptions within the family. Professor Dorothy Dinnerstein feels that even more basic parental sharing of infant care is necessary not only for equality and happiness but for the very survival of the race. Women activists are working for institutional change that will support the concept of gender equality. They point out that society's refusal to help parents care for children by such adaptations as flexible work schedules, for example, perpetuates the myth that only biological mothers are capable of child care. Mothering—or parenting—is a learned skill; research indicates that men as well as women are able to acquire it, though probably not all people want to. Though current research makes it clear that there are significant sex differences in behavior and capacity, the research also indicates that there is as wide a variance among members of the same sex as between the sexes. Gender does not determine individual limits. Because of centuries of acculturation, it is clear, however, that women today have special sensitivity to the emotional dimension of human behavior. Psychiatrist Jean Baker Miller suggests that perceiving the value of this sensitivity

will not only enable women to overcome their low self-esteem but will aid
society in overcoming the sense of alienation and despair that dominates
current attitudes.

Recent feminist literary research has resulted in new concepts important
to the study of images of women in literature. In the 1970s, studies
of almost every country and period as well as of many individual authors
have documented the predominance of negative—or at best, not affirmative—
images of women in literature by men. The fact that American fiction as
late as the 1960s portrayed women as negatively as any medieval text
illustrates literature's continuing function of conserving tradition. But
recent research shows the falsity of assuming that women have had no
alternative but to write according to the dominant male modes. Professor
Elaine Showalter sees the interrelationships among nineteenth-century
women writers in Britain as a subculture with its own style and concerns.
Professor Emily Stipes Watts shows that American women poets shared
common imagery, treatment of myth, attitudes toward marriage, nature,
and God, which differ from those of American male writers and of English
women writers. Professor Nina Baym has shown the traditional dichotomy
of the fair good heroine/dark bad one in American literature to be an
oversimplification. In hundreds of nineteenth-century novels written by
women for women, she has found a focus on strong young women who
achieve both psychic and economic independence by venturing out into the
world, much as young men did. The traditional ending of these stories with
the heroine's marriage, corresponding to the reality of life for most
nineteenth-century women, has obscured the degree of autonomy achieved
by the heroines. The "happy ending" no doubt helps account for the
continued popularity of heroic romances today, in spite of their silence about
"afterwards." But these heroines can serve as better role models than the
seduced and abandoned victims that dominate male American fiction.

Other scholars are resurrecting and reassessing previously unknown or
long-forgotten works. Diaries and letters by black women discovered in
manuscript in libraries have been edited and published. We now know of
their experiences as slaves and of their search to define personal freedom
and to find dignity through religion. Massive publishing ventures have
made us aware of the numerous works yet to be recovered. A new encyclopedia of biography and criticism, *Guide to American Women Writers,* is
a valuable tool for recovering our heritage. A series selected by Elizabeth
Hardwick for the Arno Press makes eighteen forgotten but important
nineteenth-century American novels by women again available. Already
some rediscovered works of feminist literature have achieved the status
of classics: one thinks of such treasures as Agnes Smedley's *Daughter of
Earth,* Harriet Arnow's *The Doll-maker,* Christina Stead's *The Man Who
Loved Children,* Zora Neale Hurston's *Their Eyes Were Watching God.*

Literary critics are also explaining why such works by women have
been so consistently ignored. They disappeared for the same reason women

doctors, according to Professor Walsh, disappeared in the 1880s: they were ignored or rejected by institutionalized male superiority. Professor Frank Kermode, a prominent literary critic, points out that the past century's professionalization of the teaching and criticism of literature has resulted in the establishment of a literary canon considered as sacred as the canon of books of the Bible, and as fiercely protected against change. He sees not only the canon of works to be studied but the methods of interpretation being determined by professionals—usually academic—who have been, historically, white males. Incursions by "outsiders," the uninitiated such as women and blacks, are thought to lower the standards set by literary critics; when they are considered at all, their works are dismissed with condescension or scorn as minor and crude.

The fact that such judgments are often based on sex discrimination or what Mary Ellman has called "phallic criticism" and that they persist into the 1980s may be demonstrated by the critical response to two authors separated by more than a century. Carol Ohman has shown that many critics' acclaim for Emily Brontë's *Wuthering Heights,* published in 1847 under the pseudonym "Ellis Bell," changed to pejorative when the author's female identity was disclosed. Recently, after James Tiptree, Jr., received three coveted prizes for science fiction, a male critic introduced a collection of Tiptree's short stories with high praise for the masterly masculine style that set them above all others in this field dominated by male writers. Later, in the introduction to another collection, Ursula LeGuin revealed that Tiptree is in fact Alice Sheldon. Whatever virtues her style may have, they are not based on gender. Whether her reputation will survive this disclosure remains to be seen. But the equation of *excellent* with *masculine* is clear.

Avant-garde literary theory of the 1970s seems to offer hope of new critical acceptance for literature by women because it rejects the so-called New Criticism that dominated literary theory in this country until the 1950s. This "formalist" criticism evaluated literature primarily according to standards of unity and perfection of form, the individual work's "integrity"; it minimized, even repudiated, the perspective of biographical, psychological, historical, and social context. Achievement and recognition of literary perfection were closely tied to working within the tradition under which the various forms had been established. Whether imitating or rebelling against tradition, artists were expected to have deep awareness of its specifications. Since the traditional forms, especially poetry and drama, were established by males (often in foreign languages known only by educated males), masculinity has been perceived as inherent in the forms. As late as 1959, a male critic of Emily Dickinson summed up these assumptions by "suggesting" that " 'woman poet' is a contradiction in terms." New Critics focused on short poems and discussed few women poets. At first they excluded fiction, rejecting the form to which women have made highly visible contributions particularly since the nineteenth century. When they grudgingly condescended to criticize fiction, few women were found worthy. Unfortunately more recent critics who have rejected the New Criticism have not opened doors for serious consideration of women writers. Those who emphasize the role of readers in "creating" literary texts often describe competent readers as clones of themselves, highly learned and immersed in literary traditions. Though acknowledging the social and psychological context of literature, avant-garde critics establish no norms for judging them; much of the literary evaluation that goes on is personal and limited to a narrow range of works. Few women writers are even mentioned—a fate worse perhaps than being condescendingly included. The perception that the critic shares the creative process with authors exalts the authority of established critics; they seem to speak only to each other.

An important recent work of feminist criticism does enter into the avant-garde literary dialogue. In their monumental work on nineteenth-century women writers, *The Madwoman in the Attic* (1979), Professors Sandra Gilbert and Susan Gubar measure women writers from the perspective of their reaction to Milton's *Paradise Lost,* a work viewed by the major critic Professor Harold Bloom as central to the identity of male writers in English. Gilbert and Gubar show that the major women British novelists and poets as well as Emily Dickinson take Milton's concept of woman as secondary as a point of departure for their self-concept as writers and as women. Their feelings about trying to be both writers and women elicited consistent images of enclosure, suffocation, and starvation, as well as fantasies of escape and freedom. Gilbert and Gubar intend to continue their analysis into the twentieth century; their work helps overcome the problems for feminist critics outlined by Professor Annette Kolodny in a prize-winning essay. She points out that male readers will not be able to change their perceptions and accept women's writing as a contribution to human experience until they have read enough writing by women to understand its relationship to experience and to its own traditions. The time for such a change may come in the 1980s. On the level of popular criticism, prejudice has continued undiminished: *Time* Magazine's list of ten best novels of the 1970s included none by women, even though Eudora Welty published her masterpiece *Losing Battles* in 1970 and won the Pulitzer prize in 1973 for a lesser work, *The Optimist's Daughter.*

Thus in spite of new feminist scholarship and criticism, traditional images of women persist into the 1970s and 1980s. But some women—and some men—writers are creating a body of literature that may be labeled feminist. This new literature shows fully human women characters who, like men, are in some sense self-aware and autonomous; who fail or succeed for the same reasons men do—limitation by circumstances (poverty, poor health, ignorance), by the actions of others, by narrow societal roles, lack of energy, and insight; who assume responsibility for their own acts and are thus capable of heroism and of tragedy. By showing ways in which women experience the world differently than men, feminist writers expand our knowledge of human nature. New works explore the dynamics of mother-daughter relationships, of friendship among women as a major aspect of their socialization, of sexual unions between women as valid and enriching human experiences. They establish links with women of the past and women of different classes and races; they invite women to find, by developing a sense of community with other women, ways of evaluating themselves positively. Searching for language and forms in which to express their insights, feminist writers are creating new images that not only reflect reality but reveal to women their own reality. Whether fulfilling the traditional roles associated with their biology or experimenting with new roles, women reading the works in this book will see changing, growing, fully human beings—women becoming.

PART I

TRADITIONAL IMAGES

OF WOMEN

IMAGE ONE

THE SUBMISSIVE WIFE

In a society in which males play dominant roles—
a patriarchal society—the ideal of adult womanhood is the wife who happily and submissively
passes from her father to her husband, changing
her last name in the process. Chaucer embodied this
ideal in *The Canterbury Tales* (fourteenth century) in Griselde. The daughter of a serf, Griselde
is honored when chosen by a nobleman as bride,
endures without complaint his depriving her of
her children and replacing her with a new wife,
and continues to be kind and loving to all regardless of her personal status. Although even the

pilgrims who heard this tale in Chaucer's poem knew it was only an ideal, this image has persisted in literature and life because it is an easy solution to the problem of dominance in a hierarchically organized society. Its ambiguity in a democracy—officially recognized when, only sixty years ago, women won the vote in this country—accounts for the guilt and anger in contemporary society as the reality of women's human need for self-development becomes impossible to deny. The selections here show the tensions that arise when women play the role of happy subordinate, the devices that cause women to adopt the role, and their rebellion against it.

The first story shows the submissive wife as ideally willing to be sub-servient to her husband; she chooses her role. In Sally Benson's "Little Woman," Penny emphasizes her smallness and childishness by her language and choice of clothes; as a wife she has arrested her development and tried to maintain her image of youth and beauty. She refuses to maintain any friendships or to leave her home more often than necessary, delighting in her captivity. It is this willingness of a woman to lose her identity that has been labeled the "feminine mystique" and that constitutes the primary attribute of the submissive wife stereotype. Benson makes it clear that the role is not only self-destructive for the wife but limiting to the husband. Penny's husband soon wearies of the littleness he once found so attractive and longs for a wife who is a full human being. Her role playing—living his fantasy—costs them both the real communication that should be the basis of any adult relationship.

Not all wives play the submissive role willingly. Social pressures through economics, tradition, and religion force acquiescence; women's reluctance is often repressed or unrecognized. Mrs. Grimes in "Death in the Woods" becomes the suffering servant of animals and men because circumstances force her to do so. Marrying the brutal Jake as an alternative to rape by her master-father, she stoically feeds him, their sons, the stock; she expects and gets no happiness for herself. Anderson exalts her as a Christ-like figure, ignoring the fact that she had no alternative and did not, godlike, choose her fate. She is a mystical ideal to the young boy in the story, but her life story is that of a victim. May Swenson's poem "Women" shows the limitation of Anderson's view; women who serve the purposes of men, who support them like pedestals, do so by sacrificing their own identity, becoming toylike, dolls like Penny Loomis.

Elizabeth Stuart Phelps's story "Angel Over the Right Shoulder" and Ruth Whitman's poem "Cutting the Jewish Bride's Hair" show the role religion has played in women's willing assumption of the role of submissive wife. They also reveal women's resentment of the pressure to conform. Most of Phelps's story is a realistic representation of the discontinuities that prevent women from studying and creating masterpieces. Mrs. James can find no earthly justification for the triviality of her life and the necessity to sacrifice her intellectual development; she sees herself as a failure as a wife, mother, student. But in a dream she has a vision of heavenly reward for her work; her smallest sacrifice for her family is recorded by an angel who is always "over the right shoulder." This vision causes her to give up willingly her personal ambitions and assume fully her role as wife and mother; her reward will be in heaven.

In Ruth Whitman's poem, the bride's passive submission to having her hair cut as a symbol of assuming the role of wife is presumed by the male Jews to be willing. Through subtlety of tone Ruth Whitman lets us see that her passivity comes from the pressure of the patriarchs, who view it as necessary for the stability of society. The daily prayer of Jewish men—"I thank God I was not born a woman"—makes clear their knowledge that the role is a subhuman one; but they are not willing to face change that would "shift the balance of the universe." Whitman's quiet irony lets us see the total self-centeredness of the tradition; the poem makes clear the reason for the persistence of the stereotype. Women seeking equality disturb the status quo.

Another reason the ideal persists is that it is related to hope and to the dream of romantic love. Alice Cary's speaker in "The Bridal Veil" sounds very modern as she refuses to be put on a pedestal, behind the bridal veil. She presents herself realistically as "common earth, common dew" and demands not only that she be perceived as one who will continue to grow but that her husband "grow to new heights" if she is to continue to love him. She feels that she could elude captivity, but she is willing to wear the veil—fulfill the wifely role—if love "do not fail." This age-old hope that love can transcend human limitations persists as women today try to formulate new definitions of their roles; it can be the source of energy for a will to change or an opiate for continuing traditions. It is significant that the speaker's declaration of independence occurs at a wedding. The actual experience of marriage may lead the bride to perceive that even with good will, as in Phelps's story, a good husband can do little to ameliorate the burdens of the wife's role as long as the ideal of the submissive wife prevails.

The pain and anger women feel because of the dichotomy between ideal and actuality are shown in Slesinger's story "On Being Told . . ." and Plath's poem "The Jailor." Written in the first person, Slesinger's story lets us see the cost to a woman caught in the double standard of morality. "On Being Told That Her Second Husband Has Taken His First Lover" shows that a woman has few options when her husband confesses his adultery. Cornelia realizes that she cannot retaliate effectively in kind: "for it is not true that men despise what they possess or what they have exclusive rights over; what is true is that they cannot love (in normal, masculine fashion) what they must share." Her experience has taught her that "every man has the germs of it in him somewhere, the little woman waiting at home." She reverts to the role after his announcement, casually accepting his leaving though she knows that "in a minute pain will go tearing through the veils." The sexual revolution has not been equally liberating for women and for men; Cornelia is caught in a repetitious pattern from which she sees no escape. Though written long before the current women's movement, Slesinger's story describes the dilemma of many wives today. Plath's "The Jailor" bitterly expresses her sense of entrapment. She must play the roles her husband imposes on her—cook, sex object, fantasy object; she is not even free to dream. The worst captivity is her inability to imagine a different life because she sees him as inevitably dependent upon her role playing.

The readings in this part show the submissive wife stereotype as sterile, resulting in emptiness or death for the women. Yet none of the wives—except Cary's bride—see any alternative; internalizing the image, they act out the role that cheats them of selfhood and happiness. The mythically and religiously reinforced stereotype has a tenacious hold upon the imagination. Even self-aware women like Cornelia and Plath's persona find the role playing inescapable. In fact, the more aware they are of their roles, the more they seem to suffer. One wonders if those able to live with the illusion of happiness in the traditional roles are not better off than those who have raised their consciousness. Feminist literature emphasizes that awareness and self-knowledge, however painful, are the price of being fully human—a price worth paying.

SALLY BENSON

(1900–1948) Sally Benson began her career as a journalist and ended it writing movie scripts. Two collections of her short stories, *Junior Miss* (1941) and *Meet Me in St. Louis* (1942), depict female adolescent rites of passage. Both became popular in dramatized and film versions that somewhat distorted their insights. Over one hundred of her short stories appeared in *The New Yorker*.

LITTLE WOMAN

Penny Loomis liked to look back to the day when Ralph had first seen her. It was the day she had first seen Ralph, too, but she didn't think of that. She remembered only the delighted, incredulous look in Ralph's eyes when he caught sight of her sitting in the large chair in the Matsons' living room. In the short skirts and long waists of ten years ago, she had seemed just like a doll. Later in the evening he had told her so. "I can't get over you!" he exclaimed. "You're so tiny!"

"Oh, I know! And I hate it!" she answered. "It's dreadful, really! About clothes, I mean. Why, I wear size eleven!"

"You could look taller," Louise Matson said. "Naturally, those flat-heeled shoes make you look awfully little. If you *wanted* to look taller, you could wear high heels."

Penny Loomis had surveyed her strapped, patent-leather shoes thoughtfully and then her eyes had rested for a rather long instant on Louise's substantial Size 7 brocade slippers. "It's all very well for you to talk," she replied ruefully. "Your feet are a decent size, not disgraceful little Chinese feet like mine. You have nice, *big* feet."

Taking her home that night, Ralph had commented on Louise's attitude. "She was just trying to be catty," he said. "And you were swell about it. You may be little, but you aren't *small*!"

There was nothing to it after that first evening. It was as though Ralph never knew what hit him. There were three months of being engaged, of dancing night after night, attracting attention because Ralph was so tall—over six feet—and she was so tiny. He was enchanted with her daintiness and made jokes about it. "Now where," he would ask, looking over her head and pretending he couldn't see her, "did I put that woman I had with me?"

Everybody would laugh, especially Penny. "Big silly!" she would say. "Take me home!"

Everything she did pleased and amazed him. When, the Christmas before they were married, she presented him with a scarf she had knitted, he was genuinely overwhelmed. "I don't believe it," he said, smoothing it over and over with his hands. "You're not big enough to hold the needles."

He made so much fuss about the scarf at home that his mother, who had knitted scarves, sweaters, and socks for him all his life, was inclined to be bitter. "You act as though she'd knitted that scarf with her feet," she said acidly. "And by the way, I put those golf stockings I just finished for you in your bottom bureau drawer."

His enchantment lasted long after they were married. It amused him to see her childish, round-toed shoes lying on the floor, to see her diminutive dresses hanging in the closet. Their house was full of company, too, those first months, men mostly, who marvelled with Ralph at the sight of Penny in an apron actually being able to get dinner, carrying platters of food almost bigger than she was.

They had no children, which was a pity, as Penny had fancied the idea of herself surrounded by tall, stalwart sons, but she had Ralph to flutter over and take care of. She made few friends and was content in their small apartment. Once Ralph asked her why she didn't go out more. "Do you good," he said, "to get out and play bridge or something in the afternoon. Why don't you look up Louise? You and she used to be pretty good friends."

Penny replied scornfully. Women were all right, she supposed. But she hated bridge, really. It was such a silly game. And she felt so funny going out with Louise, who was so tall. They looked ridiculous walking together.

Ralph had laughed at that. "Say, listen," he said, "I'm taller than Louise."

"You are a man," she answered. "Men are supposed to be big."

She looked so little and so pretty that Ralph agreed with her. "Louise is kind of a horse," he said.

They spent their vacations in Canada, where Ralph liked to fish. And Penny, dressed enchantingly in boys' denim trousers, checked shirt, and felt hat, lounged against cushions in the canoe while he paddled. She would scream a little, hiding her head, as he took the fish off the hooks. When they walked, Ralph carried her over the rough spots and took her arm up the hills, so that finally, although he insisted she was no trouble, he took to fishing nearer the Lodge.

Sometimes he was surprised at the number of things a man who was married to a little thing like Penny had to think of. There was the question of theatre tickets, for instance; he had to make an effort to gets seats in the first row so that Penny wouldn't have to crane her neck or sit on her coat to see the stage; he must also remember to shorten his steps when they walked together or Penny got tired and out of breath; things must be left where Penny could reach them without having to stand on a chair.

Once he had spoken to her about it. "Gosh," he said "it is kind of tough to be as little as you are! I never thought how it must be for you, not being able to do things that other people do."

The instant the words were out of his mouth, he knew he had said the wrong thing. "I'd like to know what I can't do that other women can!" she told him indignantly. "I think I manage to keep busy!"

He had to admit she did keep busy. In fact, she was never still. She was as busy, he thought, as a canary in a cage, fluttering, picking, keeping up an incessant chirping. "Sure you keep busy," he said. "Busy as a bird."

When they had been married almost ten years, he went on a business trip to Chicago. The thought of being left all alone frightened Penny and she made a great deal of it. He must put a chain lock on the front door and write down where he would be every night so that she could call him in case anything happened. Her anxious fluttering depressed him, and his depression lasted until he was safely on the train and seated in the warm, noisy dining car.

His second night in Chicago, the man he had come to see, a Mr. Merrick, asked him out to dinner. Mrs. Merrick went with them. She was a plain-looking woman, a little too stout, but there was something pleasing in the monotony of her solid brown hair that had no disturbing highlights, in her soft, friendly brown eyes, and her uninteresting brown felt hat. She had the appearance of a woman who had contemplatively set aside all personal vanity and turned to other things.

Ralph was surprised to find himself having a rather hilarious evening with them, and delighted to learn that Mr. Merrick had about decided to go back to New York with him and wind up their business for good and all. "And take me," Mrs. Merrick said.

"Oh, sure, take you," Mr. Merrick agreed.

And Ralph had added, "You bet!"

That night at the hotel, he wrote to Penny. It was a long, enthusiastic letter, and he wrote everything he could think of to please her. "They asked all about you," he wrote. "And I told them you were no bigger than a minute and as pretty as a picture. So we'll take them to dinner, when I get back, which should be about Friday. I'll wire exactly when. I miss you."

As he wrote "I miss you," he stopped and put his pen down on the desk. It struck him that he hadn't missed Penny at all, while she—well, he supposed that she was rattling around in the apartment not knowing what to do with herself. It occurred to him that she ought to have something to do, something better than fussing around with things at home. Not that he wanted her to work, he thought. Penny was far too helpless and little to be able to cope with a job. His heart softened when he remembered their evenings together with Penny curled up on his lap as he sat in the big chair, talking to him a mile a minute in her rather high, clear voice. He was ashamed of the many times he had wished she would read more, and recalled one dreadful evening when he had looked up from his paper at the sound of her nervous wandering about the room to say, "For the love of Pete, *light,* can't you?"

Thinking of these things and of the fine evening he had had with the Merricks, he picked up his pen again and underlined "I miss you."

The trip back to New York with the Merricks was great, but Penny was not at the station to meet him. "Unless we've missed her," he said gaily. "She's so darned little, she's easy to miss."

He assured the Merricks that he would just dash home, change his clothes, pick up Penny, and meet them at their hotel.

Penny was waiting for him at home. She was almost hysterically glad to see him, and he noticed that the house was shining and spotless, with fresh flowers in the vases and a wood fire burning in the grate. She was already dressed for the evening in a pale-pink taffeta dress with many ruffles, and stubby satin shoes tied with large bows. She wore a ribbon around her hair, and in the shaded lights of the living room she looked very young. It was only when she followed him to the bathroom to talk to him while he shaved that he noticed her more closely; the line of her mouth, always too thin, looked set and unhappy; the skin on her face looked drawn; and there was more than a sprinkling of gray in her black hair. The pink taffeta dress looked suddenly absurd on her, and he wished that she had worn something more suitable, something more her age. Why, Penny must be thirty-five!

She was curious about the Merricks, she said. "I never heard you make so much fuss over any two people in my life. What's she like?"

"Mrs. Merrick?" he asked, struggling with his stiff white shirt. "Oh, she's darned nice."

"Oh, I *know* that," Penny answered impatiently. "I know you think she's nice. What does she look like? Is she pretty?"

"No," he told her. "You couldn't call her pretty."

"Well, is she big, little, fat, thin?"

"She's not little," he said. "Why, she'd make two of you."

This seemed to satisfy her and she asked no more about the Merricks.

At the hotel they were told that Mr. and Mrs. Merrick were waiting for them in the main dining room. Walking through the lobby and down the long corridor, Penny was pleasantly conscious of the stir they created. She even shortened her steps a little, so that she appeared to be keeping up with Ralph by tripping at his side.

Mrs. Merrick's first words to her were what she expected. "Why, you're tiny!"

Penny laughed sweetly and looked up at Ralph. "Yes, isn't it silly?" she said. "I must look perfectly absurd beside Ralph, who is so enormous."

Mrs. Merrick's eyes took in every detail of Penny, her dress, her shoes, and the ribbon around her hair, and then she said, in almost the exact words that Louise had used so many years ago, "Do you know, with heels you'd look much taller. Why, you must be five feet one or so, and with good, high heels you'd look three inches taller. That would make you five feet four, which is a nice height. A great many movie actresses are five feet four."

Penny laughed again, but she flushed slightly.

"Now, Nellie," Mr. Merrick said, "don't go to making people over the first minute you see them. Maybe Mrs. Loomis *likes* to look small."

"Nonsense!" Mrs. Merrick exclaimed heartily. "No one wants to look like a midget! That is, no one wants to look *too* different. I know I was awfully tall for my age when I was about fifteen and I felt terribly about it. I was a sight, I can tell you."

And you're a sight now, Penny thought furiously. She chose a seat next to Mrs. Merrick and during dinner she rested her small, thin hand next to Mrs. Merrick's large, square one. She picked at her food daintily and exclaimed pleasantly when the other woman ordered ice cream with chocolate sauce for dessert. "Not that I wouldn't love it, but I just haven't *room*," she said.

Later, when the music started, she was surprised to see Ralph spring eagerly to his feet and ask Mrs. Merrick to dance.

"I haven't danced much lately," he said. "But let's go!"

He put one arm around Mrs. Merrick's waist and they started off. It was pleasant to have her face so near his own, to feel her soft, straight hair brush his forehead. She wore a dark-brown velvet dress, not very new and not very smart, but she had dignity and she moved smoothly with him across the dance floor. Over her shoulder he saw Penny dancing with Mr. Merrick. She was looking up into his face and talking brightly and animatedly. Mr. Merrick was bending down to catch what she was saying, smiling a frozen sort of smile, but he didn't look very happy.

The rest of the evening was not especially successful. Ralph tried in vain to recapture the spirit of hilarity he had felt with the Merricks in Chicago. But there was a sort of uneasiness in the air, even though Penny showed them several match tricks.

He was a little relieved, as they said good night, to learn that the Merricks had bought theatre tickets for the following evening and were leaving the day after for Chicago.

All the way home, Ralph sat in one corner of the taxi watching Penny as she talked. Her head was bent slightly to one side in the birdlike way she affected, and the white street lights flashing through the window were not kind to her. As he looked at her, she seemed to grow smaller and smaller until there was nothing much left of her but a pink taffeta dress and a pink ribbon. It had started to rain and the drops on the glass cast black dots on the pink taffeta dress, and he had the impression that it, too, might eventually disappear.

He did not notice that the cab had stopped in front of their apartment until Penny's voice gaily brought him back to earth. It was habit that made him pick her up and carry her across the wet, slippery pavement. And for such a little woman, she felt surprisingly heavy in his arms.

ELIZABETH STUART PHELPS

(1815–1852) Born in Andover, Massachusetts, Phelps was the daughter of a clergyman and later married one. She started writing stories at ten and started publishing in a religious journal at sixteen. While living in Boston, she published stories and poems. A novel based on a journal she kept about her family was a best seller in 1851 and was translated into several languages. Her daughter became a writer and took her mother's name to try to make up for her mother's premature death.

THE ANGEL OVER
THE RIGHT SHOULDER

"There! a woman's work is never done," said Mrs. James; "I thought, for once, I was through; but just look at that lamp, now! it will not burn, and I must go and spend half an hour over it."

"Don't you wish you had never been married?" said Mr. James, with a good-natured laugh.

"Yes"—rose to her lips, but was checked by a glance at the group upon the floor, where her husband was stretched out, and two little urchins with sparkling eyes and glowing cheeks, were climbing and tumbling over him, as if they found in this play the very essence of fun.

She did say, "I should like the good, without the evil, if I could have it."

"You have no evils to endure," replied her husband.

"That is just all you gentlemen know about it. What would you think, if you could not get an uninterrupted half hour to yourself, from morning till night? I believe you would give up trying to do anything."

"There is no need of that; all you want, is *system*. If you arranged your work systematically, you would find that you could command your time."

"Well," was the reply, "all I wish is, that you could just follow me around for one day, and see what I have to do. If you could reduce it all to system, I think you would show yourself a genius."

When the lamp was trimmed, the conversation was resumed. Mr. James had employed the "half hour," in meditating on this subject.

"Wife," said he, as she came in, "I have a plan to propose to you, and I wish you to promise me beforehand, that you will accede to it. It is to be an experiment, I acknowledge, but I wish it to have a fair trial. Now to please me, will you promise?"

Mrs. James hesitated. She felt almost sure that his plan would be quite impracticable, for what does a man know of a woman's work? yet she promised.

"Now I wish you," said he, "to set apart two hours of every day for your own private use. Make a point of going to your room and locking yourself in; and also make up your mind to let the work which is not done, go undone, if it must. Spend this time on just those things which will be most profitable to yourself. I shall bind you to your promise for one month— then, if it has proved a total failure, we will devise something else."

"When shall I begin?"

"To-morrow."

The morrow came. Mrs. James had chosen the two hours before dinner as being, on the whole, the most convenient and the least liable to interruption. They dined at one o'clock. She wished to finish her morning work, get dressed for the day, and enter her room at eleven.

Hearty as were her efforts to accomplish this, the hour of eleven found her with her work but half done; yet, true to her promise, she left all, retired to her room and locked the door.

With some interest and hope, she immediately marked out a course of reading and study, for these two precious hours; then, arranging her table, her books, pen and paper, she commenced a schedule of her work with much enthusiasm. Scarcely had she dipped her pen in ink, when she heard the tramping of little feet along the hall, and then a pounding at her door.

"Mamma! mamma! I cannot find my mittens, and Hannah is going to slide without me."

"Go to Amy, my dear; mamma is busy."

"So Amy busy too; she say she can't leave baby."

The child began to cry, still standing close to the fastened door. Mrs. James knew the easiest, and indeed the only way of settling the trouble, was to go herself and hunt up the missing mittens. Then a parley must be held with Frank, to induce him to wait for his sister, and the child's tears must be dried, and little hearts must be all set right before the children went out to play; and so favorable an opportunity must not be suffered to slip, without impressing on young minds the importance of having a "place for everything and everything in its place;" this took time; and when Mrs. James returned to her study, her watch told her that *half* her portion had gone. Quietly resuming her work, she was endeavoring to mend her broken train of thought, when heavier steps were heard in the hall, and the fastened door was once more besieged. Now, Mr. James must be admitted.

"Mary," said he, "cannot you come and sew a string on for me? I do believe there is not a bosom in my drawer in order, and I am in a great hurry. I ought to have been down town an hour ago."

The schedule was thrown aside, the work-basket taken, and Mrs. James followed him. She soon sewed on the tape, but then a button needed fastening—and at last a rip in his glove, was to be mended. As Mrs. James stitched away on the glove, a smile lurked in the corners of her mouth, which her husband observed.

"What are you laughing at?" asked he.

"To think how famously your plan works."

"I declare!" said he, "is this your study hour? I am sorry, but what can a man do? He cannot go down town without a shirt bosom!"

"Certainly not," said his wife, quietly.

When her liege lord was fairly equipped and off, Mrs. James returned to her room. A half an hour yet remained to her, and of this she determined to make the most. But scarcely had she resumed her pen, when there was another disturbance in the entry. Amy had returned from walking out with the baby, and she entered the nursery with him, that she might get him to sleep. Now it happened that the only room in the house which Mrs. James could have to herself with a fire, was the one adjoining the nursery. She had become so accustomed to the ordinary noise of the children, that it did not disturb her; but the very extraordinary noise which master Charley sometimes felt called upon to make, when he was fairly on his back in the cradle, did disturb the unity of her thoughts. The words which she was reading rose and fell with the screams and lulls of the child, and she felt obliged to close her book, until the storm was over. When quiet was restored in the cradle, the children came in from sliding, crying with cold fingers—and just as she was going to them, the dinner-bell rang.

"How did your new plan work this morning?" inquired Mr. James.

"Famously," was the reply, "I read about seventy pages of German, and as many more in French."

"I am sure *I* did not hinder you long."

"No—yours was only one of a dozen interruptions."

"O, well! you must not get discouraged. Nothing succeeds well the first time. Persist in your arrangement, and by and by the family will learn that if they want anything of you, they must wait until after dinner."

"But what can a man do?" replied his wife; "he cannot go down town without a shirt-bosom."

"I was in a bad case," replied Mr. James, "it may not happen again. I am anxious to have you try the month out faithfully, and then we will see what has come of it."

The second day of trial was a stormy one. As the morning was dark, Bridget over-slept, and consequently breakfast was too late by an hour. This lost hour Mrs. James could not recover. When the clock struck eleven, she seemed but to have commenced her morning's work, so much remained to be done. With mind disturbed and spirits depressed, she left her household matters "in the suds," as they were, and punctually retired to her study. She soon found, however, that she could not fix her attention upon any intellectual pursuit. Neglected duties haunted her, like ghosts around the guilty conscience. Perceiving that she was doing nothing with her books, and not wishing to lose the morning wholly, she commenced writing a letter. Bridget interrupted her before she had proceeded far on the first page.

"What, ma'am, shall we have for dinner? No marketing ha'n't come."

"Have some steaks, then."

"We ha'n't got none, ma'am."

"I will send out for some, directly."

Now there was no one to send but Amy, and Mrs. James knew it. With a sigh, she put down her letter and went into the nursery.

"Amy, Mr. James has forgotten our marketing. I should like to have you run over to the provision store, and order some beef-steaks. I will stay with the baby."

Amy was not much pleased to be sent out on this errand. She remarked, that "she must change her dress first."

"Be as quick as possible," said Mrs. James, "for I am particularly engaged at this hour."

Amy neither obeyed, nor disobeyed, but managed to take her own time, without any very deliberate intention to do so. Mrs. James, hoping to get along with a sentence or two, took her German book into the nursery. But this arrangement was not to master Charley's mind. A fig did he care for German, but "the kitties," he must have, whether or no—and kitties he would find in that particular book—so he turned its leaves over in great haste. Half of the time on the second day of trial had gone, when Amy returned and Mrs. James with a sigh, left her nursery. Before one o'clock, she was twice called into the kitchen to superintend some important dinner arrangement, and thus it turned out that she did not finish one page of her letter.

On the third morning the sun shone, and Mrs. James rose early, made every provision which she deemed necessary for dinner, and for the comfort of her family; and then, elated by her success, in good spirits, and with good courage, she entered her study precisely at eleven o'clock, and locked her door. Her books were opened, and the challenge given to a hard German lesson. Scarcely had she made the first onset, when the door-bell was heard to ring, and soon Bridget coming nearer and nearer—then tapping at the door.

"Somebodies wants to see you in the parlor, ma'am."

"Tell them I am engaged, Bridget."

"I told 'em you were to-home, ma'am, and they sent up their names, but I ha'n't got 'em, jist."

There was no help for it—Mrs. James must go down to receive her callers. She had to smile when she felt little like it—to be sociable when her thoughts were busy with her task. Her friends made a long call—they had nothing else to do with their time, and when they went, others came. In very unsatisfactory chit-chat, her morning slipped away.

On the next day, Mr. James invited company to tea, and her morning was devoted to preparing for it; she did not enter her study. On the day following, a sick-head-ache confined her to her bed, and on Saturday the care of the baby devolved upon her, as Amy had extra work to do. Thus passed the first week.

True to her promise, Mrs. James patiently persevered for a month, in her efforts to secure for herself this little fragment of her broken time, but with what success, the first week's history can tell. With its close, closed the month of December.

On the last day of the old year, she was so much occupied in her preparations for the morrow's festival, that the last hour of the day was approaching, before she made her good night's call in the nursery. She first went to the crib and looked at the baby. There he lay in his innocence and beauty, fast asleep. She softly stroked his golden hair—she kissed gently his rosy cheek—she pressed the little dimpled hand in hers, and then, carefully drawing the coverlet over it, tucked it in, and stealing yet another kiss—she left him to his peaceful dreams and sat down on her daughter's bed. She also slept sweetly, with her dolly hugged to her bosom. At this her mother smiled, but soon grave thoughts entered her mind, and these deepened into sad ones. She thought of her disappointment and the failure of her plans. To her, not only the past month but the whole past year, seemed to have been one of fruitless effort—all broken and dis-jointed—even her hours of religious duty had been encroached upon, and disturbed. She had accomplished nothing, that she could see, but to keep her house and family in order, and even this, to her saddened mind, seemed to have been but indifferently done. She was conscious of yearnings for a more earnest life than this. Unsatisfied longings for something which she had not attained, often clouded what, otherwise, would have been a bright day to her; and yet the causes of these feelings seemed to lie in a dim and misty region, which her eye could not penetrate.

What then did she need? To see some *results* from her life's work? To know that a golden cord bound her life-threads together into *unity* of purpose—notwithstanding they seemed, so often, single and broken?

She was quite sure that she felt no desire to shrink from duty, however humble, but she sighed for some comforting assurance of what *was duty*. Her employments, conflicting as they did with her tastes, seemed to her frivolous and useless. It seemed to her that there was some better way of living, which she, from deficiency in energy of character, or of principle, had failed to discover. As she leaned over her child, her tears fell fast upon its young brow.

Most earnestly did she wish, that she could shield that child from the disappointments and mistakes and self-reproach from which the mother was then suffering; that the little one might take up life where she could give it to her—all mended by her own experience. It would have been a comfort to have felt, that in fighting the battle, she had fought for both; yet she knew that so it could not be—that for ourselves must we all learn what are those things which "make for our peace."

The tears were in her eyes, as she gave the good-night to her sleeping daughter—then with soft steps she entered an adjoining room, and there fairly kissed out the old year on another chubby cheek, which nestled among the pillows. At length she sought her own rest.

Soon she found herself in a singular place. She was traversing a vast plain. No trees were visible, save those which skirted the distant horizon, and on their broad tops rested wreaths of golden clouds. Before her was a female, who was journeying towards that region of light. Little children were about her, now in her arms, now running by her side, and as they travelled, she occupied herself in caring for them. She taught them how to place their little feet—she gave them timely warnings of the pit-falls— she gently lifted them over the stumbling-blocks. When they were weary, she soothed them by singing of that brighter land, which she kept ever in view, and towards which she seemed hastening with her little flock. But what was most remarkable was, that, all unknown to her, she was constantly watched by two angels, who reposed on two golden clouds which floated above her. Before each was a golden book, and a pen of gold. One angel, with mild and loving eyes, peered constantly over her right shoulder—another kept as strict watch over her left. Not a deed, not a word, not a look, escaped their notice. When a good deed, word, look, went from her, the angel over the right shoulder with a glad smile, wrote it down in his book; when an evil, however trivial, the angel over the left shoulder recorded it in his book—then with sorrowful eyes followed the pilgrim until he observed penitence for the wrong, upon which he dropped a tear on the record, and blotted it out, and both angels rejoiced.

To the looker-on, it seemed that the traveller did nothing which was worthy of such careful record. Sometimes she did but bathe the weary feet of her little children, but the angel over the *right shoulder*—wrote it down. Sometimes she did but patiently wait to lure back a little truant who had turned his face away from the distant light, but the angel over the *right shoulder*—wrote it down. Sometimes she did but soothe an angry feeling or raise a drooping eye-lid, or kiss away a little grief; but the angel over the right shoulder—*wrote it down.*

Sometimes, her eye was fixed so intently on that golden horizon, and she became so eager to make progress thither, that the little ones, missing her care, did languish or stray. Then it was that the angel over the *left shoulder,* lifted his golden pen, and made the entry, and followed her with sorrowful eyes, until he could blot it out. Sometimes she seemed to advance rapidly, but in her haste the little ones had fallen back, and it was the sorrowing angel who recorded her progress. Sometimes so intent was she to gird up her loins and have her lamp trimmed and burning, that the little children wandered away quite into forbidden paths, and it was the angel over the *left shoulder* who recorded her diligence.

Now the observer as she looked, felt that this was a faithful and true record, and was to be kept to that journey's end. The strong clasps of gold on those golden books, also impressed her with the conviction that, when they were closed, it would only be for a future opening.

Her sympathies were warmly enlisted for the gentle traveller, and with a beating heart she quickened her steps that she might overtake her. She wished to tell her of the angels keeping watch above her—to entreat her to be faithful and patient to the end—for her life's work was all written down—every item of it—and the *results* would be known when those golden books should be unclasped. She wished to beg of her to think no duty trivial which must be done, for over her right shoulder and over her left were recording angels, who would surely take note of all!

Eager to warn the traveller of what she had seen, she touched her. The traveller turned, and she recognized or seemed to recognize *herself.* Startled and alarmed she awoke in tears. The gray light of morning struggled through the half-open shutter, the door was ajar and merry faces were peeping in.

"Wish you a happy new year, mamma,"—"Wish you a *Happy new Year,*"—"a happy noo ear."

She returned the merry greeting most heartily. It seemed to her as if she had entered upon a new existence. She had found her way through the thicket in which she had been entangled, and a light was now about her path. The *Angel over the Right Shoulder* whom she had seen in her dream, would bind up in his golden book her life's work, if it were but well done. He required of her no great deeds, but faithfulness and patience to the end of the race which was set before her. Now she could see plainly enough, that though it was right and important for her to cultivate her own mind and heart, it was equally right and equally important, to meet and perform faithfully all those little household cares and duties on which the comfort and virtue of her family depended; for into these things the angels carefully looked—and these duties and cares acquired a dignity from the strokes of that golden pen—they could not be neglected without danger.

Sad thoughts and sadder misgivings—undefined yearnings and ungratified longings seemed to have taken their flight with the Old Year, and it was with fresh resolution and cheerful hope, and a happy heart, she welcomed the *Glad* New Year. The *Angel over the Right Shoulder* would go with her, and if she were found faithful, would strengthen and comfort her to its close.

SHERWOOD ANDERSON

(1876–1941) Sherwood Anderson is an important American novelist and short story writer. In *Winesburg, Ohio* and other short story collections he probed beneath the surface of small-town life, often focusing on sexual frustration as the cause of wasted lives. In "Perhaps Women" (1931), an essay on the evils of industrialization, he wrote about women as men's hope of salvation in a technological society.

DEATH IN THE WOODS

I

She was an old woman and lived on a farm near the town in which I lived. All country and small-town people have seen such old women, but no one knows much about them. Such an old woman comes into town driving an old wornout horse or she comes afoot carrying a basket. She may own a few hens and have eggs to sell. She brings them in a basket and takes them to a grocer. There she trades them in. She gets some salt pork and some beans. Then she gets a pound or two of sugar and some flour.

Afterwards she goes to the butcher's and asks for some dog-meat. She may spend ten or fifteen cents, but when she does she asks for something. Formerly the butchers gave liver to any one who wanted to carry it away. In our family we were always having it. Once one of my brothers got a whole cow's liver at the slaughter-house near the fairgrounds in our town. We had it until we were sick of it. It never cost a cent. I have hated the thought of it ever since.

The old farm woman got some liver and a soup-bone. She never visited with any one, and as soon as she got what she wanted she lit out for home. It made quite a load for such an old body. No one gave her a lift. People drive right down a road and never notice an old woman like that.

There was such an old woman who used to come into town past our house one Summer and Fall when I was a young boy and was sick with what was called inflammatory rheumatism. She went home later carrying a heavy pack on her back. Two or three large gaunt-looking dogs followed at her heels.

The old woman was nothing special. She was one of the nameless ones that hardly any one knows, but she got into my thoughts. I have just suddenly now, after all these years, remembered her and what happened. It is a story. Her name was Grimes, and she lived with her husband and son in a small unpainted house on the bank of a small creek four miles from town.

The husband and son were a tough lot. Although the son was but twenty-one, he had already served a term in jail. It was whispered about that the woman's husband stole horses and ran them off to some other county. Now and then, when a horse turned up missing, the man had also disappeared. No one ever caught him. Once, when I was loafing at Tom Whitehead's livery-barn, the man came there and sat on the bench in front. Two or three other men were there, but no one spoke to him. He sat for a few minutes and then got up and went away. When he was leaving he turned around and stared at the men. There was a look of defiance in his eyes. "Well, I have tried to be friendly. You don't want to talk to me. It has been so wherever I have gone in this town. If, some day, one of your fine horses turns up missing, well, then what?" He did not say anything actually. "I'd like to bust one of you on the jaw," was about what his eyes said. I remember how the look in his eyes made me shiver.

The old man belonged to a family that had had money once. His name was Jake Grimes. It all comes back clearly now. His father, John Grimes, had owned a sawmill when the country was new, and had made money. Then he got to drinking and running after women. When he died there wasn't much left.

Jake blew in the rest. Pretty soon there wasn't any more lumber to cut and his land was nearly all gone.

He got his wife off a German farmer, for whom he went to work one June day in the wheat harvest. She was a young thing then and scared to death. You see, the farmer was up to something with the girl—she was, I think, a bound girl and his wife had her suspicions. She took it out on the girl when the man wasn't around. Then, when the wife had to go off to town for supplies, the farmer got after her. She told young Jake that nothing really ever happened, but he didn't know whether to believe it or not.

He got her pretty easy himself, the first time he was out with her. He wouldn't have married her if the German farmer hadn't tried to tell him where to get off. He got her to go riding with him in his buggy one night when he was threshing on the place, and then he came for her the next Sunday night.

She managed to get out of the house without her employer's seeing, but when she was getting into the buggy he showed up. It was almost dark, and he just popped up suddenly at the horse's head. He grabbed the horse by the bridle and Jake got out his buggy-whip.

They had it out all right! The German was a tough one. Maybe he didn't care whether his wife knew or not. Jake hit him over the face and shoulders with the buggy-whip, but the horse got to acting up and he had to get out.

Then the two men went for it. The girl didn't see it. The horse started to run away and went nearly a mile down the road before the girl got him stopped. Then she managed to tie him to a tree beside the road. (I wonder how I know all this. It must have stuck in my mind from small-town tales when I was a boy.) Jake found her there after he got through with the German. She was huddled up in the buggy seat, crying, scared to death. She told Jake a lot of stuff, how the German had tried to get her, how he chased her once into the barn, how another time, when they happened to be alone in the house together, he tore her dress open clear down the front. The German, she said, might have got her that time if he hadn't heard his old woman drive in at the gate. She had been off to town for supplies. Well, she would be putting the horse in the barn. The German managed to sneak off to the fields without his wife seeing. He told the girl he would kill her if she told. What could she do? She told a lie about ripping her dress in the barn when she was feeding the stock. I remember now that she was a bound girl and did not know where her father and mother were. Maybe she did not have any father. You know what I mean.

Such bound children were often enough cruelly treated. They were children who had no parents, slaves really. There were very few orphan homes then. They were legally bound into some home. It was a matter of pure luck how it came out.

2

She married Jake and had a son and daughter, but the daughter died.

Then she settled down to feed stock. That was her job. At the German's place she had cooked the food for the German and his wife. The wife was a strong woman with big hips and worked most of the time in the fields with her husband. She fed them and fed the cows in the barn, fed the pigs, the horses and the chickens. Every moment of every day, as a young girl, was spent feeding something.

Then she married Jake Grimes and he had to be fed. She was a slight thing, and when she had been married for three or four years, and after the two children were born, her slender shoulders became stooped.

Jake always had a lot of big dogs around the house, that stood near the unused sawmill near the creek. He was always trading horses when he wasn't stealing something and had a lot of poor bony ones about. Also he kept three or four pigs and a cow. They were all pastured in the few acres left of the Grimes place and Jake did little enough work.

He went into debt for a threshing outfit and ran it for several years, but it did not pay. People did not trust him. They were afraid he would steal the grain at night. He had to go a long way off to get work and it cost too much to get there. In the Winter he hunted and cut a little firewood, to be sold in some nearby town. When the son grew up he was just like the father. They got drunk together. If there wasn't anything to eat in the house when they came home the old man gave his old woman a cut over the head. She had a few chickens of her own and had to kill one of them in a hurry. When they were all killed she wouldn't have any eggs to sell when she went to town, and then what would she do?

She had to scheme all her life about getting things fed, getting the pigs fed so they would grow fat and could be butchered in the Fall. When they were butchered her husband took most of the meat off to town and sold it. If he did not do it first the boy did. They fought sometimes and when they fought the old woman stood aside trembling.

She had got the habit of silence anyway—that was fixed. Sometimes, when she began to look old—she wasn't forty yet—and when the husband and son were both off, trading horses or drinking or hunting or stealing, she went around the house and the barnyard muttering to herself.

How was she going to get everything fed?—that was her problem. The dogs had to be fed. There wasn't enough hay in the barn for the horses and the cow. If she didn't feed the chickens how could they lay eggs? Without eggs to sell how could she get things in town, things she had to have to keep the life of the farm going? Thank heaven, she did not have to feed her husband—in a certain way. That hadn't lasted long after their marriage and after the babies came. Where he went on his long trips she did not know. Sometimes he was gone from home for weeks, and after the boy grew up they went off together.

They left everything at home for her to manage and she had no money. She knew no one. No one ever talked to her in town. When it was Winter she had to gather sticks of wood for her fire, had to try to keep the stock fed with very little grain.

The stock in the barn cried to her hungrily, the dogs followed her about. In the Winter the hens laid few enough eggs. They huddled in the corners of the barn and she kept watching them. If a hen lays an egg in the barn in the Winter and you don't find it, it freezes and breaks.

One day in Winter the old woman went off to town with a few eggs and the dogs followed her. She did not get started until nearly three o'clock and the snow was heavy. She hadn't been feeling very well for several days and so she went muttering along, scantily clad, her shoulders stooped. She had an old grain bag in which she carried her eggs, tucked away down in the bottom. There weren't many of them, but in Winter the price of eggs is up. She would get a little meat in exchange for the eggs, some salt pork, a little sugar, and some coffee perhaps. It might be the butcher would give her a piece of liver.

When she had got to town and was trading in her eggs the dogs lay by the door outside. She did pretty well, got the things she needed, more than she had hoped. Then she went to the butcher and he gave her some liver and some dog-meat.

It was the first time any one had spoken to her in a friendly way for a long time. The butcher was alone in his shop when she came in and was annoyed by the thought of such a sick-looking old woman out on such a day. It was bitter cold and the snow, that had let up during the afternoon, was falling again. The butcher said something about her husband and her son, swore at them, and the old woman stared at him, a look of mild surprise in her eyes as he talked. He said that if either the husband or the son were going to get any of the liver or the heavy bones with scraps of meat hanging to them that he had put into the grain bag, he'd see him starve first.

Starve, eh? Well, things had to be fed. Men had to be fed, and horses that weren't any good but maybe could be traded off, and the poor thin cow that hadn't given any milk for three months.

Horses, cows, pigs, dogs, men.

3

The old woman had to get back before darkness came if she could. The dogs followed at her heels, sniffing at the heavy grain bag she had fastened on her back. When she got to the edge of town she stopped by a fence and tied the bag on her back with a piece of rope she had carried in her dress-pocket for just that purpose. It was hard when she had to crawl over fences and once she fell over and landed in the snow. The dogs went frisking about. She had to struggle to get to her feet again, but she made it. The point of climbing over the fences was that there was a short cut over a hill and through a woods. She might have gone around by the road, but it was a mile farther that way. She was afraid she couldn't make it. And then, besides, the stock had to be fed. There was a little hay left and a little corn. Perhaps her husband and son would bring some home when they came. They had driven off in the only buggy the Grimes family had, a rickety thing, a rickety horse hitched to the buggy, two other rickety horses led by halters. They were going to trade horses, get a little money if they could. They might come home drunk. It would be well to have something in the house when they came back.

The son had an affair on with a woman at the county seat, fifteen miles away. She was a rough enough woman, a tough one. Once, in the Summer, the son had brought her to the house. Both she and the son had been drinking. Jake Grimes was away and the son and his woman ordered the old woman about like a servant. She didn't mind much; she was used to it.

Whatever happened she never said anything. That was her way of getting along. She had managed that way when she was a young girl at the German's and ever since she had married Jake. That time her son brought his woman to the house they stayed all night, sleeping together just as though they were married. It hadn't shocked the old woman, not much. She had got past being shocked early in life.

With the pack on her back she went painfully along across an open field, wading in the deep snow, and got into the woods.

There was a path, but it was hard to follow. Just beyond the top of the hill, where the woods was thickest, there was a small clearing. Had some one once thought of building a house there? The clearing was as large as a building lot in town, large enough for a house and a garden. The path ran along the side of the clearing, and when she got there the old woman sat down to rest at the foot of a tree.

It was a foolish thing to do. When she got herself placed, the pack against the tree's trunk, it was nice, but what about getting up again? She worried about that for a moment and then quietly closed her eyes.

She must have slept for a time. When you are about so cold you can't get any colder. The afternoon grew a little warmer and the snow came thicker than ever. Then after a time the weather cleared. The moon even came out.

There were four Grimes dogs that had followed Mrs. Grimes into town, all tall gaunt fellows. Such men as Jake Grimes and his son always keep just such dogs. They kick and abuse them, but they stay. The Grimes dogs, in order to keep from starving, had to do a lot of foraging for themselves, and they had been at it while the old woman slept with her back to the tree at the side of the clearing. They had been chasing rabbits in the woods and in adjoining fields and in their ranging had picked up three other farm dogs.

After a time all the dogs came back to the clearing. They were excited about something. Such nights, cold and clear and with a moon, do things to dogs. It may be that some old instinct, come down from the time when they were wolves and ranged the woods in packs on Winter nights, comes back into them.

The dogs in the clearing, before the old woman, had caught two or three rabbits and their immediate hunger had been satisfied. They began to play, running in circles in the clearing. Round and round they ran, each dog's nose at the tail of the next dog. In the clearing, under the snow-laden trees and under the wintry moon they made a strange picture, running thus silently, in a circle their running had beaten in the soft snow. The dogs made no sound. They ran around and around in the circle.

It may have been that the old woman saw them doing that before she died. She may have awakened once or twice and looked at the strange sight with dim old eyes.

She wouldn't be very cold now, just drowsy. Life hangs on a long time.

Perhaps the old woman was out of her head. She may have dreamed of her girlhood at the German's, and before that, when she was a child and before her mother lit out and left her.

Her dreams couldn't have been very pleasant. Not many pleasant things had happened to her. Now and then one of the Grimes dogs left the running circle and came to stand before her. The dog thrust his face to her face. His red tongue was hanging out.

The running of the dogs may have been a kind of death ceremony. It may have been that the primitive instinct of the wolf, having been aroused in the dogs by the night and the running, made them somehow, afraid.

"Now we are no longer wolves. We are dogs, the servants of men. Keep alive, man! When man dies we become wolves again." When one of the dogs came to where the old woman sat with her back against the tree and thrust his nose close to her face he seemed satisfied and went back to run with the pack. All the Grimes dogs did it at some time during the evening, before she died. I knew all about it afterward, when I grew to be a man, because once in a woods in Illinois, on another Winter night, I saw a pack of dogs act just like that. The dogs were waiting for me to die as they had waited for the old woman that night when I was a child, but when it happened to me I was a young man and had no intention whatever of dying.

The old woman died softly and quietly. When she was dead and when one of the Grimes dogs had come to her and had found her dead all the dogs stopped running.

They gathered about her.

Well, she was dead now. She had fed the Grimes dogs when she was alive, what about now?

There was the pack on her back, the grain bag containing the piece of salt pork, the liver the butcher had given her, the dog-meat, the soup-bones. The butcher in town, having been suddenly overcome with a feeling of pity, had loaded her grain bag heavily. It had been a big haul for the old woman.

It was a big haul for the dogs now.

4

One of the Grimes dogs sprang suddenly out from among the others and began worrying the pack on the old woman's back. Had the dogs really been wolves that one would have been the leader of the pack. What he did, all the others did.

All of them sank their teeth into the grain bag the old woman had fastened with the ropes to her back.

They dragged the old woman's body out into the open clearing. The worn-out dress was quickly torn from her shoulders. When she was found, a day or two later, the dress had been torn from her body clear to the hips, but the dogs had not touched her body. They had got the meat out of the grain bag, that was all. Her body was frozen stiff when it was found, and the shoulders were so narrow and the body so slight that in death it looked like the body of some charming young girl.

Such things happened in towns of the Middle West, on farms near town, when I was a boy. A hunter out after rabbits found the old woman's body and did not touch it. Something, the beaten round path in the little snow-covered clearing, the silence of the place, the place where the dogs had worried the body trying to pull the grain bag away or tear it open—something startled the man and he hurried off to town.

I was in Main Street with one of my brothers who was town newsboy and who was taking the afternoon papers to the stores. It was almost night.

The hunter came into a grocery and told his story. Then he went into a hardware-shop and into a drugstore. Men began to gather on the sidewalks. Then they started out along the road to the place in the woods.

My brother should have gone on about his business of distributing papers but he didn't. Every one was going to the woods. The undertaker went and the town marshal. Several men got on a dray and rode out to where the path left the road and went into the woods, but the horses weren't very sharply shod and slid about on the slippery roads. They made no better time than those of us who walked.

The town marshal was a large man whose leg had been injured in the Civil War. He carried a heavy cane and limped rapidly along the road. My brother and I followed at his heels, and as we went other men and boys joined the crowd.

It had grown dark by the time we got to where the old woman had left the road but the moon had come out. The marshal was thinking there might have been a murder. He kept asking the hunter questions. The hunter went along with his gun across his shoulders, a dog following at his heels. It isn't often a rabbit hunter has a chance to be so conspicuous. He was taking full advantage of it, leading the procession with the town marshal. "I didn't see any wounds. She was a beautiful young girl. Her face was buried in the snow. No. I didn't know her." As a matter of fact, the hunter had not looked closely at the body. He had been frightened. She might have been murdered and some one might spring out from behind a tree and murder him. In a woods, in the late afternoon, when the trees are all bare and there is white snow on the ground, when all is silent, something creepy steals over the mind and body. If something strange or uncanny has happened in the neighborhood all you think about is getting away from there as fast as you can.

The crowd of men and boys had got to where the old woman had crossed the field and went, following the marshal and the hunter, up the slight incline and into the woods.

My brother and I were silent. He had his bundle of papers in a bag slung across his shoulder. When he got back to town he would have to go on distributing his papers before he went home to supper. If I went along, as he had no doubt already determined I should, we would both be late. Either mother or our older sister would have to warm our supper.

Well, we would have something to tell. A boy did not get such a chance very often. It was lucky we just happened to go into the grocery when the hunter came in. The hunter was a country fellow. Neither of us had ever seen him before.

Now the crowd of men and boys had got to the clearing. Darkness comes quickly on such Winter nights, but the full moon made everything clear. My brother and I stood near the tree, beneath which the old woman had died.

She did not look old, lying there in that light, frozen and still. One of the men turned her over in the snow and I saw everything. My body trembled with some strange mystical feeling and so did my brother's. It might have been the cold.

Neither of us had ever seen a woman's body before. It may have been the snow, clinging to the frozen flesh, that made it look so white and lovely, so like marble. No woman had come with the party from town; but one of the men, he was the town blacksmith, took off his overcoat and spread it over her. Then he gathered her into his arms and started off to town, all the others following silently. At that time no one knew who she was.

5

I had seen everything, had seen the oval in the snow, like a miniature racetrack, where the dogs had run, had seen how the men were mystified, had seen the white bare young-looking shoulders, had heard the whispered comments of the men.

The men were simply mystified. They took the body to the undertaker's, and when the blacksmith, the hunter, the marshal and several others had got inside they closed the door. If father had been there perhaps he could have got in, but we boys couldn't.

I went with my brother to distribute the rest of his papers and when we got home it was my brother who told the story.

I kept silent and went to bed early. It may have been I was not satisfied with the way he told it.

Later, in the town, I must have heard other fragments of the old woman's story. She was recognized the next day and there was an investigation.

The husband and son were found somewhere and brought to town and there was an attempt to connect them with the woman's death, but it did not work. They had perfect enough alibis.

However, the town was against them. They had to get out. Where they went I never heard.

I remember only the picture there in the forest, the men standing about, the naked girlish-looking figure, face down in the snow, the tracks made by the running dogs and the clear cold Winter sky above. White fragments of clouds were drifting across the sky. They went racing across the little open space among the trees.

The scene in the forest had become for me, without my knowing it, the foundation for the real story I am now trying to tell. The fragments, you see, had to be picked up slowly, long afterwards.

Things happened. When I was a young man I worked on the farm of a German. The hired-girl was afraid of her employer. The farmer's wife hated her.

I saw things at that place. Once later, I had a half-uncanny, mystical adventure with dogs in an Illinois forest on a clear, moon-lit Winter night. When I was a schoolboy, and on a Summer day, I went with a boy friend out along a creek some miles from town and came to the house where the old woman had lived. No one had lived in the house since her death. The doors were broken from the hinges; the window lights were all broken. As the boy and I stood in the road outside, two dogs, just roving farm dogs no doubt, came running around the corner of the house. The dogs were tall, gaunt fellows and came down to the fence and glared through at us, standing in the road.

The whole thing, the story of the old woman's death, was to me as I grew older like music heard from far off. The notes had to be picked up slowly one at a time. Something had to be understood.

The woman who died was one destined to feed animal life. Anyway, that is all she ever did. She was feeding animal life before she was born, as a child, as a young woman working on the farm of the German, after she married, when she grew old and when she died. She fed animal life in cows, in chickens, in pigs, in horses, in dogs, in men. Her daughter had died in childhood and with her one son she had no articulate relations. On the night when she died she was hurrying homeward, bearing on her body food for animal life.

She died in the clearing in the woods and even after her death continued feeding animal life.

You see it is likely that, when my brother told the story, that night when we got home and my mother and sister sat listening, I did not think he got the point. He was too young and so was I. A thing so complete has its own beauty.

I shall not try to emphasize the point. I am only explaining why I was dissatisfied then and have been ever since. I speak of that only that you may understand why I have been impelled to try to tell the simple story over again.

MAY SWENSON

(b. 1919) Born and educated in Utah, May Swenson has written children's books and a play, but she is best known for her poetry. Volumes include *To Mix with Time* (1963), *Half Sun Half Sleep* (1967), *Poems to Solve* (1966), *More Poems to Solve* (1970), and *Iconographs* (1970). She has won many prizes and in 1970 was elected to the National Institute of Arts and Letters. Her most recent work is *New and Selected Things Taking Place* (1978).

WOMEN

Women	Or they
should be	should be
pedestals	little horses
moving	those wooden
pedestals	sweet
moving	oldfashioned
to the	painted
motions	rocking
of men	horses

the gladdest things in the toyroom

The	feelingly
pegs	and then
of their	unfeelingly
ears	To be
so familiar	joyfully
and dear	ridden
to the trusting	rockingly
fists	ridden until
To be chafed	the restored

egos dismount and the legs stride away

Immobile   willing
 sweetlipped   to be set
   sturdy   into motion
  and smiling   Women
    women   should be
    should always   pedestals
     be waiting   to men

RUTH WHITMAN

(b. 1922) Ruth Whitman graduated from Radcliffe College in 1944 with honors in Greek and English. She has published several volumes of translations as well as four volumes of poetry, one of which, *Tamsen Donner: A Woman's Journey* (1977), re-creates the experience of a pioneer on the Oregon Trail. Her latest volume, *Permanent Address,* appeared in 1980. A winner of many awards, Ms. Whitman held a National Endowment for the Arts grant in 1974–1975. She regularly conducts poetry workshops at the Mary Bunting Institute at Radcliffe.

CUTTING THE JEWISH
BRIDE'S HAIR

It's to possess more than the skin
that those old world Jews
exacted the hair of their brides.
   Good husband, lover of the Torah,
   does the calligraphy of your bride's hair
   interrupt your page?

Before the clownish friction of flesh
creating out of nothing
a mockup of its begetters,
a miraculous puppet of God,
you must first divorce her from her vanity.

She will snip off her pride,
cut back her appetite to be devoured,
she will keep herself well braided,
her love's furniture will not endanger you,
   but this little amputation
   will shift the balance of the universe.

(1820–1871) Born on a farm near Cincinnati, Alice and her sister Phoebe were educated at home. The poems they began to publish as teen-agers were widely admired; Edgar Allan Poe considered a lyric by Alice one of the most musically perfect in English. Moving to New York City in 1850, the sisters earned a living by writing. Alice's realistic novel *Clovernook* (1852), a best seller, revealed the cultural deprivation of women. Both sisters worked for abolition of slavery and women's suffrage.

THE BRIDAL VEIL

We're married, they say, and you think you have won me,—
Well, take this white veil from my head, and look on me:
Here's matter to vex you, and matter to grieve you,
Here's doubt to distrust you, and faith to believe you,—
I am all as you see, common earth, common dew;
Be wary, and mould me to roses, not rue!

Ah! shake out the filmy thing, fold after fold,
And see if you have me to keep and to hold,—
Look close on my heart—see the worst of its sinning—
It is not yours to-day for the yesterday's winning—
The past is not mine—I am too proud to borrow—
You must grow to new heights if I love you to-morrow.

We're married! I'm plighted to hold up your praises,
As the turf at your feet does its handful of daisies;
That way lies my honor,—my pathway of pride,
But, mark you, if greener grass grow either side,
I shall know it, and keeping in body with you,
Shall walk in my spirit with feet on the dew!

THE SUBMISSIVE WIFE

We're married! Oh, pray that our love do not fail!
I have wings flattened down and hid under my veil:
They are subtle as light—you can never undo them,
And swift in their flight—you can never pursue them,
And spite of all clasping, and spite of all bands,
I can slip like a shadow, a dream, from your hands.

Nay, call me not cruel, and fear not to take me,
I am yours for my lifetime, to be what you make me,—
To wear my white veil for a sign, or a cover,
As you shall be proven my lord, or my lover;
A cover for peace that is dead, or a token
Of bliss that can never be written or spoken.

TESS SLESINGER

(1905–1945) Born in New York City, Tess Slesinger graduated from Swarthmore College and the Columbia University School of Journalism. Her short stories were collected in *Time: The Present* (1935), after publication of her novel *The Unpossessed* (1934). She wrote the screenplay for *The Good Earth* and with her husband Frank Davis screenplays for *A Day to Remember* and *A Tree Grows in Brooklyn,* before her untimely death of cancer.

ON BEING TOLD THAT HER SECOND HUSBAND HAS TAKEN HIS FIRST LOVER

Well (you think in a sprightly voice) this is no surprise, at least *essentially.* So it's nice my dear, that you are always so clever; and sad my dear that you always need to be. Time was when a thing like this was a shock that fell heavily in the pit of your stomach and gave you indigestion all at once. But you can only feel a thing like this in its entirety the first time, after that it's a weaker repetition. Nowadays you go around automatically expecting the worst all the time, so that you can only be pleasantly surprised by the exceptions. Pretty nice to be so clever, Cornelia my gal, *pretty sad too.* Now when the message is shot out to you you've got a nice little lined glove like a catcher's mitt for it to fall into, more or less painlessly, more or less soundlessly. Oh sure, the details, falling like pepper into a fresh wound, sting a bit. And of course the confirmation, the *dead-certain* confirmation, of what you were clever enough to *know* and clever enough to keep away from knowing, does wrap you round in a sort of straight-jacket for a minute . . . But no nausea comes.

No nausea. No sharp pain. A mild disgust, and a quick defensive rallying of your forces. Your wits are keyed to concert pitch, nothing can escape you, you are intensely self-conscious. You have utter and absolute control over all your nerves. You go right on lying there in his arms letting what must have gone rigid inside you with his words go rigid away inside your skin, so his arms can't sense the difference, can't feel the animal flinch that maybe after all you couldn't avoid.

You observe the lines in his face, his weakness, his male pride which even in his moment of confession he cannot hide even from himself, and at the same time you are marking infinitesimal notes on your own emotions. Implacable logic comes and sits in your head. Your associative processes, like your wits, are functioning brilliantly, you are intensely, even thrillingly alive with the tingling call to battle in all your veins. Your past thoughts and observations, fragments from his conversation, kaleidoscopic pictures of his facial muscles scarcely noted at the time yet registered indelibly somewhere deep in the consciousness, stand out like well-framed entities of a jig-saw puzzle, only they cease now to be entities, and under your courageous and all-seeing eye they fit together and form a large bold map omitting nothing.

Oh, you could talk about the thing, in Proustian vein, forever. Show him where he was weak, analyze his emotions for him, tear him to pieces like a female lion. Time was, with Jimsie (ah, *that* pain can still come, and it is not that Jimsie ever was more to you than Dill is now, it is because Jimsie was the first, and that pain was the first, his news was a blow the heart will never recover from—never), time was when you brilliantly talked, explaining away everything, for two whole days, while Jimsie stayed home from work to listen and neither of you so much as dressed nor saw another person but the boy from the delicatessen bringing sandwiches and cigarettes at intervals, and at last vichy-water when you fell to drinking. But you have learned a lesson. You know that you cannot handle these things as though you were giving a lecture course. No, no; no matter how much he acknowledges with his mind, there will be no satisfaction for you ultimately, and no sensitive revelations for him, unless you become at the same time an artist and an actress (or else of course an impulsive human being, but that is not possible). Of course, you could go on forever, apparently relieving your mind of all its stored-up bitterness and grievances (some of them you never knew you had, some of them you had only against Jimsie and not against Dill at all), but a stream like that is futile and self-multiplying; you must be a highly selective artist, Mrs. Dill Graham formerly-something-else; a gently restrained actress, *née* Cornelia North.

It is a delicate matter you have on your hands, my poor Cornelia, unless, that is, you choose to toss it down quickly with a drink and never look it in the eye again. But what's the use of doing that? Why make infidelity a painless operation and take from it its only possible lasting virtue, a possible binding closer together of the original two partners? Besides, there's something cheap in painlessness, something too modern-generationish. Go in for recriminations, gal, but on a modern scale; you can't of course go on lying there in his arms (and it's cowardice that keeps you so, even now) and mutter things about honor and weep, because you know too well that honor has nothing to do with it, and you don't feel in the least like weeping, in fact you couldn't manage it right now thanks. No, it has nothing to do with honor, it unfortunately has nothing to do with anything but human nature, and how can you take a man to task for that—not to mention *two* men?

He has the gall to ask you whether you feel "through" with him now. No, you answer, the thing has been going on right along and I've been happy enough—I'm not one to look back now that I know I've always had t.b. and say God how I have always suffered. "Well, but is it going to make any difference to you, from now on?" How in hell should I know? At the moment I have no desire but to keep my head above water and say funny things. And I can do it too, by God. (Like the time you wandered into the wrong room at a party and found him with his arms around that girl What's-her-name in no uncertain manner—ah, you put on a swell act that time, old girl! Just before being sick in the bathroom you managed a hearty laugh and said, O dear Lord, it looks so funny when you're not doing it yourself! How mad Dill was. But how he loved you for your wit. Still, if he had known about the mess in the bathroom which you so carefully cleaned up, *mightn't* he have loved you more? and *mightn't* you have prevented this other thing . . . ?) "Is it going to make a difference to you, Cornelia, now that you know?" "If you must be a gay deceiver, honey, for God's sake, be a *gay* one! My goodness, isn't adultery more fun than *that*?"

Suddenly you are filled with power which makes you light as air, which goes to your head like champagne the last night on shipboard. You have somehow got rid of something, somehow picked out his weakness in chiaroscuro. His triumph is smaller now than his guilt; his guilt you will reduce to sheepishness. I can do anything, my little man: now give me something *hard* to do. Besides, it occurs to you suddenly (elated as you are) that the thing is impossible. Simply and utterly impossible—it hasn't happened at all. Does he actually exist when he leaves your sight? Does he actually exist when . . .

Ah careful there, Cornelia; the ice is thin that way, Mrs. D. Graham; watch your step dancing on those there *particular* eggs, Miss North—for the visual inner eye is a keen thing, a sharp sadist, a talented beast of an artist, an old devil of a perverted surgeon . . . delete that diagram, my dear, quick, before it stains the heart's plate permanently . . .

And then you reason (philosophical now, the body gone cold in his cold hands, the mind gone cold in your own cold skull) it *is* impossible, elementally and fundamentally impossible—impossible on the level of real values. For you are YOU, therefore if he loves the real YOU he cannot *love* anybody else; and if, on the other hand, it is not the real YOU he has reached down and found to love, why then, the hell with him altogether—you don't want to be loved for what you have in common with other presentable women: for your decent hair, your fine teeth, your eyes, your neat little figger. No. You want to be loved, not really even for your wit, but for the whole tricky pattern of all these things and the mysterious something else besides which spells in the end YOU and you alone. So then, since he loves you in this way, Dill does (of that you are sure, both warmly and coldly), since he really *loves* you, since he loves the real YOU —what can it possibly matter if he touches her with his hands, not the real HER, and not with the real HIM, suppose he does say to her . . . laugh with her . . . kiss her . . . Ah, ah, that way the ice is thin again, that way leads not to pain but to the terrible presentiment of pain . . . Ah, cold philosophy! denying the body, consoling the brain! Philosophy is senility to the young, religion to the starving, a dictionary to a baby, a fine silk purse to a pig . . .

To hell with philosophy, in short. "But what are you going to *do*?" he says, Dill says, and you discover that he too is lying without moving, as afraid as you that if a muscle twitches or a breath catches, something, or the whole of everything, will go smashing to small pieces in this life you share. What are you going to *do*? To *do*? Why, lie here, I suppose, for the rest of our married life, in your arms gone cold, in our bed gone cold, my heart gone cold as a philosopher's. What am I going to *do*, you think. It is a good question. One of the best questions, for there is never any answer to it.

Certainly, you think, you have a legalistic right to go out and get even . . . But you did that once, you matched Jimsie amour for amour, and what happened? Why, the string between you wore out, it got like old elastic and finally, because it would never snap any more for deadness, each of you let go his end and wandered off, too empty to feel pain, too dead to feel anything. You merely destroyed something that way, Cornelia, you didn't even save your self-respect when that bank closed. No, that's painless dentistry again, remote control, the Machine Age, Watson and the reflex, the Modern Generation. To derive *full* value out of anything, one must pay the price in pain; full beauty consists of pain as well as joy —and halving the pain cuts the joy in two. Let us not compromise, you think strongly; God send me pain again, God let me feel.

"I mean, can you love me in spite of anything?" If I love you at all, you think, if there is such a thing as love at all, then I suppose it is in spite of anything. "Oh sure," you hear yourself saying like a girl scout, but it sounds like the kind of records your grandfather used to play on his gramophone. "And how about you, my gay deceiver, would you love me in spite of anything, Dill? Would you now?" Impossible, clearly, to speak without lilting; try a drop of pallid humor first thing in the morning, nothing like it to aid digestion, avoid those infidelity blues, that early-morning tremolo.

"Anything, *but no gents*," he says, with fear piled up in his eyes and a sort of anticipatory hatred. "Don't ask me why, I don't *know* why, but it's different with a man."

He says and has said and will go on saying, *But no gents* for you, my girl, one gent and I am through. He will go on saying it until there has been one gent. (And the first is the only one that counts. After that, the elastic begins to stretch and go dead—we found that out between us, Jimsie and I.) Then it is a toss-up what he will do, when there has been one gent. But one thing is clear, Cornelia, you shrewd and calculating woman, one thing is clear: one gent, and you will have lost the large part of your power over him. For it is not true that men despise what they possess or what they have exclusive rights over; what is true is that they cannot love (in normal, masculine fashion) what they must share. No, there is no point to your going and doing likewise, not as long as there is any point to your relations with this man, this philandering second husband, this gay deceiver who tells the truth and looks so far from gay about it. As long as he can lie there with fear written on his face and say to you *But no gents,* you have a power which nothing can destroy. You gain thereby an integrity which exists not merely in his eyes, but which is actual, which is a fact. You become a whole person even in your sadness, while he stands before you, however male, a split one. He will know it, you will know it.

"The old Dolly Gray complex," you say. And evidently every man has the germs of it in him somewhere, the little woman waiting at home. It is even a little perverse that he can feel this way about you when he considers you were a bum (as he called it) out and out before he met you, ever since Jimsie in fact, and realizes that you were one on the very night he met you. But that's nice; that's what appeals to him; the very perversity of these strange facts: that you were a bastard (in his own language) and that now you sit at home and wait for him. He could not bear it if you were straight-out Dolly Gray, for he is a modern young man. But you have that whole rich background (rich! and supposing you have children and then grandchildren, would that story about falling asleep in a fraternity house with two "brothers" be the kind kids would like to hear from dear old Granny?)—but you have it, and he can never quite forgive you, and this is enough to tease him and please him for the rest of his life; you can never be quite Dolly Gray in his eyes because you can never shake off your past and his memory of your complaisance (to put it mildly) on the very night on which he met you. All right, let him have the joy of reforming you, of capturing what was free and keeping it in a cage, of owning what used to belong to nobody. At least let him for the time being. See what happens. You can always go back to being a bum again. Hallelujah, bum again! "I couldn't stand it if I thought this changed things," says Dill—and of course he knows it has changed things, what he

THE SUBMISSIVE WIFE

58

means is he can't stand it if it's going to change your staying at home and waiting for him.

"Ah let's get up, nothing is changed, why should it be," you say quite gayly (and feeling it too), and spring stiffly out of his stiff arms. Well, it isn't quite the same as yesterday, it never will be. There is none of that pleasant, early-morning family-feeling now. You feel wicked a little as you run about with your pyjamas falling off one shoulder, getting breakfast but taking care to be rather attractive about it today as though you and Dill were not married yet. Ah yes, it is a very flirtatious breakfast that you have, flirtatious and a little bit precarious, for if the toast burns you might cry, and if the coffee is not done properly today he might fling it to the floor in a rage. But no, no; everything comes out all right because it *had* to come out all right, even the eggs get poached quite nicely instead of slipping out of their shells and allowing themselves to be parboiled— the toast turns out like the toast in a suave English comedy, and the coffee has never been better (you taste all this with your mind, with your weighing-machine, for your tongue has ceased to give a damn, and your alimentary canal is working like a derrick without a soul). In fact the whole thing passes off rather like a fine English play, in which the husband has just murdered the child because he found out his wife had it by the butler, the wife is scheduled to murder the butler immediately after breakfast, and meantime the butler serves them an impeccable breakfast over an impeccable table with unimpeachable manners, and the husband and the wife delicately break their toast and wonder if the season will be a good one, if the Queen has got over her cold. Oh yes, yes, yes, it is all very nice, Dill flips over the pages of *The Times* (why is he wearing his good blue jacket and his natty grey trousers, he never starts that until May and here it is only April) and Cornelia does the wifely thing, she keeps his plate stacked with fresh toast and wipes the corners of her mouth (which she has rouged before breakfast, for a change) very nicely, with the edge of the fringed napkin (which belongs to the linen set they don't usually use when they are alone).

And it is all very nice (and a little bit formal), only that the house looks queerly different to you now, no longer quite your own, it no longer holds you as it held you yesterday. Yet there have been days when those four walls were so dear to you, too dear, times when they hemmed you in until you felt like a caged animal. Today you rather wish they pressed in closer. But the walls seem all made of doors today. Now the boredom that weighed pleasantly yesterday is gone. Why did you not whisper yesterday, while there was still time, why did you not shout it yesterday while you still had the voice—that that boredom was a good thing, let us preserve it, Dill, it is good, it is warm, it is real; it cannot be said today. No, no, and a good thing too, for this is life, life as it is spoken in the Twentieth Century, will you have a little toast dear? No? really not? then how about a second cup of coffee, well for heaven's sake, those politicians! when will they leave off cutting one another's throats?—all so very delicate and stilted, all so very fine and quiet, so civilized, so neat, the corpse inside in the bedroom but the play's the thing and let's not forget our very fine modern manners. (And why, with that impossibly gay suit, has he chosen that impossibly gay tie—a bow tie, does he think it's Spring?) but why in such a hurry, Dill, Dill darling—"You've left half your coffee, it's cold, Dill, let me pour you another cup? it's still hot." And you have the specious joy of seeing him stay against his will and drink his second cup of coffee, which he clearly doesn't want.

So he wipes his mouth and puts his fancy napkin down and stands there smiling at you quite politely. This is the moment for you to rise and casually murder the butler and come back and help your husband with his coat. But you can't make the grade. For you see it all suddenly, you see it there in his face, reluctant as he is to hurt you. He does have an actual existence outside of you, and he is anxious to leave you now and enter it. You see it in his face. It is clearer than any of the things you told yourself—and he cannot help revealing it to you. He will be lost to you the minute he walks out of your sight; he will be back, of course, but this time and forever after you will know that he has been away, clean away, on his own. You see it in his face, and your heart, which had sunk to the lowest bottom, suddenly sinks lower.

"Don't go yet." It is time to murder the butler, but you walk instead— or lilt, for you cannot trust yourself to walk—to your husband, and you begin a wretched game of opening up each button of his coat after he has fastened it. You go on playing the game together, both of you laughing, it may be a little ruefully. He lets you get all the buttons undone at last, and then when you press yourself against him like a very small girl suddenly, he puts his arms around you and holds you—oh *fairly* tight, you think, but you can feel his arms relaxing, you can feel goodbye in his fingertips. You indulge yourself anyway for a mad whirling second, you steal what he doesn't want to give you, the illusion of comfort against his apocryphal chest, the illusion that he is holding you so tightly that he will never let you go. And then you give up, quite nicely, and stand back surveying him with your head on one side. Very definitely you refrain from asking him why the Spring suit, the bow tie. Quite loudly you do not ask him what time he will be home.

He tells you, though, he tells you everything. "I'll be a little late," he says; "I've got to stop off someplace for a cocktail or something." I'll be a little late, he tells you, with his gay-deceiver's troubled eyes, with his blue serge coat and light grey pants, and with the tiny pause he gives his words, I'll be a little late because I've got to stop off for a cocktail or something—with my girl; because I'm helpless, Cornelia, helpless, caught in as strong a web as your misery makes for you . . .

In a minute now the pain will go tearing and surging through the veils, drop the curtain on the polished comedy—but hold it for another moment. "Oh then," you say, reaching up, quite coy, quite gay, "you must let me fix your tie in a better bow, if you are stopping off someplace for a cocktail or something." Tweak, tweak, like an idiot, at his gay bow tie. "Which will you have, my darling, my blessing or my cake? And always remember, little one, that everything you do reflects on me," but this is bad, you realize, and turning with your hands raised in a rather silly gesture that is meant for mocking admiration, you wave him off. "There, there we are, now off with you in a cloud of dust."

B plus for that one, little sister, you tell yourself wearily, as you stand there hearing the door slam, and you wait there a minute but he doesn't come back, he isn't coming back, and if he were going to telephone you from the corner drug-store he would have done it by now, and you walk back past the laden table and you do not sweep the cups and saucers off the table, nor do you scream nor do you turn on the gas nor do you telephone the boy that used to take you dancing (though you think of all these things), nor do you fall in a heap sobbing on the empty bed (though that is what you thought you wanted to do)—you merely stand at the kitchen sink letting the hot water run to grow hotter, and you say to the cold walls reproachfully, "Oh Dill, Dill . . . oh Jimsie, Jimsie . . ." and when the doorbell rings at last you know that it is not Dill and not Jimsie but merely the man collecting last week's laundry.

(1932–1963) Born in Boston, Sylvia Plath graduated from Smith College and took her M.A. at Cambridge University in England, where she lived with her husband, poet Ted Hughes. She won many awards for poetry and the *Mademoiselle* College Fiction Contest, an experience recollected in her novel *The Bell Jar* (1963). Her many poems have been published in four volumes. Finally, unable to resolve the role conflicts involved in being a woman writer, she committed suicide.

THE JAILOR

My night sweats grease his breakfast plate.
The same placard of blue fog is wheeled into position
With the same trees and headstones.
Is that all he can come up with,
The rattler of keys?

I have been drugged and raped.
Seven hours knocked out of my right mind
Into a black sack
Where I relax, foetus or cat,
Lever of his wet dreams.

Something is gone.
My sleeping capsule, my red and blue zeppelin,
Drops me from a terrible altitude.
Carapace smashed,
I spread to the beaks of birds.

O little gimlets!
What holes this papery day is already full of!

THE SUBMISSIVE WIFE

He has been burning me with cigarettes,
Pretending I am a Negress with pink paws.
I am myself. That is not enough.

The fever trickles and stiffens in my hair.
My ribs show. What have I eaten?
Lies and smiles.
Surely the sky is not that colour,
Surely the grass should be rippling.

All day, gluing my church of burnt matchsticks,
I dream of someone else entirely.
And he, for this subversion,
Hurts me, he
With his armoury of fakery.

His high, cold masks of amnesia.
How did I get here?
Indeterminate criminal,
I die with variety—
Hung, starved, burned, hooked!

I imagine him
Impotent as distant thunder,
In whose shadow I have eaten my ghost ration.
I wish him dead or away.
That, it seems is the impossibility,

That being free. What would the dark
Do without fevers to eat?
What would the light
Do without eyes to knife, what would he
Do, do, do without me?

IMAGE TWO

THE MOTHER:

ANGEL OR "MOM"?

Whether popular stereotype or profound archetype, the image of mother is an ambivalent one. The sentimental Mother's Day vision of "the one who means the world to me" and the image of the all-powerful "Mom" who castrates her sons reflect centuries of romantic exaltation of mother and the psychological theories that acknowledge her powers while deprecating them. Both images place the responsibility for the socialization of children—of all of us—absolutely upon the mother. This awesome role is reinforced by the almost universal archetype of "The Great Mother," in whom are represented both the "Good Mother" and the "Terrible Mother"—the giver of life and all its joys and the bringer of denial, pain, and death. The power of this myth, found in the symbols and rituals of almost all societies, lies in the basic truth it represents: all human beings yearn for the free-floating comfort of complete dependence and, at the same time, for independence and assertion as individuals. The desire to "return to the womb" is a metaphor for the longing for total comfort; it is also a metaphor for what Freud referred to as the death wish, the oblivion of the individual. The association of these desires with birth and death has led to the symbolization of motherhood. The universality of "The Great Mother" image and each individual's recognition of the internalization of that image accounts for the assumption that the image is natural, a part of reality. Only recently have there been serious attempts by women scholars and writers to separate the archetype from the actual women who are mothers.

In the last few years many books about motherhood, especially about mother-daughter relationships, have questioned whether the link between good and terrible mother is inevitable. Sociologist Nancy Chodorov and psychologist Dorothy Dinnerstein suggest that the link persists because of socialization that does not separate child-bearing and child-raising. Thrust into the responsibility for both roles, mothers bear the onus for the inevitable pains of growth and maturity. Freud's metaphor for the struggle, the Oedipus complex, is taken from the Greek myth of a son who can claim his royal identity only after he has murdered his father and married his mother. Unless a son can, metaphorically, overcome this desire and channel it into the adult role of separation from both parents and marriage to an adult woman, he will be an emotional cripple. For a daughter, the Oedipal struggle is to murder the mother and marry the father. Because women can never fully outgrow their desire to be like their mothers, according to this theory, they can become adults only when they identify with their mothers by becoming mothers—Freud saw them as doomed to incomplete individuation and hence to moral inferiority to men. Chodorov and Dinnerstein accept Freud's analysis that "the reproduction of mother-hood" perpetuates women's secondary roles in society; they suggest that equal parenting by fathers and mothers especially in infancy can disrupt the cycle and allow women to be ordinary human beings instead of symbols.

The works in this section express the emotional turmoil women encounter in the role of mother. They depict the gamut of human emotions—anger, resentment, bitterness, joy, pride—that accompany the physical pain and isolation of giving birth, of having to assume the role of disciplinarian, of accepting the necessary separation from one's child. Doris Betts in "Still Life with Fruit" shows how lonely, uncertain, and guilty a woman feels when giving birth in the sterile environment of a modern hospital. Gwen is made to feel like an object, a thing being manipulated, instead of an adult going through a natural process. Even so, when she holds her child, she experiences ecstasy and love along with bitterness. Her honesty with herself and with her husband leaves the reader with an impression of her strength and maturity. One feels that she will continue to grow so that she can, like the mother in Ernest Gaines's story "The Sky Is Gray," encourage her child's growth toward adulthood. But the realism Betts uses to describe the birth process and Gwen's ambivalence let us understand why a mother might cling to her child as all she has to show for the anguish she has suffered. The castrating "Mom" is a woman caught in the weakness of the dependent role assigned to mothers in our society. A recent article identified the audience for daytime educational programs as prisoners, the handicapped, mothers at home with young children; mothers in this category find it hard to transcend their dependency.

Gwendolyn Brooks, Gaines, and Isabella Gardner point out the price mothers pay to acquire the strength they need to be fully adult. In "The Mother" Brooks repudiates the image of abortion as unnatural, as devoid of love and strongly asserts her love and sense of loss. She refuses guilt as she asserts that "even in my deliberateness I was not deliberate." She assumes full responsibility, refusing to "whine that the crime was other than mine." In "The Sky Is Gray" the mother must function as father and mother. Although she departs from the tender role expected by her minister and her sister, she insists that her son learn to cope with the realities of life regardless of his pain. In this story the child accepts both her authority and the tender help she gives him when he is suffering from a toothache; he is not ambivalent about her, seeing her both as a strong, brave adult and as a pitiful woman overburdened by poverty and loneliness. He reacts by wanting to grow up to help and protect her—perhaps an indication that Chodorov's and Dinnerstein's thesis is correct. Since the mother plays both male and female roles, she frees her son from overdependence on her.

Gaines's mother allows her son to go beyond the Oedipal relationship. Harold Brodkey's story "Verona: A Young Woman Speaks" shows the complexity of the Oedipal myth for females. The child of doting parents who share the parenting role, the daughter cannot accept her father's courtship. She feels her mother's jealousy of her father's love for her while realizing that her father's love for his wife restrains her power. The mother's limitation is both a welcome relief and a deprivation; though jealous of her mother's adult relationship with her father she rejoices in her sense of identity with her mother. She sees herself and her mother as "moons; we brighten and wane; and after a while, he comes to us, to the moons, the big one, and the little one, and we welcome him, and he is always, to my surprise, he is always surprised, as if he didn't deserve to be loved. . . ." In the battle for the child's love, "Momma was the winner"; the two are bonded by their knowledge of "how we loved men and how dangerous men were and how they stole everything from you no matter what you gave. . . ." This story illustrates men's archetypal feeling that women possess a mysterious secret that men cannot penetrate, that women are closer to a knowledge of reality because of their role as mothers. Men's sense of being excluded—that somehow they "don't deserve to be loved" wholeheartedly for themselves—sufficiently explains their fear and anger toward women. Brodkey invites us to see fathers not as domineering patriarchs but as human beings in need of love.

In the remaining selections, writers explore the mother-daughter relationship. Catherine Davis's speaker both admires her mother for her individuality and freedom and resents her own small role in her mother's life. "SHE/gave me life/ . . . and/here I am" frames a description of the mother's independent life; the daughter faces alone the responsibility of living her own life, of becoming adult. Her fear comes to us through the form of the poem, symbolized by the large letters of "SHE." Similarly, a mother's deep fears for her daughter lurk under the surface of Isabella Gardner's poem "At a Summer Hotel." She fears for the daughter's future: will she be raped as Europa was by Zeus; will she become the bride of the god of the underworld, sentenced to half a life in darkness like Persephone; or will she find happiness in love, as does Miranda in Shakespeare's *The Tempest?* Her anxiety includes her own fear of losing her daughter as she moves into adulthood. Europa and Miranda in their stories are their father's daughters, essentially motherless; Persephone's mother, the goddess Demeter, was powerless to prevent Persephone's marriage to Hades, though she did win for her the right to return to earth periodically. What will happen to the mother when her daughter leaves her? In her role as mother, she has given up her expectation of being "roused by these roses roving wild," her adult sexual role. She reflects Gwen's anxiety in "Still Life with Fruit" that motherhood is a deprivation, a loss, and the implication of "SHE" that somehow it ought to be. Gardner's poem reinforces with myth the difficulty of separating one's human need for pleasure and assertion from the selflessness that society's images of mothers project upon women.

The stories by Goldberg, Phillips, and Munro explore the deep layers of myth from a daughter's perspective. "We think back through our mothers if we are women," Virginia Woolf says in *A Room of One's Own*; she saw clearly that a woman's maturity requires coming to terms with her mother. In "Gifts" Myra Goldberg shows the tensions between a sixty-five-year-old mother and her thirty-year-old daughter; the daughter's reluctance to accept a gift symbolizes her sense of herself as a separate individual. Yet, being adult, she can see that her mother's need to give is also a symbol—of love, of recognition of aging, of her own individuality. The story asks the reader to perceive the relationship as one of *inter*dependence; as adults, the women must both give and take. Kate and her mother in Phillips's story come to the same realization. The pewter candle holders they give each other are souvenirs of their recognition of their mutual needs. Kate needs her mother to "defend [her] . . . choices"; her mother needs Kate to validate *her* choices by becoming a mother and giving her grandchildren. But the mother can receive validation by other means: "If you like yourself, I must have done something right," she says. Though her daughter is not replicating her experience as a mother, she is repeating her role as teacher. Kate and her mother communicate, without words, sharing their deepest knowledge; the honesty of their relationship contrasts with Kate's brother's reluctance to tell his mother the truth about her impending death. Phillips acknowledges the special bond between mother and daughter without reducing either to mere role playing.

In stressing the negative aspects of the mother-daughter bond, Alice Munro's "Royal Beatings" probes psychic depths seldom expressed in literature. Making Flo a stepmother gives credence to Rose's dream that a real mother would be different from the one she knows—a common childhood fantasy to relieve the resentment at powerlessness. The effectiveness of Flo's appeal to her husband to help discipline the child forces Rose to give up the Oedipal fancy that her father will be her ally. The sense all three characters have that they are acting, playing out inevitable roles that they desire and enjoy, affirms the beating as a societal necessity, even though it occurs in the privacy of the home. The shame and guilt all three characters feel symbolize the difficulty our society has had in facing up to the violence—latent or actual—inherent in our most intimate roles. The secret pleasure with which Rose has provoked the beating and with which she accepts Flo's peace offering of food is a symbol of a child's joy in experiencing itself as an individual, in rejecting the parents. Munro's story makes clear the emotional strength of social roles; but bringing to our conscious attention emotions usually hidden is at least a beginning toward removing the circumstances that perpetuate them. Since we as children need to provoke parental rejection to become adults, perhaps we can, like Myra Goldberg's persona, come to accept parental gifts as symbols of their own pain in giving us the freedom to reject them. Only if we go beyond the Oedipal situation—if both parents and children assume adulthood—can the violence that accompanies the need for dominance be diminished. To start change with our most intimate relationships may be easier and more effective, in the long run, than to try to reform the social institutions of patriarchy from the outside. If we can change the wars in the family, we might be able to rid ourselves of the need for wars outside.

DORIS BETTS

(b. 1932) Born in North Carolina, Doris Betts was educated at the University of North Carolina in Chapel Hill, where she now teaches. She has worked as a newspaper editor and has written several novels and many short stories. *Beasts of the Southern Wild and Other Stories* (1973) was nominated for a National Book Award in 1974.

STILL LIFE WITH FRUIT

Although Gwen said three times she felt fine, the Sister made her sit in a wheelchair and be rolled to the elevator like some invalid. Looking over her shoulder for Richard, she let one hand drop onto the rubber tire which scraped heat into her fingertips. Immediately Gwen repeated on the other side, for her fingers felt clammy and disconnected from the rest of her.

"Your husband can't come up for a while, dear," said the Sister, parking her neatly in one corner and pressing the Number 4 button. Sister was broad in the hip and wore a white skirt starched stiff as poster paper. "Are the pains bad?"

"No." Gwen sat rigid and cold, all the blood gone to her fingers. There was so much baby jammed toward her lungs that lifting her chest would have been ridiculous. Surely the Sister knew enough to say "contraction," and never "pain." For some women—not Gwen, of course—that could be a serious psychological mistake.

Besides, they weren't bad. Maybe not bad enough. Gwen had no fear of childbirth since she understood its stages perfectly, but to make a fool of herself with false labor? She'd never bear the embarrassment. To so misread the body's deepest messages—that would be like wetting one's pants on-stage.

She said, uneasily, "I hope they're not slowing down."

The Sister's face grew briefly alert, perhaps suspicious. "When's your due date?"

Gwen told her ten days ago, and the Sister said, "That's all right, then." Maybe if Gwen were Catholic, the Sister's face would seem kinder, even blessed. That led to the idea—quickly pushed aside—that had she been Catholic, bearing the first in a long row of unimpeded babies—the Sister would like her better.

On Ward Four she was rolled to a special room, told to put on the backless nightshirt and get into bed.

"And drink water. Drink lots of water," the Sister said, took her blood pressure, and left her with a thermometer cocked at an angle in her mouth.

Gwen couldn't recall anything in the doctor's pamphlet about drinking water. Maybe in this hospital it was sanctified? She jerked both hands to her abdomen, relieved when it tightened and hardened the way Dr. Somers had been promising for months. She hoped this new pang was on schedule; Richard's watch was still on Richard's arm, downstairs. She felt no pain, since she was a well-adjusted modern who accepted her womanhood. Two months ago, however, she'd decided not to try natural childbirth, mainly because the doctor who advocated it was male. She was drifting, then, away from everything male. Lately she had withdrawn from Everything, period. (The baby has eaten me, she sometimes thought.)

She climbed into the high bed, suddenly angry and alone, and discovered on the wall facing her a bronze statuette of Jesus wrenched on His cross, each shoulder drawn in its joint, His neck roped from pain, His face turned out with agony. It struck Gwen that Catholics might be downright insensitive. The Virgin Mary was one thing, but in this room on this day, this prince . . . this chaste bachelor on His way to God's bosom? To Gwen it seemed . . . well . . . tasteless.

Another Sister recorded her 98.6 temperature and drew an assortment of blood samples on glass slides and in phials. She sucked these up through a flexible brown tube and Gwen wondered if she ever sipped too hard and got a mouthful. The Sister also wrote down what Mrs. Gower had eaten and how recently and made her urinate into a steel bowl. "You take a nap, till the barber comes," she said. And giggled.

But Gwen, crackling with energy, doubled her pillow behind her and sat nearly upright, wide eyes fixed on the wracked form of Jesus in a loincloth. They must have already cast lots for His seamless robe (down on the cool, gray hospital tile) but at this stage in the crucifixion no one had yet buried a spear point in His side. He was skinnier than Gwen had always pictured Him.

Ah, to be skinny herself! To sleep on her flat stomach, walk lightly again on the balls of her feet. To own a navel that would be a hole and not a hill! Gwen made herself bear down once, as if on the toilet. No effect at all. Too early.

The Labor Room, pale green, was furnished in buffed aluminum. Its single chair was dull metal, straight, uncomfortable. Her clothes had been hung in a green wall locker next to Jesus, including the linen dress with the 24-inch-waist she hoped to wear home next week. On her bedside table was a pitcher of water and crushed ice, and a glass with a clear tube in it. She drank water as the Sister had ordered. Maybe it wet down the sliding-ramp where Junior, like some battleship, would be launched to the open sea. He felt to her like a battleship, plated turrets and stacks and projections, each pricking her own organs until they withdrew and gave him room. She sometimes felt as if her lungs had slipped slightly into each arm and her entrails been driven down her thighs.

The next nurse wore black religious garb, its hem nearly to the floor. With a black arm she set her covered tray on Gwen's mattress, said it was time for the first shave in Mrs. Gower's life, and flicked off the sheet. Gwen pressed into the pillow. She had never felt so naked—even after months of probes with gloved fingers and cold entries of the doctor's periscope. It must be a sign of her failing brain that one minute she saw her baby as a battleship; now there were periscopes thrust up his launching ramp. She had not thought clearly since that first sperm hit the egg and blew fuses all the way upstairs. Even her paintings showed it. Haphazard smears on canvas, with no design at all. Richard pretended, still, to admire them. He pretended the thought never crossed his mind that she might slice off one ear. She might have, too, if she could remember where the thing was growing.

It was the stare of a woman which embarrassed her. A religious. The young Sister gazed with interest between Gwen's thighs as she made ready to repeat (here Gwen giggled) what Delilah did to Sampson. She thought of asking the nun whether work in a maternity ward lent new appeal to chastity.

The nun said brightly, "Here we are."

"Here *we* are?" Gwen laughed again. I'm getting giddy. There must be dope in that water pitcher.

"You're very hairy." The Sister couldn't be over 20 years old. Perhaps she was still apprenticed, a novice. Sleeping single in her narrow bed, spending her days with women who slept double and who now brought her the ripe fruits of God. Her face looked pure and pale as if she were preparing to cross herself in some holy place. So it was a shock when she said, "All beautiful women are hairy. We had a movie star here once, miscarried on a promotion tour, and you could have combed her into ringlets."

Gwen could not match that so she lay, eyes closed, while the dull razor yanked out her pubic essence by the roots. She could no longer remember how she would look there, bald. She could recall sprouting her first scattered hairs as a girl, each lying flat and separate. Sparse, very soft in texture. Now would she grow-back prickly? Now, when she most needed to recapture Richard, would she scrape him like a cheese grater? Five o'clock shadow in the midnight place? When Gwen opened her eyes it seemed to her Jesus had been nailed at just the right height to get a good view from His cross.

At last the Sister's pan was black with sheep shearings. Black Sheep, have you any wool? One for the unborn boy, who lives up the lane? Gwen drank more water while the Sister took out the razor blade and wiped the last hairs on a cloth.

"When can my husband come?" asked Gwen. She felt her face pucker. "I don't have anything to read."

The Sister smiled, "Maybe after the enema." She carried out her wooly pan. Maybe she stuffed sofa cushions. And the blood-letting nun reclined on these and sipped Type O cocktails through her soft rubber tube. Maybe a "hair shirt" really meant . . .

Why, I'm just furious! Gwen thought, surprised. I'm almost homicidal!

The nurse with the enema must have been poised outside the door. Gwen barely had time to test her shaved skin with shocked fingers. Plucked chicken butt. She ought to keep her fingers away—Germs—had she not just lately picked her own nose? Maybe she bore some deep, subconscious hostility against her baby!

She jerked her hand away and lifted her hips as told onto the rubber sheet. She refused to hear the cheery conversation floating between her knees. Inside her the liquid burned. When she belched she feared the enema had risen all the way. She might sneeze and twin spurts jet out her ears. She gasped, "I can't, can't hold it in."

Quickly she was helped across the room to the toilet cubicle. God, she would never make it. She carried herself, a brimming bowl, with the least possible movement. Then she could let go and spew full every sewer pipe in the whole hospital. Through the plastic curtain the nun said happily, "You doing just fine, Mrs. Gower?" Now *there* was psychology!

"O.K.," she managed to say. "Can my husband come now?"

"You just sit there awhile," said the nun, and carried her equipment to the next plucked chicken down the hall.

Disgusting how clean the bathroom was. Gwen was a bad housekeeper —as Richard's parents kept hinting—but she couldn't see why. She was always at work, twenty projects underway at once; yet while she emptied the wastebasket, soap crud caked in the soap dish and flecks of toothpaste flew from nowhere onto the mirror. Nor could she keep pace with Richard's bladder. The disinfectant was hardly dry before he peed again and splattered everything. Yet, enemas and all, this place was clean as a monk's/nun's cell.

Gwen flushed the toilet but did not stand. In case. She had never felt so alone. Ever since she crossed two states to live in a house clotted with Gowers, she had been shrinking. The baby ate her. Now the baby's container was huge but Gwen, invisible, had no body to live in. Today she had been carried to the hospital like a package. This end up. Open with care.

"Ready for bed?"

She cleaned herself one more time and tottered out. The new nurse was in plain uniform, perhaps even agnostic. She set a cheap clock by the water pitcher. "How far apart are your pains now?"

Gwen had forgotten them. "I don't know." She was sleepy.

"Have you had any show?"

Gwen couldn't remember what "show" was. Some plug? Mucus. She didn't know. Was she expected to know everything? Couldn't the fool nurse look on the sheets and tell? She was probably Catholic, too, and her suit was in the cleaners.

"Your husband can visit in a minute, now. And your doctor's on the floor."

Gwen fell back on the skimpy pillow. She drowsed, one hand dropped like a fig-leaf over her cool pubis.

"How's it going?" Richard said. His voice was very loud.

"Going!" Gwen flew awake. "It's gone!" she said bitterly. "Gone down the toilet! I don't even have any phlegm left in my throat. All of it. Whoosh." Suddenly he looked a good five years younger than she, tanned, handsome. Joe College. He looked well-fed, padded with meat and vegetables and plump with his own cozy waste from meat and vegetables. "Where in hell have you been?"

"In the waiting room." He yanked his smile into a straight line. "You having a bad time?"

She stared at the ceiling. "They shaved me."

"Oh." He gave a laugh nearly dry enough for a sympathetic cluck. Give the little chicken a great big cluck. Ever since they'd moved in with his parents Gwen had been the Outsider and Richard the Hypocrite. If she talked liberal and Mr. Gower conservative, Richard said nervously they shared the same goals. When he left mornings for work, he kissed her goodbye in the bedroom and his mother in the kitchen. If Gwen fixed congealed salad and Mother Gower made tossed fruit, Richard ate heartily of both and gave equal praise. Lately Gwen had been drawing his caricature, in long black strokes, and he thought it was Janus.

He said, "I never thought about shaving, but it must be necessary. The doctor can probably see things better."

Things? Gwen turned her face away. Cruelly she said, "It's probably easier to clean off the blood."

"Hey Gwen," he said, and bent to kiss as much cheek as he could reach. She grabbed him. So hard it must have pinched his neck. Poor little man with a pinch on his neck! She stuck her tongue deep in his mouth and then bit his lower lip.

Uneasy, he sat in the metal chair and held her hand. "Whatever they're giving you, let's take some home," he said.

And go through this again? At first, in their rented room, she and Richard had lain in bed all day on Sundays. Sleeping and screwing, and screwing and sleeping. My come got lost in the baby's Coming. I don't even remember how it feels.

But Dr. Somers, when he came in, looked to Gwen for the first time virile and attractive. A little old, but he'd never be clumsy. For medical reasons alone, he'd never roll sleepily away and leave her crammed against the wall with a pillow still under her ass, swollen and hot. With Richard's parents on the other side of that wall, breathing lightly and listening.

She gave Dr. Somers a whore's smile to show him her hand lay in Richard's with no more feeling than paper in an envelope.

"You look just fine, Gwendolyn," he said. He nodded to Richard as if he could hardly believe a young squirt with no obvious merits could have put her in such a predicament. "We'll take a look now and see how far along things are. Mr. Gower?"

Richard went into the hall. She watched Dr. Somers put ooze on his rubber gloves. Talking with him down the valley of uplifted knees seemed now more normal than over the supper table to Richard. She lost her embarrassment with him. Besides, Dr. Somers liked art. He continued to talk to her as if the baby had not yet eaten her painting-hand, her eye for line and color. As if there would still be something of Gwen left when this was over.

While he fumbled around in her dampness, he often asked what she was painting now, or raved about Kandinsky. When she first went to his office with two missed menstrual periods, she mentioned the prints hung in his waiting room. "Black Lines" was Dr. Somers' favorite—he had seen the original at the Guggenheim on a convention in New York.

Gwen had not told him when, in her sixth month, her own admiration settled instead on Ivan Albright. Her taste shifted to Albright's warty, funereal textures, even while her disconnected hand continued to play with a palette knife and lampblack dribble. The few times her brain could get hold of the proper circuits, it made that hand pour together blobs of Elmer's glue, lighter fluid, and india ink. Voila! Mitosis extended! She had done also a few charcoal sketches of herself nude and pregnant, with no face at all under the wild black hair, or with a face rounded to a single, staring eye.

Oh, she was sore where he slid his finger! Politely he nodded uphill toward her head. "Glaswell has a sculpture in the lobby, did you see it?"

"We came in the other door."

"I was on the purchasing committee. It's metal and fiberglass, everything straining upward. That answered the board's request for a modern work consistent with the Christian view of man." He frowned. "You're hardly dilated at all. When did you feel the last one?"

"I stopped feeling anything right after that enema."

He thrust deeper. "False alarm, I'm afraid. But your departure date—when is it? I want you well rested before a long trip."

"In two weeks." Richard was being drafted. Once he left for the army,

Gwen would take the baby home to her parents. The Gowers expected her to stay here, of course, but she would not. Last week she had given Dr. Somers all her good reasons, one by one. When the baby came, she planned to give them to Richard. And if he dared balk, she intended to go into a post partum depression which would be a medical classic.

He laughed. "The baby's not following your schedule." His round head shook, and behind his thick glasses his eyes floated like ripe olives. "It's a false alarm, all right."

"But it happened just the way you said. An ache in the back. That cramp-feeling. And it settled down right by the clock." To her humiliation, Gwen started to cry. "I'm overdue, goddammit. He must weigh 50 pounds up there. What in hell is he waiting for?"

Dr. Somers withdrew and stripped off the glove. He looked at Jesus. thoughtfully. He scrubbed his hands in a steel pan. "Tell you what, Gwendolyn. Stop that crying now. It's suppertime anyway; let's keep you overnight. A little castor oil at bedtime. If nothing happens by morning, I'll induce labor."

"You can skip the castor oil," Gwen said, sniffing hard. "It'll go through me like . . . like a marble down a drainpipe." She did not know how he might induce labor. Some powerful uterine drug? She pictured herself convulsing, held down by a crowd of orderlies and priests. "Induce it how?"

"Puncture the membranes," he said cheerfully. He looked so merry she got an ugly superimposed picture: Boy, straight pin, balloons. "I'll just have a word with your husband."

An hour later they demoted Gwen from the Labor Room and down the hall to a plain one, where she lay alongside a woman who was pleased to announce she had just had her tubes tied. "And these old Roman biddies hate it. Anybody that screws ought to get caught at it—that's their motto."

The Roman biddy who happened to be helping Gwen into bed did not even turn, although her face blotched in uneven red. Her cheeks ripened, their anger as disconnected from her soul as Gwen's painting-hand was adrift from her brain. Among the red patches her mouth said, perfectly controlled, "I wouldn't talk too much, Mrs. Gower. I'd get my rest."

The woman in the next bed was Ramona Plumpton, and she had four babies already. With this last one she'd nearly bled to death. "This is the best hospital in town, though, and I'm a Baptist. The food's good and it's the cleanest. No staph infections." Behind one hand she added, "I hear, though, they'll save the baby first, no matter what. That puts it down to a 50–50 chance in my book. Is this your first, honey?"

"Yes. They're going to induce labor so I can travel soon. My husband's joining the army." She hoped Richard would not mention false labor, not in front of this veteran.

"You're smart to follow him from camp to camp." Perhaps to counteract her hemorrhage, Mrs. Plumpton had painted rosy apples on each cheek. "The women that hang around after soldiers! You wouldn't believe it!"

Gwen thought about that. There she'd be, home with her beard growing out, while Richard entered some curly, practiced woman. Huge breasts with nipples lined like a pair of prunes. Like Titian, she arranged the woman, adjusted the light. She made the woman cock one heavy arm so she could stipple reddish fur underneath.

"Bringing it on like that, you'll birth fast," said Mrs. Plumpton. " A dry birth, but fast. I was in labor a day and a half with my first and I've got stretch marks you wouldn't believe. Calvin says I look like the tatooed lady."

Gwen assigned Mrs. Plumpton's broad, blushing face to the prostitute in Fort Bragg and tied off her tubes with a scarlet ribbon.

Richard came by but said he wasn't allowed to stay. He'd driven all the way uptown to bring Gwen some books—one of Klee prints and a *Playboy* magazine and three paperbacks about British murders. Gwen usually enjoyed multiple murders behind the vicarage, after tea, discovered by spinsters and solved by Scotland Yard.

He kissed her very tenderly and she stared into one of his eyes. The large woman was imprinted there already, peach-colored, her heart-of-gold glowing through her naked skin.

"It's very common and you're not to feel bad about it."

She touched Richard's mouth with her fingers. Did a dry birth have anything in common with dry sex? It sounded harder. She reached beyond him and drank a whole glass of water.

". . . Dr. Somers says there's nothing to it. I'll be here tomorrow long before anything happens."

"Now don't you worry," Gwen said, just to remind him what his duty was. She got down a little more water.

Richard said his parents, downstairs, were not allowed to visit. "They send you their love. Mom's getting everything ready."

Sweeping lint from under our marriage bed. Straightening my skirts on their hangers. She can't come near my cosmetics without tightening every lid and bottle-cap.

"Mom's a little worried about induced labor. Says it doesn't seem natural." He patted her through the sheet. "They've both come to love you like a daughter."

When he had gone Ramona Plumpton said, "Well, he's good *looking.*" It wasn't much, she meant, but it was something. "Between you and him, that ought to be a pretty baby. You want a boy or a girl?"

"Girl." They had mainly discussed a son, to bear both grandfathers' names. William Everest Gower. Suddenly she did want a daughter. And she'd tell her from the first that school dances, fraternity pins, parked cars —it all led down to this. This shaved bloat in a bed with a reamed-out gut.

She read until the nurse brought castor oil, viscous between two layers of orange juice. It made her gag, but she got it down.

For a long time she could not sleep. Too many carts of metal implements were rolled down the hall; ploughshares rattled in buckets, and once a whole harvesting machine clashed out of the elevator.

When she finally drifted off she dreamed she found her baby hanging on a wall. Its brain had grown through the skull like fungus; and suspended from its wafer-head was a neckless wet sack with no limbs at all. Gwen started to cry and a priest came in carrying a delicate silver pitchfork. He told her to hush, he hadn't opened the membranes yet. When he pricked the soft bag it fell open and spilled out three perfect male babies, each of them no bigger than her hand, and with a rosebud penis tipped with one very tiny thorn. The priest began to circumcise them in the name of the Father, Son, and Holy Ghost; and when a crowd gathered Gwen was pushed to the rear where she couldn't see anything but a long row of pictures—abstracts—down a long snaky hall.

She woke when somebody put a thermometer in her mouth, straight out of the refrigerator. It was no-time, not dark or light, not late, not early. She could not even remember if the year bent toward Easter or Halloween.

Pressure bloomed suddenly in her gut. She barely made it to the toilet, still munching the glass rod. She filled the bowl with stained oil and walked carefully back to bed, rubbing her swollen abdomen for tremors. She had not wakened in the night when the baby thumped, nor once felt the long leg cramps which meant he had leaned on her femoral arteries. It came to Gwen suddenly that the baby must be dead, had smothered inside her overnight. By her bed Gwen stood first on one foot, then the other, shaking herself in case he might rattle in her like a peanut. She laid the thermometer on the table, knowing it measured her cold terror. She thumped herself. Nothing thumped back.

"Time to eat!" said Ramona Plumpton, peeling a banana from her tray. She got into bed, pressing her belly with both palms.

A tall black man brought her breakfast tray. He said it was about 6:30. She had nothing but juice and black coffee which she must not drink until a nurse checked her temperature and said it was fine. "No labor pains?"

"No. And he isn't moving!"

"He's waiting for *you* to move him," she said with a smile, and marked a failing grade on Gwen's chart. Later a resident pulled the curtain around her bed and thrust a number of fingers into her, all the wrong size. He said they'd induce at nine o'clock. She played with that awhile: induce, seduce. Reduce, produce. She folded out *Playboy's* nude Girl-of-the-Month, also hairless, with tinted foam rubber skin. There was an article which claimed Miss April read Nietzsche and collected Guatemalan postage stamps, preferred the Ruy Lopez in chess, and had once composed an oratorio. Miss April owned two glistening nipples which someone—the photographer?—had just sucked to points before the shutter clicked.

At nine, strangers rolled Gwen into what looked like a restaurant kitchen, Grade A, and strapped her feet wide into steel stirrups on each side of a hard table. The small of her back hurt. Gwen wanted to brace it with the flat of one hand, but someone tied it alongside her hip. "Don't do that!" Gwen said, flapping her left out of reach. A nurse plucked it from the air like a tame partridge. "Regular procedure," said the nurse, and tied it in place.

Through a side door came Dr. Somers, dressed in crisp lettuce-colored clothes. He talked briefly about the weather and Vietnam while he drove both hands into powdered rubber gloves.

Gwen broke in, "Is my baby dead?"

Above the gauze mask his eyes flared and shrank. "Certainly not." He sounded muffled and insincere.

Gwen let down her lids. Spider patterns of light and dark. Caught in the web, tiny sunspots and eclipses.

Someone spread her legs wider. She felt strange, cold things sliding in, one of them shaped like a mailed fist on a hard bronze forearm. The witches did that for Black Mass. Used a metal dildoe. Gwen was not frightened, only as shocked as a witch to find the devil's part icy, incapable of being warmed even there, at her deepest. She cracked her lids and saw the rapist bend, half bald beyond the white sheet which swaddled her knees.

Fine, said the gauze, *Just fine.* He called over a mummified henchman and he, too, admired the scene. Gwen felt herself the reverse of some tiny pocketpeepshow, some key charm through which men look at spread technicolor thighs, magnified and welcoming. Now she enclosed the peephole, and through their cold tube they gloated over her dimpled cervix, which throbbed in rhythm like a winking pear.

Helpless and angry she thought: Everything's filthy.

"Looks just fine," the henchman said, fidgeting in his green robe. Gwen wondered what the Sister thought as she rolled an enamel table across the room like the vicar's tea cart. Full of grace? Fruit of *whose* womb?

Dr. Somers said, "There'll be one quick pain, Gwendolyn. Don't jump."

Until then she had given up jumping, spread and tied down as she was. Now she knew at his lightest touch she would leap, shrieking, and his scalpel would pierce her through like a spear. The sweat on her upper lip ran hot into her mouth. Sour.

"Lie very still now," said the Sister.

The pain, when it came, was not great. If fluid spilled, Gwen could not tell since the sharp prick spilled her all over with exhalations, small grunts, muscles she did not even own falling loose. "Nothing to it," Dr. Somers said.

She shivered when the devil took himself out of her.

"Now we just wait awhile." He gave a mysterious message to the Sister, who injected something high in Gwen's arm. They freed her trembly hands and feet and rolled her back to the room she remembered well from yesterday.

Everything, magically, had been shifted here—Klee, clock, her magazines and mysteries. Mrs. Plumpton had even sent a choice collection from her candy box, mostly chocolate-covered cherries, which the Sister said Gwen couldn't eat yet. Overnight Jesus had moved very slightly on His cross and dropped His chin onto one shoulder. Yet, His exhaustion looked faked. Forewarned, He waited the shaking and dark. He was listening for that swift zipper rent in the veil of the tabernacle, ceiling to floor. Three days from now (Count them: three) and the great stone would roll.

Gwen stared at the Sister who helped her into bed. Was this the one who shifted the figurines? Did she carry under her habit, even now, the next distraught bronze who, when cued, would cry out about being forsaken?

Politely, Gwen asked, "You like your work here?"

"Of course. All my patients are happy. You should sleep now, Mrs. Gower, and catnap from now on. Things will happen by themselves."

Trusting no one, Gwen opened her eyes as wide as they would go. Her face was one huge wakeful eye, like a headlamp. "Is my husband outside?"

"Not yet," smiled the Sister. "Can I get you anything before I go? No? And drink water."

The baby might have died from drowning. Unbaptized, but drowned. Gwen was certain she did not sleep, yet Dr. Somers was suddenly there in a business suit, patting her arm. "You've started nicely," he said.

She felt dizzy from the hypodermic. She announced she would not give birth after all, having changed her mind. Her body felt drawn and she sat up to see if her feet had been locked into traction. Dr. Somers said Mr. Gower had come by and been sent on to work—there was plenty of time. He faded, sharpened again to say Gwendolyn was to ask the nurse when she needed it.

The next thing she noticed was a line of figures who climbed in her window, rattling aside the venetian blinds and straddling a radiator, then crossing her room and marching out into the hall. It was very peculiar, since her room was on the hospital's fourth floor. Most of the people did not speak or even notice her. A few nodded, slightly embarrassed to find her lying by their path, then drew away toward the wall and passed by like Levites on the other side.

One was a frightened young Jewish girl, hardly fourteen, whose weary face showed what a hard climb it had been up the sheer brick side of the hospital. Behind her came an aging athlete in lederhosen, drunk; he wore one wing like a swan's and was yodeling *Leda-leda-Ledal-lay.* He gave Gwen a sharp look, half-lecherous, as he went by her bed, flapping his snowy wing as if it were a nuisance he could not dislodge. A workman in coveralls climbed in next; he thrust head and shoulders back out the window and called to someone, "I tell you it's already open wide enough!" After much coaxing, the penguin followed him in and rode through the room on his shoulder, so heavy the workman tottered under the glossy weight. Several of the parade kept their rude backs to her. Angry, Gwen called them by name but they would not turn, and two of the women whispered about her when they went by.

It was noon when Gwen next looked at the clock. Richard had not come back. Instantly awake and furious, Gwen swung out of the high bed. She nearly fell. She grabbed for the metal chair—Good God!—something thudded in her middle like a piledriver. She felt curiously numb and in pain at the same time. She clumped to the doorway and hung onto the frame. There was a nun at a small desk to her right, filling out charts in a lovely, complex script.

"Going to telephone my husband," Gwen said. Her voice box had fallen and each word had to be grunted up from a long distance.

A chair was slid under her. ". . . shouldn't be out of bed . . . Quickly." The nurse balanced the telephone on Gwen's knees.

She dialed and Mrs. Gower said, "Hello?" Her voice was high and sweet as if she had just broken off some soprano melody. Gwen said nothing. "Hello? Hello? Is anybody there?"

With great effort, short of breath, she said, "May I speak to Richard Gower? Please?"

"He's eating lunch."

Gwen looked at the far wall. A niche, some figurines, a lighted candle. She took a deep breath. When she screamed full blast, no doubt, the candle would blow out twelve feet away and across town the old lady's eardrum would spatter all over the telephone. But before she got half enough air sucked in she heard, "Gwen? That's not you? Gwen, good heavens, you're not out of bed? Richard! Richard, come quick!"

Gwen could hear the chair toppling at the table, Richard's heavy shoes running down the hall and then, "Gwen? Gwen, you're all right?"

Wet and nasal, the breath blew out of her. "You just better get yourself over here, Richard Gower. That's all," she wailed. "You just quit eating and come this very minute. How can you eat at a time like this?"

Richard swore the doctor said they had hours yet. He was on his way right now and he hadn't even been *able* to eat, thinking of her.

She told him to hurry and slammed down the phone. The nun was looking at her, shaking her headdress. She half-pushed Gwen into bed. "Now you've scared him," she said gently.

Gwen shook free of her wide black sleeve. The next pain hit her and this one was pain—not a "contraction" at all. One more lie in a long line of lies. "Long-line-of-lies," she recited to herself, and got through the pain by keeping rhythm.

DORIS BETTS

81

>One more lie
>In-a
>Longline
>Of Lies.

On the next pain she remembered to breathe deep and count. She needed fourteen long breaths to get through it, and only the six gasps in the middle were really bad.

By the time Richard trotted in she was up to twenty-two breaths, and most of them were hard ones in the center without much taper on either end. He stopped dead, his mouth crooked, and Gwen knew she must look pale. Perhaps even ugly. She could no longer remember why she had wanted him there.

"Good," said Dr. Somers. "We were just taking her in."

Richard kissed her. Gwen would not say anything. He rubbed her forehead with his fingers. New wrinkles had broken there, perhaps, like Ramona's stretch marks. As they rolled her into the Delivery Room, Gwen saw that Jesus had perked up a lot, gotten His second wind. She closed her eyes counting mentally her pains in tune: One and two and three-three-three. Four-four-four. Five-five-five. Words caught up slowly with the music in her head: Mary had a little Lamb. Little Lamb. Little . . .

When they made her sit upright on the table so an anesthetic could be shot into her spine, Gwen hurt too much from the bending even to feel the puncture. They had trouble getting her spread and tied into this morning's position; she had begun to thrash around and moan. She could not help the thrashing, yet she enjoyed it, too. If they'd let go of me once, I'd flop all over this damn sterile floor like a whale on the beach. I'd bellow like an elephant.

That reminded her of something Dr. Somers had said—that in the delivery room most Negro women prayed. *Jesus, Oh Lord, Sweet Jesus!* And most white women, including the high-born, cursed. Oh you damn fool, Gwen groaned (aloud, probably). It's *all* swearing!

Oh Jesus!

Oh Hell!

They scratched at her thighs with pins and then combs and then kleenex and Dr. Somers said that proved the anesthetic was working. Gwen fell rather quickly from agony to half-death and floated loose, broken in two at the waist.

"Move your right foot," said the doctor, and somebody's right foot moved. He explained she would be able to bear down, by will, even though she would notice only the intent to do so, and not feel herself pushing. So when they said bear-down, Gwen thought about that, and somebody else bore down somewhere to suit them.

"High forceps." Two hands molded something below her navel, outside, and pressed it.

"Now," said the mummified henchman.

THE MOTHER: ANGEL OR "MOM"?

The huge overhead light had the blueness of a gas flame. She might paint it, staring, on a round canvas. She might call the painting Madonna's Eye. She might even rise up into it and float loose in the salty eye of the Blessed Damozel like a dustmote.

Suddenly the doctor was very busy and, like a magician, tugged out of nowhere a long and slimy blue-gray thing, one gut spilling from its tail. No, that was cord, umbilical cord. He dropped the mass wetly on the sheet near Gwen's waist, groped into an opening at one end. Then that blunt end of it rolled, became a soft head on a stringy neck, rolled farther and had a face, bas relief, carved shallow on one side. The mouth gave a sickly mew and, before her eyes, the whole length began to bleach and to pinken. Gwen could hardly breathe from watching while it lay loosely on her middle and somehow finished being born of its own accord, by will, finally shaped itself and assumed a new color. Ribs tiny as a bird's sprang outward—she could see their whiteness through the skin. The baby screamed and shook a fist wildly at the great surgical light.

Like electricity, that scream jolted Gwen's every cell. She vibrated all over. "That's natural," said Dr. Somers, "that little nervous chill." He finished with the cord, handed the baby to a man in a grocer's apron and began to probe atop her abdomen. "We'll let the placenta come and it's all done. He's a beautiful boy, Gwendolyn."

The pediatrician she and Richard had chosen was already busy at another table. Cleaning him, binding him, piling him into a scale for weight. Dr. Somers explained that Gwen must lie perfectly flat in bed, no pillow, so the spinal block would not give her headaches. If she'd drunk enough water, as ordered, her bladder would soon recover from the drug. Otherwise they'd use a catheter—no problem.

The Sister, her face as round as the operating light, bent over her. "Have you picked out a name?"

"No," Gwen lied. *She* needed the new name. *She* was the one who would never be the same.

". . . a small incision so you wouldn't be torn by the birth. An episiotomy. I'll take the stitches now." Dr. Somers winked between her knees. "Some women ask me to take an extra stitch. To tighten them for their husbands."

Stitch up the whole damn thing, Gwen thought. They were scraping her numb thighs with combs again.

". . . may feel like hemorrhoids for a few days . . ."

She went to sleep. When she woke there was a small glass pram alongside, and they were ready to roll her back to her room. Gwen tried to sit up but a nun leaned on her shoulder. "Flat on your back, Mrs. Gower."

"I want to see."

"Shhh." The Sister bent over the small transparent box and lifted the bundle and flew it face down at her, so Gwen could see the baby as if he floated prone in the air. His head was tomato-red, now, and the nun's starched wide sleeves flew out beyond his flaming ears. A flat, broad nose.

Gwen would never be able to get the tip of her own breast into that tiny mouth. There was peach fuzz dusted on his skull except in the top, where a hank of coarse black hair grew forward.

Gwen touched her own throat to make sure no other hand had grabbed it. Something crawled under her skin, like the spider who webbed her eyelids tightening all lines. In both her eyes the spider spilled her hot, wet eggs—those on the right for bitterness, and those on the left for joy.

GWENDOLYN BROOKS

(b. 1917) A resident of Chicago, Gwendolyn Brooks is the poet laureate of Illinois; she has won many awards, including the Pulitzer Prize, and two Guggenheim Fellowships. She has had a long and distinguished career, having written eight volumes of poetry, a novel, and in 1972 her autobiography, *Report from Part One*. She has also edited many volumes, and in 1975 *A Capsule Course in Black Poetry Writing* appeared.

THE MOTHER

Abortions will not let you forget.
You remember the children you got that you did not get,
The damp small pulps with a little or with no hair,
The singers and workers that never handled the air.
You will never neglect or beat
Them, or silence or buy with a sweet.
You will never wind up the sucking-thumb
Or scuttle off ghosts that come.
You will never leave them, controlling your luscious sigh,
Return for a snack of them, with gobbling mother-eye.

I have heard in the voices of the wind the voices of my dim killed children.
I have contracted. I have eased
My dim dears at the breasts they could never suck.
I have said, Sweets, if I sinned, if I seized
Your luck
And your lives from your unfinished reach,
If I stole your births and your names,
Your straight baby tears and your games,
Your stilted or lovely loves, your tumults, your marriages, aches, and
    your deaths,

If I poisoned the beginnings of your breaths,
Believe that even in my deliberateness I was not deliberate.
Though why should I whine,
Whine that the crime was other than mine?—
Since anyhow you are dead.
Or rather, or instead,
You were never made.
But that too, I am afraid,
Is faulty: oh, what shall I say, how is the truth to be said?
You were born, you had body, you died.
It is just that you never giggled or planned or cried.

Believe me, I loved you all.
Believe me, I knew you, though faintly, and I loved, I loved you
All.

ERNEST J. GAINES

(b. 1933) Born in Louisiana, Ernest J.
Gaines was educated in California, where he
now lives. He has written novels, novellas,
short stories, and a work for children. In his
novel *The Autobiography of Miss Jane Pitt-
man* (1971), Gaines tells the story of a slave
woman's quest for freedom. Television versions of this novel and of "The Sky Is Gray"
have won great acclaim. Gaines's most recent
works include *In My Father's House* (1978)
and *Of Love and Dust* (1979).

THE SKY IS GRAY

I

Go'n be coming in a few minutes. Coming round that bend down there
full speed. And I'm go'n get out my handkerchief and wave it down, and
we go'n get on it and go.

I keep on looking for it, but Mama don't look that way no more. She's
looking down the road where we just come from. It's a long old road, and
far's you can see you don't see nothing but gravel. You got dry weeds on
both sides, and you got trees on both sides, and fences on both sides, too.
And you got cows in the pastures and they standing close together. And
when we was coming out here to catch the bus I seen the smoke coming
out of the cows's noses.

I look at my mama and I know what she's thinking. I been with Mama
so much, just me and her, I know what she's thinking all the time. Right
now it's home—Auntie and them. She's thinking if they got enough wood—
if she left enough there to keep them warm till we get back. She's thinking
if it go'n rain and if any of them go'n have to go out in the rain. She's
thinking 'bout the hog—if he go'n get out, and if Ty and Val be able to
get him back in. She always worry like that when she leaves the house.
She don't worry too much if she leave me there with the smaller ones, 'cause
she know I'm go'n look after them and look after Auntie and everything
else. I'm the oldest and she say I'm the man.

I look at my mama and I love my mama. She's wearing that black coat and that black hat and she's looking sad. I love my mama and I want to put my arm round her and tell her. But I'm not supposed to do that. She say that's weakness and that's crybaby stuff, and she don't want no crybaby round her. She don't want you to be scared, either. 'Cause Ty's scared of ghosts and she's always whipping him. I'm scared of the dark, too, but I make 'tend I ain't. I make 'tend I ain't 'cause I'm the oldest, and I got to set a good sample for the rest. I can't ever be scared and I can't ever cry. And that's why I never said nothing 'bout my teeth. It's been hurting me and hurting me close to a month now, but I never said it. I didn't say it 'cause I didn't want act like a crybaby, and 'cause I know we didn't have enough money to go have it pulled. But, Lord, it been hurting me. And look like it wouldn't start till at night when you was trying to get yourself little sleep. Then soon's you shut your eyes—ummm-ummm, Lord, look like it go right down to your heartstring.

"Hurting, hanh?" Ty'd say.

I'd shake my head, but I wouldn't open my mouth for nothing. You open your mouth and let that wind in, and it almost kill you.

I'd just lay there and listen to them snore. Ty there, right 'side me, and Auntie and Val over by the fireplace. Val younger than me and Ty, and he sleeps with Auntie. Mama sleeps round the other side with Louis and Walker.

I'd just lay there and listen to them, and listen to that wind out there, and listen to that fire in the fireplace. Sometimes it'd stop long enough to let me get little rest. Sometimes it just hurt, hurt, hurt. Lord, have mercy.

2

Auntie knowed it was hurting me. I didn't tell nobody but Ty, 'cause we buddies and he ain't go'n tell anybody. But some kind of way Auntie found out. When she asked me, I told her no, nothing was wrong. But she knowed it all the time. She told me to mash up a piece of aspirin and wrap it in some cotton and jugg it down in that hole. I did it, but it didn't do no good. It stopped for a little while, and started right back again. Auntie wanted to tell Mama, but I told her, "Uh-uh." 'Cause I knowed we didn't have any money, and it just was go'n make her mad again. So Auntie told Monsieur Bayonne, and Monsieur Bayonne came over to the house and told me to kneel down 'side him on the fireplace. He put his finger in his mouth and made the Sign of the Cross on my jaw. The tip of Monsieur Bayonne's finger is some hard, 'cause he's always playing on that guitar. If we sit outside at night we can always hear Monsieur Bayonne playing on his guitar. Sometimes we leave him out there playing on the guitar.

Monsieur Bayonne made the Sign of the Cross over and over on my jaw, but that didn't do no good. Even when he prayed and told me to pray some, too, that tooth still hurt me.

"How you feeling?" he say.

"Same," I say.

He kept on praying and making the Sign of the Cross and I kept on praying, too.

"Still hurting?" he say.

"Yes, sir."

Monsieur Bayonne mashed harder and harder on my jaw. He mashed so hard he almost pushed me over on Ty. But then he stopped.

"What kind of prayers you praying, boy?" he say.

"Baptist," I say.

"Well, I'll be—no wonder that tooth still killing him. I'm going one way and he pulling the other. Boy, don't you know any Catholic prayers?"

"I know 'Hail Mary,' " I say.

"Then you better start saying it."

"Yes, sir."

He started mashing on my jaw again, and I could hear him praying at the same time. And, sure enough, after awhile it stopped hurting me.

Me and Ty went outside where Monsieur Bayonne's two hounds was and we started playing with them. "Let's go hunting," Ty say. "All right," I say; and we went on back in the pasture. Soon the hounds got on a trail, and me and Ty followed them all 'cross the pasture and then back in the woods, too. And then they cornered this little old rabbit and killed him, and me and Ty made them get back, and we picked up the rabbit and started on back home. But my tooth had started hurting me again. It was hurting me plenty now, but I wouldn't tell Monsieur Bayonne. That night I didn't sleep a bit, and first thing in the morning Auntie told me to go back and let Monsieur Bayonne pray over me some more. Monsieur Bayonne was in his kitchen making coffee when I got there. Soon's he seen me he knowed what was wrong.

"All right, kneel down there 'side that stove," he say. "And this time make sure you pray Catholic. I don't know nothing 'bout that Baptist, and I don't want know nothing 'bout him."

3

Last night Mama say, "Tomorrow we going to town."

"It ain't hurting me no more," I say. "I can eat anything on it."

"Tomorrow we going to town," she say.

And after she finished eating, she got up and went to bed. She always go to bed early now. 'Fore Daddy went in the Army, she used to stay up late. All of us sitting out on the gallery or round the fire. But now, look like soon's she finish eating she go to bed.

This morning when I woke up, her and Auntie was standing 'fore the fireplace. She say: "Enough to get there and get back. Dollar and a half to have it pulled. Twenty-five for me to go, twenty-five for him. Twenty-five for me to come back, twenty-five for him. Fifty cents left. Guess I get little piece of salt meat with that."

"Sure can use it," Auntie say. "White beans and no salt meat ain't white beans."

"I do the best I can," Mama say.

They was quiet after that, and I made 'tend I was still asleep.

"James, hit the floor," Auntie say.

I still made 'tend I was asleep. I didn't want them to know I was listening.

"All right," Auntie say, shaking me by the shoulder. "Come on. Today's the day."

I pushed the cover down to get out, and Ty grabbed it and pulled it back.

"You, too, Ty," Auntie say.

"I ain't getting no teef pulled," Ty say.

"Don't mean it ain't time to get up," Auntie say. "Hit it, Ty."

Ty got up grumbling.

"James, you hurry up and get in your clothes and eat your food," Auntie say. "What time y'all coming back?" she say to Mama.

"That 'leven o'clock bus," Mama say. "Got to get back in that field this evening."

"Get a move on you, James," Auntie say.

I went in the kitchen and washed my face, then I ate my breakfast. I was having bread and syrup. The bread was warm and hard and tasted good. And I tried to make it last a long time.

Ty came back there grumbling and mad at me.

"Got to get up," he say. "I ain't having no teefs pulled. What I got to be getting up for?"

Ty poured some syrup in his pan and got a piece of bread. He didn't wash his hands, neither his face, and I could see that white stuff in his eyes.

"You the one getting your teef pulled," he say. "What I got to get up for. I bet if I was getting a teef pulled, you wouldn't be getting up. Shucks; syrup again. I'm getting tired of this old syrup. Syrup, syrup, syrup. I'm go'n take with the sugar diabetes. I want me some bacon sometime."

"Go out in the field and work and you can have your bacon," Auntie say. She stood in the middle door looking at Ty. "You better be glad you got syrup. Some people ain't got that—hard's time is."

"Shucks," Ty say. "How can I be strong."

"I don't know too much 'bout your strength," Auntie say; "but I know where you go'n be hot at, you keep that grumbling up. James, get a move on you; your mama waiting."

I ate my last piece of bread and went in the front room. Mama was standing 'fore the fireplace warming her hands. I put on my coat and cap, and we left the house.

<h2 style="text-align:center">4</h2>

I look down there again, but it still ain't coming. I almost say, "It ain't coming yet," but I keep my mouth shut. 'Cause that's something else she don't like. She don't like for you to say something just for nothing. She can see it ain't coming. I can see it ain't coming, so why say it ain't coming. I don't say it, I turn and look at the river that's back of us. It's so cold the smoke's just raising up from the water. I see a bunch of pool-doos not too far out—just on the other side the lilies. I'm wondering if you can eat pool-doos. I ain't too sure, 'cause I ain't never ate none. But I done ate owls and blackbirds, and I done ate redbirds, too. I didn't want to kill the redbirds, but she made me kill them. They had two of them back there. One in my trap, one in Ty's trap. Me and Ty was go'n play with them and let them go, but she made me kill them 'cause we needed the food.

"I can't," I say. "I can't."

"Here," she say. "Take it."

"I can't," I say. "I can't. I can't kill him, Mama, please."

"Here," she say. "Take this fork, James."

"Please, Mama, I can't kill him," I say.

I could tell she was go'n hit me. I jerked back, but I didn't jerk back soon enough.

"Take it," she say.

I took it and reached in for him, but he kept on hopping to the back.

"I can't, Mama," I say. The water just kept on running down my face. "I can't," I say.

"Get him out of there," she say.

I reached in for him and he kept on hopping to the back. Then I reached in farther, and he pecked me on the hand.

"I can't, Mama," I say.

She slapped me again.

I reached in again, but he kept on hopping out my way. Then he hopped to one side and I reached there. The fork got him on the leg and I heard his leg pop. I pulled my hand out 'cause I had hurt him.

"Give it here," she say, and jerked the fork out of my hand.

She reached in and got the little bird right in the neck. I heard the fork go in his neck, and I heard it go in the ground. She brought him out and helt him right in front of me.

"That's one," she say. She shook him off and gived me the fork. "Get the other one."

"I can't, Mama," I say. "I'll do anything, but don't make me do that."

She went to the corner of the fence and broke the biggest switch over there she could find. I knelt 'side the trap, crying.

ERNEST J. GAINES

"Get him out of there," she say.

"I can't, Mama."

She started hitting me 'cross the back. I went down on the ground, crying.

"Get him," she say.

"Octavia?" Auntie say.

'Cause she had come out of the house and she was standing by the tree looking at us.

"Get him out of there," Mama say.

"Octavia," Auntie say, "explain to him. Explain to him. Just don't beat him. Explain to him."

But she hit me and hit me and hit me.

I'm still young—I ain't no more than eight; but I know now; I know why I had to do it. (They was so little, though. They was so little. I 'member how I picked the feathers off them and cleaned them and helt them over the fire. Then we all ate them. Ain't had but a little bitty piece each, but we all had a little bitty piece, and everybody just looked at me 'cause they was so proud.) Suppose she had to go away? That's why I had to do it. Suppose she had to go away like Daddy went away? Then who was go'n look after us? They had to be somebody left to carry on. I didn't know it then, but I know it now. Auntie and Monsieur Bayonne talked to me and made me see.

5

Time I see it I get out my handkerchief and start waving. It's still 'way down there, but I keep waving anyhow. Then it come up and stop and me and Mama get on. Mama tell me go sit in the back while she pay. I do like she say, and the people look at me. When I pass the little sign that say "White" and "Colored," I start looking for a seat. I just see one of them back there, but I don't take it, 'cause I want my mama to sit down herself. She comes in the back and sit down, and I lean on the seat. They got seats in the front, but I know I can't sit there, 'cause I have to sit back of the sign. Anyhow, I don't want to sit there if my mama go'n sit back here.

They got a lady sitting 'side my mama and she looks at me and smiles little bit. I smile back, but I don't open my mouth, 'cause the wind'll get in and make that tooth ache. The lady take out a pack of gum and reach me a slice, but I shake my head. The lady just can't understand why a little boy'll turn down gum, and she reach me a slice again. This time I point to my jaw. The lady understands and smiles little bit, and I smile little bit, but I don't open my mouth, though.

They got a girl sitting 'cross from me. She got on a red overcoat and her hair's plaited in one big plait. First, I make 'tend I don't see her over there, but then I start looking at her little bit. She make 'tend she don't see me, either, but I catch her looking that way. She got a cold, and every now and then she h'ist that little handkerchief to her nose. She ought to blow it, but she don't. Must think she's too much a lady or something.

Every time she h'ist that little handkerchief, the lady 'side her say something in her ear. She shakes her head and lays her hands in her lap again. Then I catch her kind of looking where I'm at. I smile at her little bit. But think she'll smile back? Uh-uh. She just turn up her little old nose and turn her head. Well, I show her both of us can turn us head. I turn mine too and look out at the river.

The river is gray. The sky is gray. They have pool-doos on the water. The water is wavy, and the pool-doos go up and down. The bus go round a turn, and you got plenty trees hiding the river. Then the bus go round another turn, and I can see the river again.

I look toward the front where all the white people sitting. Then I look at that little old gal again. I don't look right at her, 'cause I don't want all them people to know I love her. I just look at her little bit, like I'm looking out that window over there. But she knows I'm looking that way, and she kind of look at me, too. The lady sitting 'side her catch her this time, and she leans over and says something in her ear.

"I don't love him nothing," that little old gal says out loud.

Everybody back there hear her mouth, and all of them look at us and laugh.

"I don't love you, either," I say. "So you don't have to turn up your nose, Miss."

"You the one looking," she say.

"I wasn't looking at you," I say. "I was looking out that window, there."

"Out that window, my foot," she say. "I seen you. Everytime I turned round you was looking at me."

"You must of been looking yourself if you seen me all them times," I say.

"Shucks," she say, "I got me all kind of boyfriends."

"I got girlfriends, too," I say.

"Well, I just don't want you getting your hopes up," she say.

I don't say no more to that little old gal 'cause I don't want have to bust her in the mouth. I lean on the seat where Mama sitting, and I don't even look that way no more. When we get to Bayonne, she jugg her little old tongue out at me. I make 'tend I'm go'n hit her, and she duck down 'side her mama. And all the people laugh at us again.

6

Me and Mama get off and start walking in town. Bayonne is a little bitty town. Baton Rouge is a hundred times bigger than Bayonne. I went to Baton Rouge once—me, Ty, Mama, and Daddy. But that was 'way back yonder, 'fore Daddy went in the Army. I wonder when we go'n see him again. I wonder when. Look like he ain't ever coming back home. . . .

Even the pavement all cracked in Bayonne. Got grass shooting right out the sidewalk. Got weeds in the ditch, too; just like they got at home.

It's some cold in Bayonne. Look like it's colder than it is home. The wind blows in my face, and I feel that stuff running down my nose. I sniff. Mama says use that handkerchief. I blow my nose and put it back.

We pass a school and I see them white children playing in the yard. Big old red school, and them children just running and playing. Then we pass a café, and I see a bunch of people in there eating. I wish I was in there 'cause I'm cold. Mama tells me keep my eyes in front where they belong.

We pass stores that's got dummies, and we pass another café, and then we pass a shoe shop, and that bald-head man in there fixing on a shoe. I look at him and I butt into that white lady, and Mama jerks me in front and tells me stay there.

We come up to the courthouse, and I see the flag waving there. This flag ain't like the one we got at school. This one here ain't got but a handful of stars. One at school got a big pile of stars—one for every state. We pass it and we turn and there it is—the dentist office. Me and Mama go in, and they got people sitting everywhere you look. They even got a little boy in there younger than me.

Me and Mama sit on that bench, and a white lady come in there and ask me what my name is. Mama tells her and the white lady goes on back. Then I hear somebody hollering in there. Soon's that little boy hear him hollering, he starts hollering, too. His mama pats him and pats him, trying to make him hush up, but he ain't thinking 'bout his mama.

The man that was hollering in there comes out holding his jaw. He is a big old man and he's wearing overalls and a jumper.

"Got it, hanh?" another man asks him.

The man shakes his head—don't want open his mouth.

"Man, I thought they was killing you in there," the other man says. "Hollering like a pig under a gate."

The man don't say nothing. He just heads for the door, and the other man follows him.

"John Lee," the white lady says. "John Lee Williams."

The little boy juggs his head down in his mama's lap and holler more now. His mama tells him go with the nurse, but he ain't thinking 'bout his mama. His mama tells him again, but he don't even hear her. His mama picks him up and takes him in there, and even when the white lady shuts the door I can still hear little old John Lee.

"I often wonder why the Lord let a child like that suffer," a lady says to my mama. The lady's sitting right in front of us on another bench. She's got on a white dress and a black sweater. She must be a nurse or something herself, I reckon.

"Not us to question," a man says.

"Sometimes I don't know if we shouldn't," the lady says.

THE MOTHER: ANGEL OR "MOM"?

"I know definitely we shouldn't," the man says. The man looks like a preacher. He's big and fat and he's got on a black suit. He's got a gold chain, too.

"Why?" the lady says.

"Why anything?" the preacher says.

"Yes," the lady says. "Why anything?"

"Not us to question," the preacher says.

The lady looks at the preacher a little while and looks at Mama again.

"And look like it's the poor who suffers the most," she says. "I don't understand it."

"Best not to even try," the preacher says. "He works in mysterious ways —wonders to perform."

Right then little John Lee bust out hollering, and everybody turn they head to listen.

"He's not a good dentist," the lady says. "Dr. Robillard is much better. But more expensive. That's why most of the colored people come here. The white people go to Dr. Robillard. Y'all from Bayonne?"

"Down the river," my mama says. And that's all she go'n say, 'cause she don't talk much. But the lady keeps on looking at her, and so she says, "Near Morgan."

"I see," the lady says.

7

"That's the trouble with the black people in this country today," somebody else says. This one here's sitting on the same side me and Mama's sitting, and he is kind of sitting in front of that preacher. He looks like a teacher or somebody that goes to college. He's got on a suit, and he's got a book that he's been reading. "We don't question is exactly our problem," he says. "We should question and question and question—question everything."

The preacher just looks at him a long time. He done put a toothpick or something in his mouth, and he just keeps on turning it and turning it. You can see he don't like that boy with that book.

"Maybe you can explain what you mean," he says.

"I said what I meant," the boy says. "Question everything. Every stripe, every star, every word spoken. Everything."

"It 'pears to me that this young lady and I was talking 'bout God, young man," the preacher says.

"Question Him, too," the boy says.

"Wait," the preacher says, "Wait now."

"You heard me right," the boy says. "His existence as well as everything else. Everything."

The preacher just looks across the room at the boy. You can see he's getting madder and madder. But mad or no mad, the boy ain't thinking 'bout him. He looks at that preacher just's hard's the preacher looks at him.

"Is this what they coming to?" the preacher says. "Is that what we educating them for?"

"You're not educating me," the boy says. "I wash dishes at night so that I can go to school in the day. So even the words you spoke need questioning."

The preacher just looks at him and shakes his head.

"When I come in this room and seen you there with your book, I said to myself, 'There's an intelligent man.' How wrong a person can be."

"Show me one reason to believe in the existence of a God," the boy says.

"My heart tells me," the preacher says.

" 'My heart tells me,' " the boy says. " 'My heart tells me.' Sure, 'My heart tells me.' And as long as you listen to what your heart tells you, you will have only what the white man gives you and nothing more. Me, I don't listen to my heart. The purpose of the heart is to pump blood throughout the body, and nothing else."

"Who's your paw, boy?" the preacher says.

"Why?"

"Who is he?"

"He's dead."

"And your mom?"

"She's in Charity Hospital with pneumonia. Half killed herself, working for nothing."

"And 'cause he's dead and she's sick, you mad at the world?"

"I'm not mad at the world. I'm questioning the world. I'm questioning it with cold logic sir. What do words like Freedom, Liberty, God, White, Colored mean? I want to know. That's why *you* are sending us to school, to read and to ask questions. And because we ask these questions, you call us mad. No sir, it is not us who are mad."

"You keep saying 'us'?"

" 'Us.' Yes—us. I'm not alone."

The preacher just shakes his head. Then he looks at everybody in the room—everybody. Some of the people look down at the floor, keep from looking at him. I kind of look 'way myself, but soon's I know he done turn his head, I look that way again.

"I'm sorry for you," he says to the boy.

"Why?" the boy says. "Why not be sorry for yourself? Why are you so much better off than I am? Why aren't you sorry for these other people in here? Why not be sorry for the lady who had to drag her child into the dentist office? Why not be sorry for the lady sitting on that bench over there? Be sorry for them. Not for me. Some way or the other I'm going to make it."

"No, I'm sorry for you," the preacher says.

"Of course, of course," the boy says, nodding his head. "You're sorry for me because I rock that pillar you're leaning on."

"You can't ever rock the pillar I'm leaning on, young man. It's stronger than anything man can ever do."

"You believe in God because a man told you to believe in God," the boy says. "A white man told you to believe in God. And why? To keep you ignorant so he can keep his feet on your neck."

"So now we the ignorant?" the preacher says.

"Yes," the boy says. "Yes." And he opens his book again.

The preacher just looks at him sitting there. The boy done forgot all about him. Everybody else make 'tend they done forgot the squabble, too.

Then I see that preacher getting up real slow. Preacher's great big old man and he got to brace himself to get up. He comes over where the boy is sitting. He just stands there a little while looking down at him, but the boy don't raise his head.

"Get up, boy," preacher says.

The boy looks up at him, then he shuts his book real slow and stands up. Preacher just hauls back and hit him in the face. The boy falls back 'gainst the wall, but he straightens himself up and looks right back at that preacher.

"You forgot the other cheek," he says.

The preacher hauls back and hit him again on the other side. But this time the boy braces himself and don't fall.

"That hasn't changed a thing," he says.

The preacher just looks at the boy. The preacher's breathing real hard like he just run up a big hill. The boy sits down and opens his book again.

"I feel sorry for you," the preacher says. "I never felt so sorry for a man before."

The boy makes 'tend he don't even hear that preacher. He keeps on reading his book. The preacher goes back and gets his hat off the chair.

"Excuse me," he says to us. "I'll come back some other time. Y'all, please excuse me."

And he looks at the boy and goes out the room. The boy h'ist his hand up to his mouth one time to wipe 'way some blood. All the rest of the time he keeps on reading. And nobody else in there say a word.

8

Little John Lee and his mama come out the dentist office, and the nurse calls somebody else in. Then little bit later they come out, and the nurse calls another name. But fast's she calls somebody in there, somebody else comes in the place where we sitting, and the room stays full.

The people coming in now, all of them wearing big coats. One of them says something 'bout sleeting, another one says he hope not. Another one says he think it ain't nothing but rain. 'Cause, he says, rain can get awful cold this time of year.

All round the room they talking. Some of them talking to people right by them, some of them talking to people clear 'cross the room, some of them talking to anybody'll listen. It's a little bitty room, no bigger than us kitchen, and I can see everybody in there. The little old room's full of smoke, 'cause you got two old men smoking pipes over by that side door. I think I feel my tooth thumping me some, and I hold my breath and wait. I wait and wait, but it don't thump me no more. Thank God for that.

I feel like going to sleep, and I lean back 'gainst the wall. But I'm scared to go to sleep. Scared 'cause the nurse might call my name and I won't hear her. And Mama might go to sleep, too, and she'll be mad if neither one of us heard the nurse.

I look up at Mama. I love my mama. I love my mama. And when cotton come I'm go'n get her a new coat. And I ain't go'n get a black one, either. I think I'm go'n get her a red one.

"They got some books over there," I say. "Want read one of them?"

Mama looks at the books, but she don't answer me.

"You got yourself a little man there," the lady says.

Mama don't say nothing to the lady, but she must've smiled, 'cause I seen the lady smiling back. The lady looks at me a little while, like she's feeling sorry for me.

"You sure got that preacher out here in a hurry," she says to that boy.

The boy looks up at her and looks in his book again. When I grow up I want be just like him. I want clothes like that and I want keep a book with me, too.

"You really don't believe in God?" the lady says.

"No," he says.

"But why?" the lady says.

"Because the wind is pink," he says.

"What?" the lady says.

The boy don't answer her no more. He just reads in his book.

"Talking 'bout the wind is pink," that old lady says. She's sitting on the same bench with the boy and she's trying to look in his face. The boy makes 'tend the old lady ain't even there. He just keeps on reading. "Wind is pink," she says again. "Eh, Lord, what children go'n be saying next?"

The lady 'cross from us bust out laughing.

"That's a good one," she says. "The wind is pink. Yes sir, that's a good one."

"Don't you believe the wind is pink?" the boy says. He keeps his head down in the book.

"Course I believe it, honey," the lady says. "Course I do." She looks at us and winks her eye. "And what color is grass, honey?"

"Grass? Grass is black."

She bust out laughing again. The boy looks at her.

"Don't you believe grass is black?" he says.

The lady quits her laughing and looks at him. Everybody else looking at him, too. The place quiet, quiet.

"Grass is green, honey," the lady says. "It was green yesterday, it's green today, and it's go'n be green tomorrow."

"How do you know it's green?"

"I know because I know."

"You don't know it's green," the boy says. "You believe it's green because someone told you it was green. If someone had told you it was black you'd believe it was black."

"It's green," the lady says. "I know green when I see green."

"Prove it's green," the boy says.

"Sure, now," the lady says. "Don't tell me it's coming to that."

"It's coming to just that," the boy says. "Words mean nothing. One means no more than the other."

"That's what it all coming to?" the old lady says. That old lady got on a turban and she got on two sweaters. She got a green sweater under a black sweater. I can see the green sweater 'cause some of the buttons on the other sweater's missing.

"Yes ma'am," the boy says. "Words mean nothing. Action is the only thing. Doing. That's the only thing."

"Other words, you want the Lord to come down here and show Hisself to you?" she says.

"Exactly, ma'am," he says.

"You don't mean that, I'm sure?" she says.

"I do, ma'am," he says.

"Done, Jesus," the old lady says, shaking her head.

"I didn't go 'long with that preacher at first," the other lady says; "but now—I don't know. When a person say the grass is black, he's either a lunatic or something's wrong."

"Prove to me that it's green," the boy says.

"It's green because the people say it's green."

"Those same people say we're citizens of these United States," the boy says.

"I think I'm a citizen," the lady says.

"Citizens have certain rights," the boy says. "Name me one right that you have. One right, granted by the Constitution, that you can exercise in Bayonne."

The lady don't answer him. She just looks at him like she don't know what he's talking 'bout. I know I don't.

"Things changing," she says.

"Things are changing because some black men have begun to think with their brains and not their hearts," the boy says.

"You trying to say these people don't believe in God?"

ERNEST J. GAINES

99

"I'm sure some of them do. Maybe most of them do. But they don't believe that God is going to touch these white people's hearts and change things tomorrow. Things change through action. By no other way."

Everybody sit quiet and look at the boy. Nobody says a thing. Then the lady 'cross the room from me and Mama just shakes her head.

"Let's hope that not all your generation feel the same way you do," she says.

"Think what you please, it doesn't matter," the boy says. "But it will be men who listen to their heads and not their hearts who will see that your children have a better chance than you had."

"Let's hope they ain't all like you, though," the old lady says. "Done forgot the heart absolutely."

"Yes ma'am, I hope they aren't all like me," the boy says. "Unfortunately, I was born too late to believe in your God. Let's hope that the ones who come after will have your faith—if not in your God, then in something else, something definitely that they can lean on. I haven't anything. For me, the wind is pink, the grass is black."

9

The nurse comes in the room where we all sitting and waiting and says the doctor won't take no more patients till one o'clock this evening. My mama jumps up off the bench and goes up to the white lady.

"Nurse, I have to go back in the field this evening," she says.

"The doctor is treating his last patient now," the nurse says. "One o'clock this evening."

"Can I at least speak to the doctor?" my mama asks.

"I'm his nurse," the lady says.

"My little boy's sick," my mama says. "Right now his tooth almost killing him."

The nurse looks at me. She's trying to make up her mind if to let me come in. I look at her real pitiful. The tooth ain't hurting me at all, but Mama says it is, so I make 'tend for her sake.

"This evening," the nurse says, and goes on back in the office.

"Don't feel 'jected, honey," the lady says to Mama. "I been round them a long time—they take you when they want to. If you was white, that's something else; but we the wrong color."

Mama don't say nothing to the lady, and me and her go outside and stand 'gainst the wall. It's cold out there. I can feel that wind going through my coat. Some of the other people come out of the room and go up the street. Me and Mama stand there a little while and we start walking. I don't know where we going. When we come to the other street we just stand there.

"You don't have to make water, do you?" Mama says.

"No, ma'am," I say.

We go on up the street. Walking real slow. I can tell Mama don't know where she's going. When we come to a store we stand there and look at the dummies. I look at a little boy wearing a brown overcoat. He's got on brown shoes, too. I look at my old shoes and look at his'n again. You wait till summer, I say.

Me and Mama walk away. We come up to another store and we stop and look at them dummies, too. Then we go on again. We pass a café where the white people in there eating. Mama tells me keep my eyes in front where they belong, but I can't help from seeing them people eat. My stomach starts to growling 'cause I'm hungry. When I see people eating, I get hungry; when I see a coat, I get cold.

A man whistles at my mama when we go by a filling station. She makes 'tend she don't even see him. I look back and I feel like hitting him in the mouth. If I was bigger, I say; if I was bigger, you'd see.

We keep on going. I'm getting colder and colder, but I don't say nothing. I feel that stuff running down my nose and I sniff.

"That rag," Mama says.

I get it out and wipe my nose. I'm getting cold all over now—my face, my hands, my feet, everything. We pass another little café, but this'n for white people, too, and we can't go in there, either. So we just walk. I'm so cold now I'm 'bout ready to say it. If I knowed where we was going I wouldn't be so cold, but I don't know where we going. We go, we go, we go. We walk clean out of Bayonne. Then we cross the street and we come back. Same thing I seen when I got off the bus this morning. Same old trees, same old walk, same old weeds, same old cracked pave—same old everything.

I sniff again.

"That rag," Mama says.

I wipe my nose real fast and jugg that handkerchief back in my pocket 'fore my hand gets too cold. I raise my head and I can see David's hardware store. When we come up to it, we go in. I don't know why, but I'm glad.

It's warm in there. It's so warm in there you don't ever want to leave. I look for the heater, and I see it over by them barrels. Three white men standing round the heater talking in Creole. One of them comes over to see what my mama want.

"Got any axe handles?" she says.

Me, Mama and the white man start to the back, but Mama stops me when we come up to the heater. She and the white man go on. I hold my hands over the heater and look at them. They go all the way to the back, and I see the white man pointing to the axe handles 'gainst the wall. Mama takes one of them and shakes it like she's trying to figure how much it weighs. Then she rubs her hand over it from one end to the other end. She turns it over and looks at the other side, then she shakes it again, and shakes her head and puts it back. She gets another one and she does it just like she did the first one, then she shakes her head. Then she gets a brown one and do it that, too. But she don't like this one, either. Then she gets

ERNEST J. GAINES

another one, but 'fore she shakes it or anything, she looks at me. Look like she's trying to say something to me, but I don't know what it is. All I know is I done got warm now and I'm feeling right smart better. Mama shakes this axe handle just like she did the others, and shakes her head and says something to the white man. The white man just looks at his pile of axe handles, and when Mama pass him to come to the front, the white man just scratch his head and follows her. She tells me come on and we go on and start walking again.

We walk and walk, and no time at all I'm cold again. Look like I'm colder now 'cause I can still remember how good it was back there. My stomach growls and I suck it in to keep Mama from hearing it. She's walking right 'side me, and it growls so loud you can hear it a mile. But Mama don't say a word.

10

When we come up to the courthouse, I look at the clock. It's got quarter to twelve. Mean we got another hour and a quarter to be out here in the cold. We go and stand 'side a building. Something hits my cap and I look up at the sky. Sleet's falling.

I look at Mama standing there. I want stand close 'side her, but she don't like that. She say that's crybaby stuff. She say you got to stand for yourself, by yourself.

"Let's go back to that office," she says.

We cross the street. When we get to the dentist office I try to open the door, but I can't. I twist and twist, but I can't. Mama pushes me to the side and she twist the knob, but she can't open the door, either. She turns 'way from the door. I look at her, but I don't move and I don't say nothing. I done seen her like this before and I'm scared of her.

"You hungry?" she says. She says it like she's mad at me, like I'm the cause of everything.

"No, ma'am," I say.

"You want eat and walk back, or you rather don't eat and ride?"

"I ain't hungry," I say.

I ain't just hungry, but I'm cold, too. I'm so hungry and cold I want to cry. And look like I'm getting colder and colder. My feet done got numb. I try to work my toes, but I don't even feel them. Look like I'm go'n die. Look like I'm go'n stand right here and freeze to death. I think 'bout home. I think 'bout Val and Auntie and Ty and Louis and Walker. It's 'bout twelve o'clock and I know they eating dinner now. I can hear Ty making jokes. He done forgot 'bout getting up early this morning and right now he's probably making jokes. Always trying to make somebody laugh. I wish I was right there listening to him. Give anything in the world if I was home round the fire.

"Come on," Mama says.

We start walking again. My feet so numb I can't hardly feel them. We turn the corner and go on back up the street. The clock on the courthouse starts hitting for twelve.

The sleet's coming down plenty now. They hit the pave and bounce like rice. Oh, Lord; oh, Lord, I pray. Don't let me die, don't let me die, don't let me die, Lord.

II

Now I know where we going. We going back of town where the colored people eat. I don't care if I don't eat. I been hungry before. I can stand it. But I can't stand the cold.

I can see we go'n have a long walk. It's 'bout a mile down there. But I don't mind. I know when I get there I'm go'n warm myself. I think I can hold out. My hands numb in my pockets and my feet numb, too, but if I keep moving I can hold out. Just don't stop no more, that's all.

The sky's gray. The sleet keeps on falling. Falling like rain now— plenty, plenty. You can hear it hitting the pave. You can see it bouncing. Sometimes it bounces two times 'fore it settles.

We keep on going. We don't say nothing. We just keep on going, keep on going.

I wonder what Mama's thinking. I hope she ain't mad at me. When summer come I'm go'n pick plenty cotton and get her a coat. I'm go'n get her a red one.

I hope they'd make it summer all the time. I'd be glad if it was summer all the time—but it ain't. We got to have winter, too. Lord, I hate the winter. I guess everybody hate the winter.

I don't sniff this time. I get out my handkerchief and wipe my nose. My hands's so cold I can hardly hold the handkerchief.

I think we getting close, but we ain't there yet. I wonder where everybody is. Can't see a soul but us. Look like we the only two people moving round today. Must be too cold for the rest of the people to move round in.

I can hear my teeth. I hope they don't knock together too hard and make that bad one hurt. Lord, that's all I need, for that bad one to start off.

I hear a church bell somewhere. But today ain't Sunday. They must be ringing for a funeral or something.

I wonder what they doing at home. They must be eating. Monsieur Bayonne might be there with his guitar. One day Ty played with Monsieur Bayonne's guitar and broke one of the strings. Monsieur Bayonne was some mad with Ty. He say Ty wasn't go'n ever 'mount to nothing. Ty can go just like Monsieur Bayonne when he ain't there. Ty can make everybody laugh when he starts to mocking Monsieur Bayonne.

I used to like to be with Mama and Daddy. We used to be happy. But they took him in the Army. Now, nobody happy no more. . . . I be glad when Daddy comes home.

Monsieur Bayonne say it wasn't fair for them to take Daddy and give

ERNEST J. GAINES

Mama nothing and give us nothing. Auntie say, "Shhh, Etienne. Don't let them hear you talk like that." Monsieur Bayonne say, "It's God truth. What they giving his children? They have to walk three and a half miles to school hot or cold. That's anything to give for a paw? She's got to work in the field rain or shine just to make ends meet. That's anything to give for a husband?" Auntie say, "Shhh, Etienne, shhh." "Yes, you right," Monsieur Bayonne say. "Best don't say it in front of them now. But one day they go'n find out. One day." "Yes, I suppose so," Auntie say. "Then what, Rose Mary?" Monsieur Bayonne say. "I don't know, Etienne," Auntie say. "All we can do is us job, and leave everything else in His hand . . ."

We getting closer, now. We getting closer. I can even see the railroad tracks.

We cross the tracks, and now I see the café. Just to get in there, I say. Just to get in there. Already I'm starting to feel little better.

12

We go in. Ahh, it's good. I look for the heater; there 'gainst the wall. One of them little brown ones. I just stand there and hold my hands over it. I can't open my hands too wide 'cause they almost froze.

Mama's standing right 'side me. She done unbuttoned her coat. Smoke rises out of the coat, and the coat smells like a wet dog.

I move to the side so Mama can have more room. She opens out her hands and rubs them together. I rub mine together, too, 'cause this keep them from hurting. If you let them warm too fast, they hurt you sure. But if you let them warm just little bit at a time, and you keep rubbing them, they be all right every time.

They got just two more people in the café. A lady back of the counter, and a man on this side the counter. They been watching us ever since we come in.

Mama gets out the handkerchief and count up the money. Both of us know how much money she's got there. Three dollars. No, she ain't got three dollars 'cause she had to pay us way up here. She ain't got but two dollars and a half left. Dollar and a half to get my tooth pulled, and fifty cents for us to go back on, and fifty cents worth of salt meat.

She stirs the money round with her finger. Most of the money is change 'cause I can hear it rubbing together. She stirs it and stirs it. Then she looks at the door. It's still sleeting. I can hear it hitting 'gainst the wall like rice.

"I ain't hungry, Mama," I say.

"Got to pay them something for they heat," she says.

She takes a quarter out the handkerchief and ties the handkerchief up again. She looks over her shoulder at the people, but she still don't move. I hope she don't spend the money. I don't want her spending it on me.

I'm hungry, I'm almost starving I'm so hungry, but I don't want her spending the money on me.

She flips the quarter over like she's thinking. She's must be thinking 'bout us walking back home. Lord, I sure don't want walk home. If I thought it'd do any good to say something, I'd say it. But Mama makes up her own mind 'bout things.

She turns 'way from the heater right fast, like she better hurry up and spend the quarter 'fore she change her mind. I watch her go toward the counter. The man and the lady look at her. She tells the lady something and the lady walks away. The man keeps on looking at her. Her back's turned to the man, and she don't even know he's standing there.

The lady puts some cakes and a glass of milk on the counter. Then she pours up a cup of coffee and sets it 'side the other stuff. Mama pays her for the things and comes on back where I'm standing. She tells me sit down at the table 'gainst the wall.

The milk and the cakes's for me; the coffee's for Mama. I eat slow and I look at her. She's looking outside at the sleet. She's looking real sad. I say to myself, I'm go'n make all this up one day. You see, one day, I'm go'n make all this up. I want say it now; I want tell her how I feel right now; but Mama don't like for us to talk like that.

"I can't eat all this," I say.

They ain't got but just three little old cakes there. I'm so hungry right now, the Lord knows I can eat a hundred times three, But I want my mama to have one.

Mama don't even look my way. She knows I'm hungry, she knows I want it. I let it stay there a little while, then I get it and eat it. I eat just on my front teeth, though, 'cause if cake touch that back tooth I know what'll happen. Thank God it ain't hurt me at all today.

After I finish eating I see the man go to the juke box. He drops a nickel in it, then he just stand there a little while looking at the record. Mama tells me keep my eyes in front where they belong. I turn my head like she say, but then I hear the man coming toward us.

"Dance, pretty?" he says.

Mama gets up to dance with him. But 'fore you know it, she done grabbed the little man in the collar and done heaved him 'side the wall. He hit the wall so hard he stop the juke box from playing.

"Some pimp," the lady back of the counter says. "Some pimp."

The little man jumps up off the floor and starts toward my mama. 'Fore you know it, Mama done sprung open her knife and she's waiting for him.

"Come on," she says. "Come on. I'll gut you from your neighbo to your throat. Come on."

I go up to the little man to hit him, but Mama makes me come and stand 'side her. The little man looks at me and Mama and goes on back to the counter.

"Some pimp," the lady back of the counter says. "Some pimp." She starts laughing and pointing at the little man. "Yes sir, you a pimp, all right. Yes sir-ree."

13

"Fasten that coat, let's go," Mama says.

"You don't have to leave," the lady says. Mama don't answer the lady, and we right out in the cold again. I'm warm right now—my hands, my ears, my feet—but I know this ain't go'n last too long. It done sleet so much now you got ice everywhere you look.

We cross the railroad tracks, and soon's we do, I get cold. That wind goes through this little old coat like it ain't even there. I got on a shirt and a sweater under the coat, but that wind don't pay them no mind. I look up and I can see we got a long way to go. I wonder if we go'n make it 'fore I get too cold.

We cross over to walk on the sidewalk. They got just one sidewalk back here, and it's over there.

After we go just a little piece, I smell bread cooking. I look, then I see a baker shop. When we get closer, I can smell it more better. I shut my eyes and make 'tend I'm eating. But I keep them shut too long and I butt up 'gainst a telephone post. Mama grabs me and see if I'm hurt. I ain't bleeding or nothing and she turns me loose.

I can feel I'm getting colder and colder, and I look up to see how far we still got to go. Uptown is 'way up yonder. A half mile more, I reckon. I try to think of something. They say think and you won't get cold. I think of that poem, "Annabel Lee." I ain't been to school in so long—this bad weather—I reckon they done passed "Annabel Lee" by now. But passed it or not, I'm sure Miss Walker go'n make me recite it when I get there. That woman don't never forget nothing. I ain't never seen nobody like that in my life.

I'm still getting cold. "Annabel Lee" or no "Annabel Lee," I'm still getting cold. But I can see we getting closer. We getting there gradually.

Soon's we turn the corner, I seen a little old white lady up in front of us. She's the only lady on the street. She's all in black and she's got a long black rag over her head.

"Stop," she says.

Me and Mama stop and look at her. She must be crazy to be out in all this bad weather. Ain't got but a few other people out there, and all of them's men.

"Y'all done ate?" she says.

"Just finish," Mama says.

"Y'all must be cold then?" she says.

"We headed for the dentist," Mama says. "We'll warm up when we get there."

"What dentist?" the old lady says. "Mr. Bassett?"

"Yes, ma'am," Mama says.

"Come on in," the old lady says. "I'll telephone him and tell him y'all coming."

Me and Mama follow the old lady in the store. It's a little bitty store, and it don't have much in there. The old lady takes off her head rag and folds it up.

"Helena?" somebody calls from the back.

"Yes, Alnest?" the old lady says.

"Did you see them?"

"They're here. Standing beside me."

"Good. Now you can stay inside."

The old lady looks at Mama. Mama's waiting to hear what she brought us in here for. I'm waiting for that, too.

"I saw y'all each time you went by," she says. "I came out to catch you, but you were gone."

"We went back of town," Mama says.

"Did you eat?"

"Yes, ma'am."

The old lady looks at Mama a long time, like she's thinking Mama might just be saying that. Mama looks right back at her. The old lady looks at me to see what I have to say. I don't say nothing. I sure ain't going 'gainst my mama.

"There's food in the kitchen," she says to Mama. "I've been keeping it warm."

Mama turns right around and starts for the door.

"Just a minute," the old lady says. Mama stops. "The boy'll have to work for it. It isn't free."

"We don't take no handout," Mama says.

"I'm not handing out anything," the old lady says. "I need my garbage moved to the front. Ernest has a bad cold and can't go out there."

"James'll move it for you," Mama says.

"Not unless you eat," the old lady says. "I'm old, but I have my pride, too, you know."

Mama can see she ain't go'n beat this old lady down, so she just shakes her head.

"All right," the old lady says. "Come into the kitchen."

She leads the way with that rag in her hand. The kitchen is a little bitty little old thing, too. The table and the stove just 'bout fill it up. They got a little room to the side. Somebody in there layin 'cross the bed— 'cause I can see one of his feet. Must be the person she was talking to: Ernest or Alnest—something like that.

"Sit down," the old lady says to Mama. "Not you," she says to me. "You have to move the cans."

"Helena?" the man says in the other room.

"Yes, Alnest?" the old lady says.

"Are you going out there again?"

"I must show the boy where the garbage is, Alnest," the old lady says.

"Keep your shawl over your head," the old man says.

"You don't have to remind me, Alnest. Come, Boy," the old lady says.

We go out in the yard. Little old back yard ain't no bigger than the store or the kitchen. But it can sleet here just like it can sleet in any big back yard. And 'fore you know it, I'm trembling.

"There," the old lady says, pointing to the cans. I pick up one of the cans and set it right back down. The can's so light. I'm go'n see what's inside of it.

"Here," the old lady says. "Leave that can alone."

I look back at her standing there in the door. She's got that black rag wrapped round her shoulders, and she's pointing one of her little old fingers at me.

"Pick it up and carry it to the front," she says. I go by her with the can, and she's looking at me all the time. I'm sure the can's empty. I'm sure she could've carried it herself—maybe both of them at the same time. "Set it on the sidewalk by the door and come back for the other one," she says.

I go and come back, and Mama looks at me when I pass her. I get the other can and take it to the front. It don't feel a bit heavier than that first one. I tell myself I ain't go'n be nobody's fool, and I'm go'n look inside this can to see just what I been hauling. First, I look up the street, then down the street. Nobody coming. Then I look over my shoulder toward the door. That little old lady done slipped up there quiet's a mouse, watching me again. Look like she knowed what I was go'n do.

"Ehh, Lord," she says. "Children, children. Come in here, boy, and go wash your hands."

I follow her in the kitchen. She points toward the bathroom, and I go in there and wash up. Little bitty old bathroom, but it's clean, clean. I don't use any of her towels; I wipe my hands on my pants legs.

When I come back in the kitchen, the old lady done dished up the food. Rice, gravy, meat—and she even got some lettuce and tomato in a saucer. She even got a glass of milk and a piece of cake there, too. It looks so good, I almost start eating 'fore I say my blessing.

"Helena?" the old man says.

"Yes, Alnest?"

"Are they eating?"

"Yes," she says.

"Good," he says. "Now you'll stay inside."

The old lady goes in there where he is and I can hear them talking. I look at Mama. She's eating slow like she's thinking. I wonder what's the matter now. I reckon she's thinking 'bout home.

The old lady comes back in the kitchen.

"I talked to Dr. Bassett's nurse," she says. "Dr. Bassett will take you as soon as you get there."

"Thank you, ma'am," Mama says.

"Perfectly all right," the old lady says. "Which one is it?"

Mama nods toward me. The old lady looks at me real sad. I look sad, too.

"You're not afraid, are you?" she says.

"No, ma'am," I say.

"That's a good boy," the old lady says. "Nothing to be afraid of. Dr. Bassett will not hurt you."

When me and Mama get through eating, we thank the old lady again.

"Helena, are they leaving?" the old man says.

"Yes, Alnest."

"Tell them I say good-bye."

"They can hear you, Alnest."

"Good-bye both mother and son," the old man says. "And may God be with you."

Me and Mama tell the old man good-bye, and we follow the old lady in the front room. Mama opens the door to go out, but she stops and comes back in the store.

"You sell salt meat?" she says.

"Yes."

"Give me two bits worth."

"That isn't very much salt meat," the old lady says.

"That's all I have," Mama says.

The old lady goes back of the counter and cuts a big piece off the chunk. Then she wraps it up and puts it in a paper bag.

"Two bits," she says.

"That looks like awful lot of meat for a quarter," Mama says.

"Two bits," the old lady says. "I've been selling salt meat behind this counter twenty-five years. I think I know what I'm doing."

"You got a scale there," Mama says.

"What?" the old lady says.

"Weigh it," Mama says.

"What?" the old lady says. "Are you telling me how to run my business?"

"Thanks very much for the food," Mama says.

"Just a minute," the old lady says.

"James," Mama says to me. I move toward the door.

"Just one minute, I said," the old lady says.

Me and Mama stop again and look at her. The old lady takes the meat out of the bag and unwraps it and cuts 'bout half of it off. Then she wraps it up again and juggs it back in the bag and gives the bag to Mama. Mama lays the quarter on the counter.

"Your kindness will never be forgotten," she says. "James," she says to me.

We go out, and the old lady comes to the door to look at us. After we go a little piece I look back, and she's still there watching us.

The sleet's coming down heavy, heavy now, and I turn up my coat collar to keep my neck warm. My mama tells me turn it right back down.

"You not a bum," she says. "You a man."

ISABELLA GARDNER

(b. 1915) A Boston native, Isabella Gardner
started a career in acting before turning to
poetry. She has lectured and read her poetry
both in the United States and abroad. Her
works include *Birthdays from the Ocean*
(1955), *The Looking Glass* (1961), and *West
of Childhood: Poems 1950–65* (1965).

AT A SUMMER HOTEL

For my daughter, Rose Van Kirk

I am here with my beautiful bountiful womanful child
to be soothed by the sea not roused by these roses roving wild.
My girl is gold in the sun and bold in the dazzling water,
she drowses on the blond sand and in the daisy fields my daughter
dreams. Uneasy in the drafty shade I rock on the veranda
reminded of Europa Persephone Miranda.

CATHERINE DAVIS

(b. 1924) Catherine Davis grew up in Iowa and Minnesota and holds degrees from George Washington University and the University of Iowa. She has been an editor and a librarian as well as a teacher of writing in several colleges. She is the recipient of several prizes, and her poems have been published in *The Southern Review* and *The New Yorker*. At present she is working on a collection of her poems and teaching at the University of Massachusetts, Boston.

SHE

gave me life
      what a hell
              on wheels she was
                     but
drive!
      indestructible (almost)
                   down
          snaky
              pitchdark
          highways blind
curves
    hairpin
turns
     the chances she took
        (if you wouldn't dim your lights
neither would she)
        a good
              head on her shoulders
quick reflexes
     but no

THE MOTHER: ANGEL OR "MOM"?

                spare or
             no brakes at all
                      a welter of
signals and signs
            signifying
                  something to
someone else
           (too hell-
           bent
           to look)
                stopping
only to refuel
           and then drive on like mad to make up
                            for lost time
(losing
       the way) and
             always in a storm of
                  rage   laughter
torrents of
           words and
              wit
                curses and
                   tears
           (or as the song on the jukebox goes
"if you think I laugh too loud
                  you should hear me
                      cry")
oh
   the collisions
           the wrecks as if
driven
        by some demon
             lover of
                 go and
                   find and
get
    (but what?
           not money)
               the good die
               young so
        she kept going
           an unforgettable

occurrence
        tearing through
                at 3 a.m.
dangerous
        to ignore
                        no apparition
                        but a dream
awakened
        of longing in all directions
                        and the roads
                          all open
In the determined
            course of her life
                      she gave as
good
    as she got
        and
                here I am

MYRA GOLDBERG

(b. 1943) A resident of New York City, Myra Goldberg has been a draft counselor and English teacher. Her stories have appeared in such magazines as *Transatlantic Review, New England Review, Feminist Studies,* and have been presented on National Public Radio and station WBAI. "Gifts" is from a collection entitled "Goosedown," as yet unpublished.

GIFTS

My mother tells me that a gift will arrive for me by mail, from Macy's. I try to thank her, but can't, because I've asked her not to send me gifts any more, clothes especially. I'm thirty. I've got a closet full of gifts from her, have never really dressed myself. My mother is sixty-five. We're in the dressing room of the municipal pool together. Her back is to me. She's squatting. Piling clothes into her locker. She turns around, stands, looks up at me. Her small pointed face is hopeful. Her large breasts droop. She's naked.

"It's a shirt," she says.

"So you asked her not to send you gifts," I think. "She wants to send you a shirt from Macy's. Let her send you a shirt from Macy's."

"You can always return it," she says, after awhile.

"Okay. I'll return it if it isn't right."

"Fine," she says. "I'll return it for you. It's easier for me to get to Macy's: I'm not so busy." She pulls her bathing suit up, settles her breasts inside. "I would have gotten it for myself," she adds, "if they had it in my size or in a different color."

I put one foot into the leg of my leotard.

"You're not taking a shower before you go in?"

"I never do. Look, Ma, I probably won't want to return it. You have wonderful taste, usually."

"It looked like you," she says. "Simple. Not severe. But I could be wrong."

We start for the pool. The water is warm, chlorinated. She breast strokes. I crawl. She favors her right side, because her left hip was broken in a car accident and never mended. I favor my left, because my bad basketball knee won't kick. We swim back and forth, lose each other. I look around. She's holding on to the ladder, dangling. I swim up to her.

"Are you okay?"

"Fine. I was watching you. You're a strong swimmer."

"So are you."

"Grandma was stronger."

We used to watch from the beach, Grandma at the water's edge. Mrs. Handelman on one side, Mrs. Scheineman on the other. Black woolen tank suits wrinkling around their old ladies' thighs, the three women chatting, bending, scooping water from the lake. sprinkling water on their bosoms, rubbing water into their wrists, elbows, shoulderblades, like perfume, then crack—Grandma was gone, wading into the lake, thighs carrying her out, past the rope, past the lifeguard's whistling objections, breast stroking across the lake, then back to us again, bunioned feet covered with sand, water dripping on our blanket as she reached for the bathrobe that my mother held out to her, wrapped it around her, waited like a wrestler for the lifeguard to approach: "What's he so afraid of, that boy in the highchair? I'll be drowned? I can't go out alone? An old lady like me?"

"I loved her," says my mother. "But I could never talk to her." She lets go of the ladder. Her legs stir up the waters behind her. Her freckled arms part the waters in front of her. She detours around a group of splashing children, swims swiftly down the center of the pool, then lifts herself to the concrete edge at the other end, dangles her legs in the water, kicks, smiles.

I wave.

We meet in the dressing room.

I admire her haircut. She likes the way I wrap my towel around my head. We start for the subway. She's tired now. Her hip hurts her. At the turnstile, she takes two tokens out of her pocketbook. "Here. For you."

"Never mind. I can get one."

"You'll have to stand in line." She points to the token booth.

I take the token. Offer her fifty cents.

She shakes her head. "The price is terrible," she says, slipping her token into the turnstile. The machine clanks and turns, noisy, but functional. Then it's my turn.

Inside the subway car, I find an empty seat for her. She holds the pole. "Save the seat for someone who needs it," she says. I hold the same pole, think longingly of France, where subway sitting is regulated by the state, where the mutilés de guerre go first, then les âges, les enceintes, mutilés ordinaires.

"For my sake," I say, pointing to the seat.

THE MOTHER: ANGEL OR "MOM"?

116

She sits down.

I grab the strap above her. She wipes her eyes. I lean down to see what the matter is. She says the chlorine in the pool makes her eyes hurt. It's not right, what they do to the waters, the elements.

I'm sorry about your eyes, I say, but the pool is better than nothing, better than what most people have.

She's grateful, she supposes.

My stop is next.

At home, there's a package from Macy's waiting.

Unwrapped, it's the same shirt I bought four years ago, got tired of, hung on a tree outside, watched my neighbor take home with her.

No, it's not the same shirt, I see, unpinning it, unfolding it, slipping the cardboard out, holding it against me. Same material. Different cut. Softer. Not so severe.

I call my mother to thank her.

She says, "I thought it looked like you, but I wasn't sure. I worried."

"Don't worry, Ma," I say.

She's quiet.

"I love it," I say.

"I did okay?"

"You did fine, believe me."

"I'm surprised," she says. "I didn't expect it to arrive so soon."

Now we're both quiet. I follow the telephone wires across town and back. "I don't want to run up your phone bill," she says. "I'm getting off."

She gets off. The line is free again. I stand, listening to nothing. A few minutes later, I'm dialing my brother in California. I want to hear his voice. See what he sounds like. "Hello," he says. "Is that you?"

HAROLD BRODKEY

(b. 1925) Born in Staunton, Illinois, Harold Brodkey grew up in the Midwest and now lives in New York City. He has published short stories in such magazines as *The New Yorker, Esquire,* and *American Review;* a collection of his stories, *First Love and Other Sorrows,* appeared in 1958. "Verona: A Young Woman Speaks," was included in *The Best American Short Stories* for 1978.

VERONA: A YOUNG
WOMAN SPEAKS

I know a lot! I know about happiness! I don't mean the love of God, either: I mean I know the human happiness with the crimes in it.

Even the happiness of childhood.

I think of it now as a cruel, middle-class happiness.

Let me describe one time—one day, one night.

I was quite young, and my parents and I—there were just the three of us—were traveling from Rome to Salzburg, journeying across a quarter of Europe to be in Salzburg for Christmas, for the music and the snow. We went by train because planes were erratic, and my father wanted us to stop in half a dozen Italian towns and see paintings and buy things. It was absurd, but we were all three drunk with this; it was very strange: we woke every morning in a strange hotel, in a strange city. I would be the first one to wake; and I would go to the window and see some tower or palace; and then I would wake my mother and be justified in my sense of wildness and belief and adventure by the way she acted, her sense of romance at being in a city as strange as I had thought it was when I had looked out the window and seen the palace or the tower.

We had to change trains in Verona, a darkish, smallish city at the edge of the Alps. By the time we got there, we'd bought and bought our way up the Italian peninsula: I was dizzy with shopping and new possessions:

I hardly knew who I was, I owned so many new things: my reflection in any mirror or shopwindow was resplendently fresh and new, disguised even, glittering, I thought. I was seven or eight years old. It seemed to me we were almost in a movie or in the pages of a book: only the simplest and most light-filled words and images can suggest what I thought we were then. We went around shiningly: we shone everywhere. *Those clothes.* It's easy to buy a child. I had a new dress, knitted, blue and red, expensive as hell, I think; leggings, also red; a red loden-cloth coat with a hood and a knitted cap for under the hood; marvelous lined gloves; fur-lined boots and a fur purse or carryall, and a tartan skirt—and shirts and a scarf, and there was even more: a watch, a bracelet: more and more.

On the trains we had private rooms, and Momma carried games in her purse and things to eat, and Daddy sang carols off-key to me; and sometimes I became so intent on my happiness I would suddenly be in real danger of wetting myself; and Momma, who understood such emergencies, would catch the urgency in my voice and see my twisted face; and she—a large, good-looking woman—would whisk me to a toilet with amazing competence and unstoppability, murmuring to me, "Just hold on for a while," and she would hold my hand while I did it.

So we came to Verona, where it was snowing, and the people had stern, sad faces, beautiful, unlaughing faces. But if they looked at me, those serious faces would lighten, they would smile at me in my splendor. Strangers offered me candy, sometimes with the most excruciating sadness, kneeling or stooping to look directly into my face, into my eyes; and Momma or Papa would judge them, the people, and say in Italian we were late, we had to hurry, or pause, and let the stranger touch me, talk to me, look into my face for a while. I would see myself in the eyes of some strange man or woman; sometimes they stared so gently I would want to touch their eyelashes, stroke those strange, large, glistening eyes. I knew I decorated life. I took my duties with great seriousness. An Italian count in Siena said I had the manners of an English princess—at times—and then he laughed because it was true I would be quite lurid: I ran shouting in his *galleria,* a long room, hung with pictures, and with a frescoed ceiling: and I sat on his lap and wriggled: I was a wicked child, and I liked myself very much; and almost everywhere, almost every day, there was someone new to love me, briefly, while we traveled.

I understood I was special. I understood it *then.*

I knew that what we were doing, everything we did, involved money. I did not know if it involved mind or not, or style. But I knew about money somehow, checks and traveler's checks and the clink of coins. Daddy was a fountain of money: he said it was a spree; he meant for us to be amazed; he had saved money—we weren't really rich but we were to be for this trip. I remember a conservatory in a large house outside Florence and orange trees in tubs; and I ran there too. A servant, a man dressed in black, a very old man, mean-faced—he did not like being a servant anymore after the days of servants were over—and he scowled but he smiled at me, and at my mother, and even once at my father: we were clearly so separate from the griefs and wearinesses and cruelties of the world. We were at play, we were at our joys, and Momma was glad, with a terrible and naïve inner gladness, and she relied on Daddy to make it work: oh, she worked too, but she didn't know the secret of such—unreality: is that what I want to say? Of such a game, of such an extraordinary game.

There was a picture in Verona Daddy wanted to see; a painting; I remember the painter because the name Pisanello reminded me I had to go to the bathroom when we were in the museum, which was an old castle, Guelf or Ghibelline, I don't remember which; and I also remember the painting because it showed the hind end of the horse, and I thought that was not nice and rather funny, but Daddy was admiring; and so I said nothing.

He held my hand and told me a story so I wouldn't be bored as we walked from room to room in the museum/castle, and then we went outside into the snow, into the soft light when it snows, light coming through snow; and I was dressed in red and had on boots, and my parents were young and pretty and had on boots too; and we could stay out in the snow if we wanted; and we did. We went to a square, a piazza—the Scaligera, I think; I don't remember—and just as we got there, the snowing began to bellow and then subside, to fall heavily and then sparsely, and then it stopped: and it was very cold, and there were pigeons every-where in the piazza, on every cornice and roof, and all over the snow on the ground, leaving little tracks as they walked, while the air trembled in its just-after-snow and just-before-snow weight and thickness and grey seriousness of purpose. I had never seen so many pigeons or such a private and haunted place as that piazza, me in my new coat at the far rim of the world, the far rim of who knew what story, the rim of foreign beauty and Daddy's games, the edge, the white border of a season.

I was half mad with pleasure, anyway, and now Daddy brought five or six cones made of newspaper, wrapped, twisted; and they held grains of something like corn, yellow and white kernels of something; and he poured some on my hand and told me to hold my hand out; and then he backed away.

At first there was nothing, but I trusted him and I waited; and then the pigeons came. On heavy wings. Clumsy pigeony bodies. And red, unreal bird's feet. They flew at me, slowing at the last minute; they lit on my arm and fed from my hand. I wanted to flinch, but I didn't. I closed my eyes and held my arm stiffly; and felt them peck and eat—from my hand, these free creatures, these flying things. I liked that moment. I liked my happiness. If I were mistaken about life and pigeons and my own nature, it didn't matter *then*.

The piazza was very silent, with snow; and Daddy poured grains on

THE MOTHER: ANGEL OR "MOM"?

both my hands and then on the sleeves of my coat and on the shoulders of the coat, and I was entranced with yet more stillness, with this idea of his. The pigeons fluttered heavily in the heavy air, more and more of them, and sat on my arms and on my shoulders; and I looked at Momma and then at my father and then at the birds on me.

Oh. I'm sick of everything as I talk. There is happiness. It always makes me slightly ill. I lose my balance because of it.

The heavy birds, and the strange buildings, and Momma near, and Daddy too: Momma is pleased that I am happy and she is a little jealous; she is jealous of everything Daddy does; she is a woman of enormous spirit; life is hardly big enough for her; she is drenched in wastefulness and prettiness. She knows things. She gets inflexible, though, and foolish at times, and temperamental; but she is a somebody, and she gets away with a lot, and if she is near, you can feel her, you can't escape her, she's that important, that echoing, her spirit is that powerful in the space around her.

If she weren't restrained by Daddy, if she weren't in love with him, there is no knowing what she might do: she does not know. But she manages almost to be gentle because of him; he is incredibly watchful and changeable and he gets tired; he talks and charms people; sometimes, then, Momma and I stand nearby, like moons; we brighten and wane; and after a while, he comes to us, to the moons, the big one, and the little one, and we welcome him, and he is always, to my surprise, he is always surprised, as if he didn't deserve to be loved, as if it were time he was found out.

Daddy is very tall, and Momma is watching us, and Daddy anoints me again and again with the grain. I cannot bear it much longer. I feel joy or amusement or I don't know what; it is all through me, like a nausea—I am ready to scream and laugh, that laughter that comes out like magical, drunken, awful and yet pure spit or vomit or God knows what, that makes me a child mad with laughter. I become brilliant, gleaming, soft: an angel, a great bird-child of laughter.

I am ready to be like that, but I hold myself back.

There are more and more birds near me. They march around my feet and peck at falling and fallen grains. One is on my head. Of those on my arms, some move their wings, fluff those frail, feather-loaded wings, stretch them. I cannot bear it, they are so frail, and I am, at the moment, the kindness of the world that feeds them in the snow.

All at once, I let out a splurt of laughter: I can't stop myself and the birds fly away but not far; they circle around me, above me; some wheel high in the air and drop as they return; they all returned, some in clouds and clusters driftingly, some alone and angry, pecking at others; some with a blind, animal-strutting abruptness. They gripped my coat and fed themselves. It started to snow again.

I was there in my kindness, in that piazza, within reach of my mother and father.

HAROLD BRODKEY

Oh, how will the world continue? Daddy suddenly understood I'd had enough, I was at the end of my strength—Christ, he was alert—and he picked me up, and I went limp, my arm around his neck, and the snow fell. Momma came near and pulled the hood lower and said there were snowflakes in my eyelashes. She knew he had understood, and she wasn't sure she had; she wasn't sure he ever watched her so carefully. She became slightly unhappy, and so she walked like a clumsy boy beside us, but she was so pretty: she had powers, anyway.

We went to a restaurant, and I behaved very well, but I couldn't eat, and then we went to the train and people looked at us, but I couldn't smile; I was too dignified, too sated; some leftover—pleasure, let's call it—made my dignity very deep, I could not stop remembering the pigeons, or that Daddy loved me in a way he did not love Momma; and Daddy was alert, watching the luggage, watching strangers for assassination attempts or whatever; he was on duty; and Momma was pretty and alone and *happy,* defiant in that way.

And then, you see, what she did was wake me in the middle of the night when the train was chugging up a very steep mountainside; and outside the window, visible because our compartment was dark and the sky was clear and there was a full moon, were mountains, a landscape of mountains everywhere, big mountains, huge ones, impossible, all slanted and pointed and white with snow, and absurd, sticking up into an ink-blue sky and down into blue, blue shadows, miraculously deep. I don't know how to say what it was like: they were not like anything I knew: they were high things: and we were up high in the train and we were climbing higher, and it was not at all true, but it was, you see. I put my hands on the window and stared at the wild, slanting, unlikely marvels, whiteness and dizziness and moonlight and shadows cast by moonlight, not real, not familiar, not pigeons, but a clean world.

We sat a long time, Momma and I, and stared, and then Daddy woke up and came and looked too. "It's pretty," he said, but he didn't really understand. Only Momma and I did. She said to him, "When I was a child, I was bored all the time, my love—I thought nothing would ever happen to me—and now these things are happening—and you have happened." I think he was flabbergasted by her love in the middle of the night; he smiled at her, oh, so swiftly that I was jealous, but I stayed quiet, and after a while, in his silence and amazement at her, at us, he began to seem different from us, from Momma and me; and then he fell asleep again; Momma and I didn't; we sat at the window and watched all night, watched the mountains and the moon, the clean world. We watched together.

Momma was the winner.

We were silent, and in silence we spoke of how we loved men and how dangerous men were and how they stole everything from you no matter how much you gave—but we didn't say it aloud.

We looked at mountains until dawn, and then when dawn came, it was too pretty for me—there was pink and blue and gold, in the sky, and on icy places, brilliant pink and gold flashes, and the snow was colored too, and I said, "Oh," and sighed; and each moment was more beautiful than the one before; and I said, "I love you, Momma." Then I fell asleep in her arms.

That was happiness then.

JAYNE ANNE PHILLIPS

(b. 1953) Born in West Virginia, Jayne Anne
Phillips earned degrees from West Virginia
University and the University of Iowa. She
has taught in college and now writes full-
time. She has won many awards including
the 1980 Sue Kaufman Prize for First Fiction
by the American Academy and Institute of
Arts and Letters. She has held a fellowship
from the National Endowment for the Arts
and is a fellow of the Mary Bunting Institute
at Radcliffe College. Her stories have been
collected in two small press editions as well as
in *Black Tickets* (1979).

SOUVENIR

Kate always sent her mother a card on Valentine's Day. She timed the mails
from wherever she was so that the cards arrived on February 14th. Her
parents had celebrated the day in some small fashion, and since her father's
death six years before, Kate made a gesture of compensatory remembrance.
At first, she made the cards herself: collage and pressed grasses on
construction paper sewn in fabric. Now she settled for art reproductions,
glossy cards with blank insides. Kate wrote in them with colored inks,
"You have always been my Valentine," or simply "Hey, take care of
yourself." She might enclose a present as well, something small enough to
fit into an envelope; a sachet, a perfumed soap, a funny tintype of a
prune-faced man in a bowler hat.

This time, she forgot. Despite the garish displays of paper cupids and
heart-shaped boxes in drugstore windows, she let the day nearly approach
before remembering. It was too late to send anything in the mail. She
called her mother long-distance at night when the rates were low.

"Mom? How are you?"

"It's you! How are *you*?" Her mother's voice grew suddenly brighter;
Kate recognized a tone reserved for welcome company. Sometimes it took
a while to warm up.

"I'm fine," answered Kate. "What have you been doing?"

"Well, actually I was trying to sleep."

"Sleep? You should be out setting the old hometown on fire."

"The old hometown can burn up without me tonight."

"Really? What's going on?"

"I'm running in-service training sessions for the primary teachers." Kate's mother was a school superintendent. "They're driving me batty. You'd think their brains were rubber."

"They are," Kate said. "Or you wouldn't have to train them. Think of them as a salvation, they create a need for your job."

"Some salvation. Besides, your logic is ridiculous. Just because someone needs training doesn't mean they're stupid."

"I'm just kidding. But *I'm* stupid. I forgot to send you a Valentine's card."

"You did? That's bad. I'm trained to receive one. They bring me luck."

"You're receiving a phone call instead," Kate said. "Won't that do?"

"Of course," said her mother, "but this is costing you money. Tell me quick, how are you?"

"Oh, you know. Doctoral pursuits. Doing my student trip, grooving with the professors."

"The professors? You'd better watch yourself."

"It's a joke, Mom, a joke. But what about you? Any men on the horizon?"

"No, not really. A married salesman or two asking me to dinner when they come through the office. Thank heavens I never let those things get started."

"You should do what you want to," Kate said.

"Sure," said her mother. "And where would I be then?"

"I don't know. Maybe Venezuela."

"They don't even have plumbing in Venezuela."

"Yes, but their sunsets are perfect, and the villages are full of dark passionate men in blousy shirts."

"That's your department, not mine."

"Ha," Kate said, "I wish it were my department. Sounds a lot more exciting than teaching undergraduates."

Her mother laughed. "Be careful," she said. "You'll get what you want. End up sweeping a dirt floor with a squawling baby around your neck."

"A dark baby," Kate said, "to stir up the family blood."

"Nothing would surprise me," her mother said as the line went fuzzy. Her voice was submerged in static, then surfaced. "Listen," she was saying. "Write to me. You seem so far away."

They hung up and Kate sat watching the windows of the neighboring house. The curtains were transparent and flowered and none of them matched. Silhouettes of the window frames spread across them like single dark bars. Her mother's curtains were all the same, white cotton hemmed with a ruffle, tiebacks blousing the cloth into identical shapes. From the street it looked as if the house was always in order.

Kate made a cup of strong Chinese tea, turned the lights off, and sat holding the warm cup in the dark. Her mother kept no real tea in the house, just packets of instant diabetic mixture which tasted of chemical sweetener and had a bitter aftertaste. The packets sat on the shelf next to her mother's miniature scales. The scales were white. Kate saw clearly the face of the metal dial on the front, its markings and trembling needle. Her mother weighed portions of food for meals: frozen broccoli, slices of plastic-wrapped Kraft cheese, careful chunks of roast beef. A dog-eared copy of *The Diabetic Diet* had remained propped against the salt shaker for the last two years.

Kate rubbed her forehead. Often at night she had headaches. Sometimes she wondered if there were an agent in her body, a secret in her blood making ready to work against her.

The phone blared repeatedly, careening into her sleep. Kate scrambled out of bed, naked and cold, stumbling, before she recognized the striped wallpaper of her bedroom and realized the phone was right there on the bedside table, as always. She picked up the receiver.

"Kate?" said her brother's voice. "It's Robert. Mom is in the hospital. They don't know what's wrong but she's in for tests."

"Tests? What's happened? I just talked to her last night."

"I'm not sure. She called the neighbors and they took her to the emergency room around dawn." Robert's voice still had that slight twang Kate knew was disappearing from her own. He would be calling from his insurance office, nine o'clock their time, in his thick glasses and wide, perfectly knotted tie. He was a member of the million-dollar club and his picture, tiny, the size of a postage stamp, appeared in the Mutual of Omaha magazine. His voice seemed small too over the distance. Kate felt heavy and dulled. She would never make much money, and recently she had begun wearing make-up again, waking in smeared mascara as she had in high school.

"Is Mom all right?" she managed now. "How serious is it?"

"They're not sure," Robert said. "Her doctor thinks it could have been any of several things, but they're doing X rays."

"Her doctor *thinks?* Doesn't he know? Get her to someone else. There aren't any doctors in that one-horse town."

"I don't know about that," Robert said defensively. "Anyway, I can't force her. You know how she is about money."

"Money? She could have a stroke and drop dead while her doctor wonders what's wrong."

"Doesn't matter. You know you can't tell her what to do."

"Could I call her somehow?"

"No, not yet. And don't get her all worried. She's been scared enough as it is. I'll tell her what you said about getting another opinion, and I'll call you back in a few hours when I have some news. Meanwhile, she's all right, do you hear?"

The line went dead with a click and Kate walked to the bathroom to wash her face. She splashed her eyes and felt guilty about the Valentine's card. Slogans danced in her head like reprimands. *For A Special One. Dearest Mother. My Best Friend.* Despite Robert, after breakfast she would call the hospital.

She sat a long time with her coffee, waiting for minutes to pass, considering how many meals she and her mother ate alone. Similar times of day, hundreds of miles apart. Women by themselves. The last person Kate had eaten breakfast with had been someone she'd met in a bar. He was passing through town. He liked his fried eggs gelatinized in the center, only slightly runny, and Kate had studiously looked away as he ate. The night before he'd looked down from above her as he finished and she still moved under him. "You're still wanting," he'd said. "That's nice." Mornings now, Kate saw her own face in the mirror and was glad she'd forgotten his name. When she looked at her reflection from the side, she saw a faint etching of lines beside her mouth. She hadn't slept with anyone for five weeks, and the skin beneath her eyes had taken on a creamy darkness.

She reached for the phone but drew back. It seemed bad luck to ask for news, to push toward whatever was coming as though she had no respect for it.

Standing in the kitchen last summer, her mother had stirred gravy and argued with her.

"I'm thinking of your own good, not mine," she'd said. "Think of what you put yourself through. And how can you feel right about it? You were born here, I don't care what you say." Her voice broke and she looked, perplexed, at the broth in the pan.

"But, hypothetically," Kate continued, her own voice unaccountably shaking, "if I'm willing to endure whatever I have to, do you have a right to object? You're my mother. You're supposed to defend my choices."

"You'll have enough trouble without choosing more for yourself. Using birth control that'll ruin your insides, moving from one place to another. I can't defend your choices. I can't even defend myself against you." She wiped her eyes on a napkin.

"Why do you have to make me feel so guilty?" Kate said, fighting tears of frustration. "I'm not attacking you."

"You're not? Then who are you talking to?"

"Oh Mom, give me a break."

"I've tried to give you more than that," her mother said. "I know what your choices are saying to me." She set the steaming gravy off the stove. "You may feel very differently later on. It's just a shame I won't be around to see it."

"Oh? Where will you be?"

"Floating around on a fleecy cloud."

JAYNE ANNE PHILLIPS

Kate got up to set the table before she realized her mother had already done it.

The days went by. They'd gone shopping before Kate left. Standing at the cash register in an antique shop on Main Street, they bought each other pewter candle holders. "A souvenir," her mother said. "A reminder to always be nice to yourself. If you live alone you should eat by candlelight."

"Listen," Kate said, "I eat in a heart-shaped tub with bubbles to my chin. I sleep on satin sheets and my mattress has a built-in massage engine. My overnight guests are impressed. You don't have to tell me about the solitary pleasures."

They laughed and touched hands.

"Well," her mother said. "If you like yourself, I must have done something right."

Robert didn't phone until evening. His voice was fatigued and thin. "I've moved her to the university hospital," he said. "They can't deal with it at home."

Kate waited, saying nothing. She concentrated on the toes of her shoes. They needed shining. *You never take care of anything,* her mother would say.

"She has a tumor in her head." He said it firmly, as though Kate might challenge him.

"I'll take a plane tomorrow morning," Kate answered, "I'll be there by noon."

Robert exhaled. "Look," he said, "don't even come back here unless you can keep your mouth shut and do it my way."

"Get to the point."

"The point is they believe she has a malignancy and we're not going to tell her. I almost didn't tell you." His voice faltered. "They're going to operate but if they find what they're expecting, they don't think they can stop it."

For a moment there was no sound except an oceanic vibration of distance on the wire. Even that sound grew still. Robert breathed. Kate could almost see him, in a booth at the hospital, staring straight ahead at the plastic instructions screwed to the narrow rectangular body of the telephone. It seemed to her that she was hurtling toward him.

"I'll do it your way," she said.

The hospital cafeteria was a large room full of orange Formica tables. Its southern wall was glass. Across the highway, Kate saw a small park modestly dotted with amusement rides and bordered by a narrow band of river. How odd, to build a children's park across from a medical center. The sight was pleasant in a cruel way. The rolling lawn of the little park was perfectly, relentlessly green.

Robert sat down. Their mother was to have surgery in two days.

"After it's over," he said, "they're not certain what will happen. The tumor is in a bad place. There may be some paralysis."

"What kind of paralysis?" Kate said. She watched him twist the green-edged coffee cup around and around on its saucer.

"Facial. And maybe worse."

"You've told her this?"

He didn't answer.

"Robert, what is she going to think if she wakes up and—"

He leaned forward, grasping the cup and speaking through clenched teeth. "Don't you think I thought of that?" He gripped the sides of the table and the cup rolled onto the carpeted floor with a dull thud. He seemed ready to throw the table after it, then grabbed Kate's wrists and squeezed them hard.

"You didn't drive her here," he said. "She was so scared she couldn't talk. How much do you want to hand her at once?"

Kate watched the cup sitting solidly on the nubby carpet.

"We've told her it's benign," Robert said, "that the surgery will cause complications, but she can learn back whatever is lost."

Kate looked at him. "Is that true?"

"They hope so."

"We're lying to her, all of us, more and more." Kate pulled her hands away and Robert touched her shoulder.

"What do *you* want to tell her, Kate? 'You're fifty-five and you're done for'?"

She stiffened. "Why put her through the operation at all?"

He sat back and dropped his arms, lowering his head. "Because without it she'd be in bad pain. Soon." They were silent, then he looked up. "And anyway," he said softly, "we don't *know*, do we? She may have a better chance than they think."

Kate put her hands on her face. Behind her closed eyes she saw a succession of blocks tumbling over.

They took the elevator up to the hospital room. They were alone and they stood close together. Above the door red numerals lit up, flashing. Behind the illuminated shapes droned an impersonal hum of machinery.

Then the doors opened with a sucking sound. Three nurses stood waiting with a lunch cart, identical covered trays stacked in tiers. There was a hot bland smell, like warm cardboard. One of the women caught the thick steel door with her arm and smiled. Kate looked quickly at their rubber-soled shoes. White polish, the kind that rubs off. And their legs seemed only white shapes, boneless and two-dimensional, stepping silently into the metal cage.

She looked smaller in the white bed. The chrome side rails were pulled up and she seemed powerless behind them, her dark hair pushed back from her face and her forearms delicate in the baggy hospital gown. Her eyes were different in some nearly imperceptible way; she held them wider, they were shiny with a veiled wetness. For a moment the room seemed empty of all else; there were only her eyes and the dark blossoms of the flowers on the table beside her. Red roses with pine. Everyone had sent the same thing.

Robert walked close to the bed with his hands clasped behind his back, as though afraid to touch. "Where did all the flowers come from?" he asked.

"From school, and the neighbors. And Katie." She smiled.

"FTD," Kate said. "Before I left home. I felt so bad for not being here all along."

"That's silly," said her mother. "You can hardly sit at home and wait for some problem to arise."

"Speaking of problems," Robert said, "the doctor tells me you're not eating. Do I have to urge you a little?" He sat down on the edge of the bed and shook the silverware from its paper sleeve.

Kate touched the plastic tray. "Jell-O and canned cream of chicken soup. Looks great. We should have brought you something."

"They don't *want* us to bring her anything," Robert said. "This is a hospital. And I'm sure your comments make her lunch seem even more appetizing."

"I'll eat it!" said their mother in mock dismay. "Admit they sent you in here to stage a battle until I gave in."

"I'm sorry," Kate said. "He's right."

Robert grinned. "Did you hear that? She says I'm right. I don't believe it." He pushed the tray closer to his mother's chest and made a show of tucking a napkin under her chin.

"Of course you're right, dear." She smiled and gave Kate an obvious wink.

"Yeah," Robert said, "I know you two. But seriously, you eat this. I have to go make some business calls from the motel room."

Their mother frowned. "That motel must be costing you a fortune."

"No, it's reasonable," he said. "Kate can stay for a week or two and I'll drive back and forth from home. If you think this food is bad, you should see the meals in that motel restaurant." He got up to go, flashing Kate a glance of collusion. "I'll be back after supper."

His footsteps echoed down the hallway. Kate and her mother looked wordlessly at each other, relieved. Kate looked away guiltily. Then her mother spoke, apologetic. "He's so tired," she said. "He's been with me since yesterday."

She looked at Kate, then into the air of the room. "I'm in a fix," she said. "Except for when the pain comes, it's all a show that goes on without me. I'm like an invalid, or a lunatic."

Kate moved close and touched her mother's arms. "That's all right, we're going to get you through it. Someone's covering for you at work?"

"I had to take a leave of absence. It's going to take a while afterward—"

"I know. But it's the last thing to worry about, it can't be helped."

"Like spilt milk. Isn't that what they say?"

"I don't know what they say. But why didn't you tell me? Didn't you know something was wrong?"

"Yes . . . bad headaches. Migraines, I thought, or the diabetes getting worse. I was afraid they'd start me on insulin." She tightened the corner of her mouth. "Little did I know . . ."

They heard the shuffle of slippers. An old woman stood at the open door of the room, looking in confusedly. She seemed about to speak, then moved on.

"Oh," said Kate's mother in exasperation, "shut that door, please? They let these old women wander around like refugees." She sat up, reaching for a robe. "And let's get me out of this bed."

They sat near the window while she finished eating. Bars of moted yellow banded the floor of the room. The light held a tinge of spring which seemed painful because it might vanish. They heard the rattle of the meal cart outside the closed door, and the clunk-slide of patients with aluminum walkers. Kate's mother sighed and pushed away the half-empty soup bowl.

"They'll be here after me any minute. More tests. I just want to stay with you." Her face was warm and smooth in the slanted light, lines in her skin delicate, unreal; as though a face behind her face was now apparent after many years. She sat looking at Kate and smiled.

"One day when you were about four you were dragging a broom around the kitchen. I asked you what you were doing and you told me that when you got old you were going to be an angel and sweep the rotten rain off the clouds."

"What did you say to that?"

"I said that when you were old I was sure God would see to it." Her mother laughed. "I'm glad you weren't such a smart aleck then," she said. "You would have told me my view of God was paternalistic."

"Ah yes," sighed Kate. "God, that famous dude. Here I am, getting old, facing unemployment, alone, and where is He?"

"You're not alone," her mother said, "I'm right here."

Kate didn't answer. She sat motionless and felt her heart begin to open like a box with a hinged lid. The fullness had no edges.

Her mother stood. She rubbed her hands slowly, twisting her wedding rings. "My hands are so dry in the winter," she said softly, "I brought some hand cream with me but I can't find it anywhere, my suitcase is so jumbled. Thank heavens spring is early this year. . . . They told me that little park over there doesn't usually open till the end of March . . ."

She's helping me, thought Kate, I'm not supposed to let her down.

". . . but they're already running it on weekends. Even past dusk. We'll see the lights tonight. You can't see the shapes this far away, just the motion . . ."

A nurse came in with a wheelchair. Kate's mother pulled a wry face. "This wheelchair is a bit much," she said.

"We don't want to tire you out," said the nurse.

The chair took her weight quietly. At the door she put out her hand to stop, turned, and said anxiously, "Kate, see if you can find that hand cream?"

It was the blue suitcase from years ago, still almost new. She'd brought things she never used for everyday; a cashmere sweater, lace slips, silk underpants wrapped in tissue. Folded beneath was a stack of postmarked envelopes, slightly ragged, tied with twine. Kate opened one and realized that all the cards were there, beginning with the first of the marriage. There were a few photographs of her and Robert, baby pictures almost indistinguishable from each other, and then Kate's homemade Valentines, fastened together with rubber bands. Kate stared. *What will I do with these things?* She wanted air; she needed to breathe. She walked to ·the window and put the bundled papers on the sill. She'd raised the glass and pushed back the screen when suddenly, her mother's clock radio went off with a flat buzz. Kate moved to switch it off and brushed the cards with her arm. Envelopes shifted and slid, scattering on the floor of the room. A few snapshots wafted silently out the window. They dipped and turned, twirling. Kate didn't try to reach them. They seemed only scraps, buoyant and yellowed, blown away, the faces small as pennies. Somewhere far-off there were sirens, almost musical, drawn out and carefully approaching.

The nurse came in with evening medication. Kate's mother lay in bed. "I hope this is strong enough," she said. "Last night I couldn't sleep at all. So many sounds in a hospital . . ."

"You'll sleep tonight," the nurse assured her.

Kate winked at her mother. "That's right," she said, "I'll help you out if I have to."

They stayed up for an hour, watching the moving lights outside and the stationary glows of houses across the distant river. The halls grew darker, were lit with night lights, and the hospital dimmed. Kate waited. Her mother's eyes fluttered and finally she slept. Her breathing was low and regular.

Kate didn't move. Robert had said he'd be back; where was he? She felt a sunken anger and shook her head. She'd been on the point of telling her mother everything. The secrets were a travesty. What if there were things her mother wanted done, people she needed to see? Kate wanted to wake her before these hours passed in the dark and confess that she had lied. Between them, through the tension, there had always been a trusted clarity. Now it was twisted. Kate sat leaning forward, nearly touching the hospital bed.

Suddenly her mother sat bolt upright, her eyes open and her face transfixed. She looked blindly toward Kate but seemed to see nothing. "Who are you?" she whispered. Kate stood, at first unable to move. The woman in the bed opened and closed her mouth several times, as though she were gasping. Then she said loudly, "Stop moving the table. Stop it this instant!" Her eyes were wide with fright and her body was vibrating.

Kate reached her. "Mama, wake up, you're dreaming." Her mother jerked, flinging her arms out. Kate held her tightly.

"I can hear the wheels," she moaned.

"No, no," Kate said. "You're here with me."

"It's not so?"

"No," Kate said. "It's not so."

She went limp. Kate felt for her pulse and found it rapid, then regular. She sat rocking her mother. In a few minutes she lay her back on the pillows and smoothed the damp hair at her temples, smoothed the sheets of the bed. Later she slept fitfully in a chair, waking repeatedly to assure herself that her mother was breathing.

Near dawn she got up, exhausted, and left the room to walk in the corridor. In front of the window at the end of the hallway she saw a man slumped on a couch; the man slowly stood and wavered before her like a specter. It was Robert.

"Kate?" he said.

Years ago he had flunked out of a small junior college and their mother sat in her bedroom rocker, crying hard for over an hour while Kate tried in vain to comfort her. Kate went to the university the next fall, so anxious that she studied frantically, outlining whole textbooks in yellow ink. She sat in the front rows of large classrooms to take voluminous notes, writing quickly in her thick notebook. Robert had gone home, held a job in a plant that manufactured business forms and worked his way through the hometown college. By that time their father was dead, and Robert became, always and forever, the man of the house.

"Robert," Kate said, "I'll stay. Go home."

After breakfast they sat waiting for Robert, who had called and said he'd arrive soon. Kate's fatigue had given way to an intense awareness of every sound, every gesture. How would they get through the day? Her mother had awakened from the drugged sleep still groggy, unable to eat. The meal was sent away untouched and she watched the window as though she feared the walls of the room.

"I'm glad your father isn't here to see this," she said. There was a silence and Kate opened her mouth to speak. "I mean," said her mother quickly, "I'm going to look horrible for a few weeks, with my head all shaved." She pulled an afghan up around her lap and straightened the magazines on the table beside her chair.

"Mom," Kate said, "your hair will grow back."

Her mother pulled the afghan closer. "I've been thinking of your father," she said. "It's not that I'd have wanted him to suffer. But if he had to die, sometimes I wish he'd done it more gently. That heart attack, so finished; never a warning. I wish I'd had some time to nurse him. In a way, it's a chance to settle things."

"Did things need settling?"

"They always do, don't they?" She sat looking out the window, then said softly, "I wonder where I'm headed."

"You're not headed anywhere," Kate said. "I want you right here to see me settle down into normal American womanhood."

Her mother smiled reassuringly. "Where are my grandchildren?" she said. "That's what I'd like to know."

"You stick around," said Kate, "and I promise to start working on it." She moved her chair closer, so that their knees were touching and they could both see out the window. Below them cars moved on the highway and the Ferris wheel in the little park was turning.

"I remember when you were one of the little girls in the parade at the county fair. You weren't even in school yet; you were beautiful in that white organdy dress and pinafore. You wore those shiny black patent shoes and a crown of real apple blossoms. Do you remember?"

"Yes," Kate said. "That long parade. They told me not to move and I sat so still my legs went to sleep. When they lifted me off the float I couldn't stand up. They put me under a tree to wait for you, and you came, in a full white skirt and white sandals, your hair tied back in a red scarf. I can see you yet."

Her mother laughed. "Sounds like a pretty exaggerated picture."

Kate nodded. "I was little. You were big."

"You loved the county fair. You were wild about the carnivals." They looked down at the little park. "Magic, isn't it?" her mother said.

"Maybe we could go see it," said Kate. "I'll ask the doctor."

They walked across a pedestrian footbridge spanning the highway. Kate had bundled her mother into a winter coat and gloves despite the sunny weather. The day was sharp, nearly still, holding its bright air like illusion. Kate tasted the brittle water of her breath, felt for the cool handrail and thin steel of the webbed fencing. Cars moved steadily under the bridge. Beyond a muted roar of motors the park spread green and wooded, its limits clearly visible.

Kate's mother had combed her hair and put on lipstick. Her mouth was defined and brilliant; she linked arms with Kate like an escort. "I was afraid they'd tell us no," she said. "I was ready to run away!"

"I promised I wouldn't let you. And we only have ten minutes, long enough for the Ferris wheel." Kate grinned.

"I haven't ridden one in years. I wonder if I still know how."

"Of course you do. Ferris wheels are genetic knowledge."

"All right, whatever you say." She smiled. "We'll just hold on."

They drew closer and walked quickly through the sounds of the highway. When they reached the grass it was ankle-high and thick, longer and more ragged than it appeared from a distance. The Ferris wheel sat squarely near a grove of swaying elms, squat and laboring, taller than trees. Its neon lights still burned, pale in the sun, spiraling from inside like an imagined bloom. The naked elms surrounded it, their topmost branches tapping. Steel ribs of the machine were graceful and slightly rusted, squeaking faintly above a tinkling music. Only a few people were riding.

"Looks a little rickety," Kate said.

"Oh, don't worry," said her mother.

Kate tried to buy tickets but the ride was free. The old man running the motor wore an engineer's cap and patched overalls. He stopped the wheel and led them on a short ramp to an open car. It dipped gently, padded with black cushions. An orderly and his children rode in the car above. Kate saw their dangling feet, the girls' dusty sandals and gray socks beside their father's shoes and the hem of his white pants. The youngest one swung her feet absently, so it seemed the breeze blew her legs like fabric hung on a line.

Kate looked at her mother. "Are you ready for the big sky?" They laughed. Beyond them the river moved lazily. Houses on the opposite bank seemed empty, but a few rowboats bobbed at the docks. The surface of the water lapped and reflected clouds, and as Kate watched, searching for a definition of line, the Ferris wheel jerked into motion. The car rocked. They looked into the distance and Kate caught her mother's hand as they ascended.

Far away the hospital rose up white and glistening, its windows catching the glint of the sun. Directly below, the park was nearly deserted. There were a few cars in the parking lot and several dogs chasing each other across the grass. Two or three lone women held children on the teeter-totters and a wind was coming up. The forlorn swings moved on their chains. Kate had a vision of the park at night, totally empty, wind weaving heavily through the trees and children's playthings like a great black fish about to surface. She felt a chill on her arms. The light had gone darker, quietly, like a minor chord.

"Mom," Kate said, "it's going to storm." Her own voice seemed distant, the sound strained through layers of screen or gauze.

"No," said her mother, "it's going to pass over." She moved her hand to Kate's knee and touched the cloth of her daughter's skirt.

Kate gripped the metal bar at their waists and looked straight ahead. They were rising again and she felt she would scream. She tried to breathe rhythmically, steadily. She felt the immense weight of the air as they moved through it.

They came almost to the top and stopped. The little car swayed back and forth.

"You're sick, aren't you," her mother said.

Kate shook her head. Below them the grass seemed to glitter coldly, like a sea. Kate sat wordless, feeling the touch of her mother's hand. The hand moved away and Kate felt the absence of the warmth.

They looked at each other levelly.

"I know all about it," her mother said, "I know what you haven't told me."

The sky circled around them, a sure gray movement. Kate swallowed calmly and let their gaze grow endless. She saw herself in her mother's wide brown eyes and felt she was falling slowly into them.

ROYAL BEATINGS

Royal Beating. That was Flo's promise. You are going to get one Royal Beating.

The word Royal lolled on Flo's tongue, took on trappings. Rose had a need to picture things, to pursue absurdities, that was stronger than the need to stay out of trouble, and instead of taking this threat to heart she pondered: how is a beating royal? She came up with a tree-lined avenue, a crowd of formal spectators, some white horses and black slaves. Someone knelt, and the blood came leaping out like banners. An occasion both savage and splendid. In real life they didn't approach such dignity, and it was only Flo who tried to supply the event with some high air of necessity and regret. Rose and her father soon got beyond anything presentable.

Her father was king of the royal beatings. Those Flo gave never amounted to much; they were quick cuffs and slaps dashed off while her attention remained elsewhere. You get out of my road, she would say. You mind your own business. You take that look off your face.

They lived behind a store in Hanratty, Ontario. There were four of them: Rose, her father, Flo, Rose's young half brother Brian. The store was really a house, bought by Rose's father and mother when they married and set up here in the furniture and upholstery repair business. Her mother could do upholstery. From both parents Rose should have inherited clever hands, a quick sympathy with materials, an eye for the nicest turns of mending, but she hadn't. She was clumsy, and when something broke she couldn't wait to sweep it up and throw it away.

Her mother had died. She said to Rose's father during the afternoon, "I have a feeling that is so hard to describe. It's like a boiled egg in my chest, with the shell left on." She died before night, she had a blood clot on her lung. Rose was a baby in a basket at the time, so of course could not remember any of this. She heard it from Flo, who must have heard it from her father. Flo came along soon afterward, to take over Rose in the basket, marry her father, open up the front room to make a grocery store. Rose, who had known the house only as a store, who had known only Flo for a mother, looked back on the sixteen or so months her parents spent here as an orderly, far gentler and more ceremonious time, with little touches of affluence. She had nothing to go on but some egg cups her mother had bought, with a pattern of vines and birds on them, delicately drawn as if with red ink; the pattern was beginning to wear away. No books or clothes or pictures of her mother remained. Her father must have got rid of them, or else Flo would. Flo's only story about her mother, the one about her death, was oddly grudging. Flo liked the details of a death: the things people said, the way they protested or tried to get out of bed or swore or laughed (some did those things), but when she said that Rose's mother mentioned a hard-boiled egg in her chest she made the comparison sound slightly foolish, as if her mother really was the kind of person who might think you could swallow an egg whole.

Her father had a shed out behind the store, where he worked at his furniture repairing and restoring. He caned chair seats and backs, mended wickerwork, filled cracks, put legs back on, all most admirably and skill-fully and cheaply. That was his pride: to startle people with such fine work, such moderate, even ridiculous charges. During the Depression people could not afford to pay more, perhaps, but he continued the practice through the war, through the years of prosperity after the war, until he died. He never discussed with Flo what he charged or what was owing. After he died she had to go out and unlock the shed and take all sorts of scraps of paper and torn envelopes from the big wicked-looking hooks that were his files. Many of these she found were not accounts or receipts at all but records of the weather, bits of information about the garden, things he had been moved to write down.

> Ate new potatoes 25th June. Record.
> Dark Day, 1880's, nothing supernatural. Clouds of
>   ash from forest fires.
> Aug 16, 1938. Giant thunderstorm in evng. Light-
>   ning str. Pres. Church, Turberry Twp. Will of
>   God?
> Scald strawberries to remove acid.
> All things are alive. Spinoza.

Flo thought Spinoza must be some new vegetable he planned to grow, like broccoli or eggplant. He would often try some new thing. She showed the scrap of paper to Rose and asked, did she know what Spinoza was? Rose did know, or had an idea—she was in her teens by that time—but she replied that she did not. She had reached an age where she thought she could not stand to know any more, about her father, or about Flo; she pushed any discovery aside with embarrassment and dread.

There was a stove in the shed, and many rough shelves covered with cans of paint and varnish, shellac and turpentine, jars of soaking brushes and also some dark sticky bottles of cough medicine. Why should a man who coughed constantly, whose lungs took in a whiff of gas in the War (called, in Rose's earliest childhood, not the First, but the Last, War) spend all his days breathing fumes of paint and turpentine? At the time, such questions were not asked as often as they are now. On the bench outside Flo's store several old men from the neighborhood sat gossiping, drowsing, in the warm weather, and some of these old men coughed all the time too. The fact is they were dying, slowly and discreetly, of what was called, without any particular sense of grievance, "the foundry disease." They had worked all their lives at the foundry in town, and now they sat still, with their wasted yellow faces, coughing, drifting into aimless obscenity on the subject of women walking by, or any young girl on a bicycle.

From the shed came not only coughing, but speech, a continual muttering, reproachful or encouraging, usually just below the level at which separate words could be made out. Slowing down when her father was at a tricky piece of work, taking on a cheerful speed when he was doing something less demanding, sandpapering or painting. Now and then some words would break through and hang clear and nonsensical on the air. When he realized they were out, there would be a quick bit of cover-up coughing, a swallowing, an alert, unusual silence.

"Macaroni, pepperoni, Botticelli, beans—"

What could that mean? Rose used to repeat such things to herself. She could never ask him. The person who spoke these words and the person who spoke to her as her father were not the same, though they seemed to occupy the same space. It would be the worst sort of taste to acknowledge the person who was not supposed to be there; it would not be forgiven. Just the same, she loitered and listened.

The cloud-capped towers, she heard him say once.

"The cloud-capped towers, the gorgeous palaces."

That was like a hand clapped against Rose's chest, not to hurt, but astonish her, to take her breath away. She had to run then, she had to get away. She knew that was enough to hear, and besides, what if he caught her? That would be terrible.

This was something the same as bathroom noises. Flo had saved up, and had a bathroom put in, but there was no place to put it except in a corner of the kitchen. The door did not fit, the walls were only beaverboard.

The result was that even the tearing of a piece of toilet paper, the shifting of a haunch, was audible to those working or talking or eating in the kitchen. They were all familiar with each other's nether voices, not only in their more explosive moments but in their intimate sighs and growls and pleas and statements. And they were all most prudish people. So no one ever seemed to hear, or be listening, and no reference was made. The person creating the noises in the bathroom was not connected with the person who walked out.

They lived in a poor part of town. There was Hanratty and West Hanratty, with the river flowing between them. This was West Hanratty. In Hanratty the social structure ran from doctors and dentists and lawyers down to foundry workers and factory workers and draymen; in West Hanratty it ran from factory workers and foundry workers down to large improvident families of casual bootleggers and prostitutes and unsuccessful thieves. Rose thought of her own family as straddling the river, belonging nowhere, but that was not true. West Hanratty was where the store was and they were, on the straggling tail end of the main street. Across the road from them was a blacksmith shop, boarded up about the time the war started, and a house that had been another store at one time. The Salada Tea sign had never been taken out of the front window; it remained as a proud and interesting decoration though there was no Salada Tea for sale inside. There was just a bit of sidewalk, too cracked and tilted for roller-skating, though Rose longed for roller skates and often pictured herself whizzing along in a plaid skirt, agile and fashionable. There was one street light, a tin flower; then the amenities gave up and there were dirt roads and boggy places, front-yard dumps and strange-looking houses. What made the houses strange-looking were the attempts to keep them from going completely to ruin. With some the attempt had never been made. These were gray and rotted and leaning over, falling into a landscape of scrub hollows, frog ponds, cattails and nettles. Most houses, however, had been patched up with tarpaper, a few fresh shingles, sheets of tin, hammered-out stovepipes, even cardboard. This was, of course, in the days before the war, days of what would later be legendary poverty, from which Rose would remember mostly low-down things—serious-looking anthills and wooden steps, and a cloudy, interesting, problematical light on the world.

There was a long truce between Flo and Rose in the beginning. Rose's nature was growing like a prickly pineapple, but slowly, and secretly, hard pride and skepticism overlapping, to make something surprising even to herself. Before she was old enough to go to school, and while Brian was still in the baby carriage, Rose stayed in the store with both of them— Flo sitting on the high stool behind the counter, Brian asleep by the window; Rose knelt or lay on the wide creaky floorboards working with crayons on pieces of brown paper too torn or irregular to be used for wrapping.

People who came to the store were mostly from the houses around. Some country people came too, on their way home from town, and a few people from Hanratty, who walked across the bridge. Some people were always on the main street, in and out of stores, as if it was their duty to be always on display and their right to be welcomed. For instance, Becky Tyde.

Becky Tyde climbed up on Flo's counter, made room for herself beside an open tin of crumbly jam-filled cookies.

"Are these any good?" she said to Flo, and boldly began to eat one. "When are you going to give us a job, Flo?"

"You could go and work in the butcher shop," said Flo innocently. "You could go and work for your brother."

"Roberta?" said Becky with a stagey sort of contempt. "You think I'd work for him?" Her brother who ran the butcher shop was named Robert but often called Roberta, because of his meek and nervous ways. Becky Tyde laughed. Her laugh was loud and noisy like an engine bearing down on you.

She was a big-headed loud-voiced dwarf, with a mascot's sexless swagger, a red velvet tam, a twisted neck that forced her to hold her head on one side, always looking up and sideways. She wore little polished high-heeled shoes, real lady's shoes. Rose watched her shoes, being scared of the rest of her, of her laugh and her neck. She knew from Flo that Becky Tyde had been sick with polio as a child, that was why her neck was twisted and why she had not grown any taller. It was hard to believe that she had started out differently, that she had ever been normal. Flo said she was not cracked, she had as much brains as anybody, but she knew she could get away with anything.

"You know I used to live out here?" Becky said, noticing Rose. "Hey! What's-your-name! Didn't I used to live out here, Flo?"

"If you did it was before my time," said Flo, as if she didn't know anything.

"That was before the neighborhood got so downhill. Excuse me saying so. My father built his house out here and he built his slaughterhouse and we had half an acre of orchard."

"Is that so?" said Flo, using her humoring voice, full of false geniality, humility even. "Then why did you ever move away?"

"I told you, it got to be such a downhill neighborhood," said Becky. She would put a whole cookie in her mouth if she felt like it, let her cheeks puff out like a frog's. She never told any more.

Flo knew anyway, and who didn't. Everyone knew the house, red brick with the veranda pulled off and the orchard, what was left of it, full of the usual outflow—car seats and washing machines and bedsprings and junk. The house would never look sinister, in spite of what had happened in it, because there was so much wreckage and confusion all around.

Becky's old father was a different kind of butcher from her brother according to Flo. A bad-tempered Englishman. And different from Becky in the matter of mouthiness. His was never open. A skinflint, a family tyrant. After Becky had polio he wouldn't let her go back to school. She was seldom seen outside the house, never outside the yard. He didn't want people gloating. That was what Becky said, at the trial. Her mother was dead by that time and her sisters married. Just Becky and Robert at home. People would stop Robert on the road and ask him, "How about your sister, Robert? Is she altogether better now?"

"Yes."

"Does she do the housework? Does she get your supper?"

"Yes."

"And is your father good to her, Robert?"

The story being that the father beat them, had beaten all his children and beaten his wife as well, beat Becky more now because of her deformity, which some people believed he had caused (they did not understand about polio). The stories persisted and got added to. The reason that Becky was kept out of sight was now supposed to be her pregnancy, and the father of the child was supposed to be her own father. Then people said it had been born, and disposed of.

"What?"

"Disposed of," Flo said. "They used to say go and get your lamb chops at Tyde's, get them nice and tender! It was all lies in all probability," she said regretfully.

Rose could be drawn back—from watching the wind shiver along the old torn awning, catch in the tear—by this tone of regret, caution, in Flo's voice. Flo telling a story—and this was not the only one, or even the most lurid one, she knew—would incline her head and let her face go soft and thoughtful, tantalizing, warning.

"I shouldn't even be telling you this stuff."

More was to follow.

Three useless young men, who hung around the livery stable, got together—or were got together, by more influential and respectable men in town—and prepared to give old man Tyde a horsewhipping, in the interests of public morality. They blacked their faces. They were provided with whips and a quart of whiskey apiece, for courage. They were: Jelly Smith, a horse-racer and a drinker; Bob Temple, a ball-player and strongman; and Hat Nettleton, who worked on the town dray, and had his nickname from a bowler hat he wore, out of vanity as much as for the comic effect. He still worked on the dray, in fact; he had kept the name if not the hat, and could often be seen in public—almost as often as Becky Tyde—

delivering sacks of coal, which blackened his face and arms. That should have brought to mind his story, but didn't. Present time and past, the shady melodramatic past of Flo's stories, were quite separate, at least for Rose. Present people could not be fitted into the past. Becky herself, town oddity and public pet, harmless and malicious, could never match the butcher's prisoner, the cripple daughter, a white streak at the window: mute, beaten, impregnated. As with the house, only a formal connection could be made.

The young men primed to do the horsewhipping showed up late, outside Tyde's house, after everybody had gone to bed. They had a gun, but they used up their ammunition firing it off in the yard. They yelled for the butcher and beat on the door; finally they broke it down. Tyde concluded they were after his money, so he put some bills in a handkerchief and sent Becky down with them, maybe thinking those men would be touched or scared by the sight of a little wry-necked girl, a dwarf. But that didn't content them. They came upstairs and dragged the butcher out from under his bed, in his nightgown. They dragged him outside and stood him in the snow. The temperature was four below zero, a fact noted later in court. They meant to hold a mock trial but they could not remember how it was done. So they began to beat him and kept beating him until he fell. They yelled at him, *Butcher's meat!* and continued beating him while his nightgown and the snow he was lying in turned red. His son Robert said in court that he had not watched the beating. Becky said that Robert had watched at first but had run away and hid. She herself had watched all the way through. She watched the men leave at last and her father make his delayed bloody progress through the snow and up the steps of the veranda. She did not go out to help him, or open the door until he got to it. Why not? she was asked in court, and she said she did not go out because she just had her nightgown on, and she did not open the door because she did not want to let the cold into the house.

Old man Tyde then appeared to have recovered his strength. He told Robert to harness the horse, and made Becky heat water so that he could wash. He dressed and took all the money and with no explanation to his children got into the cutter and drove to Belgrave where he left the horse tied in the cold and took the early morning train to Toronto. On the train he behaved oddly, groaning and cursing as if he was drunk. He was picked up on the streets of Toronto a day later, out of his mind with fever, and was taken to a hospital, where he died. He still had all the money. The cause of death was given as pneumonia.

But the authorities got wind, Flo said. The case came to trial. The three men who did it all received long prison sentences. A farce, said Flo. Within a year they were all free, had all been pardoned, had jobs waiting for them. And why was that? It was because too many higher-ups were in on it. And it seemed as if Becky and Robert had no interest in seeing justice done. They were left well-off. They bought a house in Hanratty. Robert went into the store. Becky after her long seclusion started on a career of public sociability and display.

That was all. Flo put the lid down on the story as if she was sick of it. It reflected no good on anybody.

"Imagine," Flo said.

Flo at this time must have been in her early thirties. A young woman. She wore exactly the same clothes that a woman of fifty, or sixty, or seventy, might wear: print housedresses loose at the neck and sleeves as well as the waist; bib aprons, also of print, which she took off when she came from the kitchen into the store. This was a common costume at the time, for a poor though not absolutely poverty-stricken woman; it was also, in a way, a scornful deliberate choice. Flo scorned slacks, she scorned the outfits of people trying to be in style, she scorned lipstick and permanents. She wore her own black hair cut straight across, just long enough to push behind her ears. She was tall but fine-boned, with narrow wrists and shoulders, a small head, a pale, freckled, mobile, monkeyish face. If she had thought it worthwhile, and had the resources, she might have had a black-and-pale, fragile, nurtured sort of prettiness; Rose realized that later. But she would have to have been a different person altogether; she would have to have learned to resist making faces, at herself and others.

Rose's earliest memories of Flo were of extraordinary softness and hardness. The soft hair, the long, soft, pale cheeks, soft almost invisible fuzz in front of her ears and above her mouth. The sharpness of her knees, hardness of her lap, flatness of her front.

When Flo sang:

> Oh the buzzin' of the bees in the cigarette trees
> And the soda-*water* fountain . . .

Rose thought of Flo's old life before she married her father, when she worked as a waitress in the coffee shop in Union Station, and went with her girl friends Mavis and Irene to Centre Island, and was followed by men on dark streets and knew how pay phones and elevators worked. Rose heard in her voice the reckless dangerous life of cities, the gum-chewing sharp answers.

And when she sang:

> Then slowly, slowly, she got up
> And slowly she came nigh him
> And all she said, that she ever did say,
> Was young man I think, you're dyin'!

THE MOTHER: ANGEL OR "MOM"?

Rose thought of a life Flo seemed to have had beyond that, earlier than that, crowded and legendary, with Barbara Allen and Becky Tyde's father and all kinds of outrages and sorrows jumbled up together in it.

The royal beatings. What got them started?

Suppose a Saturday, in spring. Leaves not out yet but the doors open to the sunlight. Crows. Ditches full of running water. Hopeful weather. Often on Saturdays Flo left Rose in charge of the store—it's a few years now, these are the years when Rose was nine, ten, eleven, twelve—while she herself went across the bridge to Hanratty (going uptown they called it) to shop and see people, and listen to them. Among the people she listened to were Mrs. Lawyer Davies, Mrs. Anglican Rector Henley-Smith, and Mrs. Horse-Doctor McKay. She came home and imitated their flibberty voices. Monsters, she made them seem; of foolishness, and showiness, and self-approbation.

When she finished shopping she went into the coffee shop of the Queen's Hotel and had a sundae. What kind? Rose and Brian wanted to know when she got home, and they would be disappointed if it was only pineapple or butterscotch, pleased if it was a Tin Roof, or Black and White. Then she smoked a cigarette. She had some ready-rolled, that she carried with her, so that she wouldn't have to roll one in public. Smoking was the one thing she did that she would have called showing off in anybody else. It was a habit left over from her working days, from Toronto. She knew it was asking for trouble. Once the Catholic priest came over to her right in the Queen's Hotel, and flashed his lighter at her before she could get her matches out. She thanked him but did not enter into conversation, lest he should try to convert her.

Another time, on the way home, she saw at the town end of the bridge a boy in a blue jacket, apparently looking at the water. Eighteen, nineteen years old. Nobody she knew. Skinny, weakly looking, something the matter with him, she saw at once. Was he thinking of jumping? Just as she came up even with him, what does he do but turn and display himself, holding his jacket open, also his pants. What he must have suffered from the cold, on a day that had Flo holding her coat collar tight around her throat.

When she first saw what he had in his hand, Flo said, all she could think of was, what is he doing out here with a baloney sausage?

She could say that. It was offered as truth; no joke. She maintained that she despised dirty talk. She would go out and yell at the old men sitting in front of her store.

"If you want to stay where you are you better clean your mouths out!"

Saturday, then. For some reason Flo is not going uptown, has decided to stay home and scrub the kitchen floor. Perhaps this has put her in a bad mood. Perhaps she was in a bad mood anyway, due to people not paying their bills, or the stirring-up of feelings in spring. The wrangle with Rose has already commenced, has been going on forever, like a dream that goes back and back into other dreams, over hills and through doorways, maddeningly dim and populous and familiar and elusive. They are carting all the chairs out of the kitchen preparatory to the scrubbing, and they have also got to move some extra provisions for the store, some cartons of canned goods, tins of maple syrup, coal-oil cans, jars of vinegar. They take these things out to the woodshed. Brian who is five or six by this time is helping drag the tins.

"Yes," says Flo, carrying on from our lost starting point. "Yes, and that filth you taught to Brian."

"What filth?"

"And he doesn't know any better."

There is one step down from the kitchen to the woodshed, a bit of carpet on it so worn Rose can't ever remember seeing the pattern. Brian loosens it, dragging a tin.

"Two Vancouvers," she says softly.

Flo is back in the kitchen. Brian looks from Flo to Rose and Rose says again in a slightly louder voice, an encouraging sing-song, "Two Vancouvers—"

"Fried in snot!" finishes Brian, not able to control himself any longer.

"Two pickled arseholes—"

"—tied in a knot!"

There it is. The filth.

Two Vancouvers fried in snot!
Two pickled arseholes tied in a knot!

Rose has known that for years, learned it when she first went to school. She came home and asked Flo, what is a Vancouver?

"It's a city. It's a long ways away."

"What else besides a city?"

Flo said, what did she mean, what else? How could it be fried, Rose said, approaching the dangerous moment, the delightful moment, when she would have to come out with the whole thing.

"Two Vancouvers fried in snot!/Two pickled arseholes tied in a knot!"

"You're going to get it!" cried Flo in a predictable rage. "Say that again and you'll get a good clout!"

Rose couldn't stop herself. She hummed it tenderly, tried saying the innocent words aloud, humming through the others. It was not just the words snot and arsehole that gave her pleasure, though of course they did. It was the pickling and tying and the unimaginable Vancouvers. She saw them in her mind shaped rather like octopuses, twitching in the pan. The tumble of reason; the spark and spit of craziness.

Lately she has remembered it again and taught it to Brian, to see if it has the same effect on him, and of course it has.

"Oh, I heard you!" says Flo. "I heard that! And I'm warning you!"

So she is. Brian takes the warning. He runs away, out the woodshed door, to do as he likes. Being a boy, free to help or not, involve himself or not. Not committed to the household struggle. They don't need him anyway, except to use against each other, they hardly notice his going. They continue, can't help continuing, can't leave each other alone. When they seem to have given up they really are just waiting and building up steam.

Flo gets out the scrub pail and the brush and the rag and the pad for her knees, a dirty red rubber pad. She starts to work on the floor. Rose sits on the kitchen table, the only place left to sit, swinging her legs. She can feel the cool oilcloth, because she is wearing shorts, last summer's tight faded shorts dug out of the summer-clothes bag. They smell a bit moldy from winter storage.

Flo crawls underneath, scrubbing with the brush, wiping with the rag. Her legs are long, white and muscular, marked all over with blue veins as if somebody had been drawing rivers on them with an indelible pencil. An abnormal energy, a violent disgust, is expressed in the chewing of the brush at the linoleum, the swish of the rag.

What do they have to say to each other? It doesn't really matter. Flo speaks of Rose's smart-aleck behavior, rudeness and sloppiness and conceit. Her willingness to make work for others, her lack of gratitude. She mentions Brian's innocence, Rose's corruption. Oh, don't you think you're somebody, says Flo, and a moment later, Who do you think you are? Rose contradicts and objects with such poisonous reasonableness and mildness, displays theatrical unconcern. Flo goes beyond her ordinary scorn and self-possession and becomes amazingly theatrical herself, saying it was for Rose that she sacrificed her life. She saw her father saddled with a baby daughter and she thought, what is that man going to do? So she married him, and here she is, on her knees.

At that moment the bell rings, to announce a customer in the store. Because the fight is on, Rose is not permitted to go into the store and wait on whoever it is. Flo gets up and throws off her apron, groaning— but not communicatively, it is not a groan whose exasperation Rose is allowed to share—and goes in and serves. Rose hears her using her normal voice.

"About time! Sure is!"

She comes back and ties on her apron and is ready to resume.

"You never have a thought for anybody but your ownself! You never have a thought for what I'm doing."

"I never asked you to do anything. I wish you never had. I would have been a lot better off."

Rose says this smiling directly at Flo, who has not yet gone down on her knees. Flo sees the smile, grabs the scrub rag that is hanging on the side of the pail, and throws it at her. It may be meant to hit her in the face but instead it falls against Rose's leg and she raises her foot and catches it, swinging it negligently against her ankle.

"All right," says Flo. "You've done it this time. All right."

Rose watches her go to the woodshed door, hears her tramp through the woodshed, pause in the doorway, where the screen door hasn't yet been hung, and the storm door is standing open, propped with a brick. She calls Rose's father. She calls him in a warning, summoning voice, as if against her will preparing him for bad news. He will know what this is about.

The kitchen floor has five or six different patterns of linoleum on it. Ends, which Flo got for nothing and ingeniously trimmed and fitted together, bordering them with tin strips and tacks. While Rose sits on the table waiting, she looks at the floor, at this satisfying arrangement of rectangles, triangles, some other shape whose name she is trying to remember. She hears Flo coming back through the woodshed, on the creaky plank walk laid over the dirt floor. She is loitering, waiting, too. She and Rose can carry this no further, by themselves.

Rose hears her father come in. She stiffens, a tremor runs through her legs, she feels them shiver on the oilcloth. Called away from some peaceful, absorbing task, away from the words running in his head, called out of himself, her father has to say something. He says, "Well? What's wrong?"

Now comes another voice of Flo's. Enriched, hurt, apologetic, it seems to have been manufactured on the spot. She is sorry to have called him from his work. Would never have done it, if Rose was not driving her to distraction. How to distraction? With her back talk and impudence and her terrible tongue. The things Rose has said to Flo are such that, if Flo had said them to her mother, she knows her father would have thrashed her into the ground.

Rose tries to butt in, to say this isn't true.

What isn't true?

Her father raises a hand, doesn't look at her, says, "Be quiet."

When she says it isn't true, Rose means that she herself didn't start this, only responded, that she was goaded by Flo, who is now, she believes, telling the grossest sort of lies, twisting everything to suit herself. Rose puts aside her other knowledge that whatever Flo has said or done, whatever she herself has said or done, does not really matter at all. It is the struggle itself that counts, and that can't be stopped, can never be stopped, short of where it has got to, now.

Flo's knees are dirty, in spite of the pad. The scrub rag is still hanging over Rose's foot.

Her father wipes his hands, listening to Flo. He takes his time. He is slow at getting into the spirit of things, tired in advance, maybe, on the verge of rejecting the role he has to play. He won't look at Rose, but at any sound or stirring from Rose, he holds up his hand.

"Well we don't need the public in on this, that's for sure," Flo says, and she goes to lock the door of the store, putting in the store window the sign that says BACK SOON, a sign Rose made for her with a great deal of fancy curving and shading of letters in black and red crayon. When she comes back she shuts the door to the store, then the door to the stairs, then the door to the woodshed.

Her shoes have left marks on the clean wet part of the floor.

"Oh, I don't know," she says now, in a voice worn down from its emotional peak. "I don't know what to do about her." She looks down and sees her dirty knees (following Rose's eyes) and rubs them viciously with her bare hands, smearing the dirt around.

"She humiliates me," she says, straightening up. There it is, the explanation. "She humiliates me," she repeats with satisfaction. "She has no respect."

"I do not!"

"Quiet, you!" says her father.

"If I hadn't called your father you'd still be sitting there with that grin on your face! What other way is there to manage you?"

Rose detects in her father some objections to Flo's rhetoric, some embarrassment and reluctance. She is wrong, and ought to know she is wrong, in thinking that she can count on this. The fact that she knows about it, and he knows she knows, will not make things any better. He is beginning to warm up. He gives her a look. This look is at first cold and challenging. It informs her of his judgment, of the hopelessness of her position. Then it clears, it begins to fill up with something else, the way a spring fills up when you clear the leaves away. It fills with hatred and pleasure. Rose sees that and knows it. Is that just a description of anger, should she see his eyes filling up with anger? No. Hatred is right. Pleasure is right. His face loosens and changes and grows younger, and he holds up his hand this time to silence Flo.

"All right," he says, meaning that's enough, more than enough, this part is over, things can proceed. He starts to loosen his belt.

Flo has stopped anyway. She has the same difficulty Rose does, a difficulty in believing that what you know must happen really will happen, that there comes a time when you can't draw back.

"Oh, I don't know, don't be too hard on her." She is moving around nervously as if she has thoughts of opening some escape route. "Oh, you don't have to use the belt on her. Do you have to use the belt?"

He doesn't answer. The belt is coming off, not hastily. It is being grasped at the necessary point. *All right you.* He is coming over to Rose. He pushes her off the table. His face, like his voice, is quite out of character. He is like a bad actor, who turns a part grotesque. As if he must savor and insist on just what is shameful and terrible about this. That is not to say he is pretending, that he is acting, and does not mean it. He is acting, and he means it. Rose knows that, she knows everything about him.

She has since wondered about murders, and murderers. Does the thing have to be carried through, in the end, partly for the effect, to prove to the audience of one—who won't be able to report, only register, the lesson—that such a thing can happen, that there is nothing that can't happen, that the most dreadful antic is justified, feelings can be found to match it?

She tries again looking at the kitchen floor, that clever and comforting geometrical arrangement, instead of looking at him or his belt. How can this go on in front of such daily witnesses—the linoleum, the calendar with the mill and creek and autumn trees, the old accommodating pots and pans?

Hold out your hand!

Those things aren't going to help her, none of them can rescue her. They turn bland and useless, even unfriendly. Pots can show malice, the patterns of linoleum can leer up at you, treachery is the other side of dailiness.

At the first, or maybe the second, crack of pain, she draws back. She will not accept it. She runs around the room, she tries to get to the doors. Her father blocks her off. Not an ounce of courage or of stoicism in her, it would seem. She runs, she screams, she implores. Her father is after her, cracking the belt at her when he can, then abandoning it and using his hands. Bang over the ear, then bang over the other ear. Back and forth, her head ringing. Bang in the face. Up against the wall and bang in the face again. He shakes her and hits her against the wall, he kicks her legs. She is incoherent, insane, shrieking. *Forgive me! Oh please, forgive me!*

Flo is shrieking too. *Stop, stop!*

Not yet. He throws Rose down. Or perhaps she throws herself down. He kicks her legs again. She has given up on words but is letting out a noise, the sort of noise that makes Flo cry, *Oh, what if people can hear her?* The very last-ditch willing sound of humiliation and defeat it is, for it seems Rose must play her part in this with the same grossness, the same exaggeration, that her father displays, playing his. She plays his victim with a self-indulgence that arouses, and maybe hopes to arouse, his final, sickened contempt.

They will give this anything that is necessary, it seems, they will go to any lengths.

Not quite. He has never managed really to injure her, though there are times, of course, when she prays that he will. He hits her with an open hand, there is some restraint in his kicks.

Now he stops, he is out of breath. He allows Flo to move in, he grabs Rose up and gives her a push in Flo's direction, making a sound of disgust. Flo retrieves her, opens the stair door, shoves her up the stairs.

"Go on up to your room now! Hurry!"

Rose goes up the stairs, stumbling, letting herself stumble, letting herself fall against the steps. She doesn't bang her door because a gesture like that could still bring him after her, and anyway, she is weak. She lies on the bed. She can hear through the stovepipe hole Flo snuffling and re-monstrating, her father saying angrily that Flo should have kept quiet then, if she did not want Rose punished she should not have recommended it. Flo says she never recommended a hiding like that.

They argue back and forth on this. Flo's frightened voice is growing stronger, getting its confidence back. By stages, by arguing, they are being drawn back into themselves. Soon it's only Flo talking; he will not talk anymore. Rose has had to fight down her noisy sobbing, so as to listen to them, and when she loses interest in listening, and wants to sob some more, she finds she can't work herself up to it. She has passed into a state of calm, in which outrage is perceived as complete and final. In this state events and possibilities take on a lovely simplicity. Choices are mercifully clear. The words that come to mind are not the quibbling, seldom the conditional. Never is a word to which the right is suddenly established. She will never speak to them, she will never look at them with anything but loathing, she will never forgive them. She will punish them; she will finish them. Encased in these finalities, and in her bodily pain, she floats in curious comfort, beyond herself, beyond responsibility.

Suppose she dies now? Suppose she commits suicide? Suppose she runs away? Any of these things would be appropriate. It is only a matter of choosing, of figuring out the way. She floats in her pure superior state as if kindly drugged.

And just as there is a moment, when you are drugged, in which you feel perfectly safe, sure, unreachable, and then without warning and right next to it a moment in which you know the whole protection has fatally cracked, though it is still pretending to hold soundly together, so there is a moment now—the moment, in fact, when Rose hears Flo step on the stairs—that contains for her both present peace and freedom and a sure knowledge of the whole down-spiraling course of events from now on.

Flo comes into the room without knocking, but with a hesitation that shows it might have occurred to her. She brings a jar of cold cream. Rose is hanging on to advantage as long as she can, lying face down on the bed, refusing to acknowledge or answer.

"Oh come on," Flo says uneasily. "You aren't so bad off, are you? You put some of this on and you'll feel better."

She is bluffing. She doesn't know for sure what damage has been done. She has the lid off the cold cream. Rose can smell it. The intimate, babyish, humiliating smell. She won't allow it near her. But in order to avoid it, the big ready clot of it in Flo's hand, she has to move. She scuffles, resists, loses dignity, and lets Flo see there is not really much the matter.

"All right," Flo says. "You win. I'll leave it here and you can put it on when you like."

Later still a tray will appear. Flo will put it down without a word and go away. A large glass of chocolate milk on it, made with Vita-Malt from the store. Some rich streaks of Vita-Malt around the bottom of the glass. Little sandwiches, neat and appetizing. Canned salmon of the first quality and reddest color, plenty of mayonnaise. A couple of butter tarts from a bakery package, chocolate biscuits with a peppermint filling. Rose's favorites, in the sandwich, tart and cookie line. She will turn away, refuse to look, but left alone with these eatables will be miserably tempted, roused and troubled and drawn back from thoughts of suicide or flight by the smell of salmon, the anticipation of crisp chocolate, she will reach out a finger, just to run it around the edge of one of the sandwiches (crusts cut off!) to get the overflow, get a taste. Then she will decide to eat one, for strength to refuse the rest. One will not be noticed. Soon, in helpless corruption, she will eat them all. She will drink the chocolate milk, eat the tarts, eat the cookies. She will get the malty syrup out of the bottom of the glass with her finger, though she sniffles with shame. Too late.

Flo will come up and get the tray. She may say, "I see you got your appetite still," or, "Did you like the chocolate milk, was it enough syrup in it?" depending on how chastened she is feeling, herself. At any rate, all advantage will be lost. Rose will understand that life has started up again, that they will all sit around the table eating again, listening to the radio news. Tomorrow morning, maybe even tonight. Unseemly and unlikely as that may be. They will be embarrassed, but rather less than you might expect considering how they have behaved. They will feel a queer lassitude, a convalescent indolence, not far off satisfaction.

One night after a scene like this they were all in the kitchen. It must have been summer, or at least warm weather, because her father spoke of the old men who sat on the bench in front of the store.

"Do you know what they're talking about now?" he said, and nodded his head toward the store to show who he meant, though of course they were not there now, they went home at dark.

"Those old coots," said Flo. "What?"

There was about them both a geniality not exactly false but a bit more emphatic than was normal, without company.

Rose's father told them then that the old men had picked up the idea somewhere that what looked like a star in the western sky, the first star that came out after sunset, the evening star, was in reality an airship hovering over Bay City, Michigan, on the other side of Lake Huron. An American invention, sent up to rival the heavenly bodies. They were all in agreement about this, the idea was congenial to them. They believed it to be lit by ten thousand electric light bulbs. Her father had ruthlessly disagreed with them, pointing out that it was the planet Venus they saw, which had appeared in the sky long before the invention of an electric light bulb. They had never heard of the planet Venus.

"Ignoramuses," said Flo. At which Rose knew, and knew her father knew, that Flo had never heard of the planet Venus either. To distract them from this, or even apologize for it, Flo put down her teacup, stretched out with her head resting on the chair she had been sitting on and her feet on another chair (somehow she managed to tuck her dress modestly between her legs at the same time), and lay stiff as a board, so that Brian cried out in delight, "Do that! Do that!"

Flo was double-jointed and very strong. In moments of celebration or emergency she would do tricks.

They were silent while she turned herself around, not using her arms at all but just her strong legs and feet. Then they all cried out in triumph, though they had seen it before.

Just as Flo turned herself Rose got a picture in her mind of that airship, an elongated transparent bubble, with its strings of diamond lights, floating in the miraculous American sky.

"The planet Venus!" her father said, applauding Flo. "Ten thousand electric lights!"

There was a feeling of permission, relaxation, even a current of happiness, in the room.

Years later, many years later, on a Sunday morning, Rose turned on the radio. This was when she was living by herself in Toronto.

Well sir.

It was a different kind of place in our day. Yes it was.

It was all horses then. Horses and buggies. Buggy races up and down the main street on the Saturday nights.

"Just like the chariot races," says the announcer's, or interviewer's, smooth encouraging voice.

I never seen a one of them.

"No sir, that was the old Roman chariot races I was referring to. That was before your time."

Musta been before my time. I'm a hunerd and two years old.

"That's a wonderful age, sir."

It is so.

She left it on, as she went around the apartment kitchen, making coffee for herself. It seemed to her that this must be a staged interview, a scene from some play, and she wanted to find out what it was. The old man's voice was so vain and belligerent, the interviewer's quite hopeless and alarmed, under its practiced gentleness and ease. You were surely meant to see him holding the microphone up to some toothless, reckless, preening centenarian, wondering what in God's name he was doing here, and what would he say next?

"They must have been fairly dangerous."

What was dangerous?

"Those buggy races."

They was. Dangerous: Used to be the runaway horses. Used to be a-plenty of accidents. Fellows was dragged along on the gravel and cut their face open. Wouldna matter so much if they was dead. Heh.

Some of them horses was the high-steppers. Some, they had to have the mustard under their tail. Some wouldn step out for nothin. That's the thing it is with the horses. Some'll work and pull till they drop down dead and some wouldn pull your cock out of a pail of lard. Hehe.

It must be a real interview after all. Otherwise they wouldn't have put that in, wouldn't have risked it. It's all right if the old man says it. Local color. Anything rendered harmless and delightful by his hundred years.

Accidents all the time then. In the mill. Foundry. Wasn't the precautions.

"You didn't have so many strikes then, I don't suppose? You didn't have so many unions?"

Everybody taking it easy nowadays. We worked and we was glad to get it. Worked and was glad to get it.

"You didn't have television."

Didn't have no TV. Didn't have no radio. No picture show.

"You made your own entertainment."

That's the way we did.

"You had a lot of experiences young men growing up today will never have."

Experiences.

"Can you recall any of them for us?"

I eaten groundhog meat one time. One winter. You wouldna cared for it. Heh.

There was a pause, of appreciation, it would seem, then the announcer's voice saying that the foregoing had been an interview with Mr. Wilfred Nettleton of Hanratty, Ontario, made on his hundred and second birthday, two weeks before his death, last spring. A living link with our past. Mr. Nettleton had been interviewed in the Wawanash County Home for the Aged.

Hat Nettleton.

Horsewhipper into centenarian. Photographed on his birthday, fussed over by nurses, kissed no doubt by a girl reporter. Flash bulbs popping at him. Tape recorder drinking in the sound of his voice. Oldest resident. Oldest horsewhipper. Living link with our past.

Looking out from her kitchen window at the cold lake, Rose was longing to tell somebody. It was Flo who would enjoy hearing. She thought of her saying *Imagine!* in a way that meant she was having her worst suspicions gorgeously confirmed. But Flo was in the same place Hat Nettleton had died in, and there wasn't any way Rose could reach her. She had been there even when that interview was recorded, though she would not have heard it, would not have known about it. After Rose put her in the Home, a couple of years earlier, she had stopped talking. She had removed herself, and spent most of her time sitting in a corner of her crib, looking crafty and disagreeable, not answering anybody, though she occasionally showed her feelings by biting a nurse.

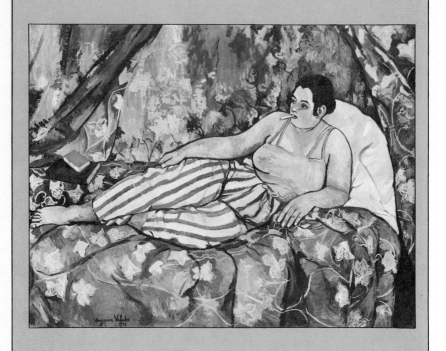

I M A G E   T H R E E

T H E   D O M I N A T I N G   W I F E :

T H E   B I T C H

As the submissive wife corresponds to the "good" mother, the dominating wife corresponds to the "terrible" mother. In the past the shrewish wife has often been viewed as comic and could be laughed at as a necessary evil: the medieval stock character Mrs. Noah who rants and raves as she orders her husband around, Chaucer's Wife of Bath who brags about her manipulation of five husbands, Shakespeare's Kate who has to be tamed by her husband. But women with strong wills, such as Lady Macbeth and Cleopatra, were often the source of tragedy. Sometimes just by being beautiful a wife could unman her husband and cause his disgrace, as in the French romance about Erèc and Enide. Though we laugh at Thurber's bossy Mrs. Mitty in "The Secret Life of Walter Mitty," a selfish, destructive alcoholic like Martha in Albee's *Who's Afraid of Virginia Woolf?* is perceived as realistic. Unlike the submissive wife and the mother about whom some ambiguous attitudes remain, the dominating wife is usually perceived with unrelieved hostility and anger. Thurber's cartoon of the little man about to be swallowed by the monstrous matriarch ruling his house seems true to life in a society that tends to ascribe a dominant role in every relationship.

Violence and death are the keynotes of the selections in this part. Images of guns, hunting, pain, suicide, murder show the effects of an unnatural woman, one who dominates men. In Eugene O'Neill's play "Before Breakfast," Mrs. Rowland dominates the scene so forcefully that we do not even see her husband, toward whom she directs her tirade of abuse and threats. She taunts him for his dependence on her and makes it clear she will never let him pursue his own happiness. Margaret Macomber in Hemingway's "The Short Happy Life of Francis Macomber" not only deprives her husband of his courage and virility but (it is strongly implied) may have been his executioner to prevent him from assuming the dominant role in their marriage. The effects of female dominance are unrelievedly disastrous. The main cause of their dominance, from a male perspective, is an unnatural lack of womanly qualities. The slovenly and prematurely old Mrs. Rowland is an alcoholic who drinks before breakfast to gain the courage to search for evidence of her husband's infidelity; an unnatural woman, she enjoys her "triumphal malignity" as a witch might. From the perspective of Wilson, the hunting guide, Margaret Macomber is typical of American women whom he sees as "the hardest in the world; the hardest, the cruelest, the most predatory and the most attractive." Wilson sees her as her husband's murderer and intends to blackmail her.

For these stories it is especially important to recognize the significance of the persona from whose perspective the story is told. As readers, we need not be limited to the attitudes of the narrative voice but can use our own experience with life and reading to go beyond the narrator's view. Since O'Neill's work is a play, we are free to judge the scenes without a narrator as guide; subtly, the play builds on our expectations, upon public stereotypes. Objectively, we can have little doubt about Mrs. Rowland's bitchiness. But her horror when she sees the full effect of her threats suggests that she did not intend anything as extreme as driving her husband to suicide. From a feminist perspective we may believe that the husband's insistence on his right to nourish his genius at her expense led to her alcoholism and rage. We know that a person who is abusive has usually been abused. Though Mrs. Rowland is given no visible redeeming qualities, it is not reasonable to suppose she is evil incarnate, as the play suggests. Similarly, in Hemingway's story we need not accept as totally reliable the view of the hunting guide, to whom the Macombers are foreigners. Our own experience of American women can help us generalize more reliably than Wilson can, though of course it is sobering to realize that anyone perceives American women so negatively. We can at least wonder about Margaret's motivation for shooting; she may indeed have tried to save him as she protests. We can question Wilson's motivation for accusing her so quickly. In any case, Hemingway invites the reader to focus on questions about Francis Macomber, not Margaret. Was he happy at all? When? By choosing Wilson as the central consciousness, Hemingway limits our information for assessing Margaret.

In Florence Cohen's "Mrs. Poe" we see how a central consciousness sympathetic to a character viewed by many as a bitch can influence a reader's perspective. Mrs. Poe is finally committed to an institution for the insane because her persistent need for truth in human relationships is counter to the moral code of her family and her society. The omniscient narrator weighs the reader's view with rich symbols. Mrs. Poe wears white clothes, a symbol of purity; her beauty and her golden hair make her seem the feminine ideal. Comparing her to a dandelion brings her down to earth; the omnipresent symbol of spring has its roots in the earth too tenaciously to be extirpated by society's view of it as a weed. The fact that Jeb Williams, the symbol of the devil, is eating pomegranate seeds reminds us of the myth in which Persephone was enticed by the god of the underworld to eat a pomegranate. As a result she had to marry him and remain in Hades for half the year, separated from her mother Demeter; for human beings her stay in hell causes winter and death. Cohen's linking of this symbol of death and destruction to a male figure counters the usual mythical identification of woman—Eve, Lilith, Pandora—as the source of evil and death in the world. Cohen's story, emphasizing the wickedness and weakness of the males bonded in the father-son relationship, invites us to understand the mother-daughter bond as an emblem of truth and justice. Though Mrs. Poe will be lost, her daughter as writer will tell her story. Cohen condemns patriarchal justice in the image of Judge Poe, patriarchal religion in the Reverend Mr. Williams, patriarchal separation of morality from everyday life in Emory Poe. Though the weight of guilt is on the male characters, women share in the system's corruption: the Sunday school teacher, all the "mattering" people are caught up in hypocrisy. The story is not anti-male; Mrs. Poe loves Rufe, the innocent black lynching victim, who significantly, has no father in his life. "Mrs. Poe" is a call for the justice best represented now in our society by female concern for human relationships and love; it stresses societal need for feminine qualities in men and women alike. It also makes terrifyingly clear the price that may be paid by those who defy the system.

EUGENE O'NEILL

(1888–1953) The first great American drama-tist, Eugene O'Neill won the Pulitzer Prize four times and the Nobel Prize in 1936. Author of a number of one-act plays, he is best known for his comedy *Ah, Wilderness* and for many great tragedies echoing Greek drama. His masterpiece, *Long Day's Jour-ney into Night,* is the story of his own family tragedy, and shows the influence of Freudian and other contemporary psycho-logical thought.

BEFORE BREAKFAST

A Play in One Act

Characters

MRS. ROWLAND
ALFRED Her husband (not seen)

Scene

A small room serving both as kitchen and dining room in a flat on Chris-topher Street, New York City. In the rear, to the right, a door leading to the outer hallway. On the left of the doorway, a sink, and a two-burner gas stove. Over the stove, and extending to the left wall, a wooden closet for dishes, etc. On the left, two windows looking out on a fire escape where several potted plants are dying of neglect. Before the windows, a table covered with oilcloth. Two cane-bottomed chairs are placed by the table. Another stands against the wall to the right of door in rear. In the right wall, rear, a doorway leading into a bedroom. Farther forward, different articles of a man's and a woman's clothing are hung on pegs. A clothes line is strung from the left corner, rear, to the right wall, forward. A man's underclothes are thrown over the line.

It is about eight-thirty in the morning of a fine, sunshiny day in the early fall.

Mrs. Rowland enters from the bedroom, yawning, her hands still busy putting the finishing touches on a slovenly toilet by sticking hairpins into her hair which is bunched up in a drab-colored mass on top of her round head. She is of medium height and inclined to a shapeless stoutness, accentuated by her formless blue dress, shabby and worn. Her face is characterless, with small regular features and eyes of a nondescript blue. There is a pinched expression about her eyes and nose and her weak, spiteful mouth. She is in her early twenties but looks much older.

She comes to the middle of the room and yawns, stretching her arms to their full length. Her drowsy eyes stare about the room with the irritated look of one to whom a long sleep has not been a long rest. She goes wearily to the clothes hanging on the right and takes an apron from a hook. She ties it about her waist, giving vent to an exasperated "damn" when the knot fails to obey her clumsy, fat fingers. Finally gets it tied and goes slowly to the gas stove and lights one burner. She fills the coffee pot at the sink and sets it over the flame. Then slumps down into a chair by the table and puts a hand over her forehead as if she were suffering from headache. Suddenly her face brightens as though she had remembered something, and she casts a quick glance at the dish closet; then looks sharply at the bedroom door and listens intently for a moment or so.

MRS. ROWLAND *(in a low voice)* Alfred! Alfred! *(There is no answer from the next room and she continues suspiciously in a louder tone)* You needn't pretend you're asleep. *(There is no reply to this from the bedroom, and, reassured, she gets up from her chair and tiptoes cautiously to the dish closet. She slowly opens one door, taking great care to make no noise, and slides out, from their hiding place behind the dishes, a bottle of Gordon gin and a glass. In doing so she disturbs the top dish, which rattles a little. At this sound she starts guiltily and looks with sulky defiance at the doorway to the next room)*
(Her voice trembling) Alfred!
(After a pause, during which she listens for any sound, she takes the glass and pours out a large drink and gulps it down; then hastily returns the bottle and glass to their hiding place. She closes the closet door with the same care as she had opened it, and, heaving a great sigh of relief, sinks down into her chair again. The large dose of alcohol she has taken has an almost immediate effect. Her features become more animated, she seems to gather energy, and she looks at the bedroom door with a hard, vindictive smile on her lips. Her eyes glance quickly about the room and are fixed on a man's coat and vest which hang from a hook at right. She moves stealthily over to the open doorway and stands there, out of sight of any one inside, listening for any movement from within)
(Calling in a half-whisper) Alfred!
(Again there is no reply. With a swift movement she takes the coat and vest from the hook and returns with them to her chair. She sits down and

takes the various articles out of each pocket but quickly puts them back again. At last, in the inside pocket of the vest, she finds a letter)
(Looking at the handwriting—slowly to herself) Hmm! I knew it. *(She opens the letter and reads it. At first her expression is one of hatred and rage, but as she goes on to the end it changes to one of triumphant malignity. She remains in deep thought for a moment, staring before her, the letter in her hands, a cruel smile on her lips. Then she puts the letter back in the pocket of the vest, and still careful not to awaken the sleeper, hangs the clothes up again on the same hook, and goes to the bedroom door and looks in)*
(In a loud, shrill voice) Alfred! *(Still louder)* Alfred! *(There is a muffled, yawning groan from the next room)* Don't you think it's about time you got up? Do you want to stay in bed all day? *(Turning around and coming back to her chair)* Not that I've got any doubts about your being lazy enough to stay in bed forever. *(She sits down and looks out of the window, irritably)* Goodness knows what time it is. We haven't even got any way of telling the time since you pawned your watch like a fool. The last valuable thing we had, and you knew it. It's been nothing but pawn, pawn, pawn, with you—anything to put off getting a job, anything to get out of going to work like a man. *(She taps the floor with her foot nervously, biting her lips)*
(After a short pause) Alfred! Get up, do you hear me? I want to make that bed before I go out. I'm sick of having this place in a continual mess on your account. *(With a certain vindictive satisfaction)* Not that we'll be here long unless you manage to get some money some place. Heaven knows I do my part—and more—going out to sew every day while you play the gentleman and loaf around bar rooms with that good-for-nothing lot of artists from the Square.
(A short pause during which she plays nervously with a cup and saucer on the table)
And where are you going to get money, I'd like to know? The rent's due this week and you know what the landlord is. He won't let us stay a minute over our time. You say you *can't* get a job. That's a lie and you know it. You never even look for one. All you do is moon around all day writing silly poetry and stories that no one will buy—and no wonder they won't. I notice I can always get a position, such as it is; and it's only that which keeps us from starving to death.
(Gets up and goes over to the stove—looks into the coffee pot to see if the water is boiling; then comes back and sits down again)
You'll have to get money to-day some place. I can't do it all, and I won't do it all. You've got to come to your senses. You've got to beg, borrow, or steal it somewheres. *(With a contemptuous laugh)* But where, I'd like to know? You're too proud to beg, and you've borrowed the limit, and you haven't the nerve to steal.
(After a pause—getting up angrily) Aren't you up yet, for heaven's sake?

THE DOMINATING WIFE: THE BITCH

It's just like you to go to sleep again, or pretend to. *(She goes to the bedroom door and looks in)* Oh, you are up. Well, it's about time. You needn't look at me like that. Your airs don't fool me a bit any more. I know you too well—better than you think I do—you and your goings-on. *(Turning away from the door—meaningly)* I know a lot of things, my dear. Nevermind what I know, now. I'll tell you before I go, you needn't worry. *(She comes to the middle of the room and stands there, frowning)*

(Irritably) Hmm! I suppose I might as well get breakfast ready—not that there's anything much to get.

(Questioningly) Unless you have some money? *(She pauses for an answer from the next room which does not come)* Foolish question! *(She gives a short, hard laugh)* I ought to know you better than that by this time. When you left here in such a huff last night I knew what would happen. You can't be trusted for a second. A nice condition you came home in! The fight we had was only an excuse for you to make a beast of yourself. What was the use pawning your watch if all you wanted with the money was to waste it in buying drink?

(Goes over to the dish closet and takes out plates, cups, etc., while she is talking)

Hurry up! It don't take long to get breakfast these days, thanks to you. All we got this morning is bread and butter and coffee; and you wouldn't even have that if it wasn't for me sewing my fingers off. *(She slams the loaf of bread on the table with a bang)*

The bread's stale. I hope you'll like it. *You* don't deserve any better, but I don't see why *I* should suffer.

(Going over to the stove) The coffee'll be ready in a minute, and you needn't expect me to wait for you.

(Suddenly with great anger) What on earth are you doing all this time? *(She goes over to the door and looks in)* Well, you're *almost* dressed at any rate. I expected to find you back in bed. That'd be just like you. How awful you look this morning! For heaven's sake, shave! You're disgusting! You look like a tramp. No wonder no one will give you a job. I don't blame them—when you don't even look half-way decent. *(She goes to the stove)* There's plenty of hot water right here. You've got no excuse. *(Gets a bowl and pours some of the water from the coffee pot into it)* Here. *(He reaches his hand into the room for it. It is a beautiful, sensitive hand with slender, tapering fingers. It trembles and some of the water spills on the floor)*

(Tauntingly) Look at your hand tremble! You'd better give up drinking. You can't stand it. It's just your kind that get the D.T.'s. *That would be* the last straw! *(Looking down at the floor)* Look at the mess you've made of this floor—cigarette butts and ashes all over the place. Why can't you put them on a plate? No, you wouldn't be considerate enough to do that. You never think of me. You don't have to sweep the room and that's all you care about.

(Takes the broom and commences to sweep viciously, raising a cloud of dust. From the inner room comes the sound of a razor being stropped) *(Sweeping)* Hurry up! It must be nearly time for me to go. If I'm late I'm liable to lose my position, and then I couldn't support you any longer. *(As an afterthought she adds sarcastically)* And then you'd have to go to work or something dreadful like that. *(Sweeping under the table)* What I want to know is whether you're going to look for a job to-day or not. You know your family won't help us any more. They've had enough of you, too. *(After a moment's silent sweeping)* I'm about sick of all this life. I've got a good notion to go home, if I wasn't too proud to let them know what a failure you've been—you, the millionaire Rowland's only son, the Harvard graduate, the poet, the catch of the town—Huh! *(With bitterness)* There wouldn't be many of them now envy my catch if they knew the truth. What has our marriage been, I'd like to know? Even before your *millionaire* father died owing every one in the world money, you certainly never wasted any of your time on your wife. I suppose you thought I'd ought to be glad you were *honorable* enough to marry me— after getting me into trouble. You were ashamed of me with your fine friends because my father's only a grocer, that's what you were. At least he's honest, which is more than any one could say about yours. *(She is sweeping steadily toward the door. Leans on her broom for a moment)* You hoped every one'd think you'd been forced to marry me, and pity you, didn't you? You didn't hesitate much about telling me you loved me, and making me believe your lies, before it happened, did you? You made me think you didn't want your father to buy me off as he tried to do. I know better now. I haven't lived with you all this time for nothing. *(Somberly)* It's lucky the poor thing was born dead, after all. What a father you'd have been!
(Is silent, brooding moodily for a moment—then she continues with a sort of savage joy)
But I'm not the only one who's got you to thank for being unhappy. There's one other, at least, and *she* can't hope to marry you now. *(She puts her head into the next room)* How about Helen? *(She starts back from the doorway, half frightened)*
Don't look at me that way! Yes, I read her letter. What about it? I got a right to. I'm your wife. And I know all there is to know, so don't lie. You needn't stare at me so. You can't bully me with your superior airs any longer. Only for me you'd be going without breakfast this very morning. *(She sets the broom back in the corner—whiningly)* You never did have any gratitude for what I've done. *(She comes to the stove and puts the coffee into the pot)* The coffee's ready. I'm not going to wait for you. *(She sits down in her chair again)*
(After a pause—puts her hand to her head—fretfully) My head aches so this morning. It's a shame I've got to go to work in a stuffy room all day in my condition. And I wouldn't if you were half a man. By rights I ought

to be lying on my back instead of you. You know how sick I've been this last year; and yet you object when I take a little something to keep up my spirits. You even didn't want me to take that tonic I got at the drug store. *(With a hard laugh)* I know you'd be glad to have me dead and out of your way; then you'd be free to run after all these silly girls that think you're such a wonderful, misunderstood person—this Helen and the others. *(There is a sharp exclamation of pain from the next room)* *(With satisfaction)* There! I knew you'd cut yourself. It'll be a lesson to you. You know you oughtn't to be running around nights drinking with your nerves in such an awful shape. *(She goes to the door and looks in)* What makes you so pale? What are you staring at yourself in the mirror that way for? For goodness sake, wipe that blood off your face! *(With a shudder)* It's horrible. *(In relieved tones)* There, that's better. I never could stand the sight of blood. *(She shrinks back from the door a little)* You better give up trying and go to a barber shop. Your hand shakes dreadfully. Why do you stare at me like that? *(She turns away from the door)* I'll give you fifteen cents—only promise you won't buy a drink with it. Are you still mad at me about that letter? *(Defiantly)* Well, I had a right to read it. I'm your wife. *(She comes to the chair and sits down again. After a pause)*

I knew all the time you were running around with some one. Your lame excuses about spending the time at the library didn't fool me. Who is this Helen, anyway? One of those artists? Or does she write poetry, too? Her letter sounds that way. I'll bet she told you your things were the best ever, and you believed her, like a fool. Is she young and pretty? I was young and pretty, too, when you fooled me with your fine, poetic talk; but life with you would soon wear anyone down. What I've been through! *(Goes over and takes the coffee off the stove)* Breakfast is ready. *(With a contemptuous glance)* Breakfast! *(Pours out a cup of coffee for herself and puts the pot on the table)* Your coffee'll be cold. What are you doing —still shaving, for heaven's sake? You'd better give it up. One of these mornings you'll give yourself a serious cut. *(She cuts off bread and butters it. During the following speeches she eats and sips her coffee)*

I'll have to run as soon as I've finished eating. One of us has got to work. *(Angrily)* Are you going to look for a job to-day or aren't you? I should think some of your fine friends would help you, if they really think you're so much. But I guess they just like to hear you talk. *(Sits in silence for a moment)*

I'm sorry for this Helen, whoever she is. Haven't you got any feelings for other people? What will her family say? I see she mentions them in her letter. What is she going to do—have the child—or go to one of those doctors? That's a nice thing. I must say. Where can she get the money? Is she rich? *(She waits for some answer to this volley of questions)* Hmm! You won't tell me anything about her, will you? Much I care. Come to think of it, I'm not so sorry for her, after all. She knew what she was doing. She isn't any schoolgirl, like I was, from the looks of her letter. Does she know you're married? Of course, she must. All your friends know about your unhappy marriage. I know they pity you, but they don't know my side of it. They'd talk different if they did.

(Too busy eating to go on for a second or so)

This Helen must be a fine one, if she knew you were married. What does she expect, then? That I'll divorce you and let her marry you? Does she think I'm crazy enough for that—after all you've made me go through? I guess not! And you can't get a divorce from me and you know it. No one can say *I've* ever done anything wrong. *(Drinks the last of her cup of coffee)* She deserves to suffer, that's all I can say. I'll tell you what I think; I think your Helen is no better than a common street-walker, that's what I think. *(There is a stifled groan of pain from the next room)*

Did you cut yourself again? Serves you right. Why don't you go to a barber shop when I offer you the money? *(Gets up and takes off her apron)* Well, I've got to run along. *(Peevishly)* This is a fine life for me to be leading! I won't stand for your loafing any longer. *(Something catches her ear and she pauses and listens intently)* There! You've overturned the water all over everything. Don't say you haven't. I can hear it dripping on the floor. *(A vague expression of fear comes over her face)* Alfred! Why don't you answer me?

(She moves slowly toward the room. There is the noise of a chair being overturned and something crashes heavily to the floor. She stands, trembling with fright)

Alfred! Alfred! Answer me! What is it you knocked over? Are you still drunk? *(Unable to stand the tension a second longer she rushes to the door of the bedroom)*

Alfred!

(She stands in the doorway looking down at the floor of the inner room, transfixed with horror. Then she shrieks wildly and runs to the other door, unlocks it and frenziedly pulls it open, and runs shrieking madly into the outer hallway.)

(The curtain falls.)

ERNEST HEMINGWAY

(1899–1961) Winner of both the Pulitzer and Nobel prizes, Hemingway has been one of the most important influences in contemporary American fiction. He wrote often about boys and men who were searching for and living by a code of behavior in the masculine world of hunting, fishing, bullfighting, and war. He became an exemplar of the legendary heroes he created and followed his own code by committing suicide when faced with incurable cancer. Collections of his short stories include *Men Without Women* (1927) and *Winner Take Nothing* (1933), titles descriptive of his work.

THE SHORT HAPPY LIFE
OF FRANCIS MACOMBER

It was now lunch time and they were all sitting under the double green fly of the dining tent pretending that nothing had happened.

"Will you have lime juice or lemon squash? Macomber asked.

"I'll have a gimlet," Robert Wilson told him.

"I'll have a gimlet too. I need something," Macomber's wife said.

"I suppose it's the thing to do," Macomber agreed. "Tell him to make three gimlets."

The mess boy had started them already, lifting the bottles out of the canvas cooling bags that sweated wet in the wind that blew through the trees that shaded the tents.

"What had I ought to give them?" Macomber asked.

"A quid would be plenty," Wilson told him. "You don't want to spoil them."

"Will the headman distribute it?"

"Absolutely."

Francis Macomber had, half an hour before, been carried to his tent from the edge of the camp in triumph on the arms and shoulders of the cook, the personal boys, the skinner and the porters. The gun-bearers had taken no part in the demonstration. When the native boys put him down at the door of his tent, he had shaken all their hands, received their congratulations, and then gone into the tent and sat on the bed until his wife came in. She did not speak to him when she came in and he left the tent at once to wash his face and hands in the portable wash basin outside and go over to the dining tent to sit in a comfortable canvas chair in the breeze and the shade.

"You've got your lion," Robert Wilson said to him, "and a damned fine one too."

Mrs. Macomber looked at Wilson quickly. She was an extremely handsome and well-kept woman of the beauty and social position which had, five years before, commanded five thousand dollars as the price of endorsing, with photographs, a beauty product which she had never used. She had been married to Francis Macomber for eleven years.

"He is a good lion, isn't he?" Macomber said. His wife looked at him now. She looked at both these men as though she had never seen them before.

One, Wilson, the white hunter, she knew she had never truly seen before. He was about middle height with sandy hair, a stubby mustache, a very red face and extremely cold blue eyes with faint white wrinkles at the corners that grooved merrily when he smiled. He smiled at her now and she looked away from his face at the way his shoulders sloped in the loose tunic he wore with the four big cartridges held in loops where the left breast pocket should have been, at his big brown hands, his old slacks, his very dirty boots and back to his red face again. She noticed where the baked red of his face stopped in a white line that marked the circle left by his Stetson hat that hung now from one of the pegs of the tent pole.

"Well, here's to the lion," Robert Wilson said. He smiled at her again and, not smiling, she looked curiously at her husband.

Francis Macomber was very tall, very well built if you did not mind that length of bone, dark, his hair cropped like an oarsman, rather thin-lipped, and was considered handsome. He was dressed in the same sort of safari clothes that Wilson wore except that his were new, he was thirty-five years old, kept himself very fit, was good at court games, had a number of big-game fishing records, and had just shown himself, very publicly, to be a coward.

"Here's to the lion," he said. "I can't ever thank you for what you did."

Margaret, his wife, looked away from him and back to Wilson.

"Let's not talk about the lion," she said.

Wilson looked over at her without smiling and now she smiled at him.

"It's been a very strange day," she said. "Hadn't you ought to put your hat on even under the canvas at noon? You told me that, you know."

"Might put it on," said Wilson.

"You know you have a very red face, Mr. Wilson," she told him and smiled again.

"Drink," said Wilson.

"I don't think so," she said. "Francis drinks a great deal, but his face is never red."

"It's red today," Macomber tried a joke.

"No," said Margaret. "It's mine that's red today. But Mr. Wilson's is always red."

"Must be racial," said Wilson. "I say, you wouldn't like to drop my beauty as a topic, would you?"

"I've just started on it."

"Let's chuck it," said Wilson.

"Conversation is going to be so difficult," Margaret said.

"Don't be silly, Margot," her husband said.

"No difficulty," Wilson said. "Got a damn fine lion."

Margot looked at them both and they saw that she was going to cry. Wilson had seen it coming for a long time and he dreaded it. Macomber was past dreading it.

"I wish it hadn't happened. Oh, I wish it hadn't happened," she said and started for her tent. She made no noise of crying but they could see that her shoulders were shaking under the rose-colored, sun-proofed shirt she wore.

"Women upset," said Wilson to the tall man. "Amounts to nothing. Strain on the nerves and one thing'n another."

"No," said Macomber. "I suppose that I rate that for the rest of my life now."

"Nonsense. Let's have a spot of the giant killer," said Wilson. "Forget the whole thing. Nothing to it anyway."

"We might try," said Macomber. "I won't forget what you did for me though."

"Nothing," said Wilson. "All nonsense."

So they sat there in the shade where the camp was pitched under some wide-topped acacia trees with a boulder-strewn cliff behind them, and a stretch of grass that ran to the bank of a boulder-filled stream in front with forest beyond it, and drank their just-cool lime drinks and avoided one another's eyes while the boys set the table for lunch. Wilson could tell that the boys all knew about it now and when he saw Macomber's personal boy looking curiously at his master while he was putting dishes on the table he snapped at him in Swahili. The boy turned away with his face blank.

"What were you telling him?" Macomber asked.

"Nothing. Told him to look alive or I'd see he got about fifteen of the best."

"What's that? Lashes?"

"It's quite illegal," Wilson said. "You're supposed to fine them."

"Do you still have them whipped?"

"Oh, yes. They could raise a row if they chose to complain. But they don't. They prefer it to the fines."

"How strange!" said Macomber.

"Not strange, really," Wilson said. "Which would you rather do? Take a good birching or lose your pay?"

Then he felt embarrassed at asking it and before Macomber could answer he went on, "We all take a beating every day, you know, one way or another."

This was no better. "Good God," he thought. "I am a diplomat, aren't I?"

"Yes, we take a beating," said Macomber, still not looking at him. "I'm awfully sorry about that lion business. It doesn't have to go any further, does it? I mean no one will hear about it, will they?"

"You mean will I tell it at the Mathaiga Club?" Wilson looked at him now coldly. He had not expected this. So he's a bloody four-letter man as well as a bloody coward, he thought. I rather liked him too until today. But how is one to know about an American?

"No," said Wilson. "I'm a professional hunter. We never talk about our clients. You can be quite easy on that. It's supposed to be bad form to ask us not to talk though."

He had decided now that to break would be much easier. He would eat, then, by himself and could read a book with his meals. They would eat by themselves. He would see them through the safari on a very formal basis—what was it the French called it? Distinguished consideration—and it would be a damn sight easier than having to go through this emotional trash. He'd insult him and make a good clean break. Then he could read a book with his meals and he'd still be drinking their whisky. That was the phrase for it when a safari went bad. You ran into another white hunter and you asked, "How is everything going?" and he answered, "Oh, I'm still drinking their whisky," and you knew everything had gone to pot.

"I'm sorry," Macomber said and looked at him with his American face that would stay adolescent until it became middle-aged, and Wilson noted his crew-cropped hair, fine eyes only faintly shifty, good nose, thin lips and handsome jaw. "I'm sorry I didn't realize that. There are lots of things I don't know."

So what could he do, Wilson thought. He was all ready to break it off quickly and neatly and here the beggar was apologizing after he had just insulted him. He made one more attempt. "Don't worry about me talking," he said. "I have a living to make. You know in Africa no woman ever misses her lion and no white man ever bolts."

"I bolted like a rabbit," Macomber said.

Now what in hell were you going to do about a man who talked like that, Wilson wondered.

Wilson looked at Macomber with his flat, blue, machine-gunner's eyes and the other smiled back at him. He had a pleasant smile if you did not notice how his eyes showed when he was hurt.

"Maybe I can fix it up on buffalo," he said. "We're after them next, aren't we?"

"In the morning if you like," Wilson told him. Perhaps he had been wrong. This was certainly the way to take it. You most certainly could not tell a damned thing about an American. He was all for Macomber again. If you could forget the morning. But, of course, you couldn't. The morning had been about as bad as they come.

"Here comes the Memsahib," he said. She was walking over from her tent looking refreshed and cheerful and quite lovely. She had a very perfect oval face, so perfect that you expected her to be stupid. But she wasn't stupid, Wilson thought, no, not stupid.

"How is the beautiful red-faced Mr. Wilson? Are you feeling better, Francis, my pearl?"

"Oh, much," said Macomber.

"I've dropped the whole thing," she said, sitting down at the table. "What importance is there to whether Francis is any good at killing lions? That's not his trade. That's Mr. Wilson's trade. Mr. Wilson is really very impressive killing anything. You do kill anything, don't you?"

"Oh, anything," said Wilson. "Simply anything." They are, he thought, the hardest in the world; the hardest, the cruelest, the most predatory and the most attractive and their men have softened or gone to pieces nervously as they have hardened. Or is it that they pick men they can handle? They can't know that much at the age they marry, he thought. He was grateful that he had gone through his education on American women before now because this was a very attractive one.

"We're going after buff in the morning," he told her.

"I'm coming," she said.

"No, you're not."

"Oh, yes, I am. Mayn't I, Francis?"

"Why not stay in camp?"

"Not for anything," she said. "I wouldn't miss something like today for anything."

When she left, Wilson was thinking, when she went off to cry, she seemed a hell of a fine woman. She seemed to understand, to realize, to be hurt for him and for herself and to know how things really stood. She is away for twenty minutes and now she is back, simply enamelled in that American female cruelty. They are the damnedest women. Really the damnedest.

"We'll put on another show for you tomorrow," Francis Macomber said.

"You're not coming," Wilson said.

"You're very mistaken," she told him. "And I want *so* to see you perform again. You were lovely this morning. That is if blowing things' heads off is lovely."

"Here's the lunch," said Wilson. "You're very merry, aren't you?"

"Why not? I didn't come out here to be dull."

"Well, it hasn't been dull," Wilson said. He could see the boulders in the river and the high bank beyond with the trees and he remembered the morning.

"Oh, no," she said. "It's been charming. And tomorrow. You don't know how I look forward to tomorrow."

"That's eland he's offering you," Wilson said.

"They're the big cowy things that jump like hares, aren't they?"

"I suppose that describes them," Wilson said.

"It's very good meat," Macomber said.

"Did you shoot it, Francis?" she asked.

"Yes."

"They're not dangerous, are they?"

"Only if they fall on you," Wilson told her.

"I'm so glad."

"Why not let up on the bitchery just a little, Margot," Macomber said, cutting the eland steak and putting some mashed potato, gravy and carrot on the down-turned fork that tined through the piece of meat.

"I suppose I could," she said, "since you put it so prettily."

"Tonight we'll have champagne for the lion," Wilson said. "It's a bit too hot at noon."

"Oh, the lion," Margot said. "I'd forgotten the lion!"

So, Robert Wilson thought to himself, she *is* giving him a ride, isn't she? Or do you suppose that's her idea of putting up a good show? How should a woman act when she discovers her husband is a bloody coward? She's damn cruel but they're all cruel. They govern, of course, and to govern one has to be cruel sometimes. Still, I've seen enough of their damn terrorism.

"Have some more eland," he said to her politely.

That afternoon, late, Wilson and Macomber went out in the motor car with the native driver and the two gun-bearers. Mrs. Macomber stayed in the camp. It was too hot to go out, she said, and she was going with them in the early morning. As they drove off Wilson saw her standing under the big tree, looking pretty rather than beautiful in her faintly rosy khaki, her dark hair drawn back off her forehead and gathered in a knot low on her neck, her face as fresh, he thought, as though she were in England. She waved to them as the car went off through the swale of high grass and curved around through the trees into the small hills of orchard bush.

In the orchard bush they found a herd of impala, and leaving the car they stalked one old ram with long, wide-spread horns and Macomber killed it with a very creditable shot that knocked the buck down at a good two hundred yards and sent the herd off bounding wildly and leaping over one another's backs in long, leg-drawn-up leaps as unbelievable and as floating as those one makes sometimes in dreams.

"That was a good shot," Wilson said. "They're a small target."

"Is it a worth-while head?" Macomber asked.

"It's excellent," Wilson told him. "You shoot like that and you'll have no trouble."

"Do you think we'll find buffalo tomorrow?"

"There's a good chance of it. They feed out early in the morning and with luck we may catch them in the open."

"I'd like to clear away that lion business," Macomber said. "It's not very pleasant to have your wife see you do something like that."

I should think it would be even more unpleasant to do it, Wilson thought, wife or no wife, or to talk about it having done it. But he said, "I wouldn't think about that any more. Any one could be upset by his first lion. That's all over."

But that night after dinner and a whisky and soda by the fire before going to bed, as Francis Macomber lay on his cot with the mosquito bar over him and listened to the night noises it was not all over. It was neither all over nor was it beginning. It was there exactly as it happened with some parts of it indelibly emphasized and he was miserably ashamed at it. But more than shame he felt cold, hollow fear in him. The fear was still there like a cold slimy hollow in all the emptiness where once his confidence had been and it made him feel sick. It was still there with him now.

It had started the night before when he had wakened and heard the lion roaring somewhere up along the river. It was a deep sound and at the end there were sort of coughing grunts that made him seem just outside the tent, and when Francis Macomber woke in the night to hear it he was afraid. He could hear his wife breathing quietly, asleep. There was no one to tell he was afraid, nor to be afraid with him, and, lying alone, he did not know the Somali proverb that says a brave man is always frightened three times by a lion; when he first sees his track, when he first hears him roar and when he first confronts him. Then while they were eating breakfast by lantern light out in the dining tent, before the sun was up, the lion roared again and Francis thought he was just at the edge of camp.

"Sounds like an old-timer," Robert Wilson said, looking up from his kippers and coffee. "Listen to him cough."

"Is he very close?"

"A mile or so up the stream."

"Will we see him?"

"We'll have a look."

"Does his roaring carry that far? It sounds as though he were right in camp."

"Carries a hell of a long way," said Robert Wilson. "It's strange the way it carries. Hope he's a shootable cat. The boys said there was a very big one about here."

"If I get a shot, where should I hit him," Macomber asked, "to stop him?"

"In the shoulders," Wilson said. "In the neck if you can make it. Shoot for bone. Break him down."

"I hope I can place it properly," Macomber said.

"You shoot very well," Wilson told him. "Take your time. Make sure of him. The first one in is the one that counts."

"What range will it be?"

"Can't tell. Lion has something to say about that. Don't shoot unless it's close enough so you can make sure."

"At under a hundred yards?" Macomber asked.

Wilson looked at him quickly.

"Hundred's about right. Might have to take him a bit under. Shouldn't chance a shot at much over that. A hundred's a decent range. You can hit him wherever you want at that. Here comes the Memsahib."

"Good morning," she said. "Are we going after that lion?"

"As soon as you deal with your breakfast," Wilson said. "How are you feeling?"

"Marvelous," she said. "I'm very excited."

"I'll just go and see that everything is ready," Wilson went off. As he left the lion roared again.

"Noisy beggar." Wilson said. "We'll put a stop to that."

"What's the matter, Francis?" his wife asked him.

"Nothing," Macomber said.

"Yes, there is," she said. "What are you upset about?"

"Nothing," he said.

"Tell me," she looked at him. "Don't you feel well?"

"It's that damned roaring," he said. "It's been going on all night, you know."

"Why didn't you wake me," she said. "I'd love to have heard it."

"I've got to kill the damned thing," Macomber said, miserably.

"Well, that's what you're out here for, isn't it?"

"Yes. But I'm nervous. Hearing the thing roar gets on my nerves."

"Well then, as Wilson said, kill him and stop his roaring."

"Yes, darling," said Francis Macomber. "It sounds easy, doesn't it?"

"You're not afraid, are you?"

"Of course not. But I'm nervous from hearing him roar all night."

"You'll kill him marvellously," she said. "I know you will. I'm awfully anxious to see it."

"Finish your breakfast and we'll be starting."

"It's not light yet," she said. "This is a ridiculous hour."

Just then the lion roared in a deep-chested moaning, suddenly gutteral, ascending vibration that seemed to shake the air and ended in a sigh and a heavy, deep-chested grunt.

"He sounds almost here," Macomber's wife said.

"My God," said Macomber. "I hate that damned noise."

"It's very impressive."

"Impressive. It's frightful."

Robert Wilson came up then carrying his short, ugly, shockingly big-bored .505 Gibbs and grinning.

"Come on," he said. "Your gun-bearer has your Springfield and the big gun. Everything's in the car. Have you solids?"

"Yes."

"I'm ready," Mrs. Macomber said.

"Must make him stop that racket," Wilson said. "You get in front. The Memsahib can sit back here with me."

They climbed into the motor car and, in the gray first daylight, moved off up the river through the trees. Macomber opened the breech of his rifle and saw he had metal-cased bullets, shut the bolt and put the rifle on safety. He saw his hand was trembling. He felt in his pocket for more cartridges and moved his fingers over the cartridges in the loops of his tunic front. He turned back to where Wilson sat in the rear seat of the doorless, box-bodied motor car beside his wife, them both grinning with excitement, and Wilson leaned forward and whispered,

"See the birds dropping. Means the old boy has left his kill."

On the far bank of the stream Macomber could see, above the trees, vultures circling and plummeting down.

"Chances are he'll come to drink along here," Wilson whispered. "Before he goes to lay up. Keep an eye out."

They were driving slowly along the high bank of the stream which here cut deeply to its boulder-filled bed, and they wound in and out through big trees as they drove. Macomber was watching the opposite bank when he felt Wilson take hold of his arm. The car stopped.

"There he is," he heard the whisper. "Ahead and to the right. Get out and take him. He's a marvelous lion."

Macomber saw the lion now. He was standing almost broadside, his great head up and turned toward them. The early morning breeze that blew toward them was just stirring his dark mane, and the lion looked huge, silhouetted on the rise of bank in the gray morning light, his shoulders heavy, his barrel of a body bulking smoothly.

"How far is he?" asked Macomber, raising his rifle.

"About seventy-five. Get out and take him."

"Why not shoot from where I am?"

"You don't shoot them from cars," he heard Wilson saying in his ear. "Get out. He's not going to stay there all day."

Macomber stepped out of the curved opening at the side of the front seat, onto the step and down onto the ground. The lion still stood looking majestically and coolly toward this object that his eyes only showed in silhouette, bulking like some super-rhino. There was no man smell carried toward him and he watched the object, moving his great head a little from side to side. Then watching the object, not afraid, but hesitating before going down the bank to drink with such a thing opposite him, he saw a man figure detach itself from it and he turned his heavy head and swung away toward the cover of the trees as he heard a cracking crash and felt the slam of a .30–06 220-grain solid bullet that bit his flank and ripped in sudden hot scalding nausea through his stomach. He trotted, heavy, big-footed, swinging wounded full-bellied, through the trees toward the tall grass and cover, and the crash came again to go past him ripping the air apart. Then it crashed again and he felt the blow as it hit his lower ribs and ripped on through, blood sudden hot and frothy in his mouth, and he galloped toward the high grass where he could crouch and not be seen and make them bring the crashing thing close enough so he could make a rush and get the man that held it.

Macomber had not thought how the lion felt as he got out of the car. He only knew his hands were shaking and as he walked away from the car it was almost impossible for him to make his legs move. They were stiff in the thighs, but he could feel the muscles fluttering. He raised the rifle, sighted on the junction of the lion's head and shoulders and pulled the trigger. Nothing happened though he pulled until he thought his finger would break. Then he knew he had the safety on and as he lowered the rifle to move the safety over he moved another frozen pace forward, and the lion seeing his silhouette now clear of the silhouette of the car, turned and started off at a trot, and, as Macomber fired, he heard a whunk that meant that the bullet was home; but the lion kept on going. Macomber shot again and everyone saw the bullet throw a spout of dirt beyond the trotting lion. He shot again, remembering to lower his aim, and they all heard the bullet hit, and the lion went into a gallop and was in the tall grass before he had the bolt pushed forward.

Macomber stood there feeling sick at his stomach, his hands that held the Springfield still cocked, shaking, and his wife and Robert Wilson were standing by him. Beside him too were the two gun-bearers chattering in Wakamba.

"I hit him," Macomber said. "I hit him twice."

"You gut-shot him and you hit him somewhere forward," Wilson said without enthusiasm. The gun-bearers looked very grave. They were silent now.

"You may have killed him," Wilson went on. "We'll have to wait a while before we go in to find out."

"What do you mean?"

"Let him get sick before we follow him up."

"Oh," said Macomber.

"He's a hell of a fine lion," Wilson said cheerfully. "He's gotten into a bad place though."

"Why is it bad?"

"Can't see him until you're on him."

"Oh," said Macomber.

"Come on," said Wilson. "The Memsahib can stay here in the car. We'll go to have a look at the blood spoor."

"Stay here, Margot," Macomber said to his wife. His mouth was very dry and it was hard for him to talk.

"Why?" she asked.

"Wilson says to."

"We're going to have a look," Wilson said. "You stay here. You can see even better from here."

"All right."

Wilson spoke in Swahili to the driver. He nodded and said, "Yes, Bwana."

Then they went down the steep bank and across the stream, climbing over and around the boulders and up the other bank, pulling up by some projecting roots, and along it until they found where the lion had been trotting when Macomber first shot. There was dark blood on the short grass that the gun-bearers pointed out with grass stems, and that ran away behind the river bank trees.

"What do we do?" asked Macomber.

"Not much choice," said Wilson. "We can't bring the car over. Bank's too steep. We'll let him stiffen up a bit then you and I'll go in and have a look for him."

"Can't we set the grass on fire?" Macomber asked.

"Too green."

"Can't we send beaters?"

Wilson looked at him appraisingly. "Of course we can," he said. "But it's just a touch murderous. You see we know the lion's wounded. You can drive an unwounded lion—he'll move on ahead of a noise—but a wounded lion's going to charge. You can't see him until you're right on him. He'll make himself perfectly flat in cover you wouldn't think would hide a hare. You can't very well send boys in there to that sort of a show. Somebody bound to get mauled."

"What about the gun-bearers?"

"Oh, they'll go with us. It's their *shauri*. You see, they signed on for it. They don't look too happy though, do they?"

"I don't want to go in there," said Macomber. It was out before he knew he'd said it.

"Neither do I," said Wilson very cheerily. "Really no choice though." Then, as an afterthought, he glanced at Macomber and saw suddenly how he was trembling and the pitiful look on his face.

"You don't have to go in, of course," he said. "That's what I'm hired for, you know. That's why I'm so expensive."

"You mean you'd go in by yourself? Why not leave him there?"

Robert Wilson, whose entire occupation had been with the lion and the problem he presented, and who had not been thinking about Macomber except to note that he was rather windy, suddenly felt as though he had opened the wrong door in a hotel and seen something shameful.

"What do you mean?"

"Why not just leave him?"

"You mean pretend to ourselves he hasn't been hit?"

"No. Just drop it."

"It isn't done."

"Why not?"

"For one thing, he's certain to be suffering. For another, some one else might run onto him."

"I see."

"But you don't have to have anything to do with it."

"I'd like to," Macomber said. "I'm just scared, you know."

"I'll go ahead when we go in," Wilson said, "with Kongoni tracking. You keep behind me and a little to one side. Chances are we'll hear him growl. If we see him we'll both shoot. Don't worry about anything. I'll keep you backed up. As a matter of fact, you know, perhaps you'd better not go. It might be much better. Why don't you go over and join the Memsahib while I just get it over with?"

"No, I want to go."

"All right," said Wilson. "But don't go in if you don't want to. This is my *shauri* now, you know."

"I want to go," said Macomber.

They sat under a tree and smoked.

"Want to go back and speak to the Memsahib while we're waiting?" Wilson asked.

"No."

"I'll just step back and tell her to be patient."

"Good," said Macomber. He sat there, sweating under his arms, his mouth dry, his stomach hollow feeling, wanting to find courage to tell Wilson to go on and finish off the lion without him. He could not know that Wilson was furious because he had not noticed the state he was in earlier and sent him back to his wife. While he sat there Wilson came up. "I have your big gun," he said. "Take it. We've given him time, I think. Come on."

Macomber took the big gun and Wilson said:

"Keep behind me and about five yards to the right and do exactly as I tell you." Then he spoke in Swahili to the two gun-bearers who looked the picture of gloom.

"Let's go," he said.

"Could I have a drink of water?" Macomber asked. Wilson spoke to the older gun-bearer, who wore a canteen on his belt, and the man unbuckled, unscrewed the top and handed it to Macomber, who took it noticing how heavy it seemed and how hairy and shoddy the felt covering was in his hand. He raised it to drink and looked ahead at the high grass with the flat-topped trees behind it. A breeze was blowing toward them and the grass rippled gently in the wind. He looked at the gun-bearer and he could see the gun-bearer was suffering too with fear.

Thirty-five yards into the grass the big lion lay flattened out along the ground. His ears were back and his only movement was a slight twitching up and down of his long, black-tufted tail. He had turned at bay as soon as he had reached this cover and he was sick with the wound through his full belly, and weakening with the wound through his lungs that brought a thin foamy red to his mouth each time he breathed. His flanks were wet and hot and flies were on the little openings the solid bullets had made in his tawny hide, and his big yellow eyes, narrowed with hate, looked straight ahead, only blinking when the pain came as he breathed, and his claws dug in the soft baked earth. All of him, pain, sickness, hatred and all of his remaining strength, was tightening into an absolute concentration for a rush. He could hear the men talking and he waited, gathering all of himself into this preparation for a charge as soon as the men would come into the grass. As he heard their voices his tail stiffened to twitch up and down, and, as they came into the edge of the grass, he made a coughing grunt and charged.

Kongoni, the old gun-bearer, in the lead watching the blood spoor, Wilson watching the grass for any movement, his big gun ready, the second gun-bearer looking ahead and listening, Macomber close to Wilson, his rifle cocked, they had just moved into the grass when Macomber heard the blood-choked coughing grunt, and saw the swishing rush in the grass. The next thing he knew he was running; running wildly, in panic in the open, running toward the stream.

He heard the *ca-ra-wong!* of Wilson's big rifle, and again in a second a crashing *carawong!* and turning saw the lion, horrible-looking now, with half his head seeming to be gone, crawling toward Wilson in the edge of the tall grass while the red-faced man worked the bolt on the short ugly rifle and aimed carefully as another blasting *carawong!* came from the muzzle, and the crawling, heavy, yellow bulk of the lion stiffened and the huge, mutilated head slid forward and Macomber, standing by himself in the clearing where he had run, holding a loaded rifle, while two black men and a white man looked back at him in contempt, knew the lion was dead. He came toward Wilson, his tallness all seeming a naked reproach, and Wilson looked at him and said:

"Want to take pictures?"

"No," he said.

That was all any one had said until they reached the motor car. Then Wilson had said:

"Hell of a fine lion. Boys will skin him out. We might as well stay here in the shade."

Macomber's wife had not looked at him nor he at her and he had sat by her in the back seat with Wilson sitting in the front seat. Once he had

reached over and taken his wife's hand without looking at her and she
had removed her hand from his. Looking across the stream to where the
gun-bearers were skinning out the lion he could see that she had been
able to see the whole thing. While they sat there his wife had reached
forward and put her hand on Wilson's shoulder. He turned and she had
leaned forward over the low seat and kissed him on the mouth.

"Oh, I say," said Wilson, going redder than his natural baked color.

"Mr. Robert Wilson," she said. "The beautiful red-faced Mr. Robert
Wilson."

Then she sat down beside Macomber again and looked away across the
stream to where the lion lay, with uplifted, white-muscled, tendon-marked
naked forearms, and white bloating belly, as the black men fleshed away
the skin. Finally the gun-bearers brought the skin over, wet and heavy,
and climbed in behind with it, rolling it up before they got in, and the
motor car started. No one had said anything more until they were back
in camp.

That was the story of the lion. Macomber did not know how the lion
had felt before he started his rush, nor during it when the unbelievable
smash of the .505 with a muzzle velocity of two tons had hit him in the
mouth, nor what kept him coming after that, when the second ripping
crash had smashed his hind quarters and he had come crawling on toward
the crashing, blasting thing that had destroyed him. Wilson knew something about it and only expressed it by saying, "Damned fine lion," but
Macomber did not know how Wilson felt about things either. He did
not know how his wife felt except that she was through with him.

His wife had been through with him before but it never lasted. He was
very wealthy, and would be much wealthier, and he knew she would not
leave him ever now. That was one of the few things that he really knew.
He knew about that, about motor cycles—that was earliest—about motor
cars, about duck-shooting, about fishing, trout, salmon and big-sea, about
sex in books, many books, too many books, about all court games, about
dogs, not much about horses, about hanging on to his money, about most
of the other things his world dealt in, and about his wife not leaving him.
His wife had been a great beauty and she was still a great beauty in Africa,
but she was not a great enough beauty any more at home to be able to
leave him and better herself and she knew it and he knew it. She had
missed the chance to leave him and he knew it. If he had been better with
women she would probably have started to worry about him getting another
new, beautiful wife; but she knew too much about him to worry about
him either. Also, he had always had a great tolerance which seemed the
nicest thing about him if it were not the most sinister.

All in all they were known as a comparatively happily married couple,
one of those whose disruption is often rumored but never occurs, and as
the society columnist put it, they were adding more than a spice of *adventure*

to their much envied and ever-enduring *Romance* by a *Safari* in what was known as *Darkest Africa* until the Martin Johnsons lighted it on so many silver screens where they were pursuing *Old Simba* the lion, the buffalo, *Tembo* and the elephant and as well collecting specimens for the Museum of Natural History. This same columnist had reported them *on the verge* at least three times in the past and they had been. But they always made it up. They had a sound basis of union. Margot was too beautiful for Macomber to divorce her and Macomber had too much money for Margot ever to leave him.

It was now about three o'clock in the morning and Francis Macomber, who had been asleep a little while after he had stopped thinking about the lion, wakened and then slept again, woke suddenly, frightened in a dream of the bloody-headed lion standing over him, and listening while his heart pounded, he realized that his wife was not in the other cot in the tent. He lay awake with that knowledge for two hours.

At the end of that time his wife came into the tent, lifted her mosquito bar and crawled cozily into bed.

"Where have you been?" Macomber asked in the darkness.

"Hello," she said. "Are you awake?"

"Where have you been?"

"I just went out to get a breath of air."

"You did, like hell."

"What do you want me to say, darling?"

"Where have you been?"

"Out to get a breath of air."

"That's a new name for it. You *are* a bitch."

"Well, you're a coward."

"All right," he said. "What of it?"

"Nothing as far as I'm concerned. But please let's not talk, darling, because I'm very sleepy."

"You think that I'll take anything."

"I know you will, sweet."

"Well, I won't."

"Please, darling, let's not talk. I'm so very sleepy."

"There wasn't going to be any of that. You promised there wouldn't be."

"Well, there is now," she said sweetly.

"You said if we made this trip that there would be none of that. You promised."

"Yes, darling. That's the way I meant it to be. But the trip was spoiled yesterday. We don't have to talk about it, do we?"

"You don't wait long when you have an advantage, do you?"

"Please let's not talk. I'm so sleepy, darling."

"I'm going to talk."

"Don't mind me then because I'm going to sleep." And she did.

At breakfast, there were all three at the table before daylight and Francis Macomber found that, of all the men that he hated, he hated Robert Wilson the most.

"Sleep well?" Wilson asked in his throaty voice, filling a pipe.

"Did you?"

"Topping," the white hunter told him.

You bastard, thought Macomber, you insolent bastard.

So she woke him when she came in, Wilson thought, looking at them both with his flat, cold eyes. Well, why doesn't he keep his wife where she belongs? What does he think I am, a bloody plaster saint? Let him keep her where she belongs. It's his own fault.

"Do you think we'll find buffalo?" Margot asked, pushing away a dish of apricots.

"Chance of it," Wilson said and smiled at her. "Why don't you stay in camp?"

"Not for anything," she told him.

"Why not order her to stay in camp?" Wilson said to Macomber.

"You order her," said Macomber coldly.

"Let's not have any ordering, nor," turning to Macomber, "any silliness, Francis," Margot said quite pleasantly.

"Are you ready to start?" Macomber asked.

"Any time," Wilson told him. "Do you want the Memsahib to go?"

"Does it make any difference whether I do or not?"

The hell with it, thought Robert Wilson. The utter complete hell with it. So this is what it's going to be like. Well, this is what it's going to be like, then.

"Makes no difference," he said.

"You're sure you wouldn't like to stay in camp with her yourself and let me go out and hunt the buffalo?" Macomber asked.

"Can't do that," said Wilson. "Wouldn't talk rot if I were you."

"I'm not talking rot. I'm disgusted."

"Bad word, disgusted."

"Francis, will you please try to speak sensibly?" his wife said.

"I speak too damned sensibly," Macomber said. "Did you ever eat such filthy food?"

"Something wrong with the food?" asked Wilson quietly.

"No more than with everything else."

"I'd pull yourself together, laddybuck," Wilson said very quietly. "There's a boy waits at table that understands a little English."

"The hell with him."

Wilson stood up and puffing on his pipe strolled away, speaking a few words in Swahili to one of the gun-bearers who was standing waiting for him. Macomber and his wife sat on at the table. He was staring at his coffee cup.

"If you make a scene I'll leave you, darling," Margot said quietly.

"No, you won't."

"You can try it and see."

"You won't leave me."

"No," she said. "I won't leave you and you'll behave yourself."

"Behave myself? That's a way to talk. Behave myself."

"Yes. Behave yourself."

"Why don't *you* try behaving?"

"I've tried it so long. So very long."

"I hate that red-faced swine," Macomber said. "I loathe the sight of him."

"He's really *very* nice."

"Oh, *shut up*," Macomber almost shouted. Just then the car came up and stopped in front of the dining tent and the driver and the two gun-bearers got out. Wilson walked over and looked at the husband and wife sitting there at the table.

"Going shooting?" he asked.

"Yes," said Macomber, standing up. "Yes."

"Better bring a woolly. It will be cool in the car," Wilson said.

"I'll get my leather jacket," Margot said.

"The boy has it," Wilson told her. He climbed into the front with the driver and Francis Macomber and his wife sat, not speaking, in the back seat.

Hope the silly beggar doesn't take a notion to blow the back of my head off, Wilson thought to himself. Women *are* a nuisance on safari.

The car was grinding down to cross the river at a pebbly ford in the gray daylight and then climbed, angling up the steep bank, where Wilson had ordered a way shovelled out the day before so they could reach the parklike wooded rolling country on the far side.

It was a good morning, Wilson thought. There was a heavy dew and as the wheels went through the grass and low bushes he could smell the odor of the crushed fronds. It was an odor like verbena and he liked this early morning smell of the dew, the crushed bracken and the look of the tree trunks showing black through the early morning mist, as the car made its way through the untracked, parklike country. He had put the two in the back seat out of his mind now and was thinking about buffalo. The buffalo that he was after stayed in the daytime in a thick swamp where it was impossible to get a shot, but in the night they fed out into an open stretch of country and if he could come between them and their swamp with the car, Macomber would have a good chance at them in the open. He did not want to hunt buff with Macomber in thick cover. He did not want to hunt buff or anything else with Macomber at all, but he was a professional hunter and he had hunted with some rare ones in his time. If they got buff today there would only be rhino to come and the poor man would have gone through his dangerous game and things might pick up. He'd have nothing more to do with the woman and Macomber would get over that too. He must have gone through plenty of that before by the look of things. Poor beggar. He must have a way of getting over it. Well, it was the poor sod's own bloody fault.

He, Robert Wilson, carried a double size cot on safari to accommodate any windfalls he might receive. He had hunted for a certain clientele, the international, fast, sporting set, where the women did not feel they were getting their money's worth unless they had shared that cot with the white hunter. He despised them when he was away from them although he liked some of them well enough at the time, but he made his living by them; and their standards were his standards as long as they were hiring him.

They were his standards in all except the shooting. He had his own standards about the killing and they could live up to them or get some one else to hunt them. He knew, too, that they all respected him for this. This Macomber was an odd one though. Damned if he wasn't. Now the wife. Well, the wife. Yes, the wife. Hm, the wife. Well he'd dropped all that. He looked around at them. Macomber sat grim and furious. Margot smiled at him. She looked younger today, more innocent and fresher and not so professionally beautiful. What's in her heart God knows, Wilson thought. She hadn't talked much last night. At that it was a pleasure to see her.

The motor car climbed up a slight rise and went on through the trees and then out into a grassy prairie-like opening and kept in the shelter of the trees along the edge, the driver going slowly and Wilson looking carefully out across the prairie and all along its far side. He stopped the car and studied the opening with his field glasses. Then he motioned to the driver to go on and the car moved slowly along, the driver avoiding wart-hog holes and driving around the mud castles ants had built. Then, looking across the opening, Wilson suddenly turned and said,

"By God, there they are!"

And looking where he pointed, while the car jumped forward and Wilson spoke in rapid Swahili to the driver, Macomber saw three huge, black animals looking almost cylindrical in their long heaviness, like big black tank cars, moving at a gallop across the far edge of the open prairie. They moved at a stiff-necked, stiff-bodied gallop and he could see the upswept wide black horns on their heads as they galloped heads out; the heads not moving.

"They're three old bulls," Wilson said. "We'll cut them off before they get to the swamp."

The car was going a wild forty-five miles an hour across the open and as Macomber watched, the buffalo got bigger and bigger until he could see the gray, hairless, scabby look of one huge bull and how his neck was a part of his shoulders and the shiny black of his horns as he galloped a little behind the others that were strung out in that steady plunging gait; and then, the car swaying as though it had just jumped a road, they drew up close and he could see the plunging hugeness of the bull, and the dust in his sparsely haired hide, the wide boss of horn and his outstretched, wide-nostrilled muzzle, and he was raising his rifle when Wilson shouted, "Not from the car, you fool!" and he had no fear, only hatred of Wilson, while the brakes clamped on and the car skidded, plowing sideways to an almost stop and Wilson was out on one side and he on the other, stumbling as his feet hit the still speeding-by of the earth, and then he was shooting at the bull as he moved away, hearing the bullets whunk into him, emptying his rifle at him as he moved steadily away, finally remembering to get his shots forward into the shoulder, and as he fumbled to reload, he saw the bull was down. Down on his knees, his big head tossing, and seeing the other two still galloping he shot at the leader and hit him. He shot again and missed and he heard the *carawonging* roar as Wilson shot and saw the leading bull slide forward onto his nose.

"Get that other," Wilson said. "Now you're shooting."

But the other bull was moving steadily at the same gallop and he missed, throwing a spout of dirt, and Wilson missed and the dust rose in a cloud and Wilson shouted, "Come on. He's too far!" and grabbed his arm and they were in the car again, Macomber and Wilson hanging on the sides and rocketing swayingly over the uneven ground, drawing up on the steady, plunging, heavy-necked, straight-moving gallop of the bull.

They were behind him and Macomber was filling his rifle, dropping shells onto the ground, jamming it, clearing the jam, then they were almost up with the bull when Wilson yelled "Stop," and the car skidded so that it almost swung over and Macomber fell forward onto his feet, slammed his bolt forward and fired as far forward as he could aim into the galloping, rounded black bull, aimed and shot again, then again, then again, and the bullets, all of them hitting, had no effect on the buffalo that he could see. Then Wilson shot, the roar deafening him, and he could see the bull stagger. Macomber shot again, aiming carefully, and down he came, onto his knees.

"All right," Wilson said. "Nice work. That's three."

Macomber felt a drunken elation.

"How many times did you shoot?" he asked.

"Just three," Wilson said. "You killed the first bull. The biggest one. I helped you finish the other two. Afraid they might have got into cover. You had them killed. I was just mopping up a little. You shot damn well."

"Let's go to the car," said Macomber. "I want a drink."

"Got to finish off that buff first," Wilson told him. The buffalo was on his knees and he jerked his head furiously and bellowed in pig-eyed roaring rage as they came toward him.

"Watch he doesn't get up," Wilson said. Then, "Get a little broadside and take him in the neck just behind the ear."

Macomber aimed carefully at the center of the huge, jerking, rage-driven neck and shot. At the shot the head dropped forward.

"That does it," said Wilson. "Got the spine. They're a hell of a looking thing, aren't they?"

ERNEST HEMINGWAY

185

"Let's get the drink," said Macomber. In his life he had never felt so good.

In the car Macomber's wife sat very white faced. "You were marvellous, darling," she said to Macomber. "What a ride."

"Was it rough?" Wilson asked.

"It was frightful. I've never been more frightened in my life."

"Let's all have a drink," Macomber said.

"By all means," said Wilson. "Give it to the Memsahib." She drank the neat whisky from the flask and shuddered a little when she swallowed. She handed the flask to Macomber who handed it to Wilson.

"It was frightfully exciting," she said. "It's given me a dreadful headache. I didn't know you were allowed to shoot them from cars though."

"No one shot from cars," said Wilson coldly.

"I mean chase them from cars."

"Wouldn't ordinarily," Wilson said. "Seemed sporting enough to me though while we were doing it. Taking more chance driving that way across the plain full of holes and one thing and another than hunting on foot. Buffalo could have charged us each time we shot if he liked. Gave him every chance. Wouldn't mention it to any one though. It's illegal if that's what you mean."

"It seemed very unfair to me" Margot said, "chasing those big helpless things in a motor car."

"Did it?" said Wilson.

"What would happen if they heard about it in Nairobi?"

"I'd lose my license for one thing. Other unpleasantnesses," Wilson said, taking a drink from the flask. "I'd be out of business."

"Really?"

"Yes, really."

"Well," said Macomber, and he smiled for the first time all day. "Now she has something on you."

"You have such a pretty way of putting things, Francis," Margot Macomber said. Wilson looked at them both. If a four-letter man marries a five-letter woman, he was thinking, what number of letters would their children be? What he said was, "We lost a gun-bearer. Did you notice it?"

"My God, no," Macomber said.

"Here he comes," Wilson said. "He's all right. He must have fallen off when we left the first bull."

Approaching them was the middle-aged gun-bearer, limping along in his knitted cap, khaki tunic, shorts and rubber sandals, gloomy-faced and disgusted looking. As he came up he called out to Wilson in Swahili and they all saw the change in the white hunter's face.

"What does he say?" asked Margot.

"He says the first bull got up and went into the bush," Wilson said with no expression in his voice.

"Oh," said Macomber blankly.

"Then it's going to be just like the lion," said Margot, full of anticipation.

"It's not going to be a damned bit like the lion," Wilson told her. "Did you want another drink, Macomber?"

"Thanks, yes," Macomber said. He expected the feeling he had had about the lion to come back but it did not. For the first time in his life he really felt wholly without fear. Instead of fear he had a feeling of definite elation.

"We'll go and have a look at the second bull," Wilson said. "I'll tell the driver to put the car in the shade."

"What are you going to do?" asked Margaret Macomber.

"Take a look at the buff," Wilson said.

"I'll come."

"Come along."

The three of them walked over to where the second buffalo bulked blackly in the open, head forward on the grass, the massive horns swung wide.

"He's a very good head," Wilson said. "That's close to a fifty-inch spread."

Macomber was looking at him with delight.

"He's hateful looking," said Margot. "Can't we go into the shade?"

"Of course," Wilson said. "Look," he said to Macomber, and pointed. "See that patch of bush?"

"Yes."

"That's where the first bull went in. The gun-bearer said when he fell off the bull was down. He was watching us helling along and the other two buff galloping. When he looked up there was the bull up and looking at him. Gun-bearer ran like hell and the bull went off slowly into that bush."

"Can we go in after him now?" asked Macomber eagerly.

Wilson looked at him appraisingly. Damned if this isn't a strange one, he thought. Yesterday he's scared sick and today he's a ruddy fire eater.

"No, we'll give him a while."

"Let's please go into the shade," Margot said. Her face was white and she looked ill.

They made their way to the car where it stood under a single, wide-spreading tree and all climbed in.

"Chances are he's dead in there," Wilson remarked. "After a little we'll have a look."

Macomber felt a wild unreasonable happiness that he had never known before.

"By God, that was a chase," he said. "I've never felt any such feeling. Wasn't it marvellous, Margot?"

"I hated it."

"Why?"

"I hated it," she said bitterly. "I loathed it."

"You know I don't think I'd ever be afraid of anything again," Macomber said to Wilson. "Something happened in me after we first saw the buff and started after him. Like a dam bursting. It was pure excitement."

"Cleans out your liver," said Wilson. "Damn funny things happen to people."

Macomber's face was shining. "You know something did happen to me," he said. "I feel absolutely different."

His wife said nothing and eyed him strangely. She was sitting far back in the seat and Macomber was sitting forward talking to Wilson who turned sideways talking over the back of the front seat.

"You know, I'd like to try another lion," Macomber said. "I'm really not afraid of them now. After all, what can they do to you?"

"That's it," said Wilson. "Worst one can do is kill you. How does it go? Shakespeare. Damned good. See if I can remember. Oh, damned good. Used to quote it to myself at one time. Let's see. 'By my troth, I care not; a man can die but once; we owe God a death and let it go which way it will, he that dies this year is quit for the next.' Damned fine, eh?"

He was very embarrassed, having brought out this thing he had lived by, but he had seen men come of age before and it always moved him. It was not a matter of their twenty-first birthday.

It had taken a strange chance of hunting, a sudden precipitation into action without opportunity for worrying beforehand, to bring this about with Macomber, but regardless of how it had happened it had most certainly happened. Look at the beggar now, Wilson thought. It's that some of them stay little boys so long, Wilson thought. Sometimes all their lives. Their figures stay boyish when they're fifty. The great American boy-men. Damned strange people. But he liked this Macomber now. Damned strange fellow. Probably meant the end of cuckoldry too. Well, that would be a damned good thing. Damn good thing. Beggar had probably been afraid all his life. Don't know what started it. But over now. Hadn't had time to be afraid with the buff. That and being angry too. Motor car too. Motor cars made it familiar. Be a damn fire eater now. He'd seen it in the war work the same way. More of a change than any loss of virginity. Fear gone like an operation. Something else grew in its place. Main thing a man had. Made him into a man. Women knew it too. No bloody fear.

From the far corner of the seat Margaret Macomber looked at the two of them. There was no change in Wilson. She saw Wilson as she had seen him the day before when she had first realized what his great talent was. But she saw the change in Francis Macomber now.

"Do you have that feeling of happiness about what's going to happen?" Macomber asked, still exploring his new wealth.

"You're not supposed to mention it," Wilson said, looking in the other's face. "Much more fashionable to say you're scared. Mind you, you'll be scared too, plenty of times."

"But you *have* a feeling of happiness about action to come?"

"Yes," said Wilson. "There's that. Doesn't do to talk too much about all this. Talk the whole thing away. No pleasure in anything if you mouth it up too much."

"You're both talking rot," said Margot. "Just because you've chased some helpless animals in a motor car you talk like heroes."

"Sorry," said Wilson. "I have been gassing too much." She's worried about it already, he thought.

"If you don't know what we're talking about why not keep out of it?" Macomber asked his wife.

"You've gotten awfully brave, awfully suddenly," his wife said contemptuously, but her contempt was not secure. She was afraid of something.

Macomber laughed, a very natural hearty laugh. "You know I *have*," he said. "I really have."

"Isn't it sort of late?" Margot said bitterly. Because she had done the best she could for many years back and the way they were together now was no one person's fault.

"Not for me," said Macomber.

Margot said nothing but sat back in the corner of the seat.

"Do you think we've given him time enough?" Macomber asked Wilson cheerfully.

"We might have a look," Wilson said. "Have you any solids left?"

"The gun-bearer has some."

Wilson called in Swahili and the older gun-bearer, who was skinning out one of the heads, straightened up, pulled a box of solids out of his pocket and brought them over to Macomber, who filled his magazine and put the remaining shells in his pocket.

"You might as well shoot the Springfield," Wilson said. "You're used to it. We'll leave the Mannlicher in the car with the Memsahib. Your gun-bearer can carry your heavy gun. I've this damned cannon. Now let me tell you about them." He had saved this until the last because he did not want to worry Macomber. "When a buff comes he comes with his head high and thrust straight out. The boss of the horns covers any sort of a brain shot. The only shot is straight into the nose. The only other shot is into his chest or, if you're to one side, into the neck or the shoulders. After they've been hit once they take a hell of a lot of killing. Don't try anything fancy. Take the easiest shot there is. They've finished skinning out that head now. Should we get started?"

He called to the gun-bearers, who came up wiping their hands, and the older one got into the back.

"I'll only take Kongoni," Wilson said. "The other can watch to keep the birds away."

As the car moved slowly across the open space toward the island of brushy trees that ran in a tongue of foliage along a dry water course that cut the open swale, Macomber felt his heart pounding and his mouth was dry again, but it was excitement, not fear.

ERNEST HEMINGWAY

189

"Here's where he went in," Wilson said. Then to the gun-bearer in Swahili, "Take the blood spoor."

The car was parallel to the patch of bush. Macomber, Wilson and the gun-bearer got down. Macomber, looking back, saw his wife, with the rifle by her side, looking at him. He waved to her and she did not wave back.

The brush was very thick ahead and the ground was dry. The middle-aged gun-bearer was sweating heavily and Wilson had his hat down over his eyes and his red neck showed just ahead of Macomber. Suddenly the gun-bearer said something in Swahili to Wilson and ran forward.

"He's dead in there," Wilson said. "Good work," and he turned to grip Macomber's hand and as they shook hands, grinning at each other, the gun-bearer shouted wildly and they saw him coming out of the bush side-ways, fast as a crab, and the bull coming, nose out, mouth tight closed, blood dripping, massive head straight out, coming in a charge, his little pig eyes bloodshot as he looked at them. Wilson, who was ahead, was kneeling shooting, and Macomber, as he fired, unhearing his shot in the roaring of Wilson's gun, saw fragments like slate burst from the huge boss of the horns, and the head jerked, he shot again at the wide nostrils and saw the horns jolt again and fragments fly, and he did not see Wilson now and, aiming carefully, shot again with the buffalo's huge bulk almost on him and his rifle almost level with the on-coming head, nose out, and he could see the little wicked eyes and the head started to lower and he felt a sudden white-hot, blinding flash explode inside his head and that was all he ever felt.

Wilson had ducked to one side to get in a shoulder shot. Macomber had stood solid and shot for the nose, shooting a touch high each time and hitting the heavy horns, splintering and chipping them like hitting a slate roof, and Mrs. Macomber, in the car, had shot at the buffalo with the 6.5 Mannlicher as it seemed about to gore Macomber and had hit her husband about two inches up and a little to one side of the base of his skull.

Francis Macomber lay now, face down, not two yards from where the buffalo lay on his side and his wife knelt over him with Wilson beside her.

"I wouldn't turn him over," Wilson said.

The woman was crying hysterically.

"I'd get back in the car," Wilson said. "Where's the rifle?"

She shook her head, her face contorted. The gun-bearer picked up the rifle.

"Leave it as it is," said Wilson. Then, "Go get Abdulla so that he may witness the manner of the accident."

He knelt down, took a handkerchief from his pocket, and spread it over Francis Macomber's crew-cropped head where it lay. The blood sank into the dry, loose earth.

Wilson stood up and saw the buffalo on his side, his legs out, his thinly-haired belly crawling with ticks. "Hell of a good bull," his brain registered automatically. "A good fifty inches, or better. Better." He called to the driver and told him to spread a blanket over the body and stay by it. Then he walked over to the motor car where the woman sat crying in the corner.

"That was a pretty thing to do," he said in a toneless voice. "He *would* have left you too."

"Stop it," she said.

"Of course it's an accident," he said. "I know that."

"Stop it," she said.

"Don't worry," he said. "There will be a certain amount of unpleasantness but I will have some photographs taken that will be very useful at the inquest. That's the testimony of the gun-bearers and the driver too. You're perfectly all right."

"Stop it," she said.

"There's a hell of a lot to be done," he said. "And I'll have to send a truck off to the lake to wireless for a plane to take the three of us into Nairobi. Why didn't you poison him? That's what they do in England."

"Stop it. Stop it. Stop it," the woman cried.

Wilson looked at her with his flat blue eyes.

"I'm through now," he said. "I was a little angry. I'd begun to like your husband."

"Oh, please stop it," she said. "Please, please stop it."

"That's better," Wilson said. "Please is much better. Now I'll stop."

FLORENCE COHEN

(b. 1927) Born in Pittsburgh, Florence Cohen
lives in Wilmette, Illinois, and teaches creative writing at Northwestern University.
Though many of her stories have been cited
in *Best American Short Stories* over the years,
The Monkey Puzzle Tree (1979) is her first
collection. Many of Cohen's stories reflect her
interest in Israel and Arab-Jewish relationships. Some of her best stories have a rural
or small-town mid-America locale.

MRS. POE

No one in the Poe family would say when Mrs. Poe's queerness started, but
some of them in Leesville linked it up with the time she began wearing
yellow. Morning, noon, and evening, all her clothes were yellow. Not that
they did not become her considering her hair was white, and her skin
as white as cornstarch. The yellow clothes stood out. The men who knew
her husband Henry said she married him to cure his liver which had soured
from whiskey. Henry Poe was not the match Leesville had expected for
the daughter of Judge Fowler. But Mrs. Poe was always taking something
on. Like dressing down the deputy when he came out when Rufe, her
colored woman's boy, was caught thumbing his nose and showing his
tongue at folks all over town. No one in Leesville ever figured Mrs. Poe
at all except to put it down to her peculiarities, which boiled down to just
plain queerness. Soon after the judge died and she married Henry, she
began making little speeches about judges and justice and mixed them
all up together.

Mrs. Poe was a little woman, but she had strength about her, too.
She was like a dandelion, all yellow and strong with a stem made of so
many threads you couldn't hardly break it.

Mrs. Poe had Thanksgiving dinner on Sunday. No one knew exactly
how she reckoned it. People in Leesville that mattered were not a bit put
out, since they hadn't had an invitation from the Poes from the time she

brought Henry home. It was a shame how the big gray house with its broad verandah, once such a center of things, was closed to everyone except their daughter, Janice, who lived there, and on mighty rare occasions, their son, Emory.

Janice, on the verge of being a spinster, spent most of her time in her room, Lord knows why. Someone said she was writing about Leesville folks, but no one ever saw a word of what she wrote or did they see much of Janice except when she went down for the marketing. Even then, she would only smile and go about her business, carrying the big straw basket their colored woman, Dilly Mae, had made for her. Janice held her bright blond head up as though she had to keep a crown from falling off. Folks would turn around and look after her, as though she had come that day, a stranger, to Leesville. She was too fancy stiff for Leesville blood. Sometimes, though, if you passed the Poe house at evening, you would hear the two of them, Janice playing the piano and Mrs. Poe singing in her canary voice.

As for Emory, Thanksgiving Sunday was the only day of the year he brought his wife, Grace, and his daughter, Emma Lynn, to visit his family. Emory had taken over his Poppa's lumber mill when the old man's liver gave out and he took to the porch rocker; Emory did not want the mattering people of Leesville to think he had broken with the family completely. Then, too, Grace was president of the Bethany Bible Club, and it would never do to rift out in the open. Thanksgiving Sunday saved all their faces.

The mattering people of Leesville kept close account of those dinners and it was easy, since all they had to do was ask Emma Lynn. Mostly it was old Mrs. George who did the asking. She was principal of Bethany Sunday School, but she knew a whole lot more than what was in the scriptures.

Mrs. George would ask Emma Lynn at Sunday School, "Emma Lynn, did you go down to your grandma's for Thanksgiving Sunday?"

"Yes, ma'am, I did."

"And your poppa, Emma Lynn? Did he go too?"

"Yes ma'am, he did."

"Well that's nice, Emma Lynn. The Poes are keeping up right nice."

"Yes ma'am, we are."

Mrs. George would give Emma Lynn a smiling nod, and her face, which was all speckled over with red blood vessels (they said it came from a high blood pressure) would look appeased as if she had gotten something off her mind for another year to come.

Mrs. George wasn't the only one. Everyone waited for things to break between Emory and Mrs. Poe. Emory could always twist his poppa whichever way he wanted; he could not twist Mrs. Poe. When she set her mind to something, she shot ahead without looking around her twice. Like the time she tried to send Dilly Mae and Rufe to Hendricksville for good. Dilly Mae had been doing the Poe housework for years. She had come to Mrs. Poe, a girl of fifteen, and Mrs. Poe had taken her right along with Rufe, that illegal black baby of hers. It was a scandal how Mrs. Poe doted on those two, eating right up to the kitchen table with them. Yes, she'd been caught red-handed at it more than once. She passed the best of everything to Dilly Mae's bastard Rufe, and it appeared as though she had as much feeling for him as she had for her own son, Emory. Emory hated Rufe for that, had a downright aversion to him.

When Mrs. Poe put out Dilly Mae, Rufe was ten and Emory was almost grown. Rufe was as sassy a boy as walked in Georgia. Mrs. Poe could be blamed for that, too, giving him the run of the house, letting him take cookies out of the jar without even so much as a please.

Dilly Mae wept like a willow tree that day Mrs. Poe caught her by the arm after the wash was done and all folded up. Mrs. Poe said, "You've got to leave here, Dilly Mae. Emory has had his fill of Rufe. He's jealous mad. Lord knows my heart is big enough for both of them, but Emory won't stand my loving your black boy. Trouble's brewing. You mark my word."

She gave Dilly Moe a hundred dollars and a ticket to Hendricksville where Dilly Mae had kin. Poor Dilly Mae. She tried to give the money back, but Mrs. Poe shook her head, and said Dilly Mae was to keep it for the day she knew was coming. Dilly Mae cajoled and carried on, but Mrs. Poe would not have Rufe in the same house with Emory any more. In the end, she got the boys at the lumber yard to build Dilly Mae a cabin way down by the edge of the Poe land that borders on the swamp; and after that Dilly Mae walked three miles to work, back and forth every day.

Emory would never say much about his momma. Even as a child, to hear speak of her made him mad. When he was small, she would stand out by the gate with him for all of Leesville to see, and put her arms around him before he went to school, and she'd give him an apple and whisper loud at his ear about an apple a day keeping germs away.

Emory would go on to school holding the apple with the tickle of his momma's secret chilly in his ear. He would carry the apple till he got to the creek, and then he would stand on the bridge and lean over, holding the apple high over his head. Then he'd drop it . . . plunk! There must have been something about the sound of that plunk that pleased Emory and made him smile. Each time he would hold the apple higher so it would plunk higher and deeper.

The story about Mrs. Poe visiting the Sunday School causes Emory to redden up and bristle to this very day. Just before class let out the teacher asked if Mrs. Poe enjoyed herself, and Mrs. Poe with no coaxing whatsoever, got up.

"I did indeed," she chirped. "I did indeed. I want to say to all you children: Listen well and learn the truth in gospel. We need you strong and bent on justice . . ."

Well, it would have gone on if it weren't that the teacher knew about Mrs. Poe's speeches and she put an end to it by pulling on Mrs. Poe's yellow sleeve and saying quick, "Why, thank you, Mrs. Poe. It's fine to see folks showing interest. Yes indeed."

She said later that she pretended not to notice all the giggling, but then the spitball came. It came from the back row where Emory and Jeb Williams, the reverend's son, were sitting. It came fast and landed square on Mrs. Poe's forehead. Everyone knew it was Jeb who threw it, with Emory watching, but Emory would never tell on Jeb. He said he would die before he would tell on Jeb.

Emory and Jeb Williams were the best of friends. Emory hung on to Jeb like moss to the cypress tree. Jeb played with Lucifer was what they said, and they reckoned it no more than natural for a preacher's son to carry on a bit. But Reverend Williams never could do a thing with Jeb since his momma died. Jeb's red temper shouted down the scriptures and stalked the quiet parish house, while Reverend Williams sat back and feared Jeb more than sin. He bore Jeb like a cross, and Leesville knew the weight of it with Jeb's corn likker, his carousing, and his evil tongue. Leesville carried the reverend's cross and considered him the better preacher, for so long as the reverend harbored Jeb, Leesville's sons were due the same salvation.

Emory loved Jeb Williams, and as they grew, they put aside their wads of chewing gum—chewed tobacco instead—and traded in the spitballs for shotguns they bought at the hardware store. They would go out to the swamp to shoot duck, and Emory would cock his shotgun, lift it, and aim. "Crack!" The sound of "crack" made Emory's face glow with pleasure, and he and Jeb would laugh and make the guns go, "Crack, crack . . ." Rufe followed them every time he could steal away from the cabin where Dilly Mae had his chores laid out like Sunday clothes. He would wade down in the swamp to watch, poking his head out over the reeds, shielding his eyes from the sun, following the ducks as they fell, down, down, flapping and staggering out of the sky, and Rufe would whistle through his teeth as each one dropped, "Wow—Wee . . ."

All the while, Reverend Williams read the scriptures. Mrs. Poe developed an eye tic. Blink, blink, blink. It was hard to keep from doing it back at her. Her speeches got short, quick as gunshot. Almost everywhere, at the grocer's or at the butcher's, you'd hear her say all of a sudden, like lightning flash, "We need you strong and bent on justice . . ."

Jeb and Emory went shooting every Sunday, and that's what made Emory all the crankier about Mrs. Poe's twisting around Thanksgiving. It meant he would miss a duck shoot with Jeb.

This one Thanksgiving Sunday, Grace had a fight with Emory before they went down to Mrs. Poe's for dinner. Emory said he wouldn't go.

"Grace," he said, "Take Emma Lynn to dinner by yourself. I'm not going to put up with Momma's Thanksgiving no more. There isn't a man standing at the courthouse that don't know her speech by heart—Be strong and bent on justice—She's clear out of her head. Get on down there now, Grace, because I'm not going."

Grace straightened her stocking and told Emma Lynn she looked all right. Then she wheeled around to Emory. "You listen here. Don't you pass your soft-minded family off on me. We've got position, Emory, and I've got responsibility to the Bible Club. I won't have folks chewing on my family affairs, or taking it out on Emma Lynn. First thing, they'll say I'm not a fit president. Once a year, at your Momma's Thanksgiving Sunday nonsense, you'll be there. Else I'll throw Jeb Williams out next time he comes around."

Emory laughed in that loud cawcaw of his and nipped Grace's rear end. He told her she had spunk and guts like Jeb had, and the three of them were the proper pride of Leesville. He reckoned it would be a fine idea to ask Jeb over for Thanksgiving Sunday, too. Then he laughed again. Like someone playing dixie on his ribs.

Thanksgiving dinner was on the table. Janice was coming out of the kitchen when Emory, Grace and Emma Lynn walked in. Janice hugged Emma Lynn but hardly had a smile for Emory. He was four years older than she and all the time they were growing up there had been trouble between them. Jeb told the story all over town about the time Janice was just twelve and Emory had scared her near to death. She had come out of the house to swing on the tire her poppa had hung from the cypress tree. Emory and Jeb, who had been playing in the yard, swaggered over.

"Stand up next to the tree, Janice," said Jeb.

"Whatever for, Jeb?"

"You do what I tell you to."

"Don't you touch me, Jeb. I'll call Mama . . ."

Emory clapped his hands over her mouth, pushed her up against the tree, and held her there.

"You do like Jeb wants you to," he said.

Jeb lifted her dress and her petticoat. He lifted them high and poked her square in the middle of her stomach, while Emory held her mouth and her eyes got wide as moons.

"If you ever tell," Emory whispered in her ear. "If you ever tell . . ."

Jeb roared with laughter. "She's gonna have a black belly button," he howled. "She'll have one just like Rufe. She dotes on Rufe, don't she, Emory? Let her go. Maybe she can marry Rufe, get herself a black baby."

On this Thanksgiving Sunday, though, they were all grown up. But

Janice nursed her grudge; at least Grace said so. Whenever Janice smiled at them it was no more than a pinched up squint.

Mrs. Poe was seated at the table when Henry came in from the back porch, his drawn face spread out in a flabby smile. "Well, now," he said, "right nice to have you here." When they were seated Henry bowed his head to pray before the meal. His gray hair stood out all over his head in wisps like puffed out milkweed ready to blow.

"We thank thee Lord this day, for all the blessings Thou dost give."

Then Mrs. Poe got up in her starched yellow dress and the blink in her eye.

"And now my prayer," she said.

Emory gnashed his teeth and turned sideways in his chair. "Oh my Lord, it's coming now," he said.

"Dear Lord," sang Mrs. Poe, ignoring Emory, "deliver us from weakness. Deliver us from fear. Make us strong and bent on justice."

"Momma," Emory said, chuckling and pointing at her. "I call you downright greedy. Why, here it is Thanksgiving. You're supposed to be thanking God for what you got already. Not asking for more. Now, Momma, I call that downright greedy."

"Emory," said Mrs. Poe, "I'm praying for you. And I'm praying for folks like Dilly Mae down there in the cabin sick from scrubbing all her life. I'm praying for that sassy boy of hers. Oh Lord, I'm worried about that boy."

Then Mrs. Poe's blink went on and off like the sign at the cafe, and her face got all worked up as if the mention of Dilly Mae's boy was like reaching down into a well and pulling up a bucket of grief.

"What do you do down there in the swamp, Emory?" she asked. "You and that pariah, Jeb? Drink corn likker and hunt duck down there in the swamp? Hunt duck and Lord, what else . . ."

Emory shot to his feet. "Listen here!" he yelled. "Are you through with preaching? Do you want to eat or preach?" He wheeled around to Henry. "Start carving, Pa . . ."

As for Janice, she just sat there. Nervous like her Momma. Next thing you know, Janice might be making speeches. Why, she was enough like Mrs. Poe to worry anyone with the likeness. A dandelion weed, just like her mother. Push down Mrs. Poe, and up pops Janice.

Henry went on with the carving. Not another word was spoken until the time Grace and Emma Lynn muttered their goodbyes at the door.

A day afterward, Mrs. Poe was taking the air out on the back verandah and reading the *Leesville News* when suddenly she jumped to her feet and yelled. She hollered loud enough to set the dogs to barking. Then she swept the paper up again and her head rolled around as though she couldn't read it fast enough. Most of them in Leesville had known all day about the young colored man dragged out of the swamp with a shotgun wound through his head. He had been messed up so bad they couldn't tell who he was, but they had found him in the very place where Emory and Jeb Williams did their duck shooting and had their blinds set up. But the sheriff had not detained either of the boys. Emory had been at Mrs. Poe's Thanksgiving on the day of the murder, and Jeb Williams according to what Emory swore, had been there too.

Mrs. Poe started hollering again, waving her arms around like she had gone blind and couldn't find her way into the house. "Janice! Janice!"

Janice was out there in a flash holding her mother round the shoulders and setting her back on the chair. The newspaper was all crumpled up around her feet.

"Hush, Momma," Janice said. "You can't do a thing. Emory was here." Janice's voice was praying and pleading. "Emory has Poppa scared enough to swear that Jeb was here to dinner. There is nothing you can do. I can't either. They won't hear a word we say."

Mrs. Poe sat staring straight ahead. She looked like she was seeing hell right there beyond the cypress tree where the rubber tire still swung easy in the breeze.

"Who was the boy?" she wailed.

No one would ever believe that Janice's fancy voice could sound so squashed. "I was down to the cabin an hour ago . . ." Mrs. Poe's hand shot up to her chest. She began to moan an awful tune. "Dilly's boy," she sang. "Dilly Mae's boy . . ."

They stayed there, the two of them, Janice clasping her momma around the knees and Mrs. Poe staring past the cypress tree. A few minutes later, Janice got up, straightened her hair, dabbed a handkerchief to her eyes, and went in.

Henry, Emory, Grace, and Steven Knowles, the sheriff, were already inside, waiting.

"Well now," Steven said, "It's Miss Janice. Mighty nice to see you."

"How do you do, Sheriff Knowles," Janice said, twisting her handkerchief around like she was going to knot a noose in it.

"I do just fine, Miss Janice," Steven said. "Just fine. And I won't be bothering you all more than just a minute. I want to know about Jeb's being here to dinner. Not that I'm in any doubt . . . why, Jeb and Emory are friends of mine . . . but it's my job."

"I know," said Janice, getting stiff again.

"Well now, we'll just get on with it. Yesterday, you all had Thanksgiving Sunday here." Steven smiled when he said "Thanksgiving Sunday."

Janice nodded.

"Let's try it this way," he went on. "I'll go around this room and ask all of you to tell me who was here to dinner. I can't think of anything as short and sweet as that . . ."

Steven nodded at Henry to begin, and Henry, his jaw hanging loose and trembling, looked around to Emory sitting with his legs crossed in a chair, and Grace fidgeting on the sofa, and Janice pulling at her handkerchief. He looked back at Emory again and said quick without further hesitation, "There was Emory and Grace . . . Emma Lynn and Janice . . . Mrs. P-p—." It seemed that his tongue got tied and he started coughing. Emory got out of his chair, pulled a handkerchief out of his pocket and handed it to him. Henry held it to his mouth, glanced up at Emory again and then went on. "There was . . . uh . . . Jeb. He was right here as our guest . . ."

"That's fine," Steven said. "Now it's your turn, Grace . . ."

"Just exactly like Poppa says, sheriff. Jeb was Mrs. Poe's guest. He ate a pile of turkey, too. Jeb loves turkey. I always say to Emory, are you going to invite Jeb for dinner again? Why, he'll eat Mrs. Poe right out of house and home."

The sheriff laughed. "He's a mighty big man to fill, Jeb is. Your turn now, Miss Janice . . ."

Janice started to say something but she did not get far along. Mrs. Poe had come in softly through the back door and took them by surprise. She came round in front of them, stood straight and pointed at Emory.

"Evil!" she crowed. "Lucifer could be no worse!"

Then she crept around to Henry. She was all hunched over like a yellow witch. "Fool!" she cried at him and Henry shrunk up like a fig. She turned back to Emory. "Evil is in the marrow of you, but I'll have no lies. I'll have no devil's lies . . ."

Then she came up to the sheriff, close enough to breathe on him. Her eye was blinking and her voice was cracked, and she began to wring her hands like the niggers taken with the spirit at the revival tent. "It's a lie!" she yelled. "I would not have Jeb Williams in my house. I would not let Jeb Williams share my meal. He was never here. Not that pariah in my house. Lord! Do you hear? Rufe is shot to death and they are telling lies . . ."

Janice, flustered beyond anything Leesville'd ever seen, tried to lead her off, but Mrs. Poe wrenched herself free and would not move. She grabbed the sheriff's hand and started pressing it. That clammy palm of hers rubbing sweat around in his. Then all of a sudden she went soft. She put her hand to Steven's hair and smoothed it like a momma would do to a child. "Boy," she said, "I'm here to save you. Oh Lord, I never thought to say it but my father was a judge and did no justice. He told me that before he died. He said, Caroline, I did no justice for the fear of them. I've got to save you, boy. I've got to make you strong and bent on justice."

The sheriff wrung himself away from her; he nodded to Emory, but she had seen him. In a whisk, Mrs. Poe turned and she was out of the house. Janice started after her but Emory held her back. Henry sat there, shriveled up.

FLORENCE COHEN

"Now there, Janice," Emory said. "Don't you worry about Momma. Momma's sick. She needs me. I know where she's going. You leave Momma to me."

Mrs. Poe ran with Emory after her. She ran down Fowler Avenue around the bend to River Clearing until she got to Reverend Williams' house. At the front porch she saw him leaning against the door waiting; as though he had been there all night, doing nothing but waiting for Mrs. Poe. He helped her up the steps and Emory followed them inside the house. Jeb was there, sitting in the reverend's swivel chair, peeling a pomegranate. Mrs. Poe with hardly any breath left at all, reeled around to face the reverend. "You know they're telling lies," she gasped. "You know I would not have him in my house or at my table . . ." Then her voice got small and sad. "You've known all these years that Jeb would do a terrible thing . . . God help you . . . My heart pains for you . . .But Jeb's done murder."

"Hush, Mrs. Poe!" The reverend took out his handkerchief and wiped his neck with it. "Hush!" he repeated, turning his head to Emory, then to Jeb, then all over the room as though Mrs. Poe's accusations would seep into the walls and the furniture and the prayer books on the shelves.

"The truth!" shrieked Mrs. Poe. "The truth!"

The reverend's hands were shaking and beads of sweat trickled off his temples. He tried to calm her, hold her up, but she caught hold of his coat and shook him hard. Reverend Williams closed his eyes and began to pray. "Mercy, Father, mercy on us all . . ." But Mrs. Poe was shouting over him, "You're breathing down the devil's neck!"

Neither Emory nor Jeb had made a move toward them. Jeb was spitting pomegranate seeds into a saucer when Emory finally moved in and took his mother's hands off the reverend's coat. He put his arms around her and held her so she couldn't get away from him. And Mrs. Poe stopped raving. She just stood there with Emory's arms around her, weeping soft, simpering cries on his shoulder.

"Reverend," Emory said softly, "I'm mighty apologetic about this trouble. Momma's sick. Why, we're going to have to call the doctors in. The sheriff's about to swear she's gone clear out of her mind. Reverend? Are you about to swear it, too? I wouldn't worry about Janice. You know how she is when it comes to Momma—she'd lie—do anything . . ."

Reverend Williams was froze to the floor. Emory had to lean over and repeat it near his ear. "Reverend? Are you about to swear it, too?"

It wasn't long before Leesville knew how Mrs. Poe had danced around the sheriff pulling on his arms and petting his face, while Grace, president of the Bethany Bible Club, sat there saying her prayers. Janice, of course, told lies, they said, to save her mother; and finally, Mrs. Poe had called the reverend wicked names and had even tried to choke him. The reverend himself would not testify to his being choked, but they said that preachers should not be expected to condemn, but pray for souls. When Emory brought Mrs. Poe back to the house that evening, she was all wild and crazy. She kept yelling at Janice to be strong and bent on justice. Then the doctors came and Janice made a fuss again while old Henry slouched weeping in his chair. But they took her. Sure enough, they took her.

IMAGE FOUR

WOMAN ON A PEDESTAL

Women in the Western world have higher status and more freedom than women elsewhere in the world. This fact is usually connected with the Christian tradition in the twelfth century, which exalted Mary as Queen of Heaven and raised great Gothic cathedrals to honor her. Simultaneously with Maryology secular women were idealized in stories about knights and their pursuit of honor; in this so-called courtly love tradition, women were both the inspiration and the reward for men of high achievement. It is hard to see the noble woman of this tradition as dehumanized in any way; yet it is perhaps the most effective stereotype in causing women to perceive themselves as other than fully human beings. Instead, they try to live up to the ideal of nobility; reinforced by its religious form, the secular ideal is very far removed from reality. It fulfills the human need to find and strive for a symbol for the value of life as does the comparable male ideal of the hero. But in most literature male heroes who fall short of the dream are viewed as autonomous agents and their failure, tragic. Women who fall short are viewed as either not autonomous or as unnatural; they are perceived as pathetic rather than tragic. Exceptions come to mind, of course. But Antigone, the Greek heroine who defied the ruling powers to perform funeral rites for her brothers, is seen by scholars as a projection of male virtues, with no relationship to the reality of the life of Greek women. Lady Macbeth asks to be "unsexed" to goad her husband to murder. By and large, the women who serve as inspirations to noble action do so because of their beauty, not because of any action or achievement of their own. Since beauty cannot be understood on human terms, it is feared; a beautiful woman often becomes a symbol of the greatest human fear, death.

The righteous elders in Crapsey's quintain "Susanna and the Elders" "devise/evil" against the beautiful girl. Though in the Biblical story she is completely innocent of causing them any real harm, her beauty reminds them that righteousness will not be sufficient to save them from death. Their fear and hatred for her find counterparts in the stories of many societies documented by anthropologists.

Other works in this section show the process by which a specific living woman is made into a symbol of mystery, usually of evil and death. In Jean Toomer's story "Fern" the process of symbolization begins when a man perceives a woman's beauty as unfathomable. When the narrator looks into Fern's eyes, he finds them magnetically attractive but baffling; he does not see in them any "obvious and tangible desire." Like Freud, who asked "What do women want?", the observer is mystified because he cannot understand what she wants from him and from life. Yet he acknowledges her power over all the men who have known her; her influence makes them transcend physical desire and want to do something great and noble for her. The narrator comes to understand that her appeal is superhuman. In her eyes he sees God, who possesses her as He did the oracles of Greek myth, speaking through her tortured body paradoxical answers to existential questions.

Fern, a humble black woman, is exalted in this story. Though a prostitute, she has a beneficent and ennobling effect on men. But her lovers' noble resolutions to help her never come to fruition: "Nothing ever came to Fern." Their exaltation of her is a self-delusory attempt to deal with their own sexual appetites and with their knowledge of mortality. In other literature in this section a mysteriously beautiful woman is even more directly linked with deleterious effects on men; instead of inspiring them, however briefly, she entices them to shame and death. Keats's "La Belle Dame sans Merci" shows a woman who seems to symbolize Death itself. Her wild eyes, strange language, and fairylike song have made corpses of many men. The appearance of their ghosts in a dream causes her most recent victim to realize that what he thinks is the sleep of love is really deathlike and destructive; he awakens completely disoriented.

Keats uses the poetic tradition of intercourse and sleep as metaphors for death. The Knight's love for the mysterious woman testifies to the strength of the death wish, which seems stronger than his will to live. The image of a lover as a helpless victim of overpowering emotion parallels that of the beautiful woman as superhuman, like a goddess on a pedestal to be propiated, if not worshipped. Edgar Allan Poe said that for a poet the best subject is the death of a beautiful woman. The image of a delicate, doomed, pure, but powerful creature underlies the courtship rites of romantic love, with the male suitor as the humble supplicant bringing rich gifts.

Heine's "The Loreley" emphasizes the fatal power of women but also reveals their innocence in using this power. The mermaid is merely combing her hair and singing an old song when sailors crash on her rock; like that of Fern and "La Belle Dame," her mysterious power is a fantasy of the males who encounter her. In Blake's poem the fantasy of a princely lover reduces his beloved to a caged automaton, a toy for his pleasure. Gorky's story "26 Men and a Girl" makes clear the role of men in projecting the image of evil onto a woman. Gorky vividly shows that the brutalization of men by poverty and class barriers is the source of their fantasy of a beautiful woman as salvation. Their idea of Tanya has no relation to her human qualities and forces a feeling of guilt upon her when they discover her humanity. She reciprocates with anger when they violently express their disillusionment; she becomes full of "pride and contempt" toward them. Gorky lets us feel compassion for all the characters, but the story is a comment on the destructive power of ideals divorced from reality.

Howells's story "Editha" shows the persistence of the courtly love ideal. The picture of Editha urging her lover to overcome his and his mother's pacifism and go off to a noble death in war clashes with our modern concept of the feminine influence on both men and women to avoid war. Today it is easy to forget that Americans did not perceive war as evil until the reaction to Vietnam in the 1970s; war had always been legitimized by patriotism. Even today a uniform may arouse female admiration, especially if it is that of an officer. The courtly love tradition, as well as the association of love and war as ennobling, has been a class-bound concept. But the romantic concept lingers on in the stereotype of the pure, noble woman sheltered from the brutality of life in the real world of competition and struggle; too good for the world of public life, she is both the inspiration for the struggle and the reward after a hard day's work. Fulfilling this ideal removes a woman from her human qualities; like Tanya, she may become bitter and contemptuous of men for being so foolishly gullible. Behind all the wild eyes is the desire men seldom respond to: let me be your equal, experiencing struggle, achievement, joy, and failure.

Kate Wilhelm in "Baby, You Were Great!" and Helene Davis in "Affair" make clear that goddesses are made, not born. Their willingness to adapt themselves to male fantasies stems from their own human emotions of love, desire for status, greed. Though Anne Beaumont in Wilhelm's story is perceived as if she were a goddess, she is more like the humanized goddesses of the Greeks than the frozen statues of the courtly tradition. Unlike Aphrodite and Hera, however, human goddesses do not retain their divine power. Anne Beaumont is trapped into continuing to play the role of superhuman outlet for others' fantasies and emotions; the victim of electronic thought control, she cannot escape playing out her role to the death. In this human world, the men involved, though powerful enough to determine women's fate, are also caught. "Shaped by centuries of civilization" into becoming like a stalactite—incapable of warm emotions—John has made his world a hell of fear and violence for all the characters. The most startling aspect of Wilhelm's story is that women are the main audience for Anne's experiences of rape, terror, torture; their vicarious masochism removes them from "boredom and frustration," "a life of work, kids, bills." Through Anne they live the Cinderella myth.

Wilhelm has pinpointed the psychological explanation for the overwhelming popularity of romances written by women for women, of soap operas on television. The need to escape from the reality of their lives is as pressing as that of Gorky's bakers. But both stories show that to live in a world of fantasy is dehumanizing for all concerned. Only by outgrowing such dreams can men and women find alternatives to Wilhelm's grim vision of the future.

ADELAIDE CRAPSEY

(1878–1914) Born in Rochester, New York, Adelaide Crapsey studied at Vassar and later taught in preparatory schools and at Smith College. Some of her poems and a major book on English metrics were published after her death by tuberculosis; her complete poems were published along with a biography in 1977. She invented a new poetic form, the cinquain, a five-line form akin to the Japanese *haiku* and *tanka*.

SUSANNA AND THE ELDERS

"Why do
You thus devise
Evil against her?" "For that
She is beautiful, delicate:
Therefore."

JEAN TOOMER

(1894–1967) A Georgian who also lived in New York, Toomer wrote of the struggles of blacks—male and female, rural and urban—to achieve a sense of human dignity. *Cane* (1923), called a novel though it is also a collection of short stories and poems, was acclaimed as a contribution to the Harlem Renaissance, but only recently, with the republication of *Cane* in 1969 and the appearance of an anthology of other works in 1978, has Toomer's achievement been fully appreciated.

FERN

Face flowed into her eyes. Flowed in soft cream foam and plaintive ripples, in such a way that wherever your glance may momentarily have rested, it immediately thereafter wavered in the direction of her eyes. The soft suggestion of down slightly darkened, like the shadow of a bird's wing might, the creamy brown color of her upper lip. Why, after noticing it, you sought her eyes, I cannot tell you. Her nose was aquiline, Semitic. If you have heard a Jewish cantor sing, if he has touched you and made your own sorrow seem trivial when compared with his, you will know my feeling when I follow the curves of her profile, like mobile rivers, to their common delta. They were strange eyes. In this, that they sought nothing —that is, nothing that was obvious and tangible and that one could see, and they gave the impression that nothing was to be denied. When a woman seeks, you will have observed, her eyes deny. Fern's eyes desired nothing that you could give her; there was no reason why they should withhold. Men saw her eyes and fooled themselves. Fern's eyes said to them that she was easy. When she was young, a few men took her, but got no joy from it. And then, once done, they felt bound to her (quite unlike their hit and run with other girls), felt as though it would take them a lifetime to fulfill an obligation which they could find no name for. They became attached to her, and hungered after finding the barest trace of what she might desire. As she grew up, new men who came to town felt as almost everyone did who ever saw her: that they would not be denied.

Men were everlastingly bringing her their bodies. Something inside of her got tired of them, I guess, for I am certain that for the life of her she could not tell why or how she began to turn them off. A man in fever is no trifling thing to send away. They began to leave her, baffled and ashamed, yet vowing to themselves that some day they would do some fine thing for her: send her candy every week and not let her know whom it came from, watch out for her wedding-day and give her a magnificent something with no name on it, buy a house and deed it to her, rescue her from some unworthy fellow who had tricked her into marrying him. As you know, men are apt to idolize or fear that which they cannot understand, especially if it be a woman. She did not deny them, yet the fact was that they were denied. A sort of superstition crept into their consciousness of her being somehow above them. Being above them meant that she was not to be approached by anyone. She became a virgin. Now a virgin in a small southern town is by no means the usual thing, if you will believe me. That the sexes were made to mate is the practice of the South. Particularly, black folks were made to mate. And it is black folks whom I have been talking about thus far. What white men thought of Fern I can arrive at only by analogy. They let her alone.

Anyone, of course, could see her, could see her eyes. If you walked up the Dixie Pike most any time of day, you'd be most like to see her resting listless-like on the railing of her porch, back propped against a post, head tilted a little forward because there was a nail in the porch post just where her head came which for some reason or other she never took the trouble to pull out. Her eyes, if it were sunset, rested idly where the sun, molten and glorious, was pouring down between the fringe of pines. Or maybe they gazed at the gray cabin on the knoll from which an evening folk-song was coming. Perhaps they followed a cow that had been turned loose to roam and feed on cotton-stalks and corn leaves. Like as not they'd settle on some vague spot above the horizon, though hardly a trace of wistfulness would come to them. If it were dusk, then they'd wait for the search-light of the evening train which you could see miles up the track before it flared across the Dixie Pike, close to her home. Wherever they looked, you'd follow them and then waver back. Like her face, the whole countryside seemed to flow into her eyes. Flowed into them with the soft listless cadence of Georgia's South. A young Negro, once, was looking at her, spellbound, from the road. A white man passing in a buggy had to flick him with his whip if he was to get by without running him over. I first saw her on her porch. I was passing with a fellow whose crusty numbness (I was from the North and suspected of being prejudiced and stuck-up) was melting as he found me warm. I asked him who she was. "That's Fern," was all I could get from him. Some folks already thought that I was given to nosing around; I let it go at that, so far as questions were concerned. But at first sight of her I felt as if I heard a Jewish cantor sing. As if his

singing rose above the unheard chorus of a folk-song. And I felt bound
to her. I too had my dreams: something I would do for her. I have knocked
about from town to town too much not to know the futility of mere change
of place. Besides, picture if you can, this cream-colored solitary girl
sitting at a tenement window looking down on the indifferent throngs
of Harlem. Better that she listens to folk-songs at dusk in Georgia, you
would say, and so would I. Or, suppose she came up North and married.
Even a doctor or a lawyer, say, one who would be sure to get along—
that is, make money. You and I know, who have had experience in such
things, that love is not a thing like prejudice which can be bettered by
changes of town. Could men in Washington, Chicago, or New York, more
than the men of Georgia, bring her something left vacant by the bestowal
of their bodies? You and I who know men in these cities will have to say,
they could not. See her out and out a prostitute along State Street in
Chicago. See her move into a southern town where white men are more
aggressive. See her become a white man's concubine . . . Something I must
do for her. There was myself. What could I do for her? Talk, of course.
Push back the fringe of pines upon new horizons. To what purpose? and
what for? Her? Myself? Men in her case seem to lose their selfishness.
I lost mine before I touched her. I ask you, friend (it makes no difference
if you sit in the Pullman or the Jim Crow as the train crosses her road),
what thoughts would come to you—that is, after you'd finished with the
thoughts that leap into men's minds at the sight of a pretty woman who
will not deny them; what thoughts would come to you, had you seen her
in a quick flash, keen and intuitively, as she sat there on her porch when
your train thundered by? Would you have got off at the next station and
come back for her to take her where? Would you have completely forgotten
her as soon as you reached Macon, Atlanta, Augusta, Pasadena, Madison,
Chicago, Boston, or New Orleans? Would you tell your wife or sweetheart about a girl you saw? Your thoughts can help me, and I would like
to know. Something I would do for her . . .

One evening I walked up the Pike on purpose, and stopped to say hello.
Some of her family were about, but they moved away to make room for
me. Damn if I knew how to begin. Would you? Mr. and Miss So-and-So,
people, the weather, the crops, the new preacher, the frolic, the church
benefit, rabbit and possum hunting, the new soft drink they had at old
Pap's store, the schedule of the trains, what kind of town Macon was,
Negro's migration north, boll-weevils, syrup, the Bible—to all these things
she gave a yassur or nassur, without further comment. I began to wonder
if perhaps my own emotional sensibility had played one of its tricks on
me. "Let's take a walk," I at last ventured. The suggestion, coming after so
long an isolation, was novel enough, I guess, to surprise. But it wasn't
that. Something told me that men before me had said just that, as a pre-
lude to the offering of their bodies. I tried to tell her with my eyes. I think

she understood. The thing from her that made my throat catch, vanished. Its passing left her visible in a way I'd thought, but never seen. We walked down the Pike with people on all the porches gaping at us. "Doesn't it make you mad?" She meant the row of petty gossiping people. She meant the world. Through a canebreak that was ripe for cutting, the branch was reached. Under a sweet-gum tree, and where reddish leaves had dammed the creek a little, we sat down. Dusk, suggesting the almost imperceptible procession of giant trees, settled with a purple haze about the cane. I felt strange, as I always do in Georgia, particularly at dusk. I felt that things unseen to men were tangibly immediate. It would not have surprised me had I had a vision. People have them in Georgia more often than you would suppose. A black woman once saw the mother of Christ and drew her in charcoal on the courthouse wall . . . When one is on the soil of one's ancestors, most anything can come to one . . . From force of habit, I suppose, I held Fern in my arms—that is, without at first noticing it. Then my mind came back to her. Her eyes, unusually weird and open, held me. Held God. He flowed in as I've seen the countryside flow in. Seen men. I must have done something—what, I don't know, in the confusion of my emotion. She sprang up. Rushed some distance from me. Fell to her knees, and began swaying, swaying. Her body was tortured with something it could not let out. Like boiling sap it flooded arms and fingers till she shook them as if they burned her. It found her throat, and spattered inarticulately in plaintive, convulsive sounds, mingled with calls to Christ Jesus. And then she sang, brokenly. A Jewish cantor singing with a broken voice. A child's voice, uncertain, or an old man's. Dusk hid her; I could hear only her song. It seemed to me as though she were pounding her head in anguish upon the ground. I rushed to her. She fainted in my arms.

There was talk about her fainting with me in the canefield. And I got one or two ugly looks from town men who'd set themselves up to protect her. In fact, there was talk of making me leave town. But they never did. They kept a watch-out for me, though. Shortly after, I came back North. From the train window I saw her as I crossed her road. Saw her on her porch, head tilted a little forward where the nail was, eyes vaguely focused on the sunset. Saw her face flow into them, the countryside and something that I call God, flowing into them . . . Nothing ever really happened. Nothing ever came to Fern, not even I. Something I would do for her. Some fine unnamed thing . . . And, friend, you? She is still living, I have reason to know. Her name, against the chance that you might happen down that way, is Fernie May Rosen.

JEAN TOOMER

JOHN KEATS

(1795–1821) The famous English Romantic poet John Keats studied medicine before embarking on his all too brief career as a poet. His poems reflect his love for Greek myth, for nature, and for the supernatural, often personified as woman.

LA BELLE DAME
SANS MERCI

Ah, what can ail thee, wretched wight,
  Alone and palely loitering;
The sedge is wither'd from the lake,
  And no birds sing.

Ah, what can ail thee, wretched wight,
  So haggard and so woe-begone?
The squirrel's granary is full,
  And the harvest's done.

I see a lilly on thy brow,
  With anguish moist and fever dew;
And on thy cheek a fading rose
  Fast withereth too.

I met a Lady in the meads,
  Full beautiful, a fairy's child;
Her hair was long, her foot was light,
  And her eyes were wild.

I set her on my pacing steed,
    And nothing else saw all day long;
For sideways would she lean, and sing
    A faery's song.

I made a garland for her head,
    And bracelets too, and fragrant zone,
She look'd at me as she did love,
    And made sweet moan.

She found me roots of relish sweet,
    And honey wild, and manna dew,
And sure in language strange she said,
    I love thee true.

She took me to her elfin grot,
    And there she gaz'd and sighed deep,
And there I shut her wild sad eyes—
    So kiss'd to sleep.

And there we slumber'd on the moss,
    And there I dream'd, ah woe betide
The latest dream I ever dream'd
    On the cold hill side.

I saw pale kings, and princes too,
    Pale warriors, death-pale were they all;
Who cry'd—"La belle Dame sans merci
    Hath thee in thrall."

I saw their starv'd lips in the gloom
    With horrid warning gaped wide,
And I awoke, and found me here
    On the cold hill side.

And this is why I sojourn here
    Alone and palely loitering,
Though the sedge is wither'd from the lake,
    And no birds sing.

HEINRICH HEINE

(1797–1856) A well-known German writer, Heinrich Heine voluntarily exiled himself in Paris in 1831 to escape the rigid political regime of his native Prussia. His early works, including the famous "Loreley," were romantic; later he satirized the Romantic movement and wrote political and philosophical works in prose.

THE LORELEY

Ich weiss nicht, was soll es bedeuten

I cannot tell why this imagined
    Despair has fallen on me;
The ghost of an ancient legend
    That will not let me be:

The air is cool, and twilight
    Flows down the quiet Rhine;
A mountain alone in the high light
    Still holds the faltering shine.

The last peak rosily gleaming
    Reveals, enthroned in air,
A maiden, lost in dreaming,
    Who combs her golden hair.

Combing her hair with a golden
    Comb in her rocky bower.
She sings the tune of an olden
    Song that has magical power.

WOMAN ON A PEDESTAL

The boatman has heard; it has bound him
  In throes of a strange, wild love;
Blind to the reefs that surround him,
  He sees but the vision above.

And lo, hungry waters are springing—
  Boat and boatsman are gone. . . .
Then silence. And this, with her singing,
  The Loreley has done.

WILLIAM BLAKE

(1757–1827) Usually considered a Romantic poet, William Blake was such an individual that it is hard to label him. He was essentially a revolutionary in politics and in philosophy, and his long mystical poems have had many interpretations. His own beautiful engravings illustrate and help to explain many of his poems. Blake was as ardent a women's liberationist as was his contemporary, Mary Wollstonecraft.

SONG

How sweet I roam'd from field to field
And tasted all the summer's pride,
Till I the Prince of Love beheld
Who in the sunny beams did glide!

He show'd me lilies for my hair,
And blushing roses for my brow;
He led me through his gardens fair
Where all his golden pleasures grow.

With sweet May dews my wings were wet,
And Phoebus fir'd my vocal rage;
He caught me in his silken net,
And shut me in his golden cage.

He loves to sit and hear me sing,
Then, laughing, sports and plays with me;
Then stretches out my golden wing,
And mocks my loss of liberty.

MAXIM GORKY

※

(1868–1936) The name "Gorky," a pseudonym chosen by Alexei Maximovich Peshkov,
means "bitter." Of humble birth, Gorky experienced the turmoil that led to the Russian
Revolution and tried to write of the "bitter"
destiny of common people without despair-
ing of their ultimate success. He is famous
for his mix of realism, especially in dialogue,
and romantic optimism evident in many
novels, plays, and short stories.

TWENTY-SIX MEN AND A GIRL

There were six and twenty of us—twenty-six animated machines, cooped up
in a damp basement where, making butter pretzels and cracknels, we
kneaded dough from morning till night. The windows of our basement
were on the level of a hole that had been excavated and then built over
with now moldy brick; the window frames were barred on the outside
with a fine iron screen, and the light of the sun could not penetrate to us
through panes clotted with flour. Our boss had iron-barred the windows
in order to make it impossible for us to hand out morsels of bread to
beggars or those of our comrades who were out of work and starving. Our
boss called us swindlers and gave us putrid offal instead of meat for our
midday meals.

It was stifling and stuffy living in that stone box under the low, smoke-
yellow ceiling completely covered with soot and cobwebs. We felt depressed
and sickened inside the stout walls splotched with stains of filth and
mold. . . . We used to get up at five in the morning without our fair share of
sleep, and by six o'clock—dull-witted and lethargic—we were already sitting
down at a table to fashion butter pretzels from dough prepared overnight
for us by other assistants. All day long, from early morning till ten at
night, some of us sat at the table with sleeves rolled up, kneading the tough
dough and rocking our bodies to fight the creeping stiffness; others,
in the meantime, were busy mixing flour and water. All day long the water,
bubbling in the big cauldron where the pretzels were being boiled, purred

in a mournful, melancholy way, and our baker's wooden shovel scuffled in quick and fierce thrusts to and fro on the floor of the oven furnace, throwing slippery lumps of boiled dough onto the red-hot brick. From morning till night logs burned in one section of the oven, and the red reflections of the flame quivered on one of the walls of the bakery as if in mute mockery of us. The huge oven resembled the deformed head of a fabled monster. It seemed to project from under the floor, its gaping jaws bristling with bright fire, to breathe scorching heat upon us, watching our endless labors through a pair of black, hollow vents above the mouth of the oven. These two deep hollows were like the eyes—the pitiless and dispassionate eyes—of a monster: they always stared at us with the same dark gaze, as if tired of watching slaves at work and expecting nothing human from them; and they hated the slaves with all the frigid contempt of wisdom.

Day after day, covered in flour, spattered with the mud our boots brought in from the outside, we kneaded dough and made pretzels saturated with our sweat in that thick, badly smelling, overheated atmosphere; we detested our work with a keen hatred, and never ate what came from our hands, preferring black rye bread. Sitting opposite one another at a long table—nine men on each side—we moved our hands and fingers mechanically for hours on end, and we had grown so accustomed to our work that we no longer kept track of our movements. We had seen each other so often that we knew all the wrinkles on each other's faces. We had nothing to talk about and were used to that, and kept our mouths shut unless we swore—for there is always a reason for abusing a man and especially a comrade. But we abused each other very rarely—for what can a man be blamed if he is half dead, or if he is like a stone statue, all his feelings crushed by the burden of his labor? But silence terrifies and torments only those who have already spoken all they had to say and have nothing left to add; on the other hand, silence is simple and easy for those who have not yet begun to speak. Sometimes we sang, and our song would begin as follows: in the middle of work, someone would suddenly sigh deeply like an exhausted hack and would then softly take up one of those long-drawn-out, plaintively tender airs that always lighten the pressure on the singer's soul. One of us would sing, and we would listen at first in silence to his single song as it died away and faded under the oppressive basement ceiling, like the flickering flame of a bonfire in the steppes on a damp autumn night when the gray skies blot out the earth with their leaden roof. Then another singer would join in, and there would now be two voices floating gently and nostalgically in the stifling atmosphere of our stuffy hole. Next, several voices in unison would suddenly pick up the song—it would swell like a wave, growing stronger and louder, and shift apart the damp, massive walls of our stone prison. . . .

All twenty-six of us would be singing now. The loud, well-practiced voices filled the bakery; the song, hemmed in, beat against the stone walls, moaned, sobbed, and stirred our hearts with a gently tickling pain, making old wounds smart, and awakening our longing. . . . The singers would utter deep, heavy sighs; one of them would unexpectedly break off his song and listen for a long while to his comrades' singing, then pour his voice again into the general wave. Another, dismally exclaiming "Ekh!" would sing with his eyes closed; and the dense, broad wave of sounds would, perhaps, loom before him like a road, brightly illumined by the sun, stretching somewhere into the far distance—a spacious road along which he saw himself walking. . . .

The flame in the oven furnace would still be throbbing, the baker's wooden shovel would still be scraping on brick, the water in the kettle would be purring, and the reflections of the fire on the wall would be flickering as always, mocking us in silence. . . . And we would go on singing our blunted sorrow in words composed by other men, expressive of the heavy longing of living men deprived of the sun, the longing of slaves. That is how we lived, the twenty-six of us, in the basement of a large stone house; and our life was so oppressive that all the three stories of this house might well have been built right on top of our shoulders. . . .

But, besides our songs, we possessed something else that was good, that we loved, that was, perhaps, a substitute for the sun. There was a gold-embroidery workshop on the second floor of our house and there, among the many seamstresses, lived Tanya, a sixteen-year-old housemaid. Every morning, her small rosy little face with its light-blue twinkling eyes would be glued to the pane of a small window cut in the door to the entrance hall, and she would shout to us in her tender voice: "Little convicts! Let me have my little pretzels!"

We all turned at the sound of this clear voice, gazing with pleasure and good nature at this pure, girlish face smiling so gloriously at us. It gave us pleasure to see her nose squashed against the glass and her small, white teeth glittering between her rosy lips parted in a smile. We rushed to open the door for her, pushing each other, and she, the bright darling, would take a step forward and hold out her apron, standing before us with her head slightly to one side and smiling all the time. The long thick plait of her chestnut hair fell over one shoulder and rested on her breast. We, dirty, ignorant, deformed men, looked up at her from below—the threshold of the door was four steps higher than the floor—we looked up at her with raised heads and greeted her with "Good morning!" and spoke some very special words to her—words we had found only for her. Our voices were softer and our jokes lighter when we talked to her. Everything we gave her was very special. The baker pulled out a shovelful of the crispest, most golden pretzels from the oven furnace and tossed them deftly into Tanya's apron.

MAXIM GORKY

"Be careful and don't let the boss see you!" we warned her. She only laughed mischievously and shouted gaily as she disappeared swiftly, like a little mouse: "Good-by, my little convicts!"

That was all. . . . But long after her departure we discussed her pleasantly amongst us; and we repeated the same things we had said yesterday and the day before, because she, and we, and everything around us, were the same as they had been the previous day and the day before. . . . It is a hard and torturing thing when a man goes on living and nothing around him ever changes; and if that fails to kill his soul, then the immobility of his environment becomes all the more tormenting to him. . . . We always spoke of women in a way that was repugnant even to ourselves when we heard our coarse, shameless, lewd talk; and that was understandable because the women we knew may, perhaps, have deserved no better comment. But our references to Tanya were never lewd; not one of us ever allowed himself even to put a hand on her, still less to utter a dirty joke in her presence. Perhaps this was due to the fact that she never stayed with us any length of time: like a falling star she would flash before our gaze and then vanish; and, perhaps, it was also due to her being so small and so very beautiful, for every form of beauty evokes respect even from the coarsest people. Moreover, even though our hard, convictlike labor had made us as dull as oxen, we yet managed to remain human beings and, like all human beings, could not live without having something to worship. We had no one better than Tanya, and no one but she had ever paid any attention to us stuck in that basement—no one at all, even though dozens of other people lived in the house. And finally, and this is probably the main reason, we regarded her as something very personal, something that existed only thanks to our pretzels. We had made it our duty to give her freshly baked ones every day, and that was the daily sacrifice we offered to our idol; it became an almost sacred ritual and with every day it bound us even more closely to her. Besides the pretzels we gave Tanya many pieces of advice—to dress more warmly, not to run up and down stairs so fast, not to carry any heavy loads of logs. She listened to our advice with a smile, replied to it with a laugh, and never heeded us, but this did not offend us: we only wanted to show that we were concerned about her.

She often turned to us with various requests, asking us, for example, to open the heavy door of the ice-cellar and to chop wood for her. We did this, and anything else she asked, not only with delight, but with a sort of pride as well.

But when one of us asked her to repair his only shirt she replied with a contemptuous snort: "What more! You expect me to do that!"

We laughed a lot over this odd fellow, and no one ever asked her to do anything again. We loved her—that was the long and the short of it. Man always desires to impose his love upon someone, even if it becomes a crushing burden sometimes or proves soiling; with his love he may poison the life of one he holds most dear, because, in loving, he fails to respect the beloved. We were obliged to love Tanya because we had nobody else to love.

At times one of us would suddenly, and for some reason, begin to argue as follows: "And why are we spoiling this girl? What's she got? Eh? We're too stuck on her!"

The man who ventured to say such things was swiftly and rudely put in his place. We needed to have something to love: we had found it, and we loved it; and what we loved, all twenty-six of us, must be as permanent as a holy of holies to any one of us; and everyone who went against us in this was our declared enemy. We loved what was, perhaps, not so very beneficial for us; but since there were six and twenty of us, we always wished for this very reason to ensure that the rest of us also held sacred what was precious to each of us individually.

Our love weighs no less than our hatred, and, for this very reason perhaps, certain proud characters affirm that our hatred is more flattering than our love. . . . But why do they not run away from us in that case?

In addition to the pretzel bakehouse our boss also had a bakery for rolls; it was situated in the same house, with only a wall dividing it from our hole; but the bakers who made rolls—there were four of them—held themselves aloof; regarding their work as cleaner than ours, and themselves as our superiors, they avoided our premises and sniggered contemptuously whenever they met us in the yard. We did not visit them either; our boss forbade us to do so for fear we might steal some of the white rolls. We disliked these bakers because we envied them: their work was easier than ours, they received more pay, they were better fed, they had bright spacious premises, and they were all so very clean, healthy, and repugnant. We ourselves looked a sort of dirty yellow-and-gray; three of us were syphilitic, several had the itch, and one was completely twisted with rheumatism. On holidays, and in their spare time, the bakers of rolls wore jackets and creaking boots; a couple of them owned accordions; and they all used to go promenading in the park. We, on the contrary, were dressed in filthy rags, shoes made of bast or worn-out leather, and the police would not admit us into the park. So how could we like the bakers?

We learned one day that their chief baker had gone on the booze; the boss had dismissed him and engaged a substitute, a former soldier, who walked about in a satin vest and with a gold watch and chain. We were very anxious to see such a dandy; in the hope of catching sight of him we began taking turns to run out into the yard.

But he paid us a visit in person. Kicking open the door and leaving it ajar, he paused on the threshold and called out with a smile: "God bless! A fine day to you, lads!"

The frosty air, bursting through the door in a cloud of steam, wreathed around his feet as he stood on the threshold looking us up and down; a row of large yellow teeth glittered from under his fair, smartly twirled

mustaches. The vest he wore was, indeed, very unusual: blue and embroidered with flowers, it shone brightly, and its buttons were of some sort
of red stone. There was a gold chain too. . . .

He was handsome, this soldier, tall, healthy, pink-cheeked; and his large
bright eyes—amiable and clear—made a good impression. On his head
he wore a white, stiffly starched baker's conical hat, while the tips of a
pair of pointed, fashionable, highly polished boots peeped from underneath
his spotlessly clean apron.

Our baker respectfully requested him to shut the door; this he did without
haste and then started to question us about the boss. Interrupting each
other, we told him that our boss was a cunning rogue, a scoundrel, a
rascal and a bloodsucker—all the things that we could and should say
about the boss, but that cannot all be reported here. The soldier listened,
his mustaches quivering, and scrutinized us with his soft, clear gaze.

"And do you have many girls here?" he suddenly inquired.

Several of us tittered respectfully; others made sweet faces, and one of us
finally explained that there were nine girls in the house. . . .

"D'you profit by them?" the soldier asked with a wink.

We laughed again, not very loudly, in an embarrassed way. . . . Many
of us would have liked to show ourselves as devil-may-care as this baker,
but none of us, not a single one, could carry it off. Someone even admitted
this, saying quietly: "That's not for us. . . ."

"Y-yes, it's difficult for you!" the soldier commented with assurance,
examining us closely. "There's something . . . not quite so . . . about
you . . . You haven't got the bearing . . . a decent manner . . . appearance, I mean! And as for women—they love a man's appearance! The body
frame has to be just right for her . . . so that everything . . . is in its place!
And moreover she respects strength. . . . A man's arm must be . . . like
this!"

The soldier thereupon pulled out his right hand from his pocket and
showed us his arm with sleeve rolled up to the elbow. . . . His arm was
white, muscular, and covered with glistening golden hair.

"The leg, the chest—they should all be firm. . . . And again—a man
should be dressed according to form . . . as the beauty of things demands.
The women—they just love me. I don't call or lure them—they just come
five at a time and hang around my neck. . . ."

He sat down on a sack of flour and gave us a detailed account of how
much women loved him and how cavalierly he treated them. Then he
departed. When the creaking door had shut behind him, we were speechless
for a long while, pondering on him and his stories. Then, of a sudden, we
all began to talk, and it became clear that all of us had taken a liking to
him. He was so simple and friendly—he had come in, sat about, and
chatted. No one had ever visited us, no one had ever talked to us in such an
amiable manner. . . . And we continued to discuss him and his future
exploits with the women embroiderers, who, whenever they met us in the

yard, either avoided us with pursed lips or marched right past us as if we did not exist. We had always admired them as they passed by our windows—in the winter, wearing some sort of special hats and fur-lined coats, and, in the summer, dressed in flowered hats and carrying bright parasols. But, in private among ourselves, we spoke of those girls in a way that, had they heard us, would have made them furious with shame and a sense of outrage.

"However, I hope he doesn't spoil our Tanya!" the baker suddenly exclaimed with concern.

We stopped talking, flabbergasted at these words. Somehow we had forgotten about our Tanya: the soldier's sturdy, handsome figure had fenced her from us. A heated discussion followed: some argued that Tanya would never sink so low; others affirmed that she would be unable to resist the soldier; others again suggested that, if the soldier tried to annoy her, we'd break his ribs. Finally, we all resolved to keep an eye on both of them, and to warn the girl to be on her guard against him. . . . This ended the discussion.

About a month elapsed. The soldier went on baking bread, walking out with the women embroiderers, dropping in quite often to see us, but now he made no mention of his conquests and only twirled his mustaches and smacked his lips.

Each morning Tanya came to fetch her "little pretzels" and, as always, she was cheerful, tender, and affectionate toward us. We tried to talk to her about the soldier, but she merely referred to him as "a pop-eyed calf" and bestowed many other funny nicknames on him, which reassured us. We took pride in "our" girl. Observing how much fuss the women embroiderers made over the soldier, we felt elevated by Tanya's attitude to him and, as if guided by her attitude, began to treat the soldier with scorn. As a result we loved her all the more, welcoming her with even greater joy and amiability in the morning.

But one day the soldier came to see us a little the worse for drink; he sat down and began to laugh. When we inquired as to the cause of his laughter, he explained:

"Two of them—Lydka and Grushka—had a fight over me. . . . They really damaged themselves! Ha-ha-ha! One of them pulled the other's hair, got her down on the floor in the passage, and then sat on top of her. . . . Ha-ha-ha-ha! They clawed each other's faces and ripped their clothes— you'd die laughing to see it! And why can't women fight fair? Why do they scratch, tell me that?"

He sat on the bench there, in the pink of health, clean-cut, beaming— sat there and couldn't stop laughing. We remained silent. On this occasion we found him unpleasant.

"Say, don't I have all the luck with the girls, eh? I'll die laughing. I need only wink, and the girl's ready! The devil!"

He raised and then let drop his white hands with their glistening hair with a loud slap upon his knees. And he stared at us with a look of delighted astonishment as if genuinely puzzled at being always so lucky in his affairs with women. His pink, stolid dial of a face shone with uninhibited self-satisfaction and happiness as he smacked his lips with juicy gusto.

With violent fury our baker thrust his shovel into the hearth of the oven and remarked with sudden irony: "It doesn't need great strength to topple a sapling, but just you try toppling a full grown pine. . . ."

"What do you mean? Are you talking to me?" the soldier asked.

"And you . . ."

"What are you saying?"

"Nothing . . . it's passed!"

"No, just a minute! What is it about? What pine?"

Our baker made no reply as he worked rapidly with his shovel in the oven: into it he would thrust the boiled dough of the pretzels, hook the already baked ones out, and noisily chuck them on the floor for his young assistants, who then threaded them on bast strips. He seemed to have forgotten the soldier and his conversation with him. But the soldier grew very restless of a sudden. He rose to his feet and stepped toward the oven, at the risk of running his chest against the end of the handle of our baker's shovel, which was feverishly darting in and out of the oven.

"Now, tell me . . . who's she? You annoy me . . . I? Not one of them can shake me off, no! And you're casting such aspersions . . ."

He seemed genuinely hurt. Evidently he had no reason to respect himself except for his ability to seduce women. Perhaps this ability of his was the only vital virtue he possessed and it alone qualified him to feel himself alive.

There are people who cherish some disease of mind or body as their greatest and highest asset in life. They put up with the disease all their lives, and it provides them with their only vitality; suffering from it, they nourish themselves upon it, complain of it to others, and in this way attract the attention of their neighbors. In this way they exact the compassion of others, and it is all they have. Deprive them of their disease, cure them, and they will feel very unhappy; they will thus lose their only reason for living— they will become empty. Sometimes a man's life is so wretched that he is involuntarily compelled to value some particular vice of his and to live by it; and it can also be said that boredom makes such people vicious.

The soldier, offended, pushed against our baker, yelling: "No, you tell me—who?"

"Want me to tell you?" the baker asked, turning suddenly.

"Well?"

"D'you know Tanya?"

"Well?"

"That's it! Try her. . . ."

"I?"

"You!"

"Her? For me—that's nothing!"

"We'll see!"

"You'll see! Ha-ha!"

"She'll fix you. . . ."

"A month is all I need!"

"You're a real braggart, soldier!"

"Two weeks, then! I'll show you! Who's she? Tanka! Tfu! . . ."

"Now off with you. . . . You're getting in the way!"

"A couple of weeks and the thing will be done! Ah, you . . ."

"Off with you, I say. . . ."

Our baker, suddenly furious, raised his shovel. The soldier backed away in astonishment, glared at us, and, after a short silence, exclaimed in a sinister tone, "Very well then!" and left us.

Fascinated, we had not said a word during the dispute.

But when the soldier was gone, we all began to talk with noisy animation.

Some shouted to the baker: "That wasn't a good thing you started, Pavel!"

"Get on with your work!"

We felt that the soldier had been hurt to the quick, and that danger now threatened Tanya. We felt this, but at the same time we were gripped by a burning, pleasing curiosity as to the outcome. What would come of it? Would Tanya hold out against the soldier? Almost all of us declared with conviction:

"Tanya? She'll hold out. You can't take her with bare hands!"

We were terribly eager to test the fortitude of our idol: with great intensity we demonstrated to each other that our idol was a strong idol, that it would emerge victorious from this conflict. In the end, we began to think that we had not baited the soldier enough, that he would forget the dispute, and that we should try to arouse his vanity more thoroughly. From that day we began to live a very peculiar, highly strung, nervous life, such as we had never lived before. For whole days we argued with each other, became more intelligent, all of us, and began to talk better and at greater length. It seemed we were playing some sort of a game with the devil, with Tanya as our big stake. And when we learned from the bread bakers that the soldier had begun "to try and make" our Tanya, we felt elated and so glad to be alive that we failed to notice that our boss, profiting by our excitement, had added an extra five hundred pounds of dough a day for us to knead. Work did not even seem to tire us. Tanya's name was on our tongue all day. And every morning we awaited her arrival with a very particular impatience. Sometimes we imagined her entering—no longer the same Tanya, but somehow a very different person.

However, we never told her of our dispute. We asked no questions, and treated her as before, with every affectionate regard. But a new element alien to our former feelings had already crept into our attitude toward Tanya—and this new element was a keen curiosity, cold and sharp as steel. . . .

"Brothers! Time's running out today!" the baker announced one morning as he began work.

We knew this very well ourselves even without being reminded, but we were now on the alert.

"Look closely at her . . . when she comes in . . . as she will in a moment!" the baker suggested.

Someone exclaimed with regret: "But can you spot anything with your eyes! . . ."

Again a lively, noisy argument broke out between us. This day we would finally learn how pure and unsullied was the vessel into which we had poured our best. For the first time that morning we suddenly felt that we were actually playing for big stakes, that our idol's test of purity might also prove her undoing in our eyes. In all these past days we had heard that the soldier had been pursuing Tanya persistently, closely, and without any letup but, for some reason, none of us had questioned her as to her attitude. And she had continued to call on us punctually every morning for her order of pretzels, and she looked the same as ever.

It was not long before we heard her voice: "Little convicts! Here I am. . . ."

We hastened to let her in, and as she entered we met her—contrary to our custom—in silence. With all our eyes fixed upon her, we were at a loss what to say and what to ask. And we stood facing her, an opaque, silent crowd. She was evidently surprised at this unaccustomed confrontation, and we suddenly saw her turn pale and nervous. Fidgeting on one spot, she asked in a suppressed voice: "What's the matter with you all?"

"And with you?" the baker asked sullenly, without removing his eyes from her.

"What do you mean—I?"

"N-nothing . . ."

"Well, let me have the pretzels quickly. . . ."

She had never been impatient with us before.

"You've time enough!" our baker said, without budging or taking his eyes off her face.

Then, of a sudden, she turned and vanished through the door.

The baker picked up his shovel and, turning his back to us as he faced the oven, exclaimed in a low voice: "It's done! Ah, that soldier! . . . The scoundrel!"

Jostling each other like a flock of sheep, we made for the table, sat down quietly, and set to work without any vim. Very soon someone remarked: "And maybe, still . . ."

"No, now! You can talk!"

We all knew that he was an intelligent man, more intelligent than the rest of us. And we understood his exclamation to mean that he was convinced the soldier had won. . . . We felt dejected and disquieted. . . .

During the midday meal the soldier came in. As always he was clean and dapper, and as always he looked us straight in the eye. We felt awkward returning his gaze.

"Well, honest sirs, would you like me to give you an example of soldierly valor?" he asked with a proud smile. "Then go out into the entrance hall and peep through the cracks. . . . D'you understand?"

We went out and, huddling together, fixed our eyes to the cracks in the wooden wall of the entrance hall giving on the yard. We did not have long to wait. . . . Very soon Tanya, with hurried step and troubled face, walked across the yard, jumping over the puddles of mud and thawing snow. She disappeared behind the door to the ice-cellar. Then the soldier, whistling, followed her there without haste. His hands were thrust deep in his pockets and his mustaches quivered.

It was raining, and we watched the raindrops falling into the puddles and the puddles wrinkling under their impact. It was a damp, gray day— a very dreary day. Snow still lay on the roofs, and dark muddy patches had appeared on the ground. The snow on the roofs was also covered with a dirty brown deposit. The rain fell slowly, making a dismal sound. We felt chilled, and it was unpleasant waiting. . . .

The soldier was the first to emerge from the cellar; he walked slowly the length of the yard, his mustaches quivering, his hands in his pockets. He looked the same as usual.

Then Tanya came out. Her eyes . . . her eyes were shining with joy and happiness and her lips were smiling. And she walked as if in her sleep, with staggering, uncertain steps.

This we could not quietly accept. We, all of us, made a dash for the door, leapt out into the yard and began loudly and savagely to whistle our spite at her.

She gave a start on catching sight of us and then stopped as though rooted in the mud at her feet. We crowded around her and wickedly, without restraint, started to swear at and abuse her with lewd words.

We did so without shouting or haste, for having barred her way and surrounded her we could mock her to our hearts' content. I shall never know why we did not beat her up. She stood in our midst, turning her head here and there, listening to our insults. And with ever increasing violence we pelted her with the mud and venom of our words.

The color had left her face. Her light-blue eyes, shining happily a minute before, were now wide open, her breath came with an effort, and her lips quivered.

And we, who had surrounded her, took our revenge because she had robbed us. She had belonged to us, we had spent our very best on her; and even though our "very best" was no more than a beggar's crumbs, yet there were six and twenty of us and she was all alone, and, for that reason, no

MAXIM GORKY

torture was adequate for her! How we insulted her! She had not uttered a word, staring at us with wild eyes and trembling all over.

We laughed, roared, growled. . . . Other people came running up. . . . One of us snatched at the sleeve of Tanya's blouse. . . .

Suddenly her eyes flashed. Without undue haste she raised her hands to her head and, tidying her hair, addressed us very coolly and distinctly, looking us straight in the face: "Ah, you unhappy convicts!"

And then she walked straight at us, just walked as if we were not standing there at all in front of her, as if we were not barring her way. Thus, none of us did actually bar her way.

Having broken out of the encirclement, she, without turning around, exclaimed in a loud voice tinged with pride and contempt: "Ah, you rabble, you vipers!"

And she went off—upright, beautiful, and proud.

We were left standing in the middle of the yard, in the mud, beneath the rain and the gray sunless sky.

Then we went back in sullen silence to our bricked-in hole. As before, the sun never looked into our windows, and Tanya came visiting no more—never again!

WILLIAM DEAN HOWELLS

(1837–1920) Largely self-taught as a poor boy in Ohio, William Dean Howells became one of the most influential writers in America in his roles as novelist, critic, and editor of *The Atlantic Monthly*. In his many works of fiction, Howells tried to be completely realistic about ordinary people.

EDITHA

The air was thick with the war feeling, like the electricity of a storm which has not yet burst. Editha sat looking out into the hot spring afternoon, with her lips parted, and panting with the intensity of the question whether she could let him go. She had decided that she could not let him stay, when she saw him at the end of the still leafless avenue, making slowly up towards the house, with his head down and his figure relaxed. She ran impatiently out on the veranda, to the edge of the steps, and imperatively demanded greater haste of him with her will before she called aloud to him: "George!"

He had quickened his pace in mystical response to her mystical urgence, before he could have heard her; now he looked up and answered, "Well?"

"Oh, how united we are!" she exulted, and then she swooped down the steps to him. "What is it?" she cried.

"It's war," he said, and he pulled her up to him and kissed her.

She kissed him back intensely, but irrelevantly, as to their passion, and uttered from deep in her throat, "How glorious!"

"It's war," he repeated, without consenting to her sense of it; and she did not know just what to think at first. She never knew what to think of him; that made his mystery, his charm. All through their courtship, which was contemporaneous with the growth of the war feeling, she had been puzzled by his want of seriousness about it. He seemed to despise it even more than he abhorred it. She could have understood his abhorring any sort of bloodshed; that would have been a survival of his old life when he thought he would be a minister, and before he changed and took up the law. But making light of a cause so high and noble seemed to show a want of earnestness at the core of his being. Not but that she felt herself able to cope with a congenital defect of that sort, and make his love for her save him from himself. Now perhaps the miracle was already wrought in him. In the presence of the tremendous fact that he announced, all triviality seemed to have gone out of him; she began to feel that. He sank down on the top step, and wiped his forehead with his handkerchief, while she poured out upon him her question of the origin and authenticity of his news.

All the while, in her duplex emotioning, she was aware that now at the very beginning she must put a guard upon herself against urging him, by any word or act, to take the part that her whole soul willed him to take, for the completion of her ideal of him. He was very nearly perfect as he was, and he must be allowed to perfect himself. But he was peculiar, and he might very well be reasoned out of his peculiarity. Before her reasoning went her emotioning: her nature pulling upon his nature, her womanhood upon his manhood, without her knowing the means she was using to the end she was willing. She had always supposed that the man who won her would have done something to win her; she did not know what, but something. George Gearson had simply asked her for her love, on the way home from a concert, and she gave her love to him, without, as it were, thinking. But now, it flashed upon her, if he could do something worthy to *have* won her—be a hero, *her* hero—it would be even better than if he had done it before asking her; it would be grander. Besides, she had believed in the war from the beginning.

"But don't you see, dearest," she said, "that it wouldn't have come to this if it hadn't been in the order of Providence? And I call any war glorious that is for the liberation of people who have been struggling for years against the cruelest oppression. Don't you think so, too?"

"I suppose so," he returned, languidly. "But war! Is it glorious to break the peace of the world?"

"That ignoble peace! It was no peace at all, with that crime and shame at our very gates." She was conscious of parroting the current phrases of the newspapers, but it was no time to pick and choose her words. She must sacrifice anything to the high ideal she had for him, and after a good deal of rapid argument she ended with the climax: "But now it doesn't matter about the how or why. Since the war has come, all that is gone. There are no two sides any more. There is nothing now but our country."

He sat with his eyes closed and his head leant back against the veranda, and he remarked, with a vague smile, as if musing aloud, "Our country— right or wrong."

"Yes, right or wrong!" she returned, fervidly. "I'll go and get you some lemonade." She rose rustling, and whisked away; when she came back with two tall glasses of clouded liquid on a tray, and the ice clicking in them, he still sat as she had left him, and she said, as if there had been no interruption: "But there is no question of wrong in this case. I call it a sacred war. A war for liberty and humanity, if ever there was one. And I know you will see it just as I do, yet."

He took half the lemonade at a gulp, and he answered as he set the glass down: "I know you always have the highest ideal. When I differ from you I ought to doubt myself."

A generous sob rose in Editha's throat for the humility of a man, so very nearly perfect, who was willing to put himself below her.

Besides, she felt, more subliminally, that he was never so near slipping through her fingers as when he took that meek way.

"You shall not say that! Only, for once I happen to be right." She seized his hand in her two hands, and poured her soul from her eyes into his. "Don't you think so?" she entreated him.

He released his hand and drank the rest of his lemonade, and she added, "Have mine, too," but he shook his head in answering, "I've no business to think so, unless I act so, too."

Her heart stopped a beat before it pulsed on with leaps that she felt in her neck. She had noticed that strange thing in men: they seemed to feel bound to do what they believed, and not think a thing was finished when they said it, as girls did. She knew what was in his mind, but she pretended not, and she said, "Oh, I am not sure," and then faltered.

He went on as if to himself, without apparently heeding her: "There's only one way of proving one's faith in a thing like this."

She could not say that she understood, but she did understand.

He went on again. "If I believed—if I felt as you do about the war—Do you wish me to feel as you do?"

Now she was really not sure; so she said: "George, I don't know what you mean."

He seemed to muse away from her as before. "There is a sort of fascination in it. I suppose that at the bottom of his heart every man would like at times to have his courage tested, to see how he would act."

"How can you talk in that ghastly way?"

"It *is* rather morbid. Still, that's what it comes to, unless you're swept away by ambition or driven by conviction. I haven't the conviction or the ambition, and the other thing is what it comes to with me. I ought to have been a preacher, after all; then I couldn't have asked it of myself as I must, now I'm a lawyer. And you believe it's a holy war, Editha?" he suddenly addressed her. "Oh, I know you do! But you wish me to believe so, too?"

She hardly knew whether he was mocking or not, in the ironical way he always had with her plainer mind. But the only thing was to be out-spoken with him.

WILLIAM DEAN HOWELLS

"George, I wish you to believe whatever you think is true, at any and every cost. If I've tried to talk you into anything, I take it all back."

"Oh, I know that, Editha. I know how sincere you are, and how—I wish I had your undoubting spirit! I'll think it over; I'd like to believe as you do. But I don't, now; I don't, indeed. It isn't this war alone; though this seems peculiarly wanton and needless; but it's every war—so stupid; it makes me sick. Why shouldn't this thing have been settled reasonably?"

"Because," she said, very throatily again, "God meant it to be war."

"You think it was God? Yes, I suppose that is what people will say."

"Do you suppose it would have been war if God hadn't meant it?"

"I don't know. Sometimes it seems as if God had put this world into men's keeping to work it as they pleased."

"Now, George, that is blasphemy."

"Well, I won't blaspheme. I'll try to believe in your pocket Providence," he said, and then he rose to go.

"Why don't you stay to dinner?" Dinner at Balcom's Works was at one o'clock.

"I'll come back to supper, if you'll let me. Perhaps I shall bring you a convert."

"Well, you may come back, on that condition."

"All right. If I don't come, you'll understand."

He went away without kissing her, and she felt it a suspension of their engagement. It all interested her intensely; she was undergoing a tremendous experience, and she was being equal to it. While she stood looking after him, her mother came out through one of the long windows onto the veranda, with a catlike softness and vagueness.

"Why didn't he stay to dinner?"

"Because—because—war has been declared," Editha pronounced, without turning.

Her mother said, "Oh, my!" and then said nothing more until she had sat down in one of the large Shaker chairs and rocked herself for some time. Then she closed whatever tacit passage of thought there had been in her mind with the spoken words: "Well, I hope *he* won't go."

"And *I* hope he *will*," the girl said, and confronted her mother with a stormy exaltation that would have frightened any creature less unimpressionable than a cat.

Her mother rocked herself again for an interval of cogitation. What she arrived at in speech was: "Well, I guess you've done a wicked thing, Editha Balcom."

The girl said, as she passed indoors through the same window her mother had come out by: "I haven't done anything—yet."

In her room, she put together all her letters and gifts from Gearson, down to the withered petals of the first flower he had offered, with that timidity of his veiled in that irony of his. In the heart of the packet she enshrined her engagement ring which she had restored to the pretty box he had brought it her in. Then she sat down, if not calmly yet strongly, and wrote:

"George:—I understood when you left me. But I think we had better emphasize your meaning that if we cannot be one in everything we had better be one in nothing. So I am sending these things for your keeping till you have made up your mind.

"I shall always love you, and therefore I shall never marry anyone else. But the man I marry must love his country first of all, and be able to say to me,

> " 'I could not love thee, dear, so much,
> Loved I not honor more.'

"There is no honor above America with me. In this great hour there is no other honor.

"Your heart will make my words clear to you. I had never expected to say so much, but it has come upon me that I must say the utmost.

Editha"

She thought she had worded her letter well, worded it in a way that could not be bettered; all had been implied and nothing expressed.

She had it ready to send with the packet she had tied with red, white, and blue ribbon, when it occurred to her that she was not just to him, that she was not giving him a fair chance. He said he would go and think it over, and she was not waiting. She was pushing, threatening, compelling. That was not a woman's part. She must leave him free, free, free. She could not accept for her country or herself a forced sacrifice.

In writing her letter she had satisfied the impulse from which it sprang; she could well afford to wait till he had thought it over. She put the packet and the letter by, and rested serene in the consciousness of having done what was laid upon her by her love itself to do, and yet used patience, mercy, justice.

She had her reward. Gearson did not come to tea, but she had given him till morning, when, late at night there came up from the village the sound of a fife and drum, with a tumult of voices, in shouting, singing, and laughing. The noise drew nearer and nearer; it reached the street end of the avenue; there it silenced itself, and one voice, the voice she knew best, rose over the silence. It fell; the air was filled with cheers; the fife and drum struck up, with the shouting, singing, and laughing again, but now retreating; and a single figure came hurrying up the avenue.

She ran down to meet her lover and clung to him. He was very gay, and he put his arms round her with a boisterous laugh. "Well, you must call me Captain now; or Cap, if you prefer; that's what the boys call me. Yes, we've had a meeting at the town hall, and everybody has volunteered; and they selected me for captain, and I'm going to the war, the big war, the glorious war, the holy war ordained by the pocket Providence that blesses butchery. Come along: let's tell the whole family about it. Call them from their downy beds, father, mother, Aunt Hitty, and all the folks!"

But when they mounted the veranda steps he did not wait for a larger audience; he poured the story out upon Editha alone.

"There was a lot of speaking, and then some of the fools set up a shout for me. It was all going one way, and I thought it would be a good joke to sprinkle a little cold water on them. But you can't do that with a crowd that adores you. The first thing I knew I was sprinkling hell-fire on them. 'Cry havoc, and let slip the dogs of war.' That was the style. Now that it had come to the fight, there were no two parties; there was one country, and the thing was to fight to a finish as quick as possible. I suggested volunteering then and there, and I wrote my name first of all on the roster. Then they elected me—that's all. I wish I had some ice-water."

She left him walking up and down the veranda, while she ran for the ice-pitcher and a goblet, and when she came back he was still walking up and down, shouting the story he had told her to her father and mother, who had come out more sketchily dressed than they commonly were by day. He drank goblet after goblet of the ice-water without noticing who was giving it, and kept on talking, and laughing through his talk wildly. "It's astonishing," he said, "how well the worse reason looks when you try to make it appear the better. Why, I believe I was the first convert to the war in that crowd tonight! I never thought I should like to kill a man; but now I shouldn't care; and the smokeless powder lets you see the man drop that you kill. It's all for the country! What a thing it is to have a country that *can't* be wrong, but if it is, is right, anyway."

Editha had a great, vital thought, an inspiration. She set down the ice-pitcher on the veranda floor, and ran upstairs and got the letter she had written him. When at last he noisily bade her father and mother, "Well, good-night. I forgot I woke you up: I shan't want any sleep myself," she followed him down the avenue to the gate. There, after the whirling words that seemed to fly away from her thoughts and refuse to serve them, she made a last effort to solemnize the moment that seemed so crazy, and pressed the letter she had written upon him.

"What's this?" he said. "Want me to mail it?"

"No, no. It's for you. I wrote it after you went this morning. Keep it—keep it—and read it sometime—" She thought, and then her inspiration came: "Read it if ever you doubt what you've done, or fear that I regret your having done it. Read it after you've started."

They strained each other in embraces that seemed as ineffective as their words, and he kissed her face with quick, hot breaths that were so unlike him, that made her feel as if she had lost her old lover and found a stranger in his place. The stranger said: "What a gorgeous flower you are, with your red hair, and your blue eyes that look black now, and your face with the color painted out by the white moonshine! Let me hold you under the chin, to see whether I love blood, you tiger-lily!" Then he laughed Gearson's laugh, and released her, scared and giddy. Within her wilfulness she had been frightened by a sense of subtler force in him, and mystically mastered as she had never been before.

She ran all the way back to the house, and mounted the steps panting. Her mother and father were talking of the great affair. Her mother said: "Wa'n't Mr. Gearson in rather of an excited state of mind? Didn't you think he acted curious?"

"Well, not for a man who'd just been elected captain and had set 'em up for the whole of Company A," her father chuckled back.

"What in the world do you mean, Mr. Balcom? Oh! There's Editha!" She offered to follow the girl indoors.

"Don't come, mother!" Editha called, vanishing.

Mrs. Balcom remained to reproach her husband. "I don't see much of anything to laugh at."

"Well, it's catching. Caught it from Gearson. I guess it won't be much of a war, and I guess Gearson don't think so, either. The other fellows will back down as soon as they see we mean it. I wouldn't lose any sleep over it. I'm going back to bed, myself."

Gearson came again next afternoon, looking pale and rather sick, but quite himself, even to his languid irony. "I guess I'd better tell you, Editha, that I consecrated myself to your god of battles last night by pouring too many libations to him down my own throat. But I'm all right now. One has to carry off the excitement, somehow."

"Promise me," she commanded, "that you'll never touch it again!"

"What! Not let the cannikin clink? Not let the soldier drink? Well, I promise."

"You don't belong to yourself now; you don't even belong to *me*. You belong to your country, and you have a sacred charge to keep yourself strong and well for your country's sake. I have been thinking, thinking all night and all day long."

"You look as if you had been crying a little, too," he said, with his queer smile.

"That's all past. I've been thinking, and worshipping *you*. Don't you suppose I know all that you've been through, to come to this? I've followed you every step from your old theories and opinions."

"Well, you've had a long row to hoe."

"And I know you've done this from the highest motives—"

"Oh, there won't be much pettifogging to do till this cruel war is—"

"And you haven't simply done it for my sake. I couldn't respect you if you had."

WILLIAM DEAN HOWELLS

235

"Well, then we'll say I haven't. A man that hasn't got his own respect intact wants the respect of all the other people he can corner. But we won't go into that. I'm in for the thing now, and we've got to face our future. My idea is that this isn't going to be a very protracted struggle; we shall just scare the enemy to death before it comes to a fight at all. But we must provide for contingencies, Editha. If anything happens to me—"

"Oh, George!" She clung to him, sobbing.

"I don't want you to feel foolishly bound to my memory. I should hate that, wherever I happened to be."

"I am yours, for time and eternity—time and eternity." She liked the words; they satisfied her famine for phrases.

"Well, say eternity; that's all right; but time's another thing; and I'm talking about time. But there is something! My mother! If anything happens—"

She winced, and he laughed. "You're not the bold soldier-girl of yesterday!" Then he sobered. "If anything happens, I want you to help my mother out. She won't like my doing this thing. She brought me up to think war a fool thing as well as a bad thing. My father was in the Civil War; all through it; lost his arm in it." She thrilled with the sense of the arm round her; what if that should be lost? He laughed as if divining her: "Oh, it doesn't run in the family, as far as I know!" Then he added, gravely: "He came home with misgivings about war, and they grew on him. I guess he and mother agreed between them that I was to be brought up in his final mind about it; but that was before my time. I only know him from my mother's report of him and his opinions; I don't know whether they were hers first; but they were hers last. This will be a blow to her. I shall have to write and tell her—"

He stopped, and she asked: "Would you like me to write, too, George?"

"I don't believe that would do. No, I'll do the writing. She'll understand a little if I say that I thought the way to minimize it was to make war on the largest possible scale at once—that I felt I must have been helping on the war somehow if I hadn't helped keep it from coming, and I knew I hadn't; when it came, I had no right to stay out of it."

Whether his sophistries satisfied him or not, they satisfied her. She clung to his breast, and whispered, with closed eyes and quivering lips: "Yes, yes, yes!"

"But if anything should happen, you might go to her and see what you could do for her. You know? It's rather far off; she can't leave her chair—"

"Oh, I'll go, if it's the ends of the earth! But nothing will happen! Nothing can! I—"

She felt herself lifted with his rising, and Gearson was saying, with his arm still round her, to her father: "Well, we're off at once, Mr. Balcom. We're to be formally accepted at the capital, and then bunched up with the rest somehow, and sent into camp somewhere, and go to the front as soon as possible. We all want to be in the van, of course; we're the first company to report to the Governor. I came to tell Editha, but I hadn't got round to it."

She saw him again for a moment at the capital, in the station, just before the train started southward with his regiment. He looked well, in his uniform, and very soldierly, but somehow girlish, too, with his clean-shaven face and slim figure. The manly eyes and the strong voice satisfied her, and his preoccupation with some unexpected details of duty flattered her. Other girls were weeping and bemoaning themselves, but she felt a sort of noble distinction in the abstraction, the almost unconsciousness, with which they parted. Only at the last moment he said: "Don't forget my mother. It mayn't be such a walk-over as I supposed," and he laughed at the notion.

He waved his hand to her as the train moved off—she knew it among a score of hands that were waved to other girls from the platform of the car, for it held a letter which she knew was hers. Then he went inside the car to read it, doubtless, and she did not see him again. But she felt safe for him through the strength of what she called her love. What she called her God, always speaking the name in a deep voice and with the implication of a mutual understanding, would watch over him and keep him and bring him back to her. If with an empty sleeve, then he should have three arms instead of two, for both of hers should be his for life. She did not see, though, why she should always be thinking of the arm his father had lost.

There were not many letters from him, but they were such as she could have wished, and she put her whole strength into making hers such as she imagined he could have wished, glorifying and supporting him. She wrote to his mother glorifying him as their hero, but the brief answer she got was merely to the effect that Mrs. Gearson was not well enough to write herself, and thanking her for her letter by the hand of someone who called herself "Yrs truly, Mrs. W. J. Andrews."

Editha determined not to be hurt, but to write again quite as if the answer had been all she expected. Before it seemed as if she could have written, there came news of the first skirmish, and in the list of the killed, which was telegraphed as a trifling loss on our side, was Gearson's name. There was a frantic time of trying to make out that it might be, must be, some other Gearson; but the name and the company and the regiment and the State were too definitely given.

Then there was a lapse into depths out of which it seemed as if she never could rise again; then a lift into clouds far above all grief, black clouds, that blotted out the sun, but where she soared with him, with George—George! She had the fever that she expected of herself, but she did not die in it; she was not even delirious, and it did not last long. When she was well enough to leave her bed, her one thought was of George's mother, of his strangely worded wish that she should go to her and see what she could do for her. In the exaltation of the duty laid upon her—it buoyed her up instead of burdening her—she rapidly recovered.

Her father went with her on the long railroad journey from Northern New York to Western Iowa; he had business out at Davenport, and he said he could just as well go then as any other time; and he went with her to the little country town where George's mother lived in a little house on the edge of the illimitable cornfields, under trees pushed to a top of the rolling prairie. George's father had settled there after the Civil War, as so many other old soldiers had done; but they were Eastern people, and Editha fancied touches of the East in the June rose overhanging the front door, and the garden with early summer flowers stretching from the gate of the paling fence.

It was very low inside the house, and so dim, with the closed blinds, that they could scarcely see one another: Editha tall and black in her crapes which filled the air with the smell of their dyes; her father standing decorously apart with his hat on his forearm, as at funerals; a woman rested in a deep armchair, and the woman who had let the strangers in stood behind the chair.

The seated woman turned her head round and up, and asked the woman behind the chair: "*Who* did you say?"

Editha, if she had done what she expected of herself, would have gone down on her knees at the feet of the seated figure and said, "I am George's Editha," for answer.

But instead of her own voice she heard that other woman's voice, saying: "Well, I don't know as I *did* get the name just right. I guess I'll have to make a little more light in here," and she went and pushed two of the shutters ajar.

Then Editha's father said, in his public will-now-address-a-few-remarks tone: "My name is Balcom, ma'am—Junius H. Balcom, of Balcom's Works, New York; my daughter—"

"Oh!" the seated woman broke in, with a powerful voice, the voice that always surprised Editha from Gearson's slender frame. "Let me see you. Stand round where the light can strike on your face," and Editha dumbly obeyed. "So, you're Editha Balcom," she sighed.

"Yes," Editha said, more like a culprit than a comforter.

"What did you come for?" Mrs. Gearson asked.

Editha's face quivered and her knees shook. "I came—because—because George—" She could go no further.

"Yes," the mother said, "he told me he had asked you to come if he got killed. You didn't expect that, I suppose, when you sent him."

"I would rather have died myself than done it!" Editha said, with more truth in her deep voice than she ordinarily found in it. "I tried to leave him free—"

"Yes, that letter of yours, that came back with his other things, left him free."

Editha saw now where George's irony came from.

"It was not to be read before—unless—until—I told him so," she faltered.

"Of course, he wouldn't read a letter of yours, under the circumstances, till he thought you wanted him to. Been sick?" the woman abruptly demanded.

"Very sick," Editha said, with self-pity.

"Daughter's life," her father interposed, "was almost despaired of, at one time."

Mrs. Gearson gave him no heed. "I suppose you would have been glad to die, such a brave person as you! I don't believe *he* was glad to die. He was always a timid boy, that way; he was afraid of a good many things; but if he was afraid he did what he made up his mind to. I suppose he made up his mind to go; but I knew what it cost him by what it cost me when I heard of it. I had been through *one* war before. When you sent him you didn't expect he would get killed."

The voice seemed to compassionate Editha, and it was time. "No," she huskily murmured.

"No, girls don't; women don't, when they give their men up to their country. They think they'll come marching back, somehow, just as gay as they went, or if it's an empty sleeve, or even an empty pantaloon, it's all the more glory, and they're so much the prouder of them, poor things!"

The tears began to run down Editha's face; she had not wept till then; but it was now such a relief to be understood that the tears came.

"No, you didn't expect him to get killed," Mrs. Gearson repeated, in a voice which was startlingly like George's again. "You just expected him to kill someone else, some of those foreigners, that weren't there because they had any say about it, but because they had to be there, poor wretches— conscripts, or whatever they call 'em. You thought it would be all right for my George, *your* George, to kill the sons of those miserable mothers and the husbands of those girls that you would never see the faces of." The woman lifted her powerful voice in a psalmlike note. "I thank my God he didn't live to do it! I thank my God they killed him first, and that he ain't livin' with their blood on his hands!" She dropped her eyes, which she had raised with her voice, and glared at Editha. "What you got that black on for?" She lifted herself by her powerful arms so high that her helpless body seemed to hang limp its full length. "Take it off, take it off, before I tear it from your back!"

The lady who was passing the summer near Balcom's Works was sketching Editha's beauty, which lent itself wonderfully to the effects of a colorist. It had come to that confidence which is rather apt to grow between artist and sitter, and Editha had told her everything.

"To think of your having such a tragedy in your life!" the lady said. She added: "I suppose there are people who feel that way about war. But when you consider the good this war has done—how much it has done

WILLIAM DEAN HOWELLS

239

for the country! I can't understand such people, for my part. And when you had come all the way out there to console her—got up out of a sickbed! Well!"

"I think," Editha said, magnanimously, "she wasn't quite in her right mind; and so did papa."

"Yes," the lady said, looking at Editha's lips in nature and then at her lips in art, and giving an empirical touch to them in the picture. "But how dreadful of her! How perfectly—excuse me—how *vulgar!*"

A light broke upon Editha in the darkness which she felt had been without a gleam of brightness for weeks and months. The mystery that had bewildered her was solved by the word; and from that moment she rose from groveling in shame and self-pity, and began to live again in the ideal.

KATE WILHELM

(b. 1928) Born in Ohio, Kate Wilhelm now
lives in Florida. She has published many
novels and two volumes of short stories,
mainly science fiction. In 1968 she won the
Nebula Award of Science Fiction Writers of
America for one of her short stories. Her
most recent volumes include *City of Cain*
(1978), *Fault Lines* (1978), and *Somerset
Dreams and Other Fictions* (1978).

BABY, YOU WERE GREAT!

John Lewisohn thought that if one more door slammed, or one more bell
rang, or one more voice asked if he was all right, his head would explode.
Leaving his laboratories, he walked through the carpeted hall to the
elevator that slid wide to admit him noiselessly, was lowered, gently, two
floors, where there were more carpeted halls. The door he shoved open
bore a neat sign, AUDITIONING STUDIO. Inside, he was waved on through the
reception room by three girls who knew better than to speak to him unless
he spoke first. They were surprised to see him; it was his first visit there
in seven or eight months. The inner room where he stopped was darkened,
at first glance appearing empty, revealing another occupant only after
his eyes had time to adjust to the dim lighting.

John sat in the chair next to Herb Javits, still without speaking. Herb
was wearing the helmet and gazing at a wide screen that was actually
a one-way glass panel permitting him to view the audition going on in the
next room. John lowered a second helmet to his head. It fit snugly and
immediately made contact with the eight prepared spots on his skull.
As soon as he turned it on, the helmet itself was forgotten.

A girl had entered the other room. She was breathtakingly lovely, a
long-legged honey blonde with slanting green eyes and apricot skin. The
room was furnished as a sitting room with two couches, some chairs, end
tables and a coffee table, all tasteful and lifeless, like an ad in a furniture
trade publication. The girl stopped at the doorway and John felt her

indecision, heavily tempered with nervousness and fear. Outwardly she appeared poised and expectant, her smooth face betraying none of her emotions. She took a hesitant step toward the couch, and a wire showed trailing behind her. It was attached to her head. At the same time a second door opened. A young man ran inside, slamming the door behind him; he looked wild and frantic. The girl registered surprise, mounting nervousness; she felt behind her for the door handle, found it and tried to open the door again. It was locked. John could hear nothing that was being said in the room; he only felt the girl's reaction to the unexpected interruption. The wild-eyed man was approaching her, his hands slashing through the air, his eyes darting glances all about them constantly. Suddenly he pounced on her and pulled her to him, kissing her face and neck roughly. She seemed paralyzed with fear for several seconds, then there was something else, a bland nothing kind of feeling that accompanied boredom sometimes, or too-complete self-assurance. As the man's hands fastened on her blouse in the back and ripped it, she threw her arms about him, her face showing passion that was not felt anywhere in her mind or in her blood.

"Cut!" Herb Javits said quietly.

The man stepped back from the girl and left her without a word. She looked about blankly, her torn blouse hanging about her hips, one shoulder strap gone. She was very beautiful. The audition manager entered, followed by a dresser with a gown that he threw about her shoulders. She looked startled; waves of anger mounted to fury as she was drawn from the room, leaving it empty. The two watching men removed their helmets.

"Fourth one so far," Herb grunted. "Sixteen yesterday; twenty the day before . . . All nothing." He gave John a curious look. "What's got you stirred out of your lab?"

"Anne's had it this time," John said. "She's been on the phone all night and all morning."

"What now?"

"Those damn sharks! I told you that was too much on top of the airplane crash last week. She can't take much more of it."

"Hold it a minute, Johnny," Herb said. "Let's finish off the next three girls and then talk." He pressed a button on the arm of his chair and the room beyond the screen took their attention again.

This time the girl was slightly less beautiful, shorter, a dimply sort of brunette with laughing blue eyes and upturned nose. John liked her. He adjusted his helmet and felt with her.

She was excited; the audition always excited them. There was some fear and nervousness, not too much. Curious about how the audition would go, probably. The wild young man ran into the room, and her face paled. Nothing else changed. Her nervousness increased, not uncomfortably. When he grabbed her, the only emotion she registered was the nervousness.

"Cut," Herb said.

The next girl was also brunette, with gorgeously elongated legs. She was very cool, a real professional. Her mobile face reflected the range of emotions to be expected as the scene played through again, but nothing inside her was touched. She was a million miles away from it all.

The next one caught John with a slam. She entered the room slowly, looking about with curiosity, nervous, as they all were. She was younger than the other girls, less poised. She had pale gold hair piled in an elaborate mound of waves on top of her head. Her eyes were brown, her skin nicely tanned. When the man entered, her emotions changed quickly to fear, then to terror. John didn't know when he closed his eyes. He was the girl, filled with unspeakable terror; his heart pounded, adrenalin pumped into his system; he wanted to scream but could not. From the dim unreachable depths of his psyche there came something else, in waves, so mixed with terror that the two merged and became one emotion that pulsed and throbbed and demanded. With a jerk he opened his eyes and stared at the window. The girl had been thrown down to one of the couches, and the man was kneeling on the floor beside her, his hands playing over her bare body, his face pressed against her skin.

"Cut!" Herb said. His voice was shaken. "Hire her," he said. The man rose, glanced at the girl, sobbing now, and then quickly bent over and kissed her cheek. Her sobs increased. Her golden hair was down, framing her face; she looked like a child. John tore off the helmet. He was perspiring.

Herb got up, turned on the lights in the room, and the window blanked out, blending with the wall. He didn't look at John. When he wiped his face, his hand was shaking. He rammed it in his pocket.

"When did you start auditions like that?" John asked, after a few moments of silence.

"Couple of months ago. I told you about it. Hell, we had to, Johnny. That's the six hundred nineteenth girl we've tried out! Six hundred nineteen! All phonies but one! Dead from the neck up. Do you have any idea how long it was taking us to find that out! Hours for each one. Now it's a matter of minutes."

John Lewisohn sighed. He knew. He had suggested it, actually, when he had said, "Find a basic anxiety for the test." He hadn't wanted to know what Herb had come up with.

He said, "Okay, but she's only a kid. What about her parents, legal rights, all that?"

"We'll fix it. Don't worry. What about Anne?"

"She's called me five times since yesterday. The sharks were too much. She wants to see us, both of us, this afternoon."

"You're kidding! I can't leave here now!"

"Nope. Kidding I'm not. She says no plug-up if we don't show. She'll take pills and sleep until we get there."

"Good Lord! She wouldn't dare!"

"I've booked seats. We take off at twelve-thirty-five." They stared at one another silently for another moment, when Herb shrugged. He was a short man, not heavy but solid. John was over six feet, muscular, with a temper that he knew he had to control. Others suspected that when he did let it go, there would be bodies lying around afterward, but he controlled it.

Once it had been a physical act, an effort of body and will to master that temper; now it was done so automatically that he couldn't recall occasions when it even threatened to flare anymore.

"Look, Johnny, when we see Anne, let me handle it. Right? I'll make it short."

"What are you going to do?"

"Give her an earful. If she's going to start pulling temperament on me, I'll slap her down so hard she'll bounce a week." He grinned. "She's had it all her way up to now. She knew there wasn't a replacement if she got bitchy. Let her try it now. Just let her try." Herb was pacing back and forth with quick, jerky steps.

John realized with a shock that he hated the stocky, red-faced man. The feeling was new; it was almost as if he could taste the hatred he felt, and the taste was unfamiliar and pleasant.

Herb stopped pacing and stared at him for a moment. "Why'd she call you? Why does she want you down, too? She knows you're not mixed up with this end of it."

"She knows I'm a full partner, anyway," John said.

"Yeah, but that's not it." Herb's face twisted in a grin. "She thinks you're still hot for her, doesn't she? She knows you tumbled once, in the beginning, when you were working on her, getting the gimmick working right." The grin reflected no humor then. "Is she right, Johnny, baby? Is that it?"

"We made a deal," John said. "You run your end, I run mine. She wants me along because she doesn't trust you, or believe anything you tell her anymore. She wants a witness."

"Yeah, Johnny. But you be sure you remember our agreement." Suddenly Herb laughed. "You know what it was like, Johnny, seeing you and her? Like a flame trying to snuggle up to an icicle."

At three-thirty they were in Anne's suite in the Skyline Hotel in Grand Bahama. Herb had a reservation to fly back to New York on the 6 P.M. flight. Anne would not be off until four, so they made themselves comfortable in her rooms and waited. Herb turned her screen on, offered a helmet to John, who shook his head, and they both seated themselves. John watched the screen for several minutes; then he, too, put on a helmet.

Anne was looking at the waves far out at sea where they were long, green, undulating; then she brought her gaze in closer, to the blue-green and quick seas, and finally in to where they stumbled on the sandbars, breaking into foam that looked solid enough to walk on. She was peaceful, swaying with the motion of the boat, the sun hot on her back, the fishing rod heavy in her hands. It was like being an indolent animal at peace with its world, at home in the world, being one with it. After a few seconds she put down the rod and turned, looking at a tall smiling man in swimming trunks. He held out his hand and she took it. They entered the cabin of the boat where drinks were waiting. Her mood of serenity and happiness ended abruptly, to be replaced by shocked disbelief, and a start of fear.

"What the hell . . .?" John muttered, adjusting the audio. You seldom needed audio when Anne was on.

". . . Captain Brothers had to let them go. After all, they've done nothing yet—" the man was saying soberly.

"But why do you think they'll try to rob me?"

"Who else is here with a million dollars' worth of jewels?"

John turned it off and said, "You're a fool! You can't get away with something like that!"

Herb stood up and crossed to the window wall that was open to the stretch of glistening blue ocean beyond the brilliant white beaches. "You know what every woman wants? To own something worth stealing." He chuckled, a sound without mirth. "Among other things, that is. They want to be roughed up once or twice, and forced to kneel. . . . Our new psychologist is pretty good, you know? Hasn't steered us wrong yet. Anne might kick some, but it'll go over great."

"She won't stand for an actual robbery." Louder, emphatically, he added, "I won't stand for that."

"We can dub it," Herb said. "That's all we need, Johnny, plant the idea, and then dub the rest."

John stared at his back. He wanted to believe that. He needed to believe it. His voice was calm when he said, "It didn't start like this, Herb. What happened?"

Herb turned then. His face was dark against the glare of light behind him. "Okay, Johnny, it didn't start like this. Things accelerate, that's all. You thought of a gimmick, and the way we planned it, it sounded great, but it didn't last. We gave them the feeling of gambling, or learning to ski, of automobile racing, everything we could dream up, and it wasn't enough. How many times can you take the first ski jump of your life? After a while you want new thrills, you know? For you it's been great, hasn't it? You bought yourself a shiny new lab and closed the door. You bought yourself time and equipment and when things didn't go right, you could toss it out and start over, and nobody gave a damn. Think of what it's been like for me, kid! I gotta keep coming up with something new, something that'll give Anne a jolt and through her all those nice little people who aren't even alive unless they're plugged in. You think it's been easy? Anne was a green kid. For her everything was new and exciting, but it isn't like that now, boy. You better believe it is *not* like that now. You know what she told me last month? She's sick and tired of men. Our little hot-box Annie! Tired of men!"

John crossed to him and pulled him around toward the light. "Why didn't you tell me?"

"Why, Johnny? What would you have done that I didn't do? I looked harder for the right guy. What would you do for a new thrill for her? I worked for them, kid. Right from the start you said for me to leave you alone. Okay. I left you alone. You ever read any of the memos I sent? You initialed them, kiddo. Everything that's been done, we both signed. Don't give me any of that why didn't I tell you stuff. It won't work!" His face was ugly red and a vein bulged in his neck. John wondered if he had high blood pressure, if he would die of a stroke during one of his flash rages.

John left him at the window. He had read the memos. Herb was right; all he had wanted was to be left alone. It had been his idea; after twelve years of work in a laboratory on prototypes he had shown his—gimmick— to Herb Javits. Herb had been one of the biggest producers on television then; now he was the biggest producer in the world.

The gimmick was simple enough. A person fitted with electrodes in his brain could transmit his emotions, which in turn could be broadcast and picked up by the helmets to be felt by the audience. No words or thoughts went out, only basic emotions—fear, love, anger, hatred . . . That, tied in with a camera showing what the person saw, with a voice dubbed in, and you were the person having the experience, with one important difference—you could turn it off if it got to be too much. The "actor" couldn't. A simple gimmick. You didn't really need the camera and the sound track; many users never turned them on at all, but let their own imaginations fill in the emotional broadcast.

The helmets were not sold, only leased or rented after a short, easy fitting session. A year's lease cost fifty dollars, and there were over thirty-seven million subscribers. Herb had created his own network when the demand for more hours squeezed him out of regular television. From a one-hour weekly show, it had gone to one hour nightly, and now it was on the air eight hours a day live, with another eight hours of taped programming.

What had started out as A DAY IN THE LIFE OF ANNE BEAUMONT was now a life in the life of Anne Beaumont and the audience was insatiable.

Anne came in then, surrounded by the throng of hangers-on that mobbed her daily—hairdressers, masseurs, fitters, script men . . . She looked tired. She waved the crowd out when she saw John and Herb were there. "Hello, John," she said, "Herb."

"Anne, baby, you're looking great!" Herb said. He took her in his arms and kissed her solidly. She stood still, her hands at her sides.

She was tall, very slender, with wheat-colored hair and gray eyes. Her cheekbones were wide and high, her mouth firm and almost too large. Against her deep red-gold suntan her teeth looked whiter than John remembered. Although too firm and strong ever to be thought of as pretty, she was a very beautiful woman. After Herb released her, she turned to John, hesitated only a moment, then extended a slim, sun-browned hand. It was cool and dry in his.

"How have you been, John? It's been a long time."

He was very glad she didn't kiss him, or call him darling. She smiled only slightly and gently removed her hand from his. He moved to the bar as she turned to Herb.

"I'm through, Herb." Her voice was too quiet. She accepted a whiskey sour from John, but kept her gaze on Herb.

"What's the matter, honey? I was just watching you, baby. You were great today, like always. You've still got it, kid. It's coming through like always."

"What about this robbery? You must be out of your mind . . .".

"Yeah, that. Listen, Anne baby, I swear to you I don't know a thing about it. Laughton must have been giving you the straight goods on that. You know we agreed that the rest of this week you just have a good time, remember? That comes over too, baby. When you have a good time and relax, thirty-seven million people are enjoying life and relaxing. That's good. They can't be stimulated all the time. They like the variety." Wordlessly John held out a glass, scotch and water. Herb took it without looking.

Anne was watching him coldly. Suddenly she laughed. It was a cynical, bitter sound. "You're not a damn fool, Herb. Don't try to act like one." She sipped her drink again, staring at him over the rim of the glass. "I'm warning you, if anyone shows up here to rob me, I'm going to treat him like a real burglar. I bought a gun after today's broadcast, and I learned how to shoot when I was ten. I still know how. I'll kill him, Herb, whoever it is."

"Baby," Herb started, but she cut him short.

"And this is my last week. As of Saturday, I'm through."

"You can't do that, Anne," Herb said. John watched him closely, searching for a sign of weakness; he saw nothing. Herb exuded confidence. "Look around, Anne, at this room, your clothes, everything. . . . You are the richest woman in the world, having the time of your life, able to go anywhere, do anything . . ."

"While the whole world watches—"

"So what? It doesn't stop you, does it?" Herb started to pace, his steps jerky and quick. "You knew that when you signed the contract. You're a rare girl, Anne, beautiful, emotional, intelligent. Think of all those women who've got nothing but you. If you quit them, what do they do? Die? They might, you know. For the first time in their lives they're able to feel like they're living. You're giving them what no one ever did before, what was only hinted at in books and films in the old days. Suddenly they know what it feels like to face excitement, to experience love, to feel contented and peaceful. Think of them, Anne, empty, with nothing in their lives but you, what you're able to give them. Thirty-seven million drabs, Anne, who never felt anything but boredom and frustration until you gave them life. What do they have? Work, kids, bills. You've given them the world, baby! Without you they wouldn't even want to live anymore."

She wasn't listening. Almost dreamily she said, "I talked to my lawyers, Herb, and the contract is meaningless. You've already broken it over and over. I agreed to learn a lot of new things. I did. My God! I've climbed mountains, hunted lions, learned to ski and water-ski, but now you want me to die a little bit each week . . . That airplane crash, not bad, just enough to terrify me. Then the sharks. I really do think it was having sharks brought in when I was skiing that did it, Herb. You see, you will kill me. It will happen, and you won't be able to top it, Herb. Not ever."

There was a hard, waiting silence following her words. *No!* John shouted soundlessly. He was looking at Herb. He had stopped pacing when she started to talk. Something flicked across his face—surprise, fear, something not readily identifiable. Then his face went blank and he raised his glass and finished the scotch and water, replacing the glass on the bar. When he turned again, he was smiling with disbelief.

"What's really bugging you, Anne? There have been plants before. You knew about them. Those lions didn't just happen by, you know. And the avalanche needed a nudge from someone. You know that. What else is bugging you?"

"I'm in love, Herb."

Herb waved that aside impatiently. "Have you ever watched your own show, Anne?" She shook her head. "I thought not. So you wouldn't know about the expansion that took place last month, after we planted that new transmitter in your head. Johnny boy's been busy, Anne. You know these scientist-types, never satisfied, always improving, changing. Where's the camera, Anne? Do you ever know where it is anymore? Have you ever seen a camera in the past couple of weeks, or a recorder of any sort? You have not, and you won't again. You're on now, honey." His voice was quite low, amused almost. "In fact the only time you aren't on is when you're sleeping. I know you're in love. I know who he is. I know how he makes you feel. I even know how much money he makes a week. I should know, Anne baby. I pay him." He had come closer to her with each word, finishing with his face only inches from hers. He didn't have a chance to duck the flashing slap that jerked his head around, and before either of them realized it, he had hit her back, knocking her into a chair.

The silence grew, became something ugly and heavy, as if words were being born and dying without utterance because they were too brutal for the human spirit to bear. There was a spot of blood on Herb's mouth where Anne's diamond ring had cut him. He touched it and looked at his finger. "It's all being taped now, honey, even this," he said. He turned his back on her and went to the bar.

There was a large red print on her cheek. Her gray eyes had turned black with rage.

"Honey, relax," Herb said after a moment. "It won't make any difference to you, in what you do, or anything like that. You know we can't use most of the stuff, but it gives the editors a bigger variety to pick from. It was getting to the point where most of the interesting stuff was going on after you were off. Like buying the gun. That's great stuff there, baby. You weren't blanketing a single thing, and it'll all come through like pure gold." He finished mixing his drink, tasted it, and then swallowed half of it. "How many women have to go out and buy a gun to protect themselves? Think of them all, feeling that gun, feeling the things you felt when you picked it up, looked at it . . ."

"How long have you been tuning in all the time?" she asked. John felt a stirring along his spine, a tingle of excitement. He knew what was going out over the miniature transmitter, the rising crests of emotion she was feeling. Only a trace of them showed on her smooth face, but the raging interior torment was being recorded faithfully. Her quiet voice and quiet body were lies; the tapes never lied.

Herb felt it too. He put his glass down and went to her, kneeling by the chair, taking her hand in both of his. "Anne, please, don't be that angry with me. I was desperate for new material. When Johnny got this last wrinkle out, and we knew we could record around the clock, we had to try it, and it wouldn't have been any good if you'd known. That's no way to test anything. You knew we were planting the transmitter . . ."

"How long?"

"Not quite a month."

"And Stuart? He's one of your men? He is transmitting also? You hired him to . . . to make love to me? Is that right?"

Herb nodded. She pulled her hand free and averted her face. He got up then and went to the window. "But what difference does it make?" he shouted. "If I introduced the two of you at a party, you wouldn't think anything of it. What difference if I did it this way? I knew you'd like each other. He's bright, like you, likes the same sort of things you do. Comes from a poor family, like yours . . . Everything said you'd get along."

"Oh, yes," she said almost absently. "We get along." She was feeling in her hair, her fingers searching for the scars.

"It's all healed by now," John said. She looked at him as if she had forgotten he was there.

"I'll find a surgeon," she said, standing up, her fingers white on her glass. "A brain surgeon—"

"It's a new process," John said slowly. "It would be dangerous to go in after them."

KATE WILHELM

She looked at him for a long time. "Dangerous?"

He nodded.

"You could take it back out."

He remembered the beginning, how he had quieted her fear of the electrodes and wires. Her fear was that of a child for the unknown and the unknowable. Time and again he had proved to her that she could trust him, that he wouldn't lie to her. He hadn't lied to her, then. There was the same trust in her eyes, the same unshakable faith. She would believe him. She would accept without question whatever he said. Herb had called him an icicle, but that was wrong. An icicle would have melted in her fires. More like a stalactite, shaped by centuries of civilization, layer by layer he had been formed until he had forgotten how to bend, forgotten how to find release for the stirrings he felt somewhere in the hollow, rigid core of himself. She had tried and, frustrated, she had turned from him, hurt, but unable not to trust one she had loved. Now she waited. He could free her, and lose her again, this time irrevocably. Or he could hold her as long as she lived.

Her lovely gray eyes were shadowed with fear, and the trust that he had given to her. Slowly he shook his head.

"I can't," he said. "No one can."

"I see," she murmured, the black filling her eyes. "I'd die, wouldn't I? Then you'd have a lovely sequence, wouldn't you, Herb?" She swung around, away from John. "You'd have to fake the story line, of course, but you are so good at that. An accident, emergency brain surgery needed, everything I feel going out to the poor little drabs who never will have brain surgery done. It's very good," she said admiringly. Her eyes were black. "In fact, anything I do from now on, you'll use, won't you? If I kill you, that will simply be material for your editors to pick over. Trial, prison, very dramatic . . . On the other hand, if I kill myself . . ."

John felt chilled; a cold, hard weight seemed to be filling him. Herb laughed. "The story line will be something like this," he said. "Anne has fallen in love with a stranger, deeply, sincerely in love with him. Everyone knows how deep that love is, they've all felt it, too, you know. She finds him raping a child, a lovely little girl in her early teens. Stuart tells her they're through. He loves the little nymphet. In a passion she kills herself. You are broadcasting a real storm of passion, right now, aren't you, honey? Never mind, when I run through this scene, I'll find out." She hurled her glass at him, ice cubes and orange slices flying across the room. Herb ducked, grinning.

"That's awfully good, baby. Corny, but after all, they can't get too much corn, can they? They'll love it, after they get over the shock of losing you. And they will get over it, you know. They always do. Wonder if it's true about what happens to someone experiencing a violent death?" Anne's teeth bit down on her lip, and slowly she sat down again, her eyes closed tight. Herb watched her for a moment, then said, even more cheerfully,

"We've got the kid already. If you give them a death, you've got to give them a new life. Finish one with a bang. Start one with a bang. We'll name the kid Cindy, a real Cinderella story after that. They'll love her, too."

Anne opened her eyes, black, dulled now; she was so full of tension that John felt his own muscles contract. He wondered if he would be able to stand the tape she was transmitting. A wave of excitement swept him and he knew he would play it all, feel it all, the incredibly contained rage, fear, the horror of giving a death to them to gloat over, and finally, anguish. He would know it all. Watching Anne, he wished she would break now. She didn't. She stood up stiffly, her back rigid, a muscle hard ridged in her jaw. Her voice was flat when she said, "Stuart is due in half an hour. I have to dress." She left them without looking back.

Herb winked at John and motioned toward the door. "Want to take me to the plane, kid?" In the cab he said, "Stick close to her for a couple of days, Johnny. There might be an even bigger reaction later when she really understands just how hooked she is." He chuckled again. "By God! It's a good thing she trusts you, Johnny boy!"

As they waited in the chrome and marble terminal for the liner to unload its passengers, John said, "Do you think she'll be any good after this?"

"She can't help herself. She's too life-oriented to deliberately choose to die. She's like a jungle inside, raw, wild, untouched by that smooth layer of civilization she shows on the outside. It's a thin layer, kid, real thin. She'll fight to stay alive. She'll become more wary, more alert to danger, more excited and exciting . . . She'll really go to pieces when he touches her tonight. She's primed real good. Might even have to do some editing, tone it down a little." His voice was very happy. "He touches her where she lives, and she reacts. A real wild one. She's one; the new kid's one; Stuart . . . They're few and far between, Johnny. It's up to us to find them. God knows we're going to need all of them we can get." His expression became thoughtful and withdrawn. "You know, that really wasn't such a bad idea of mine about rape and the kid. Who ever dreamed we'd get that kind of reaction from her? With the right sort of buildup . . ." He had to run to catch his plane.

John hurried back to the hotel, to be near Anne if she needed him. But he hoped she would leave him alone. His fingers shook as he turned on his screen; suddenly he had a clear memory of the child who had wept, and he hoped Stuart was on from six until twelve, and he already had missed almost an hour of the show. He adjusted the helmet and sank back into a deep chair. He left the audio off, letting his own words form, letting his own thoughts fill in the spaces.

Anne was leaning toward him, sparkling champagne raised to her lips, her eyes large and soft. She was speaking, talking to him, John, calling him by name. He felt a tingle start somewhere deep inside him, and his glance was lowered to rest on her tanned hand in his, sending electricity through him. Her hand trembled when he ran his fingers up her palm, to her wrist where a blue vein throbbed. The slight throb became a pounding that grew and when he looked into her eyes, they were dark and very deep. They danced and he felt her body against his, yielding, pleading. The room darkened and she was an outline against the window, her gown floating down about her. The darkness grew denser, or he closed his eyes, and this time when her body pressed against his, there was nothing between them, and the pounding was everywhere.

In the deep chair, with the helmet on his head, John's hand clenched, opened, clenched, again and again.

HELENE DAVIS

(b. 1945) Born in Providence, Rhode Island,
Helene Davis studied art at Boston University
and English at the University of Massachusetts, Boston, where she is now a graduate
student. A student of Ruth Whitman at the
poetry workshop of Radcliffe College, she
has published poems in several journals, including the *Southern Poetry Review* and
Ploughshares. Her first collection, *Nightblind,*
appeared in 1976. She teaches poetry in ele-
mentary schools and works as a waitress.

AFFAIR

Together our hands find no indifferent touch.
We are one kind, a dark breed who must love
for sheer breath.

> *In the old story, leaning against the lamplight,*
> *the woman is electric, happy,*
> *never cries.*

You move back into stone eyes. With your darkhaired words
you press illusion in fine volumes,
for keepsakes.

> *The woman owns no name—mistress, mother, kind*
> *friend or lover—a velvet backdrop*
> *in his quiet life.*

Without you my flesh becomes bone dry and breaks
easily, my face invisible as moss
on gravestones.

> *The woman must, like earth, be able to change*
> *size: a spot of dust, a rose half grown, a room*
> *full of music.*

I M A G E F I V E

THE SEX OBJECT

A woman is confused about how to respond to wolf calls and whistles: should she smile and accept them as efforts to humanize existence, or should she haughtily ignore them because they reduce her from person to thing, a sexual object? Often fear rules her response more than reason: behind the most casual approach of a male may lurk every woman's nightmare, the rapist-murderer. Whether preceded by courtship or not, to a woman sexual intercourse is the equivalent of rape if her partner's purpose is to use her for his own pleasure, to reify or make an object of her.

In Irwin Shaw's "The Girls in Their Summer Dresses," Michael's girl-watching seems a very slight offense and his wife's anger seems possessive and out of proportion, until one realizes that he sees her just as he does other pretty girls. To him she is an object, and he admits that probably a more attractive object will replace her. Both Michael and Frances accept his roving eye as part of his nature and the unhappiness it causes as inevitable. Michael could well quote the lines of W. B. Yeats's poem "For Anne Gregory": ". . . only God, my dear, /Could love you for yourself alone." Frances's acceptance of her role after her brief rebellion' makes her not only a sex object but also a submissive wife.

In Rona Jaffe's "Rima, the Bird Girl" Rima Allen is overwhelmingly eager to assume the submissive wife role. As the paramour of a succession of men, Rima changes to fit their images of a desirable mate—or, ironically, the images of their wives—and repeatedly gives herself to men who use her and discard her. As she goes from one liaison to another, it is apparent that the price of giving herself is the loss of that self; she can only play roles. More subtly, Jaffe shows us that the narrator through whom we perceive Rima, an old college friend, has played the same role. Though she "missed zoology and hated typing and filing," the narrator is happy to give up zoology for wifehood: she has cleaned her husband's apartment, "read his magazines, his books, played his records, and waited for him to come home to eat the dinners [she] cooked." These two educated women are eager to be submissive. Sergius O'Shaugnessy, Mailer's persona in "The Time of her Time," expects Denise, a college girl who has had the nerve to argue with him, to be submissive. Her courage in asserting her literary opinion makes him want to use against her "the avenger of . . . [his] crotch, . . . to prong her right then and there." Sergius is trying to find an identity for himself through conquest of any kind—bull fighting, a brawl with a macho street boss, sexual dominance. His determination to bring Denise to orgasm stems not from any desire for pleasure that either of them might experience, but from the necessity to "prove" himself. When Denise has the last word at the end of the story, she reminds the reader of the fate of the macho knife expert for whom one defeat is the end of his reign as champion. In spite of the numbers of women Sergius's "avenger" has conquered, this one defeat symbolizes the loss of his manhood and his failure to find meaning in life. Failure in sexual domination is the sign of the beginning of the end for the aging athlete.

In Joyce Carol Oates's story "The Girl," lack of meaning in a world in which women are sex objects is symbolized by the fact that none of the characters has a name; all are playacting, making life a game totally removed from reality. At the end the girl is not sure whether she has actually been a victim of rape or whether she "really" was playing the victim for the camera. Her uncertainty corresponds to the difficulty many rape victims have in getting people to believe their stories; they are always suspected of having invited the violence they experienced. Ntozake Shange in "With No Immediate Cause" uses repetition and concrete, vivid images to establish the reality of rape and violence toward women. Her poem rules out any illusion of love or even sexual desire as the motivation for rape. The object of violence may be children or old women. Atwood's poem about Circe bitterly shows that the reification of women into the "essentials" of sexuality denies them individuality and humanity. Made of mud by men, a woman lacks any distinction from the natural world. Atwood questions whether either men or women want such a reduction to mere physicality. The enchantress Circe, the "I" of the poem, comments on the relationship between the superhuman woman and the sex object.

Alberto Moravia's "The Chase" treats a woman's physical desire as a symbol of the human need for freedom. Man's jealous possessiveness is symbolized by his role of a hunter who does not need to kill: in refusing to deny his wife her freedom to be wild and self-assertive, the husband denies the validity of the usual male role. He is mature enough to perceive her actions objectively. They are part of her own need, and are not directed at him; he does not perceive her rejection as a denial of his masculinity. His letting her go frees him from rigid role playing.

Doris Lessing's "One Off the Short List" shows a woman who, like the husband in Moravia's story, can be objective about sex. Barbara Coles does not equate sexual surrender with self-surrender; she can even allow her attacker the cheap satisfaction of publicly seeming to be the victor. Like Sergius O'Shaugnessy in Mailer's story, Graham Spence thinks of sex as a battle of wills; he maps his campaign to entrap Barbara Coles as if he were a general planning a campaign. Thinking of him only as a colleague, Barbara does not put up any defenses until it is too late to get out of his trap with dignity. She refuses to cry rape, to be a victim. Rightly perceiving that physical gratification is not his goal, she contemptuously allows him his cheap victory, knowing that in so doing she is denying him his real goal, a feeling of superiority. Lessing's story should not be seen as advocating "when rape is inevitable, relax and enjoy it"; Barbara does not need Graham, either for physical or ego gratification. Rather, the story makes an important point that is often overlooked because the sexual revolution and women's liberation have been chronologically linked: sexuality is only a part of self-definition. The story also validates women's fear that the most civilized exterior may hide a rapist. In a society where male dominance is considered necessary and where violence is condoned on many levels, such fear is self-protective.

IRWIN SHAW

(b. 1913) Born in New York, Irwin Shaw has
lived much of his adult life abroad. He has
written radio and movie scripts as well as
plays, novels, and short stories. His best-
known novel is *The Young Lions* (1948); his
most recent is *The Top of the Hill* (1979).
His latest collection of short stories is *Short
Stories of Five Decades* (1978).

THE GIRLS IN THEIR
SUMMER DRESSES

Fifth Avenue was shining in the sun when they left the Brevoort. The sun
was warm, even though it was February, and everything looked like
Sunday morning—the buses and the well-dressed people walking slowly in
couples and the quiet buildings with the windows closed.

Michael held Frances' arm tightly as they walked toward Washington
Square in the sunlight. They walked lightly, almost smiling, because they
had slept late and had a good breakfast and it was Sunday. Michael
unbuttoned his coat and let it flap around him in the mild wind.

"Look out," Frances said as they crossed Eighth Street. "You'll break
your neck."

Michael laughed and Frances laughed with him.

"She's not so pretty," Frances said. "Anyway, not pretty enough to take a
chance of breaking your neck."

Michael laughed again. "How did you know I was looking at her?"

Frances cocked her head to one side and smiled at her husband under
the brim of her hat. "Mike, darling," she said.

"O.K.," he said. "Excuse me."

Frances patted his arm lightly and pulled him along a little faster
toward Washington Square. "Let's not see anybody all day," she said. "Let's

just hang around with each other. You and me. We're always up to our neck in people, drinking their Scotch or drinking our Scotch; we only see each other in bed. I want to go out with my husband all day long. I want him to talk only to me and listen only to me."

"What's to stop us?" Michael asked.

"The Stevensons. They want us to drop by around one o'clock and they'll drive us into the country."

"The cunning Stevensons," Mike said. "Transparent. They can whistle. They can go driving in the country by themselves."

"Is it a date?"

"It's a date."

Frances leaned over and kissed him on the tip of the ear.

"Darling," Michael said, "this is Fifth Avenue."

"Let me arrange a program," Frances said. "A planned Sunday in New York for a young couple with money to throw away."

"Go easy."

"First let's go to the Metropolitan Museum of Art," Frances suggested, because Michael had said during the week he wanted to go. "I haven't been there in three years and there're at least ten pictures I want to see again. Then we can take the bus down to Radio City and watch them skate. And later we'll go down to Cavanaugh's and get a steak as big as a blacksmith's apron, with a bottle of wine, and after that there's a French picture at the Filmarte that everybody says—say, are you listening to me?"

"Sure," he said. He took his eyes off the hatless girl with the dark hair, cut dancer-style like a helmet, who was walking past him.

"That's the program for the day," Frances said flatly. "Or maybe you'd just rather walk up and down Fifth Avenue."

"No," Michael said. "Not at all."

"You always look at other women," Frances said. "Everywhere. Every damned place we go."

"No, darling," Michael said, "I look at everything. God gave me eyes and I look at women and men and subway excavations and moving pictures and the little flowers of the field. I casually inspect the universe."

"You ought to see the look in your eye," Frances said, "as you casually inspect the universe on Fifth Avenue."

"I'm a happily married man." Michael pressed her elbow tenderly. "Example for the whole twentieth century—Mr. and Mrs. Mike Loomis. Hey, let's have a drink," he said, stopping.

"We just had breakfast."

"Now listen, darling," Mike said, choosing his words with care, "it's a nice day and we both felt good and there's no reason why we have to break it up. Let's have a nice Sunday."

"All right. I don't know why I started this. Let's drop it. Let's have a good time."

They joined hands consciously and walked without talking among the baby carriages and the old Italian men in their Sunday clothes and the young women with Scotties in Washington Square Park.

"At least once a year everyone should go to the Metropolitan Museum of Art," Frances said after a while, her tone a good imitation of the tone she had used at breakfast and at the beginning of their walk. "And it's nice on Sunday. There're a lot of people looking at the pictures and you get the feeling maybe Art isn't on the decline in New York City, after all—"

"I want to tell you something," Michael said very seriously. "I have not touched another woman. Not once. In all the five years."

"All right," Frances said.

"You believe that, don't you?"

"All right."

They walked between the crowded benches, under the scrubby city-park trees.

"I try not to notice it," Frances said, "but I feel rotten inside, in my stomach, when we pass a woman and you look at her and I see that look in your eye and that's the way you looked at me the first time. In Alice Maxwell's house. Standing there in the living room, next to the radio, with a green hat on and all those people."

"I remember the hat," Michael said.

"The same look," Frances said. "And it makes me feel bad. It makes me feel terrible."

"Sh-h-h, please, darling, sh-h-h."

"I think I would like a drink now," Frances said.

They walked over to a bar on Eighth Street, not saying anything. Michael automatically helping her over curbstones and guiding her past automobiles. They sat near a window in the bar and the sun streamed in and there was a small, cheerful fire in the fireplace. A little Japanese waiter came over and put down some pretzels and smiled happily at them.

"What do you order after breakfast?" Michael asked.

"Brandy, I suppose," Frances said.

"Courvoisier," Michael told the waiter. "Two Courvoisiers."

The waiter came with the glasses and they sat drinking the brandy in the sunlight. Michael finished half his and drank a little water.

"I look at women," he said. "Correct. I don't say it's wrong or right. I look at them. If I pass them on the street and I don't look at them, I'm fooling you, I'm fooling myself."

"You look at them as though you want them," Frances said, playing with her brandy glass. "Every one of them."

"In a way," Michael said, speaking softly and not to his wife, "in a way that's true. I don't do anything about it, but it's true."

"I know it. That's why I feel bad."

"Another brandy," Michael called. "Waiter, two more brandies."

He sighed and closed his eyes and rubbed them gently with his fingertips.

"I love the way women look. One of the things I like best about New York is the battalions of women. When I first came to New York from Ohio that was the first thing I noticed, the million wonderful women, all over the city. I walked around with my heart in my throat."

"A kid," Frances said. "That's a kid's feeling."

"Guess again," Michael said. "Guess again. I'm older now. I'm a man getting near middle age, putting on a little fat and I still love to walk along Fifth Avenue at three o'clock on the east side of the street between Fiftieth and Fifty-seventh Streets. They're all out then, shopping, in their furs and their crazy hats, everything all concentrated from all over the world into seven blocks—the best furs, the best clothes, the handsomest women, out to spend money and feeling good about it."

The Japanese waiter put the two drinks down, smiling with great happiness.

"Everything is all right?" he asked.

"Everything is wonderful," Michael said.

"If it's just a couple of fur coats," Frances said, "and forty-five-dollar hats—"

"It's not the fur coats. Or the hats. That's just the scenery for that particular kind of woman. Understand," he said, "you don't have to listen to this."

"I want to listen."

"I like the girls in the offices. Neat, with their eyeglasses, smart, chipper, knowing what everything is about. I like the girls on Forty-fourth Street at lunchtime, the actresses, all dressed up on nothing a week. I like the salesgirls in the stores, paying attention to you first because you're a man, leaving lady customers waiting. I got all this stuff accumulated in me because I've been thinking about it for ten years and now you've asked for it and here it is."

"Go ahead," Frances said.

"When I think of New York City, I think of all the girls on parade in the city. I don't know whether it's something special with me or whether every man in the city walks around with the same feeling inside him, but I feel as though I'm at a picnic in this city. I like to sit near the women in the theatres, the famous beauties who've taken six hours to get ready and look it. And the young girls at the football games, with the red cheeks, and when the warm weather comes, the girls in their summer dresses." He finished his drink. "That's the story."

Frances finished her drink and swallowed two or three times extra. "You say you love me?"

"I love you."

"I'm pretty, too," Frances said. "As pretty as any of them."

"You're beautiful," Michael said.

"I'm good for you," Frances said, pleading. "I've made a good wife, a good housekeeper, a good friend. I'd do any damn thing for you."

"I know," Michael said. He put his hand out and grasped hers.

"You'd like to be free to—" Frances said.

"Sh-h-h."

"Tell the truth." She took her hand away from under his.

Michael flicked the edge of his glass with his finger. "O.K.," he said gently. "Sometimes I feel I would like to be free."

"Well," Frances said, "any time you say."

"Don't be foolish." Michael swung his chair around to her side of the table and patted her thigh.

She began to cry silently into her handkerchief, bent over just enough so that nobody else in the bar would notice. "Someday," she said, crying, "you're going to make a move."

Michael didn't say anything. He sat watching the bartender slowly peel a lemon.

"Aren't you?" Frances asked harshly. "Come on, tell me. Talk. Aren't you?"

"Maybe," Michael said. He moved his chair back again. "How the hell do I know?"

"You know," Frances persisted. "Don't you know?"

"Yes," Michael said after a while, "I know."

Frances stopped crying then. Two or three snuffles into the handkerchief and she put it away and her face didn't tell anything to anybody. "At least do me one favor," she said.

"Sure."

"Stop talking about how pretty this woman is or that one. Nice eyes, nice breasts, a pretty figure, good voice." She mimicked his voice. "Keep it to yourself. I'm not interested."

Michael waved to the waiter. "I'll keep it to myself," he said.

Frances flicked the corners of her eyes. "Another brandy," she told the waiter.

"Two," Michael said.

"Yes, Ma'am, yes sir," said the waiter, backing away.

Frances regarded Michael coolly across the table. "Do you want me to call the Stevensons?" she asked. "It'll be nice in the country."

"Sure," Michael said. "Call them."

She got up from the table and walked across the room toward the telephone. Michael watched her walk, thinking what a pretty girl, what nice legs.

RONA JAFFE

(b. 1932) A graduate of Radcliffe College, Rona Jaffe has written often about the life of career girls in New York City. Her frankness about women as sex objects in *The Best of Everything* (1958) made her a forerunner of the "second wave" of women's liberation. Recent works are *The Other Woman* (1972), *Family Secrets* (1975), *The Last Chance* (1976), and *Class Reunion* (1979).

RIMA THE BIRD GIRL

I don't remember the day we first met, but my first memory of her is of a wraithlike dark-haired girl sitting in the corner of the living room of our dormitory at college, reciting poetry—no, almost shouting it—she and a friend in unison. And it seemed to me then as if poetry should always be shouted in this inspired, almost orgiastic, way, for it was really music. "O love is the crooked thing,/-There is nobody wise enough/To find out all that is in it, . . ./Ah, penny, brown penny, brown penny,/-One cannot begin it too soon."

Her name was Rima Allen, and she came from a small town in Pennsylvania which had neither the distinction of being a grimy coal town nor Main Line, but just a town. Her mother had been reading *Green Mansions* when her daughter was born, and she felt it would give her child some individuality to be named Rima. Her father was a tax accountant, a vague man who spent his life bent over records of other people's lives. He thought Rima was a silly name, but his wife overruled him, and later it was she who chose Radcliffe for Rima, and so we met.

There was a fireplace at one end of the living room in our dormitory, and beside it a nook, wood paneled and cushioned in velvet. Rima was sitting in that nook with her temporary friend, a lumpy debutante from New York who powdered her face like a Kabuki dancer and had once brought a copy of the Social Register into dinner to point out her own name in it. That frightened and graceless snob (whose registered name I have forgotten) was the last person on earth you would expect to find chanting Yeats with such obvious joy, yet Rima had made her memorize dozens of his poems. I knew at once that Rima was a special girl, a girl people gravitated toward to find their dream, their opposite, whatever it was they could not find alone.

"An aged man is but a paltry thing,/A tattered coat upon a stick, unless/Soul clap its hands and sing, and louder sing/For every tatter in its mortal dress."

Rima was a tall girl who always looked very small and fragile, until you noticed her standing next to someone else and realized with surprise that she was big. She had narrow shoulders and small bones, a delicate way of moving, and a soft, child's voice. Her face, in those years of our late teens, was a white blur, as I suppose all our faces were, for we did not yet know who we were. I have a photograph of her sitting on the library steps, a pretty, pale, no-face child of seventeen, all wonder, her arms held out to the wan New England sun.

Every one of us owned several bottles of cologne; Rima had none, but she had one bottle of perfume. We all had many party dresses; Rima had only one, but it was orange, with a swirly skirt, and it had cost a hundred dollars. I remember her always hiding in her room, the shades down, studying, or reading the poetry she loved, and then the sound of the phone bell . . . and ten minutes later she emerged—a swirl of orange skirt, a cloud of Arpege drifting after her, as if she had suddenly been told she existed.

That's all I remember of her from those days; it was, after all, fifteen years ago, and her story had not begun. When we graduated, four of us went to Washington to work in offices, share a house, and find husbands. I had been a zoology major in college, studying such unfeminine things as mollusks, but when we went to Washington I decided to become a secretary along with the others, because we were almost twenty-one and not getting any younger. Everyone knew you found nothing among the mollusks but shells and a lot of ugly old men. We had decided on Washington instead of New York because the other two girls said that was where the bright young men were. A few months after the four of us settled in rooms in a Greek Revival style mansion turned into a rooming house, the two who had brought us to this city of romance began going steady with two boys they had known back at Harvard, and I realized why we had come.

I missed zoology and hated typing and filing; but missing one's work takes an odd form in girls, I think—I was less conscious of the loss than I was of what replaced it, a ferocious need to be loved. I needed someone to inflict all that creative energy on, it didn't matter much who. Of the four of us, it was only Rima who seemed to enjoy being a secretary; who preferred staying home and listening to old Noel Coward records to going out with a new prospect; who went to bed early and got up early, eagerly, without resentment; and who went to the office in her prettiest clothes.

I soon discovered it was because she was in love with someone she had met
at work.

It was one of those impossibly romantic meetings that occur only in bad
movies and real life. The man was attached to the State Department, one
of those career diplomats whose work is so important and confidential
that you can talk to him for an hour at a cocktail party and realize afterward he has not said a word about himself. He was American, forty-five
years old, very attractive, totally sophisticated and, of course, married. Rima
had been dispatched to take some papers to his office. There she was, in the
doorway—his secretary was in the powder room—and he was alone behind
the largest desk she had ever seen. She looked at him, knowing only
vaguely who he was and how important he was, thinking only that he was
a grownup and extraordinarily attractive. She was wearing her neat little
college-girl suit, her hair tied back with a ribbon, her face all admiration
and awe. She thought as girls do in the darkness of movie theaters without
any sense of further reality: I'd love to go out with him! No one knows
what he thought. But the next day he took her to the country for lunch.

She did not tell me who her mysterious lover was for several months,
and she never told our other two roommates at all. She saved newspaper
clippings about glittering Washington parties he had attended, but because
diplomatic amours are very diplomatic in Washington, she had little
else in the way of souvenirs, not even a matchbook from a restaurant. I
did not know how they managed to meet during those first few months,
but I always knew when she was meeting him because again, as in our
college days, there was a swirl of brightly colored skirt running down the
stairs, a faint cloud of perfume (Joy this time instead of Arpege), and the
air around her was charged with life. When she finally told me his name,
it was only after they had both decided they were in love.

Rima had had crushes on boys at Harvard, had even cried over a few
missed phone calls, but it was nothing like this. As for him, he had played
around with little interest with a few predatory wives, but he had never
had a real love affair with anyone since his marriage. Rima was so young,
so full of confidence in a future in which she would always be young and
he would always care for her, that she never even thought of asking him
to get a divorce. It was a courtship. They planned how they would meet,
when they would meet, how she could see him most often, how she could
get along. He could not bear for her to be poor; even the thought that she
was spending part of her $60 salary on taxis to meet him appalled him,
he wanted to make everything up to her, but how? She refused to go out
with any of the boys (we still called them that) who phoned, and he knew
it. Suddenly, one day, our freezer was full of steaks, the refrigerator was
filled with splits of champagne, and our house was so filled with flowers
I thought someone had died.

I went with Rima one day to help her sell her jewelry so that she could buy him a birthday present. Her charm bracelet with the gold disk that said "Sweet Sixteen," her college ring . . . whatever she could not sell she pawned. None of it meant anything to her. "I want to get him gold cuff links," she said. "He wears French cuffs." I thought of the O. Henry story about the gift of the Magi, but it was not the same, because he was not giving up anything for her, and what she was giving up for him was only bits of metal and chips of gems that belonged to an already fading past.

That summer, when our first year of independence drew to a close, our two roommates married the boys they had come to Washington to pursue, and Rima and I had two whole rooms to ourselves. Summers in Washington are very hot. An air conditioner mysteriously appeared in our bedroom window, installed by a man from the air-conditioning company whom neither of us had sent for. On the first cool fall day, for the first time, I was allowed to meet the diplomat. He came to our house for tea and sat on the edge of one of our frayed chairs, very elegant in his hand-tailored suit and Sulka tie. He even wore a vest. I thought he looked like our uncle; not our father—he was too young, too glamorous, too much from another world. But there was something fatherly in the way he looked around at our landlady's furniture with amusement and yet a little annoyance— was it clean enough, good enough, for his child—the way he smiled with adult pride at everything Rima said, as if she were a precious being from another planet. I could hardly believe any of this was happening; I think, in a way, neither could he. Yet they were obviously in love with each other.

He went to New York on several business trips that fall and winter and took Rima with him, meeting her as if by accident on the train, where he had taken a private bedroom for the short trip and Rima had a ticket in the parlor car. They had rooms in the same hotel on different floors. At Buccellati's he bought her a gold and emerald ring, which she wore on her left hand, but they entered and left the shop by the back door. When they returned to Washington after the last trip, his wife met him at the station, and Rima alighted from a different car and stood staring on the station platform as her love drove off in a silver-gray foreign automobile with someone who was suddenly flesh and blood, an actuality, a force, a monster.

"I saw her, the old hag," Rima said to me that night, almost in tears. "I wish I could kill her. She's very sophisticated . . . she was wearing a real Chanel suit, and the Chanel shoes and bag too . . . she's too thin, she chain-smokes and uses a holder . . . she's one of those terribly chic, tense women who knows everybody and always says and does the right things. You could tell. She's unhappy, though . . . she must know he loves some-one else. Women as nervous as that always know they aren't loved. He told me he doesn't love her any more. He'd leave her if it weren't for his career; a scandal—zip!" She drew her finger across her throat. "He's so proper and old-fashioned in his way, nobody is like him any more. If it weren't for her he could marry me and we'd both be happy. I hate her, the old hag."

"She doesn't sound like an old hag," I said.

"She is!"

"All right, she is."

"And ugly, too."

"Well, at least she's ugly."

"No, she's not ugly," Rima said. "I wish she were. She must have something if he won't leave her for me. If he really didn't love her, he'd leave her, no matter what he says. How could he marry me? I couldn't be a hostess, I couldn't run two homes the way she does. I don't know anything about being a diplomat's wife. I *know* he loves me, but he won't leave *her*. . . ."

So she did want to marry him after all. It had been inevitable. The courtship had been beautiful; the five-minute meetings in hallways, the stolen afternoons and weekends—all had been part of the discovery and wonder of love. But after a year and a half the champagne of secrecy had gone flat. I suspected that Rima had wanted to marry him long before this but had never dared say the words until she saw his wife and realized bitterly that someone had married him, someone was sharing all of his life except those stolen afternoons; for someone it was possible.

All lovers make near-fatal mistakes in their relationships; it is part of the pleasure of love, illicit or not, to tempt providence. So when, one weekend when his wife was away, the diplomat took Rima to his home, it seemed to me merely one of the fatal mistakes some lovers have to make. It was not fatal in any immediate sense, for they were not caught, no one saw them, the servants were away, his wife did not return unexpectedly with a detective or a gun. On his part, it was only a further avowal of his love for Rima; he wanted her to see where and how he lived, he didn't want her to be an outsider. He wanted her to approve of him, of the beautiful things with which he filled his life. He wanted to give her a setting to picture when she dreamed of him, a background for her lonely fantasies; perhaps he also wanted to be able to imagine her in his home when she was no longer there and he was sitting through a dull diplomatic dinner party. The mistake was fatal because Rima did approve of his home . . . she approved of it too much.

She told me about it that night in detail, and I could picture her scampering through those huge rooms like a child, touching each piece of antique furniture as her lover told her what famous person might have sat in this chair, dined from that plate (now an ashtray), or what skill distinguished the weaving of this piece of cloth from any other. She peered into every closet, learning about the heirloom silver, the china, the crystal; she even tried on some of his wife's clothes. To him, Rima was a child, wistful, amusing, and filled with amazement, so he let her try on the

Chanels, the Diors, stroke the furs, wave the lapis cigarette holder in the air as if it held a cigarette and she were a grownup at the ball. When she returned home to the Greek Revival rooming house, the photographic mind that had gotten A's at Radcliffe was a living archive of memorabilia.

The bulging scrapbooks of souvenirs and photographs from our college days, which still amused us on Sunday afternoons, were shipped home to her parents. In their place appeared glossy magazines that looked more like books, with names like "Antiquaries," and "A History of Battersea Boxes." One of them was even in French. The diplomat collected Battersea boxes, and also tiny silver boxes with crests on them, so Rima began to scour back street antique shops for a collection exactly like his. Real Battersea boxes were too expensive, but on her twenty-third birthday the diplomat gave her one, topped with white china, on which was written in fine script: "A Trifle From a Friend."

"He wanted to give me a coat," she told me, "but this coat will go another year. I just had to have a real Battersea box."

There was a one-of-a-kind pair of Louis XV chairs in the diplomat's living room. But there turned out to be, surprisingly, an identical pair, for Rima discovered it on a trip to New York, and she began putting away part of her salary every month to buy them. "A hundred dollars a month forever. . . ." Our landlady's frayed chairs were sent to the basement, and the two Louis XV chairs took their place in front of our fireplace that December, for the diplomat had added the frighteningly large difference for a Christmas present. But he seemed disappointed with the gift she had chosen for him to give her, because he surprised her with an additional present, a beige and white fox fur coat. She looked young and rich and daring in the coat, but as for the chairs, I was afraid to sit on them.

One night Rima packed all her career-girl clothes in a large box and sent them to charity, for she was the new owner of a real Chanel suit with the shoes and bag to match. She bought a cigarette holder and began to smoke; she said it would help her lose weight, for she had suddenly decided she was too fat. When her lover told her she was getting too thin, she cried all night, but she did not stop smoking, for the excuse was it would help her stop biting her nails. The collection of tiny silver boxes with crests grew larger and covered the entire top of a spindly-legged antique table Rima had found, which was by coincidence exactly like the one in the bedroom of the diplomat and his wife. The real Chanel suit was joined, in a few months, by another, and a white Dior evening gown, which Rima wore at home in the evening, alone, while she sipped sherry from a certain crystal wineglass, chain-smoked, and wrote letters to a certain firm in Paris asking if it was possible to obtain ten yards of a certain brocaded fabric which had been specially made at one time for another American client, and a tiny sample of which she happened to have snipped from the underside of that client's sofa.

When the fabric finally arrived, the sofa it would cover had arrived too, a gift for Rima's twenty-fourth birthday. I reminded her we were still paying rent for a furnished apartment, although it now looked like a museum, and our landlady's basement looked like a warehouse. Rima looked at me with the nervous, near-tearful look she had acquired during the past year, which somehow made her look rather tragic and mysterious. "We're too old to live like pigs anymore," she said. "Don't you want a real home?"

I did, and I wanted something more, something elusive but wonderful, which I felt must surely be beyond the next corner, or at the next party, or on the threshold of our front door tomorrow night. . . It had to be, or I felt I would disappear. So one fall evening, when the doorbell rang, announcing the arrival of perhaps the hundredth blind date I would have had in Washington, I decided: If he's anything better than a monster, whoever he is, *this one* I will fall in love with.

He was far from a monster, and he had green eyes and a sense of humor —my two fatal weaknesses—so while he sat in my living room talking and trying to make me like him he never knew he needn't have bothered, because I already loved him. He talked all night, and at dawn, when he remembered he had invited me to his apartment after dinner to make a pass at me, and now it was too late because it was day and we had to go to our offices, he decided he was in love with me, too.

"How could I not love you?" he asked (this young man who was already destined to become my first husband). "You are me. If I didn't love you, it would be like not loving myself."

My decision to marry him seemed as mad and romantic as my decision to fall in love with him. We were in his car at the curb in front of a restaurant. It was that first night, before his apartment, at our first restaurant together, the first time I had been in his car. I wanted to invent some test for destiny, something simple, arbitrary and irrevocable, therefore magic. "If he comes around to my side to open the door, I'll marry him. If he doesn't, he'll never know." He came around to open the door.

Rima gave a cocktail party for us when we announced our engagement, one of many parties she had begun to give. She had become a polished hostess, entertaining a mélange of people: minor politicians, intellectuals, an artist, a writer, an actress, a few foreigners who spoke no English at all but whose languages Rima had studied in college and perfected during the past few years of her diplomatic education. Her diplomat was not there, of course, and she had hidden her half-dozen tiny framed photographs of him in the dresser drawer, but his presence hovered in the rooms throughout the party, for it was now his home, done in his taste, filled with the objects of his pleasures, and the hostess who presided over it all with infinite charm might as well have been his wife. I had a brief irreverent fantasy of the diplomat coming here one night by accident, and panicking, not knowing which home he had come to.

At the party there was a visitor from New York, a young advertising executive. He was thirty-four, married twelve years to his high school sweetheart, and had two children. He was in Washington on business and obviously had never seen anyone like Rima at such close range. He was almost childishly infatuated with her after ten minutes. She flirted with him, named him Heathcliff (for that was rather whom he resembled), and although she obviously enjoyed playing with him, she seemed unaware of her new power. When she was moving about the room talking to her other guests he did not take his eyes off her.

"You need some more champagne, Heathcliff," Rima said, touching his arm lightly as she drifted past. "I want you to get good and drunk. 'Wine comes in at the mouth and love comes in at the eye; That's all we shall know for truth before we grow old and die.'"

"'I lift the glass to my mouth,'" he finished, "'I look at you, and I sigh.'" She stopped dead and stared at him.

He smiled. There was something about him both boyish and wire-strong, a man who would piously refuse to deceive anyone and yet who was destined to deceive many people throughout his life because they would mistake him for someone simple. He raised his champagne glass at Rima. "'A mermaid found a swimming lad, picked him for her own, pressed her body to his body, laughed; and plunging down forgot in cruel happiness that even lovers drown.'"

"I don't think anyone could drown you," she said. "Heathcliff. . . ."

"Lady Brett Ashley . . . ." he said, transfixed.

"Me?" Rima laughed. *"Me?"*

He asked her to have dinner with him, as he was alone in this city, but she refused, explaining that she was in love with someone and never went out with anyone else.

"Where is he?" the advertising man asked, looking around the crowded room.

"He's not here."

"Oh. Married."

"Aren't you?" she replied sweetly, and drifted away to her guests.

My husband's work took him to New York, where we lived in a three-room apartment that I cleaned carefully every day. I went to the grocery store, read his magazines, his books, played his records, and waited for him to come home to eat the dinners I cooked. He did not like his work very much, and I did not work at all, so in the evenings we talked about the past, our childhoods, our friends; and when we were bored with that we talked about the future, although that seemed more like a game than reality. Sometimes we talked about Rima, who he said was neurotic. He said her life was going to end badly. "If I weren't married to you, I would save her from that man."

"Really? What makes you think she'd want you?" And at that moment, only six months after we had vowed to stay together forever, I wondered why I wanted him, either. I was beginning to look the way Rima had: nervous, lost, a bird girl who appeared out of a tree in the jungle to answer someone's dream and then disappeared at dawn . . . or was it he who disappeared, back into the real world, while the bird girl waited, invisible, for his return, for his summons, for her moments of reality?

Rima wrote to me quite regularly during those months. She had nothing else to do in the evenings, for the decorating job on her apartment was completed, and for some reason the diplomat was not seeing her as often as he used to. He was overworked, she wrote to me, and when he did manage a little time with her he usually spent it falling asleep.

"For the first time in my life," she wrote, "I feel old. I feel like a wife. But I want to marry him, and I know this isn't what our life would be like if I were really his wife. Then we'd share everything. But now he acts as if it isn't a romance any more. I don't know why. Do you remember in the beginning, when the house was full of flowers? He hasn't taken me out to lunch in four months."

They had their first serious fight, "He called me extravagant, said I cared too much about clothes," Rima wrote. "He used to tell me she was extravagant (the old hag) and I told him never to dare compare me with her. He said, 'In some ways you are like her,' and the way he said it was like an insult. He refused to explain. What more does he want from me? I can't be perfect, I need love, I can't help that. Why can't he love me enough to leave her? What's wrong with me that he can't love me enough to choose me over someone he doesn't love at all?"

The day after her fifth anniversary with the diplomat, Rima arrived at my apartment in New York. It seems they had been planning their fifth anniversary celebration for months; she had saved for and bought a new white Dior gown, had her hair done at eight in the morning in order to be at the office on time, and then at five o'clock—an hour before they were to meet to celebrate—he had phoned to say he had to go to an important dinner party, his wife would not understand if she had to attend alone, there was nothing he could do. Rima had gotten tremendously drunk on the bottle of Taittinger Blanc de Blancs 1953 she had been chilling in her refrigerator, given the Malossol caviar to the cleaning woman, thrown the white Dior on the closet floor, and taken the morning train to New York. He had promised to make it up to her, perhaps even a whole weekend away somewhere . . . but she could not wait.

"Wait!" she cried to me, tears pouring down her face as if she were a marble statue in a fountain. "Wait! Wait! All I have ever done is wait."

When my husband came home he flirted with Rima all evening—to save her?—as if I were invisible, and she took an instant dislike to it. When he started to talk about a girl he had known before he met me, Rima stood up. "If I ever get married," she said coldly, "my husband will never talk about other women in my presence. Nor will he ever flirt with other women when I am in the room. It's insulting. I am going to be the first in his life, not just something that's *there,* and if I ever find there's someone else I'm going to leave."

"Isn't that a little too much to ask of a man?" I said, wishing I had her courage.

"It's what I will ask," Rima said.

"Well, Rima," he said, cheerfully nasty, "you ought to know."

I don't remember her ever speaking to my husband again, for that was the way Rima was. She drifted in and out of rooms during the two days she stayed with us, graceful and silent as a cat, always pleasant, but whenever he began to talk she suddenly wasn't there. The afternoon of the second day, when she was feeling repentant toward the diplomat, who did not know where she had gone, I went with Rima to Gucci's where she bought him a wallet. It was elegant, expensive, and impersonal—no, thank you, she would not wait to have it initialed—the kind of gift one had to give a man whose wife noticed all his personal possessions. Coming out of the store we saw the advertising man who had been at Rima's party, or rather, he saw us, for she did not recognize him.

He was so excited he called out to stop us; he shook her gloved hand with both his hands, and then he blushed, as if he had attacked her in my presence. Rima laughed, and then he laughed, too, and invited us both for a drink.

We went to the Plaza (Rima's choice), where Heathcliff had one Scotch (his limit, he told us) and Rima had champagne. She was wearing the beige and white fox coat over a pale wool dress, she had a long gold cigarette holder, her beige alligator handbag and the little package from Gucci were on the table, and she did indeed look like Lady Brett Ashley, or someone equally golden and fictional. We sat in the dark wood-paneled room, watching the sunset through the windows that overlooked the park, laughing, happy; and I thought that people from out of town who saw her here must be thinking she was a real New Yorker, on her way somewhere exciting for the evening. The advertising man evidently thought so, too, when he got up reluctantly, almost jealously, to catch his train to Old Greenwich.

There was a row of taxis at the curb. He helped us into the first, gave her a mischievous look and kissed her hand. When their eyes met, I had the feeling he had done some investigating about her friend in Washington. As we watched him walk away to the second taxi he seemed to change, grow firmer, more stubborn, as if preparing himself for an everyday life he had momentarily forgotten.

"He makes me feel young," Rima said wistfully. She smiled. "He makes me want to go to the country and throw snowballs."

She went back to Washington that night, and we did not see each other again until spring. In the meantime I had gotten what is known as a friendly divorce, and custody of the three-room apartment. There had been only two short letters from Rima during the intervening months. The first said, "I'm too depressed to write, everything is lousy."

The second said, "I have begun to realize that people don't break up because of one unforgivable incident, but rather, because of hopelessness. I used to think love could be killed with a mortal blow, but that's not true. Love goes on and on, until one day you wake up and realize that the hopelessness is stronger than the love. I've done everything I could think of, and it was not enough. He sees me once a week, for twenty minutes. How many more ways can I change? He says he loves me, but somehow that doesn't mean anything any more; they're just words. I hear them and I don't remember what they used to mean."

One morning Rima packed all her clothes and the collection of tiny antique boxes, and left Washington forever. She did not say goodbye to the diplomat, she simply disappeared into the dawn. She left every stick of antique furniture—his, hers, theirs, whatever it was—and I imagine the rooms in the Greek Revival style mansion must have looked very strange, as if the occupant had only gone out for a walk. She came to stay with me, and the first thing she did was give me her precious collection.

"I remember you used to admire them. Just consider them a house gift."

The second thing she did was get another secretarial job, because she insisted on paying half the rent. I had decided to go back to zoology and was taking a Master's degree at night and working days as a receptionist so I could study my textbooks behind the potted plant that stood on my glossy desk. I was much happier than I had expected to be. Rima surprised me by her resiliency. I had resigned myself nervously to having to nurse a potential suicide, but what I found was a convalescent who was grateful to have survived.

We went to a few cocktail parties, to dinner with a few old friends, and introduced each other to the few single men we found in our respective offices who were not nineteen. It was a restful existence, and the weeks drifted by almost without notice. Then, one afternoon, Rima rushed back early from the office, and when I came home the scent of bath oil filled the entire apartment. She had put her newest Chanel suit on the bed and was washing her emerald ring with a nail brush.

"Guess what I did today! I just felt like doing something crazy, like we used to do when we were at college, so I called Heathcliff at his office and said, 'Here I am in New York!' He had a moment of conscience—I could hear it over the phone, almost like a gulp—and then he asked me to dinner."

"Dinner? Where's his wife?"

"Evidently she's a Den Mother, whatever that is, and they have a meeting. He was going to stay and work late at the office. He says he works late at the office once or twice a week anyway, and he has to eat somewhere, so—oh, you should have heard the stammering, the excuses. He's terrified of me. Of *me*, the girl who never got anybody in her life!"

They went to an Italian restaurant where Rima had often gone with the diplomat, and where the advertising man had never been in his life. The headwaiter recognized her, with obvious respect. The menu was not only in Italian but in handwriting, and Rima took pains to explain innocently to the old Italian waiter what a certain simple dish consisted of, so that Heathcliff could stammer, "Make it two."

He missed the nine-o'clock train, and before the nine-forty-two he had bought her a white orchid. "An orchid," Rima laughed, showing it to me. "An *orchid!* I haven't had an orchid since the Senior prom. I didn't think they made them any more."

But she put it carefully into a glass of champagne in the refrigerator, the alchemy that we had believed in our Senior Prom days would keep an orchid fresh for a week.

She had been almost silent about her affair with the diplomat, as if the gravity of first love had stunned her, but she bubbled over with her delight in Heathcliff, and I knew she had fallen in love with him before she did. "He's so square," she would say, laughing, and then add, "But he's a fox— oh, smart—watch out! I really think I'm the only one who sees the other side of him, the humor. In the advertising business they're just afraid of him, because he's so young and shrewd and on the way up. His wife's name is Dorlee—can you imagine?—and she's the same age he is, of course, because they've known each other all their lives. The old hag."

One of Rima's casual beaus, a plump young man who was also in advertising, took her to a cocktail party where Heathcliff appeared with Dorlee. "She just stood in the corner and talked to the wives," Rima told me afterward. "She looks as if she has steel fillings in her teeth. I don't think she ever shortened a dress in her life; she just wears them the way they come from the store. I heard her telling somebody that in Old Greenwich she has a TV room decorated like the inside of a ship. When she started talking about how they had to have plastic covers on everything I had to run out of the room because I nearly choked."

Heathcliff's commuting hours were irregular, for he often worked late and his two children were old enough to stay up in the TV room decorated like a ship until the captain came home to say good night. He met Rima after work several times a week. He seemed to have a calming effect on her in one way, for she stopped smoking and gave her long gold cigarette holder to our cleaning woman, who had admired it. It was a romance confined to furtive handholding, for he was consumed by guilt and told Rima often that she was "dangerous."

"Dangerous!" she told me in delight. "Dangerous! Me, the failure, dangerous! Isn't he beautiful?"

A letter arrived from our former Washington landlady informing Rima she was not running a storage company, and then several huge crates arrived, Railway Express collect. Rima and I stared at them with dismay.

"It's either storage or my own apartment," she said, "and I think at this point, an apartment of my own might be a good idea."

She found an apartment in a new, modern building, a block from Grand Central Station. "And believe me," she said, "an apartment a block from Grand Central is not easy to find." The choice of this location was logical to her—Heathcliff could stop by for a drink every evening on his way to his train. It seems several times he had mentioned, as if he were talking about an impossible dream, that such an arrangement would be the height of bliss.

The beautiful old furniture took some of the coldness away from the boxlike rooms of this glass-and-steel monstrosity, whose only redeeming feature was that it had a working fireplace; and when I went to visit her I found the rooms once again filled with flowers. The only strange note was a small bottle with a ship inside it, which perched on the center of her spindly-legged table.

"He collects them," she said. "He gave it to me. It's kind of pretty, don't you think?"

The next time I visited Rima's apartment a block from Grand Central it was a month later. There was a man's bathrobe hanging on the hook on the bathroom door, and a can of shaving cream on the tole shelf next to the sink. A small photograph of Heathcliff stood on the table beside her bed, framed in rope.

"It's so wonderful being in love with a man near my own age," she said. "He's thirty-four, I'm twenty-six—that means when I'm seventy, he'll be only seventy-eight."

"And commuting?"

"No, of course not," she said, touching his photograph reverently. "He's never been in love before, he never cheated on her in all those years, and do you know they were both virgins when they got married? Him, too. He has a very strong sense of honor. He said he wished she would find out about us so she would do something terrible to him, because he feels he deserves it; and then he said I ought to leave him, because he deserves that; and then he said if I did leave him he might as well be dead."

"He sounds happy," I said.

"It's just his sense of honor," Rima said. "It's a man like that who makes decisions. Men *do* leave their wives, you know, but only because of great love or great guilt. And he has both. I'm glad I didn't get married last time, because I was so young I mistook romance for love. This is real love: planning a life together, being able to help someone, making someone feel alive for the first time. Before he met me, his whole life was encased in plastic, just like that horrible chintz furniture of his in the country."

Men did leave their wives, as I well knew, and lovers left lovers, but it was neither for great love nor great guilt. Rima had been right the first time, in her letter to me: people part because of hopelessness. The death of love leads to the rebirth of another love, for love is a phoenix. A greater love does not kill a small one; it only adds pomp to the funeral.

During the following year, Rima and her advertising man tried to break up three times, but each time he came back to her, vowing he loved her more than ever and felt guiltier. She had already proposed to him several times, pretending it was only a joke, but at the end of their second year of afternoons before the train, she proposed to him seriously, and he answered her.

"How could I marry you?" he asked, tears in his eyes. "I'd bore you. You'd get tired of me. You're my elusive golden girl, and I'm just a husband and father."

"But that's what I *want*," Rima said.

"No. . . . I see you in front of the fire on a snowy night . . . I see you in that white fur coat, your eyes shining, going into the Plaza to meet an ambassador or a movie star. . . . I just don't see you in a gingham dress at the supermarket."

"Where do you think I get my food, out of flowers?"

"Yes," he answered. "And I will always bring them to you."

The transformation of Rima began that night. The next day, printed cotton slipcovers appeared on the Louis XV chairs. She bought a huge Early American object she informed me was called an Entertainment Center, containing a 19-inch television set, a stereo phonograph with four speakers, and a radio, with a long flat surface on top that was soon covered with a collection of ships in bottles. Her Chanels and Diors were sent to a thrift shop (tax deductible) and she replaced them with tweed skirts, cashmere sweater sets, and flowered, sleeveless cotton blouses. She had pawned her emerald ring to buy the Entertainment Center, and now she wore a single strand of imitation pearls. She learned to cook tuna fish casserole with potato chips on top, and in time even a peanut butter soufflé. She saved trading stamps and redeemed them for a hobnail glass lamp with a ruffly shade, and gave her 1850 tole lamp to the cleaning woman, who ventured she'd just as soon have had the nice new one.

She washed and set her hair herself, because it was obvious Dorlee had, and she used the money thus saved to buy books called *The Sexually Satisfied Housewife,* and *The Problems of the Adolescent Stepchild,* which she piled on top of the spindly-legged antique table until it broke and she replaced it with something that had formerly been a butter churn.

Her triumph came on Heathcliff's birthday. He had left his office early, and a light snow had begun to fall. At four-thirty, in the winter's early darkness, he arrived at Rima's apartment. There was snow on his coat, and he was carrying a gold-wrapped package that later turned out to contain champagne. Rima was sitting in front of the roaring fire, wearing blue jeans and toasting marshmallows.

He looked around the room as if he had never really noticed it before, still wearing his coat, still clutching the bottle of champagne in his arms. The air was fragrant with the scent of detergent and meat loaf.

"Happy birthday, honey," Rima said.

"Thank you. . . ." he murmured. "I'd better hang my coat in the bathroom; it's wet."

"Wait till you see your present! I made it."

When he came out of the bathroom he seemed more composed. He opened his present: a ship in a bottle. Rima had put the ship inside, herself. "You see," she said, "to get it in, the sails lie flat, and then I pull the string . . ."

"I know."

"Look at the marshmallow," she said. "When it's burned black like that, with the little red lights inside, it looks the way New York used to look to me at night, when I first came here—all dark and mysterious, with just those millions of little lights."

"Oh, Rima," Heathcliff whispered, holding the two bottles in his hands, the one with the ship and the one with the champagne, "I wish you had written me a poem."

She did write him a poem, the following summer, but she never gave it to him. Instead, she read it to me on the telephone. I had not seen very much of her during the winter and spring, because I had gotten a new job doing research (and my Master's degree), and she had spent most of her time in her apartment waiting for him to visit her, although the visits were fewer and farther between. We were both going to be thirty, but now it no longer seemed to matter that when Rima was thirty Heathcliff would be only thirty-eight.

"Send him the poem," I told her. "It's beautiful."

"No," she said. "I'm going to push it into one of his revolting little bottles and I'm going to toss it into the Greenwich Sound, or whatever the name is of that river he lives on. Then when he's walking in front of his split-level saying Yo-Ho-Ho he can find it, and see what he lost. Four years. . . . Well, last time it was five, so you can't say I'm not improving. At least it doesn't take me as long to find out I'm doomed. I am doomed, you know. I'm the girl they recite poetry to, and then in the mornings they always go back to their wives. It must be me, because I fell in love with two completely different men and neither of them wanted to stay with me."

"It's not you," I said. "Neither of them really knew what you were like. If they had, they would have loved you."

I don't know if she ever threw the bottle into the Sound, but she might have tossed it into the lake in Central Park, because all that summer Rima was addicted to long, lonely walks. Perhaps she was trying to figure things out; perhaps she was only still in her fantasy of the country wife, and the streets of the summer city were her Old Greenwich roads. I felt guilty not spending more time with her, but this time I had met someone I loved.

RONA JAFFE

277

I had not met him among the mollusks and the octogenarians; I had met him at a cocktail party. He was a producer, but he did not think lady zoologists were freaks, and I certainly did not think producers were freaks, although I had never met one before, either.

While I was occupied with the extraordinary miracle of my second (and present) love, Rima became involved in what, to her, seemed only an ordinary meeting. She had been on a long walk, it was about midnight, and she was passing Grand Central Station on her way back to her apartment when she saw a man fall down in the street. The few passers-by thought he was drunk and avoided him, but Rima went closer to see if he was ill, and discovered that he was indeed drunk. She also discovered, with delight and dismay, that he was one of her favorite authors.

"What are you doing, lying there on the curb?" she said sternly. "A great writer does not lie on the curb."

"He does if he's drunk," the author answered. He was trying to go to sleep, his cheek nestled on the sidewalk.

"You get up this minute." Rima pulled him to his feet, which was not too difficult as he was a short, wiry man, about her height, quite under-nourished from too much wine, women and song. He was, she remembered reading, only four years older than she was, and she felt maternal toward him.

"Have to go Bennington," he murmured. "Where the hell is Bennington? Have to be there in the morning."

"Bennington, Vermont?"

"Little girls' school . . . college. Lecture. Where's my train?"

"You can't lecture at Bennington like this," Rima said. She inspected his soiled clothing and bleary face with distaste. "Those girls idolize you. If they see you like this, it might ruin the rest of their lives."

"I'm . . . going to be sick."

"Good."

He decided not to be sick. "Who are you?"

"A former English major at Radcliffe, and an admirer of yours—although not at the moment. Come with me, I live around the corner." She was already leading him, his arm about her shoulders.

The writer stared at the sleeveless flowered cotton blouse, the chino walking skirt, the little strand of pearls. "Funniest-looking streetwalker I ever saw . . ." Rima slapped him.

She then took him to her apartment, a block from Grand Central, where she forced him to eat scrambled eggs and drink three cups of black coffee, and then spot-cleaned and pressed his suit while he cursed at her from a cold shower. She scanned the timetable while the writer looked around her apartment.

"You in the Waves?"

"Very funny. You can take the two-thirty train to Boston, and then there's probably a connection."

"You've even got a timetable."

"Purely for sentimental reasons," Rima said. "Here, take this aspirin and these vitamins; you'll need them later."

"You have any children?"

"No. Do you?"

"I'm not married," he said.

Suddenly, he became more than an idol or an invalid—he became a person. "You're *not?*"

"Divorced," he said.

"So am I," Rima said, "sort of."

"That's too bad. You'd make a wonderful wife. Very homey apartment. It reminds me of my mother's. You wouldn't think I had a mother, would you? Well, I do."

"You need her," Rima said. "Or a nurse. How could you possibly have gotten so drunk when you have an appointment tomorrow—or today, I should say."

"Oh!" he said, looking wildly for his jacket. "Where's the train?"

"At the station. Where are your lecture notes? Good. Your aspirin? Good. Now, take these cookies, in case you get tempted on the way."

The writer took hold firmly of Rima's arm. "You're coming with me."

"Are you crazy?"

"Yes. Come with me. I need you. I'll only be there one day, and then we'll go to St. Thomas. I live in St. Thomas; you'll like it."

Rima looked around her apartment, the cozy, chintzy, friendly room filled with its memories of love and failure. " 'Be not afeard. The isle is full of noises, sounds and sweet airs, that give delight and hurt not.' "

"Come with Caliban," he said.

"No," Rima said, following him docilely to the door, "no, not Caliban . . . Shakespeare."

When she came back from Bennington she came to visit me, to bring me her collection of ships in bottles and to say goodbye. "When you marry that divine man you're going with, you'll have a little boy someday, and he'll like these."

"Are you really going away with him?" I asked stupidly.

"Imagine—St. Thomas! He can write his books, and I can keep house. I'll walk on the beach, and I'll send you shells if you like, if I find anything they don't have anywhere else. Imagine—he's not married—at last! He's so brilliant; I've always adored his work. I've read everything he ever wrote, and do you know what? Once, when we were in college and he had his first story published, I cut his picture out of the magazine and kept it for a year."

"Listen," I said, hating myself for it, "I read in *Time* magazine that he travels around with a Great and Good Friend. She lives in St. Thomas with him. What happened to her?"

"Oh, her!" Rima said. "He hates her. She just happens to live in St.

RONA JAFFE

279

Thomas, that's all. He says she's not a girlfriend, she's a friend girl. I saw that picture in *Time;* she looks like a squaw. She's got a braid down her back and she had this leather thong around her neck with a big tooth attached to it. I'll bet it came out of her mouth. No wonder he drank before he met me."

"He's stopped drinking?"

"One Scotch before dinner, like Heathcliff used to. Oh, I'm a reformer now." She laughed at herself, the reformer, and I wondered if life would at last be kind to her, she who could never be kind to herself.

She left the apartment, the furniture, her winter clothes, everything, and she and the writer went to St. Thomas. I went to her apartment two days before my wedding, suddenly taken by the absurdly sentimental thought that I must sell that Early American Entertainment Center and get Rima's emerald ring out of the pawn shop, if it was still there, and send it to her. I don't know why that ring seemed so important to me—perhaps because I was going to be married and I was happy, and I couldn't bear the thought of a ring Rima had worn for five years on the third finger of her left hand being misused by some stranger. But the landlord had taken possession of all the furniture in lieu of the rent she had never sent from St. Thomas, and the apartment had been sublet. Well, I thought, caught up again in my own happiness, we've both learned enough from the past, and that ring doesn't mean anything any more.

So I was married, and two years later we did have a little boy who will like the collection of ships in bottles, when he's old enough not to break them to get the ships out. Our apartment is filled with scripts, books, records, theatrical posters, an aquarium, shells, textbooks, toys; but still there is room on the piano for Rima's collection of Battersea boxes. She had written me two happy postcards the first year, and then, nothing. I wondered if she was still in St. Thomas. Five years after she had left New York, I took a chance and wrote to her at her last address to tell her that my husband and I were going to take a winter vacation in St. Thomas, and was she still alive? She wrote back immediately.

"Yes," her letter said, "I'm still alive. Alive and single. Surprise. Look for me in the bar at your hotel any night at about ten o'clock. I'll be the one seated at the right hand of the Bard."

We arrived in St. Thomas in the afternoon. When we went down to the hotel bar that night at ten, Rima was not there. There were some pink-broiled American tourists, and a party of Italians from a large yacht that was moored in the harbor; the owner, very rich, very clean in a blue blazer, two teen-aged starlets who sat toying with the speared fruit in their drinks, two rather sinister-looking young men, and two contessas with streaks in their hair and a lot of diamonds. The Calypso trio played on a small bandstand, and the starlets got up to do whatever dance it was teen-aged starlets were doing that winter in the jet set. The contessas and their escorts looked bored because they were supposed to, and the Italian millionaire looked bored because he was. I was afraid Rima wasn't going to show up after all.

Then, at half past twelve, she arrived. She was, indeed at the right hand of the Bard, and the Bard was very, very drunk. At the left hand of the Bard, helping to support him, was a young woman the same age as Rima, with a long black braid down her back, a turtleneck T-shirt, a peasant skirt, no makeup, and a silver-and-turquoise ornament the size of a breast-plate dangling from a chain around her neck. Rima had let her hair grow to her waist and braided it, her face was scrubbed and tanned, she was dressed in an almost identical village outfit, and the only difference between the two Squaw Twins was that Rima was the prettier one.

Rima let go of the writer's hand and ran over to our table. Liberated, he pulled free of the other lady and went to the bar.

"Oh, I'm so glad to see you!" Rima said. "Look how pale you are—you'll have to come to the beach with me." She held her arm, the color of glistening walnut, against mine.

My husband was transfixed by the object dangling from a thong around Rima's neck. "Whose tooth is that?"

She shrugged. "I don't know. It's Olive's; we trade."

"How is everything?" I asked lamely.

"Don't ask that. I want to be happy tonight. No, it's all right, really. I'm content; I mean, I'm over him, I just stay with him because he needs me."

"Who's Olive?"

Rima glanced at her Squaw Twin. "Remember the girlfriend he said was only a friend girl? That's her. Actually, I'd go insane if I didn't have her to talk to. He's so drunk lately. And, do you know, in the beginning I really hated her? She has great individuality, though, and a crystalline intellect. She's above such things as jealousy and animosity, she really believes in the purity of non-thought. . . . Oh, hell, she bores me to death."

The writer had taken the sticks away from the Calypso drummer and was crashing them on every cymbal, drum, and any surface in sight. The musicians and waiters ignored him as if he was a nightly fixture. Olive was watching him inscrutably. The Italians from the yacht looked amused.

"If I had his talent . . ." Rima said. "If I had *any* talent. . . . Tell me about New York! Tell me about the world, is it still there?"

We ordered drinks and told her about people she had known, and then we ordered more drinks and she made us tell her about people she didn't know. She was insatiable. The world, the world, what was happening outside this tiny island, this paradisiacal prison? The American tourists went up to bed, the Calypso trio disappeared, the writer and Olive were now sitting with the party of Italians from the yacht. The millionaire glanced over at us and bent toward him to whisper a question; the writer shook his head.

"How old is your baby?" Rima asked suddenly.

"Three years old."

"I'm thirty-five," Rima said. "Do I look it? Don't answer. Look—the sun's coming up, I'm going to walk on the beach."

She ran out of the bar, across the patio, across the sand, and was gone. I was afraid she might be going to drown herself and was going to run after her, but then I saw her again, wandering among the sea-grape trees, sad and alone. The writer had fallen asleep at the table, his head between the empty glasses. Olive was watching over him, totally still, a little smile at the corner of her mouth. The Italian millionaire excused himself to the group and went out to the beach.

I could see his silhouette in the pink-and-gold dawn, bowing slightly to Rima's silhouette, and then, after a moment, walking slowly beside it through the silhouettes of the sea-grape trees. The sea was all blue and gold and silver now, and in the distance the Italian's yacht rocked gently at anchor, all white.

We went up to our room. Then, suddenly, I felt one of those obsessive, extrasensory calls that are like a shout in the mind. "I'll be right back," I said, and ran down the stairs to the lobby.

The bar was closed, chairs piled on top of the tables. The Italians had all gone, and in a corner of the lobby Olive was asleep in a big chair. A yawning porter handed me a hotel envelope with my name on it, and went back behind the desk. The writer, despite his hangover, was milling around like twelve people. "Where is she? Where is she? *Rima . . . !*"

I tore open the envelope, and the tooth on the leather thong fell into my hand. There was a note, in Rima's impeccable script: " 'When such as I cast out remorse so great a sweetness flows into the breast we must laugh and we must sing. We are blest by everything. Everything we look upon is blest.' *La donna è mobile*. Goodbye, and love."

I looked out to sea, where the yacht was only a tiny toy ship on the horizon, and then I went up to our room.

So she was gone again, with the Italian millionaire, and his starlets, and his contessas with the streaked hair. Soon, I knew, she would fall in love, and cut her braid, and toss her pueblo jewelry into the sea. She would paint her eyelids and enamel her toenails, and disappear. Once again, as always, a man who had fallen in love with a fantasy that had been created for another man would lose that fantasy, consuming it in the fire of his love. I remembered that the Rima of *Green Mansions,* for whom Rima Allen had been named, had been killed in a fire that destroyed her hiding-tree. It seemed to me, that lonely morning in St. Thomas, that the Rima I knew had been killed in many fires, rising again from the ashes of each one like a bright bird to sing the song of some wanderer's need. Had there ever been a real Rima? Born and reborn to a splendid image, she had never looked for her self, nor had anyone else. Being each man's dream of love, she had eventually failed him, and so he had failed her, and so, finally, she had failed herself.

THE SEX OBJECT

282

NORMAN MAILER

(b. 1923) Like Ernest Hemingway, Norman Mailer has come to epitomize an age as much in his highly publicized personal life as in his fiction. His most famous novel, written about World War II, is *The Naked and the Dead* (1948). In *The Prisoner of Sex* (1971) he discusses his ideas about male-female relationships. His most recent work, *The Executioner's Song: A True Life Novel* (1979), for which he won a Pulitzer Prize in 1980, is written in the mode of the New Journalism that blends fiction and fact.

THE TIME OF HER TIME

I

I was living in a room one hundred feet long and twenty-five feet wide, and it had nineteen windows staring at me from three of the walls and part of the fourth. The floor planks were worn below the level of the nails which held them down, except for the southern half of the room where I had laid a rough linoleum which gave a hint of sprinkled sand, conceivably an aid to the footwork of my pupils. For one hundred dollars I had the place whitewashed; everything; the checkerboard of tin ceiling plates one foot square with their fleurs-de-lis stamped into the metal, the rotted sashes on the window frames (it took twelve hours to scrape the calcimine from the glass), even parts of the floor had white drippings (although that was scuffed into dust as time went on) and yet it was worth it: when I took the loft it stank of old machinery and the paint was a liverish brown—I had tried living with that color for a week, my old furniture, which had been moved by a mover friend from the Village and me, showed the scars of being bumped and dragged and flung up six flights of stairs, and the view of it sprawled over twenty-five hundred feet of living space, three beat old day beds, some dusty cushions, a broken-armed easy chair, a cigarette-scarred coffee table made from a door, a kitchen table, some peeled enamel chairs which thumped like a wooden-legged pirate when one sat in them, the bookshelves of unfinished pine butted by bricks, yes, all of this, my purview, this grand vista, the New York sunlight greeting me in the morning through the double filter of the smog-yellow sky and the nineteen dirt-frosted windows, inspired me with so much content, especially those liver-brown walls, that I fled my pad like the plague, and in the first week, after a day of setting the furniture to rights, I was there for four hours of sleep a night, from five in the morning when I maneuvered in from the last closed Village bar and the last coffee-klatsch of my philosopher friends' for the night to let us say nine in the morning when I awoke with a partially destroyed brain and the certainty that the sore vicious growl of my stomach was at least the onset of an ulcer and more likely the first gone cells of a thorough-going cancer of the duodenum. So I lived it that way for a week, and then following the advice of a bar-type who was the friend of a friend, I got myself up on the eighth morning, boiled my coffee on a hot-plate while I shivered in the October air (neither the stove nor the gas heaters had yet been bought) and then I went down-stairs and out the front door of the warehouse onto Monroe Street, picking my way through the garbage-littered gutter which always made me think of the gangs on this street, the Negroes on the east end of the block, the Puerto Ricans next to them, and the Italians and Jews to the west— those gangs were going to figure a little in my life, I suspected that, I was anticipating those moments with no quiet bravery considering how hung was my head in the morning, for the worst clue to the gangs was the six-year-olds. They were the defilers of the garbage, knights of the ordure, and here, in this province of a capital Manhattan, at the southern tip of the island, with the overhead girders of the Manhattan and Brooklyn bridges the only noble structures for a mile of tenement jungle, yes here the barbarians ate their young, and any type who reached the age of six without being altogether mangled by father, mother, family or friends, was a pint of iron man, so tough, so ferocious, so sharp in the teeth that the wildest alley cat would have surrendered a freshly caught rat rather than contest the meal. They were charming, these six-year-olds, as I told my uptown friends, and they used to topple the overloaded garbage cans, strew them through the street, have summer snowball fights with orange peel, coffee grounds, soup bones, slop, they threw the discus by scaling the raw tin rounds from the tops of cans, their pillow fights were with loaded socks of scum, and a debauch was for two of them to scrub a third around the inside of a twenty-gallon pail still warm with the heat of its emptied treasures. I heard that the Olympics took place in summer when they were out of school and the streets were so thick with the gum of old detritus, alluvium and dross that the mash made by passing car tires fermented in the sun. Then the parents and the hoods and the debs and the grandmother dowagers cheered them on and promised them murder and the garbage flew all day, but I was there in fall and the scene was quiet from nine to three. So I picked my way through last night's stew of rubble on this eighth morning of my hiatus on Monroe Street, and went half down the block to a tenement on the boundary between those two bandit republics of the Negroes and the Puerto Ricans, and with a history or two of knocking on the wrong door, and with a nose full of the smells of the sick overpeppered bowels of the poor which seeped and oozed out of every leaking pipe in every communal crapper (only as one goes north does the word take on the Protestant propriety of john), I was able finally to find my man, and I was an hour ahead of him—he was still sleeping off his last night's drunk. So I spoke to his wife, a fat masculine Negress with the face and charity of a Japanese wrestler, and when she understood that I was neither a junk-peddler nor fuzz, that I sold no numbers, carried no bills, and was most certainly not a detective (though my Irish face left her dubious of that) but instead had come to offer her husband a job of work, I was admitted to the first of three dark rooms, face to face with the gray luminescent eye of the television set going its way in a dark room on a bright morning, and through the hall curtains I could hear them talking in the bedroom.

"Get up, you son of a bitch," she said to him.

He came to work for me, hating my largesse, lugging his air compressor up my six flights of stairs, and after a discussion in which his price came down from two hundred to one, and mine rose from fifty dollars to meet his, he left with one of my twenty-dollar bills, the air compressor on the floor as security, and returned in an hour with so many sacks of whitewash that I had to help him up the stairs. We worked together that day, Charley Thompson his name was, a small lean Negro maybe forty years old, and conceivably sixty, with a scar or two on his face, one a gouge on the cheek, the other a hairline along the bridge of his nose, and we got along not too badly, working in sullen silence until the hangover was sweated out, and then starting to talk over coffee in the Negro hashhouse on the corner where the bucks bridled a little when I came in, and then ignored me. Once the atmosphere had become neutral again, Thompson was willing to talk.

"Man," he said to me, "what you want all that space for?"

"To make money."

"Out of which?"

I debated not very long. The people on the block would know my business sooner or later—the reward of living in a slum is that everyone knows everything which is within reach of the senses—and since I would be nailing a sign over my mailbox downstairs for the pupils to know which floor they would find me on, and the downstairs door would have to be open since I had no bell, the information would be just as open. But for that matter I was born to attract attention; given my height and my blond hair, the barbarians would notice me, they noticed everything, and so it was wiser to come on strong than to try to sidle in.

"Ever hear of an *Escuela de Torear?*" I asked him without a smile.

He laughed with delight at the sound of the words, not even bothering to answer.

"That's a bullfighter's school," I told him. "I teach bullfighting."

"You know that?"

"I used to do it in Mexico."

"Man, you can get killed."

"Some do." I let the exaggeration of a cooled nuance come into my voice. It was true after all; some do get killed. But not so many as I was suggesting, maybe one in fifty of the successful, and one in five hundred of the amateurs like me who fought a few bulls, received a few wounds, and drifted away.

Charley Thompson was impressed. So were others—the conversation was being overheard after all, and I had become a cardinal piece on the chaotic chessboard of Monroe Street's sociology—I felt the clear bell-like adrenalins of clean anxiety, untainted by weakness, self-interest, neurotic habit, or the pure yellows of the liver. For I had put my poker money on the table, I was the new gun in a frontier saloon, and so I was asking for it, not today, not tomorrow, but come sooner come later something was likely to follow from this. The weak would leave me alone, the strong would have respect, but be it winter or summer, sunlight or dark, there would come an hour so cold or so hot that someone, somebody, some sexed-up head, very strong and very weak, would be drawn to discover a new large truth about himself and the mysteries of his own courage or the lack of it. I knew. A year before, when I had first come to New York, there was a particular cat I kept running across in the bars of the Village, an expert with a knife, or indeed to maintain the salts of accuracy, an expert with two knives. He carried them everywhere—he had been some sort of hothead instructor in the Marines on the art of fighting with the knife, and he used to demonstrate nice fluid poses, his elbows in, the knives out, the points of those blades capering free of one another—he could feint in any direction with either hand, he was an artist, he believed he was better with a knife than any man in all of New York, and night after night in bar after bar he sang the love-song of his own prowess, begging for the brave type who would take on his boast and leave him confirmed or dead.

It is mad to take on the city of New York, there is too much talent waiting on line; this cat was calling for every hoodlum in every crack gang and clique who fancies himself with the blade, and one night, drunk and on the way home, he was greeted by another knife, a Puerto Rican cat who was defective in school and spent his afternoons and nights shadow-knifing in the cellar clubhouse of his clique, a real contender, long-armed for a Latin, thin as a Lehmbruck, and fast as a hungry wolf; he had practiced for two months to meet the knife of New York.

So they went into an alley, the champion drunk, a fog of vanity blanketing the point of all his artistic reflexes, and it turned out to be not too much of a fight: the Puerto Rican caught it on the knuckles, the lip, and above the knee, but they were only nicks, and the champion was left in bad shape, bleeding from the forearm, the belly, the chest, the neck, and the face: once he was down, the Puerto Rican had engraved a double oval, labium majorum and minorum on the skin of the cheek, and left him there, having the subsequent consideration or fright to make a telephone call to the bar in which our loser had been drinking. The ex-champion, a bloody cat, was carried to his pad which was not far away (a bit of belated luck) and in an hour, without undue difficulty the brother-in-law doctor of somebody or other was good enough to take care of him. There were police reports, and as our patois goes, the details were a drag, but what makes my story sad is that our ex-champion was through. He mended by sorts and shifts, and he still bragged in the Village bars, and talked of finding the Puerto Rican when he was sober and in good shape, but the truth was that he was on the alcoholic way, and the odds were that he would stay there. He had been one of those gamblers who saw his life as a single bet, and he had lost. I often thought that he had been counting on a victory to put some charge below his belt and drain his mouth of all that desperate labial libido.

Now I was following a modest parallel, and as Thompson kept asking me some reasonable if openly ignorant questions about the nature of the bullfight, I found myself shaping every answer as carefully as if I were writing dialogue, and I was speaking particularly for the black-alerted senses of three Negroes who were sitting behind me, each of them big in his way (I had taken my glimpse as I came in) with a dull, almost Chinese, sullenness of face. They could have been anything. I had seen faces like theirs on boxers and ditch diggers, and I had seen such faces by threes and fours riding around in Cadillacs through the Harlem of the early-morning hours. I was warning myself to play it carefully, and yet I pushed myself a little further than I should, for I became ashamed of my caution and therefore was obliged to brag just the wrong bit. Thompson, of course, was encouraging me—he was a sly old bastard—and he knew even better than me the character of our audience.

"Man, you can take care of yourself," he said with glee.

"I don't know about that," I answered, obeying the formal minuet of the *macho*. "I don't like to mess with anybody," I told him. "But a man messes with me—well, I wouldn't want him to go away feeling better than he started."

"Oh, yeah, ain't that a fact. I hears just what you hear." He talked like an old-fashioned Negro—probably Southern. "What if four or five of them comes on and gangs you?"

We had come a distance from the art of the *corrida*. "That doesn't happen to me," I said. "I like to be careful about having some friends." And

part for legitimate emphasis, and part to fulfill my image of the movie
male lead—that blond union of the rugged and the clean-cut (which would
after all be *their* image as well)—I added, "Good friends, you know."

There we left it. My coffee cup was empty, and in the slop of the saucer
a fly was drowning. I was thinking idly and with no great compassion that
wherever this fly had been born it had certainly not expected to die in a
tan syrupy ring-shaped pond, struggling for the greasy hot-dogged air of
a cheap Negro hashhouse. But Thompson rescued it with a deft flip of his
fingers.

"I always save," he told me seriously. "I wouldn't let nothing be killed.
I'm a preacher."

"Real preacher?"

"Was one. Church and devoted congregation." He said no more. He
had the dignified sadness of a man remembering the major failure of his
life.

As we got up to go, I managed to turn around and get another look at
the three spades in the next booth. Two of them were facing me. Their
eyes were flat, the whites were yellow and flogged with red—they stared
back with no love. The anxiety came over me again, almost nice—I had
been so aware of them, and they had been so aware of me.

2

That was in October, and for no reason I could easily discover, I found
myself thinking of that day as I awoke on a spring morning more than
half a year later with a strong light coming through my nineteen windows.
I had fixed the place up since then, added a few more pieces of furniture,
connected a kitchen sink and a metal stall shower to the clean water
outlets in the john, and most noticeably I had built a wall between the
bullfight studio and the half in which I lived. That was more necessary than
one might guess—I had painted the new wall red; after Thompson's job
of whitewash I used to feel as if I were going snow-blind; it was no easy
pleasure to get up each morning in a white space so blue with cold that
the chill of a mountain peak was in my blood. Now, when I opened my
eyes, I could choose the blood of the wall in preference to the ice slopes
of Mt. O'Shaugnessy, where the sun was always glinting on the glaciers
of the windows.

But on this particular morning, when I turned over a little more, there
was a girl propped on one elbow in the bed beside me, no great surprise,
because this was the year of all the years in my life when I was scoring
three and four times a week, literally combing the pussy out of my hair,
which was no great feat if one knew the Village and the scientific temperament of the Greenwich Village mind. I do not want to give the false
impression that I was one of the lustiest to come adventuring down the
pike—I was cold, maybe by birth, certainly by environment: I grew up in
a Catholic orphanage—and I had had my little kinks and cramps, difficulties

enough just a few years ago, but I had passed through that, and I was going now on a kind of disinterested but developed competence; what it came down to was that I could go an hour with the average girl without destroying more of the vital substance than a good night's sleep could repair, and since that sort of stamina seems to get advertised, and I had my good looks, my blond hair, my height, build and bullfighting school, I suppose I became one of the Village equivalents of an Eagle Scout badge for the girls. I was one of the credits needed for a diploma in the sexual humanities, I was par for a good course, and more than one of the girls and ladies would try me on an off-evening like comparison-shoppers to shop the value of their boy friend, lover, mate, or husband against the certified professionalism of Sergius O'Shaugnessy.

Now if I make this sound bloodless, I am exaggerating a bit—even an old habit is livened once in a while with color, and there were girls I worked to get and really wanted, and nights when the bull was far from dead in me. I even had two women I saw at least once a week, each of them, but what I am trying to emphasize is that when you screw too much and nothing is at stake, you begin to feel like a saint. It was a hell of a thing to be holding a nineteen-year-old girl's ass in my hands, hefting those young kneadables of future power, while all the while the laboratory technician in my brain was deciding that the experiment was a routine success—routine because her cheeks looked and felt just about the way I had thought they would while I was sitting beside her in the bar earlier in the evening, and so I still had come no closer to understanding my scientific compulsion to verify in the retort of the bed how accurately I had predicted the form, texture, rhythm and surprise of any woman who caught my eye.

Only an ex-Catholic can achieve some of the rarer amalgams of guilt, and the saint in me deserves to be recorded. I always felt an obligation—some noblesse oblige of the kindly cocksman—to send my women away with no great wounds to their esteem, feeling at best a little better than when they came in, I wanted to be friendly (what vanity of the saint!). I was the messiah of the one-night stand, and so I rarely acted like a pig in bed, I wasn't greedy, I didn't grind all my tastes into their mouths, I even abstained from springing too good a lay when I felt the girl was really in love with her man, and was using me only to give love the benefit of new perspective. Yes, I was a good sort, I probably gave more than I got back, and the only real pains for all those months in the loft, for my bullfighting classes, my surprisingly quiet time (it had been winter after all) on Monroe Street, my bulging portfolio of experiments—there must have been fifty girls who spent at least one night in the loft—my dull but doggedly advancing scientific data, even the cold wan joys of my saintliness demanded for their payment only one variety of the dead hour: when I woke in the morning, I could hardly wait to get the latest mouse out of my bed and out of my lair. I didn't know why, but I would awaken with the deadliest of depressions, the smell of the woman had gone very stale for me, and the armpits, the ammonias and dead sea life of old semen and old snatch, the sour fry of last night's sweat, the whore scent of over-exercised perfume, became an essence of the odious, all the more remarkable because I clung to women in my sleep, I was one Don John who hated to sleep alone, I used to feel as if my pores were breathing all the maternal (because sleeping) sweets of the lady, wet or dry, firm or flaccid, plump, baggy, or lean who was handled by me while we dreamed. But on awakening, hung with my head—did I make love three times that year without being drunk?—the saint was given his hour of temptation, for I would have liked nothing more than to kick the friendly ass out of bed, and dispense with the coffee, the good form, my depression and often hers, and start the new day by lowering her in a basket out of my monk-ruined retreat six floors down to the garbage pile (now blooming again in the freshets of spring), wave my hand at her safe landing and get in again myself to the blessed isolations of the man alone.

But of course that was not possible. While it is usually a creep who generalizes about women, I think I will come on so heavy as to say that the cordial tone of the morning after is equally important to the gymkhana of the night before—at least if the profit made by a nice encounter is not to be lost. I had given my working hours of the early morning to dissolving a few of the inhibitions, chilled reflexes and dampened rhythms of the corpus before me, but there is not a restraint in the world which does not have to be taken twice—once at night on a steam-head of booze, and once in daylight with the grace of a social tea. To open a girl up to the point where she loves you or It or some tremor in her sexual baggage, and then to close her in the morning is to do the disservice which the hateful side of women loves most—you have fed their cold satisfied distrust of a man. Therefore my saint fought his private churl, and suffering all the detail of abusing the sympathetic nervous system, I made with the charm in the daylight and was more of a dear than most.

It was to be a little different this morning, however. As I said, I turned over in my bed, and looked at the girl propped on her elbow beside me. In her eyes there was a flat hatred which gave no ground—she must have been staring like this at my back for several minutes, and when I turned, it made no difference—she continued to examine my face with no embarrassment and no delight.

That was sufficient to roll me around again, my shoulder blades bare to her inspection, and I pretended that the opening of my eyes had been a false awakening. I felt deadened then with all the diseases of the dull—making love to her the night before had been a little too much of a marathon. She was a Jewish girl and she was in her third year at New York University, one of those harsh alloys of a self-made bohemian from a middle-class home (her father was a hardware wholesaler), and I was remembering how her voice had irritated me each time I had seen her, an ugly New York accent with a cultured overlay. Since she was still far from formed, there had been all sorts of Lesbian hysterias in her shrieking laugh and they warred with that excess of strength, complacency and deprecation which I found in many Jewish women—a sort of "Ech" of disgust at the romantic and mysterious All. This one was medium in size and she had dark long hair which she wore like a Village witch in two extended braids which came down over her flat breasts, and she had a long thin nose, dark eyes, and a kind of lean force, her arms and square shoulders had shown the flat thin muscles of a wiry boy. All the same, she was not bad, she had a kind of Village chic, a certain snotty elegance of superiority, and when I first came to New York I had dug girls like her—Jewesses were strange to me—and I had even gone with one for a few months. But this new chick had been a mistake—I had met her two weeks ago at a party, she was on leave from her boy friend, and we had had an argument about T. S. Eliot, a routine which for me had become the quintessence of corn, but she said that Eliot was the apotheosis of manner, he embodied the ecclesiasticism of classical and now futureless form, she adored him she said, and I was tempted to tell her how little Eliot would adore the mannerless yeasts of the Brooklyn from which she came, and how he might prefer to allow her to appreciate his poetry only in step to the transmigration of her voice from all urgent Yiddish nasalities to the few high English analities of relinquished desire. No, she would not make that other world so fast—nice society was not cutting her crumpets thus quickly because she was gone on Thomas Sterns Eeeee. Her college-girl snobbery, the pity for me of eighty-five other honey-pots of the Village aesthetic whose smell I knew all too well, so inflamed the avenger of my crotch, that I wanted to prong her then and there, right on the floor of the party, I was a primitive for a prime minute, a gorged gouge of a working-class phallus, eager to ram into all her nasty little tensions. I had the message again, I was one of the millions on the bottom who had the muscles to move the sex which kept the world alive, and I would grind it into her, the healthy hearty inches and the sweat of the cost of acquired culture when you started low and you wanted to go high. She was a woman, what! she sensed that moment, she didn't know if she could handle me, and she had the guts to decide to find out. So we left the party and we drank and (leave it to a Jewish girl to hedge the bet) she drained the best half of my desire in conversation because she was being psychoanalyzed, what a predictable pisser! and she was in that stage where the jargon had the totalitarian force of all vocabularies of mechanism, and she could only speak of her infantile relations to men, and the fixations and resistances of unassimilated penis-envy with all the smug gusto of a female commissar. She was enthusiastic about her analyst, he was also Jewish (they were working now on Jewish self-hatred), he was really an integrated guy,

Stanford Joyce, he belonged to the same mountain as Eliot, she loved the doers and the healers of life who built on the foundationless prevalence of the void those islands of proud endeavor.

"You must get good marks in school," I said to her.

"Of course."

How I envied the jazzed-up grain of the Jews. I was hot for her again, I wanted the salts of her perspiration in my mouth. They would be acrid perhaps, but I would digest them, and those intellectual molecules would rise to my brain.

"I know a girl who went to your bullfighting school," she said to me. She gave her harsh laugh. "My friend thought you were afraid of her. She said you were full of narcissistic anxieties."

"Well, we'll find out," I said.

"Oh, you don't want me. I'm very inadequate as a lover." Her dark hard New York eyes, bright with appetite, considered my head as if I were a delicious and particularly sour pickle.

I paid the check then, and we walked over to my loft. As I had expected, she made no great fuss over the back-and-forth of being seduced—to the contrary. Once we were upstairs, she prowled the length of my loft twice, looked at the hand-made bullfighting equipment I had set up along one wall of the studio, asked me a question or two about the killing machine, studied the swords, asked another question about the cross-guard on the descabellar, and then came back to the living-room—bedroom—dining-room—kitchen of the other room, and made a face at the blood-red wall. When I kissed her she answered with a grinding insistence of her mouth upon mine, and a muscular thrust of her tongue into my throat, as direct and unfeminine as the harsh force of her voice.

"I'd like to hang my clothes up," she said.

It was not all that matter-of-fact when we got to bed. There was nothing very fleshy about the way she made love, no sense of the skin, nor smell, nor touch, just anger, anger at her being there, and another anger which was good for my own, that rage to achieve . . . just what, one cannot say. She made love as if she were running up an inclined wall so steep that to stop for an instant would slide her back to disaster. She hammered her rhythm at me, a hard driving rhythm, an all but monotonous drum, pound into pound against pound into pound until that moment when my anger found its way back again to that delayed and now recovered Time when I wanted to prong her at the party. I had been frustrated, had waited, had lost the anger, and so been taken by her. That finally got me— all through the talk about T. S. Eliot I had been calculating how I would lay waste to her little independence, and now she was alone, with me astride her, going through her paces, teeth biting the pillow, head turned away, using me as the dildoe of a private gallop. So my rage came back, and my rhythm no longer depended upon her drive, but found its own life, and we made love like two club fighters in an open exchange, neither giving ground, rhythm to rhythm, even to even, hypnotic, knowing neither the pain of punishment nor the pride of pleasure, and the equality of this, as hollow as the beat of the drum, seemed to carry her into some better deep of desire, and I had broken through, she was following me, her muscular body writhed all about me with an impersonal abandon, the wanton whip-thrash of a wounded snake, she was on fire and frozen at the same time, and then her mouth was kissing me with a rubbery greedy compulsion so avid to use all there was of me, that to my distant surprise, not in character for the saint to slip into the brutal, my hand came up and clipped her mean and openhanded across the face which brought a cry from her and broke the piston of her hard speed into something softer, wetter, more sly, more warm, I felt as if her belly were opening finally to receive me, and when her mouth kissed me again with a passing tender heat, warm-odored with flesh, and her body sweetened into some feminine embrace of my determination driving its way into her, well, I was gone, it was too late. I had driven right past her in that moment she turned, and I had begun to come, I was coming from all the confluences of my body toward that bud of sweetness I had plucked from her, and for a moment she was making it, she was a move back and surging to overtake me, and then it was gone, she made a mistake, her will ordered all temptings and rhythms to mobilize their march, she drove into the hard stupidities of a marching-band's step, and as I was going off in the best for many a month, she was merely going away, she had lost it again. As I ebbed into what should have been the contentments of a fine after-pleasure, warm and fine, there was one little part of me remaining cold and murderous because she had deprived me, she had fled the domination which was liberty for her, and the rest of the night was bound to be hell.

Her face was ugly. "You're a bastard, do you know that?" she asked me.

"Let it go. I feel good."

"Of course you feel good. Couldn't you have waited one minute?"

I disliked this kind of thing. My duty was reminding me of how her awakened sweets were souring now in the belly, and her nerves were sharpening into the gone electric of being just nowhere.

"I hate inept men," she said.

"Cool it." She could, at least, be a lady. Because if she didn't stop, I would give her back a word or two.

"You did that on purpose," she nagged at me, and I was struck with the intimacy of her rancor—we might as well have been married for ten years to dislike each other so much at this moment.

"Why," I said, "you talk as if this were something unusual for you."

"It is."

"Come on," I told her, "you've never made it in your life."

"How little you know," she said. "This is the first time I've missed in months."

If she had chosen to get my message, I could have been preparing now for a good sleep. Instead I would have to pump myself up again—and as if some ghost of the future laid the squeak of a tickle on my back, I felt an odd dread, not for tonight so much as for some ills of the next ten years whose first life was stirring tonight. But I lay beside her, drew her body against mine, feeling her trapped and irritable heats jangle me as much as they roused me, and while I had no fear that the avenger would remain asleep, still he stirred in pain and in protest, he had supposed his work to be done, and he would claim the wages of overtime from my reserve. That was the way I thought it would go, but Junior from New York University, with her hard body and her passion for proper poetry, gave a lewd and angry old grin as her face stared boldly into mine, and with the practical bawdiness of the Jew she took one straight utilitarian finger, smiled a deceptive girlish pride, and then she jabbed, fingernail and all, into the tight defended core of my clenched buttocks. One wiggle of her knuckle and I threw her off, grunting a sound between rage and surprise, to which she laughed and lay back and waited for me.

Well, she had been right, that finger tipped the balance, and three-quarters with it, and one-quarter hung with the mysteries of sexual ambition, I worked on her like a beaver for forty-odd minutes or more, slapping my tail to build her next, and she worked along while we made the round of the positions, her breath sobbing the exertions, her body as alive as a charged wire and as far from rest.

I gave her all the Time I had in me and more besides, I was weary of her, and the smell which rose from her had so little of the sea and so much of the armpit, that I breathed the stubborn wills of the gymnasium where the tight-muscled search for grace, and it was like that, a hard punishing session with pulley weights, stationary bicycle sprints, and ten breath-seared laps around the track. Yes, when I caught that smell, I knew she would not make it, and so I kept on just long enough to know she was exhausted in body, exhausted beyond the place where a ten-minute rest would have her jabbing that finger into me again, and hating her, hating women who could not take their exercise alone, I lunged up over the hill with my heart pounding past all pleasure, and I came, but with hatred, tight, electric, and empty, the spasms powerful but centered in my heart and not from the hip, the avenger taking its punishment even at the end, jolted clear to the seat of my semen by the succession of rhythmic blows which my heart drummed back to my feet.

For her, getting it from me, it must have been impressive, a convoluted, smashing, and protracted spasm, a hint of the death throe in the animal male which cannot but please the feminine taste for the mortal wound. "Oh, you're lucky," she whispered in my ear as I lay all collapsed beside her, alone in my athlete's absorption upon the whisperings of damage in the unlit complexities of my inner body. I was indeed an athlete, I knew my body was my future, and I had damaged it a bit tonight by most certainly doing it no good. I disliked her for it with the simple dislike we know for the stupid.

"Want a cigarette?" she asked.

I could wait, my heart would have preferred its rest, but there was something tired in her voice beyond the fatigue of what she had done. She too had lost after all. So I came out of my second rest to look at her, and her face had the sad relaxation (and serenity) of a young whore who has finished a hard night's work with the expected lack of issue for herself, content with no more than the money and the professional sense of the hard job dutifully done.

"I'm sorry you didn't make it," I said to her.

She shrugged. There was a Jewish tolerance for the expected failures of the flesh. "Oh, well, I lied to you before," she said.

"You never have been able to, have you?"

"No." She was fingering the muscles of my shoulder, as if in unconscious competition with my strength. "You're pretty good," she said grudgingly.

"Not really inept?" I asked.

"*Sans façons*," said the poetess in an arch change of mood which irritated me. "Sandy has been illuminating those areas where my habits make for destructive impulses."

"Sandy is Doctor Joyce?" She nodded. "You make him sound like your navigator," I told her.

"Isn't it a little obvious to be hostile to psychoanalysis?"

Three minutes ago we had been belaboring each other in the nightmare of the last round, and now we were close to cozy. I put the sole of my foot on her sharp little knee.

"You know the first one we had?" she asked me. "Well, I wanted to tell you. I came close—I guess I came as close as I ever came."

"You'll come closer. You're only nineteen."

"Yes, but this evening has been disturbing to me. You see I get more from you than I get from my lover."

Her lover was twenty-one, a senior at Columbia, also Jewish—which lessened interest, she confessed readily. Besides, Arthur was too passive— "Basically, it's very comprehensible," said the commissar, "an aggressive female and a passive male—we complement one another, and that's no good." Of course it was easy to find satisfaction with Arthur, "via the oral perversions. That's because, vaginally, I'm anaesthetized—a good phallic narcissist like you doesn't do enough for me."

In the absence of learned credentials, she was setting out to bully again. So I thought to surprise her. "Aren't you mixing your language a little?" I began. "The phallic narcissist is one of Wilhelm Reich's categories."

"Therefore?"

"Aren't you a Freudian?"

"It would be presumptuous of me to say," she said like a seminar student working for his pee-aitch-dee. "But Sandy is an eclectic. He accepts a lot of Reich—you see, he's very ambitious, he wants to arrive at his own synthesis." She exhaled some smoke in my face, and gave a nice tough little grin which turned her long serious young witch's face into something indeed less presumptuous. "Besides," she said, "you are a phallic narcissist. There's an element of the sensual which is lacking in you."

"But Arthur possesses it?"

"Yes, he does. And you . . . you're not very juicy."

"I wouldn't know what you mean."

"I mean this." With the rich cruel look of a conquistador finding a new chest of Indian gold, she bent her head and gave one fleeting satiric half-moon of a lick to the conjugation of my balls. "That's what I mean," she said, and was out of the bed even as I was recognizing that she was finally not without art. "Come back," I said.

But she was putting her clothes on in a hurry. "Shut up. Just don't give me your goddamned superiority."

I knew what it was: she had been about to gamble the reserves which belonged to Arthur, and the thought of possibly wasting them on a twenty-seven-year-old connoisseur like myself was too infuriating to take the risk.

So I lay in bed and laughed at her while she dressed—I did not really want a go at things again—and besides, the more I laughed, the angrier she would be, but the anger would work to the surface, and beneath it would be resting the pain that the evening had ended on so little.

She took her leisure going to the door, and I got up in time to tell her to wait—I would walk her to the subway. The dawn had come, however, and she wanted to go alone, she had had a bellyful of me, she could tell me that.

My brain was lusting its own private futures of how interesting it would be to have this proud, aggressive, vulgar, tense, stiff and arrogant Jewess going wild on my bottom—I had turned more than one girl on, but never a one of quite this type. I suppose she had succeeded instead of me; I was ready to see her again and improve the message.

She turned down all dates, but compromised by giving me her address and the number of her telephone. And then glaring at me from the open door, she said, "I owe you a slap in the face."

"Don't go away feeling unequal."

I might have known she would have a natural punch. My jaw felt it for half an hour after she was gone and it took another thirty minutes before I could bring myself back to concluding that she was one funny kid.

All of that added up to the first night with the commissar, and I saw her two more times over this stretch, the last on the night when she finally agreed to sleep over with me, and I came awake in the morning to see her glaring at my head. So often in sex, when the second night wound itself up with nothing better in view than the memory of the first night, I was reminded of Kafka's *Castle,* that tale of the search of a man for his apocalyptic orgasm: in the easy optimism of a young man, he almost captures the castle on the first day, and is never to come so close again. Yes, that was the saga of the nervous system of a man as it was bogged into the defeats, complications, and frustrations of middle age. I still had my future before me of course—the full engagement of my will in some go-for-broke I considered worthy of myself was yet to come, but there were times in that loft when I knew the psychology of an old man, and my second night with Denise—for Denise Gondelman was indeed her name—left me racked for it amounted to so little that we could not even leave it there—the hangover would have been too great for both of us—and so we made a date for a third night. Over and over in those days I used to compare the bed to the bullfight, sometimes seeing myself as the matador and sometimes as the bull, and this second appearance, if it had taken place, in the Plaza Mexico, would have been a *fracaso* with kapok seat cushions jeering down on the ring, and a stubborn cowardly bull staying in *querencia* before the doubtful prissy overtures, the gloomy trim technique of a veteran and mediocre *torero* on the worst of days when he is forced to wonder if he has even his *pundonor* to sustain him. It was a gloomy deal. Each of us knew it was possible to be badly worked by the other, and this seemed so likely that neither of us would gamble a finger. Although we got into bed and had a perfunctory ten minutes, it was as long as an hour in a coffee shop when two friends are done with one another.

By the third night we were ready for complexities again; to see a woman three times is to call on the dialectic of an affair. If the waves we were making belonged less to the viper of passion than the worm of inquiry, still it was obvious from the beginning that we had surprises for one another. The second night we had been hoping for more, and so got less; this third night, we each came on with the notion to wind it up, and so got involved in more.

For one thing, Denise called me in the afternoon. There was studying she had to do, and she wondered if it would be all right to come to my place at eleven instead of meeting me for drinks and dinner. Since that would save me ten dollars she saw no reason why I should complain. It was a down conversation. I had been planning to lay siege to her, dispense a bit of elixir from my vast reservoirs of charm, and instead she was going to keep it *in camera*. There was a quality about her I could not locate, something independent—abruptly, right there, I knew what it was. In a year she would have no memory of me, I would not exist for her unless . . . and then it was clear . . . unless I could be the first to carry her stone of no-orgasm up the cliff, all the way, over and out into the sea. That was the kick I could find, that a year from now, five years from now, down all the seasons to the hours of her old age, I would be the one she would be forced to remember, and it would nourish me a little over the years, thinking of that grudged souvenir which could not die in her, my blond hair, my blue eyes, my small broken nose, my clean mouth and chin, my height, my boxer's body, my parts—yes, I was getting excited at the naked image of me in the young-old mind of that sour sexed-up dynamo of black-pussied frustration.

A phallic narcissist she had called me. Well, I was phallic enough, a Village stickman who could muster enough of the divine It on the head of his will to call forth more than one becoming out of the womb of feminine Time, yes a good deal more than one from my fifty new girls a year, and when I failed before various prisons of frigidity, it mattered little. Experience gave the cue that there were ladies who would not be moved an inch by a year of the best, and so I looked for other things in them, but this one, this Den-of-Ease, she was ready, she was entering the time of her Time, and if not me, it would be another—I was sick in advance at the picture of some bearded Negro cat who would score where I had missed and thus cuckold me in spirit, deprive me of those telepathic waves of longing (in which I obviously believed) speeding away to me from her over the years to balm the hours when I was beat, because I had been her psychic bridegroom, had plucked her ideational diddle, had led her down the walk of her real wedding night. Since she did not like me, what a feat to pull it off.

In the hours I waited after dinner, alone, I had the sense—which I always trusted—that tonight this little victory or defeat would be full of leverage, magnified beyond its emotional matter because I had decided to bet on myself that I would win, and a defeat would bring me closer to a general depression, a fog bank of dissatisfaction with myself which I knew could last for months or more. Whereas a victory would add to the panoplies of my ego some peculiar (but for me, valid) ingestion of her arrogance, her stubbornness, and her will—those necessary ingredients of which I could not yet have enough for my own ambition.

When she came in she was wearing a sweater and dungarees which I had been expecting, but there was a surprise for me. Her braids had been clipped, and a short cropped curled Italian haircut decorated her head, moving her severe young face across the spectrum from the austerities of a poetess to a hint of all those practical and promiscuous European girls who sold their holy hump to the Germans and had been subsequently punished by shaved heads—how attractive the new hair proved; once punished, they were now free, free to be wild, the worst had happened and they were still alive with the taste of the first victor's flesh enriching the sensual curl of the mouth.

Did I like her this way? Denise was interested to know. Well, it was a shock, I admitted, a pleasant shock. If it takes you so long to decide, you must be rigid, she let me know. Well, yes, as a matter of fact I was rigid, rigid for her with waiting.

The nun of severity passed a shade over her. She hated men who were uncool, she thought she would tell me.

"Did your analyst tell you it's bad to be uncool?"

She had taken off her coat, but now she gave me a look as if she were ready to put it on again. "No, he did not tell me that." She laughed spitefully. "But he told me a couple of revealing things about you."

"Which you won't repeat."

"Of course not."

"I'll never know," I said, and gave her the first kiss of the evening. Her mouth was heated—it was the best kiss I had received from her, and it brought me on too quickly—"My fruit is ready to be plucked," said the odors of her mouth, betraying that perfume of the ducts which, against her will no doubt, had been plumping for me. She was changed tonight. From the skin of her face and the glen of her neck came a new smell, sweet, sweaty, and tender, the smell of a body which had been used and had enjoyed its uses. It came to me nicely, one of the nicest smells in quite some time, so different from the usual exudations of her dissatisfied salts that it opened a chain of reflexes in me, and I was off in all good speed on what Denise would probably have called the vertical foreplay. I suppose I went at her like a necrophiliac let loose upon a still-warm subject, and as I gripped her, grasped her, groped her, my breath a bellows to blow her into my own flame, her body remained unmoving, only her mouth answering my call, those lips bridling hot adolescent kisses back upon my face, the smell almost carrying me away—such a fine sweet sweat.

Naturally she clipped the rhythm. As I started to slip up her sweater, she got away and said a little huskily, "I'll take my own clothes off." Once again I could have hit her. My third eye, that athlete's inner eye which probed its vision into all the corners, happy and distressed of my body whole, was glumly cautioning the congestion of the spirits in the coils of each teste. They would have to wait, turn rancid, maybe die of delay.

Off came the sweater and the needless brassière, her economical breasts swelled just a trifle tonight, enough to take on the convexities of an Amazon's armor. Open came the belt and the zipper of her dungarees, zipped from the front which pleased her not a little. Only her ass, a small masterpiece, and her strong thighs, justified this theatre. She stood there naked, quite psychicly clothed, and lit a cigarette.

If a stiff prick has no conscience, it has also no common sense. I stood there like a clown, trying to coax her to take a ride with me on the bawdy car, she out of her clothes, I in all of mine, a muscular little mermaid to melt on my knee. She laughed, one harsh banker's snort—she was giving no loans on my idiot's collateral.

"You didn't even ask me," Denise thought to say, "of how my studying went tonight."

"What did you study?"

"I didn't. I didn't study." She gave me a lovely smile, girlish and bright. "I just spent the last three hours with Arthur."

"You're a dainty type," I told her.

But she gave me a bad moment. That lovely flesh-spent smell, scent of the well used and the tender, that avatar of the feminine my senses had accepted so greedily, came down now to no more than the rubbings and the sweats of what was probably a very nice guy, passive Arthur with his Jewish bonanzas of mouth-love.

The worst of it was that it quickened me more. I had the selfish wisdom to throw such evidence upon the mercy of my own court. For the smell of Arthur was the smell of love, at least for me, and so from man or woman, it did not matter—the smell of love was always feminine—and if the man in Denise was melted by the woman in Arthur, so Arthur might have flowered that woman in himself from the arts of a real woman, his mother? —it did not matter—that voiceless message which passed from the sword of the man into the cavern of the woman was carried along from body to body, and if it was not the woman in Denise I was going to find tonight, at least I would be warmed by the previous trace of another. ·

But that was a tone poem to quiet the toads of my doubt. When Denise —it took five more minutes—finally decided to expose herself on my clumped old mattress, the sight of her black pubic hair, the feel of the foreign but brotherly liquids in her unembarrassed maw, turned me into a jackrabbit of pissy tumescence, the quicks of my excitement beheaded from the resonances of my body, and I wasn't with her a half-minute before I was over, gone, and off. I rode not with the strength to reap the harem of her and her lover, but spit like a pinched little boy up into black forested hills of motherly contempt, a passing picture of the nuns of my childhood to drench my piddle spurtings with failures of gloom. She it was who proved stronger than me, she the he to my silly she.

All considered, Denise was nice about it. Her harsh laugh did not crackle over my head, her hand in passing me the after-cigarette settled for no more than a nudge of my nose, and if it were not for the contempt of her tough grin, I would have been left with no more than the alarm to the sweepers of my brain to sweep this failure away.

"Hasn't happened in years," I said to her, the confession coming out of me with the cost of the hardest cash.

"Oh, shut up. Just rest." And she began to hum a mocking little song. I lay there in a state, parts of me jangled for forty-eight hours to come, and yet not altogether lost to peace. I knew what it was. Years ago in the air force, as an enlisted man, I had reached the light-heavyweight finals on my air base. For two weeks I trained for the championship, afraid of the other man all the way because I had seen him fight and felt he was better than me; when my night came, he took me out with a left hook to the liver which had me conscious on the canvas but unable to move, and as the referee was counting, which I could hear all too clearly, I knew the same kind of peace, a swooning peace, a clue to that kind of death in which an old man slips away—nothing mattered except that my flesh was vulnerable and I had a dim revery, lying there with the yells of the air force crowd in my ears, there was some far-off vision of green fields and me lying in them, giving up all ambition to go back instead to another, younger life of the senses, and I remember at that moment I watered the cup of my boxer's jock, and then I must have slipped into something new, for as they picked me off the canvas the floor seemed to recede from me at a great rate as if I were climbing in an airplane.

A few minutes later, the nauseas of the blow to my liver had me retching into my hands, and the tension of three weeks of preparation for that fight came back. I knew through the fading vistas of my peace, and the oncoming spasms of my nausea, that the worst was yet to come, and it would take me weeks to unwind, and then years, and maybe never to overcome the knowledge that I had failed completely at a moment when I wanted very much to win.

A ghost of this peace, trailing intimations of a new nausea, was passing over me again, and I sat up in bed abruptly, as if to drive these weaknesses back into me. My groin had been simmering for hours waiting for Denise, and it was swollen still, but the avenger was limp, he had deserted my cause, I was in a spot if she did not co-operate.

Co-operate she did. "My God, lie down again, will you," she said, "I was thinking that finally I had seen you relax."

And then I could sense that the woman in her was about to betray her victory. She sat over me, her little breasts budding with their own desire, her short hair alive and flowering, her mouth ready to taste her gentleman's defeat. I had only to raise my hand, and push her body in the direction she wished it to go, and then her face was rooting in me, her angry tongue and voracious mouth going wild finally as I had wished it, and I knew the sadness of sour timing, because this was a prize I could not enjoy as I would have on the first night, and yet it was good enough—not art, not the tease and languor of love on a soft mouth, but therapy, therapy for her, the quick exhaustions of the tension in a harsh throat, the beseechment of an ugly voice going down into the expiation which would be its beauty. Still it was good, practically it was good, my ego could bank the hard cash that this snotty head was searching me, the act served its purpose, anger traveled from her body into mine, the avenger came to attention, cold and furious, indifferent to the trapped doomed pleasure left behind in my body on that initial and grim piddle spurt, and I was ready, not with any joy nor softness nor warmth nor care, but I was ready finally to take her tonight, I was going to beat new Time out of her if beat her I must, I was going to teach her that she was only a child, because if at last I could not take care of a nineteen-year-old, then I was gone indeed. And so I took her with a cold calculation, the rhythms of my body corresponding to no more than a metronome in my mind, tonight the driving mechanical beat would come from me, and blind to nerve-raddlings in my body, and blood pressures in my brain, I worked on her like a riveter, knowing her resistances were made of steel, I threw her a fuck the equivalent of a fifteen-round fight, I wearied her, I brought her back, I drove my fingers into her shoulders and my knees into her hips, I went, and I went, and I went, I bore her high and thumped her hard, I sprinted, I paced, I lay low, eyes all closed, under sexual water, like a submarine listening for the distant sound of her ship's motors, hoping to steal up close and trick her rhythms away.

And she was close. Oh, she was close so much of the time. Like a child on a merry-go-round the touch of the colored ring just evaded the tips of her touch, and she heaved and she hurdled, arched and cried, clawed me, kissed me, even gave a shriek once, and then her sweats running down and her will weak, exhausted even more than me, she felt me leave and lie beside her. Yes, I did that with a tactician's cunning, I let the depression of her failure poison what was left of her will never to let me succeed, I gave her slack to mourn the lost freedoms and hate the final virginity for which she fought, I even allowed her baffled heat to take its rest and attack her nerves once more, and then, just as she was beginning to fret against me in a new and unwilling appeal, I turned her over suddenly on her belly, my avenger wild with the mania of the madman, and giving her no chance, holding her prone against the mattress with the strength of my weight, I drove into the seat of all stubbornness, tight as a vise, and I wounded her, I knew it, she thrashed beneath me like a trapped little animal, making not a sound, but fierce not to allow me this last of the liberties, and yet caught, forced to give up millimeter by millimeter the bridal ground of her symbolic and therefore real vagina. So I made it, I made it all the way—it took ten minutes and maybe more, but as the avenger rode down to his hilt and tunneled the threshold of sexual home all those inches closer into the bypass of the womb, she gave at last a little cry of farewell, and I could feel a new shudder which began as a ripple and rolled into a wave, and then it rolled over her, carrying her along, me hardly moving for fear of damping this quake from her earth, and then it was gone, but she was left alive with a larger one to follow.

So I turned her once again on her back, and moved by impulse to love's first hole. There was an odor coming up, hers at last, the smell of the sea, and none of the armpit or a dirty sock, and I took her mouth and kissed it, but she was away, following the wake of her own waves which mounted, fell back, and in new momentum mounted higher and should have gone over, and then she was about to hang again, I could feel it, that moment of hesitation between the past and the present, the habit and the adventure, and I said into her ear, "You dirty little Jew."

That whipped her over. A first wave kissed, a second spilled, and a third and a fourth and a fifth came breaking over, and finally she was away, she was loose in the water for the first time in her life, and I would have liked to go with her, but I was blood-throttled and numb, and as she had the first big moment in her life, I was nothing but a set of aching balls and a congested cock, and I rode with her wistfully, looking at the contortion of her face and listening to her sobbing sound of "Oh, Jesus, I made it, oh Jesus, I did."

"Compliments of T. S. Eliot," I whispered to myself, and my head was aching, my body was shot. She curled against me, she kissed my sweat, she nuzzled my eyes and murmured in my ear, and then she was slipping away into the nicest of weary sweet sleep.

"Was it good for you too?" she whispered half-awake, having likewise read the works of The Hemingway, and I said, "Yeah, fine," and after she was asleep, I disengaged myself carefully, and prowled the loft, accepting the hours it would take for my roiled sack to clean its fatigues and know a little sleep. But I had abused myself too far, and it took till dawn and half a fifth of whisky before I dropped into an unblessed stupor. When I awoke, in that moment before I moved to look at her, and saw her glaring at me, I was off on a sluggish masculine debate as to whether the kick of studying this Denise for another few nights—now that I had turned the key—would be worth the danger of deepening into some small real feeling. But through my hangover and the knowledge of the day and the week and the month it would take the different parts of all of me to repair, I was also knowing the taste of a reinforced will—finally, I had won. At no matter what cost, and with what luck, and with a piece of charity from her, I had won nonetheless, and since all real pay came from victory, it was more likely that I would win the next time I gambled my stake on something more appropriate for my ambition.

Then I turned, saw the hatred in her eyes, turned over again, and made believe I was asleep while a dread of the next few minutes weighed a leaden breath over the new skin of my ego.

"You're awake, aren't you?" she said.

I made no answer.

"All right, I'm going then. I'm getting dressed." She whipped out of bed, grabbed her clothes, and began to put them on with all the fury of waiting for me to get the pronouncement. "That was a lousy thing you did last night," she said by way of a start.

In truth she looked better than she ever had. The severe lady and the tough little girl of yesterday's face had put forth the first agreements on what would yet be a bold chick.

"I gave you what you could use," I made the mistake of saying.

"Just didn't you," she said, and was on her way to the door. "Well, cool it. You don't do anything to me." Then she smiled. "You're so impressed with what you think was such a marvelous notch you made in me, listen, Buster, I came here last night thinking of what Sandy Joyce told me about you, and he's right, oh man is he right." Standing in the open doorway, she started to light a cigarette, and then threw the matches to the floor. From thirty feet away I could see the look in her eyes, that unmistakable point for the kill that you find in the eyes of very few bullfighters, and then having created her pause, she came on for her moment of truth by saying, "He told me your whole life is a lie, and you do nothing but run away from the homosexual that is you."

And like a real killer, she did not look back, and was out the door before I could rise to tell her that she was a hero fit for me.

JOYCE CAROL OATES

(b. 1938) Born in Lockport, New York, Joyce Carol Oates was educated at Syracuse University and the University of Wisconsin. After teaching for several years at the University of Detroit, she became a professor at the University of Windsor, Canada, where she now lives. Productive and versatile since publishing her first novel in 1963, she has written short stories, novels, plays, poetry, and a great deal of literary criticism, for which she has received much acclaim and many awards.

THE GIRL

I Background Material

Came by with a truck, The Director and Roybay and a boy I didn't know. Roybay leaned out the window, very friendly. I got in and we drove around for a while. The Director telling us about his movie-vision, all speeded-up because his friend, his contact, had lent him the equipment from an educational film company in town, and it had to be back Sunday P.M. The Director said: "It's all a matter of art and compromise." He was very excited. I knew him from before, a few days before; his name was DePinto or DeLino, something strange, but he was called The Director. He was in the third person most of the time.

Roybay, two hundred fifty pounds, very cheerful and easy and my closest friend of all of them, was The Motorcyclist. They used his motorcycle for an authentic detail. It didn't work; it was broken down. But they propped it up in the sand and it looked very real.

A boy with a scruffy face, like an explorer's face, was The Cop.

I was The Girl.

The Director said: "Oh Jesus honey your tan, your tanned legs, your feet, my God even your feet your toes, are tan, tanned, you're so lovely. . . ." And he stared at me, he stared. When we met before, he had not stared like this. His voice was hoarse, his eyebrows ragged. It was all music with him, his voice and his way of moving, the life inside him. "I mean, look at her! Isn't she—? Isn't it?"

"Perfect," Roybay said.

The boy with the scruffy face, wedged in between Roybay the driver and The Director, with me on The Director's lap and my legs sort of on his lap, stared at me and turned out to be a kid my age. I caught a look of his but rejected it. I never found out his name.

Later they said to me: "What were their names? Don't you know? Can't you remember? Can't you—?"

They were angry. They said: "Describe them."

But.

The Director. The Motorcyclist. The Cop. The Girl.

I thought there were more, more than that. If you eliminate The Girl. If you try to remember. More? More than two? Oh, I believe a dozen or two, fifty, any large reasonable number tramping down the sand. There was the motorcycle, broken. They hauled it out in the back of the truck with the film equipment and other stuff. I could describe the Santa Monica Freeway if I wanted to. But not them. I think there were more than three but I don't know. Where did they come from? Who were they? The reason I could describe the Freeway is that I knew it already, not memorized but in pieces, the way you know your environment.

I was The Girl. No need to describe. Anyone studying me, face to face, would be in my presence and would not need a description. I looked different. The costume didn't matter, the bright red and green shapes— cats and kittens—wouldn't show anyway. The film was black-and-white. It was a short-skirted dress, a top that tied in back, looped around and tied in back like a halter, the material just cotton or anything, bright shapes of red and green distortions in the material. It came from a Miss Chelsea shop in Van Nuys. I wasn't wearing anything else, anything underneath.

Someone real said to me later, a real policeman: ". . . need your cooperation. . . ."

The Director explained that he needed everyone's cooperation. He had assisted someone making a film once, or he had watched it happen, he said how crucial it is to cooperate; he wouldn't have the footage for re-takes and all the equipment had to be returned in eighteen hours. Had a sharkish skinny glamourish face, a wide-brimmed hat perched on his head. Wore sunglasses. We all did. The beach was very bright at three in the afternoon. I had yellow-lensed glasses with white plastic wrap-around frames, like goggles. It wasn't very warm. The wind came in from the ocean, chilly.

The way up, I got hypnotized by the expressway signs and all the names of the towns and beaches and the arrows pointing up off to the right, always up off to the right and off the highway and off the map.

"Which stretch of beach? Where? How far up the coast? Can't you identify it, can't you remember? We need your cooperation, can't you cooperate?"

On film, any stretch of beach resembles any stretch of beach. They called it The Beach.

II   *The Rehearsal*

The Director moved us around, walked with us; put his hands on me and turned me, stepped on my bare feet, scratched his head up beneath the straw-colored hat, made noises with his mouth, very excited, saying to himself little words: "Here—yeah—like this—this—this way—" The Motorcyclist, who was Roybay, straddled the motorcycle to wait. Had a sunny broad face with red-blond-brown hair frizzy all around it. Even his beard was frizzy. It wasn't hot but he looked hot. Was six foot three or four, taller than my father, who is or was six foot exactly. That is my way of telling if a man is tall: taller than my father, then he's *tall*; shorter than my father, *not tall*. The world could be divided that way.

No, I haven't seen my father for a while. But the world is still there.

The Director complained about the setting. The beach was beautiful but empty. "Got to imagine people crowding in, people in the place of boulders and rocks and scrubby damn flowers and sand dunes and eucalyptus and all this crap, it's hobbling to the eye," he said. He had wanted a city movie. He had wanted the movie to take place in the real world. "Really wanted Venice Beach on a Sunday, packed, but room for the motorcycle, and the whole world crowded in . . . a miscellaneous flood of people, souls, to represent the entire world . . . and the coming-together of the world in my story. In The Girl. Oh look at her," he said dreamily, looking at me, "couldn't the world come together in her? It could. But this place is so empty . . . it's wild here, a wild innocent natural setting, it's too beautiful, it could be a travelogue. . . ."

The Cop asked about splicing things together. Couldn't you—?

The Director waved him away. It was hard to concentrate.

The Cop giggled and whispered to me: "Jeeze, these guys are something, huh? How'd you meet them? I met them this morning. Where do you go to school? You go to school? Around here?"

I snubbed him, eye-to-eye.

He blushed. He was about sixteen, behind his bushy hair and sunglasses and policeman's hat. It had a tin badge on it. The Director had bought it at a costume store. The Cop had only a hat. The rest of him was a T-shirt and jeans. A club two feet long and maybe an inch and a half in diameter, but no gun. The Director had found the club in a garbage can, he said, months ago. He carried it everywhere with him. It had generated his need for a film, he said; he kept taking it from The Cop and using it to make lines in the sand.

The Director's mind was always going. It was white-hot. His body never stopped, his knees jerked as if keeping time to something. I felt the energy in him, even when he wasn't touching me. Only when he held the camera in his hands, between his hands, was he calmed down.

After a while, Roybay said, sounding nervous: "What do we do? What do I do? Somebody might come along here, huh?—we better hurry it up, huh?"

"This can't be hurried," The Director said.

The Motorcyclist was the only one of them I knew. His name was *Roybay*. Or *Robbie*. Or maybe it was *Roy Bean* (?) . . . sometimes just *Roy* or *Ray*. Said he came over from Trinidad, Colorado—I think. Or someone else his size said that, some other day. Had a big worried forehead tanned pink-red. You don't tan dark, with a complexion like that. He wore a crash helmet and goggles and a leather jacket, the sleeves a little short for his arms. The night I met him, he was explaining the fact that vegetables are not meek and passive, as people think, but exert great pressure in forcing themselves up through the soil . . . and think about vines, twisting tendrils, feelers that could choke large animals to death or pull them down into quicksand. . . . He was a vegetarian, but he scorned meekness. Believed in strength. Up at 7 A.M. for two hours of weight-lifting, very slow, Yoga-slow, and a careful diet of vegetables and vegetable juices. Said fruit was too acid, too sharp. Explained that an ox's muscles were extremely powerful and that the carnivores of the world could learn from the ox.

Or his name could have been something like *Roy baby, Roy, baby* if someone called out and slurred the words together.

The Director placed rocks on the sand. Kicked dents in the sand. He cleared debris out of the way, tossing things hand over hand, then he found a child's toy—a fire truck—and stood with it, spinning the little wheels, thinking, then he moved one of the rocks a few inches and said to me: "You walk to this point. Try it."

They watched.

The Director said that I was a sweet girl. He said that now I should practice running, from the rock out to the water. He followed alongside me. He told me when to stop. He kissed my forehead and said I was very sweet, this was part of the tragedy. He tossed the toy fire truck off to the side. Rubbed his hands together, excited. I could smell it on him, the excitement.

"I'm an orphan," he said suddenly. "I'm from a Methodist orphanage up in Seattle."

The Motorcyclist laughed. The Cop grinned stupidly; he was still standing where The Director had placed him.

"You don't get many chances in life," The Director said, "so I would hate to mess this up. It would make me very angry if something went wrong . . . if one of you went wrong . . . But you're not going to, huh, are you? Not even you?" he said, looking at me. As if I was special. He had a sharkish look caused by one tooth, I think—a side tooth that was a little longer than the rest of his teeth. If you glanced at him you wouldn't notice that tooth, not really; but somehow you would start to think of a shark a few seconds later.

In a magical presence. I knew. I knew but I was outside, not on film. The Director walked with me along the beach, his feet in ankle-high boots and mine bare, talking to me, stroking my arms, saying . . . saying. . . . *What did he say? Don't remember?* No, the noise was too much. The waves. Gulls. Birds. Words come this way and that, I don't catch them all, try to ease with the feeling, the music behind them. I took music lessons once. Piano lessons with Miss Dorsey, three blocks from my grandmother's house; from ten until thirteen. Could memorize. Could count out a beat one two three, *one* two three, one *two* three, a habit to retain throughout life. When The Director told me what to do I listened to the beat of his voice. I knew I was in a magical presence, he was not an ordinary man, but I was outside him, outside waiting. I was not yet The Girl. I was The Girl later.

It was a movie, a movie-making! I screamed. When I woke for the half-dozenth time, snatching at someone's wrist. I clawed, had to make contact. I didn't want to sink back again. I said: *It was real, it was a movie, there was film in the camera!*

You mean someone filmed it? Filmed that? Someone had a camera?

The Director carried it in his hands. Had to adjust it, squinted down into it, made noises with his mouth; he took a long time. The Cop, licking his lips, said to me: "Hey, I thought the movie cameras were real big. Pushed around on wheels. With some moving parts, like a crane or something . . . ? Where are you from?"

"You couldn't push wheels in the sand," I told him.

The Director looked over at us. "What are you two talking about? Be quiet. You," he said to The Cop, "you, you're not in the script yet, you're off-camera, go stand on the other side of that hill. Don't clutter my mind."

He walked out to the surf, stood there, was very agitated. I looked at Roybay, who was looking at me. Our eyes didn't come together; he was looking at me like on film. The Girl. Over there, straddling the broken-down rusty-handle-barred motorcycle, was The Motorcyclist. He was not from Trinidad, Colorado, or from anywhere. I saw The Cop's cap disappear over a hill behind some spiky weeds and ridges of sand.

The Director came back. He said to The Motorcyclist, "What this is, maybe, it's a poem centered in the head of The Cop, but I had it off-center; I was imagining it in The Girl. But . . . but . . . it wasn't working. It's a test of The Cop. I don't know him. Do you? I don't know who the hell he is. It will be an experiment. He rushes in to the rescue . . . and sees the scene and . . . the test is upon him. The audience will see it too. I've been dreaming this for so long, this tiny eight-minute poem," he said, putting his arm around my shoulder now, excited, "I can't miss my chance. It's not just that it's crowding my head, but people are going to be very interested in this; I know certain people who are going to pay a lot to see it. Look, it's a poem, honey. The parts must cooperate. Nothing unripe or resisting. All parts in a poem . . . in a work of art. . . . Please, do you understand, do you?"

So sensitive. It was a sensitive moment. Staring eye-to-eye with me, dark green lenses and yellow lenses, shatter-proof.

I told him yes. I had to say yes. And it was almost true; some of his words caught in me, snagged, like the rough edge of a fingernail in your clothing.

The Director said softly: "What it is . . . is . . . it's a vision, it can't be resisted. Why resist? Resist? Resist anything? If a vision comes up from the inside of the earth, it must be sacred, or down out of the sky— even, equal—because the way up is the same as the way down, the sky is a mirror and vice versa. Right? I wanted The Girl to resist The Motorcyclist and I wanted The Cop to use the club like a Zen master's stick but now I see it differently, with the scene all set. It goes the way it must. You can't control a vision. It's like going down a stairway and you're cautious and frightened and then the stairway breaks, the last step gives way, and you fall and yet you're not afraid, you're not afraid after all, you're saved. You don't understand me, I know, but you'll feel it, you'll understand in a while. Don't resist," he said to me. "If you deny the way things must operate, you turn yourself and everyone else into a phantom. We'll all be here together. One thing. We'll be sacred. Don't doubt. Now I'll talk to The Cop, the Savior . . . he's the Savior. . . . I wonder can he bear the weight of the testing?"

III   The Performance

Space around me. Hair blowing, back toward shore an arrow out of sight. The air is cold. Nervous, but doing O.K.

The Director says in a whisper-shout: "Okay. Okay. No, slow down . . . slow . . . slow down. . . . Look over here. . . . The other way. . . ." It is very easy now that the camera is working. It is very easy. I am The Girl watching the film of The Girl walking on a beach watching the water. Now The Girl watching The Girl turning The Girl in black-and-white approached by a shape, a dark thing, out of the corner of the eye. The eye must be the camera. The dark thing must be a shape with legs, with arms, with a white-helmeted head.

Now the film speeds up.

A surprise, how light you become on film! You are very graceful. It's a suspension of gravity. The Director calls to me, yells to me: *Run. Run.* But I can't. I am too light, and then too heavy; the hand on my shoulder weighs me down. I think I am giggling. *Hurry up! Hurry up!*

The marker is a real rock.

Scream! cries The Director.

But I can't, I can't get breath. They are at me. I scramble up onto my feet. But. But I have lost hold. I can't see. The Director is very close to us, right beside us. *Turn her around, make her scream—hurry up—do it like this, like this, do it fast like this—come on—*

The film is speeded up. Too fast. I have lost hold of it, can't see. I am being driven backwards, downwards, burrowed-into, like a hammer being hammered being hammered against all at once. Do I see noseholes, eyeholes, mouthholes?

Something being pounded into flesh like meat.

IV A Sequel

I was babbling, hanging onto someone's wrist. Not the doctor, who was in a hurry on his rounds, but a nurse. I said: "Did they find them? The police? Did it get in the newspapers? Was the movie shown? Was it—?"

What? What? At the important instant I lost sight of her, one adult face like another. Then it contracted into someone's regular-sized face. The ceiling above him seemed to open behind his face and to glow, fluorescent lighting as if for a stage, a studio. Why, this must be someone who knows me! He is looking at me without disgust. I don't know him. But I pretend. I ask him if they were caught, if—He says not to think about it right now. He says not to think about it. He says: "The police, they won't find them anyway . . . they don't give a damn about you . . . don't torture yourself."

But, but.

Raw reddened meat, scraped raw, hair yanked out in handfuls. A scalp bleeding and sandy. Sandy grit in my mouth. It was a jelly, a transformation. But I wanted to know. Wanted. I reached for his wrist but couldn't get it.

You can be real, but you can be stronger than real; speeded-up, lighted-up. It does take a camera. The Director helped them drag me back saying *Oh it was beautiful . . . it was beautiful . . .* and there were tears in the creases around his mouth. I strained to get free, to break the shape out of my head and into his. Strained, twisted. But there was too much noise. The back of my head was hurt and emptied out. Too much battered into me, I couldn't tell them apart, there were two of them but maybe two hundred or two thousand, I couldn't know.

But I couldn't talk right. The man tried to listen politely but here is what I said: ". . . rockhand, two of them, bird-burrow, truck, toy, wheel, the arrow, the exit, the way out. . . ." Another man, also in the room, tried to interrupt. Kept asking "Who were they? How many? Five, six, a dozen? Twenty? Where did it happen? Where did you meet them? Who are you?" but I kept on talking, babbling, now I was saying saints' names

that got into my head somehow . . . the names of saints like beads on
a rosary, but I didn't know them, the saints had terrible names to twist
my head out of shape: ". . . Saint Camarillo, Saint Oxnard, Saint . . .
Saint Ventura . . . Saint Ynez . . . Saint Goleta . . . Saint Gaviota
. . . Saint Jalama . . . Saint Casmalia . . . Saint Saint Saint. . . ."

V The Vision

A rainy wintry day, and I crossed Carpenter Street and my eye drifted right
onto someone. The Director. I stared at him and started to run after him.
He turned around, staring. Didn't recognize me. Didn't know. Behind
him a laundromat, some kids playing in the doorway, yelling. Too much
confusion. The Director walked sideways, sideways staring at me, trying to
remember. He hadn't any sunglasses now. His skin was sour-looking.

I ran up to him. I said: "Don't you remember? Don't you—?"

I laughed.

I forgave him, he looked so sick. He was about twenty-eight, thirty
years old. Edgy, cautious. Creases down both sides of his mouth.

He stared at me.

Except for the rain and a bad cold, my eyes reddened, I was pretty
again and recovered. I laughed but started to remember something out
of the corner of my eye. Didn't want to remember. So I smiled, grinned at
him, and he tried to match the way I looked.

"I'm new here, I just came here . . . I'm from. . . . I'm from up the
coast, from Seattle. . . . I don't know you. . . ."

A kind of shutter clicked in his head. Showing in his eyes. He was
walking sideways and I reached out for his wrist, a bony wrist, and he
shook me loose. His lips were thin and chalk-colored, chalky cheesy sour-
colored. One of his nostrils was bigger than the other and looked sore.
That single shark tooth was greenish. He said: " . . . just in for a day,
overnight, down from Seattle and . . . uh . . . I don't know you. . . .
Don't remember. I'm confused. I'm not well, my feet are wet, I'm from
out of town."

"What happened to the movie?" I asked.

He watched me. A long time passed. Someone walked by him on the
pavement, in the rain, the way passersby walk in a movie, behind the
main actors. They are not in focus and that person was not in focus either.

"Was it a real movie? Did it have film, the camera?" I asked. Beginning
to be afraid. Beginning. But I kept it back, the taste in my mouth. Kept
smiling to show him no harm. "Oh hey look," I said, "look, it had film,
didn't it? I mean it had film? I mean you made a real movie, didn't you?
I mean—"

Finally he began to see me. The creases around his mouth turned into
a smile. It was like a crucial scene now; he put his hand on my shoulder
and kissed my forehead, in the rain. He said: "Honey oh yeah. Yeah.

Don't you ever doubt that. I mean, did you doubt that? All these months? You should never have doubted that. I mean, that's the whole thing. That's it. That's the purpose, the center, the reason behind it, all of it, the focus, the. . . . You know what I mean? The Vision?"

I knew what he meant.

So I was saved.

NTOZAKE SHANGE

(b. 1948) Born Paulette Williams in Trenton, New Jersey, Shange took her pseudonym as an expression of her anger at the dilemma of being a black woman. In Zulu the name means "she who comes with her own things" /"she who walks like a lion." Educated at Barnard College and the University of Southern California, Shange has taught women's studies in college. Since 1975 she has been experimenting with poetic drama both as performer and playwright. Her first "choreo-poem," *For Colored Girls Who Have Considered Suicide/When the Rainbow Is Enuf*, moved to Broadway in 1976 and has been widely produced. Two other plays were produced in 1977; collections of poems appeared in 1977 and 1978.

WITH NO IMMEDIATE CAUSE

every 3 minutes a woman is beaten
every five minutes a
woman is raped/every ten minutes
a lil girl is molested
yet i rode the subway today
i sat next to an old man who
may have beaten his old wife
3 minutes ago or 3 days/30 years ago
he might have sodomized his
daughter but i sat there
cuz the young men on the train
might beat some young women
later in the day or tomorrow
i might not shut my door fast
enuf/push hard enuf
every 3 minutes it happens
some woman's innocence
rushes to her cheeks/pours from her mouth
like the betsy wetsy dolls have been torn

apart/their mouths
menses red & split/every
three minutes a shoulder
is jammed through plaster and the oven door/
chairs push thru the rib cage/hot water or
boiling sperm decorate her body
i rode the subway today
& bought a paper from a
man who might
have held his old lady onto
a hot pressing iron/i dont know
maybe he catches lil girls in the
park & rips open their behinds
with steel rods/i can't decide
what he might have done i only
know every 3 minutes
every 5 minutes every 10 minutes/so
i bought the paper
looking for the announcement
the discovery/of the dismembered
woman's body/the
victims have not all been
identified/today they are
naked and dead/refuse to
testify/one girl out of 10's not
coherent/i took the coffee
& spit it up/i found an
announcement/not the woman's
bloated body in the river/floating
not the child bleeding in the
59th street corridor/not the baby
broken on the floor/
    "there is some concern
    that alleged battered women
    might start to murder their
    husbands & lovers with no
    immediate cause"
i spit up i vomit i am screaming
we all have immediate cause
every 3 minutes
every 5 minutes
every 10 minutes

NTOZAKE SHANGE

every day
women's bodies are found
in alleys & bedrooms/at the top of the stairs
before i ride the subway/buy a paper/drink
coffee/i must know/
have you hurt a woman today
did you beat a woman today
throw a child across a room
   are the lil girl's panties
   in yr pocket
did you hurt a woman today

i have to ask these obscene questions
the authorities require me to
establish
immediate cause

every three minutes
every five minutes
every ten minutes
every day.

MARGARET ATWOOD

(b. 1939) Margaret Atwood studied at the University of Toronto in her native Canada and at Harvard; her home is in Alliston, Ontario, although since 1964 she has taught in various universities across Canada. She has published seven volumes of poetry, two of which won prestigious awards Her novel *Surfacing* (1972) was widely acclaimed; her most recent novel, *Life Before Man* (1980), establishes her as a major writer of our time.

from CIRCE—MUD POEMS

This story was told to me by another traveller, just passing through. It took place in a foreign country, as everything does.

When he was young he and another boy constructed a woman out of mud. She began at the neck and ended at the knees and elbows: they stuck to the essentials. Every sunny day they would row across to the island where she lived, in the afternoon when the sun had warmed her, and make love to her, sinking with ecstasy into her soft moist belly, her brown wormy flesh where small weeds had already rooted. They would take turns, they were not jealous, she preferred them both. Afterwards they would repair her, making her hips more spacious, enlarging her breasts with their shining stone nipples.

His love for her was perfect, he could say anything to her, into her he spilled his entire life. She was swept away in a sudden flood. He said no woman since then has equalled her.

Is this what you would like me to be, this mud woman? Is this what I would like to be? It would be so simple.

ALBERTO MORAVIA

(b. 1907) Alberto Moravia is the pseudonym
of the Italian novelist Alberto Pincherle.
Known as a realist, Moravia has written often
and sympathetically about women. Among
his translated works are *Conjugal Love*
(1949), *The Time of Indifference* (1953),
Lady Godiva and Other Stories (1975), and
Time of Desecration (1980), a novel about
the connection between loveless sex and political violence.

THE CHASE

I have never been a sportsman—or, rather, I have been a sportsman only
once, and that was the first and last time. I was a child, and one day, for
some reason or other, I found myself together with my father, who was
holding a gun in his hand, behind a bush, watching a bird that had
perched on a branch not very far away. It was a large, gray bird—or perhaps
it was brown—with a long—or perhaps a short—beak; I don't remember.
I only remember what I felt at that moment as I looked at it. It was
like watching an animal whose vitality was rendered more intense by the
very fact of my watching it and of the animal's not knowing that I
was watching it.

At that moment, I say, the notion of wildness entered my mind, never
again to leave it: everything is wild which is autonomous and unpredictable and does not depend upon us. Then all of a sudden there was an
explosion; I could no longer see the bird and I thought it had flown
away. But my father was leading the way, walking in front of me through
the undergrowth. Finally he stooped down, picked up something and put
it in my hand. I was aware of something warm and soft and I lowered my
eyes: there was the bird in the palm of my hand, its dangling, shattered
head crowned with a plume of already-thickening blood. I burst into
tears and dropped the corpse on the ground, and that was the end of my
shooting experience.

I thought again of this remote episode in my life this very day after watching my wife, for the first and also the last time, as she was walking through the streets of the city. But let us take things in order.

What had my wife been like; what was she like now? She once had been, to put it briefly, "wild"—that is, entirely autonomous and unpredictable; latterly she had become "tame"—that is, predictable and dependent. For a long time she had been like the bird that, on that far-off morning in my childhood, I had seen perching on the bough; latterly, I am sorry to say, she had become like a hen about which one knows everything in advance—how it moves, how it eats, how it lays eggs, how it sleeps, and so on.

Nevertheless I would not wish anyone to think that my wife's wildness consisted of an uncouth, rough, rebellious character. Apart from being extremely beautiful, she is the gentlest, politest, most discreet person in the world. Rather her wildness consisted of the air of charming unpredictability, of independence in her way of living, with which during the first years of our marriage she acted in my presence, both at home and abroad. Wildness signified intimacy, privacy, secrecy. Yes, my wife as she sat in front of her dressing table, her eyes fixed on the looking glass, passing the hairbrush with a repeated motion over her long, loose hair, was just as wild as the solitary quail hopping forward along a sun-filled furrow or the furtive fox coming out into a clearing and stopping to look around before running on. She was wild because I, as I looked at her, could never manage to foresee when she would give a last stroke with the hairbrush and rise and come toward me; wild to such a degree that sometimes when I went into our bedroom the smell of her, floating in the air, would have something of the acrid quality of a wild beast's lair.

Gradually she became less wild, tamer. I had had a fox, a quail, in the house, as I have said; then one day I realized that I had a hen. What effect does a hen have on someone who watches it? It has the effect of being, so to speak, an automaton in the form of a bird; automatic are the brief, rapid steps with which it moves about; automatic its hard, terse pecking; automatic the glance of the round eyes in its head that nods and turns; automatic its ready crouching down under the cock; automatic the dropping of the egg wherever it may be and the cry with which it announces that the egg has been laid. Good-by to the fox; good-by to the quail. And her smell—this no longer brought to my mind, in any way, the innocent odor of a wild animal; rather I detected in it the chemical suavity of some ordinary French perfume.

Our flat is on the first floor of a big building in a modern quarter of the town; our windows look out on a square in which there is a small public garden, the haunt of nurses and children and dogs. One day I was standing at the window, looking in a melancholy way at the garden. My wife, shortly before, had dressed to go out; and once again, watching her, I had noticed the irrevocable and, so to speak, invisible character of her gestures and personality: something which gave one the feeling of a thing already seen and already done and which therefore evaded even the most determined observation. And now, as I stood looking at the garden and at the same time wondering why the adorable wildness of former times had so completely disappeared, suddenly my wife came into my range of vision as she walked quickly across the garden in the direction of the bus stop. I watched her and then I almost jumped for joy; in a movement she was making to pull down a fold of her narrow skirt and smooth it over her thigh with the tips of her long, sharp nails, in this movement I recognized the wildness that in the past had made me love her. It was only an instant, but in that instant I said to myself: She's become wild again because she's convinced that I am not there and am not watching her. Then I left the window and rushed out.

But I did not join her at the bus stop; I felt that I must not allow myself to be seen. Instead I hurried to my car, which was standing nearby, got in and waited. A bus came and she got in together with some other people; the bus started off again and I began following it. Then there came back to me the memory of that one shooting expedition in which I had taken part as a child, and I saw that the bus was the undergrowth with its bushes and trees, my wife the bird perching on the bough while I, unseen, watched it living before my eyes. And the whole town, during this pursuit, became, as though by magic, a fact of nature like the countryside: the houses were hills, the streets valleys, the vehicles hedges and woods, and even the passers-by on the pavements had something unpredictable and autonomous—that is, wild—about them. And in my mouth, behind my clenched teeth, there was the acrid, metallic taste of gunfire; and my eyes, usually listless and wandering, had become sharp, watchful, attentive.

These eyes were fixed intently upon the exit door when the bus came to the end of its run. A number of people got out, and then I saw my wife getting out. Once again I recognized, in the manner in which she broke free of the crowd and started off toward a neighboring street, the wildness that pleased me so much. I jumped out of the car and started following her.

She was walking in front of me, ignorant of my presence, a tall woman with an elegant figure, long-legged, narrow-hipped, broad-backed, her brown hair falling on her shoulders.

Men turned around as she went past; perhaps they were aware of what I myself was now sensing with an intensity that quickened the beating of my heart and took my breath away: the unrestricted, steadily increasing, irresistible character of her mysterious wildness.

She walked hurriedly, having evidently some purpose in view, and even the fact that she had a purpose of which I was ignorant added to her wildness; I did not know where she was going, just as on that far-off morning I had not known what the bird perching on the bough was about to do. Moreover I thought the gradual, steady increase in this quality of wildness came partly from the fact that as she drew nearer to the object of this mysterious walk there was an increase in her—how shall I express it?—of biological tension, of existential excitement, of vital effervescence. Then, unexpectedly, with the suddenness of a film, her purpose was revealed.

A fair-haired young man in a leather jacket and a pair of corduroy trousers was leaning against the wall of a house in that ancient, narrow street. He was idly smoking as he looked in front of him. But as my wife passed close to him, he threw away his cigarette with a decisive gesture, took a step forward and seized her arm. I was expecting her to rebuff him, to move away from him, but nothing happened: evidently obeying the rules of some kind of erotic ritual, she went on walking beside the young man. Then after a few steps, with a movement that confirmed her own complicity, she put her arm around her companion's waist and he put his around her.

I understood then that this unknown man who took such liberties with my wife was also attracted by wildness. And so, instead of making a conventional appointment with her, instead of meeting in a café with a handshake, a falsely friendly and respectful welcome, he had preferred, by agreement with her, to take her by surprise—or, rather, to pretend to do so—while she was apparently taking a walk on her own account. All this I perceived by intuition, noticing that at the very moment when he stepped forward and took her arm her wildness had, so to speak, given an upward bound. It was years since I had seen my wife so alive, but alas, the source of this life could not be traced to me.

They walked on thus entwined and then, without any preliminaries, just like two wild animals, they did an unexpected thing: they went into one of the dark doorways in order to kiss. I stopped and watched them from a distance, peering into the darkness of the entrance. My wife was turned away from me and was bending back with the pressure of his body, her hair hanging free. I looked at that long, thick mane of brown hair, which as she leaned back fell free of her shoulders, and I felt at that moment her vitality reached its diapason, just as happens with wild animals when they couple and their customary wildness is redoubled by the violence of love. I watched for a long time and then, since the kiss went on and on and in fact seemed to be prolonged beyond the limits of my power of endurance, I saw that I would have to intervene.

I would have to go forward, seize my wife by the arm—or actually by that hair, which hung down and conveyed so well the feeling of feminine passivity—then hurl myself with clenched fists upon the blond young man. After this encounter I would carry off my wife, weeping, mortified, ashamed, while I was raging and broken-hearted, upbraiding her and pouring scorn upon her.

ALBERTO MORAVIA

But what else would this intervention amount to but the shot my father fired at that free, unknowing bird as it perched on the bough? The disorder and confusion, the mortification, the shame, that would follow would irreparably destroy the rare and precious moment of wildness that I was witnessing inside the dark doorway. It was true that this wildness was directed against me; but I had to remember that wildness, always and everywhere, is directed against everything and everybody. After the scene of my intervention it might be possible for me to regain control of my wife, but I should find her shattered and lifeless in my arms like the bird that my father placed in my hand so that I might throw it into the shooting bag.

The kiss went on and on: well, it was a kiss of passion—that could not be denied. I waited until they finished, until they came out of the doorway, until they walked on again still linked together. Then I turned back.

DORIS LESSING

(b. 1919) Born in Persia, Doris Lessing has
lived in Southern Rhodesia and England. Her
fiction has as its major theme the dehumanizing effects of violence in our time. *Children
of Violence* (1952–1965) and *The Golden
Notebook* (1962) focus on women as the central consciousnesses through whom society is
perceived, many of them "free women" independent of men. In *The Summer Before the
Dark* (1973) Lessing reaffirms the difficulty
of trying to become "free." In 1979 and 1980
she published two volumes of science fiction
envisioning life after an apocalypse such as
that she portrayed in *The Memoirs of a Sur-
vivor* (1975).

ONE OFF THE SHORT LIST

When he had first seen Barbara Coles, some years before, he only noticed
her because someone said: "That's Johnson's new girl." He certainly had
not used of her the private erotic formula: *Yes, that one.* He even wondered
what Johnson saw in her. "She won't last long," he remembered thinking,
as he watched Johnson, a handsome man, but rather flushed with drink,
flirting with some unknown girl while Barbara stood by a wall looking
on. He thought she had a sullen expression.

She was a pale girl, not slim, for her frame was generous, but her figure
could pass as good. Her straight yellow hair was parted on one side in a
way that struck him as gauche. He did not notice what she wore. But
her eyes were all right, he remembered: large, and solidly green, square-
looking because of some trick of the flesh at their corners. Emeraldlike
eyes in the face of a schoolgirl, or young schoolmistress who was watching
her lover flirt and would later sulk about it.

Her name sometimes cropped up in the papers. She was a stage
decorator, a designer, something on those lines.

Then a Sunday newspaper had a competition for stage design and she
won it. Barbara Coles was one of the "names" in the theatre, and her
photograph was seen about. It was always serious. He remembered having
thought her sullen.

One night he saw her across the room at a party. She was talking with a well-known actor. Her yellow hair was still done on one side, but now it looked sophisticated. She wore an emerald ring on her right hand that seemed deliberately to invite comparison with her eyes. He walked over and said: "We have met before, Graham Spence." He noted, with discomfort, that he sounded abrupt. "I'm sorry, I don't remember, but how do you do?" she said, smiling. And continued her conversation.

He hung around a bit, but soon she went off with a group of people she was inviting to her home for a drink. She did not invite Graham. There was about her an assurance, a carelessness, that he recognised as the signature of success. It was then, watching her laugh as she went off with her friends, that he used the formula: *"Yes, that one."* And he went home to his wife with enjoyable expectation, as if his date with Barbara Coles were already arranged.

His marriage was twenty years old. At first it had been stormy, painful, tragic—full of partings, betrayals and sweet reconciliations. It had taken him at least a decade to realise that there was nothing remarkable about this marriage that he had lived through with such surprise of the mind and the senses. On the contrary, the marriages of most of the people he knew, whether they were first, second or third attempts, were just the same. His had run true to form even to the serious love affair with the young girl for whose sake he had *almost* divorced his wife—yet at the last moment had changed his mind, letting the girl down so that he must have her for always (not unpleasurably) on his conscience. It was with humiliation that he had understood that this drama was not at all the unique thing he had imagined. It was nothing more than the experience of everyone in his circle. And presumably in everybody else's circle too?

Anyway, round about the tenth year of his marriage he had seen a good many things clearly, a certain kind of emotional adventure went from his life, and the marriage itself changed.

His wife had married a poor youth with a great future as a writer. Sacrifices had been made, chiefly by her, for that future. He was neither unaware of them, nor ungrateful; in fact he felt permanently guilty about it. He at last published a decently successful book, then a second which now, thank God, no one remembered. He had drifted into radio, television, book reviewing.

He understood he was not going to make it; that he had become—not a hack, no one could call him that—but a member of that army of people who live by their wits on the fringes of the arts. The moment of realisation was when he was in a pub one lunchtime near the B.B.C. where he often dropped in to meet others like himself: he understood that was why he went there—they *were* like him. Just as that melodramatic marriage had turned out to be like everyone else's—except that it had been shared with one woman instead of with two or three—so it had turned out that his unique talent, his struggles as a writer had led him here, to this pub and the half dozen pubs like it, where all the men in sight had the same history. They all had their novel, their play, their book of poems, a moment of fame, to their credit. Yet here they were, running television programmes about which they were cynical (to each other or to their wives) or writing reviews about other people's books. Yes, that's what he had become, an impresario of other people's talent. These two moments of clarity, about his marriage and about his talent, had roughly coincided: and (perhaps not by chance) had coincided with his wife's decision to leave him for a man younger than himself who had a future, she said, as a playwright. Well, he had talked her out of it. For her part she had to understand he was not going to be the T. S. Eliot or Graham Greene of our time—but after all, how many were? She must finally understand this, for he could no longer bear her awful bitterness. For his part he must stop coming home drunk at five in the morning, and starting a new romantic affair every six months which he took so seriously that he made her miserable because of her implied deficiencies. In short he was to be a good husband. (He had always been a dutiful father.) And she a good wife. And so it was: the marriage became stable, as they say.

The formula: *Yes, that one* no longer implied a necessarily sexual relationship. In its more mature form, it was far from being something he was ashamed of. On the contrary, it expressed a humorous respect for what he was, for his real talents and flair, which had turned out to be not artistic after all, but to do with emotional life, hard-earned experience. It expressed an ironical dignity, a proving to himself not only: I can be honest about myself, but also: I have earned the best in *that* field whenever I want it.

He watched the field for the women who were well known in the arts, or in politics; looked out for photographs, listened for bits of gossip. He made a point of going to see them act, or dance, or orate. He built up a not unshrewd picture of them. He would either quietly pull strings to meet her or—more often, for there was a gambler's pleasure in waiting—bide his time until he met her in the natural course of events, which was bound to happen sooner or later. He would be seen out with her a few times in public, which was in order, since his work meant he had to entertain well-known people, male and female. His wife always knew, he told her. He might have a brief affair with this woman, but more often than not it was the appearance of an affair. Not that he didn't get pleasure from other people envying him—he would make a point, for instance, of taking this woman into the pubs where his male colleagues went. It was that his real pleasure came when he saw her surprise at how well she was understood by him. He enjoyed the atmosphere he was able to set up between an intelligent woman and himself: a humorous complicity which had in it much that was unspoken, and which almost made sex irrelevant.

Onto the list of women with whom he planned to have this relationship went Barbara Coles. There was no hurry. Nex week, next month, next year, they would meet at a party. The world of well-known people in London is a small one. Big and little fishes, they drift around, nose each other, flirt their fins, wriggle off again. When he bumped into Barbara Coles, it would be time to decide whether or not to sleep with her.

Meanwhile he listened. But he didn't discover much. She had a husband and children, but the husband seemed to be in the background. The children were charming and well brought up, like everyone else's children. She had affairs, they said; but while several men he met sounded familiar with her, it was hard to determine whether they had slept with her, because none directly boasted of her. She was spoken of in terms of her friends, her work, her house, a party she had given, a job she had found someone. She was liked, she was respected, and Graham Spence's self-esteem was flattered because he had chosen her. He looked forward to saying in just the same tone: "Barbara Coles asked me what I thought about the set and I told her quite frankly. . . ."

Then by chance he met a young man who did boast about Barbara Coles; he claimed to have had the great love affair with her, and recently at that; and he spoke of it as something generally known. Graham realised how much he had already become involved with her in his imagination because of how perturbed he was now, on account of the character of this youth, Jack Kennaway. He had recently become successful as a magazine editor—one of those young men who, not as rare as one might suppose in the big cities, are successful from sheer impertinence, effrontery. Without much talent or taste, yet he had the charm of his effrontery. "Yes, I'm going to succeed, because I've decided to; yes, I may be stupid, but not so stupid that I don't know my deficiencies. Yes, I'm going to be successful because you people with integrity, etc., etc., simply don't believe in the possibility of people like me. You are too cowardly to stop me. Yes, I've taken your measure and I'm going to succeed because I've got the courage, not only to be unscrupulous, but to be quite frank about it. And besides, you admire me, you must, or otherwise you'd stop me. . . ." Well, that was young Jack Kennaway, and he shocked Graham. He was a tall, languishing young man, handsome in a dark melting way, and, it was quite clear, he was either asexual or homosexual. And this youth boasted of the favours of Barbara Coles; boasted, indeed, of her love. Either she was a raving neurotic with a taste for neurotics; or Jack Kennaway was a most accomplished liar; or she slept with anyone. Graham was intrigued. He took Jack Kennaway out to dinner in order to hear him talk about Barbara Coles. There was no doubt the two were pretty close—all those dinners, theatres, weekends in the country—Graham Spence felt he had put his finger on the secret pulse of Barbara Coles; and it was intolerable that he must wait to meet her; he decided to arrange it.

It became unnecessary. She was in the news again, with a run of luck. She had done a successful historical play, and immediately afterwards a modern play, and then a hit musical. In all three, the sets were remarked on. Graham saw some interviews in newspapers and on television. These all centered around the theme of her being able to deal easily with so many different styles of theatre; but the real point was, of course, that she was a woman, which naturally added piquancy to the thing. And now Graham Spence was asked to do a half-hour radio interview with her. He planned the questions he would ask her with care, drawing on what people had said of her, but above all on his instinct and experience with women. The interview was to be at nine-thirty at night; he was to pick her up at six from the theatre where she was currently at work, so that there would be time, as the letter from the B.B.C. had put it, "for you and Miss Coles to get to know each other."

At six he was at the stage door, but a message from Miss Coles said she was not quite ready, could he wait a little. He hung about, then went to the pub opposite for a quick one, but still no Miss Coles. So he made his way backstage, directed by voices, hammering, laughter. It was badly lit, and the group of people at work did not see him. The director, James Poynter, had his arm around Barbara's shoulders. He was newly well-known, a carelessly good-looking young man reputed to be intelligent. Barbara Coles wore a dark blue overall, and her flat hair fell over her face so that she kept pushing it back with the hand that had the emerald on it. These two stood close, side by side. Three young men, stagehands, were on the other side of a trestle which had sketches and drawings on it. They were studying some sketches. Barbara said, in a voice warm with energy: "Well, so I thought if we did *this*—do you see, James? What do you think, Steven?" "Well, love," said the young man she called Steven, "I see your idea, but I wonder if . . ." "I think you're right, Babs," said the director. "Look," said Barbara, holding one of the sketches toward Steven, "look, let me show you." They all leaned forward, the five of them, absorbed in the business.

Suddenly Graham couldn't stand it. He understood he was shaken to his depths. He went off stage, and stood with his back against a wall in the dingy passage that led to the dressing room. His eyes were filled with tears. He was seeing what a long way he had come from the crude, uncompromising, admirable young egomaniac he had been when he was twenty. That group of people there—working, joking, arguing, yes, that's what he hadn't known for years. What bound them was the democracy of respect for each other's work, a confidence in themselves and in each other. They looked like people banded together against a world which they—no, not despised, but which they measured, understood, would fight to the death, out of respect for what *they* stood for, for what *it* stood for. It was a long time since he felt part of that balance. And he understood that he had seen Barbara Coles when she was most herself, at ease with a group of people she worked with. It was then, with the tears drying on his eyelids, which felt old and ironic, that he decided he would sleep with Barbara Coles. It was a necessity for him. He went back through the door onto the stage, burning with this single determination.

The five were still together. Barbara had a length of blue gleaming stuff which she was draping over the shoulder of Steven, the stagehand. He was showing it off, and the others watched. "What do you think, James?" she asked the director. "We've got that sort of dirty green, and I thought . . ." "Well," said James, not sure at all, "well, Babs, well . . ."

Now Graham went forward so that he stood beside Barbara, and said: "I'm Graham Spence, we've met before." For the second time she smiled socially and said: "Oh I'm sorry, I don't remember." Graham nodded at James, whom he had known, or at least had met off and on, for years. But it was obvious James didn't remember him either.

"From the B.B.C.," said Graham to Barbara, again sounding abrupt, against his will. "Oh I'm sorry, I'm sorry, I forgot all about it. I've got to be interviewed," she said to the group. "Mr. Spence is a journalist." Graham allowed himself a small smile ironical of the word journalist, but she was not looking at him. She was going on with her work. "We should decide tonight," she said. "Steven's right." "Yes, I am right," said the stagehand. "She's right, James, we need that blue with that sludge-green everywhere." "James," said Barbara, "James, what's wrong with it? You haven't said." She moved forward to James, passing Graham. Remembering him again, she became contrite. "I'm sorry," she said, "we can none of us agree. Well, look"—she turned to Graham—"you advise us, we've got so involved with it that . . ." At which James laughed, and so did the stagehands. "No, Babs," said James, "of course Mr. Spence can't advise. He's just this moment come in. We've got to decide. Well I'll give you till tomorrow morning. Time to go home, it must be six by now."

"It's nearly seven," said Graham, taking command.

"It isn't!" said Barbara, dramatic. "My God, how terrible, how appalling, how could I have done such a thing. . . ." She was laughing at herself. "Well, you'll have to forgive me, Mr. Spence, because you haven't got any alternative."

They began laughing again: this was clearly a group joke. And now Graham took his chance. He said firmly, as if he were her director, in fact copying James Poynter's manner with her: "No, Miss Coles, I won't forgive you, I've been kicking my heels for nearly an hour." She grimaced, then laughed and accepted it. James said: "There, Babs, that's how you ought to be treated. We spoil you." He kissed her on the cheek, she kissed him on both his, the stagehands moved off. "Have a good evening, Babs," said James, going, and nodding to Graham, who stood concealing his pleasure with difficulty. He knew, because he had had the courage to be firm, indeed, peremptory, with Barbara, that he had saved himself hours of maneuvering. Several drinks, a dinner—perhaps two or three evenings of drinks and dinners—had been saved because he was now on this footing with Barbara Coles, a man who could say: "No, I won't forgive you, you've kept me waiting."

She said: "I've just got to . . ." and went ahead of him. In the passage she hung her overall on a peg. She was thinking, it seemed, of something else, but seeing him watching her, she smiled at him, companionably: he realised with triumph it was the sort of smile she would offer one of the stagehands, or even James. She said again: "Just one second . . ." and went to the stage-door office. She and the stage doorman conferred. There was some problem. Graham said, taking another chance: "What's the trouble, can I help?"—as if he could help, as if he expected to be able to. "Well . . ." she said, frowning. Then, to the man: "No, it'll be all right. Goodnight." She came to Graham. "We've got ourselves into a bit of a fuss because half the set's in Liverpool and half's here and—but it will sort itself out." She stood, at ease, chatting to him, one colleague to another. All this was admirable, he felt; but there would be a bad moment when they emerged from the special atmosphere of the theatre into the street. He took another decision, grasped her arm firmly, and said: "We're going to have a drink before we do anything at all, it's a terrible evening out." Her arm felt resistant, but remained within his. It was raining outside, luckily. He directed her, authoritative: "No, not that pub, there's a nicer one around the corner." "Oh, but I like this pub," said Barbara, "we always use it."

"Of course you do," he said to himself. But in that pub there would be the stagehands, and probably James, and he'd lose contact with her. He'd become a *journalist* again. He took her firmly out of danger around two corners, into a pub he picked at random. A quick look around—no, they weren't there. At least, if there were people from the theatre, she showed no sign. She asked for a beer. He ordered her a double Scotch, which she accepted. Then, having won a dozen preliminary rounds already, he took time to think. Something was bothering him—what? Yes, it was what he had observed backstage, Barbara and James Poynter. Was she having an affair with him? Because if so, it would all be much more difficult. He made himself see the two of them together, and thought with a jealousy surprisingly strong: *Yes, that's it.* Meantime he sat looking at her, seeing himself look at her, *a man gazing in calm appreciation at a woman:* waiting for her to feel it and respond. She was examining the pub. Her white woollen suit was belted, and had a not unprovocative suggestion of being a uniform. Her flat yellow hair, hastily pushed back after work, was untidy. Her clear white skin, without any colour, made her look tired. Not very exciting, at the moment, thought Graham, but maintaining his appreciative pose for when she would turn and see it. He knew what she would see: he was relying not only on the "warm kindly" beam of his gaze, for this was merely a reinforcement of the impression he knew he made. He had black hair, a little greyed. His clothes were loose and bulky—

masculine. His eyes were humorous and appreciative. He was not, never had been, concerned to lessen the impression of being settled, dependable: the husband and father. On the contrary, he knew women found it reassuring.

When she at last turned she said, almost apologetic: "Would you mind if we sat down? I've been lugging great things around all day." She had spotted two empty chairs in a corner. So had he, but rejected them, because there were other people at the table. "But my dear, of course!" They took the chairs, and then Barbara said: "If you'll excuse me a moment." She had remembered she needed make-up. He watched her go off, annoyed with himself. She was tired; and he could have understood, protected, sheltered. He realised that in the other pub, with the people she had worked with all day, she would not have thought: "I must make myself up, I must be on show." That was for outsiders. She had not, until now, considered Graham an outsider, because of his taking his chance to seem one of the working group in the theatre; but now he had thrown his opportunity away. She returned armoured. Her hair was sleek, no longer defenceless. And she had made up her eyes. Her eyebrows were untouched, pale gold streaks above the brilliant green eyes whose lashes were blackened. Rather good, he thought, the contrast. Yes, but the moment had gone when he could say: Did you know you had a smudge on your cheek? Or—my dear girl!—pushing her hair back with the edge of a brotherly hand. In fact, unless he was careful, he'd be back at starting point.

He remarked: "That emerald is very cunning"—smiling into her eyes.

She smiled politely, and said: "It's not cunning, it's an accident, it was my grandmother's." She flirted her hand lightly by her face, though, smiling. But that was something she had done before, to a compliment she had had before, and often. It was all social, she had become social entirely. She remarked: "Didn't you say it was half past nine we had to record?"

"My dear Barbara, we've got two hours. We'll have another drink or two, then I'll ask you a couple of questions, then we'll drop down to the studio and get it over, and then we'll have a comfortable supper."

"I'd rather eat now, if you don't mind. I had no lunch, and I'm really hungry."

"But my dear, of course." He was angry. Just as he had been surprised by his real jealousy over James, so now he was thrown off balance by his anger: he had been counting on the long quiet dinner afterwards to establish intimacy. "Finish your drink and I'll take you to Nott's." Nott's was expensive. He glanced at her assessingly as he mentioned it. She said: "I wonder if you know Butler's? It's good and it's rather close." Butler's was good, and it was cheap, and he gave her a good mark for liking it. But Nott's it was going to be. "My dear, we'll get into a taxi and be at Nott's in a moment, don't worry."

She obediently got to her feet: the way she did it made him understand how badly he had slipped. She was saying to herself: Very well, he's like that, then all right, I'll do what he wants and get it over with. . . .

Swallowing his own drink he followed her, and took her arm in the pub doorway. It was polite within his. Outside it drizzled. No taxi. He was having bad luck now. They walked in silence to the end of the street. There Barbara glanced into a side street where a sign said: BUTLER'S. Not to remind him of it, on the contrary, she concealed the glance. And here she was, entirely at his disposal, they might never have shared the comradely moment in the theatre.

They walked half a mile to Nott's. No taxis. She made conversation: this was, he saw, to cover any embarrassment he might feel because of a half-mile walk through rain when she was tired. She was talking about some theory to do with the theatre, with designs for theatre building. He heard himself saying, and repeatedly: Yes, yes, yes. He thought about Nott's, how to get things right when they reached Nott's. There he took the head-waiter aside, gave him a pound, and instructions. They were put in a corner. Large Scotches appeared. The menus were spread. "And now, my dear," he said, "I apologise for dragging you here, but I hope you'll think it's worth it."

"Oh, it's charming, I've always liked it. It's just that . . ." She stopped herself saying: it's such a long way. She smiled at him, raising her glass, and said: "It's one of my very favorite places, and I'm glad you dragged me here." Her voice was flat with tiredness. All this was appalling; he knew it; and he sat thinking how to retrieve his position. Meanwhile she fingered the menu. The headwaiter took the order, but Graham made a gesture which said: Wait a moment. He wanted the Scotch to take effect before she ate. But she saw his silent order; and, without annoyance or reproach, leaned forward to say, sounding patient: "Graham, please, I've got to eat, you don't want me drunk when you interview me, do you?"

"They are bringing it as fast as they can," he said, making it sound as if she were greedy. He looked neither at the headwaiter nor at Barbara. He noted in himself, as he slipped further and further away from contact with her, a cold determination growing in him; one apart from, apparently, any conscious act of will, that come what may, if it took all night, he'd be in her bed before morning. And now, seeing the small pale face, with the enormous green eyes, it was for the first time that he imagined her in his arms. Although he had said: *Yes, that one,* weeks ago, it was only now that he imagined her as a sensual experience. Now he did, so strongly that he could only glance at her, and then away towards the waiters who were bringing food.

"Thank the Lord," said Barbara, and all at once her voice was gay and intimate. "Thank heavens. Thank every power that is. . . ." She was making fun of her own exaggeration; and, as he saw, because she wanted to put him at his ease after his boorishness over delaying the food. (She hadn't been taken in, he saw, humiliated, disliking her.) "Thank all the gods of Nott's," she went on, "because if I hadn't eaten inside five minutes I'd have died, I tell you." With which she picked up her knife and fork and began on her steak. He poured wine, smiling with her, thinking that *this* moment of closeness he would not throw away. He watched her frank hunger as she ate, and thought: Sensual—it's strange I hadn't wondered whether she would be or not.

"Now," she said, sitting back, having taken the edge off her hunger: "Let's get to work."

He said: "I've thought it over very carefully—how to present you. The first thing seems to me, we must get away from that old chestnut: Miss Coles, how extraordinary for a woman to be so versatile in her work . . . I hope you agree?" This was his trump card. He had noted, when he had seen her on television, her polite smile when this note was struck. (The smile he had seen so often tonight.) This smile said: All right, if you *have* to be stupid, what can I do?

Now she laughed and said: "What a relief. I was afraid you were going to do the same thing."

"Good, now you eat and I'll talk."

In his carefully prepared monologue he spoke of the different styles of theatre she had shown herself mistress of, but not directly: he was flattering her on the breadth of her experience; the complexity of her character, as shown in her work. She ate, steadily, her face showing nothing. At last she asked: "And how did you plan to introduce this?"

He had meant to spring that on her as a surprise, something like: Miss Coles, a surprisingly young woman for what she has accomplished (she was thirty? thirty-two?) and a very attractive one. . . . "Perhaps I can give you an idea of what she's like if I say she could be taken for the film star Marie Carletta. . . ." The Carletta was a strong earthy blonde, known to be intellectual. He now saw he could not possibly say this: he could imagine her cool look if he did. She said: "Do you mind if we get away from all that—my manifold talents, et cetera. . . ." He felt himself stiffen with annoyance; particularly because this was not an accusation, he saw she did not think him worth one. She had assessed him: This is the kind of man who uses this kind of flattery and therefore. . . . It made him angrier that she did not even trouble to say: Why did you do exactly what you promised you wouldn't? She was being invincibly polite, trying to conceal her patience with his stupidity.

"After all," she was saying, "it is a stage designer's job to design what comes up. Would anyone take, let's say Johnnie Cranmore" (another stage designer) "onto the air or television and say: How very versatile you are because you did that musical about Java last month and a modern play about Irish labourers this?"

He battened down his anger. "My dear Barbara, I'm sorry. I didn't realise that what I said would sound just like the mixture as before. So what shall we talk about?"

"What I was saying as we walked to the restaurant: can we get away from the personal stuff?"

Now he almost panicked. Then, thank God, he laughed from nervousness, for she laughed and said: "You didn't hear one word I said."

"No, I didn't. I was frightened you were going to be furious because I made you walk so far when you were tired."

They laughed together, back to where they had been in the theatre. He leaned over, took her hand, kissed it. He said: "Tell me again." He thought: Damn, now she's going to be earnest and intellectual.

But he understood he had been stupid. He had forgotten himself at twenty—or, for that matter, at thirty; forgotten one could live inside an idea, a set of ideas, with enthusiasm. For in talking about her ideas (also the ideas of the people she worked with) for a new theatre, a new style of theatre, she was as she had been with her colleagues over the sketches or the blue material. She was easy, informal, almost chattering. This was how, he remembered, one talked about ideas that were a breath of life. The ideas, he thought, were intelligent enough; and he would agree with them, with her, if he believed it mattered a damn one way or another, if any of these enthusiasms mattered a damn. But at least he now had the key; he knew what to do. At the end of not more than half an hour, they were again two professionals, talking about ideas they shared, for he remembered caring about all this himself once. *When? How many years ago was it that he had been able to care?*

At last he said: "My dear Barbara, do you realise the impossible position you're putting me in? Margaret Ruyen who runs this programme is determined to do you personally, the poor woman hasn't got a serious thought in her head."

Barbara frowned. He put his hand on hers, teasing her for the frown: "No, wait, trust me, we'll circumvent her." She smiled. In fact Margaret Ruyen had left it all to him, had said nothing about Miss Coles.

"They aren't very bright—the brass," he said. "Well, never mind: we'll work out what we want, do it, and it'll be a *fait accompli.*"

"Thank you, what a relief. How lucky I was to be given you to interview me." She was relaxed now, because of the whisky, the food, the wine, above all because of this new complicity against Margaret Ruyen. It would all be easy. They worked out five or six questions, over coffee, and took a taxi through rain to the studios. He noted that the cold necessity to have her, to make her, to beat her down, had left him. He was even seeing himself, as the evening ended, kissing her on the cheek and going home to his wife. This comradeship was extraordinarily pleasant. It was balm to the wound he had not known he carried until that evening, when he had had to accept the justice of the word *journalist*. He felt he could talk forever about the state of the theatre, its finances, the stupidity of the government, the philistinism of . . .

At the studios he was careful to make a joke so that they walked in on the laugh. He was careful that the interview began at once, without conversation with Margaret Ruyen; and that from the moment the green light went on, his voice lost its easy familiarity. He made sure that not one personal note was struck during the interview. Afterwards, Margaret Ruyen, who was pleased, came forward to say so; but he took her aside to say that Miss Coles was tired and needed to be taken home at once: for he knew this must look to Barbara as if he were squaring a producer who had been expecting a different interview. He led Barbara off, her hand held tight in his against his side. "Well," he said, "we've done it, and I don't think she knows what hit her."

"Thank you," she said, "it really was pleasant to talk about something sensible for once."

He kissed her lightly on the mouth. She returned it, smiling. By now he felt sure that the mood need not slip again, he could hold it.

"There are two things we can do," he said. "You can come to my club and have a drink. Or I can drive you home and you can give me a drink. I have to go past you."

"Where do you live?"

"Wimbledon." He lived, in fact, at Highgate; but she lived in Fulham. He was taking another chance, but by the time she found out, they would be in a position to laugh over his ruse.

"Good," she said. "You can drop me home then. I have to get up early." He made no comment. In the taxi he took her hand; it was heavy in his, and he asked: "Does James slave-drive you?"

"I didn't realize you knew him—no, he doesn't."

"Well I don't know him intimately. What's he like to work with?"

"Wonderful," she said at once. "There's no one I enjoy working with more."

Jealousy spurted in him. He could not help himself: "Are you having an affair with him?"

She looked: what's it to do with you? but said: "No, I'm not."

"He's very attractive," he said, with a chuckle of worldly complicity. She said nothing, and he insisted: "If I were a woman I'd have an affair with James."

It seemed she might very well say nothing. But she remarked: ""He's married."

His spirits rose in a swoop. It was the first stupid remark she had made. It was a remark of such staggering stupidity that . . . he let out a humoring snort of laughter, put his arm around her, kissed her, said: "My dear little Babs."

She said: "Why Babs?"

"Is that the prerogative of James. And of the stagehands?" he could not prevent himself adding.

"I'm only called that at work." She was stiff inside his arm.

THE SEX OBJECT

334

"My dear Barbara, then . . ." He waited for her to enlighten and explain, but she said nothing. Soon she moved out of his arm, on the pretext of lighting a cigarette. He lit it for her. He noted that his determination to lay her and at all costs, had come back. They were outside her house. He said quickly: "And now, Barbara, you can make me a cup of coffee and give me a brandy." She hesitated; but he was out of the taxi, paying, opening the door for her. The house had no lights on, he noted. He said: "We'll be very quiet so as not to wake the children."

She turned her head slowly to look at him. She said, flat, replying to his real question: "My husband is away. As for the children, they are visiting friends tonight." She now went ahead of him to the door of the house. It was a small house, in a terrace of small and not very pretty houses. Inside a little, bright, intimate hall, she said: "I'll go and make some coffee. Then, my friend, you must go home because I'm very tired."

The *my friend* struck him deep, because he had become vulnerable during their comradeship. He said gabbling: "You're annoyed with me—oh, please don't, I'm sorry."

She smiled, from a cool distance. He saw, in the small light from the ceiling, her extraordinary eyes. "Green" eyes are hazel, are brown with green flecks, are even blue. Eyes are chequered, flawed, changing. Hers were solid green, but really, he had never seen anything like them before. They were like very deep water. They were like—well, emeralds; or the absolute clarity of green in the depths of a tree in summer. And now, as she smiled almost perpendicularly up at him, he saw a darkness come over them. Darkness swallowed the clear green. She said: "I'm not in the least annoyed." It was as if she had yawned with boredom. "And now I'll get the things . . . in there." She nodded at a white door and left him. He went into a long, very tidy white room, that had a narrow bed in one corner, a table covered with drawings, sketches, pencils. Tacked to the walls with drawing pins were swatches of coloured stuffs. Two small chairs stood near a low round table: an area of comfort in the working room. He was thinking: I wouldn't like it if my wife had a room like this. I wonder what Barbara's husband . . .? He had not thought of her till now in relation to her husband, or to her children. Hard to imagine her with a frying pan in her hand, or for that matter, cosy in the double bed.

A noise outside: he hastily arranged himself, leaning with one arm on the mantelpiece. She came in with a small tray that had cups, glasses, brandy, coffeepot. She looked abstracted. Graham was on the whole flattered by this: it probably meant she was at ease in his presence. He realised he was a little tight and rather tired. Of course, she was tired too, that was why she was vague. He remembered that earlier that evening he had lost a chance by not using her tiredness. Well now, if he were intelligent . . . She was about to pour coffee. He firmly took the coffeepot out of her hand, and nodded at a chair. Smiling, she obeyed him. "That's better," he said. He poured coffee, poured brandy, and pulled the table towards her. She watched him. Then he took her hand, kissed it, patted it, laid it down gently. Yes, he thought, I did that well.

Now, a problem. He wanted to be closer to her, but she was fitted into a damned silly little chair that had arms. If he were to sit by her on the floor . . .? But no, for him, the big bulky reassuring man, there could be no casual gestures, no informal postures. Suppose I scoop her out of the chair onto the bed? He drank his coffee as he plotted. Yes, he'd carry her to the bed, but not yet.

"Graham," she said, setting down her cup. She was, he saw with annoyance, looking tolerant. "Graham, in about half an hour I want to be in bed and asleep."

As she said this, she offered him a smile of amusement at this situation—man and woman maneuvering, the great comic situation. And with part of himself he could have shared it. Almost, he smiled with her, laughed. (Not till days later he exclaimed to himself: Lord what a mistake I made, not to share the joke with her then: that was where I went seriously wrong.) But he could not smile. His face was frozen, with a stiff pride. Not because she had been watching him plot; the amusement she now offered him took the sting out of that; but because of his revived determination that he was going to have his own way, he was going to have her. He was not going home. But he felt that he held a bunch of keys, and did not know which one to choose.

He lifted the second small chair opposite to Barbara, moving aside the coffee table for this purpose. He sat in this chair, leaned forward, took her two hands, and said: "My dear, don't make me go home yet, don't, I beg you." The trouble was, nothing had happened all evening that could be felt to lead up to these words and his tone—simple, dignified, human being pleading with human being for surcease. He saw himself leaning forward, his big hands swallowing her small ones; he saw his face, warm with the appeal. And he realised he had meant the words he used. They were nothing more than what he felt. He wanted to stay with her because she wanted him to, because he was her colleague, a fellow worker in the arts. He needed this desperately. But she was examining him, curious rather than surprised, and from a critical distance. He heard himself saying: "If James were here, I wonder what you'd do?" His voice was aggrieved; he saw the sudden dark descend over her eyes, and she said: "Graham, would you like some more coffee before you go?"

He said: "I've been wanting to meet you for years. I know a good many people who know you."

She leaned forward, poured herself a little more brandy, sat back, holding the glass between her two palms on her chest. An odd gesture: Graham felt that this vessel she was cherishing between her hands was herself. A patient, long-suffering gesture. He thought of various men who had mentioned her. He thought of Jack Kennaway, wavered, panicked, said: "For instance, Jack Kennaway."

And now, at the name, an emotion lit her eyes—what was it? He went on, deliberately testing this emotion, adding to it: "I had dinner with him last week—oh, quite by chance!—and he was talking about you."

"Was he?"

He remembered he had thought her sullen, all those years ago. Now she seemed defensive, and she frowned. He said: "In fact he spent most of the evening talking about you."

She said in short, breathless sentences, which he realised were due to anger: "I can very well imagine what he says. But surely you can't think I enjoy being reminded that . . ." She broke off, resenting him, he saw, because he forced her down onto a level she despised. But it was not his level either: it was all her fault, all hers! He couldn't remember not being in control of a situation with a woman for years. Again he felt like a man teetering on a tightrope. He said, trying to make good use of Jack Kennaway, even at this late hour: "Of course, he's a charming boy, but not a man at all."

She looked at him, silent, guarding her brandy glass against her breasts.

"Unless appearances are totally deceptive, of course." He could not resist probing, even though he knew it was fatal.

She said nothing.

"Do you know you are supposed to have had the great affair with Jack Kennaway?" he exclaimed, making this an amused expostulation against the fools who could believe it.

"So I am told." She set down her glass. "And now," she said, standing up, dismissing him. He lost his head, took a step forward, grabbed her in his arms, and groaned: "Barbara!"

She turned her face this way and that under his kisses. He snatched a diagnostic look at her expression—it was still patient. He placed his lips against her neck, groaned "Barbara" again, and waited. She would have to do something. Fight free, respond, something. She did nothing at all. At last she said: "For the Lord's sake, Graham!" She sounded amused: he was again being offered amusement. But if he shared it with her, it would be the end of his chance to have her. He clamped his mouth over hers, silencing her. She did not fight him off so much as blow him off. Her mouth treated his attacking mouth as a woman blows and laughs in water, puffing off waves or spray with a laugh, turning aside her head. It was a gesture half annoyance, half humour. He continued to kiss her while she moved her head and face about under the kisses as if they were small attacking waves.

And so began what, when he looked back on it afterwards, was the most embarrassing experience of his life. Even at the time he hated her for his ineptitude. For he held her there for what must have been nearly half an hour. She was much shorter than he, he had to bend, and his neck ached. He held her rigid, his thighs on either side of hers, her arms clamped to her side in a bear's hug. She was unable to move, except for her head. When his mouth ground hers open and his tongue moved and writhed inside it, she still remained passive. And he could not stop himself. While with his intelligence he watched this ridiculous scene, he was determined to go on, because sooner or later her body must soften in wanting his. And he could not stop because he could not face the horror of the moment when he set her free and she looked at him. And he hated her more, every moment. Catching glimpses of her great green eyes, open and dismal beneath his, he knew he had never disliked anything more than those "jewelled" eyes. They were repulsive to him. It occurred to him at last that even if by now she wanted him, he wouldn't know it, because she was not able to move at all. He cautiously loosened his hold so that she had an inch or so leeway. She remained quite passive. As if, he thought derisively, she had read or been told that the way to incite men maddened by lust was to fight them. He found he was thinking: Stupid cow, so you imagine I find you attractive, do you? You've got the conceit to think that!

The sheer, raving insanity of this thought hit him, opened his arms, his thighs, and lifted his tongue out of her mouth. She stepped back, wiping her mouth with the back of her hand, and stood dazed with incredulity. The embarrassment that lay in wait for him nearly engulfed him, but he let anger postpone it. She said positively apologetic, even, at this moment, humorous: "You're crazy, Graham. What's the matter, are you drunk? You don't seem drunk. You don't even find me attractive."

The blood of hatred went to his head and he gripped her again. Now she had got her face firmly twisted away so that he could not reach her mouth, and she repeated steadily as he kissed the parts of her cheeks and neck that were available to him: "Graham, let me go, do let me go, Graham." She went on saying this; he went on squeezing, grinding, kissing and licking. It might go on all night: it was a sheer contest of wills, nothing else. He thought: It's only a really masculine woman who wouldn't have given in by now out of sheer decency of the flesh! One thing he knew, however: that she would be in that bed, in his arms, and very soon. He let her go, but said: "I'm going to sleep with you tonight, you know that, don't you?"

She leaned with hand on the mantelpiece to steady herself. Her face was colourless, since he had licked all the makeup off. She seemed quite different: small and defenceless with her large mouth pale now, her smudged green eyes fringed with gold. And now, for the first time, he felt what it might have been supposed (certainly by her) he felt hours ago. Seeing the small damp flesh of her face, he felt kinship, intimacy with her, he felt intimacy of the flesh, the affection and good humour of sensuality. He felt she was flesh of his flesh, his sister in the flesh. He felt

THE SEX OBJECT

338

desire for her, instead of the will to have her; and because of this, was ashamed of the farce he had been playing. Now he desired simply to take her into bed in the affection of his senses.

She said: "What on earth am I supposed to do? Telephone for the police, or what?" He was hurt that she still addressed the man who had ground her into sulky apathy; she was not addressing *him* at all.

She said: "Or scream for the neighbours, is that what you want?"

The gold-fringed eyes were almost black, because of the depth of the shadow of boredom over them. She was bored and weary to the point of falling to the floor, he could see that.

He said: "I'm going to sleep with you."

"But how can you possibly want to?"—a reasonable, a civilised demand addressed to a man who (he could see) she believed would respond to it. She said: "You know I don't want to, and I know you don't really give a damn one way or the other."

He was stung back into being the boor because she had not the intelligence to see that the boor no longer existed; because she could not see that this was a man who wanted her in a way which she must respond to.

There she stood, supporting herself with one hand, looking small and white and exhausted, and utterly incredulous. She was going to turn and walk off out of simple incredulity, he could see that. "Do you think I don't mean it?" he demanded, grinding this out between his teeth. She made a movement—she was on the point of going away. His hand shot out on its own volition and grasped her wrist. She frowned. His other hand grasped her other wrist. His body hove up against hers to start the pressure of a new embrace. Before it could, she said: "Oh Lord, no, I'm not going through all that again. Right, then."

"What do you mean—right, then?" he demanded.

She said: "You're going to sleep with me. O.K. Anything rather than go through that again. Shall we get it over with?"

He grinned, saying in silence: "No darling, oh no you don't, I don't care what words you use, I'm going to have you now and that's all there is to it."

She shrugged. The contempt, the weariness of it, had no effect on him, because he was now again hating her so much that wanting her was like needing to kill something or someone.

She took her clothes off, as if she were going to bed by herself: her jacket, skirt, petticoat. She stood in white bra and panties, a rather solid girl, brown-skinned still from the summer. He felt a flash of affection for the brown girl with her loose yellow hair as she stood naked. She got into bed and lay there, while the green eyes looked at him in civilised appeal: Are you really going through with this? Do you have to? Yes, his eyes said back: I do have to. She shifted her gaze aside, to the wall, saying silently: Well, if you want to take me without any desire at all on my part, then go ahead, if you're not ashamed. He was not ashamed, because he was maintaining the flame of hate for her which he knew quite well was all that stood between him and shame. He took off his clothes, and got into bed beside her. As he did so, knowing he was putting himself in the position of raping a woman who was making it elaborately clear he bored her, his flesh subsided completely, sad, and full of reproach because a few moments ago it was reaching out for his sister whom he could have made happy. He lay on his side by her, secretly at work on himself, while he supported himself across her body on his elbow, using the free hand to manipulate her breasts. He saw that she gritted her teeth against his touch. At least she could not know that after all this fuss he was not potent.

In order to incite himself, he clasped her again. She felt his smallness, writhed free of him, sat up and said: "Lie down."

While she had been lying there, she had been thinking: The only way to get this over with is to make him big again, otherwise I've got to put up with him all night. His hatred of her was giving him a clairvoyance: he knew very well what went on through her mind. She had switched on, with the determination to *get it all over with,* a sensual good humour, a patience. He lay down. She squatted beside him, the light from the ceiling blooming on her brown shoulders, her flat fair hair falling over her face. But she would not look at his face. Like a bored, skilled wife, she was: or like a prostitute. She administered to him, she was setting herself to please him. Yes, he thought, she's sensual, or she could be. Meanwhile she was succeeding in defeating the reluctance of his flesh, which was the tender token of a possible desire for her, by using a cold skill that was the result of her contempt for him. Just as he decided: Right, it's enough, now I shall have her properly, she made him come. It was not a trick, to hurry or cheat him, what defeated him was her transparent thought: Yes, that's what he's worth.

Then, having succeeded, and waited for a moment or two, she stood up, naked, the fringes of gold at her loins and in her armpits speaking to him a language quite different from that of her green, bored eyes. She looked at him and thought, showing it plainly: What sort of man is it who . . .? He watched the slight movement of her shoulders: a just-checked shrug. She went out of the room: then the sound of running water. Soon she came back in a white dressing gown, carrying a yellow towel. She handed him the towel, looking away in politeness as he used it. "Are you going home now?" she enquired hopefully, at this point.

"No, I'm not." He believed that now he would have to start fighting her again, but she lay down beside him, not touching him (he could feel the distaste of her flesh for his) and he thought: Very well, my dear, but there's a lot of the night left yet. He said aloud: "I'm going to have you properly tonight." She said nothing, lay silent, yawned. Then she remarked consolingly, and he could have laughed outright from sheer surprise: "Those were hardly conducive circumstances for making love." She was *consoling* him. He hated her for it. A proper little slut: I force her into bed, she doesn't want me, but she still has to make me feel good, like a prostitute. But even while he hated her he responded in kind, from the habit of sexual generosity. "It's because of my admiration for you, because . . . after all, I was holding in my arms one of the thousand women."

A pause. "The thousand?" she enquired, carefully.

"The thousand especial women."

"In Britain or in the world? You choose them for their brains, their beauty—what?"

"Whatever it is that makes them outstanding," he said, offering her a compliment.

"Well," she remarked at last, inciting him to be amused again: "I hope that at least there's a short list you can say I am on, for politeness' sake."

He did not reply for he understood he was sleepy. He was still telling himself that he must stay awake when he was slowly waking and it was morning. It was about eight. Barbara was not there. He thought: My God! What on earth shall I tell my wife? Where was Barbara? He remembered the ridiculous scenes of last night and nearly succumbed to shame. Then he thought, reviving anger: If she didn't sleep beside me here I'll never forgive her. . . . He sat up, quietly, determined to go through the house until he found her and, having found her, to possess her, when the door opened and she came in. She was fully dressed in a green suit, her hair done, her eyes made up. She carried a tray of coffee, which she set down beside the bed. He was conscious of his big loose hairy body, half uncovered. He said to himself that he was not going to lie in bed, naked, while she was dressed. He said: "Have you got a gown of some kind?" She handed him, without speaking, a towel, and said: "The bathroom's second on the left." She went out. He followed, the towel around him. Everything in this house was gay, intimate—not at all like her efficient working room. He wanted to find out where she had slept, and opened the first door. It was the kitchen, and she was in it, putting a brown earthenware dish into the oven. "The next door," said Barbara. He went hastily past the second door, and opened (he hoped quietly) the third. It was a cupboard full of linen. "This door," said Barbara, behind him.

"So all right then, where did you sleep?"

"What's it to do with you? Upstairs, in my own bed. Now, if you have everything, I'll say goodbye, I want to get to the theatre."

"I'll take you," he said at once.

He saw again the movement of her eyes, the dark swallowing the light in deadly boredom. "I'll take you," he insisted.

"I'd prefer to go by myself," she remarked. Then she smiled: "However, you'll take me. Then you'll make a point of coming right in, so that James and everyone can see—that's what you want to take me for, isn't it?"

He hated her, finally, and quite simply, for her intelligence; that not once had he got away with anything, that she had been watching, since they had met yesterday, every movement of his campaign for her. However, some fate or inner urge over which he had no control made him say sentimentally: "My dear, you must see that I'd like at least to take you to your work."

"Not at all, have it on me," she said, giving him the lie direct. She went past him to the room he had slept in. "I shall be leaving in ten minutes," she said.

He took a shower, fast. When he returned, the workroom was already tidied, the bed made, all signs of the night gone. Also, there were no signs of the coffee she had brought in for him. He did not like to ask for it, for fear of an outright refusal. Besides, she was ready, her coat on, her handbag under her arm. He went, without a word, to the front door, and she came after him, silent.

He could see that every fibre of her body signalled a simple message: Oh God, for the moment when I can be rid of this boor! She was nothing but a slut, he thought.

A taxi came. In it she sat as far away from him as she could. He thought of what he should say to his wife.

Outside the theatre she remarked: "You could drop me here, if you liked." It was not a plea, she was too proud for that. "I'll take you in," he said, and saw her thinking: Very well, I'll go through with it to shame him. He was determined to take her in and hand her over to her colleagues, he was afraid she would give him the slip. But far from playing it down, she seemed determined to play it his way. At the stage door, she said to the doorman: "This is Mr. Spence, Tom—do you remember, Mr. Spence from last night?" "Good morning Babs," said the man, examining Graham, politely, as he had been ordered to do.

Barbara went to the door to the stage, opened it, held it open for him. He went in first, then held it open for her. Together they walked into the cavernous, littered, badly lit place and she called out: "James, James!" A man's voice called out from the front of the house: "Here, Babs, why are you so late?"

The auditorium opened before them, darkish, silent, save for an early-morning busyness of charwomen. A vacuum cleaner roared, smally, somewhere close. A couple of stagehands stood looking up at a drop which had a design of blue and green spirals. James stood with his back to the auditorium, smoking. "You're late, Babs," he said again. He saw Graham behind her, and nodded. Barbara and James kissed. Barbara said, giving allowance to every syllable: "You remember Mr. Spence from last night?" James nodded: How do you do? Barbara stood beside him, and they looked together up at the blue-and-green backdrop. Then Barbara looked again at Graham, asking silently: All right now, isn't that enough? He could see her eyes, sullen with boredom.

He said: "Bye, Babs. Bye, James. I'll ring you, Babs." No response, she ignored him. He walked off slowly, listening for what might be said.

For instance: "Babs, for God's sake, what are you doing with him?" Or she might say: "Are you wondering about Graham Spence? Let me explain."

Graham passed the stagehands who, he could have sworn, didn't recognise him. Then at last he heard James's voice to Barbara: "It's no good, Babs, I know you're enamoured of that particular shade of blue, but do have another look at it, there's a good girl. . . ." Graham left the stage, went past the office where the stage doorman sat reading a newspaper. He looked up, nodded, went back to his paper. Graham went to find a taxi, thinking: I'd better think up something convincing, then I'll telephone my wife.

Luckily he had an excuse not to be at home that day, for this evening he had to interview a young man (for television) about his new novel.

IMAGE SIX

WOMAN ALONE

Women without men are usually assumed to be
so involuntarily. Both in life and in literature
they are generally considered to be odd, pitiable, or
laughable—and sometimes all three. Edna O'Brien
in "The Call" paints the stereotype of a woman
alone, waiting for a man to take the initiative.
Being passive as her lover and our society expects
her to be, she can only accept the pain his rejection has caused her. O'Brien does not emphasize
her heroine's situation as ludicrous; she leaves her
with dignity, though fully aware of her weakness
and vulnerability. O'Brien's persona learns from

her experience that she can start over. As readers we hope that she will not simply repeat her experience with another man. As long as women accept society's verdict that they have no status except through their relationships with men, they will continue to put themselves into the position of being victims. Women will see their need for men without perceiving men's equal need for them, a need calling for free communication instead of pretending to wait to be asked. Because of society's heavy condemnation of women without men, resisting the traditional courtship role of the coy lady waiting to be swept off her feet will be difficult; self-assertion and self-definition will be elusive goals for women.

Women who have never "belonged" to a man—old maids—are perceived as ahuman, peculiar beings outside the world of human relations. Auden's Miss Gee and Freeman's Louisa Ellis in "A New England Nun" have missed out on life; they are observers, not participants. Miss Gee turns her head away as she passes lovers who do not ask her to stay; Louisa turns with relief from the prospect of marriage, happy to see her fiancé in love with a younger woman. The cancer that consumes Miss Gee and the dog that Louisa keeps chained up, feeding him on bread, symbolize these women's "foiled creative fire" and invite the reader's pity. Yet the reader is also asked to see these women as absurd. The images of Miss Gee bicycling to church as if pursued by a bull and of Louisa sweeping up after Joe are ludicrous as well as pathetic. They seem beyond human charity. The Oxford Groupers, members of a religious organization teaching the original Christian doctrine of charity, dissect the body of Miss Gee. Images of narrowness and waste—sewing and resewing a seam—invite us to see Louisa's decision to live alone as a refusal really to live. Yet Louisa's choice can be viewed as the beginning of a richer life. Though she "dies to the world" as a nun does upon taking her vows, it is arrogant to conclude that being herself and living on her own terms in a world she has created for herself is a diminishment of life. Many an overworked wife living with a demanding mother-in-law as Louisa's successor does would envy her her freedom. One could hardly envy Miss Gee; yet to imply that a childless woman is comparable to a retired man—both are subject to cancer—is to assert that motherhood is the only means for a woman to achieve humanity, that to be flat-chested, sterile, and unwanted by men is not to live at all. Auden's poem is a clear statement that, for women, anatomy is destiny.

Colette's story "The Other Wife" shows that, from a woman's perspective, life without a man can indeed be attractive. Alice cannot feel pity for or superiority toward her divorced husband's first wife, whom she sees sitting alone in a busy restaurant. Though the first wife is "not having a gayly mad time," as Alice is, Alice sees her as "a superior woman" because she has left a husband she disliked living with. Alice begins to doubt her own good fortune in having married him; she sees the first wife's freedom as desirable and her own position as inferior. James

Tiptree, Jr. (Alice Sheldon) sees living apart from men as an alternative chosen by "The Women Men Don't See," those who quietly do the work of the world. Returning to earth only so that the daughter can find a man by whom she can become pregnant, the mother and daughter prefer life on a distant planet to playing their secondary role on earth. The male narrator finds such a choice incredible, though he marveled at the self-sufficiency and competence of the women when their plane crashed. This story expresses a major fear about women's liberation: that if they become independent, women will desert men. The fear seems well grounded if women are limited to their traditional roles.

In William Carlos Williams's "The Widow's Lament in Springtime" and Kate Chopin's "The Story of an Hour," neither of the widows fits the stereotype of the pitiful, inadequate woman. Though she is the traditional image of the long-married widow desolated by her husband's death, Williams's widow is too dignified, too strong in her emotions to allow pity—an attitude that always involves a sense of superiority, of contempt. Chopin's heroine, discontent in her marriage, is happy only in the one hour when she thinks her husband dead. To many readers this reaction may seem inhuman and unnatural; certainly it casts doubt on the universality of the kind of grief suffered by the widow in Williams's poem. The quality and degree of that grief are likely to depend on the quality of the marriage. Many a widow might be happy to live with the independence of Myrtle Reeves, the central character in Elizabeth Schultz's "Bone." Myrtle remains close to her roots, enjoying simple pleasures like visiting and gardening, too wise to be motivated by others' concerns. Women alone—whether single, divorced, or widowed—must be seen not as stereotypes but as individuals, capable of meeting life on their own terms.

EDNA O'BRIEN

(b. 1932) Born in County Clare, Ireland, Edna O'Brien studied pharmacy in Dublin. After moving to London she began to write fiction. Since 1960, a novel, play, or collection of short stories has appeared about every other year. Some of these have been filmed and she herself has written movie and television scripts. Known first for her comic bawdiness, she has become increasingly concerned about women's dilemmas, both sexual and personal. Her most recent collection of stories is *A Rose in the Heart* (1979). A play about Virginia Woolf opened in 1980.

THE CALL

She would be, or so she thought, over it—over the need and over the hope and over the certainty of that invisible bond that linked them—when suddenly it would come back. It was like a storm. She would start to shake. One morning, this frenzy made her almost blind, so that she could hardly see the design on the teacup she was washing, and even the simple suds in the aluminum sink seemed to enclose a vast pool of woe. When she saw two pigeons in the plane tree outside, it smote her heart because they were cooing and because they were close. Then her telephone rang in the other room. Going to answer it, with the tea cloth in her hand, she prayed, "Oh, God, let it be him," and in a sense her prayers were answered, though she could not be sure, because by the time she got to it whoever it was had rung off. She waited, trembling. It—he—would ring again.

There was sun on the trees in the garden outside, and the varying greenness of each tree was singled out and emphasized in the brightness. There was a dark green, which emitted a gloom that seemed to come from its very interior; there was a pale green, which spoke of happiness and limes; and there was the holly leaf so shiny it might have just been polished. There was the lilac, shedding and rusted because of the recent heavy rain, and the hanging mauve blooms gave the effect of having dropsy. And all of these greens seemed to tell her of her condition—of how it varied, of how sometimes she was not rallying and then again sometimes she would pass to another state, a relatively bright and buoyant state, and sometimes, indeed, she had dropsy. Yet he was not ringing back. But why? Ah, yes. She knew why. He did not care to lose face, and by ringing immediately it would be evident that it had been him. So she busied herself with little chores. She drained the dishes and then dried them thoroughly. Her face on their shining surfaces looked distorted. Just as well he was not coming! She took the loose fallen petals of sweet pea from a vase on the window ledge and squeezed them as if to squeeze the last bit of color and juice out of them. After twenty minutes of devoting herself to pointless trivia, to errands into which she read talismanic import, she decided that he was not going to ring, and so to put herself out of her misery she must ring him. He had lately given her the number. He had repeated it twice and when last leaving he had said it again. For six months he had kept it a secret. It was his work number. He would not, of course, give her his home number, since it was also his wife's. So why not ring? Why not? Because she found herself shaking before even attempting to dial. She foresaw how she would speak rapidly and hurriedly and ask him to lunch, and suppose he said no. She would wait for half an hour and then she would ring.

In that half hour, her whole body seemed to lose its poise and its strength. She felt sick and ashamed, as if she had done some terrible wrong— some childish wrong like wetting or soiling her bed—and she sought to find the root of this pointless notion of wrongdoing that was connected with an excruciating wait. She thought of previous times when she had been spurned by others and tried to marshal in herself the pride, the fury, the common sense that would cause her not to lay herself at his feet. She thought of the day when she would learn to get by—maybe learn to swim—and for an instant she saw herself thrashing through a pool and kicking and conquering. She said, "If I ring, does it not make me the stronger one?" Her words were hollow to herself. The sun shone, yet her house had a coldness—the coldness of a vault, the coldness when you press yourself on the tiled floor of an empty dark country chapel and beg your Maker to help you in these straits—and for no reason there crowded in on her mind images of a wedding, a slow procession down the aisle, a baptismal font with a rim of rust on its marble base, religious booklets about keeping company, and in the chapel porch an umbrella with one spoke protruding. In imagination she went out the gravelled path under the yew trees and smelled their solemn, permeating perfume. She thought, Yesterday I could do without him, today I can't. And then she remonstrated, You can.

She was going on a train that afternoon, to the country, and once on the train, no matter how great her unhappiness, she could not succumb to a frenzy. She thought, too, that if she rang him once she might ring him at all hours, she might make a habit of it. If only he would sit opposite her, take her hand, and tell her that he had no interest in her, then she believed that she would be free to let him go. . . . Or was he going? Was she herself becoming narked? She saw him once a fortnight, but that was not enough. These clandestine visits were the crumbs of the marriage table. The making do with nearly nothing. Where was the bounty of it? Where the abandon?

"You are what you are," she said. But did others have to suffer so? Did others lie down and almost expire under such longing? No. Others swam; others went far out to sea, others dived, others put oxygen flagons on their backs and went down into the depths of the ocean and saw the life there—the teeming, impersonal life—and detached themselves from the life up above. She feared that her love of nature—her love of woodland, her love of sun on hillside and meadow, her love of wild flowers and dog roses and cow parsley, her love of the tangled hedgerows—was only an excuse, a solace. Mortal love was what she craved.

She imagined how he would come and pass her by in the hall, being too shy to shake hands, and walk around the room inhaling her while also trying to observe by the jug of fresh flowers or the letters on her desk who had been here recently, and if perhaps she had found a lover. He had commanded her to, and had also commanded her not to. Always when he lay above her, about to possess her, he seemed to be surveying his pasture, to sniff like a bloodhound, making sure that no other would pass through to his burrow, making sure that she would be secret and sweet, and solely for him.

Ah, would that they were out on hillside, or in the orchards of her youth, away from telephone calls or no telephone calls, away from suspicions, where he believed she wore perfume deliberately so his wife would guess his guilty secret. She was watching the face of her telephone, following with her eye the circle of congealed dust about the digits, where fingernail never reached nor duster ever strove; watching and praying. She heard a letter being pushed through her box and she ran to get it. Any errand was a mercy, a distraction, a slender way of postponing what she would do but must not do.

The letter was from a stranger. It bore a scape of a blue sea, a high craggy cliff, and a flying bird. The message said, "I thought this to be the bluebird of happiness but fear it might only be a common pigeon." It wished her happiness and to be well. It was signed, "A WELL-WISHER, MALE." She thought, Oh, Christ, the whole world knows of my stew, and she wondered calmly if this union she craved was something that others, wiser ones, had forgone—had left behind at their mothers' breasts, never to be retasted—and she thought of her dead mother with her hair tautly pinned up and of the wall of unvoiced but palpable hostility that had grown between them. She hoped then that she would be the same toward her man one day, withdrawn, cut off from him. Her mother's visage brought tears to her eyes. They were different tears from the ones she had been shedding earlier. They were a hot burst of uncontrolled grief that within minutes had sluiced her face and streamed over into her temples and wet her hair.

The half hour had passed in which she promised herself that she would ring him, and now she was talking to herself as to an addict, saying could she not wait a bit longer, could her longing not be diverted by work or a walk, could she not assuage the lump inside her throat by swallowing warmed honey on it, so that the syrup would slide down and soothe her. The needless pain there seemed to be intensified, as if a sharp current were passing through her. Could she not put it off until the morrow?

There is no stopping a galloping horse.

She went toward the telephone, and, as she did, it began to ring. It rang loudly. It rang like some tutelary ogre, telling her to pick it up quickly, telling her that it was the master of her fate, of her every moment, of the privacy of her room, of the tangle of her thoughts, of the weight of her desire, and of the enormity of her hope. She did not answer it. She did not know why she did not answer it. She simply knew that she could not answer it, and that she waited for its ringing to die down the way one waits for the ambulance siren to move out of one's hearing, to pass to the next street.

"Is this love?" she asked herself, admitting that she had wanted so much to answer it. The longing to see him, communicate with him, clasp her fingers in his, feed him, humor him, and watch him while he ran a comb through his hair was as strong and as candescent as it had ever been.

"You had better go out now," she said aloud, and quickly, but with a certain ceremony, she put an embroidered shawl over the phone, to muffle its sound.

It would be three days before she came back, and she saw a strip of water that would get wider and wider. Green and turbulent it was, and in time, she knew, it would swell into a vast sea, impassable and with no shore in sight. Time would sever them, but as yet it was love, and hard to banish.

W. H. AUDEN

(1907–1973) Born in England, Auden became an American citizen in 1939 and divided his time between the two countries and a summer home in Austria. A major American poet, Auden turned from his early interest in Marxism to a deep commitment to Christianity; his long poem *For the Time Being* (1941) expresses his belief in the need for faith in our time. His poems, many of which are light in tone, reflect a wide interest in politics, literature, and music. His last poems, *Thank You, Fog,* were published posthumously in 1975.

MISS GEE

Let me tell you a little story
    About Miss Edith Gee;
She lived in Clevedon Terrace
    At Number 83.

She'd a slight squint in her left eye,
    Her lips they were thin and small,
She had narrow sloping shoulders
    And she had no bust at all.

She'd a velvet hat with trimmings,
    And a dark-grey serge costume;
She lived in Clevedon Terrace
    In a small bed-sitting room.

She'd a purple mac for wet days,
    A green umbrella too to take,
She'd a bicycle with shopping basket
    And a harsh back-pedal brake.

The Church of Saint Aloysius
    Was not so very far;
She did a lot of knitting,
    Knitting for that Church Bazaar.

Miss Gee looked up at the starlight
    And said: 'Does anyone care
That I live in Clevedon Terrace
    On one hundred pounds a year?'

She dreamed a dream one evening
    That she was the Queen of France
And the Vicar of Saint Aloysius
    Asked Her Majesty to dance.

But a storm blew down the palace,
    She was biking through a field of corn,
And a bull with the face of the Vicar
    Was charging with lowered horn.

She could feel his hot breath behind her,
    He was going to overtake;
And the bicycle went slower and slower
    Because of that back-pedal brake.

Summer made the trees a picture,
    Winter made them a wreck;
She bicycled to the evening service
    With her clothes buttoned up to her neck.

She passed by the loving couples,
    She turned her head away;
She passed by the loving couples
    And they didn't ask her to stay.

Miss Gee sat down in the side-aisle,
    She heard the organ play;
And the choir it sang so sweetly
    At the ending of the day,

Miss Gee knelt down in the side-aisle,
    She knelt down on her knees;
'Lead me not into temptation
    But make me a good girl, please.'

The days and nights went by her
    Like waves round a Cornish wreck;
She bicycled down to the doctor
    With her clothes buttoned up to her neck.

She bicycled down to the doctor,
    And rang the surgery bell;
'O, doctor, I've a pain inside me,
    And I don't feel very well.'

Doctor Thomas looked her over,
    And then he looked some more;
Walked over to his wash-basin,
    Said, 'Why didn't you come before?'

Doctor Thomas sat over his dinner,
    Though his wife was waiting to ring;
Rolling his bread into pellets,
    Said, 'Cancer's a funny thing.

'Nobody knows what the cause is,
    Though some pretend they do;
It's like some hidden assassin
    Waiting to strike at you.

'Childless women get it,
    And men when they retire;
It's as if there had to be some outlet
    For their foiled creative fire.'

His wife she rang for the servant,
    Said, 'Don't be so morbid, dear,'
He said; 'I saw Miss Gee this evening
    And she's a goner, I fear.'

They took Miss Gee to the hospital,
    She lay there a total wreck,
Lay in the ward for women
    With the bedclothes right up to her neck.

They laid her on the table,
    The students began to laugh;
And Mr. Rose the surgeon
    He cut Miss Gee in half.

Mr. Rose he turned to his students,
    Said; 'Gentlemen, if you please,
We seldom see a sarcoma
    As far advanced as this.'

They took her off the table,
    They wheeled away Miss Gee
Down to another department
    Where they study Anatomy.

They hung her from the ceiling,
    Yes, they hung up Miss Gee;
And a couple of Oxford Groupers
    Carefully dissected her knee.

W. H. AUDEN

MARY E. WILKINS FREEMAN

(1852–1930) Mary E. Wilkins Freeman wrote many novels and short stories about the frustrations of life in New England small towns, a subject she knew firsthand. Her short-story collections include *A Humble Romance and Other Stories* (1887), *A New England Nun and Other Stories* (1891), and *The Wind in the Rose Bush* (1903). Many of these and several of her novels, such as *Jane Field* (1893), depict realistically the everyday life of women.

A NEW ENGLAND NUN

It was late in the afternoon, and the light was waning. There was a difference in the look of the tree shadows out in the yard. Somewhere in the distance cows were lowing and a little bell was tinkling; now and then a farm-wagon tilted by, and the dust flew; some blue-shirted laborers with shovels over their shoulders plodded past; little swarms of flies were dancing up and down before the people's faces in the soft air. There seemed to be a gentle stir arising over everything for the mere sake of subsidence— a very premonition of rest and hush and night.

This soft diurnal commotion was over Louisa Ellis also. She had been peacefully sewing at her sitting-room window all the afternoon. Now she quilted her needle carefully into her work, which she folded precisely, and laid in a basket with her thimble and thread and scissors. Louisa Ellis could not remember that ever in her life she had mislaid one of these little feminine appurtenances, which had become, from long use and constant association, a very part of her personality.

Louisa tied a green apron round her waist, and got out a flat straw hat with a green ribbon. Then she went into the garden with a little blue crockery bowl, to pick some currants for her tea. After the currants were picked she sat on the back door-step and stemmed them, collecting the stems carefully in her apron, and afterward throwing them into the hen-coop. She looked sharply at the grass beside the step to see if any had fallen there.

Louisa was slow and still in her movements; it took her a long time to prepare her tea; but when ready it was set forth with as much grace as if she had been a veritable guest to her own self. The little square table stood exactly in the centre of the kitchen, and was covered with a starched linen cloth whose border pattern of flowers glistened. Louisa had a damask napkin on her tea-tray, where were arranged a cut-glass tumbler full of teaspoons, a silver cream-pitcher, a china sugar-bowl, and one pink china cup and saucer. Louisa used china every day—something which none of her neighbors did. They whispered about it among themselves. Their daily tables were laid with common crockery, their sets of best china stayed in the parlor closet, and Louisa Ellis was no richer nor better bred than they. Still she would use the china. She had for her supper a glass dish full of sugared currants, a plate of little cakes, and one of light white biscuits. Also a leaf or two of lettuce, which she cut up daintily. Louisa was very fond of lettuce, which she raised to perfection in her little garden. She ate quite heartily, though in a delicate, pecking way; it seemed almost surprising that any considerable bulk of the food should vanish.

After tea she filled a plate with nicely baked thin corn-cakes, and carried them out into the back-yard.

"Caesar!" she called. "Caesar! Caesar!"

There was a little rush, and the clank of a chain, and a large yellow-and-white dog appeared at the door of his tiny hut, which was half hidden among the tall grasses and flowers. Louisa patted him and gave him the corn-cakes. Then she returned to the house and washed the tea-things, polishing the china carefully. The twilight had deepened; the chorus of the frogs floated in at the open window wonderfully loud and shrill, and once in a while a long sharp drone from a tree-toad pierced it. Louisa took off her green gingham apron, disclosing a shorter one of pink-and-white print. She lighted her lamp, and sat down again with her sewing.

In about half an hour Joe Dagget came. She heard his heavy step on the walk, and rose and took off her pink-and-white apron. Under that was still another—white linen with a little cambric edging on the bottom; that was Louisa's company apron. She never wore it without her calico sewing apron over it unless she had a guest. She had barely folded the pink and white one with methodical haste and laid it in a table-drawer when the door opened and Joe Dagget entered.

He seemed to fill up the whole room. A little yellow canary that had been asleep in his green cage at the south window woke up and fluttered wildly, beating his little yellow wings against the wires. He always did so when Joe Dagget came into the room.

"Good-evening," said Louisa. She extended her hand with a kind of solemn cordiality.

"Good-evening, Louisa," returned the man, in a loud voice.

She placed a chair for him, and they sat facing each other, with the table between them. He sat bolt-upright, toeing out his heavy feet squarely,

MARY E. WILKINS FREEMAN

glancing with a good-humored uneasiness around the room. She sat gently erect, folding her slender hands in her white-linen lap.

"Been a pleasant day," remarked Dagget.

"Real pleasant," Louisa assented softly. "Have you been haying?" she asked, after a little while.

"Yes, I've been haying all day, down in the ten-acre lot. Pretty hot work."

"It must be."

"Yes, it's pretty hot work in the sun."

"Is your mother well to-day?"

"Yes, mother's pretty well."

"I suppose Lily Dyer's with her now?"

Dagget colored. "Yes, she's with her," he answered slowly.

He was not very young, but there was a boyish look about his large face. Louisa was not quite as old as he, her face was fairer and smoother, but she gave people the impression of being older.

"I suppose she's a good deal of help to your mother," she said, further.

"I guess she is; I don't know how mother'd get along without her," said Dagget, with a sort of embarrassed warmth.

"She looks like a real capable girl. She's pretty-looking too," remarked Louisa.

"Yes, she is pretty fair looking."

Presently Dagget began fingering the books on the table. There was a square red autograph album, and a Young Lady's Gift-Book which had belonged to Louisa's mother. He took them up one after the other and opened them; then laid them down again, the album on the Gift-Book.

Louisa kept eying them with mild uneasiness. Finally she rose and changed the position of the books, putting the album underneath. That was the way they had been arranged in the first place.

Dagget gave an awkward little laugh. "Now what difference did it make which book was on top?" said he.

Louisa looked at him with a deprecating smile. "I always keep them that way," murmured she.

"You do beat everything," said Dagget, trying to laugh again. His large face was flushed.

He remained about an hour longer, then rose to take leave. Going out, he stumbled over a rug, and trying to recover himself, hit Louisa's work-basket on the table, and knocked it on the floor.

He looked at Louisa, then at the rolling spools; he ducked himself awkwardly toward them, but she stopped him. "Never mind," said she; "I'll pick them up after you're gone."

She spoke with a mild stiffness. Either she was a little disturbed, or his nervousness affected her, and made her seem constrained in her effort to reassure him.

When Joe Dagget was outside he drew in the sweet evening air with a sigh, and felt much as an innocent and perfectly well-intentioned bear might after his exit from a china shop.

Louisa, on her part, felt much as the kind-hearted, long-suffering owner of the china shop might have done after the exit of the bear.

She tied on the pink, then the green apron, picked up all the scattered treasures and replaced them in her work-basket, and straightened the rug. Then she set the lamp on the floor, and began sharply examining the carpet. She even rubbed her fingers over it, and looked at them.

"He's tracked in a good deal of dust," she murmured. "I thought he must have."

Louisa got a dust-pan and brush, and swept Joe Dagget's track carefully.

If he could have known it, it would have increased his perplexity and uneasiness, although it would not have disturbed his loyalty in the least. He came twice a week to see Louisa Ellis, and every time, sitting there in her delicately sweet room, he felt as if surrounded by a hedge of lace. He was afraid to stir lest he should put a clumsy foot or hand through the fairy web, and he had always the consciousness that Louisa was watching fearfully lest he should.

Still the lace and Louisa commanded perforce his perfect respect and patience and loyalty. They were to be married in a month, after a singular courtship which had lasted for a matter of fifteen years. For fourteen out of the fifteen years the two had not once seen each other, and they had seldom exchanged letters. Joe had been all those years in Australia, where he had gone to make his fortune, and where he had stayed until he made it. He would have stayed fifty years if it had taken so long, and come home feeble and tottering, or never come home at all, to marry Louisa.

But the fortune had been made in the fourteen years, and he had come home now to marry the woman who had been patiently and unquestioningly waiting for him all that time.

Shortly after they were engaged he had announced to Louisa his determination to strike out into new fields, and secure a competency before they should be married. She had listened and assented with the sweet serenity which never failed her, not even when her lover set forth on that long and uncertain journey. Joe, buoyed up as he was by his sturdy determination, broke down a little at the last, but Louisa kissed him with a mild blush, and said good-by.

"It won't be for long," poor Joe had said, huskily; but it was for fourteen years.

In that length of time much had happened. Louisa's mother and brother had died, and she was all alone in the world. But greatest happening of all—a subtle happening which both were too simple to understand—Louisa's feet had turned into a path, smooth maybe under a calm, serene sky, but so straight and unswerving that it could only meet a check at the grave, and so narrow that there was no room for any one at her side.

MARY E. WILKINS FREEMAN

Louisa's first emotion when Joe Dagget came home (he had not apprised her of his coming) was consternation, although she would not admit it to herself, and he never dreamed of it. Fifteen years ago she had been in love with him—at least she considered herself to be. Just at that time, gently acquiescing with and falling into the natural drift of girlhood, she had seen marriage ahead as a reasonable feature and a probable desirability of life. She had listened with calm docility to her mother's views upon the subject. Her mother was remarkable for her cool sense and sweet, even temperament. She talked wisely to her daughter when Joe Dagget presented himself, and Louisa accepted him with no hesitation. He was the first lover she had ever had.

She had been faithful to him all these years. She had never dreamed of the possibility of marrying any one else. Her life, especially for the last seven years, had been full of a pleasant peace, she had never felt discontented nor impatient over her lover's absence; still she had always looked forward to his return and their marriage as the inevitable conclusion of things. However, she had fallen into a way of placing it so far in the future that it was almost equal to placing it over the boundaries of another life.

When Joe came she had been expecting him, and expecting to be married for fourteen years, but she was as much surprised and taken aback as if she had never thought of it.

Joe's consternation came later. He eyed Louisa with an instant confirmation of his old admiration. She had changed but little. She still kept her pretty manner and soft grace, and was, he considered, every whit as attractive as ever. As for himself, his stint was done; he had his face turned away from fortune-seeking, and the old winds of romance whistled as loud and sweet as ever through his ears. All the song which he had been wont to hear in them was Louisa; he had for a long time a loyal belief that he heard it still, but finally it seemed to him that although the winds sang always that one song, it had another name. But for Louisa the wind had never more than murmured; now it had gone down, and everything was still. She listened for a little while with half-wistful attention; then she turned quietly away and went to work on her wedding clothes.

Joe had made some extensive and quite magnificent alterations in his house. It was the old homestead; the newly-married couple would live there, for Joe could not desert his mother, who refused to leave her old home. So Louisa must leave hers. Every morning, rising and going about among her neat maidenly possessions, she felt as one looking her last upon the faces of dear friends. It was true that in a measure she could take them with her, but, robbed of their old environments, they would appear in such new guises that they would almost cease to be themselves. Then there were some peculiar features of her happy solitary life which she would probably be obliged to relinquish altogether. Sterner tasks than these graceful but half-needless ones would probably devolve upon her. There would be a large house to care for; there would be company to entertain; there would be Joe's rigorous and feeble old mother to wait upon; and it would be contrary to all thrifty village traditions for her to keep more than one servant. Louisa had a little still, and she used to occupy herself pleasantly in summer weather with distilling the sweet aromatic essences from roses and peppermint and spearmint. By-and-by her still must be laid away. Her store of essences was already considerable, and there would be no time for her to distil for the mere pleasure of it. Then Joe's mother would think it foolishness; she had already hinted her opinion in the matter. Louisa dearly loved to sew a linen seam, not always for use, but for the simple, mild pleasure which she took in it. She would have been loath to confess how more than once she had ripped a seam for the mere delight of sewing it together again. Sitting at her window during long sweet afternoons, drawing her needle gently through the dainty fabric, she was peace itself. But there was small chance of such foolish comfort in the future. Joe's mother, domineering, shrewd old matron that she was even in her old age, and very likely even Joe himself, with his honest masculine rudeness, would laugh and frown down all these pretty but senseless old maiden ways.

Louisa had almost the enthusiasm of an artist over the mere order and cleanliness of her solitary home. She had throbs of genuine triumph at the sight of the window-panes which she had polished until they shone like jewels. She gloated gently over her orderly bureau-drawers, with their exquisitely folded contents redolent with lavender and sweet clover and very purity. Could she be sure of the endurance of even this? She had visions, so startling that she half repudiated them as indelicate, of coarse masculine belongings strewn about in endless litter; of dust and disorder arising necessarily from a coarse masculine presence in the midst of all this delicate harmony.

Among her forebodings of disturbance, not the least was with regard to Caesar. Caesar was a veritable hermit of a dog. For the greater part of his life he had dwelt in his secluded hut, shut out from the society of his kind and all innocent canine joys. Never had Caesar since his early youth watched at a woodchuck's hole; never had he known the delights of a stray bone at a neighbor's kitchen door. And it was all on account of a sin committed when hardly out of his puppyhood. No one knew the possible depth of remorse of which this mild-visaged, altogether innocent-looking old dog might be capable; but whether or not he had encountered remorse, he had encountered a full measure of righteous retribution. Old Caesar seldom lifted up his voice in a growl or a bark; he was fat and sleepy; there were yellow rings which looked like spectacles around his dim old eyes; but there was a neighbor who bore on his hand the imprint of several of Caesar's sharp white youthful teeth, and for that he had lived at the end of a chain, all alone in a little hut, for fourteen years. The neighbor, who was choleric and smarting with the pain of his wound, had demanded either Caesar's death or complete ostracism. So Louisa's brother, to whom the dog had belonged, had built him his little kennel and tied him up. It was now fourteen years since, in a flood of youthful spirits, he had inflicted that memorable bite, and with the exception of short excursions, always at the end of the chain, under the strict guardianship of his master or Louisa, the old dog had remained a close prisoner. It is doubtful if, with his limited ambition, he took much pride in the fact, but it is certain that he was possessed of considerable cheap fame. He was regarded by all the children in the village and by many adults as a very monster of ferocity. St. George's dragon could hardly have surpassed in evil repute Louisa Ellis's old yellow dog. Mothers charged their children with solemn emphasis not to go too near to him, and the children listened and believed greedily, with a fascinated appetite for terror, and ran by Louisa's house stealthily, with many sidelong glances at the terrible dog. If perchance he sounded a hoarse bark, there was a panic. Wayfarers chancing into Louisa's yard eyed him with respect, and inquired if the chain were stout. Caesar at large might have seemed a very ordinary dog, and excited no comment whatever; chained, his reputation overshadowed him, so that he lost his own proper outlines and looked darkly vague and enormous. Joe Dagget, however, with his good-humored sense and shrewdness, saw him as he was. He strode valiantly up to him and patted him on the head, in spite of Louisa's soft clamor of warning, and even attempted to set him loose. Louisa grew so alarmed that he desisted, but kept announcing his opinion in the matter quite forcibly at intervals. "There ain't a better-natured dog in town," he would say, "and it's downright cruel to keep him tied up there. Some day I'm going to take him out."

Louisa had very little hope that he would not, one of these days, when their interests and possessions should be more completely fused in one. She pictured to herself Caesar on the rampage through the quiet and unguarded village. She saw innocent children bleeding in his path. She was herself very fond of the old dog, because he had belonged to her dead brother, and he was always very gentle with her; still she had great faith in his ferocity. She always warned people not to go too near him. She fed him on ascetic fare of corn-mush and cakes, and never fired his dangerous temper with heating and sanguinary diet of flesh and bones. Louisa looked at the old dog munching his simple fare, and thought of her approaching marriage and trembled. Still no anticipation of disorder and confusion in lieu of sweet peace and harmony, no forebodings of Caesar on the rampage, no wild fluttering of her little yellow canary, were sufficient to turn her a hair's breadth. Joe Dagget had been fond of her and working for her all these years. It was not for her, whatever came to pass, to prove untrue and break his heart. She put the exquisite little stitches into her wedding-garments, and the time went on till it was only a week before her wedding-day. It was a Tuesday evening, and the wedding was to be a week from Wednesday.

There was a full moon that night. About nine o'clock Louisa strolled down the road a little way. There were harvest-fields on either hand, bordered by low stone walls. Luxuriant clumps of bushes grew beside the wall, and trees—wild cherry and old apple trees—at intervals. Presently Louisa sat down on the wall and looked about her with mildly sorrowful reflectiveness. Tall shrubs of blueberry and meadowsweet, all woven together and tangled with blackberry vines and horse-briers, shut her in on either side. She had a little clear space between them. Opposite her, on the other side of the road, was a spreading tree; the moon shone between its boughs, and the leaves twinkled like silver. The road was bespread with a beautiful shifting dapple of silver and shadow; the air was full of a mysterious sweetness. "I wonder if it's wild grapes?" murmured Louisa. She sat there some time. She was just thinking of rising, when she heard footsteps and low voices, and remained quiet. It was a lonely place, and she felt a little timid. She thought she would keep still in the shadow and let the persons, whoever they might be, pass her.

But just before they reached her the voices ceased, and the footsteps. She understood that their owners had also found seats upon the stone wall. She was wondering if she could not steal away unobserved, when the voice broke the stillness. It was Joe Dagget's. She sat still and listened.

The voice was announced by a loud sigh, which was as familiar as itself. "Well," said Dagget, "you've made up your mind, then, I suppose?"

"Yes," returned another voice; "I'm going day after to-morrow."

"That's Lily Dyer," thought Louisa to herself. The voice embodied itself in her mind. She saw a girl tall and full-figured, with a firm, fair face, looking fairer and firmer in the moonlight, her strong yellow hair braided in a close knot. A girl full of calm rustic strength and bloom, with a masterful way which might have beseemed a princess. Lily Dyer was a favorite with the village folk; she had just the qualities to arouse the admiration. She was good and handsome and smart. Louisa had often heard her praises sounded.

"Well," said Joe Dagget, "I ain't got a word to say."

"I don't know what you could say," returned Lily Dyer.

"Not a word to say," repeated Joe, drawing out the words heavily. Then there was a silence. "I ain't sorry," he began at last, "that that happened yesterday—that we kind of let on how we felt to each other. I guess it's just as well we knew. Of course I can't do anything any different. I'm going right on an' get married next week. I ain't going back on a woman that's waited for me fourteen years, an' break her heart."

"If you should jilt her to-morrow, I wouldn't have you," spoke up the girl, with sudden vehemence.

"Well, I ain't going to give you the chance," said he; "but I don't believe you would, either."

"You'd see I wouldn't. Honor's honor, an' right's right. An' I'd never think anything of any man that went against 'em for me or any other girl; you'd find that out, Joe Dagget."

"Well, you'll find out fast enough that I ain't going against 'em for you or any other girl," returned he. Their voices sounded almost as if they were angry with each other. Louisa was listening eagerly.

"I'm sorry you feel as if you must go away," said Joe, "but I don't know but it's best."

"Of course it's best. I hope you and I have got common-sense."

"Well, I suppose you're right." Suddenly Joe's voice got an undertone of tenderness. "Say, Lily," he said, "I'll get along well enough myself, but I can't bear to think—You don't suppose you're going to fret much about it?"

"I guess you'll find out I sha'n't fret much over a married man."

"Well, I hope you won't—I hope you won't, Lily. God knows I do. And —I hope—one of these days—you'll—come across somebody else—"

"I don't see any reason why I shouldn't." Suddenly her tone changed. She spoke in a sweet, clear voice, so loud that she could have been heard across the street. "No, Joe Dagget," said she, "I'll never marry any other man as long as I live. I've got good sense, an' I ain't going to break my heart nor make a fool of myself; but I'm never going to be married, you can be sure of that. I ain't that sort of a girl to feel this way twice."

Louisa heard an exclamation and a soft commotion behind the bushes; then Lily spoke again—the voice sounded as if she had risen. "This must be put a stop to," said she. "We've stayed here long enough. I'm going home."

Louisa sat there in a daze, listening to their retreating steps. After a while she got up and slunk softly home herself. The next day she did her housework methodically; that was as much a matter of course as breathing; but she did not sew on her wedding-clothes. She sat at her window and meditated. In the evening Joe came. Louisa Ellis had never known that she had any diplomacy in her, but when she came to look for it that night she found it, although meek of its kind, among her little feminine weapons. Even now she could hardly believe that she had heard aright, and that she would not do Joe a terrible injury should she break her troth-plight. She wanted to sound him without betraying too soon her own inclinations in the matter. She did it successfully, and they finally came to an understanding; but it was a difficult thing, for he was as afraid of betraying himself as she.

She never mentioned Lily Dyer. She simply said that while she had no cause of complaint against him, she had lived so long in one way that she shrank from making a change.

"Well, I never shrank, Louisa," said Dagget. "I'm going to be honest enough to say that I think maybe it's better this way; but if you'd wanted to keep on, I'd have stuck to you till my dying day. I hope you know that."

"Yes, I do," said she.

That night she and Joe parted more tenderly than they had done for a long time. Standing in the door, holding each other's hands, a last great wave of regretful memory swept over them.

"Well, this ain't the way we've thought it was all going to end, is it, Louisa?" said Joe.

She shook her head. There was a little quiver on her placid face.

"You let me know if there's ever anything I can do for you," said he. "I ain't ever going to forget you, Louisa." Then he kissed her, and went down the path.

Louisa, all alone by herself that night, wept a little, she hardly knew why; but the next morning, on waking, she felt like a queen who, after fearing lest her domain be wrested away from her, sees it firmly insured in her possession.

Now the tall weeds and grasses might cluster around Caesar's little hermit hut, the snow might fall on its roof year in and year out, but he never would go on a rampage through the unguarded village. Now the little canary might turn itself into a peaceful yellow ball night after night, and have no need to wake and flutter with wild terror against its bars. Louisa could sew linen seams, and distil roses, and dust and polish and fold away in lavender, as long as she listed. That afternoon she sat with her needle-work at the window, and felt fairly steeped in peace. Lily Dyer, tall and erect and blooming, went past; but she felt no qualm. If Louisa Ellis had sold her birthright she did not know it, the taste of the pottage was so delicious, and had been her sole satisfaction for so long. Serenity and placid narrowness had become to her as the birthright itself. She gazed ahead through a long reach of future days strung together like pearls in a rosary, every one like the others, and all smooth and flawless and innocent, and her heart went up in thankfulness. Outside was the fervid summer afternoon; the air was filled with the sounds of the busy harvest of men and birds and bees; there were halloos, metallic clatterings, sweet calls, and long hummings. Louisa sat, prayerfully numbering her days, like an uncloistered nun.

COLETTE

(1873–1954) Colette is the pen name of the French novelist Sidonie Gabrielle Claudine Colette, who collaborated with her husband under the pen name Colette Willy in writing the *Claudine* books. She is best known for her works about women, especially *Chéri* (translated 1951) and *Gigi* (translated 1953).

THE OTHER WIFE

'For two? This way, Monsieur and Madame, there's still a table by the bay window, if Madame and Monsieur would like to enjoy the view.'

Alice followed the *maître d'hôtel.*

'Oh, yes, come on Marc, we'll feel we're having lunch on a boat at sea . . .'

Her husband restrained her, passing his arm through hers.

'We'll be more comfortable there.'

'There? In the middle of all those people? I'd much prefer . . .'

'Please, Alice.'

He tightened his grip in so emphatic a way that she turned round.

'What's the matter with you?'

He said 'sh' very quietly, looking at her intently, and drew her towards the table in the middle.

'What is it, Marc?'

'I'll tell you, darling. Let me order lunch. Would you like shrimps? Or eggs in aspic?'

'Whatever *you* like, as you know.'

They smiled at each other, wasting the precious moments of an overworked, perspiring *maître d'hôtel* who stood near to them, suffering from a kind of St. Vitus's dance.

'Shrimps,' ordered Marc. 'And then eggs and bacon. And cold chicken with cos lettuce salad. Cream cheese? *Spécialité de la maison?* We'll settle for the *spécialité*. Two very strong coffees. Please give lunch to my chauffeur, we'll be leaving again at two o'clock. Cider? I don't trust it. . . . Dry champagne.'

He sighed as though he had been moving a wardrobe, gazed at the pale noonday sea, the nearly white sky, then at his wife, finding her pretty in her little Mercury-type hat with its long hanging veil.

'You're looking well, darling. And all this sea-blue colour gives you green eyes, just imagine! And you put on weight when you travel. . . . It's nice, up to a point, but only up to a point!'

Her rounded bosom swelled proudly as she leant over the table.

'Why did you stop me taking that place by the bay window?'

It did not occur to Marc Séguy to tell a lie.

'Because you'd have sat next to someone I know.'

'And whom I don't know?'

'My ex-wife.'

She could not find a word to say and opened her blue eyes wider.

'What of it, darling? It'll happen again. It's not important.'

Alice found her tongue again and asked the inevitable questions in their logical sequence.

'Did she see you? Did she know that you'd seen her? Point her out to me.'

'Don't turn round at once, I beg you, she must be looking at us. A lady with dark hair, without a hat, she must be staying at this hotel. . . . On her own, behind those children in red . . .'

'Yes, I see.'

Sheltered behind broad-brimmed seaside hats, Alice was able to look at the woman who fifteen months earlier had still been her husband's wife. 'Incompatibility,' Marc told her. 'Oh, it was total incompatibility! We divorced like well-brought-up people, almost like friends, quietly and quickly. And I began to love you, and you were able to be happy with me. How lucky we are that in our happiness there haven't been any guilty parties or victims!'

The woman in white, with her smooth, lustrous hair over which the seaside light played in blue patches, was smoking a cigarette, her eyes half closed. Alice turned back to her husband, took some shrimps and butter and ate composedly.

'Why didn't you ever tell me,' she said after a moment's silence, 'that she had blue eyes too?'

'But I'd never thought about it!'

He kissed the hand that she stretched out to the bread basket and she blushed with pleasure. Dark-skinned and plump, she might have seemed slightly earthy, but the changing blue of her eyes, and her wavy golden hair, disguised her as a fragile and soulful blonde. She showed overwhelming gratitude to her husband. She was immodest without knowing it and her entire person revealed over-conspicuous signs of extreme happiness.

They ate and drank with good appetite and each thought that the other had forgotten the woman in white. However, Alice sometimes laughed too loudly and Marc was careful of his posture, putting his shoulders back and holding his head up. They waited some time for coffee, in silence. An incandescent stream, a narrow reflection of the high and invisible sun, moved slowly over the sea and shone with unbearable brilliance.

'She's still there, you know,' Alice whispered suddenly.

'Does she embarrass you? Would you like to have coffee somewhere else?'

'Not at all! It's she who ought to be embarrassed! And she doesn't look as though she's having a madly gay time, if you could see her . . .'

'It's not necessary. I know that look of hers.'

'Oh, was she like that?'

He breathed smoke through his nostrils and wrinkled his brows.

'Was she like that? No. To be frank, she wasn't happy with me.'

'Well, my goodness!'

'You're delightfully generous, darling, madly generous. . . . You're an angel, you're. . . . You love me . . . I'm so proud, when I see that look in your eyes . . . yes, the look you have now. . . . She. . . . No doubt I didn't succeed in making her happy. That's all there is to it, I didn't succeed.'

'She's hard to please!'

Alice fanned herself irritably, and cast brief glances at the woman in white who was smoking, her head leaning against the back of the cane chair, her eyes closed with an expression of satisfied lassitude.

Marc shrugged his shoulders modestly.

'That's it,' he admitted. 'What can one do? We have to be sorry for people who are never happy. As for us, we're so happy. . . . Aren't we, darling?'

She didn't reply. She was looking with furtive attention at her husband's face, with its good colour and regular shape, at his thick hair, with its occasional thread of white silk, at his small, well-cared-for hands. She felt dubious for the first time, and asked herself: 'What more did she want, then?'

And until they left, while Marc was paying the bill, asking about the chauffeur and the route, she continued to watch, with envious curiosity, the lady in white, that discontented, hard-to-please, superior woman. . . .

JAMES TIPTREE, JR.

(b. 1918?) Embarrassed by the praise for
"The Women Men Don't See" as an example
of how well a man could write about women,
James Tiptree, Jr., disclosed in 1974 that she
is Alice Sheldon. A semiretired psychologist,
Sheldon has received four prizes since 1968
for science fiction writing. Widely traveled,
she lives—or at least receives her mail—at
McLean, Virginia. Ursula LeGuin introduced
Sheldon's most recent collection, *Star Songs
of an Old Primate* (1978).

THE WOMEN MEN DON'T SEE

I see her first while the Mexicana 727 is barreling down to Cozumel Island.
I come out of the can and lurch into her seat, saying "Sorry," at a double
female blur. The near blur nods quietly. The younger one in the window
seat goes on looking out. I continue down the aisle, registering nothing.
Zero. I never would have looked at them or thought of them again.

Cozumel airport is the usual mix of panicky Yanks dressed for the
sand pile and calm Mexicans dressed for lunch at the Presidente. I am a
used-up Yank dressed for serious fishing; I extract my rods and duffel from
the riot and hike across the field to find my charter pilot. One Captain
Estéban has contracted to deliver me to the bonefish flats of Belize three
hundred kilometers down the coast.

Captain Estéban turns out to be four-feet nine of mahogany Mayan *puro*.
He is also in a somber Maya snit. He tells me my Cessna is grounded
somewhere and his Bonanza is booked to take a party to Chetumal.

Well, Chetumal is south; can he take me along and go on to Belize
after he drops them off? Gloomily he concedes the possibility—*if* the other
party permits, and *if* there are not too many *equipajes*.

The Chetumal party approaches. It's the woman and her young companion—daughter?—neatly picking their way across the gravel and yucca
apron. Their Ventura two-suiters, like themselves, are small, plain and
neutral-colored. No problem. When the captain asks if I may ride along,
the mother says mildly "Of course," without looking at me.

I think that's when my inner tilt-detector sends up its first faint click. How come this woman has already looked me over carefully enough to accept on her plane? I disregard it. Paranoia hasn't been useful in my business for years, but the habit is hard to break.

As we clamber into the Bonanza, I see the girl has what could be an attractive body if there was any spark at all. There isn't. Captain Estéban folds a serape to sit on so he can see over the cowling and runs a meticulous check-down. And then we're up and trundling over the turquoise Jello of the Caribbean into a stiff south wind.

The coast on our right is the territory of Quintana Roo. If you haven't seen Yucatán, imagine the world's biggest absolutely flat green-gray rug. An empty-looking land. We pass the white ruin of Tulum and the gash of the road to Chichén Itzá, a half-dozen coconut plantations, and then nothing but reef and low scrub jungle all the way to the horizon, just about the way the conquistadors saw it four centuries back.

Long strings of cumulus are racing at us, shadowing the coast. I have gathered that part of our pilot's gloom concerns the weather. A cold front is dying on the henequen fields of Mérida to the west, and the south wind has piled up a string of coastal storms: what they call *llovisnos*. Estéban detours methodically around a couple of small thunderheads. The Bonanza jinks, and I look back with a vague notion of reassuring the women. They are calmly intent on what can be seen of Yucatán. Well, they were offered the copilot's view, but they turned it down. Too shy?

Another *llovisno* puffs up ahead. Estéban takes the Bonanza upstairs, rising in his seat to sight his course. I relax for the first time in too long, savoring the latitudes between me and my desk, the week of fishing ahead. Our captain's classic Maya profile attracts my gaze: forehead sloping back from his predatory nose, lips and jaw stepping back below it. If his slant eyes had been any more crossed, he couldn't have made his license. That's a handsome combination, believe it or not. On the little Maya chicks in their minishifts with iridescent gloop on those cockeyes, it's also highly erotic. Nothing like the oriental doll thing; these people have stone bones. Captain Estéban's old grandmother could probably tow the Bonanza . . .

I'm snapped awake by the cabin hitting my ear. Estéban is barking into his headset over a drumming racket of hail; the windows are dark gray.

One important noise is missing—the motor. I realize Estéban is fighting a dead plane. Thirty-six hundred; we've lost two thousand feet!

He slaps tank switches as the storm throws us around; I catch something about *gasolina* in a snarl that shows his big teeth. The Bonanza reels down. As he reaches for an overhead toggle, I see the fuel gauges are high. Maybe a clogged gravity feed line; I've heard of dirty gas down here. He drops the set; it's a million to one nobody can read us through the storm at this range anyway. Twenty-five hundred—going down.

His electric feed pump seems to have cut in: the motor explodes—quits—explodes—and quits again for good. We are suddenly out of the bottom of the clouds. Below us is a long white line almost hidden by rain: the reef. But there isn't any beach behind it, only a big meandering bay with a few mangrove flats—and it's coming up at us fast.

This is going to be bad, I tell myself with great unoriginality. The women behind me haven't made a sound. I look back and see they've braced down with their coats by their heads. With a stalling speed around eighty, all this isn't much use, but I wedge myself in.

Estéban yells some more into his set, flying a falling plane. He is doing one jesus job, too—as the water rushes up at us he dives into a hair-raising turn and hangs us into the wind—with a long pale ridge of sandbar in front of our nose.

Where in hell he found it I never know. The Bonanza mushes down, and we belly-hit with a tremendous tearing crash—bounce—hit again—and everything slews wildly as we flat-spin into the mangroves at the end of the bar. Crash! Clang! The plane is wrapping itself into a mound of strangler fig with one wing up. The crashing quits with us all in one piece. And no fire. Fantastic.

Captain Estéban pries open his door, which is now in the roof. Behind me a woman is repeating quietly, "Mother. Mother." I climb up the floor and find the girl trying to free herself from her mother's embrace. The woman's eyes are closed. Then she opens them and suddenly lets go, sane as soap. Estéban starts hauling them out. I grab the Bonanza's aid kit and scramble out after them into brilliant sun and wind. The storm that hit us is already vanishing up the coast.

"Great landing, Captain."

"Oh, yes! It was beautiful." The women are shaky, but no hysteria. Estéban is surveying the scenery with the expression his ancestors used on the Spaniards.

If you've been in one of these things, you know the slow-motion inanity that goes on. Euphoria, first. We straggle down the fig tree and out onto the sandbar in the roaring hot wind, noting without alarm that there's nothing but miles of crystalline water on all sides. It's only a foot or so deep, and the bottom is the olive color of silt. The distant shore around us is all flat mangrove swamp, totally uninhabitable.

"Bahía Espiritu Santo." Estéban confirms my guess that we're down in that huge water wilderness. I always wanted to fish it.

"What's all that smoke?" The girl is pointing at the plumes blowing around the horizon.

"Alligator hunters," says Estéban. Maya poachers have left burn-offs in the swamps. It occurs to me that any signal fires we make aren't going to be too conspicuous. And I now note that our plane is well-buried in the mound of fig. Hard to see it from the air.

Just as the question of how the hell we get out of here surfaces in my mind, the older woman asks composedly, "If they didn't hear you, Captain, when will they start looking for us? Tomorrow?"

"Correct," Estéban agrees dourly. I recall that air-sea rescue is fairly informal here. Like, keep an eye open for Mario, his mother says he hasn't been home all week.

It dawns on me we may be here quite some while.

Furthermore, the diesel-truck noise on our left is the Caribbean piling back into the mouth of the bay. The wind is pushing it at us, and the bare bottoms on the mangroves show that our bar is covered at high tide. I recall seeing a full moon this morning in—believe it, St. Louis—which means maximal tides. Well, we can climb up in the plane. But what about drinking water?

There's a small splat! behind me. The older woman has sampled the bay. She shakes her head, smiling ruefully. It's the first real expression on either of them; I take it as the signal for introductions. When I say I'm Don Fenton from St. Louis, she tells me their name is Parsons, from Bethesda, Maryland. She says it so nicely I don't at first notice we aren't being given first names. We all compliment Captain Estéban again.

His left eye is swelled shut, an inconvenience beneath his attention as a Maya, but Mrs. Parsons spots the way he's bracing his elbow in his ribs.

"You're hurt, Captain."

"*Roto*—I think is broken." He's embarrassed at being in pain. We get him to peel off his Jaime shirt, revealing a nasty bruise in his superb dark-bay torso.

"Is there tape in that kit, Mr. Fenton? I've had a little first-aid training."

She begins to deal competently and very impersonally with the tape. Miss Parsons and I wander to the end of the bar and have a conversation which I am later to recall acutely.

"Roseate spoonbills," I tell her as three pink birds flap away.

"They're beautiful," she says in her tiny voice. They both have tiny voices. "He's a Mayan Indian, isn't he? The pilot, I mean."

"Right. The real thing, straight out of the Bonampak murals. Have you seen Chichén and Uxmal?"

"Yes. We were in Mérida. We're going to Tikal in Guatemala . . . I mean, we were."

"You'll get there." It occurs to me the girl needs cheering up. "Have they told you that Maya mothers used to tie a board on the infant's forehead to get that slant? They also hung a ball of tallow over its nose to make the eyes cross. It was considered aristocratic."

She smiles and takes another peek at Estéban. "People seem different in Yucatán," she says thoughtfully. "Not like the Indians around Mexico City. More, I don't know, independent."

"Comes from never having been conquered. Mayas got massacred and chased a lot, but nobody ever really flattened them. I bet you didn't know that the last Mexican-Maya war ended with a negotiated truce in nineteen thirty-five?"

"No!" Then she says seriously, "I like that."

"So do I."

"The water is really rising very fast," says Mrs. Parsons gently from behind us.

It is, and so is another *llovisno*. We climb back into the Bonanza. I try to rig my parka for a rain catcher, which blows loose as the storm hits fast and furious. We sort a couple of malt bars and my bottle of Jack Daniels out of the jumble in the cabin and make ourselves reasonably comfortable. The Parsons take a sip of whiskey each, Estéban and I considerably more. The Bonanza begins to bump soggily. Estéban makes an ancient one-eyed Mayan face at the water seeping into his cabin and goes to sleep. We all nap.

When the water goes down, the euphoria has gone with it, and we're very, very thirsty. It's also damn near sunset. I get to work with a bait-casting rod and some treble hooks and manage to foul-hook four small mullets. Estéban and the women tie the Bonanza's midget life raft out in the mangroves to catch rain. The wind is parching hot. No planes go by.

Finally another shower comes over and yields us six ounces of water apiece. When the sunset envelops the world in golden smoke, we squat on the sandbar to eat wet raw mullet and Instant Breakfast crumbs. The women are now in shorts, neat but definitely not sexy.

"I never realized how refreshing raw fish is," Mrs. Parsons says pleasantly. Her daughter chuckles, also pleasantly. She's on Mamma's far side away from Estéban and me. I have Mrs. Parsons figured now; Mother Hen protecting only chick from male predators. That's all right with me. I came here to fish.

But something is irritating me. The damn women haven't complained once, you understand. Not a peep, not a quaver, no personal manifestations whatever. They're like something out of a manual.

"You really seem at home in the wilderness, Mrs. Parsons. You do much camping?"

"Oh goodness no." Diffident laugh. "Not since my girl scout days. Oh, look—are those man-of-war birds?"

Answer a question with a question. I wait while the frigate birds sail nobly into the sunset.

"Bethesda . . . Would I be wrong in guessing you work for Uncle Sam?"

"Why yes. You must be very familiar with Washington, Mr. Fenton. Does your work bring you there often?"

Anywhere but on our sandbar the little ploy would have worked. My hunter's gene twitches.

"Which agency are you with?"

She gives up gracefully. "Oh, just GSA records. I'm a librarian."

Of course. I know her now, all the Mrs. Parsonses in records divisions, accounting sections, research branches, personnel and administration offices. Tell Mrs. Parsons we need a recap on the external service contracts for fiscal '73. So Yucatán is on the tours now? Pity . . . I offer her the tired little joke. "You know where the bodies are buried."

She smiles deprecatingly and stands up. "It does get dark quickly, doesn't it?"

Time to get back into the plane.

A flock of ibis are circling us, evidently accustomed to roosting in our fig tree. Estéban produces a machete and a Mayan string hammock. He proceeds to sling it between tree and plane, refusing help. His machete stroke is noticeably tentative.

The Parsons are taking a pee behind the tail vane. I hear one of them slip and squeal faintly. When they come back over the hull, Mrs. Parsons asks, "Might we sleep in the hammock, Captain?"

Estéban splits an unbelieving grin. I protest about rain and mosquitoes.

"Oh, we have insect repellent and we do enjoy fresh air."

The air is rushing by about force five and colder by the minute.

"We have our raincoats," the girl adds cheerfully.

Well, okay, ladies. We dangerous males retire inside the damp cabin. Through the wind I hear the women laugh softly now and then, apparently cosy in their chilly ibis roost. A private insanity, I decide. I know myself for the least threatening of men; my non-charisma has been in fact an asset jobwise, over the years. Are they having fantasies about Estéban? Or maybe they really are fresh-air nuts . . . Sleep comes for me in invisible diesels roaring by on the reef outside.

We emerge dry-mouthed into a vast windy salmon sunrise. A diamond chip of sun breaks out of the sea and promptly submerges in cloud. I go to work with the rod and some mullet bait while two showers detour around us. Breakfast is a strip of wet barracuda apiece.

The Parsons continue stoic and helpful. Under Estéban's direction they set up a section of cowling for a gasoline flare in case we hear a plane, but nothing goes over except one unseen jet droning toward Panama. The wind howls, hot and dry and full of coral dust. So are we.

"They look first in the sea." Estéban remarks. His aristocratic frontal slope is beaded with sweat; Mrs. Parsons watches him concernedly. I watch the cloud blanket tearing by above, getting higher and dryer and thicker. While that lasts nobody is going to find us, and the water business is now unfunny.

Finally I borrow Estéban's machete and hack a long light pole. "There's a stream coming in back there, I saw it from the plane. Can't be more than two, three miles."

"I'm afraid the raft's torn." Mrs. Parsons shows me the cracks in the orange plastic; irritatingly, it's a Delaware label.

"All right," I hear myself announce. "The tide's going down. If we cut the good end of that air tube, I can haul water back in it. I've waded flats before."

Even to me it sounds crazy.

"Stay by plane," Estéban says. He's right, of course. He's also clearly running a fever. I look at the overcast and taste grit and old barracuda. The hell with the manual.

When I start cutting up the raft, Estéban tells me to take the serape. "You stay one night." He's right about that, too; I'll have to wait out the tide.

"I'll come with you," says Mrs. Parsons calmly.

I simply stare at her. What new madness has got into Mother Hen? Does she imagine Estéban is too battered to be functional? While I'm being astounded, my eyes take in the fact that Mrs. Parsons is now quite rosy around the knees, with her hair loose and a sunburn starting on her nose. A trim, in fact a very neat shading-forty.

"Look, that stuff is horrible going. Mud up to your ears and water over your head."

"I'm really quite fit and I swim a great deal. I'll try to keep up. Two would be much safer, Mr. Fenton, and we can bring more water."

She's serious. Well, I'm about as fit as a marshmallow at this time of winter, and I can't pretend I'm depressed by the idea of company. So be it.

"Let me show Miss Parsons how to work this rod."

Miss Parsons is even rosier and more windblown, and she's not clumsy with my tackle. A good girl, Miss Parsons, in her nothing way. We cut another staff and get some gear together. At the last minute Estéban shows how sick he feels: he offers me the machete. I thank him, but, no; I'm used to my Wirkkala knife. We tie some air into the plastic tube for a float and set out along the sandiest looking line.

Estéban raises one dark palm. *"Buen viaje."* Miss Parsons has hugged her mother and gone to cast from the mangrove. She waves. We wave.

An hour later we're barely out of waving distance. The going is surely god-awful. The sand keeps dissolving into silt you can't walk on or swim through, and the bottom is spiked with dead mangrove spears. We flounder from one pothole to the next, scaring up rays and turtles and hoping to god we don't kick a moray eel. Where we're not soaked in slime, we're desiccated, and we smell like the Old Cretaceous.

Mrs. Parsons keeps up doggedly. I only have to pull her out once. When I do so, I notice the sandbar is now out of sight.

Finally we reach the gap in the mangrove line I thought was the creek. It turns out to open into another arm of the bay, with more mangroves ahead. And the tide is coming in.

"I've had the world's lousiest idea."

Mrs. Parsons only says mildly, "It's so different from the view from the plane."

I revise my opinion of the girl scouts, and we plow on past the mangroves toward the smoky haze that has to be shore. The sun is setting in our faces, making it hard to see. Ibises and herons fly up around us, and once a big permit spooks ahead, his fin cutting a rooster tail. We fall into more potholes. The flashlights get soaked. I am having fantasies of the mangrove as universal obstacle; it's hard to recall I ever walked down a street, for instance, without stumbling over or under or through mangrove roots. And the sun is dropping down, down.

Suddenly we hit a ledge and fall over it into a cold flow.

"The stream! It's fresh water!"

We guzzle and garble and douse our heads; it's the best drink I remember. "Oh my, oh my—!" Mrs. Parsons is laughing right out loud.

"That dark place over to the right looks like real land."

We flounder across the flow and follow a hard shelf, which turns into solid bank and rises over our heads. Shortly there's a break beside a clump of spiny bromels, and we scramble up and flop down at the top, dripping and stinking. Out of sheer reflex my arm goes around my companion's shoulder—but Mrs. Parsons isn't there; she's up on her knees peering at the burnt-over plain around us.

"It's so good to see land one can walk on!" The tone is too innocent. *Noli me tangere.*

"Don't try it." I'm exasperated; the muddy little woman, what does she think? "That ground out there is a crush of ashes over muck, and it's full of stubs. You can go in over your knees."

"It seems firm here."

"We're in an alligator nursery. That was the slide we came up. Don't worry, by now the old lady's doubtless on her way to be made into handbags."

"What a shame."

"I better set a line down in the stream while I can still see."

I slide back down and rig a string of hooks that may get us breakfast. When I get back Mrs. Parsons is wringing muck out of the serape.

"I'm glad you warned me, Mr. Fenton. It *is* treacherous."

"Yeah." I'm over my irritation; god knows I don't want to *tangere* Mrs. Parsons, even if I weren't beat down to mush. "In its quiet way, Yucatán is a tough place to get around in. You can see why the Mayas built roads. Speaking of which—look!"

The last of the sunset is silhouetting a small square shape a couple of kilometers inland; a Maya *ruina* with a fig tree growing out of it.

"Lot of those around. People think they were guard towers."

"What a deserted-feeling land."

"Let's hope it's deserted by mosquitoes."

We slump down in the 'gator nursery and share the last malt bar, watching the stars slide in and out of the blowing clouds. The bugs aren't too bad; maybe the burn did them in. And it isn't hot any more, either—

in fact, it's not even warm, wet as we are. Mrs. Parsons continues tranquilly interested in Yucatán and unmistakably uninterested in togetherness.

Just as I'm beginning to get aggressive notions about how we're going to spend the night if she expects me to give her the serape, she stands up, scuffs at a couple of hummocks and says, "I expect this is as good a place as any, isn't it, Mr. Fenton?"

With which she spreads out the raft bag for a pillow and lies down on her side in the dirt with exactly half the serape over her and the other corner folded neatly open. Her small back is toward me.

The demonstration is so convincing that I'm halfway under my share of serape before the preposterousness of it stops me.

"By the way. My name is Don."

"Oh, of course." Her voice is graciousness itself, "I'm Ruth."

I get in not quite touching her, and we lie there like two fish on a plate, exposed to the stars and smelling the smoke in the wind and feeling things underneath us. It is absolutely the most intimately awkward moment I've had in years.

The woman doesn't mean one thing to me, but the obtrusive recessiveness of her, the defiance of her little rump eight inches from my fly— for two pesos I'd have those shorts down and introduce myself. If I were twenty years younger. If I wasn't so bushed . . . But the twenty years and the exhaustion are there, and it comes to me wryly that Mrs. Ruth Parsons has judged things to a nicety. If I *were* twenty years younger, she wouldn't be here. Like the butterfish that float around a sated barracuda, only to vanish away the instant his intent changes, Mrs. Parsons knows her little shorts are safe. Those firmly filled little shorts, so close . . .

A warm nerve stirs in my groin—and just as it does I become aware of a silent emptiness beside me. Mrs. Parsons is imperceptibly inching away. Did my breathing change? Whatever, I'm perfectly sure that if my hand reached, she'd be elsewhere—probably announcing her intention to take a dip. The twenty years bring a chuckle to my throat, and I relax.

"Good night, Ruth."

"Good night, Don."

And believe it or not, we sleep, while the armadas of the wind roar overhead.

Light wakes me—a cold white glare.

My first thought is 'gator hunters. Best to manifest ourselves as *turistas* as fast as possible. I scramble up, noting that Ruth has dived under the bromel clump.

"*Quién estás? A secorro!* Help, *señores!*"

No answer except the light goes out, leaving me blind.

I yell some more in a couple of languages. It stays dark. There's a vague scrabbling, whistling sound somewhere in the burn-off. Liking everything less by the minute, I try a speech about our plane having crashed and we need help.

A very narrow pencil of light flicks over us and snaps off.

"Eh-ep," says a blurry voice and something metallic twitters. They for sure aren't locals. I'm getting unpleasant ideas.

"Yes, help!"

Something goes *crackle-crackle whish-whish,* and all sounds fade away.

"What the holy hell!" I stumble toward where they were.

"Look." Ruth whispers behind me. "Over by the ruin."

I look and catch a multiple flicker which winks out fast.

"A camp?"

And I take two more blind strides. My leg goes down through the crust, and a spike spears me just where you stick the knife in to unjoint a drumstick. By the pain that goes through my bladder I recognize that my trick kneecap has caught it.

For instant basket-case you can't beat kneecaps. First you discover your knee doesn't bend any more, so you try putting some weight on it, and a bayonet goes up your spine and unhinges your jaw. Little grains of gristle have got into the sensitive bearing surface. The knee tries to buckle and can't, and mercifully you fall down.

Ruth helps me back to the serape.

"What a fool, what a god-forgotten imbecile—"

"Not at all, Don. It was perfectly natural." We strike matches; her fingers push mine aside, exploring. "I think it's in place, but it's swelling fast. I'll lay a wet handkerchief on it. We'll have to wait for morning to check the cut. Were they poachers, do you think?"

"Probably," I lie. What I think they were is smugglers.

She comes back with a soaked bandanna and drapes it on. "We must have frightened them. That light . . . it seemed so bright."

"Some hunting party. People do crazy things around here."

"Perhaps they'll come back in the morning."

"Could be."

Ruth pulls up the wet serape, and we say goodnight again. Neither of us are mentioning how we're going to get back to the plane without help.

I lie staring south where Alpha Centauri is blinking in and out of the overcast and cursing myself for the sweet mess I've made. My first idea is giving way to an even less pleasing one.

Smuggling, around here, is a couple of guys in an outboard meeting a shrimp boat by the reef. They don't light up the sky or have some kind of swamp buggy that goes whoosh. Plus a big camp . . . paramilitary-type equipment?

I've seen a report of Guevarista infiltrators operating on the British Honduran border, which is about a hundred kilometers—sixty miles—south of here. Right under those clouds. If that's what looked us over, I'll be more than happy if they don't come back . . .

I wake up in pelting rain, alone. My first move confirms that my leg is as expected—a giant misplaced erection bulging out of my shorts. I raise up painfully to see Ruth standing by the bromels, looking over the bay. Solid wet nimbus is pouring out of the south.

"No planes today."

"Oh, good morning, Don. Should we look at that cut now?"

"It's minimal." In fact the skin is hardly broken, and no deep puncture. Totally out of proportion to the havoc inside.

"Well, they have water to drink," Ruth says tranquilly. "Maybe those hunters will come back. I'll go see if we have a fish—that is, can I help you in any way, Don?"

Very tactful. I emit an ungracious negative, and she goes off about her private concerns.

They certainly are private, too; when I recover from my own sanitary efforts, she's still away. Finally I hear splashing.

"It's a big fish!" More splashing. Then she climbs up the bank with a three-pound mangrove snapper—and something else.

It isn't until after the messy work of filleting the fish that I begin to notice.

She's making a smudge of chaff and twigs to singe the fillets, small hands very quick, tension in that female upper lip. The rain has eased off for the moment; we're sluicing wet but warm enough. Ruth brings me my fish on a mangrove skewer and sits back on her heels with an odd breathy sigh.

"Aren't you joining me?"

"Oh, of course." She gets a strip and picks at it, saying quickly, "We either have too much salt or too little, don't we? I should fetch some brine." Her eyes are roving from nothing to noplace.

"Good thought." I hear another sigh and decide the girl scouts need an assist. "Your daughter mentioned you've come from Mérida. Have you seen much of Mexico?"

"Not really. Last year we went to Mazatlán and Cuernavaca . . ." She puts the fish down, frowning.

"And you're going to see Tikal. Going to Bonampak too?"

"No." Suddenly she jumps up brushing rain off her face. "I'll bring you some water, Don."

She ducks down the slide, and after a fair while comes back with a full bromel stalk.

"Thanks." She's standing above me, staring restlessly round the horizon.

"Ruth, I hate to say it, but those guys are not coming back and it's probably just as well. Whatever they were up to, we looked like trouble. The most they'll do is tell someone we're here. That'll take a day or two to get around, we'll be back at the plane by then."

"I'm sure you're right, Don." She wanders over to the smudge fire.

"And quit fretting about your daughter. She's a big girl."

"Oh, I'm sure Althea's all right . . . They have plenty of water now." Her fingers drum on her thigh. It's raining again.

JAMES TIPTREE, JR.

"Come on, Ruth. Sit down. Tell me about Althea. Is she still in college?"

She gives that sighing little laugh and sits. "Althea got her degree last year. She's in computer programming."

"Good for her. And what about you, what do you do in GSA records?"

"I'm in Foreign Procurement Archives." She smiles mechanically, but her breathing is shallow. "It's very interesting."

"I know a Jack Wittig in Contracts, maybe you know him?"

It sounds pretty absurd, there in the 'gator slide.

"Oh, I've met Mr. Wittig. I'm sure he wouldn't remember me."

"Why not?"

"I'm not very memorable."

Her voice is factual. She's perfectly right, of course. Who was that woman, Mrs. Jannings, Janny, who coped with my per diem for years? Competent, agreeable, impersonal. She had a sick father or something. But dammit, Ruth is a lot younger and better-looking. Comparatively speaking.

"Maybe Mrs. Parsons doesn't want to be memorable."

She makes a vague sound, and I suddenly realize Ruth isn't listening to me at all. Her hands are clenched around her knees, she's staring inland at the ruin.

"Ruth. I tell you our friends with the light are in the next country by now. Forget it, we don't need them."

Her eyes come back to me as if she'd forgotten I was there, and she nods slowly. It seems to be too much effort to speak. Suddenly she cocks her head and jumps up again.

"I'll go look at the line, Don. I thought I heard something—" She's gone like a rabbit.

While she's away I try getting up onto my good leg and the staff. The pain is sickening; knees seem to have some kind of hot line to the stomach. I take a couple of hops to test whether the Demerol I have in my belt would get me walking. As I do so, Ruth comes up the bank with a fish flapping in her hands.

"Oh, no, Don! *No!*" She actually clasps the snapper to her breast.

"The water will take some of my weight. I'd like to give it a try."

"You mustn't!" Ruth says quite violently and instantly modulates down. "Look at the bay, Don. One can't see a thing."

I teeter there, tasting bile and looking at the mingled curtains of sun and rain driving across the water. She's right, thank god. Even with two good legs we could get into trouble out there.

"I guess one more night won't kill us."

I let her collapse me back onto the gritty plastic, and she positively bustles around, finding me a chunk to lean on, stretching the serape on both staffs to keep rain off me, bringing another drink, grubbing for dry tinder.

"I'll make us a real bonfire as soon as it lets up, Don. They'll see our smoke, they'll know we're all right. We just have to wait." Cheery smile. "Is there any way we can make you more comfortable?"

Holy Saint Sterculius: playing house in a mud puddle. For a fatuous moment I wonder if Mrs. Parsons has designs on me. And then she lets out another sigh and sinks back onto her heels with that listening look. Unconsciously her rump wiggles a little. My ear picks up the operative word: *wait*.

Ruth Parsons is waiting. In fact, she acts as if she's waiting so hard it's killing her. For what? For someone to get us out of here, what else? . . . But why was she so horrified when I got up to try to leave? Why all this tension?

My paranoia stirs. I grab it by the collar and start idly checking back. Up to when whoever it was showed up last night, Mrs. Parsons was, I guess, normal. Calm and sensible, anyway. Now she's humming like a high wire. And she seems to want to stay here and wait. Just as an intellectual pastime, why?

Could she have intended to come here? No way. Where she planned to be was Chetumal, which is on the border. Come to think, Chetumal is an odd way round to Tikal. Let's say the scenario was that she's meeting somebody in Chetumal. Somebody who's part of an organization. So now her contact in Chetumal knows she's overdue. And when those types appeared last night, something suggests to her that they're part of the same organization. And she hopes they'll put one and one together and come back for her?

"May I have the knife, Don? I'll clean the fish."

Rather slowly I pass the knife, kicking my subconscious. Such a decent ordinary little woman, a good girl scout. My trouble is that I've bumped into too many professional agilities under the careful stereotypes. *I'm not very memorable . . .*

What's in Foreign Procurement Archives? Wittig handles classified contracts. Lots of money stuff; foreign currency negotiations, commodity price schedules, some industrial technology. Or—just as a hypothesis—it could be as simple as a wad of bills back in that modest beige Ventura, to be exchanged for a packet from say, Costa Rica. If she were a courier, they'd want to get at the plane. And then what about me and maybe Estéban? Even hypothetically, not good.

I watch her hacking at the fish, forehead knotted with effort, teeth in her lip. Mrs. Parsons of Bethesda, this thrumming, private woman. How crazy can I get? *They'll see our smoke . . .*

"Here's your knife, Don. I washed it. Does the leg hurt very badly?"

I blink away the fantasies and see a scared little woman in a mangrove swamp.

"Sit down, rest. You've been going all out."

She sits obediently, like a kid in a dentist chair.

"You're stewing about Althea. And she's probably worried about you. We'll get back tomorrow under our own steam, Ruth."

"Honestly I'm not worried at all, Don." The smile fades; she nibbles her lip, frowning out at the bay.

"You know, Ruth, you surprised me when you offered to come along. Not that I don't appreciate it. But I rather thought you'd be concerned about leaving Althea alone with our good pilot. Or was it only me?"

This gets her attention at last.

"I believe Captain Estéban is a very fine type of man."

The words surprise me a little. Isn't the correct line more like "I trust Althea," or even, indignantly, "Althea is a good girl?"

"He's a man. Althea seemed to think he was interesting."

She goes on staring at the bay. And then I notice her tongue flick out and lick that prehensile upper lip. There's a flush that isn't sunburn around her ears and throat too, and one hand is gently rubbing her thigh. What's she seeing, out there in the flats?

Oho.

Captain Estéban's mahogany arms clasping Miss Althea Parsons' pearly body. Captain Estéban's archaic nostrils snuffling in Miss Parsons' tender neck. Captain Estéban's copper buttocks pumping into Althea's creamy upturned bottom . . . The hammock, very bouncy. Mayas know all about it.

Well, well. So Mother Hen has her little quirks.

I feel fairly silly and more than a little irritated. *Now* I find out . . . But even vicarious lust has much to recommend it, here in the mud and rain. I settle back, recalling that Miss Althea the computer programmer had waved good-bye very composedly. Was she sending her mother to flounder across the bay with me so she can get programmed in Maya? The memory of Honduran mahogany logs drifting in and out of the opalescent sand comes to me. Just as I am about to suggest that Mrs. Parsons might care to share my rain shelter, she remarks serenely, "The Mayas seem to be a very fine type of people. I believe you said so to Althea."

The implications fall on me with the rain. *Type.* As in breeding, bloodline, sire. Am I supposed to have certified Estéban not only as a stud but as a genetic donor?

"Ruth, are you telling me you're prepared to accept a half-Indian grandchild?"

"Why, Don, that's up to Althea, you know."

Looking at the mother, I guess it is. Oh, for mahogany gonads.

Ruth has gone back to listening to the wind, but I'm not about to let her off that easy. Not after all that *noli me tangere* jazz.

"What will Althea's father think?"

Her face snaps around at me, genuinely startled.

"Althea's father?" Complicated semismile. "He won't mind."

"He'll accept it too, eh?" I see her shake her head as if a fly were bothering her, and add with a cripple's malice: "Your husband must be a very fine type of a man."

Ruth looks at me, pushing her wet hair back abruptly. I have the impression that mousy Mrs. Parsons is roaring out of control, but her voice is quiet.

"There isn't any Mr. Parsons, Don. There never was. Althea's father was a Danish medical student . . . I believe he has gained considerable prominence."

"Oh." Something warns me not to say I'm sorry. "You mean he doesn't know about Althea?"

"No." She smiles, her eyes bright and cuckoo.

"Seems like rather a rough deal for her."

"I grew up quite happily under the same circumstances."

Bang, I'm dead. Well, well, well. A mad image blooms in my mind: generations of solitary Parsons women selecting sires, making impregnation trips. Well, I hear the world is moving their way.

"I better look at the fish line."

She leaves. The glow fades. *No.* Just no, no contact. Good-bye, Captain Estéban. My leg is very uncomfortable. The hell with Mrs. Parsons' long-distance orgasm.

We don't talk much after that, which seems to suit Ruth. The odd day drags by. Squall after squall blows over us. Ruth singes up some more fillets, but the rain drowns her smudge; it seems to pour hardest just as the sun's about to show.

Finally she comes to sit under my sagging serape, but there's no warmth there. I doze, aware of her getting up now and then to look around. My subconscious notes that she's still twitchy. I tell my subconscious to knock it off.

Presently I wake up to find her penciling on the water-soaked pages of a little notepad.

"What's that, a shopping list for alligators?"

Automatic polite laugh. "Oh, just an address. In case we—I'm being silly, Don."

"Hey," I sit up, wincing, "Ruth, quit fretting. I mean it. We'll all be out of this soon. You'll have a great story to tell."

She doesn't look up. "Yes . . . I guess we will."

"Come on, we're doing fine. There isn't any real danger here, you know. Unless you're allergic to fish?"

Another good-little-girl laugh, but there's a shiver in it.

"Sometimes I think I'd like to go . . . really far away."

To keep her talking I say the first thing in my head.

"Tell me, Ruth. I'm curious why you would settle for that kind of lonely life, there in Washington? I mean, a woman like you—"

"Should get married?" She gives a shaky sigh, pushing the notebook back in her wet pocket.

JAMES TIPTREE, JR.

383

"Why not? It's the normal source of companionship. Don't tell me you're trying to be some kind of professional man-hater."

"Lesbian, you mean?" Her laugh sounds better. "With my security rating? No, I'm not."

"Well, then. Whatever trauma you went through, these things don't last forever. You can't hate all men."

The smile is back. "Oh, there wasn't any trauma, Don, and I *don't* hate men. That would be as silly as—as hating the weather." She glances wryly at the blowing rain.

"I think you have a grudge. You're even spooky of me."

Smooth as a mouse bite she says, "I'd love to hear about your family, Don?"

Touché. I give her the edited version of how I don't have one any more, and she says she's sorry, how sad. And we chat about what a good life a single person really has, and how she and her friends enjoy plays and concerts and travel, and one of them is head cashier for Ringling Brothers, how about that?

But it's coming out jerkier and jerkier like a bad tape, with her eyes going round the horizon in the pauses and her face listening for something that isn't my voice. What's wrong with her? Well, what's wrong with any furtively unconventional middle-aged woman with an empty bed. And a security clearance. An old habit of mind remarks unkindly that Mrs. Parsons represents what is known as the classic penetration target.

"—so much more opportunity now." Her voice trails off.

"Hurrah for women's lib, eh?"

"The lib?" Impatiently she leans forward and tugs the serape straight. "Oh, that's doomed."

The apocalyptic word jars my attention.

"What do you mean, doomed?"

She glances at me as if I weren't hanging straight either and says vaguely, "Oh . . ."

"Come on, why doomed? Didn't they get that equal rights bill?"

Long hesitation. When she speaks again her voice is different.

"Women have no rights, Don, except what men allow us. Men are more aggressive and powerful, and they run the world. When the next real crisis upsets them, our so-called rights will vanish like—like that smoke. We'll be back where we always were: property. And whatever has gone wrong will be blamed on our freedom, like the fall of Rome was. You'll see."

Now all this is delivered in a gray tone of total conviction. The last time I heard that tone, the speaker was explaining why he had to keep his file drawers full of dead pigeons.

"Oh, come on. You and your friends are the backbone of the system; if you quit, the country would come to a screeching halt before lunch."

No answering smile.

"That's fantasy." Her voice is still quiet. "Women don't work that way.

We're a—a toothless world." She looks around as if she wanted to stop talking. "What women do is survive. We live by ones and twos in the chinks of your world-machine."

"Sounds like a guerrilla operation." I'm not really joking, here in the 'gator den. In fact, I'm wondering if I spent too much thought on mahogany logs.

"Guerrillas have something to hope for." Suddenly she switches on a jolly smile. "Think of us as opossums, Don. Did you know there are opossums living all over? Even in New York City."

I smile back with my neck prickling. I thought I was the paranoid one.

"Men and women aren't different species, Ruth. Women do everything men do."

"Do they?" Our eyes meet, but she seems to be seeing ghosts between us in the rain. She mutters something that could be "My Lai" and looks away. "All the endless wars . . ." Her voice is a whisper. "All the huge authoritarian organizations for doing unreal things. Men live to struggle against each other; we're just part of the battlefields. It'll never change unless you change the whole world. I dream sometimes of—of going away—" She checks and abruptly changes voice. "Forgive me, Don, it's so stupid saying all this."

"Men hate wars too, Ruth," I say as gently as I can.

"I know." She shrugs and climbs to her feet. "But that's your problem, isn't it?"

End of communication. Mrs. Ruth Parsons isn't even living in the same world with me.

I watch her move around restlessly, head turning toward the ruins. Alienation like that can add up to dead pigeons, which would be GSA's problem. It could also lead to believing some joker who's promising to change the whole world. Which could just probably be my problem if one of them was over in that camp last night, where she keeps looking. *Guerrillas have something to hope for . . .?*

Nonsense. I try another position and see that the sky seems to be clearing as the sun sets. The wind is quieting down at last too. Insane to think this little woman is acting out some fantasy in this swamp. But that equipment last night was no fantasy; if those lads have some connection with her, I'll be in the way. You couldn't find a handier spot to dispose of the body . . . Maybe some Guevarista is a fine type of man?

Absurd. Sure . . . The only thing more absurd would be to come through the wars and get myself terminated by a mad librarian's boyfriend on a fishing trip.

A fish flops in the stream below us. Ruth spins around so fast she hits the serape. "I better start the fire," she says, her eyes still on the plain and her head cocked, listening.

All right, let's test.

"Expecting company?"

It rocks her. She freezes, and her eyes come swiveling around at me like a film take captioned Fright. I can see her decide to smile.

"Oh, one never can tell!" She laughs weirdly, the eyes not changed. "I'll get the—the kindling." She fairly scuttles into the brush.

Nobody, paranoid or not, could call *that* a normal reaction.

Ruth Parsons is either psycho or she's expecting something to happen—and it has nothing to do with me; I scared her pissless.

Well, she could be nuts. And I could be wrong, but there are some mistakes you only make once.

Reluctantly I unzip my body belt, telling myself that if I think what I think, my only course is to take something for my leg and get as far as possible from Mrs. Ruth Parsons before whoever she's waiting for arrives.

In my belt also is a .32 caliber asset Ruth doesn't know about—and it's going to stay there. My longevity program leaves the shoot-outs to TV and stresses being somewhere else when the roof falls in. I can spend a perfectly safe and also perfectly horrible night out in one of those mangrove flats . . . Am I insane?

At this moment Ruth stands up and stares blatantly inland with her hand shading her eyes. Then she tucks something into her pocket, buttons up and tightens her belt.

That does it.

I dry-swallow two 100 mg tabs, which should get me ambulatory and still leave me wits to hide. Give it a few minutes. I make sure my compass and some hooks are in my own pocket and sit waiting while Ruth fusses with her smudge fire, sneaking looks away when she thinks I'm not watching.

The flat world around us is turning into an unearthly amber and violet light show as the first numbness sweeps into my leg. Ruth has crawled under the bromels for more dry stuff; I can see her foot. Okay. I reach for my staff.

Suddenly the foot jerks, and Ruth yells—or rather, her throat makes that *Uh-uh-hhh* that means pure horror. The foot disappears in a rattle of bromel stalks.

I lunge upright on the crutch and look over the bank at a frozen scene.

Ruth is crouching sideways on the ledge, clutching her stomach. They are about a yard below, floating on the river in a skiff. While I was making up my stupid mind, her friends have glided right under my ass. There are three of them.

They are tall and white. I try to see them as men in some kind of white jumpsuits. The one nearest the bank is stretching out a long white arm toward Ruth. She jerks and scuttles further away.

The arm stretches after her. It stretches and stretches. It stretches two yards and stays hanging in the air. Small black things are wiggling from its tip.

I look where their faces should be and see black hollow dishes with vertical stripes. The stripes move slowly . . .

There is no more possibility of their being human—or anything else I've ever seen. What has Ruth conjured up?

The scene is totally silent. I blink, blink—this cannot be real. The two in the far end of the skiff are writhing those arms around an apparatus on a tripod. A weapon? Suddenly I hear the same blurry voice I heard in the night.

"Guh-give," it groans. "G-give . . ."

Dear god, it's real, whatever it is. I'm terrified. My mind is trying not to form a word.

And Ruth—Jesus, of course—Ruth is terrified too; she's edging along the bank away from them, gaping at the monsters in the skiff, who are obviously nobody's friends. She's hugging something to her body. Why doesn't she get over the bank and circle back behind me?

"G-g-give." That wheeze is coming from the tripod. "Pee-eeze give." The skiff is moving upstream below Ruth, following her. The arm undulates out at her again, its black digits looping. Ruth scrambles to the top of the bank.

"Ruth!" My voice cracks. "Ruth, get over here behind me!"

She doesn't look at me, only keeps sidling farther away. My terror detonates into anger.

"Come back here!" With my free hand I'm working the .32 out of my belt. The sun has gone down.

She doesn't turn but straightens up warily, still hugging the thing. I see her mouth working. Is she actually trying to *talk* to them?

"Please . . ." She swallows. "Please speak to me. I need your help."

"RUTH!!"

At this moment the nearest white monster whips into a great S-curve and sails right onto the bank at her, eight feet of snowy rippling horror.

And I shoot Ruth.

I don't know that for a moment—I've yanked the gun up so fast that my staff slips and dumps me as I fire. I stagger up, hearing Ruth scream "No! No! No!"

The creature is back down by his boat, and Ruth is still farther away, clutching herself. Blood is running down her elbow.

"Stop it, Don! They aren't attacking you!"

"For god's sake! Don't be a fool, I can't help you if you won't get away from them!"

No reply. Nobody moves. No sound except the drone of a jet passing far above. In the darkening stream below me the three white figures shift uneasily; I get the impression of radar dishes focusing. The word spells itself in my head: *Aliens.*

Extraterrestrials.

What do I do, call the President? Capture them single-handed with my peashooter? . . . I'm alone in the arse end of nowhere with one leg and my brain cuddled in meperidine hydrochloride.

"Prrr-eese," their machine blurs again. "Wa-wat hep . . ."

"Our plane fell down," Ruth says in a very distinct, eerie voice. She points up at the jet, out towards the bay. "My—my child is there. Please take us *there* in your boat."

Dear god. While she's gesturing, I get a look at the thing she's hugging in her wounded arm. It's metallic, like a big glimmering distributor head. What—?

Wait a minute. This morning: when she was gone so long, she could have found that thing. Something they left behind. Or dropped. And she hid it, not telling me. That's why she kept going under that bromel clump—she was peeking at it. Waiting. And the owners came back and caught her. They want it. She's trying to bargain, by god.

"—Water," Ruth is pointing again. "Take us. Me. And him."

The black faces turn toward me, blind and horrible. Later on I may be grateful for that "us." Not now.

"Throw your gun away, Don. They'll take us back." Her voice is weak.

"Like hell I will. You—who are you? What are you doing here?"

"Oh god, does it matter? He's frightened," she cries to them. "Can you understand?"

She's as alien as they, there in the twilight. The beings in the skiff are twittering among themselves. Their box starts to moan.

"Ss-stu-dens," I make out. "S-stu-ding . . . not—huh-arm-ing . . . w-we . . . buh . . ." It fades into garble and then says "G-give . . . we . . . g-go . . ."

Peace-loving cultural-exchange students—on the interstellar level now. Oh, no.

"Bring that thing here, Ruth—right now!"

But she's starting down the bank toward them saying, "Take me."

"Wait! You need a tourniquet on that arm."

"I know. Please put the gun down, Don."

She's actually at the skiff, right by them. They aren't moving.

"Jesus Christ." Slowly, reluctantly, I drop the .32. When I start down the slide, I find I'm floating; adrenaline and Demerol are a bad mix.

The skiff comes gliding toward me, Ruth in the bow clutching the thing and her arm. The aliens stay in the stern behind their tripod, away from me. I note the skiff is camouflaged tan and green. The world around us is deep shadowy blue.

"Don, bring the water bag!"

As I'm dragging down the plastic bag, it occurs to me that Ruth really is cracking up, the water isn't needed now. But my own brain seems to have gone into overload. All I can focus on is a long white rubbery arm with black worms clutching the far end of the orange tube, helping me fill it. This isn't happening.

"Can you get in, Don?" As I hoist my numb legs up, two long white pipes reach for me. *No you don't.* I kick and tumble in beside Ruth. She moves away.

A creaky hum starts up, it's coming from a wedge in the center of the skiff. And we're in motion, sliding toward dark mangrove files.

I stare mindlessly at the wedge. Alien technological secrets? I can't see any, the power source is under that triangular cover, about two feet long. The gadgets on the tripod are equally cryptic, except that one has a big lens. Their light?

As we hit the open bay, the hum rises and we start planing faster and faster still. Thirty knots? Hard to judge in the dark. Their hull seems to be a modified trihedral much like ours, with a remarkable absence of slap. Say twenty-two feet. Schemes of capturing it swirl in my mind. I'll need Estéban.

Suddenly a huge flood of white light fans out over us from the tripod, blotting out the aliens in the stern. I see Ruth pulling at a belt around her arm still hugging the gizmo.

"I'll tie that for you."

"It's all right."

The alien device is twinkling or phosphorescing slightly. I lean over to look, whispering, "Give that to me, I'll pass it to Estéban."

"No!" She scoots away, almost over the side. "It's theirs, they need it!"

"What? Are you crazy?" I'm so taken aback by this idiocy I literally stammer. "We have to, we—"

"They haven't hurt us. I'm sure they could." Her eyes are watching me with feral intensity; in the light her face has a lunatic look. Numb as I am, I realize that the wretched woman is poised to throw herself over the side if I move. With the alien thing.

"I think they're gentle," she mutters.

"For Christ's sake, Ruth, they're *aliens!*"

"I'm used to it," she says absently. "There's the island! Stop! Stop here!"

The skiff slows, turning. A mound of foliage is tiny in the light. Metal glints—the plane.

"Althea! Althea! Are you all right?"

Yells, movement on the plane. The water is high, we're floating over the bar. The aliens are keeping us in the lead with the light hiding them. I see one pale figure splashing toward us and a dark one behind, coming more slowly. Estéban must be puzzled by that light.

"Mr. Fenton is hurt, Althea. These people brought us back with the water. Are you all right?"

"A-okay." Althea flounders up, peering excitedly. "You all right? Whew, that light!" Automatically I start handing her the idiotic water bag.

"Leave that for the captain," Ruth says sharply. "Althea, can you climb in the boat? Quickly, it's important."

"Coming."

"No, no!" I protest, but the skiff tilts as Althea swarms in. The aliens twitter, and their voice box starts groaning. "Gu-give . . . now . . . give . . ."

"*Que llega?*" Estéban's face appears beside me, squinting fiercely into the light.

"Grab it, get it from her—that thing she has—" but Ruth's voice rides over mine. "Captain, lift Mr. Fenton out of the boat. He's hurt his leg. Hurry, please."

"Goddamn it, wait!" I shout, but an arm has grabbed my middle. When a Maya boosts you, you go. I hear Althea saying, "Mother, your arm!" and fall onto Estéban. We stagger around in water up to my waist; I can't feel my feet at all.

When I get steady, the boat is yards away. The two women are head-to-head, murmuring.

"Get them!" I tug loose from Estéban and flounder forward. Ruth stands up in the boat facing the invisible aliens.

"Take us with you. Please. We want to go with you, away from here."

"Ruth! Estéban, get that boat!" I lunge and lose my feet again. The aliens are chirruping madly behind their light.

"Please take us. We don't mind what your planet is like; we'll learn—we'll do anything! We won't cause any trouble. Please. Oh *please.*" The skiff is drifting farther away.

"Ruth! Althea! Are you crazy? Wait—" But I can only shuffle night-marelike in the ooze, hearing that damn voice box wheeze, "N-not come . . . more . . . not come . . ." Althea's face turns to it, open-mouthed grin.

"Yes, we understand," Ruth cries. "We don't want to come back. Please take us with you!"

I shout and Estéban splashes past me shouting too, something about radio.

"Yes-s-s" groans the voice.

Ruth sits down suddenly, clutching Althea. At that moment Estéban grabs the edge of the skiff beside her.

"Hold them, Estéban! Don't let her go."

He gives me one slit-eyed glance over his shoulder, and I recognize his total uninvolvement. He's had a good look at that camouflage paint and the absence of fishing gear. I make a desperate rush and slip again. When I come up Ruth is saying, "We're going with these people, Captain. Please take your money out of my purse, it's in the plane. And give this to Mr. Fenton."

She passes him something small; the notebook. He takes it slowly.

"Estéban! No!"

He has released the skiff.

"Thank you so much," Ruth says as they float apart. Her voice is shaky; she raises it. "There won't be any trouble, Don. Please send this cable. It's to a friend of mine, she'll take care of everything." Then she adds the craziest touch of the entire night. "She's a grand person; she's director of nursing training at N.I.H."

As the skiff drifts, I hear Althea add something that sounds like "Right on."

Sweet Jesus . . . Next minute the humming has started; the light is receding fast. The last I see of Mrs. Ruth Parsons and Miss Althea Parsons is two small shadows against that light, like two opossums. The light snaps off, the hum deepens—and they're going, going, gone away.

In the dark water beside me Estéban is instructing everybody in general to *chingarse* themselves.

"Friends, or something," I tell him lamely. "She seemed to want to go with them."

He is pointedly silent, hauling me back to the plane. He knows what could be around here better than I do, and Mayas have their own longevity program. His condition seems improved. As we get in I notice the hammock has been repositioned.

In the night—of which I remember little—the wind changes. And at seven thirty next morning a Cessna buzzes the sandbar under cloudless skies.

By noon we're back in Cozumel, Captain Estéban accepts his fees and departs laconically for his insurance wars. I leave the Parsons' bags with the Caribe agent, who couldn't care less. The cable goes to a Mrs. Priscilla Hayes Smith, also of Bethesda. I take myself to a medico and by three PM I'm sitting on the Cabañas terrace with a fat leg and a double margharita, trying to believe the whole thing.

The cable said, *Althea and I taking extraordinary opportunity for travel. Gone several years. Please take charge our affairs. Love, Ruth.*

She'd written it that afternoon, you understand.

I order another double, wishing to hell I'd gotten a good look at that gizmo. Did it have a label. Made by Betelgeusians? No matter how weird it was, *how* could a person be crazy enough to imagine—?

Not only that but to hope, to plan? *If I could only go away* . . . That's what she was doing, all day. Waiting, hoping, figuring how to get Althea. To go sight unseen to an alien world . . .

With the third margharita I try a joke about alienated women, but my heart's not in it. And I'm certain there won't be any bother, any trouble at all. Two human women, one of them possibly pregnant, have departed for, I guess, the stars; and the fabric of society will never show a ripple. I brood: do all Mrs. Parsons' friends hold themselves in readiness for any eventuality, including leaving Earth? And will Mrs. Parsons somehow one day contrive to send for Mrs. Priscilla Hayes Smith, that grand person?

I can only send for another cold one, musing on Althea. What suns will Captain Estéban's sloe-eyed offspring, if any, look upon? "Get in, Althea, we're taking off for Orion." "A-okay, Mother." Is that some system of upbringing? *We survive by ones and twos in the chinks of your world-machine . . . I'm used to aliens* . . . She'd meant every word. Insane. How could a woman choose to live among unknown monsters, to say good-bye to her home, her world?

As the margharitas take hold, the whole mad scenario melts down to the image of those two small shapes sitting side by side in the receding alien glare.

Two of our opossums are missing.

WILLIAM CARLOS WILLIAMS

(1883–1963) Although he was a hard-working New Jersey physician, William Carlos Williams managed to write over twenty-five volumes of poetry and fiction. His epic poem *Paterson* (1946–1958) reflects his knowledge of and compassion for people, his sense of history, and his use of the language and rhythms of speech.

THE WIDOW'S LAMENT
IN SPRINGTIME

Sorrow is my own yard
where the new grass
flames as it has flamed
often before but not
with the cold fire
that closes round me this year.
Thirtyfive years
I lived with my husband.
The plumtree is white today
with masses of flowers.
Masses of flowers
load the cherry branches
and color some bushes
yellow and some red
but the grief in my heart
is stronger than they
for though they were my joy
formerly, today I notice them
and turned away forgetting.

Today my son told me
that in the meadows,
at the edge of the heavy woods
in the distance, he saw
trees of white flowers.
I feel that I would like
to go there
and fall into those flowers
and sink into the marsh near them.

(1851–1904) In the past decade Kate Chopin has been rediscovered. Her novel *The Awakening* (1899) has had several editions, and recently Per Seyersted edited her collected works and a selection, *The Storm and Other Stories,* for The Feminist Press (1974). Chopin shows the difficulties a woman trying to be herself faces in a traditional society such as New Orleans. She wrote most of her works while a widow caring for six children.

THE STORY OF AN HOUR

Knowing that Mrs. Mallard was afflicted with a heart trouble, great care was taken to break to her as gently as possible the news of her husband's death.

It was her sister Josephine who told her, in broken sentences; veiled hints that revealed in half concealing. Her husband's friend Richards was there, too, near her. It was he who had been in the newspaper office when intelligence of the railroad disaster was received, with Brently Mallard's name leading the list of "killed." He had only taken the time to assure himself of its truth by a second telegram, and had hastened to forestall any less careful, less tender friend in bearing the sad message.

She did not hear the story as many women have heard the same, with a paralyzed inability to accept its significance. She wept at once, with sudden, wild abandonment, in her sister's arms. When the storm of grief had spent itself she went away to her room alone. She would have no one follow her.

There stood, facing the open window, a comfortable, roomy armchair. Into this she sank, pressed down by a physical exhaustion that haunted her body and seemed to reach into her soul.

She could see in the open square before her house the tops of trees that were all aquiver with the new spring life. The delicious breath of rain was in the air. In the street below a peddler was crying his wares. The notes of a distant song which some one was singing reached her faintly, and countless sparrows were twittering in the eaves.

There were patches of blue sky showing here and there through the clouds that had met and piled one above the other in the west facing her window.

She sat with her head thrown back upon the cushion of the chair, quite motionless, except when a sob came up into her throat and shook her, as a child who has cried itself to sleep continues to sob in its dreams.

She was young, with a fair, calm face, whose lines bespoke repression and even a certain strength. But now there was a dull stare in her eyes, whose gaze was fixed away off yonder on one of those patches of blue sky. It was not a glance of reflection, but rather indicated a suspension of intelligent thought.

There was something coming to her and she was waiting for it, fearfully. What was it? She did not know; it was too subtle and elusive to name. But she felt it, creeping out of the sky, reaching toward her through the sounds, the scents, the color that filled the air.

Now her bosom rose and fell tumultuously. She was beginning to recognize this thing that was approaching to possess her, and she was striving to beat it back with her will—as powerless as her two white slender hands would have been.

When she abandoned herself a little whispered word escaped her slightly parted lips. She said it over and over under her breath: "free, free, free!" The vacant stare and the look of terror that had followed it went from her eyes. They stayed keen and bright. Her pulses beat fast, and the coursing blood warmed and relaxed every inch of her body.

She did not stop to ask if it were or were not a monstrous joy that held her. A clear and exalted perception enabled her to dismiss the suggestion as trivial.

She knew that she would weep again when she saw the kind, tender hands folded in death; the face that had never looked save with love upon her, fixed and gray and dead. But she saw beyond that bitter moment a long procession of years to come that would belong to her absolutely. And she opened and spread her arms out to them in welcome.

There would be no one to live for her during those coming years; she would live for herself. There would be no powerful will bending hers in that blind persistence with which men and women believe they have a right to impose a private will upon a fellow-creature. A kind intention or a cruel intention made the act seem no less a crime as she looked upon it in that brief moment of illumination.

And yet she had loved him—sometimes. Often she had not. What did it matter! What could love, the unsolved mystery, count for in face of this possession of self-assertion which she suddenly recognized as the strongest impulse of her being!

"Free! Body and soul free!" she kept whispering.

Josephine was kneeling before the closed door with her lips to the keyhole, imploring for admission. "Louise, open the door! I beg; open the door—you will make yourself ill. What are you doing, Louise? For heaven's sake open the door."

"Go away. I am not making myself ill." No; she was drinking in a very elixir of life through that open window.

Her fancy was running riot along those days ahead of her. Spring days, and summer days, and all sorts of days that would be her own. She breathed a quick prayer that life might be long. It was only yesterday she had thought with a shudder that life might be long.

She rose at length and opened the door to her sister's importunities. There was a feverish triumph in her eyes, and she carried herself unwittingly like a goddess of Victory. She clasped her sister's waist, and together they descended the stairs. Richards stood waiting for them at the bottom.

Some one was opening the front door with a latchkey. It was Brently Mallard who entered, a little travel-stained, composedly carrying his grip-sack and umbrella. He had been far from the scene of the accident, and did not even know there had been one. He stood amazed at Josephine's piercing cry; at Richards' quick motion to screen him from the view of his wife.

But Richards was too late.

When the doctors came they said she had died of heart disease—of joy that kills.

ELIZABETH SCHULTZ

(b. 1936) A professor at the University of
Kansas at Lawrence, Elizabeth Schultz has
been teaching and writing about American, Afro-American, Asian-American, Native
American, and Japanese literature for more
than twenty years. She has had a Fulbright
Fellowship to Japan and a National Endowment for the Humanities Fellowship for the
study of U.S. Ethnic Minorities. She is associate editor of the scholarly journal *American
Studies*. Her essays, short stories, translations,
and reviews have appeared in a variety of
journals.

BONE

Myrtle Reeves was half-Indian and half-Irish—the Indian from her mother
who was a full-blooded Hupa and the Irish from her father who came
into the valley with Ulysses S. Grant and the American Army. She was
astonished by her daughter-in-law who said that, for herself, she was an
American and proud of it.

Myrtle Reeves' son had gotten this girl from down around Berkeley
when he was there looking for a job. When he couldn't get a job, he came
back to the valley with the girl. Two weeks ago she had returned to the
city. To take a summer vacation, she said. Now she was back in the
valley again. In the afternoon on Monday she came over to see Myrtle
Reeves to tell her about the vacation.

Myrtle Reeves lived on the long road that the timber trucks took up
out of the valley to the high forests. At the beginning of the road, where
it ditched off from the main route, the soil was coarse with sandstone bits.
Some people had set up trailers on this coarse land, but Myrtle Reeves'
house was halfway up the road, about where the valley started to disappear
into the Sisikiyous. The ground here, back from the main route before
it became mountain rock, was sponge-soft and good for growing things.
Behind the house was a water spot and a willow, its slips of leaves always
slightly stirring. Close around the front and sides of Myrtle Reeves' house
was a flat-slatted fence, with all the space inside the fence in flowers and

garden. Stems and leaves meshed together in a greenness so dense there seemed to be no solid soil. They tangled through the fence and through each other, some columbine tangling over and around the wires Myrtle Reeves had rigged from fence to house, its tendrils loose and twisting down.

A gate was set in the fence. The daughter-in-law lifted off the ring of rubber tubing latching the gate. It hung heavy on its hinges, and she had to nudge it open, grating it across the ground. At the same time, she was calling. "You-who-You-who-You-who! Where are you, Mother Reeves? Where are you, Mother Reeves?" And then, "Oh, there, I see you on the porch. I'll be right up."

Myrtle Reeves was at home on her porch. "How are you, daughter-in-law?" she asked. Inside the fence, the great greenness surrounded the daughter-in-law. Here the shadows shed from the Sisikiyous merged with the sharpness of the sun in moisture. With the poppies, the jewel lilies, the marigolds, the scarlet gilia, the daughter-in-law seemed to glow orange and golden out of the greenness. But only momentarily before she moved toward the porch.

"Did you bring me a present?" asked Myrtle Reeves.

"I brought myself," said the daughter-in-law. "On this simply sizzling day." She went on, "You know we have air-conditioning in Berkeley. In all the houses."

"Air-conditioning," mused Myrtle Reeves, amazed at this daughter-in-law. She had been in air-conditioning once in the movie-theater in Eureka when her son had taken her.

The daughter-in-law sat on the corner of the porch day-bed. She crossed her knees. "Whew! I'd almost forgotten how really bad it can be around here. And since I've been back there's been nothing to do except be hot. And make sandwiches for Sam's lunch. For him to take up to the woods. Peanut butter and lettuce. Peanut butter and jelly. Peanut butter plain. In Berkeley we had steak once in a while for supper."

Trumpet vines had been trained to twine about the porch posts and to stretch along the rim of the roof. A Japanese wind-chime was tied up from a place under the vine, and when the air moved, the flat pieces of glass made a small shattering sound against each other. Myrtle Reeves was sitting in an overstuffed brocade chair. With the day-bed and the chair, the porch was crowded. Lying around were years of well-creased movie magazines. Before the daughter-in-law came over, Myrtle Reeves had felt free in only a slip, all the fine lines pulled into her skin by the settling of her breasts showing. But knowing the daughter-in-law was coming, she had shaken herself into something decent. The pink dress with three little bows on the bodice and, of course, the gold earrings which the daughter-in-law had given her for Christmas. It pleased Myrtle Reeves to have these bright ornaments; they set off her face. She had also had time to cover over the smatterings of freckles with a pink-white powder.

ELIZABETH SCHULTZ

"You had a good time in Berkeley?" Myrtle Reeves asked. In the garden the heat was steady and shimmering, but on the porch it seemed to shift a little.

"A simply gorgeous time," said the daughter-in-law. "Something doing all the time. And like I said, since I've been back here there's been nothing doing except to be hot. Hot-hot-hot. Nights in Berkeley we would go over to some people's like Betty's and Arty's. I went to school with Betty all the way through the eleventh grade, and anyways we'd go to the movies or something." She stopped. "Hey, you got some new movie mags since I been gone."

"I be liking to read these days," said Myrtle Reeves. She smoothed out the shiny cover of a magazine with a large smiling face on it. "In the magazines you can go for miles away. I never have all that schooling you got. I only have four years and that when they sent us out to school in Pennsylvania. We went on lines of horses, across the rivers until we all got on the train and got to Pennsylvania. Then we came back to the valley after four years." The pieces of glass in the Japanese wind-chime were twirling on their strings.

"School's all right, I guess," said the daughter-in-law. She scratched herself under her arm. "So in the afternoons I used to go shopping downtown. This time of year there were lotsa sales for dresses, but the bathing suits hadn't come on yet. Once when I was down with Betty—she knows about Sam being some Indian and all—she takes me to this museum where there was some Indian stuff. White deerskins for a special dance and some old woodpecker heads. And there were some displays-like, showing how to make acorn soup. It was pretty interesting, I guess."

"They got those old things down there?" Myrtle Reeves thought about Abraham Hardrock and Rachel Little. If they knew about that, they wouldn't like it much. "I ain't got any of those old things. No baskets even. My old mother taught me how to do them, but I just forgot." Myrtle Reeves got up to get some Koolaid from inside the house.

"Anyways," the daughter-in-law said, "I got a new dress. It's sort of crinkly." Myrtle Reeves came back to the porch with a pitcher.

"I like a new dress," she said. She poured the sweet purple water out first for the daughter-in-law. The daughter-in-law swallowed it straight down. And then the girl said she had to be going.

After the daughter-in-law left, Myrtle Reeves kept sipping the Koolaid. Sometimes she tipped the glass up so that the ice cubes slid down and clinked against her teeth. She was confused about Berkeley and the white deerskins being there. Myrtle Reeves had watched the special dance with the sacred skins suspended from sticks held high in the air. She was listening now, and through the sounds of the wind-chime and the garden insects, she heard the shrill whistling sound which the old men at the white deerskin dance made on the heron-leg flutes. The whistling became a worshipping song, and the old men pressed their obsidian spears against their chests and sighed. A stillness settled into the valley, but Myrtle Reeves could not think of what to do now.

She went into the garden and stood surrounded by its steaminess. She had her shoes off, and her feet were splayed. Specks of sweat began to show out of the powder. Myrtle Reeves never spent time in the garden straightening things because there was always one more place to be planted, and she'd rather do that. She knew now she had some sunflower seeds saved under the porch. She crouched down to see into the dank darkness. Other things she had also stored there. Mostly old things that the house could no longer hold, like picture frames and jars, a shovel, a cradle, besides the sunflower seeds on a shelf. She huddled the seeds in her hand awhile before she decided where they should go in the garden.

Myrtle Reeves spent the rest of the afternoon setting in the sunflower seeds along the fence, every eighth slat. When they were grown, they would nod out over the fence. She dug the holes with a big toe. The wide shade was beginning to spread down from the Sisikiyous, and slender shadows were beginning to shoot out from under the leaves in the garden when her son stopped off at the house. He shouted to her while he was screeching the gears of the truck to a halt out in front and the red road dust was still rising up. "Hey, old lady! Guess what!"

The son had always been a sort of joker. He got out of the truck and came to speak to her across the fence. He had a load of logs on the truck, so he couldn't stay long and besides some of the boys who worked in the woods were with him. "Just wait till you see what me and the boys brought you back!"

With the shadows there was a mossy moistness about the garden now. Myrtle Reeves waited by the fence. Against her ankles the garden grasses were slivers of coolness. "Did you bring me a present?" she wanted to know.

One of her son's friends said, "You bet we did. Sam's always saying about you being interested in things."

The other friend brought a big something out of the truck. "Bone from the mountain," he said.

"Mastodon bone," the son said.

"Foreman says they've got plenty of mastodons these days," said the second friend.

Sam explained, "We had the caterpiller and were shovin' up some stumps. Then there was this thing sitting there. Sort of in this stump. Sitting right there. So I said shucks and brought it along. Couldn't leave it just sitting there. Didn't do anything just sitting there. I guess there must've been some other bones too." They came inside the fence and set the bone down on one of the steps to Myrtle Reeves' house. "Keep it polished," the son said. "See you tomorrow at the square dance," he said.

The bone bulked big on the step. Made bigger by the shadows from the half-day. It was a possession. Its substance was a stippled white, and at its sides were outspread wings. Drawn down toward the center of its shape were sharp lines which might have told how old it was. Myrtle Reeves mused on the bone. "Mastodon," she sounded to herself. Made when the mountains were made. Before the old men. And the rest of the mastodon still caught in the stump roots. Massive and unmoving. Myrtle Reeves let the bone with its outspread wings sit by itself on the step. She sat on the step below it.

In the evening on Tuesday, Myrtle Reeves went down to the square dance at the school in the Square where they had the Bureau of Indian Affairs. Every Tuesday she went down to sit along the sides and see the young people and the Square people and to have someone serve her small cookies on a plate. This Tuesday Myrtle Reeves wore her yellow satiny dress and her silver necklace. She appeared quite proper. Wallace Batterson was there finding tunes on his violin. He stood solidly on one foot with the other one tapping in time to the tunes. Whenever something sounded wrong, he put the bow between his teeth and leaned over the violin to tighten the wires. Ruby Jarnagan, who played on the accordion, was sitting behind him. These two had some Indian in them. Then there were the Hickman boys, who had come up from Arkansas to saw sugar pine in the valley. They had steel guitars and had set up microphones and magnaboxes everywhere so the sheer sounds of their guitars would slash through the crowd.

Myrtle Reeves sat by herself in the center of a bench to wait and see. Rachel Little had come only once to the square dance. She had said to Myrtle Reeves about how she did not like the new kind of songs. More people were coming in. The young girls in fuchsia skirts with little lockets on slender chains on the smooth skin of their chests. The boys in slim black suits were there with their black hair clipped on top into bristles and brushed back long on the sides. And the Square people, and Indians like Jimmie Jackson who made sure the logs were sliced right at the sugar pine mill. Myrtle Reeves' son and her daughter-in-law in her new dress came and went around saying hello to everybody. But things didn't get going until Mr. Ralph Gordon of the Bureau of Indian Affairs arrived. He wasn't long in getting there.

He grasped one of the Hickmans' microphones in his hand. "Grab your partners. Now's the time. Let's go-go-go. GO, Everybody!" and soon they were all swing-swing-swinging. The girls' skirts swirled out, and their shoes swung off out over the floor. The little lockets lunged forward. "Dig for the oyster! Duck for the clam!" Ruby Jarnagan was making wide sweeps with the accordian, and the Hickmans were really stomping the floor. "Promenade-promenade-promenade. Everybody home for some lemonade," called out Mr. Ralph Gordon on the microphone. The clashing colors slowed to a stop, and there was a sweaty pause from the clattering sounds before they all began again. All the time Ike Spender, the old Indian who was always drunk these days, was looking through the window from the outside. Sometimes the scrawny dogs which were always lying around the Square would leap up past him, over the sill, and run in crazy circles around the dancers.

People began to get tired halfway through and came over to sit on the bench by Myrtle Reeves. They passed out the cookies halfway through, too, and Myrtle Reeves made her hands small in her lap. Under the white glare of the school lights, her silver necklace gleamed. By the main door of the school there was a thick yellow light to keep the bugs away, but because of the white light inside, they kept rasping against the screens. Myrtle Reeves' son and daughter-in-law came up to her now.

"Hey, old lady," the son said, "tell them about what we got in the woods yesterday."

"Mrs. Reeves," said someone who lived in the Square, "you must drop in to see us. Not just for the square dance, you know."

"What did Sam give you, Mrs. Reeves?" somebody else asked, and offered a cookie.

Myrtle Reeves smiled because she had the beautiful feeling of knowing that the big bone belonged to her. "He brought me a bone," she told them.

"Really?"

"Mastodon," said Myrtle Reeves.

"Mastodon?" asked someone else.

"Mastodon bone in our woods?" asked Jimmie Jackson.

"And it's all bone," the son said.

"Whereabouts in the woods? Were there other bones? How many? Why didn't you notify someone? Who was with you?" These were the questions Jimmie Jackson asked. But Myrtle Reeves just sat smiling in the center of the bench so the son had to do all the explaining.

"The foreman said they've got plenty of mastodons these days."

Myrtle Reeves, no longer feeling alone, said, "It's a big bone he brought me. You must drop in to see it." People moved in to hear what was being said and moved out again.

Mr. Ralph Gordon moved in. "Mastodon bone," he said. "Miz Myrtle's got a mastodon bone, has she? Mastodon bones belong in museums. For the American people."

"The foreman said—" her son began.

"Sam," said Mr. Ralph Gordon, "I don't care what he said. He don't know what he said. But I know anything up in the woods is the property of the American government. I say that bone is property of the American government."

Myrtle Reeves said, "That bone is mine."

"Now," the son said, sidetracking, "I guess we can let that bone go. Just an old bone. Like any old bone. Just brought it back cause it wasn't doing any good sitting there."

The daughter-in-law said, "In Berkeley we put the old steak bones in the garbage every night. Couldn't very well keep them sitting around the house forever. One time I heard about ptomaine coming from having old bones around."

"That's right," said Mr. Ralph Gordon. "Think of it now—" and he stepped outside the circle around the bench where Myrtle Reeves was sitting. He took up the microphone again and tilted it up to him so his voice would blare through the school. "Think of it now—in headlines three inches high. Mastodon bone found here. Here in this valley. I can just imagine. In headlines three inches high." He stopped. "Does everybody here know Miz Myrtle Reeves has got a mastodon bone? A gen-u-ine A-mer-i-can bone!"

Myrtle Reeves understood the questions now. She kept her hands small in her lap, but the specks of sweat started to show through her powder. "She's going to give it to us, and there'll be headlines three inches high," Mr. Ralph Gordon said, and when his voice stopped searing her ears, Myrtle Reeves left the school. They had started in swinging their partners again. "Birdie-in-the-cage. Circle-circle-three hands 'round!"

On the long road to the high forest, past the trailers and toward her house, the night lay motionless. The small sounds of insects speckled the silence and then disappeared into it. Myrtle Reeves walked with her shoes off. Bats folded themselves through the stillness, and everything seemed only a shadow of itself.

In the garden the shadows lay undisturbed beneath the leaves of the flowers. But Myrtle Reeves had to disturb this quiet in order to move the bone. It was still on the step with its wings outspread. Myrtle Reeves bent down to wrap her arms around it. As she carried it, its wings protruded over her shoulders. She placed the big bone under the porch with the other still precious things. She would let it stay there. The quiet returned and settled in.

When they came down in the morning from the Square, Myrtle Reeves was sitting in the center of the day-bed on the porch, over the place where the big bone rested with its outspread wings.

PART II

WOMAN BECOMING

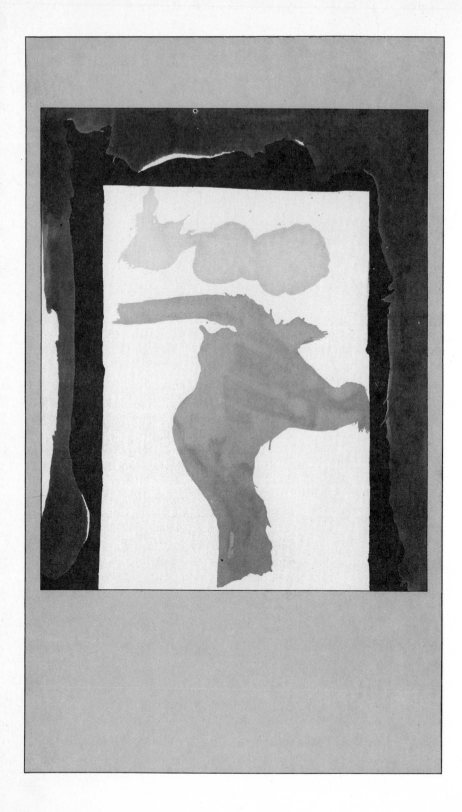

WOMAN BECOMING

But every contradiction
Has the condition of resolving
Itself through the process
Through the process
Through the process of
Becoming, becoming, becoming,
Becoming, BECOMING!
                        —Megan Terry,
                        Approaching Simone

Three major approaches characterize the attempts of women writers to show that their characters may transcend their social roles to become fully human beings who respond with joy and anguish to their experience of the world. Many writers realistically record their experience as women to show its commonality with that of other women and to validate it. Such writing helps women overcome their feeling of isolation and encourages them to stop internalizing their failures as purely individual. It promotes sisterhood, and it offers male readers a basis for comparing their experience. Other writers concentrate on frank explorations of the "problem that has no name"—Betty Friedan's words for women's unease about their socially imposed roles. They describe the women's feelings, often realistically, and suggest that the very act of describing and recognizing the problem will lead to its solution. And, realizing the deep emotional grounding of women's roles, many writers are rewriting old myths from a feminine perspective. All three of these approaches empha-size *process* more than achievement. Women are seen finding ways to be self-creators, distinguishing between themselves as objects of others' perceptions and as perceiving, imagining individuals capable of making their own worlds.

The various literary genres lend themselves to these different approaches in different ways. The novel, traditionally close to realism, most frequently records daily life over a period of time for a multitude of characters. Through stream-of-consciousness and symbolism, it reveals attitudes and feelings toward experience and assesses the significance of these reactions. Unfortunately, some novelists' revelations about female sexuality prove to be so titillating that critics fail to see their revelations about the need for personal liberation. Erica Jong's *Fear of Flying,* for instance, was greeted excitedly as an exposé of female lust; most critics failed to comment on its exposé of the heroine Isadora's desperation in her roles as submissive wife, amateur poet, incomplete human being. Jong, like other contem-porary women novelists, has employed novelistic forms traditionally used to show masculine quests for identity. The picaresque novel of adventure and the novel of development (*bildungsroman*) are used to show women as agents in their own fate, as individuals with their own life stories and need for autonomy. But successful users of these forms adapt them to the reality of female situations and psychological needs. Tillie Olsen in *Yonnondio* (1974), for example, links a mother's walk with her children into a different neighborhood where trees are in blossom to the depths of mother-daughter conflict. Margaret Atwood in *Surfacing* (1972) turns a daughter's real trip to solve the mystery of her father's death into a mythical journey into the depths of the self, made possible only after she recognizes her bond with both father and mother. Lisa Alther in *Kinflicks* (1974) combines the picaresque and the bildungsroman in linking, with great wit, a daughter's sexual and psychic adventures with her need to receive her mother's blessing before she can become fully herself. These and many other novels undergird a convincing surface realism with insights into the center of personality.

Representative drama and "confessional" poetry also record women's experience realistically. Lorraine Hansberry's *A Raisin in the Sun* (1959), for example, explodes stereotypes about the superhuman black mother. Sylvia Plath's poetry makes the suicide she recorded in her novel *The Bell Jar* (1963) and acted out in her own life totally understandable. But both the drama and the poetry of the 1970s have emphasized women's symbolic inner journey and their need to rewrite myth.

Women dramatists, historically rare because of the public nature of theatre and its need for cooperation and capital not usually available to women, have been turning to the remote origins of drama to find new modes of expression. Poetic ritual, song, and ceremony appear in such works as Ntozake Shange's *For Colored Girls Who Have Considered Suicide/When the Rainbow is Enuf* and Megan Terry's *Approaching Simone*. Choral recitation and the assumption of many roles by one actor are characteristic techniques in the more than two hundred plays by women published since the 1960s and in the many others that have been presented in semiprofessional and amateur productions without being published. Eve Merriam's *Out of Our Father's House* brings together authentic voices from the diaries and letters of women separated in time and space. Susan Griffin's *Voices* shows women who are a community because of their shared experience. These techniques are dramatically effective; they are also political statements of women's need to share in history. Today feminist theater is one of the most vibrant art forms; because drama is the most public of literary genres, it promises to maintain the vitality of the feminist perspective.

Contemporary lyric poetry shares some of the characteristics of drama; both published and unpublished poets read their work in libraries and coffee houses as well as in public halls. The voice of the poet is heard also in print through the proliferation of small publishing houses and magazines that welcome experimentation. The contemporary movement away from established verse forms toward the rhythms of speech has been hospitable to women poets; their central concern is for a language capable of expressing their insights. An excerpt from Denise Levertov's *Relearning the Alphabet* emphasizes this need.

> Relearn the alphabet,
> relearn the world, the world
> understood anew only in doing, under-
> stood only as
> looked-up-into out of earth,
> the heart of an eye looking,
> the heart of a root
> planted in earth.
> Transmutation is not
> under the will's rule.

In order to communicate a sense of self, a woman poet must present herself as a subject, as active, as in process. To communicate her deep knowledge of the world, perceived with the heart's eye "planted in earth"— or, as another of Levertov's titles indicates, *With Eyes at the Back of Her Head*—she needs to find words free of their connotations to male knowledge of the world. In "Unlearning to Not Speak," Marge Piercy emphasizes that women must learn to speak in the first person, singular and plural, to express "her own true hunger/and pleasure/and rage." In "Artemis" Olga Broumas speaks of "decoding" a "curviform alphabet" to describe joy in the body; vowels have new depths of meaning, "beginning with O, the O-/mega, horseshoe, the cave of sound"—and, significantly, the initial of the poet who is speaking through the goddess-persona. Like fiction and drama feminist poetry emphasizes through realism, expression of emotion, and new myths the need of women for a sense of identity, of community, of full humanity.

Works in Part II of this Anthology

The selections that follow supplement those in earlier sections, which described and went beyond the major stereotypes of women. They show women undergoing change, in the process of self-creation. Though honestly showing the pain that accompanies such change, the works share a sense of women's autonomy and of their joy in discovering their humanity. The selections are arranged to parallel both an individual's emerging awareness of feminine possibility and the group experience of the Women's Movement.

Emily Dickinson wrote "A Prison Gets to be a Friend—" in 1862 after she withdrew from society to discover her own voice. The range of interpretation, for this and Dickinson's work in general, indicates how feminine response to the human condition can expand tradition. Her profound understanding of the subtle appeal of captivity explains not only why women have accepted their secondary status but also why victims in general so often cooperate in their own oppression. Psychological factors— the appeal of safety, the comfort of the familiar, the illusory nature of freedom—seduce the adult from the memory of joy as a reality, a possibility. Long before Freud, Dickinson perceived the submergence of our deepest consciousness during adult life. The "Phantasm Steel" is as immovable as the stereotypes and archetypes buried in the subconscious. This poem vividly conveys the need for liberation; it offers no solutions, but in doubting that Heaven will compensate for the earthly fate, it encourages us to explore human alternatives. Its consciousness of reality is the first step in the process of change, a step necessary for each individual as well as for society.

In Tillie Olsen's "Tell Me a Riddle" a dying old woman, bitter about the discontinuity forced upon her by her roles of wife and mother, experiences a deep sense of continuity with her younger and inner self. Olsen's poetic prose evokes feelings of anguish and waste, not only for Eva but for her husband and children who are also limited by their socially imposed roles. "Tell Me a Riddle" eloquently underlines a frequent theme of feminist writing: that liberation of women is part of the liberation of all human beings. It exemplifies the expansion of human experience possible through focusing on the neglected experience of half the human race. The poignancy of having one's consciousness raised only when close to death makes the tone of "Tell Me a Riddle" almost elegiac. The story commemorates women in generations past and present to whom the possibility of liberation has not even occurred. Other works show women in more hopeful stages of liberation. Michele Murray's little poem "Coming to Self" asserts the normality of self-discovery for a woman. Marge Piercy's "Unlearning to Not Speak," a call for a sense of community, implies that it can be achieved.

Susan Glaspell's play *Trifles* shows not only the effectiveness of sisterhood but also women who are capable of the same kind of deductive logic usually attributed to men. The title ironically emphasizes the differences in male-female perceptions, a difference that makes honesty impossible if comparison is to prevail. This humorous play has a serious point: institutions such as law need the corrective of female insight, a point also made by Susan Griffin in her poem about the heroic slave liberator, Harriet Tubman. The short stories by Alice Adams and Jane Rule stress, with different emphases, female bonding. In "Roses, Rhododendron," seeing peers who contribute to female development removes some of the Freudian stress on socialization by the mother alone; friends and mothers who refuse to confine themselves to their roles help establish a range of role models. Both Adams and Rule establish a slightly ironic tone so that the main characters' introspection seems casual, normal. Rule in "Middle Children" calmly suggests that lesbianism is a normal and rational outcome of the psychological situation of the middle child. In "Joy in Provence" May Sarton shows a woman who shares with another the intellectual insights and wisdom she gained from living and suffering; her images and language make the admonition "Rejoice" seem inevitable. And Denise Levertov's persona in "Stepping Westward" exults in the joy of accepting her womanhood as a basis for growth and altruism. Lucille Clifton and Susan Griffin realistically show the price of heroism but also invite readers to share its pains and joys with their role models.

Like Harriet Tubman, Martha Collins' persona in "Homecoming" declares her independence and need for her own space. In "Tuesday Night" Ann Beattie's heroine finds that a similar assertion leaves her unsure of how to use her freedom, a common human dilemma that women have had little experience in resolving; learning how to use freedom is part of the process of becoming fully human. Speaking without respect to gender, Anne Stanford's persona in "The Descent" exults in the Platonic sense of sharing humanity with the divine, of being alive in a human way, of experiencing "the earth with all its destinies." Though the morning is "harsh in the sun," the speaker rejoices in the human condition, in being a part of the world of becoming, of "growing into light." Stanford, like the twentieth-century philosophers Suzanne Langer and Simone Weil, can think about abstractions in a way usually described as masculine. Her poem refuses to see women as secondary human beings. Alice Walker's "Beyond What" shows human beings as they "reach for destinies beyond/ what we have come to know/"; men and women alike see the world completely and individually, and love dictates their choices.

Adrienne Rich's poem "Diving into the Wreck" and Megan Terry's play *Approaching Simone* encompass several of the themes and attitudes of feminist literature. Rich's persona and Terry's central character undertake demanding tasks by preparing themselves with knowledge, skills, and tools. Like the heroes of ancient epics, they venture into the unknown, fully aware of the danger, in order to complete themselves. Rich's lonely voyage to watery depths symbolizes a search for origins, beyond history; a "book of myths" is a poor guide at best, especially since in it "our names do not appear." The diver must learn to accept the support of the water instead of trying to overcome it; the decision to accept the universe proves to be effective strategy and allows the inspection of the wreck. Searching for reality rather than its story, the diver, away from earthly limitations and familiar environment, becomes androgynous, a representative of all humanity, present and past; the wreck is the wreck of time, the sum of all human experience. Whether the motive is "cowardice or courage," what matters is the confrontation with reality, which the camera may record; the images it catches may revise the book of myths and the diver's name may become part of history when she/he surfaces. The dive may become a new myth. Whatever the results, the poem implies that the quest is worthwhile, necessary; there is hope of change.

Like Harriet Tubman, Simone Weil (1909–1943) was an activist who sought, as her life work, ways of benefiting humanity. But it was not her work as a teacher, factory worker, or fighter for freedom before World War II that moved playwright Megan Terry to make her the hero of *Approaching Simone*. It was Weil's heroic inner journey, her mystical perceptions, and her philosophical writings; Terry saw her as a woman comparable to Christ in her humanity and in her transcendence of the human. Like Rich's diver, Simone risks her life to understand life— and herself. Significantly, although she is highly independent, she does not achieve her mystical goal alone: her friends absorb her bodily pain and support her so that she can have her union with a God who is Love. Although at her self-imposed death Simone had not been able to prevent war, she dies confident that her work will have its fruition through others. Like those of other heroes who suffer, her tragedy can purge us of our pity and fear—for all who suffer, for ourselves; it can give us the courage to go beyond the discouragement and frustration that inevitably accompany the process of becoming, of change. Significantly, Terry's title suggests a relationship between Simone and the audience for the play, for us as readers: *approaching* Simone—learning about her life, understanding it, sharing her feelings and ideas—is what is required. We are not asked to *become* Simone, to live her life or die her death; but through her image we can gain light for our own self-concept and extend its boundaries.

The works in this section offer striking images of women who are acting, doing, achieving; they counteract the old image of women as passive, as acted upon. Dickinson's view of comfortable acceptance of traditional roles—"the narrow Round"—as the avoidance of liberty, of natural childlike joy, places the responsibility for diminished life upon the prisoner and rejects the hope of miraculous escape. The poem implies that only autonomous action—toward which self-awareness is the first step— can resist the lure of familiar bonds. In other works some images explicitly deny old role expectations. "Unlearning to not speak," "No melting. No squeezing/into One," "Never again to be forced to move to the rhythms of others," resolve the speakers. The emphasis is not on reaction but action. "These things shall be," asserts Eva in "Tell Me a Riddle"; "Still she believed," her husband marvels as she gasps "Lift high banner of reason justice freedom light." Perceiving heroism in a seemingly destroyed old woman, a speaker is inspired to "stand up"; thinking of Harriet Tubman, who "led an army/and won a battle/and defied the laws," a speaker gains courage for a battle for justice that she sees as "beginning." We hear women speaking admiringly of other women: "She was nothing if not enterprising"; "She taught me to read"; "she was going to knot it"; "seasoned and sweetened by loss,/She thrives." We hear them speak of their closeness to each other: "I like to think of Harriet Tubman"; "We shared the sun-drenched hours"; "the picture that moved me most . . . was . . . of you and me. . . . Going somewhere"; "She felt sorry for me. With someone on my side, I felt new courage. . . ."; ". . . alone together we could find no reason not to make love."

But whether denying old restrictions or celebrating new-found female community, most authors stress the need for, the anguish of, and the joy in self-discovery. In "Coming to Self," Michele Murray's metaphor "as iron comes by fire/from the ore" expresses the difficulty of the process and "as gold washes clean in the stream" affirms its value; both metaphors are of human processes that come close to the inevitability of natural processes. The simplicity of the poem's assertion underlines the certainty of "Coming to Self." Equal assurance comes through in the wit of Martha Collins's final line, "I am making myself at home"; the process of self-creation happens, appropriately enough for a woman, at home, but the persona will feel at home in a new way now that she has claimed her space. Denise Levertov rejoices even while aging; she is "glad to be/what, woman/and who, myself/I am."

The women who wrote the works in this section demonstrate through literature their skill and will to share with others their experience, their fantasies, their hopes. Our response should be to participate actively in making their texts live through our sympathetic reading.

EMILY DICKINSON

(1830–1886) Famous as a recluse, Emily Dickinson spent her entire life in Amherst, Massachusetts, except for a year at Mount Holyoke Female Seminary. At her death over 900 poems were found in manuscript, only 7 of which had been published. An additional 900 poems have since been discovered, many not published until 1945. Now recognized as a major poet, Dickinson wrote of love, death, God, and nature. Unconventional both in form and content, her work seems very modern. Her letters were published in three volumes in 1958.

A PRISON GETS TO BE
A FRIEND

A Prison gets to be a friend–
Between its Ponderous face
And Ours–a Kinsmanship express–
And in its narrow Eyes–

We come to look with gratitude
For the appointed Beam
It deal us–stated as our food–
And hungered for–the same–

We learn to know the Planks–
That answer to Our feet–
So miserable a sound–at first–
Nor ever now–so sweet–

As plashing in the Pools–
When Memory was a Boy–
But a Demurer Circuit–
A Geometric Joy–

The Posture of the Key
That interrupt the Day
To Our Endeavor–Not so real
The Cheek of Liberty–

As this Phantasm Steel–
Whose features–Day and Night–
Are present to us–as Our Own–
And as escapeless–quite–

The narrow Round–the Stint–
The slow exchange of Hope–
For something passiver–Content
Too steep for looking up–

The Liberty we knew
Avoided–like a Dream–
Too wide for any Night but Heaven–
If That–indeed–redeem–

TILLIE OLSEN
(b. 1913) Born in Nebraska, Tillie Olsen has
lived most of her adult life in San Francisco.
A Depression high-school dropout self-taught
in public libraries, she wrote and published
when young, but the necessity of raising and
supporting four children silenced her for
twenty years. *Tell Me a Riddle,* a collection
of short stories first published in 1962, is now
regarded as a classic. Her novel *Yonnondio:
From the Thirties,* "lost" for forty years, was
published in 1974, and *Silences,* a collection
of essays on human creativity, appeared in
1978. In recent years Tillie Olsen has received
many awards and honors and has taught and
lectured widely.

TELL ME A RIDDLE

"These Things Shall Be"

I

For forty-seven years they had been married. How deep back the stubborn,
gnarled roots of the quarrel reached, no one could say—but only now,
when tending to the needs of others no longer shackled them together,
the roots swelled up visible, split the earth between them, and the tearing
shook even to the children, long since grown.

Why now, why now? wailed Hannah.

As if when we grew up weren't enough, said Paul.

Poor Ma. Poor Dad. It hurts so for both of them, said Vivi. They never
had very much; at least in old age they should be happy.

Knock their heads together, insisted Sammy; tell 'em: you're too old
for this kind of thing; no reason not to get along now.

Lennie wrote to Clara: They've lived over so much together; what
could possibly tear them apart?

Something tangible enough.

Arthritic hands, and such work as he got, occasional. Poverty all his life, and there was little breath left for running. He could not, could not turn away from this desire: to have the troubling of responsibility, the fretting with money, over and done with; to be free, to be *care*free where success was not measured by accumulation, and there was use for the vitality still in him.

There was a way. They could sell the house, and with the money join his lodge's Haven, cooperative for the aged. Happy communal life, and was he not already an official; had he not helped organize it, raise funds, served as a trustee?

But she—would not consider it.

"What do we need all this for?" he would ask loudly, for her hearing aid was turned down and the vacuum was shrilling. "Five rooms" (pushing the sofa so she could get into the corner) "furniture" (smoothing down the rug) "floors and surfaces to make work. Tell me, why do we need it?" And he was glad he could ask in a scream.

"Because I'm use't."

"Because you're use't. This is a reason, Mrs. Word Miser? Used to can get unused!"

"Enough unused I have to get used to already. . . . Not enough words?" turning off the vacuum a moment to hear herself answer. "Because soon enough we'll need only a little closet, no windows, no furniture, nothing to make work, but for worms. Because now I want room. . . . Screech and blow like you're doing, you'll need that closet even sooner. . . . Ha, again!" for the vacuum bag wailed, puffed half up, hung stubbornly limp. "This time fix it so it stays; quick before the phone rings and you get too important busy."

But while he struggled with the motor, it seethed in him. Why fix it? Why have to bother? And if it can't be fixed, have to wring the mind with how to pay the repair? At the Haven they come in with their own machines to clean your room or your cottage; you fish, or play cards, or make jokes in the sun, not with knotty fingers fight to mend vacuums.

Over the dishes, coaxingly: "For once in your life, to be free, to have everything done for you, like a queen."

"I never liked queens."

"No dishes, no garbage, no towel to sop, no worry what to buy, what to eat."

"And what else would I do with my empty hands? Better to eat at my own table when I want, and to cook and eat how I want."

"In the cottages they buy what you ask, and cook it how you like. *You* are the one who always used to say: better mankind born without mouths and stomachs than always to worry for money to buy, to shop, to fix, to cook, to wash, to clean."

"How cleverly you hid that you heard. I said it then because eighteen hours a day I ran. And you never scraped a carrot or knew a dish towel sops. Now—for you and me—who cares? A herring out of a jar is enough. But when *I* want, and nobody to bother." And she turned off her ear button, so she would not have to hear.

But as *he* had no peace, juggling and rejuggling the money to figure: how will I pay for this now?; prying out the storm windows (there they take care of this); jolting in the streetcar on errands (there I would not have to ride to take care of this or that); fending the patronizing relatives just back from Florida (at the Haven it matters what one is, not what one can afford), he gave *her* no peace.

"Look! In their bulletin. A reading circle. Twice a week it meets."

"Haumm," her answer of not listening.

"A reading circle. Chekhov they read that you like, and Peretz. Cultured people at the Haven that you would enjoy."

"Enjoy!" She tasted the word. "Now, when it pleases you, you find a reading circle for me. And forty years ago when the children were morsels and there was a Circle, did you stay home with them once so I could go? Even once? You trained me well. I do not need others to enjoy. Others!" Her voice trembled. "Because *you* want to be there with others. Already it makes me sick to think of you always around others. Clown, grimacer, floormat, yesman, entertainer, whatever they want of you."

And now it was he who turned on the television loud so he need not hear.

Old scar tissue ruptured and the wounds festered anew. Chekhov indeed. She thought without softness of that young wife, who in the deep night hours while she nursed the current baby, and perhaps held another in her lap, would try to stay awake for the only time there was to read. She would feel again the weather of the outside on his cheek when, coming late from a meeting, he would find her so, and stimulated and ardent, sniffing her skin, coax: "I'll put the baby to bed, and you—put the book away, don't read, don't read."

That had been the most beguiling of all the "don't read, put your book away" her life had been. Chekhov indeed!

"Money?" She shrugged him off. "Could we get poorer than once we were? And in America, who starves?"

But as still he pressed:

"Let me alone about money. Was there ever enough? Seven little ones— for every penny I had to ask—and sometimes, remember, there was nothing. But always *I* had to manage. Now *you* manage. Rub your nose in it good."

But from those years she had had to manage, old humiliations and terrors rose up, lived again, and forced her to relive them. The children's needings; that grocer's face or this merchant's wife she had had to beg credit from when credit was a disgrace; the scenery of the long blocks walked around when she could not pay; school coming, and the desperate going over the old to see what could yet be remade; the soups of meat bones begged "for-the-dog" one winter. . . .

Enough. Now they had no children. Let *him* wrack his head for how they would live. She would not exchange her solitude for anything. *Never again to be forced to move to the rhythms of others.*

For in this solitude she had won to a reconciled peace.

Tranquillity from having the empty house no longer an enemy, for it stayed clean—not as in the days when it was her family, the life in it, that had seemed the enemy: tracking, smudging, littering, dirtying, engaging her in endless defeating battle—and on whom her endless defeat had been spewed.

The few old books, memorized from rereading; the pictures to ponder (the magnifying glass superimposed on her heavy, eyeglasses). Or if she wishes, when he is gone, the phonograph, that if she turns up very loud and strains, she can hear: the ordered sounds and the struggling.

Out in the garden, growing things to nurture. Birds to be kept out of the pear tree, and when the pears are heavy and ripe, the old fury of work, for all must be canned, nothing wasted.

And her one social duty (for she will not go to luncheons or meetings) the boxes of old clothes left with her, as with a life-practised eye for finding what is still wearable within the worn (again the magnifying glass superimposed on the heavy glasses) she scans and sorts—this for rag or rummage, that for mending and cleaning, and this for sending away.

Being able at last to live within, and not move to the rhythms of others, as life had forced her to: denying; removing; isolating; taking the children one by one; then deafening, half-blinding—and at last, presenting her solitude.

And in it she had won to a reconciled peace.

Now he was violating it with his constant campaigning: *Sell the house and move to the Haven.* (You sit, you sit—there too you could sit like a stone.) He was making of her a battleground where old grievances tore. (Turn on your ear button—I am talking.) And stubbornly she resisted —so that from wheedling, reasoning, manipulation, it was bitterness he now started with.

And it came to where every happening lashed up a quarrel.

"I will sell the house anyway," he flung at her one night. "I am putting it up for sale. There will be a way to make you sign."

The television blared, as always it did on the evenings he stayed home, and as always it reached her only as noise. She did not know if the tumult was in her or outside. Snap! she turned the sound off. "Shadows," she whispered to him, pointing to the screen, "look, it is only shadows." And in a scream: "Did you say that you will sell the house? Look at me, not at that. I am no shadow. You cannot sell without me."

"Leave on the television. I am watching."

"Like Paulie, like Jenny, a four-year-old. Staring at shadows. *You cannot sell the house.*"

"I will. We are going to the Haven. There you would not hear the television when you do not want it. I could sit in the social room and watch. You could lock yourself up to smell your unpleasantness in a room by yourself—for who would want to come near you?"

"No, no selling." A whisper now.

"The television is shadows. Mrs. Enlightened! Mrs. Cultured! A world comes into your house—and it is shadows. People you would never meet in a thousand lifetimes. Wonders. When you were four years old, yes, like Paulie, like Jenny, did you know of Indian dances, alligators, how they use bamboo in Malaya? No, you scratched in your dirt with the chickens and thought Olshana was the world. Yes, Mrs. Unpleasant, I will sell the house, for there better can we be rid of each other than here."

She did not know if the tumult was outside, or in her. Always a ravening inside, a pull to the bed, to lie down, to succumb.

"Have you thought maybe Ma should let a doctor have a look at her?" asked their son Paul after Sunday dinner, regarding his mother crumpled on the couch, instead of, as was her custom, busying herself in Nancy's kitchen.

"Why not the President too?"

"Seriously, Dad. This is the third Sunday she's lain down like that after dinner. Is she that way at home?"

"A regular love affair with the bed. Every time I start to talk to her."

Good protective reaction, observed Nancy to herself. The workings of hos-til-ity.

"Nancy could take her. I just don't like how she looks. Let's have Nancy arrange an appointment."

"You think she'll go?" regarding his wife gloomily. "All right, we have to have doctor bills, we have to have doctor bills." Loudly: "Something hurts you?"

She startled, looked to his lips. He repeated: "Mrs. Take It Easy, something hurts?"

"Nothing. . . . Only you."

"A woman of honey. That's why you're lying down?"

"Soon I'll get up to do the dishes, Nancy."

"Leave them, Mother, I like it better this way."

"Mrs. Take It Easy, Paul says you should start ballet. You should go to see a doctor and ask: how soon can you start ballet?"

"A doctor?" she begged. "Ballet?"

"We were talking, Ma," explained Paul, "you don't seem any too well. It would be a good idea for you to see a doctor for a checkup."

"I get up now to do the kitchen. Doctors are bills and foolishness, my son. I need no doctors."

"At the Haven," he could not resist pointing out, "a doctor is *not* bills. He lives beside you. You start to sneeze, he is there before you open up a Kleenex. You can be sick there for free, all you want."

"Diarrhea of the mouth, is there a doctor to make you dumb?"

"Ma. Promise me you'll go. Nancy will arrange it."

"It's all of a piece when you think of it," said Nancy, "the way she attacks my kitchen, scrubbing under every cup hook, doing the inside of the oven so I can't enjoy Sunday dinner, knowing that half-blind or not, she's going to find every speck of dirt. . . ."

"Don't, Nancy, I've told you—it's the only way she knows to be useful. What did the *doctor* say?"

"A real fatherly lecture. Sixty-nine is young these days. Go out, enjoy life, find interests. Get a new hearing aid, this one is antiquated. Old age is sickness only if one makes it so. Geriatrics, Inc."

"So there was nothing physical."

"Of course there was. How can you live to yourself like she does without there being? Evidence of a kidney disorder, and her blood count is low. He gave her a diet, and she's to come back for follow-up and lab work. . . . But he was clear enough: Number One prescription—start living like a human being. . . . When I think of your dad, who could really play the invalid with that arthritis of his, as active as a teenager, and twice as much fun. . . ."

"You didn't tell me the doctor says your sickness is in you, how you live." He pushed his advantage. "Life and enjoyments you need better than medicine. And this diet, how can you keep it? To weigh each morsel and scrape away each bit of fat, to make this soup, that pudding. There, at the Haven, they have a dietician, they would do it for you."

She is silent.

"You would feel better there, I know it," he says gently. "There there is life and enjoyments all around."

"What is the matter, Mr. Importantbusy, you have no card game or meeting you can go to?"—turning her face to the pillow.

For a while he cut his meetings and going out, fussed over her diet, tried to wheedle her into leaving the house, brought in visitors:

"I should come to a fashion tea. I should sit and look at pretty babies in clothes I cannot buy. This is pleasure?"

"Always you are better than everyone else. The doctor said you should go out. Mrs. Brem comes to you with goodness and you turn her away."

"Because *you* asked her to, she asked me."

"They won't come back. People you need, the doctor said. Your own cousins I asked; they were willing to come and make peace as if nothing had happened. . . ."

"No more crushers of people, pushers, hypocrites, around me. No more in *my* house. You go to them if you like."

"Kind he is to visit. And you, like ice."
"A babbler. All my life around babblers. Enough!"

"She's even worse, Dad? Then let her stew a while," advised Nancy. "You can't let it destroy you; it's a psychological thing, maybe too far gone for any of us to help."

So he let her stew. More and more she lay silent in bed, and sometimes did not even get up to make the meals. No longer was the tongue-lashing inevitable if he left the coffee cup where it did not belong, or forgot to take out the garbage or mislaid the broom. The birds grew bold that summer and for once pocked the pears, undisturbed.

A bellyfull of bitterness and every day the same quarrel in a new way and a different old grievance the quarrel forced her to enter and relive. And the new torment: I am not really sick, the doctor said it, then why do I feel so sick?

One night she asked him: "You have a meeting tonight? Do not go. Stay . . . with me."

He had planned to watch "This Is Your Life," but half sick himself from the heavy heat, and sickening therefore the more after the brooks and woods of the Haven, with satisfaction he grated:

"Hah, Mrs. Live Alone And Like It wants company all of a sudden. It doesn't seem so good the time of solitary when she was a girl exile in Siberia. 'Do not go. Stay with me.' A new song for Mrs. Free As A Bird. Yes, I am going out, and while I am gone chew this aloneness good, and think how you keep us both from where if you want people, you do not need to be alone."

"Go, go. All your life you have gone without me."

After him she sobbed curses he had not heard in years, old-country curses from their childhood: Grow, oh shall you grow like an onion, with your head in the ground. Like the hide of a drum shall you be, beaten in life, beaten in death. Oh shall you be like a chandelier, to hang, and to burn. . . .

She was not in their bed when he came back. She lay on the cot on the sun porch. All week she did not speak or come near him; nor did he try to make peace or care for her.

He slept badly, so used to her next to him. After all the years, old harmonies and dependencies deep in their bodies; she curled to him, or he coiled to her, each warmed, warming, turning as the other turned, the nights a long embrace.

It was not the empty bed or the storm that woke him, but a faint singing.

She was singing. Shaking off the drops of rain, the lightning riving her lifted face, he saw her so; the cot covers on the floor.

"This is a private concert?" he asked. "Come in, you are wet."

"I can breathe now," she answered; "my lungs are rich." Though indeed the sound was hardly a breath.

"Come in, come in." Loosing the bamboo shades. "Look how wet you are." Half helping, half carrying her, still faint-breathing her song.

A Russian love song of fifty years ago.

He had found a buyer, but before he told her, he called together those children who were close enough to come. Paul, of course, Sammy from New Jersey, Hannah from Connecticut, Vivi from Ohio.

With a kindling of energy for her beloved visitors, she arrayed the house, cooked and baked. She was not prepared for the solemn after-dinner conclave, they too probing in and tearing. Her frightened eyes watched from mouth to mouth as each spoke.

His stories were eloquent and funny of her refusal to go back to the doctor; of the scorned invitations; of her stubborn silence or the bile "like a Niagara"; of her contrariness: "If I clean it's no good how I cleaned; if I don't clean, I'm still a master who thinks he has a slave."

(Vinegar he poured on me all his life; I am well marinated; how can I be honey now?)

Deftly he marched in the rightness for moving to the Haven; their money from social security free for visiting the children, not sucked into daily needs and into the house; the activities in the Haven for him; but mostly the Haven for *her:* her health, her need of care, distraction, amusement, friends who shared her interests.

"This does offer an outlet for Dad," said Paul; "he's always been an active person. And economic peace of mind isn't to be sneezed at, either. I could use a little of that myself."

But when they asked: "And you, Ma, how do you feel about it?" could only whisper:

"For him it is good. It is not for me. I can no longer live between people."

"You lived all your life *for* people," Vivi cried.

"Not with." Suffering doubly for the unhappiness on her children's faces.

"You have to find some compromise," Sammy insisted. "Maybe sell the house and buy a trailer. After forty-seven years there's surely some way you can find to live in peace."

"There is no help, my children. Different things we need."

"Then live alone!" He could control himself no longer. "I have a buyer for the house. Half the money for you, half for me. Either alone or with me to the Haven. You think I can live any longer as we are doing now?"

"Ma doesn't have to make a decision this minute, however you feel,

Dad," Paul said quickly, "and you wouldn't want her to. Let's let it lay a few months, and then talk some more."

"I think I can work it out to take Mother home with me for a while," Hannah said. "You both look terrible, but especially you, Mother. I'm going to ask Phil to have a look at you."

"Sure," cracked Sammy. "What's the use of a doctor husband if you can't get free service out of him once in a while for the family? And absence might make the heart . . . you know."

"There was something after all," Paul told Nancy in a colorless voice. "That was Hannah's Phil calling. Her gall bladder. . . . Surgery."

"Her *gall* bladder. If that isn't classic. 'Bitter as gall'—talk of psychosom——"

He stepped closer, put his hand over her mouth, and said in the same colorless, plodding voice. "We have to get Dad. They operated at once. The cancer was everywhere, surrounding the liver, everywhere. They did what they could . . . at best she has a year. Dad . . . we have to tell him."

2

Honest in his weakness when they told him, and that she was not to know. "I'm not an actor. She'll know right away by how I am. Oh that poor woman. I am old too, it will break me into pieces. Oh that poor woman. She will spit on me: 'So my sickness was how I live.' Oh Paulie, how she will be, that poor woman. Only she should not suffer. . . . I can't stand sickness, Paulie, I can't go with you."

But went. And play-acted.

"A grand opening and you did not even wait for me. . . . A good thing Hannah took you with her."

"Fashion teas I needed. They cut out what tore in me; just in my throat something hurts yet. . . . Look! so many flowers, like a funeral. Vivi called, did Hannah tell you? And Lennie from San Francisco, and Clara; and Sammy is coming." Her gnome's face pressed happily into the flowers.

It is impossible to predict in these cases, but once over the immediate effects of the operation, she should have several months of comparative well-being.

The money, where will come the money?

Travel with her, Dad. Don't take her home to the old associations. The other children will want to see her.

The money, where will I wring the money?

Whatever happens, she is not to know. No, you can't ask her to sign papers to sell the house; nothing to upset her. Borrow instead, then after. . . .

I had wanted to leave you each a few dollars to make life easier, as other fathers do. There will be nothing left now. (Failure! you and your "business is exploitation." Why didn't you make it when it could be made?——Is that what you're thinking, Sammy?)

Sure she's unreasonable, Dad——but you have to stay with her; if there's to be any happiness in what's left of her life, it depends on you.

Prop me up, children, think of me, too. Shuffled, chained with her, bitter woman. No Haven, and the little money going. . . . How happy she looks, poor creature.

The look of excitement. The straining to hear everything (the new hearing aid turned full). Why are you so happy, dying woman?

How the petals are, fold on fold, and the gladioli color. The autumn air.

Stranger grandsons, tall above the little gnome grandmother, the little spry grandfather. Paul in a frenzy of picture-taking before going.

She, wandering the great house. Feeling the books; laughing at the maple shoemaker's bench of a hundred years ago used as a table. The ear turned to music.

"Let us go home. See how good I walk now." "One step from the hospital," he answers, "and she wants to fly. Wait till Doctor Phil says."

"Look—the birds too are flying home. Very good Phil is and will not show it, but he is sick of sickness by the time he comes home."

"Mrs. Telepathy, to read minds," he answers; "read mine what it says: when the trunks of medicines become a suitcase, then we will go."

The grandboys, they do not know what to say to us. . . . Hannah, she runs around here, there, when is there time for herself?

Let us go home. Let us go home.

Musing; gentleness—*but for the incidents of the rabbi in the hospital, and of the candles of benediction.*

Of the rabbi in the hospital:

Now tell me what happened, Mother.

From the sleep I awoke, Hannah's Phil, and he stands there like a devil in a dream and calls me by name. I cannot hear. I think he prays. Go away, please, I tell him, I am not a believer. Still he stands, while my heart knocks with fright.

You scared *him,* Mother. He thought you were delirious.

Who sent him? Why did he come to me?

It is a custom. The men of God come to visit those of their religion they might help. The hospital makes up the list for them—race, religion— and you are on the Jewish list.

Not for rabbis. At once go and make them change. Tell them to write: Race, human; Religion, none.

And of the candles of benediction:

Look how you have upset yourself, Mrs. Excited Over Nothing. Pleasant memories you should leave.

Go in, go back to Hannah and the lights. Two weeks I saw candles and said nothing. But she asked me.

So what was so terrible? She forgets you never did, she asks you to light the Friday candles and say the benediction like Phil's mother when she visits. If the candles give her pleasure, why shouldn't she have the pleasure?

Not for pleasure she does it. For emptiness. Because his family does. Because all around her do.

That is not a good reason too? But you did not hear her. For heritage, she told you. For the boys, from the past they should have tradition.

Superstition! From our ancestors, savages, afraid of the dark, of themselves: mumbo words and magic lights to scare away ghosts.

She told you: how it started does not take away the goodness. For centuries, peace in the house it means.

Swindler! does she look back on the dark centuries? Candles bought instead of bread and stuck into a potato for a candlestick? Religion that stifled and said: in Paradise, woman, you will be the footstool of your husband, and in life—poor chosen Jew—ground under, despised, trembling in cellars. And cremated. And cremated.

This is religion's fault? You think you are still an orator of the 1905 revolution? Where are the pills for quieting? Which are they?

Heritage. How have we come from our savage past, how no longer to be savages—this to teach. To look back and learn what humanizes— this to teach. To smash all ghettos that divide us—not to go back, not to go back—this to teach. Learned books in the house, will humankind live or die, and she gives to her boys—superstition.

Hannah that is so good to you. Take your pill, Mrs. Excited For Nothing, swallow.

Heritage! But when did I have time to teach? Of Hannah I asked only hands to help.

Swallow.

Otherwise—musing; gentleness.

Not to travel. To go home.

The children want to see you. We have to show them you are as thorny a flower as ever.

Not to travel.

Vivi wants you should see her new baby. She sent the tickets—airplane tickets—a Mrs. Roosevelt she wants to make of you. To Vivi's we have to go.

A new baby. How many warm, seductive babies. She holds him stiffly, *away* from her, so that he wails. And a long shudder begins, and the sweat beads on her forehead.

TILLIE OLSEN

427

"Hush, shush," croons the grandfather, lifting him back. "You should forgive your grandmamma, little prince, she has never held a baby before, only seen them in glass cases. Hush, shush."

"You're tired, Ma," says Vivi. "The travel and the noisy dinner. I'll take you to lie down."

(A long travel from, to, what the feel of a baby evokes.)

In the airplane, cunningly designed to encase from motion (no wind, no feel of flight), she had sat severely and still, her face turned to the sky through which they cleaved and left no scar.

So this was how it looked, the determining, the crucial sky, and this was how man moved through it, remote above the dwindled earth, the concealed human life. Vulnerable life, that could scar.

There was a steerage ship of memory that shook across a great, circular sea: clustered, ill human beings; and through the thick-stained air, tiny fretting waters in a window round like the airplane's—sun round, moon round. (The round thatched roofs of Olshana.) Eye round—like the smaller window that framed distance the solitary year of exile when only her eyes could travel, and no voice spoke. And the polar winds hurled themselves across snows trackless and endless and white—like the clouds which had closed together below and hidden the earth.

Now they put a baby in her lap. Do not ask me, she would have liked to beg. Enough the worn face of Vivi, the remembered grandchildren. I cannot, cannot. . . .

Cannot what? Unnatural grandmother, not able to make herself embrace a baby.

She lay there in the bed of the two little girls, her new hearing aid turned full, listening to the sound of the children going to sleep, the baby's fretful crying and hushing, the clatter of dishes being washed and put away. They thought she slept. Still she rode on.

It was not that she had not loved her babies, her children. The love—the passion of tending—had risen with the need like a torrent; and like a torrent drowned and immolated all else. But when the need was done—oh the power that was lost in the painful damming back and drying up of what still surged, but had nowhere to go. Only the thin pulsing left that could not quiet, suffering over lives one felt, but could no longer hold nor help.

On that torrent she had borne them to their own lives, and the riverbed was desert long years now. Not there would she dwell, a memoried wraith. Surely that was not all, surely there was more. Still the springs, the springs were in her seeking. Somewhere an older power that beat for life. Somewhere coherence, transport, meaning. If they would but leave her in the air now stilled of clamor, in the reconciled solitude, to journey on.

And they put a baby in her lap. Immediacy to embrace, and the breath of *that* past: warm flesh like this that had claims and nuzzled away all else and with lovely mouths devoured; hot-living like an animal— intensely and now; the turning maze; the long drunkenness; the drowning into needing and being needed. Severely she looked back—and the shudder seized her again, and the sweat. Not that way. Not there, not now could she, not yet. . . .

And all that visit, she could not touch the baby.

"Daddy, is it the . . . sickness she's like that?" asked Vivi. "I was so glad to be having the baby—for her. I told Tim, it'll give her more happiness than anything, being around a baby again. And she hasn't played with him once."

He was not listening, "Aahh little seed of life, little charmer," he crooned, "Hollywood should see you. A heart of ice you would melt. Kick, kick. The future you'll have for a ball. In 2050 still kick. Kick for your grandaddy then."

Attentive with the older children; sat through their performances (command performance; we command you to be the audience); helped Ann sort autumn leaves to find the best for a school program; listened gravely to Richard tell about his rock collection, while her lips mutely formed the words to remember: *igneous, sedimentary, metamorphic;* looked for missing socks, books, and bus tickets; watched the children whoop after their grandfather who knew how to tickle, chuck, lift, toss, do tricks, tell secrets, make jokes, match riddle for riddle. (Tell me a riddle, Grammy. I know no riddles, child.) Scrubbed sills and woodwork and furniture in every room; folded the laundry; straightened drawers; emptied the heaped baskets waiting for ironing (while he or Vivi or Tim nagged: You're supposed to rest here, you've been sick) but to none tended or gave food—and could not touch the baby.

After a week she said: "Let us go home. Today call about the tickets."

"You have important business, Mrs. Inahurry? The President waits to consult with you?" He shouted, for the fear of the future raced in him. "The clothes are still warm from the suitcase, your children cannot show enough how glad they are to see you, and you want home. There is plenty of time for home. We cannot be with the children at home."

"Blind to around you as always: the little ones sleep four in a room because we take their bed. We are two more people in a house with a new baby, and no help."

"Vivi is happy so. The children should have their grandparents a while, she told to me. I should have my mommy and daddy. . . ."

"Babbler and blind. Do you look at her so tired? How she starts to talk and she cries? I am not strong enough yet to help. Let us go home."

(To reconciled solitude.)

For it seemed to her the crowded noisy house was listening to her, listening for her. She could feel it like a great ear pressed under her heart. And everything knocked: quick constant raps: let me in, let me in.

How was it that soft reaching tendrils also became blows that knocked?

C'mon, Grandma, I want to show you. . . .

Tell me a riddle, Grandma. (*I know no riddles.*)

Look, Grammy, he's so dumb he can't even find his hands. (Dody and the baby on a blanket over the fermenting autumn mould.)

I made them—for you. (Ann) (Flat paper dolls with aprons that lifted on scalloped skirts that lifted on flowered pants; hair of yarn and great ringed questioning eyes.)

Watch me, Grandma. (Richard snaking up the tree, hanging exultant, free, with one hand at the top. Below Dody hunching over in pretend-cooking.) (*Climb too, Dody, climb and look.*)

Be my nap bed, Grammy. (The "No!" too late.) Morty's abandoned heaviness, while his fingers ladder up and down her hearing-aid cord to his drowsy chant: eentsiebeentsiespider. (*Children trust.*)

It's to start off your own rock collection, Grandma. That's a trilobite fossil, 200 million years old (millions of years on a boy's mouth) and that one's obsidian, black glass.

Knocked and knocked.

Mother, I *told* you the teacher said we had to bring it back all filled out this morning. Didn't you even ask Daddy? Then tell *me* which plan and I'll check it: evacuate or stay in the city or wait for you to come and take me away. (Seeing the look of straining to hear.) It's for Disaster, Grandma. (*Children trust.*)

Vivi in the maze of the long, the lovely drunkenness. The old old noises: baby sounds; screaming of a mother flayed to exasperation; children quarreling; children playing; singing; laughter.

And Vivi's tears and memories, spilling so fast, half the words not understood.

She had started remembering out loud deliberately, so her mother would know the past was cherished, still lived in her.

Nursing the baby: My friends marvel, and I tell them, oh it's easy to be such a cow. I remember how beautiful my mother seemed nursing my brother, and the milk just flows. . . . Was that Davy? It must have been Davy. . . .

Lowering a hem: How did you ever . . . when I think how you made everything we wore . . . Tim, just think, seven kids and Mommy sewed everything . . . do I remember you sang while you sewed? That white dress with the red apples on the skirt you fixed over for me, was it Hannah's or Clara's before it was mine?

Washing sweaters: Ma, I'll never forget, one of those days so nice you washed clothes outside; one of the first spring days it must have been. The bubbles just danced while you scrubbed, and we chased after, and you stopped to show us how to blow our own bubbles with green onion stalks . . . you always. . . .

"Strong onion, to still make you cry after so many years," her father said, to turn the tears into laughter.

While Richard bent over his homework: Where is it now, do we still have it, the Book of the Martyrs? It always seemed so, well—exalted, when you'd put it on the round table and we'd all look at it together; there was even a halo from the lamp. The lamp with the beaded fringe you could move up and down; they're in style again, pulley lamps like that, but without the fringe. You know the book I'm talking about, Daddy, the Book of the Martyrs, the first picture was a bust of Spartacus . . . Socrates? I wish there was something like that for the children, Mommy, to give them what you. . . . (And the tears splashed again.)

(What I intended and did not? Stop it, daughter, stop it, leave that time. And he, the hypocrite, sitting there with tears in his eyes—it was nothing to you then, nothing.)

. . . The time you came to school and I almost died of shame because of your accent and because I knew you knew I was ashamed; how could I? . . . Sammy's harmonica and you danced to it once, yes you did, you and Davy squealing in your arms. . . . That time you bundled us up and walked us down to the railway station to stay the night 'cause it was heated and we didn't have any coal, that winter of the strike, you didn't think I remembered that, did you, Mommy? . . . How you'd call us out to see the sunsets. . . .

Day after day, the spilling memories. Worse now, questions, too. Even the grandchildren: Grandma, in the olden days, when you were little. . . .

It was the afternoons that saved.

While they thought she napped, she would leave the mosaic on the wall (of children's drawings, maps, calendars, pictures, Ann's cardboard dolls with their great ringed questioning eyes) and hunch in the girls' closet on the low shelf where the shoes stood, and the girls' dresses covered.

For that while she would painfully sheathe against the listening house, the tendrils and noises that knocked, and Vivi's spilling memories. Sometimes it helped to braid and unbraid the sashes that dangled, or to trace the pattern on the hoop slips.

Today she had jacks and children under jet trails to forget. Last night, Ann and Dody silhouetted in the window against a sunset of flaming man-made clouds of jet trail, their jacks ball accenting the peaceful noise of dinner being made. Had she told them, yes she had told them of how they played jacks in her village though there was no ball, no jacks. Six stones, round and flat, toss them out, the seventh on the back of the hand, toss, catch and swoop up as many as possible, toss again. . . .

Of stones (repeating Richard) there are three kinds: earth's fire jetting; rock of layered centuries; crucibled new out of the old (*igneous, sedimentary, metamorphic*). But there was that other—frozen to black glass, never to transform or hold the fossil memory . . . (let not my seed fall on stone). There was an ancient man who fought to heights a great rock that crashed back down eternally—eternal labor, freedom, labor . . . (stone will perish, but the word remain). And you, David, who with a stone slew, screaming: Lord, take my heart of stone and give me flesh.

Who was screaming? Why was she back in the common room of the prison, the sun motes dancing in the shafts of light, and the informer being brought in, a prisoner now, like themselves. And Lisa leaping, yes, Lisa, the gentle and tender, biting at the betrayer's jugular. Screaming and screaming.

No, it is the children screaming. Another of Paul and Sammy's terrible fights?

In Vivi's house. Severely: you are in Vivi's house.

Blows, screams, a call: "Grandma!" For her? Oh please not for her. Hide, hunch behind the dresses deeper. But a trembling little body hurls itself beside her—surprised, smothered laughter, arms surround her neck, tears rub dry on her cheek, and words too soft to understand whisper into her ear (Is this where you hide too, Grammy? It's my secret place, we have a secret now).

And the sweat beads, and the long shudder seizes.

It seemed the great ear pressed inside now, and the knocking. "We have to go home," she told him, "I grow ill here."

"It's your own fault, Mrs. Bodybusy, you do not rest, you do too much." He raged, but the fear was in his eyes. "It was a serious operation, they told you to take care. . . . All right, we will go to where you can rest."

But where? Not home to death, not yet. He had thought to Lennie's, to Clara's; beautiful visits with each of the children. She would have to rest first, be stronger. If they could but go to Florida—it glittered before him, the never-realized promise of Florida. California: of course. (The money, the money, dwindling!) Los Angeles first for sun and rest, then to Lennie's in San Francisco.

He told her the next day. "You saw what Nancy wrote: snow and wind back home, a terrible winter. And look at you—all bones and a swollen belly. I called Phil: he said: 'A prescription, Los Angeles sun and rest.'"

She watched the words on his lips. "You have sold the house," she cried, "that is why we do not go home. That is why you talk no more of the Haven, why there is money for travel. After the children you will drag me to the Haven."

"The Haven! Who thinks of the Haven any more? Tell her, Vivi, tell Mrs. Suspicious: a prescription, sun and rest, to make you healthy. . . . And how could I sell the house without *you?*"

At the place of farewells and greetings, of winds of coming and winds of going, they say their good-byes.

They look back at her with the eyes of others before them: Richard with her own blue blaze; Ann with the nordic eyes of Tim; Morty's dreaming brown of a great-grandmother he will never know; Dody with the laughing eyes of him who had been her springtide love (who stands beside her now); Vivi's, all tears.

The baby's eyes are closed in sleep.

Good-bye, my children.

3

It is to the back of the great city he brought her, to the dwelling places of the cast-off old. Bounded by two lines of amusement piers to the north and to the south, and between a long straight paving rimmed with black benches facing the sand—sands so wide the ocean is only a far fluting.

In the brief vacation season, some of the boarded stores fronting the sands open, and families, young people and children, may be seen. A little tasselled tram shuttles between the piers, and the lights of roller coasters prink and tweak over those who come to have sensation made in them.

The rest of the year it is abandoned to the old, all else boarded up and still; seemingly empty, except the occasional days and hours when the sun, like a tide, sucks them out of the low rooming houses, casts them onto the benches and sandy rim of the walk—and sweeps them into decaying enclosures once again.

A few newer apartments glint among the low bleached squares. It is in one of these Lennie's Jeannie has arranged their rooms. "Only a few miles north and south people pay hundreds of dollars a month for just this gorgeous air, Grandaddy, just this ocean closeness."

She had been ill on the plane, lay ill for days in the unfamiliar room. Several times the doctor came by—left medicine she would not take. Several times Jeannie drove in the twenty miles from work, still in her Visiting Nurse uniform, the lightness and brightness of her like a healing.

"Who can believe it is winter?" he asked one morning. "Beautiful it is outside like an ad. Come, Mrs. Invalid, come to taste it. You are well enough to sit in here, you are well enough to sit outside. The doctor said it too."

But the benches were encrusted with people, and the sands at the sidewalk's edge. Besides, she had seen the far ruffle of the sea: "there take me," and though she leaned against him, it was she who led.

Plodding and plodding, sitting often to rest, he grumbling. Patting the sand so warm. Once she scooped up a handful, cradling it close to her better eye; peered, and flung it back. And as they came almost to the brink and she could see the glistening wet, she sat down, pulled off her shoes and stockings, left him and began to run. "You'll catch cold," he screamed, but the sand in his shoes weighed him down—he who had always been the agile one—and already the white spray creamed her feet.

He pulled her back, took a handkerchief to wipe off the wet and the sand. "Oh no," she said, "the sun will dry," seized the square and smoothed it flat, dropped on it a mound of sand, knotted the kerchief corners and tied it to a bag—"to look at with the strong glass" (for the first time in years explaining an action of hers)—and lay down with the little bag against her cheek, looking toward the shore that nurtured life as it first crawled toward consciousness the millions of years ago.

He took her one Sunday in the evil-smelling bus, past flat miles of blister houses, to the home of relatives. Oh what is this? she cried as the light began to smoke and the houses to dim and recede. Smog, he said, everyone knows but you. . . . Outside he kept his arms about her, but she walked with hands pushing the heavy air as if to open it, whispered: who has done this? sat down suddenly to vomit at the curb and for a long while refused to rise.

One's age as seen on the altered face of those known in youth. Is this they he has come to visit? This Max and Rose, smooth and pleasant, introducing them to polite children, disinterested grandchildren, "the whole family, once a month on Sundays. And why not? We have the room, the help, the food."

Talk of cars, of houses, of success: this son that, that daughter this. And *your* children? Hastily skimped over, the intermarriages, the obscure work—"my doctor son-in-law, Phil"—all he has to offer. She silent in a corner. (Car-sick like a baby, he explains.) Years since he has taken her to visit anyone but the children, and old apprehensions prickle: "no incidents," he silently begs, "no incidents." He itched to tell them. "A very sick woman," significantly, indicating her with his eyes, "a very sick woman." Their restricted faces did not react. "Have you thought maybe she'd do better at Palm Springs?" Rose asked. "Or at least a nicer section of the beach, nicer people, a pool." Not to have to say "money" he said instead: "would she have sand to look at through a magnifying glass?" and went on, detail after detail, the old habit betraying of parading the queerness of her for laughter.

After dinner—the others into the living room in men- or women-clusters, or into the den to watch TV—the four of them alone. She sat close to him, and did not speak. Jokes, stories, people they had known, beginning of reminiscence, Russia fifty-sixty years ago. Strange words across the Duncan Phyfe table: *hunger; secret meetings; human rights; spies; betrayals; prison; escape*—interrupted by one of the grandchildren: "Commercial's on; any Coke left? Gee, you're missing a real hair-raiser." And then a granddaughter (Max proudly: "look at her, an American queen") drove them home on her way back to U.C.L.A. No incident—except there had been no incidents.

The first few mornings she had taken with her the magnifying glass, but he would sit only on the benches, so she rested at the foot, where slatted bench shadows fell, and unless she turned her hearing aid down, other voices invaded.

Now on the days when the sun shone and she felt well enough, he took her on the tram to where the benches ranged in oblongs, some with tables for checkers or cards. Again the blanket on the sand in the striped shadows, but she no longer brought the magnifying glass. He played cards, and she lay in the sun and looked towards the waters; or they walked—two blocks down to the scaling hotel, two blocks back—past chili-hamburger stands, open-doored bars, Next -to- New and perpetual rummage sale stores.

Once, out of the aimless walkers, slow and shuffling like themselves, someone ran unevenly towards them, embraced, kissed, wept: "dear friends, old friends." A friend of *hers,* not his: Mrs. Mays who had lived next door to them in Denver when the children were small.

Thirty years are compressed into a dozen sentences; and the present, not even in three. All is told: the children scattered; the husband dead; she lives in a room two blocks up from the sing hall—and points to the domed auditorium jutting before the pier. The leg? phlebitis; the heavy breathing? that, one does not ask. She, too, comes to the benches each day to sit. And tomorrow, tomorrow, are they going to the community sing? Of course he would have heard of it, everybody goes—the big doings they wait for all week. They have never been? She will come to them for dinner tomorrow and they will all go together.

So it is that she sits in the wind of the singing, among the thousand various faces of age.

She had turned off her hearing aid at once they came into the auditorium. —as she would have wished to turn off sight.

One by one they streamed by and imprinted on her—and though the savage zest of their singing came voicelessly soft and distant, the faces still roared—the faces densened the air—chorded into

> children-chants, mother-croons, singing of the chained
> love serenades, Beethoven storms, mad Lucia's scream
> drunken joy-songs, keens for the dead, work-singing

*while from floor to balcony to dome a bare-footed sore-covered little
girl threaded the sound-thronged tumult, danced her ecstasy
of grimace to flutes that scratched at a cross-roads village wedding*

*Yes, faces became sound, and the sound became faces; and faces and sound
became weight—pushed, pressed*

"Air"—her hands claw his.

"Whenever I enjoy myself. . . ." Then he saw the gray sweat on her
face. "Here. Up. Help me, Mrs. Mays," and they support her out to where
she can gulp the air in sob after sob.

"A doctor, we should get for her a doctor."

"Tch, it's nothing," says Ellen Mays, "I get it all the time. You've
missed the tram; come to my place. Fix your hearing aid, honey . . .
close . . . tea. My view. See, she *wants* to come. Steady now, that's how."
Adding mysteriously: "Remember your advice, easy to keep your head
above water, empty things float. Float."

The singing a fading march for them, tall woman with a swollen leg,
weaving little man, and the swollen thinness they help between.

The stench in the hall: mildew? decay? "We sit and rest then climb.
My gorgeous view. We help each other and here we are."

The stench along into the slab of room. A washstand for a sink, a box
with oilcloth tacked around for a cupboard, a three-burner gas plate.
Artificial flowers, colorless with dust. Everywhere pictures foaming:
wedding, baby, party, vacation, graduation, family pictures. From the narrow
couch under a slit of window, sure enough the view: lurching rooftops and
a scallop of ocean heaving, preening, twitching under the moon.

"While the water heats. Excuse me . . . down the hall." Ellen Mays has
gone.

"You'll live?" he asks mechanically, sat down to feel his fright; tried
to pull her alongside.

She pushed him away. "For air," she said; stood clinging to the dresser.
Then, in a terrible voice:

After a lifetime of room. Of many rooms.

Shhh.

You remember how she lived. Eight children. And now one room like
a coffin.

She pays rent!

Shrinking the life of her into one room like a coffin Rooms and
rooms like this I lie on the quilt and hear them talk

Please, Mrs. Orator-without-Breath.

Once you went for coffee I walked I saw A Balzac a Chekhov to
write it Rummage Alone On scraps

Better old here than in the old country!

On scraps Yet they sang like like Wondrous! *Humankind one has to believe* So strong for what? To rot not grow?

Your poor lungs beg you. They sob between each word.

Singing. Unused the life in them. She in this poor room with her pictures Max You The children Everywhere unused the life And who has meaning? Century after century still all in us not to grow?

Coffins, rummage, plants: sick woman. Oh lay down. We will get for you the doctor.

"And when will it end. Oh, *the end*." *That* nightmare thought, and this time she writhed, crumpled against him, seized his hand (for a moment again the weight, the soft distant roaring of humanity) and on the strangled-for breath, begged: "Man . . . we'll destroy ourselves?"

And looking for answer—in the helpless pity and fear for her (for *her*) that distorted his face—she understood the last months, and knew that she was dying.

4

"Let us go home," she said after several days.

"You are in training for a cross-country run? That is why you do not even walk across the room? Here, like a prescription Phil said, till you are stronger from the operation. You want to break doctor's orders?"

She saw the fiction was necessary to him, was silent; then: "At home I will get better. If the doctor here says?"

"And winter? And the visits to Lennie and to Clara? All right," for he saw the tears in her eyes, "I will write Phil, and talk to the doctor."

Days passed. He reported nothing. Jeannie came and took her out for air, past the boarded concessions, the hooded and tented amusement rides, to the end of the pier. They watched the spent waves feeding the new, the gulls in the clouded sky; even up where they sat, the wind-blown sand stung.

She did not ask to go down the crooked steps to the sea.

Back in her bed, while he was gone to the store, she said: "Jeannie, this doctor, he is not one I can ask questions. Ask him for me, can I go home?"

Jeannie looked at her, said quickly: "Of course, poor Granny. You want your own things around you, don't you? I'll call him tonight. . . . Look, I've something to show you," and from her purse unwrapped a large cookie, intricately shaped like a little girl. "Look at the curls—can you hear me well, Granny?—and the darling eyelashes. I just came from a house where they were baking them."

"The dimples, there in the knees," she marveled, holding it to the better light, turning, studying, "like art. Each singly they cut, or a mold?"

"Singly," said Jeannie, "and if it is a child only the mother can make

them. Oh Granny, it's the likeness of a real little girl who died yesterday—
Rosita. She was three years old. *Pan del Muerto,* the Bread of the Dead.
It was the custom in the part of Mexico they came from."

Still she turned and inspected. "Look, the hollow in the throat, the
little cross necklace. . . . I think for the mother it is a good thing to be
busy with such bread. You know the family?"

Jeannie nodded. "On my rounds. I nursed. . . . Oh Granny, it is like a
party; they play songs she liked to dance to. The coffin is lined with pink
velvet and she wears a white dress. There are candles. . . ."

"In the house?" Surprised, "They keep her in the house?"

"Yes," said Jeannie, "and it is against the health law. The father said it
will be sad to bury her in this country; in Oaxaca they have a feast night
with candles each year; everyone picnics on the graves of those they loved
until dawn."

"Yes, Jeannie, the living must comfort themselves." And closed her
eyes.

"You want to sleep, Granny?"

"Yes, tired from the pleasure of you. I may keep the Rosita? There
stand it, on the dresser, where I can see; something of my own around me."

In the kitchenette, helping her grandfather unpack the groceries,
Jeannie said in her light voice:

"I'm resigning my job, Grandaddy."

"Ah, the lucky young man. Which one is he?"

"Too late. You're spoken for." She made a pyramid of cans, unstacked,
and built again.

"Something is wrong with the job?"

"With me. I can't be"—she searched for the word—"What they call professional enough. I let myself feel things. And tomorrow I have to report
a family. . . ." The cans clicked again. "It's not that, either. I just don't
know what I want to do, maybe go back to school, maybe go to art school. I
thought if you went to San Francisco I'd come along and talk it over with
Momma and Daddy. But I don't see how you can go. She wants to go
home. She asked me to ask the doctor."

The doctor told her himself. "Next week you may travel, when you
are a little stronger." But next week there was the fever of an infection,
and by the time that was over, she could not leave the bed—a rented hospital
bed that stood beside the double bed he slept in alone now.

Outwardly the days repeated themselves. Every other afternoon and
evening he went out to his newfound cronies, to talk and play cards. Twice
a week, Mrs. Mays came. And the rest of the time, Jeannie was there.

By the sickbed stood Jeannie's FM radio. Often into the room the shapes of music came. She would lie curled on her side, her knees drawn up, intense in listening (Jeannie sketched her so, coiled, convoluted like an ear), then thresh her hand out and abruptly snap the radio mute—still to lie in her attitude of listening, concealing tears.

Once Jeannie brought in a young Marine to visit, a friend from high-school days she had found wandering near the empty pier. Because Jeannie asked him to, gravely, without self-consciousness, he sat himself cross-legged on the floor and performed for them a dance of his native Samoa.

Long after they left, a tiny thrumming sound could be heard where, in her bed, she strove to repeat the beckon, flight, surrender of his hands, the fluttering footbeats, and his low plaintive calls.

Hannah and Phil sent flowers. To deepen her pleasure, he placed one in her hair. "Like a girl," he said, and brought the hand mirror so she could see. She looked at the pulsing red flower, the yellow skull face; a desolate, excited laugh shuddered from her, and she pushed the mirror away—but let the flower burn.

The week Lennie and Helen came, the fever returned. With it the excited laugh, and incessant words. She, who in her life had spoken but seldom and then only when necessary (never having learned the easy, social uses of words), now in dying, spoke incessantly.

In a half-whisper: "Like Lisa she is, your Jeannie. Have I told you of Lisa who taught me to read? Of the highborn she was, but noble in herself. I was sixteen; they beat me; my father beat me so I would not go to her. It was forbidden, she was a Tolstoyan. At night, past dogs that howled, terrible dogs, my son, in the snows of winter to the road, I to ride in her carriage like a lady, to books. To her, life was holy, knowledge was holy, and she taught me to read. They hung her. Everything that happens one must try to understand. She killed one who betrayed many. Because of betrayal, betrayed all she lived and believed. In one minute she killed, before my eyes (there is so much blood in a human being, my son), in prison with me. All that happens, one must try to understand.

"The name?" Her lips would work. "The name that was their pole star; the doors of the death houses fixed to open on it; I read of it my year of penal servitude. Thuban!" very excited, "Thuban, in ancient Egypt the pole star. Can you see, look out to see it, Jeannie, if it swings around *our* pole star that seems to *us* not to move.

"Yes, Jeannie, at your age my mother and grandmother had already buried children . . . yes, Jeannie, it is more than oceans between Olshana and you . . . yes, Jeannie, they danced, and for all the bodies they had they might as well be chickens, and indeed, they scratched and flapped their arms and hopped.

"And Andrei Yefimitch, who for twenty years had never known of it and never wanted to know, said as if he wanted to cry: but why my dear friend this malicious laughter?" Telling to herself half-memorized phrases from her few books. "Pain I answer with tears and cries, baseness with indignation, meanness with repulsion . . . for life may be hated or wearied of, but never despised."

Delirious: "Tell me, my neighbor, Mrs. Mays, the pictures never lived, but what of the flowers? Tell them who ask: no rabbis, no ministers, no priests, no speeches, no ceremonies: ah, false—let the living comfort themselves. Tell Sammy's boy, he who flies, tell him to go to Stuttgart and see where Davy has no grave. And what? . . . And what? where millions have no graves—save air."

In delirium or not, wanting the radio on; not seeming to listen, the words still jetting, wanting the music on. Once, silencing it abruptly as of old, she began to cry, unconcealed tears this time. "You have pain, Granny?" Jeannie asked.

"The music," she said, "still it is there and we do not hear; knocks, and our poor human ears too weak. What else, what else we do not hear?"

Once she knocked his hand aside as he gave her a pill, swept the bottles from her bedside table: "no pills, let me feel what I feel," and laughed as on his hands and knees he groped to pick them up.

Nighttimes her hand reached across the bed to hold his.

A constant retching began. Her breath was too faint for sustained speech now, but still the lips moved:

> *When no longer necessary   to injure others*
> *Pick   pick pick   Blind chicken*
> *As a human being   responsibility*

"David!" imperious, "Basin!" and she would vomit, rinse her mouth, the wasted throat working to swallow, and begin the chant again.

She will be better off in the hospital now, the doctor said.

He sent the telegrams to the children, was packing her suitcase, when her hoarse voice startled. She had roused, was pulling herself to sitting.

"Where now?" she asked. "Where now do you drag me?"

"You do not even have to have a baby to go this time," he soothed, looking for the brush to pack. "Remember, after Davy you told me—worthy to have a baby for the pleasure of the ten day rest in the hospital?"

"Where now? Not home yet?" Her voice mourned. "Where *is* my home?"

He rose to ease her back. "The doctor, the hospital," he started to explain, but deftly, like a snake, she had slithered out of bed and stood swaying, propped behind the night table.

"Coward," she hissed, "runner."

"You stand," he said senselessly.

"To take me there and run. Afraid of a little vomit."

He reached her as she fell. She struggled against him, half slipped from his arms, pulled herself up again.

"Weakling," she taunted, "to leave me there and run. Betrayer. All your life you have run."

He sobbed, telling Jeannie. "A Marilyn Monroe to run for her virtue. Fifty-nine pounds she weighs, the doctor said, and she beats at me like a Dempsey. Betrayer, she cries, and I running like a dog when she calls; day and night, running to her, her vomit, the bedpan. . . ."

"She needs you, Grandaddy," said Jeannie. "Isn't that what they call love? I'll see if she sleeps, and if she does, poor worn-out darling, we'll have a party, you and I: I brought us rum babas."

They did not move her. By her bed now stood the tall hooked pillar that held the solutions—blood and dextrose—to feed her veins. Jeannie moved down the hall to take over the sickroom, her face so radiant, her grandfather asked her once: "you are in love?" (Shameful the joy, the pure overwhelming joy from being with her grandmother; the peace, the serenity that breathed.) "My darling escape," she answered incoherently, "my darling Granny"—as if that explained.

Now one by one the children came, those that were able. Hannah, Paul, Sammy. Too late to ask: and what did you learn with your living, Mother, and what do we need to know?

Clara, the eldest, clenched:

> *Pay me back, Mother, pay me back for all you took from me. Those others you crowded into your heart. The hands I needed to be for you, the heaviness, the responsibility.*
>
> *Is this she? Noises the dying make, the crablike hands crawling over the covers. The ethereal singing.*
>
> *She hears that music, that singing from childhood; forgotten sound— not heard since, since. . . . And the hardness breaks like a cry: Where did we lose each other, first mother, singing mother?*
>
> *Annulled: the quarrels, the gibing, the harshness between; the fall into silence and the withdrawal.*
>
> *I do not know you, Mother. Mother, I never knew you.*

Lennie, suffering not alone for her who was dying, but for that in her which never lived (for that which in him might never live). From him too, unspoken words: *good-bye Mother who taught me to mother myself.*

Not Vivi, who must stay with her children; not Davy, but he is already here, having to die again with *her* this time, for the living take their dead with them when they die.

Light she grew, like a bird, and, like a bird, sound bubbled in her throat while the body fluttered in agony. Night and day, asleep or awake (though indeed there was no difference now) the songs and the phrases leaping.

TILLIE OLSEN

And he, who had once dreaded a long dying (from fear of himself, from horror of the dwindling money) now desired her quick death profoundly, for *her* sake. He no longer went out, except when Jeannie forced him; no longer laughed, except when, in the bright kitchenette, Jeannie coaxed his laughter (and she, who seemed to hear nothing else, would laugh too, conspiratorial wisps of laughter).

Light, like a bird, the fluttering body, the little claw hands, the beaked shadow on her face; and the throat, bubbling, straining.

He tried not to listen, as he tried not to look on the face in which only the forehead remained familiar, but trapped with her the long nights in that little room, the sounds worked themselves into his consciousness, with their punctuation of death swallows, whimpers, gurglings.

Even in reality (swallow) *life's lack of it*
Slaveships   deathtrains   clubs   eeenough
The bell   summon   what enables
78,000 in one minute (whisper of a scream) *78,000 human beings   we'll*
destroy ourselves?

"Aah, Mrs. Miserable," he said, as if she could hear, "all your life working, and now in bed you lie, servants to tend, you do not even need to call to be tended, and still you work. Such hard work it is to die? Such hard work?"

The body threshed, her hand clung in his. A melody, ghost-thin, hovered on her lips, and like a guilty ghost, the vision of her bent in listening to it, silencing the record instantly he was near. Now, heedless of his presence, she floated the melody on and on.

"Hid it from me," he complained, "how many times you listened to remember it so?" And tried to think when she had first played it, or first begun to silence her few records when he came near—but could reconstruct nothing. There was only this room with its tall hooked pillar and its swarm of sounds.

No man one   except through others
Strong   with the not yet   in the now
Dogma dead   war dead   one country

"It helps, Mrs. Philosopher, words from books? It helps?" And it seemed to him that for seventy years she had hidden a tape recorder, infinitely microscopic, within her, that it had coiled infinite mile on mile, trapping every song, every melody, every word read, heard, and spoken— and that maliciously she was playing back only what said nothing of him, of the children, of their intimate life together.

"Left us indeed, Mrs. Babbler," he reproached, "you who called others babbler and cunningly saved your words. A lifetime you tended and loved, and now not a word of us, for us. Left us indeed? Left me."

And he took out his solitaire deck, shuffled the cards loudly, slapped them down.

Lift high banner of reason (tatter of an orator's voice) *justice freedom light*

Humankind life worthy capacities

Seeks (blur of shudder) *belong human being*

"Words, words," he accused, "and what human beings did *you* seek around you, Mrs. Live Alone, and what humankind think worthy?"

Though even as he spoke, he remembered she had not always been isolated, had not always wanted to be alone (as he knew there had been a voice before this gossamer one; before the hoarse voice that broke from silence to lash, make incidents, shame him—a girl's voice of eloquence that spoke their holiest dreams). But again he could reconstruct, image, nothing of what had been before, or when, or how, it had changed.

Ace, queen, jack. The pillar shadow fell, so, in two tracks; in the mirror depths glistened a moonlike blob, the empty solution bottle. And it worked in him: *of reason and justice and freedom . . . Dogma dead:* he remembered the full quotation, laughed bitterly. "Hah, good you do not know what you say; good Victor Hugo died and did not see it, his twentieth century."

Deuce, ten, five. Dauntlessly she began a song of their youth of belief:

> *These things shall be, a loftier race*
> *than e'er the world hath known shall rise*
> *with flame of freedom in their souls*
> *and light of knowledge in their eyes*

King, four, jack "In the twentieth century, hah!"

> *They shall be gentle, brave and strong*
> *to spill no drop of blood, but dare*
> *all . . .*
>
> *on earth and fire and sea and air*

"To spill no drop of blood, hah! So, cadaver, and you too, cadaver Hugo, 'in the twentieth century ignorance will be dead, dogma will be dead, war will be dead, and for all mankind one country—of fulfilment?' Hah!"

> *And every life* (long strangling cough) *shall*
> *be a song*

The cards fell from his fingers. Without warning, the bereavement and betrayal he had sheltered—compounded through the years—hidden even from himself—revealed itself,

uncoiled,
released,
sprung

and with it the monstrous shapes of what had actually happened in the century.

A ravening hunger or thirst seized him. He groped into the kitchenette, switched on all three lights, piled a tray—"you have finished your night snack, Mrs. Cadaver, now I will have mine." And he was shocked at the tears that splashed on the tray.

"Salt tears. For free. I forgot to shake on salt?"

Whispered: "Lost, how much I lost."

Escaped to the grandchildren whose childhoods were childish, who had never hungered, who lived unravaged by disease in warm houses of many rooms, had all the school for which they cared, could walk on any street, stood a head taller than their grandparents, towered above—beautiful skins, straight backs, clear straightforward eyes. "Yes, you in Olshana," he said to the town of sixty years ago, "they would be nobility to you."

And was this not the dream then, come true in ways undreamed? he asked.

And are there no other children in the world? he answered, as if in her harsh voice.

And the flame of freedom, the light of knowledge?

And the drop, to spill no drop of blood?

And he thought that at six Jeannie would get up and it would be his turn to go to her room and sleep, that he could press the buzzer and she would come now; that in the afternoon Ellen Mays was coming, and this time they would play cards and he could marvel at how rouge can stand half an inch on the cheek; that in the evening the doctor would come, and he could beg him to be merciful, to stop the feeding solutions, to let her die.

To let her die, and with her their youth of belief out of which her bright, betrayed words foamed; stained words, that on her working lips came stainless.

Hours yet before Jeannie's turn. He could press the buzzer and wake her to come now; he could take a pill, and with it sleep; he could pour more brandy into his milk glass, though what he had poured was not yet touched.

Instead he went back, checked her pulse, gently tended with his knotty fingers as Jeannie had taught.

She was whimpering; her hand crawled across the covers for his. Compassionately he enfolded it, and with his free hand gathered up the cards again. Still was there thirst or hunger ravening in him.

That world of their youth—dark, ignorant, terrible with hate and disease—how was it that living in it, in the midst of corruption, filth, treachery, degradation, they had not mistrusted man nor themselves; had believed so beautifully, so . . . falsely?

"Aaah, children," he said out loud, "how we believed, how we belonged." And he yearned to package for each of the children, the grandchildren, for everyone, *that joyous certainty, that sense of mattering, of moving and being moved, of being one and indivisible with the great of the past, with all that freed, ennobled.* Package it, stand on corners, in front of stadiums and on crowded beaches, knock on doors, give it as a fabled gift.

"And why not in cereal boxes, in soap packages?" he mocked himself. "Aah. You have taken my senses, cadaver."

Words foamed, died unsounded. Her body writhed; she made kissing motions with her mouth. (Her lips moving as she read, poring over the Book of the Martyrs, the magnifying glass superimposed over the heavy eyeglasses.) *Still she believed?* "Eva!" he whispered. "Still you believed? You lived by it? These Things Shall Be?"

"One pound soup meat," she answered distinctly, "one soup bone."

"My ears heard you. Ellen Mays was witness: 'Humankind . . . one has to believe.'" Imploringly: "Eva!"

"Bread, day-old." She was mumbling. "Please, in a wooden box . . . for kindling. The thread, hah, the thread breaks. Cheap thread"—and a gurgling, enormously loud, began in her throat.

"I ask for stone; she gives me bread—day-old." He pulled his hand away, shouted: "Who wanted questions? Everything you have to wake?" Then dully, "Ah, let me help you turn, poor creature."

Words jumbled, cleared. In a voice of crowded terror:

"Paul, Sammy, don't fight.

"Hannah, have I ten hands?

"How can I give it, Clara, how can I give it if I don't have?"

"You lie," he said sturdily, "there was joy too." Bitterly: "Ah how cheap you speak of us at the last."

As if to rebuke him, as if her voice had no relationship with her flailing body, she sang clearly, beautifully, a school song the children had taught her when they were little; begged:

"Not look   my hair   where they cut. . . ."

(The crown of braids shorn.) And instantly he left the mute old woman poring over the Book of the Martyrs; went past the mother treading at the sewing machine, singing with the children; past the girl in her wrinkled prison dress, hiding her hair with scarred hands, lifting to him her awkward, shamed, imploring eyes of love; and took her in his arms, dear, personal, fleshed, in all the heavy passion he had loved to rouse from her.

"Eva!"

Her little claw hand beat the covers. How much, how much can a man stand? He took up the cards, put them down, circled the beds, walked to the dresser, opened, shut drawers, brushed his hair, moved his hand bit by bit over the mirror to see what of the reflection he could blot out with each move, and felt that at any moment he would die of what was unendurable. Went to press the buzzer to wake Jeannie, looked down, saw on Jeannie's sketch pad the hospital bed, with *her;* the double bed alongside, with him; the tall pillar feeding into her veins, and their hands, his and hers, clasped, feeding each other. And as if he had been instructed he went to his bed, lay down, holding the sketch (as if it could shield against the monstrous shapes of loss, of betrayal, of death) and with his free hand took hers back into his.

So Jeannie found them in the morning.

That last day the agony was perpetual. Time after time it lifted her almost off the bed, so they had to fight to hold her down. He could not endure and left the room; wept as if there never would be tears enough.

Jeannie came to comfort him. In her light voice she said: Grandaddy, Grandaddy don't cry. She is not there, she promised me. On the last day, she said she would go back to when she first heard music, a little girl on the road of the village where she was born. She promised me. It is a wedding and they dance, while the flutes so joyous and vibrant tremble in the air. Leave her there. Grandaddy, it is all right. She promised me. Come back, come back and help her poor body to die.

For two of that generation
Seevya and Genya
Infinite, dauntless, incorruptible

Death deepens the wonder

MICHELE MURRAY

(1934–1974) Born in Brooklyn, Michele Murray grew up in New York and earned degrees from the New School for Social Research and the University of Connecticut. She was a college teacher and for many years a book reviewer for major journals; she published two novels for children and edited an anthology on images of women. Her poems appeared in many journals before being collected in *The Great Mother and Other Poems* (1974), published after her untimely death of cancer.

COMING TO SELF

after these years
as iron comes by fire
from the ore
as gold washes clean in the stream
the dross
sifted and sifted
falling away
into the clear water

MARGE PIERCY

(b. 1936) Marge Piercy was born in Detroit and was the first in her family to attend college. She has published four volumes of poetry including *Breaking Camp* (1968), *Hard Loving* (1969), and *Living in the Open* (1976); and five novels, the latest of which are *Woman on the Edge of Time* (1976) and *Vida* (1980). An ardent feminist, Piercy presents her women characters realistically but tenderly.

UNLEARNING TO NOT SPEAK

Blizzards of paper
in slow motion
sift through her.
In nightmares she suddenly recalls
a class she signed up for
but forgot to attend.
Now it is too late.
Now it is time for finals:
losers will be shot.
Phrases of men who lectured her
drift and rustle in piles:
Why don't you speak up?
Why are you shouting?
You have the wrong answer,
wrong line, wrong face.
They tell her she is womb-man,
babymachine, mirror image, toy,
earth mother and penis-poor,
a dish of synthetic strawberry icecream
rapidly melting.

She grunts to a halt.
She must learn again to speak
starting with *I*
starting with *We*
starting as the infant does
with her own true hunger
and pleasure
and rage.

SUSAN GLASPELL

(1882–1948) Perhaps best known as a dramatist and a founder of the Provincetown Players, Susan Glaspell won a Pulitzer Prize in 1930 for her play *Alison's House*, based on the life of Emily Dickinson. She wrote several novels and short stories, of which "A Jury of Her Peers" is the most famous; it was reprinted in *The Best Short Stories of 1917*. "Trifles" is Glaspell's dramatic version of that story.

TRIFLES

Scene

The kitchen in the now abandoned farm-house of John Wright, a gloomy kitchen, and left without having been put in order—unwashed pans under the sink, a loaf of bread outside the bread-box, a dish-towel on the table—other signs of incompleted work. At the rear the outer door opens and the SHERIFF *comes in followed by the* COUNTY ATTORNEY *and* HALE. *The* SHERIFF *and* HALE *are men in middle life, the* COUNTY ATTORNEY *is a young man; all are much bundled up and go at once to the stove. They are followed by the two women—the Sheriff's wife first; she is a slight wiry woman, with a thin nervous face.* MRS. HALE *is larger and would ordinarily be called more comfortable looking, but she is disturbed now and looks fearfully about as she enters. The women have come in slowly, and stand close together near the door.*

COUNTY ATTORNEY *(rubbing his hands)* This feels good. Come up to the fire, ladies.

MRS. PETERS *(after taking a step forward)* I'm not—cold.

SHERIFF *(unbuttoning his overcoat and stepping away from the stove as if to mark the beginning of official business)* Now, Mr. Hale, before we move things about, you explain to Mr. Henderson just what you saw when you came here yesterday morning.

COUNTY ATTORNEY   By the way, has anything been moved? Are things just as you left them yesterday?

SHERIFF *(looking about)* It's just the same. When it dropped below zero last night I thought I'd better send Frank out this morning to make a fire for us—no use getting pneumonia with a big case on, but I told him not to touch anything except the stove—and you know Frank.

COUNTY ATTORNEY   Somebody should have been left here yesterday.

SHERIFF   Oh—yesterday. When I had to send Frank to Morris Center for that man who went crazy—I want you to know I had my hands full yesterday. I knew you could get back from Omaha by to-day and as long as I went over everything here myself—

COUNTY ATTORNEY   Well, Mr. Hale, tell just what happened when you came here yesterday morning.

HALE   Harry and I had started to town with a load of potatoes. We came along the road from my place and as I got here I said, "I'm going to see if I can't get John Wright to go in with me on a party telephone." I spoke to Wright about it once before and he put me off, saying folks talked too much anyway, and all he asked was peace and quiet—I guess you know about how much he talked himself; but I thought maybe if I went to the house and talked about it before his wife, though I said to Harry that I didn't know as what his wife wanted made much difference to John—

COUNTY ATTORNEY   Let's talk about that later, Mr. Hale. I do want to talk about that, but tell now just what happened when you got to the house.

HALE   I didn't hear or see anything; I knocked at the door, and still it was all quiet inside. I knew they must be up, it was past eight o'clock. So I knocked again, and I thought I heard somebody say "Come in." I wasn't sure, I'm not sure yet, but I opened the door—this door *(indicating the door by which the two women are still standing)* and there in that rocker— *(pointing to it)* sat Mrs. Wright.
(They all look at the rocker.)

COUNTY ATTORNEY   What—was she doing?

HALE   She was rockin' back and forth. She had her apron in her hand and was kind of—pleating it.

COUNTY ATTORNEY   And how did she—look?

HALE   Well, she looked queer.

COUNTY ATTORNEY   How do you mean—queer?

HALE Well, as if she didn't know what she was going to do next. And kind of done up.

COUNTY ATTORNEY How did she seem to feel about your coming?

HALE Why, I don't think she minded—one way or other. She didn't pay much attention. I said, "How do, Mrs. Wright, it's cold, ain't it?" And she said "Is it?"—and went on kind of pleating at her apron. Well, I was surprised; she didn't ask me to come up to the stove, or to set down, but just sat there, not even looking at me, so I said, "I want to see John." And then she—laughed. I guess you would call it a laugh. I thought of Harry and the team outside, so I said a little sharp: "Can't I see John?" "No," she says, kind o' dull like. "Ain't he home?" says I. "Yes," says she, "he's home." "Then why can't I see him?" I asked her out of patience. "'Cause he's dead," says she. *"Dead?"* says I. She just nodded her head, not getting a bit excited, but rockin' back and forth. "Why—where is he?" says I, not knowing what to say. She just pointed upstairs—like that *(himself pointing to the room above).* I got up, with the idea of going up there. I walked from there to here—then I says, "Why, what did he die of?" "He died of a rope round his neck," says she, and just went on pleatin' at her apron. Well, I went out and called Harry. I thought I might—need help. We went upstairs and there he was lyin'—

COUNTY ATTORNEY I think I'd rather have you go into that upstairs, where you can point it all out. Just go on now with the rest of the story.

HALE Well, my first thought was to get that rope off. It looked . . . *(Stops, his face twitches.)* . . . but Harry, he went up to him, and he said, "No, he's dead all right, and we'd better not touch anything." So we went back down stairs. She was still sitting that same way. "Has anybody been notified?" I asked. "No," says she, unconcerned. "Who did this, Mrs. Wright?" said Harry. He said it business-like—and she stopped pleatin' of her apron. "I don't know," she says. "You don't *know?*" says Harry. "No," says she. "Weren't you sleepin' in the bed with him?" says Harry. "Yes," says she, "but I was on the inside." "Somebody slipped a rope round his neck and strangled him and you didn't wake up?" says Harry. "I didn't wake up," she said after him. We must 'a looked as if we didn't see how that could be, for after a minute she said, "I sleep sound." Harry was going to ask her more questions, but I said maybe we ought to let her tell her story first to the coroner, or the sheriff, so Harry went fast as he could to Rivers' place, where there's a telephone.

COUNTY ATTORNEY And what did Mrs. Wright do when she knew that you had gone for the coroner?

HALE She moved from that chair to this over here . . . *(Pointing to a small chair in the corner.)* . . . and just sat there with her hands held together and looking down. I got a feeling that I ought to make some conversation, so I said I had come in to see if John wanted to put in a telephone, and at that she started to laugh, and then she stopped and looked at me—scared. *(The* COUNTY ATTORNEY, *who has had his notebook out, makes a note.)* I dunno, maybe it wasn't scared. I wouldn't like to say it was. Soon Harry got back, and then Dr. Lloyd came, and you, Mr. Peters, and so I guess that's all I know that you don't.

COUNTY ATTORNEY *(looking around)* I guess we'll go upstairs first—and then out to the barn and around there. *(To the* SHERIFF.*)* You're convinced that there was nothing important here—nothing that would point to any motive?

SHERIFF Nothing here but kitchen things.
(The COUNTY ATTORNEY, *after again looking around the kitchen, opens the door of a cupboard closet. He gets up on a chair and looks on a shelf. Pulls his hand away, sticky.)*

COUNTY ATTORNEY Here's a nice mess.
(The women draw nearer.)

MRS. PETERS *(to the other woman)* Oh, her fruit; it did freeze. *(To the Lawyer.)* She worried about that when it turned so cold. She said the fire'd go out and her jars would break.

SHERIFF Well, can you beat the women! Held for murder and worryin' about her preserves.

COUNTY ATTORNEY I guess before we're through she may have something more serious than preserves to worry about.

HALE Well, women are used to worrying over trifles.
(The two women move a little closer together.)

COUNTY ATTORNEY *(with the gallantry of a young politician)* And yet, for all their worries, what would we do without the ladies? *(The women do not unbend. He goes to the sink, takes a dipperful of water from the pail and, pouring it into a basin, washes his hands. Starts to wipe them on the roller-towel, turns it for a cleaner place.)* Dirty towels! *(Kicks his foot against the pans under the sink.)* Not much of a housekeeper, would you say, ladies?

MRS. HALE *(stiffly)* There's a great deal of work to be done on a farm.

COUNTY ATTORNEY To be sure. And yet . . . *(With a little bow to her.)* . . . I know there are some Dickson county farmhouses which do not have such roller towels.
(He gives it a pull to expose its full length again.)

MRS. HALE Those towels get dirty awful quick. Men's hands aren't always as clean as they might be.

COUNTY ATTORNEY Ah, loyal to your sex, I see. But you and Mrs. Wright were neighbors. I suppose you were friends, too.

MRS. HALE *(shaking her head)* I've not seen much of her of late years. I've not been in this house—it's more than a year.

COUNTY ATTORNEY And why was that? You didn't like her?

MRS. HALE I like her all well enough. Farmers' wives have their hands full, Mr. Henderson. And then—

COUNTY ATTORNEY Yes—?

MRS. HALE *(looking about)* It never seemed a very cheerful place.

COUNTY ATTORNEY No—it's not cheerful. I shouldn't say she had the homemaking instinct.

MRS. HALE Well, I don't know as Wright had, either.

COUNTY ATTORNEY You mean that they didn't get on very well?

MRS. HALE No, I don't mean anything. But I don't think a place'd be any cheerful for John Wright's being in it.

COUNTY ATTORNEY I'd like to talk more of that a little later. I want to get the lay of things upstairs now.
(He goes to the left, where three steps lead to a stair door.)

SHERIFF I suppose anything Mrs. Peters does'll be all right. She was to take in some clothes for her, you know, and a few little things. We left in such a hurry yesterday.

COUNTY ATTORNEY Yes, but I would like to see what you take, Mrs. Peters, and keep an eye out for anything that might be of use to us.

MRS. PETERS Yes, Mr. Henderson.
(The women listen to the men's steps on the stairs, then look about the kitchen.)

MRS. HALE I'd hate to have men coming into my kitchen, snooping around and criticizing.
(She arranges the pans under sink which the Lawyer had shoved out of place.)

MRS. PETERS Of course it's no more than their duty.

MRS. HALE Duty's all right, but I guess that deputy sheriff that came out to make the fire might have got a little of this on. *(Gives the roller towel a pull.)* Wish I'd thought of that sooner. Seems mean to talk about her for not having things slicked up when she had to come away in such a hurry.

MRS. PETERS *(who has gone to a small table in the left rear corner of the room, and lifted one end of a towel that covers a pan)* She had bread set. *(Stands still.)*

MRS. HALE *(eyes fixed on a loaf of bread beside the bread-box, which is on a low shelf at the other side of the room. Moves slowly toward it.)* She was going to put this in there. *(Picks up loaf, then abruptly drops it. In a manner of returning to familiar things.)* It's a shame about her fruit. I wonder if it's all gone. *(Gets up on the chair and looks.)* I think there's some here that's all right, Mrs. Peters. Yes—here; *(Holding it toward the window.)* this is cherries, too. *(Looking again.)* I declare I believe that's the only one. *(Gets down, bottle in her hand. Goes to the sink and wipes it off on the outside.)* She'll feel awful bad after all her hard work in the hot weather. I remember the afternoon I put up my cherries last summer. *(She puts the bottle on the big kitchen table, center of the room, front table. With a sigh, is about to sit down in the rocking-chair. Before she is seated realizes what chair it is: with a slow look at it, steps back. The chair which she has touched rocks back and forth.)*

MRS. PETERS Well, I must get those things from the front room closet. *(She goes to the door at the right, but after looking into the other room, steps back.)* You coming with me, Mrs. Hale? You could help me carry them.
(They go in the other room: reappear, MRS. PETERS carrying a dress and skirt, MRS. HALE following with a pair of shoes.)

MRS. PETERS My, it's cold in there.
(She puts the clothes on the big table, and hurries to the stove.)

MRS. HALE *(examining the skirt)* Wright was close. I think maybe that's why she kept so much to herself. She didn't even belong to the Ladies' Aid. I suppose she felt she couldn't do her part, and then you don't enjoy things when you feel shabby. She used to wear pretty clothes and be lively, when she was Minnie Foster, one of the town girls singing in the choir. But that—oh, that was thirty years ago. This all you was to take in?

MRS. PETERS She said she wanted an apron. Funny thing to want, for there isn't much to get you dirty in jail, goodness knows. But I suppose just to make her feel more natural. She said they was in the top drawer in this cupboard. Yes, here. And then her little shawl that always hung behind the door. *(Opens stair door and looks.)* Yes, here it is.
(Quickly shuts door leading upstairs.)

MRS. HALE *(abruptly moving toward her)* Mrs. Peters?

MRS. PETERS Yes, Mrs. Hale?

MRS. HALE Do you think she did it?

MRS. PETERS (in a frightened voice) Oh, I don't know.

MRS. HALE Well, I don't think she did. Asking for an apron and her little shawl. Worrying about her fruit.

MRS. PETERS (starts to speak, glances up, where footsteps are heard in the room above. In a low voice) Mr. Peters says it looks bad for her. Mr. Henderson is awful sarcastic in a speech and he'll make fun of her sayin' she didn't wake up.

MRS. HALE Well, I guess John Wright didn't wake when they was slipping that rope under his neck.

MRS PETERS No, it's strange. It must have been done awful crafty and still. They say it was such a—funny way to kill a man, rigging it all up like that.

MRS. HALE That's just what Mr. Hale said. There was a gun in the house. He says that's what he can't understand.

MRS. PETERS Mr. Henderson said coming out that what was needed for the case was a motive; something to show anger, or—sudden feeling.

MRS. HALE (who is standing by the table) Well, I don't see any signs of anger around here. (She puts her hand on the dish towel which lies on the table, stands looking down at table, one half of which is clean, the other half messy.) It's wiped here. (Makes a move as if to finish work, then turns and looks at loaf of bread outside the bread-box. Drops towel. In that voice of coming back to familiar things.) Wonder how they are finding things upstairs? I hope she had it a little more red-up up there. You know, it seems kind of sneaking. Locking her up in town and then coming out here and trying to get her own house to turn against her!

MRS. PETERS But, Mrs. Hale, the law is the law.

MRS. HALE I s'pose 'tis. (Unbuttoning her coat.) Better loosen up your things, Mrs. Peters. You won't feel them when you go out.

(MRS. PETERS takes off her fur tippet, goes to hang it on hook at back of room, stands looking at the under part of the small corner table.)

MRS. PETERS She was piecing a quilt. (She brings the large sewing basket and they look at the bright pieces.)

MRS. HALE It's log cabin pattern. Pretty, isn't it? I wonder if she was goin' to quilt it or just knot it?
(Footsteps have been heard coming down the stairs. The SHERIFF enters, followed by HALE and the COUNTY ATTORNEY.)

SHERIFF They wonder if she was going to quilt it or just knot it.
(The men laugh, the women look abashed.)

COUNTY ATTORNEY *(rubbing his hands over the stove)* Frank's fire didn't do much up there, did it? Well, let's go out to the barn and get that cleared up.
(The men go outside.)

MRS. HALE *(resentfully)* I don't know as there's anything so strange, our takin' up our time with little things while we're waiting for them to get the evidence. *(She sits down at the big table smoothing out a block with decision.)* I don't see as it's anything to laugh about.

MRS. PETERS *(apologetically)* Of course they've got awful important things on their minds.
(Pulls up a chair and joins MRS. HALE at the table.)

MRS. HALE *(examining another block)* Mrs. Peters, look at this one. Here, this is the one she was working on, and look at the sewing! All the rest of it has been so nice and even. And look at this! It's all over the place! Why, it looks as if she didn't know what she was about!
(After she has said this they look at each other, then start to glance back at the door. After an instant MRS. HALE has pulled at a knot and ripped the sewing.)

MRS. PETERS Oh, what are you doing, Mrs. Hale?

MRS. HALE *(mildly)* Just pulling out a stitch or two that's not sewed very good. *(Threading a needle.)* Bad sewing always made me fidgety.

MRS. PETERS *(nervously)* I don't think we ought to touch things.

MRS. HALE I'll just finish up this end. *(Suddenly stopping and leaning forward.)* Mrs. Peters?

MRS. PETERS Yes, Mrs. Hale?

MRS. HALE What do you suppose she was so nervous about?

MRS. PETERS Oh—I don't know. I don't know as she was nervous. I sometimes sew awful queer when I'm just tired. *(MRS. HALE starts to say something, looks at MRS. PETERS, then goes on sewing.)* Well, I must get these things wrapped up. They may be through sooner than we think. *(Putting apron and other things together.)* I wonder where I can find a piece of paper, and string.

MRS. HALE In that cupboard, maybe.

MRS. PETERS *(looking in cupboard)* Why, here's a bird-cage. *(Holds it up.)* Did she have a bird, Mrs. Hale?

MRS. HALE Why, I don't know whether she did or not—I've not been here for so long. There was a man around last year selling canaries cheap, but I don't know as she took one; maybe she did. She used to sing real pretty herself.

MRS. PETERS *(glancing around)* Seems funny to think of a bird here. But she must have had one, or why should she have a cage? I wonder what happened to it?

MRS. HALE I s'pose maybe the cat got it.

MRS. PETERS No, she didn't have a cat. She's got that feeling some people have about cats—being afraid of them. My cat got in her room and she was real upset and asked me to take it out.

MRS. HALE My sister Bessie was like that. Queer, ain't it?

MRS. PETERS *(examining the cage)* Why, look at this door. It's broke. One hinge is pulled apart.

MRS. HALE *(looking too)* Looks as if some one must have been rough with it.

MRS. PETERS Why, yes.
(She brings the cage forward and puts it on the table.)

MRS. HALE I wish if they're going to find any evidence they'd be about it. I don't like this place.

MRS. PETERS But I'm awful glad you came with me, Mrs. Hale. It would be lonesome for me sitting here alone.

MRS. HALE It would, wouldn't it? *(Dropping her sewing.)* But I tell you what I do wish, Mrs. Peters. I wish I had come over some times when *she* was here. I—*(Looking around the room.)*—wish I had.

MRS. PETERS But of course you were awful busy, Mrs. Hale—your house and your children.

MRS. HALE I could've come. I stayed away because it weren't cheerful—and that's why I ought to have come. I—I've never liked this place. Maybe because it's down in a hollow and you don't see the road. I dunno what it is, but it's a lonesome place and always was. I wish I had come over to see Minnie Foster sometimes. I can see now—
(Shakes her head.)

MRS. PETERS Well, you mustn't reproach yourself, Mrs. Hale. Somehow we just don't see how it is with other folks until—something comes up.

MRS. HALE Not having children makes less work—but it makes a quiet house, and Wright out to work all day, and no company when he did come in. Did you know John Wright, Mrs. Peters?

MRS. PETERS Not to know him; I've seen him in town. They say he was a good man.

MRS. HALE Yes—good; he didn't drink, and kept his word as well as most,

I guess, and paid his debts. But he was a hard man, Mrs. Peters. Just to pass the time of day with him. *(Shivers.)* Like a raw wind that gets to the bone. *(Pauses, her eye falling on the cage.)* I should think she would 'a wanted a bird. But what do you suppose went with it?

MRS. PETERS   I don't know, unless it got sick and died.
(She reaches over and swings the broken door, swings it again, both women watch it.)

MRS. HALE   You weren't raised round here, were you? (MRS. PETERS *shakes her head.*) You didn't know—her?

MRS. PETERS   Not till they brought her yesterday.

MRS. HALE   She—come to think of it, she was kind of like a bird herself—real sweet and pretty, but kind of timid and—fluttery. How—she—did—change. *(Silence; then as if struck by a happy thought and relieved to get back to every day things.)* Tell you what, Mrs. Peters, why don't you take the quilt in with you? It might take up her mind.

MRS. PETERS   Why, I think that's a real nice idea, Mrs. Hale. There couldn't possibly be any objection to it, could there? Now, just what would I take? I wonder if her patches are in here—and her things.
(They look in the sewing basket.)

MRS. HALE   Here's some red. I expect this has got sewing things in it. *(Brings out a fancy box.)* What a pretty box. Looks like something somebody would give you. Maybe her scissors are in here. *(Opens box. Suddenly puts her hand to her nose.)* Why—(MRS. PETERS *bends nearer, then turns her face away.)* There's something wrapped up in this piece of silk.

MRS. PETERS   Why, this isn't her scissors.

MRS. HALE *(lifting the silk)*   Oh, Mrs. Peters—it's—
(MRS. PETERS *bends closer.*)

MRS. PETERS   It's the bird.

MRS. HALE *(jumping up)*   But, Mrs. Peters—look at it. It's neck! Look at its neck! It's all—other side *to.*

MRS. PETERS   Somebody—wrung—it's neck.
(Their eyes meet. A look of growing comprehension, of horror. Steps are heard outside. MRS. HALE *slips box under quilt pieces, and sinks into her chair. Enter* SHERIFF *and* COUNTY ATTORNEY. MRS. PETERS *rises.)*

COUNTY ATTORNEY *(as one turning from serious things to little pleasantries)* Well, ladies, have you decided whether she was going to quilt it or knot it?

MRS. PETERS   We think she was going to—knot it.

COUNTY ATTORNEY Well, that's interesting, I'm sure. *(Seeing the bird-cage.)* Has the bird flown?

MRS. HALE *(putting more quilt pieces over the box)* We think the—cat got it.

COUNTY ATTORNEY *(preoccupied)* Is there a cat?
(MRS. HALE glances in a quick covert way at MRS. PETERS.)

MRS. PETERS Well, not now. They're superstitious, you know. They leave.

COUNTY ATTORNEY *(to SHERIFF PETERS, continuing an interrupted conversation)* No sign at all of any one having come from the outside. Their own rope. Now let's go up again and go over it piece by piece. *(They start upstairs.)* It would have to have been some one who knew just the— *(MRS. PETERS sits down. The two women sit there not looking at one another, but as if peering into something and at the same time holding back. When they talk now it is in the manner of feeling their way over strange ground, as if afraid of what they are saying, but as if they can not help saying it.)*

MRS. HALE She liked the bird. She was going to bury it in that pretty box.

MRS. PETERS *(in a whisper)* When I was a girl—my kitten—there was a boy took a hatchet, and before my eyes—and before I could get there—*(Covers her face an instant.)* If they hadn't held me back I would have—*(Catches herself, looks upstairs where steps are heard, falters weakly)*—hurt him.

MRS. HALE *(with a slow look around her)* I wonder how it would seem never to have had any children around. *(Pause.)* No, Wright wouldn't like the bird—a thing that sang. She used to sing. He killed that, too.

MRS. PETERS *(moving uneasily)* We don't know who killed the bird.

MRS. HALE I knew John Wright.

MRS. PETERS It was an awful thing was done in this house that night, Mrs. Hale. Killing a man while he slept, slipping a rope around his neck that choked the life out of him.

MRS. HALE His neck. Choked the life out of him.
(Her hand goes out and rests on the bird-cage.)

MRS. PETERS *(with rising voice)* We don't know who killed him. We don't know.

MRS. HALE *(her own feeling not interrupted)* If there'd been years and years of nothing, then a bird to sing to you, it would be awful—still, after the bird was still.

MRS. PETERS *(something within her speaking)* I know what stillness is.

When we homesteaded in Dakota, and my first baby died—after he was two years old, and me with no other then—

MRS. HALE *(moving)* How soon do you suppose they'll be through, looking for the evidence?

MRS. PETERS I know what stillness is. *(Pulling herself back.)* The law has got to punish crime, Mrs. Hale.

MRS. HALE *(not as if answering that)* I wish you'd seen Minnie Foster when she wore a white dress with blue ribbons and stood up there in the choir and sang. *(A look around the room.)* Oh, I *wish* I'd come over here once in a while. That was a crime! That was a crime! Who's going to punish that?

MRS. PETERS *(looking upstairs)* We mustn't—take on.

MRS. HALE I might have known she needed help! I know how things can be—for women. I tell you, it's queer, Mrs. Peters. We live close together and we live far apart. We all go through the same things—it's all just a different kind of the same thing. *(Brushes her eyes, noticing the bottle of fruit, reaches out for it.)* If I was you I wouldn't tell her her fruit was gone. Tell her it *ain't*. Tell her it's all right. Take this in to prove it to her. She—she may never know whether it was broke or not.

MRS. PETERS *(takes the bottle, looks about for something to wrap it in; takes petticoat from the clothes brought from the other room, very nervously begins winding this around the bottle. In a false voice)* My, it's a good thing the men couldn't hear us. Wouldn't they just laugh. Getting all stirred up over a little thing like a—dead canary. As if that could have anything to do with—with—wouldn't they *laugh!*
(The men are heard coming down stairs.)

MRS. HALE *(under her breath)* Maybe they would—maybe they wouldn't.

COUNTY ATTORNEY No, Peters, it's all perfectly clear except a reason for doing it. But you know juries when it comes to women. If there was some definite thing. Something to show—something to make a story about—a thing that would connect up with this strange way of doing it.
(The women's eyes meet for an instant. Enter HALE from outer door.)

HALE Well, I've got the team around. Pretty cold out there.

COUNTY ATTORNEY I'm going to stay here a while by myself. *(To the SHERIFF.)* You can send Frank out for me, can't you? I want to go over everything. I'm not satisfied that we can't do better.

SHERIFF Do you want to see what Mrs. Peters is going to take in?
(The Lawyer goes to the table, picks up the apron, laughs.)

COUNTY ATTORNEY   Oh, I guess they're not very dangerous things the ladies have picked out. *(Moves a few things about, disturbing the quilt pieces which cover the box. Steps back.)* No, Mrs. Peters doesn't need supervising. For that matter, a sheriff's wife is married to the law. Ever think of it that way, Mrs. Peters?

MRS. PETERS   Not—just that way.

SHERIFF *(chuckling)*   Married to the law. *(Moves toward the other room.)* I just want you to come in here a minute, George. We ought to take a look at these windows.

COUNTY ATTORNEY *(scoffingly)*   Oh, windows!

SHERIFF   We'll be right out, Mr. Hale.
(HALE goes outside. The SHERIFF follows the COUNTY ATTORNEY into the other room. Then MRS. HALE rises, hands tight together, looking intensely at MRS. PETERS, whose eyes make a slow turn, finally meeting MRS. HALE's. A moment MRS. HALE holds her, then her own eyes point the way to where the box is concealed. Suddenly MRS. PETERS throws back quilt pieces and tries to put the box in the bag she is wearing. It is too big. She opens box, starts to take bird out, cannot touch it, goes to pieces, stands there helpless. Sound of a knob turning in the other room. MRS. HALE snatches the box and puts it in the pocket of her big coat. Enter COUNTY ATTORNEY and SHERIFF.)

COUNTY ATTORNEY *(facetiously)*   Well, Henry, at least we found out that she was not going to quilt it. She was going to—what is it you call it, ladies?

MRS. HALE *(her hand against her pocket)*   We call it—knot it, Mr. Henderson.

(Curtain)

ALICE ADAMS

(b. 1926) A native of Fredericksburg, Virginia, Alice Adams was educated at Radcliffe College. After holding several clerical jobs, Adams became a full-time writer. Her first novel, *Careless Love,* appeared in 1966. She has published two other novels, one based on the life of the singer Billie Holiday, and many short stories, some of which are collected in *Beautiful Girl* (1979). She now lives in San Francisco.

ROSES, RHODODENDRON

One dark and rainy Boston spring of many years ago, I spent all my after-school and evening hours in the living room of our antique-crammed Cedar Street flat, writing down what the Ouija board said to my mother. My father, a spoiled and rowdy Irishman, a sometime engineer, had run off to New Orleans with a girl, and my mother hoped to learn from the board if he would come back. Then, one night in May, during a crashing black thunderstorm (my mother was both afraid and much in awe of such storms), the board told her to move down South, to North Carolina, taking me and all the antiques she had been collecting for years, and to open a store in a small town down there. That is what we did, and shortly thereafter, for the first time in my life, I fell violently and permanently in love: with a house, with a family of three people, and with an area of countryside.

Perhaps too little attention is paid to the necessary preconditions of "falling in love"—I mean the state of mind or place that precedes one's first sight of the loved person (or house or land). In my own case, I remember the dark Boston afternoons as a precondition of love. Later on, for another important time, I recognized boredom in a job. And once the fear of growing old.

In the town that she had chosen, my mother, Margot (she picked out her own name, having been christened Margaret), rented a small house on a pleasant back street. It had a big surrounding screened-in porch,

ALICE ADAMS

463

where she put most of the antiques, and she put a discreet sign out in the front yard: "Margot—Antiques." The store was open only in the afternoons. In the mornings and on Sundays, she drove around the countryside in our ancient and spacious Buick, searching for trophies among the area's country stores and farms and barns. (She is nothing if not enterprising; no one else down there had thought of doing that before.)

Although frequently embarrassed by her aggression—she thought nothing of making offers for furniture that was in use in a family's rooms—I often drove with her during those first few weeks. I was excited by the novelty of the landscape. The red clay banks that led up to the thick pine groves, the swollen brown creeks half hidden by flowering tangled vines. Bare, shaded yards from which rose gaunt, narrow houses. Chickens that scattered, barefoot children.

"Hello there. I'm Mrs. John Kilgore—Margot Kilgore—and I'm interested in buying old furniture. Family portraits. Silver."

Margot a big brassily bleached blonde in a pretty flowered-silk dress and high-heeled patent sandals. A hoarse and friendly voice. Me a scrawny, pale, curious girl, about ten, in a blue linen dress with smocking across the bodice. (Margot has always had a passionate belief in good clothes, no matter what.)

On other days, Margot would say, "I'm going to look over my so-called books. Why don't you go for a walk or something, Jane?"

And I would walk along the sleepy, leafed-over streets, on the unpaved sidewalks, past houses that to me were as inviting and as interesting as unread books, and I would try to imagine what went on inside. The families. Their lives.

The main street, where the stores were, interested me least. Two-story brick buildings—dry-goods stores, with dentists' and lawyers' offices above. There was also a drugstore, with round marble tables and wire-backed chairs, at which wilting ladies sipped at their Cokes (this was to become a favorite haunt of Margot's). I preferred the civic monuments: a pre-Revolutionary Episcopal chapel of yellowish cracked plaster, and several tall white statues to the Civil War dead—all of them quickly overgrown with ivy or Virginia creeper.

These were the early nineteen-forties, and in the next few years the town was to change enormously. Its small textile factories would be given defense contracts (parachute silk); a Navy preflight school would be established at a neighboring university town. But at that moment it was a sleeping village. Untouched.

My walks were not a lonely occupation, but Margot worried that they were, and some curious reasoning led her to believe that a bicycle would help. (Of course, she turned out to be right.) We went to Sears, and she bought me a big new bike—blue, with balloon tires—on which I began to explore the outskirts of town and the countryside.

WOMAN BECOMING

464

The house I fell in love with was about a mile out of town, on top of a hill. A small stone bank that was all overgrown with tangled roses led up to its yard, and pink and white roses climbed up a trellis to the roof of the front porch—the roof on which, later, Harriet and I used to sit and exchange our stores of erroneous sexual information. Harriet Farr was the daughter of the house. On one side of the house, there was what looked like a newer wing, with a bay window and a long side porch, below which the lawn sloped down to some flowering shrubs. There was a yellow rosebush, rhododendron, a plum tree, and beyond were woods—pines, and oak and cedar trees. The effect was rich and careless, generous and somewhat mysterious. I was deeply stirred.

As I was observing all this, from my halted bike on the dusty white hilltop, a small, plump woman, very erect, came out of the front door and went over to a flower bed below the bay window. She sat down very stiffly. (Emily, who was Harriet's mother, had some terrible, never diagnosed trouble with her back; she generally wore a brace.) She was older than Margot, with very beautiful white hair that was badly cut in that butchered nineteen-thirties way.

From the first, I was fascinated by Emily's obvious dissimilarity to Margot. I think I was also somehow drawn to her contradictions—the shapeless body held up with so much dignity, even while she was sitting in the dirt. The lovely chopped-off hair. (There were greater contradictions, which I learned of later—she was a Virginia Episcopalian who always voted for Norman Thomas, a feminist who always delayed meals for her tardy husband.)

Emily's hair was one of the first things about the Farr family that I mentioned to Margot after we became friends, Harriet and Emily and I, and I began to spend most of my time in that house.

"I don't think she's ever dyed it," I said, with almost conscious lack of tact.

Of course, Margot was defensive. "I wouldn't dye mine if I thought it would be a decent color on its own."

But by that time Margot's life was also improving. Business was fairly good, and she had finally heard from my father, who began to send sizable checks from New Orleans. He had found work with an oil company. She still asked the Ouija board if she would see him again, but her question was less obsessive.

The second time I rode past that house, there was a girl sitting on the front porch, reading a book. She was about my age. She looked up. The next time I saw her there, we both smiled. And the time after that (a Saturday morning in late June) she got up and slowly came out to the road, to where I had stopped, ostensibly to look at the view—the sweep of fields, the white highway, which wound down to the thick greenery bordering the creek, the fields and trees that rose in dim and distant hills.

"I've got a bike exactly like that," Harriet said indifferently, as though to deny the gesture of having come out to meet me.

For years, perhaps beginning then, I used to seek my antithesis in friends. Inexorably following Margot, I was becoming a big blonde, with some of her same troubles. Harriet was cool and dark, with long, gray eyes. A girl about to be beautiful.

"Do you want to come in? We've got some lemon cake that's pretty good."

Inside, the house was cluttered with odd mixtures of furniture. I glimpsed a living room, where there was a shabby sofa next to a pretty, "antique" table. We walked through a dining room that contained a decrepit mahogany table surrounded with delicate fruitwood chairs. (I had a horrifying moment of imagining Margot there, with her accurate eye—making offers in her harsh Yankee voice.) The walls were crowded with portraits and with nineteenth-century oils of bosky landscapes. Books overflowed from rows of shelves along the walls. I would have moved in at once.

We took our lemon cake back to the front porch and ate it there, overlooking that view. I can remember its taste vividly. It was light and tart and sweet, and a beautiful lemon color. With it, we drank cold milk, and then we had seconds and more milk, and we discussed what we liked to read.

We were both at an age to begin reading grownup books, and there was some minor competition between us to see who had read more of them. Harriet won easily, partly because her mother reviewed books for the local paper, and had brought home Steinbeck, Thomas Wolfe, Virginia Woolf, and Elizabeth Bowen. But we also found in common an enthusiasm for certain novels about English children. (Such snobbery!)

"It's the best cake I've ever had!" I told Harriet. I had already adopted something of Margot's emphatic style.

"It's very good," Harriet said judiciously. Then, quite casually, she added, "We could ride our bikes out to Laurel Hill."

We soared dangerously down the winding highway. At the bridge across the creek, we stopped and turned onto a narrow, rutted dirt road that followed the creek through woods as dense and as alien as a jungle would have been—thick pines with low sweeping branches, young leafed-out maples, peeling tall poplars, elms, brambles, green masses of honeysuckle. At times, the road was impassable, and we had to get off our bikes and push them along, over crevices and ruts, through mud or sand. And with all that we kept up our somewhat stilted discussion of literature.

"I love Virginia Woolf!"

"Yes, she's very good. Amazing metaphors."

I thought Harriet was an extraordinary person—more intelligent, more poised, and prettier than any girl of my age I had ever known. I felt that she could become anything at all—a writer, an actress, a foreign correspondent (I went to a lot of movies). And I was not entirely wrong; she eventually became a sometimes-published poet.

We came to a small beach, next to a place where the creek widened and ran over some shallow rapids. On the other side, large gray rocks rose steeply. Among the stones grew isolated, twisted trees, and huge bushes with thick green leaves. The laurel of Laurel Hill. Rhododendron. Harriet and I took off our shoes and waded into the warmish water. The bottom squished under our feet, making us laugh, like the children we were, despite all our literary talk.

Margot was also making friends. Unlike me, she seemed to seek her own likeness, and she found a sort of kinship with a woman named Dolly Murray, a rich widow from Memphis who shared many of Margot's superstitions—fear of thunderstorms, faith in the Ouija board. About ten years older than Margot, Dolly still dyed her hair red; she was a noisy, biassed, generous woman. They drank gin and gossiped together, they met for Cokes at the drugstore, and sometimes they drove to a neighboring town to have dinner in a restaurant (in those days, still a daring thing for unescorted ladies to do).

I am sure that the Farrs, outwardly a conventional family, saw me as a neglected child. I was so available for meals and overnight visits. But that is not how I experienced my life—I simply felt free. And an important thing to be said about Margot as a mother is that she never made me feel guilty for doing what I wanted to do. And of how many mothers can that be said?

There must have been a moment of "meeting" Emily, but I have forgotten it. I remember only her gentle presence, a soft voice, and my own sense of love returned. Beautiful white hair, dark deep eyes, and a wide mouth, whose corners turned and moved to express whatever she felt— amusement, interest, boredom, pain. I have never since seen such a vulnerable mouth.

I amused Emily; I almost always made her smile. She must have seen me as something foreign—a violent, enthusiastic Yankee (I used forbidden words, like "God" and "damn"). Very unlike the decorous young Southern girl that she must have been, that Harriet almost was.

She talked to me a lot; Emily explained to me things about the South that otherwise I would not have picked up. "Virginians feel superior to everyone else, you know," she said, in her gentle (Virginian) voice. "Some people in my family were quite shocked when I married a man from North Carolina and came down here to live. And a Presbyterian at that! Of course, that's nowhere near as bad as a Baptist, but only Episcopalians really count." This was all said lightly, but I knew that some part of Emily agreed with the rest of her family.

ALICE ADAMS

"How about Catholics?" I asked her, mainly to prolong the conversation. Harriet was at the dentist's, and Emily was sitting at her desk answering letters. I was perched on the sofa near her, and we both faced the sweeping green view. But since my father, Johnny Kilgore, was a lapsed Catholic, it was not an entirely frivolous question. Margot was a sort of Christian Scientist (her own sort).

"We hardly know any Catholics." Emily laughed, and then she sighed. "I do sometimes still miss Virginia. You know, when we drive up there I can actually feel the difference as we cross the state line. I've met a few people from South Carolina," she went on, "and I understand that people down there feel the same way Virginians do." (Clearly, she found this unreasonable.)

"West Virginia? Tennessee?"

"They don't seem Southern at all. Neither do Florida and Texas—not to me."

("Dolly says that Mrs. Farr is a terrible snob," Margot told me, inquiringly.

"In a way," I spoke with a new diffidence that I was trying to acquire from Harriet.

"Oh.")

Once, I told Emily what I had been wanting to say since my first sight of her. I said, "Your hair is so beautiful. Why don't you let it grow?"

She laughed, because she usually laughed at what I said, but at the same time she looked surprised, almost startled. I understood that what I had said was not improper but that she was totally unused to attentions of that sort from anyone, including herself. She didn't think about her hair. In a puzzled way, she said, "Perhaps I will."

Nor did Emily dress like a woman with much regard for herself. She wore practical, seersucker dresses and sensible, low shoes. Because her body had so little shape, no indentations (this must have been at least partly due to the back brace), I was surprised to notice that she had pretty, shapely legs. She wore little or no makeup on her sun- and wind-weathered face.

And what of Lawrence Farr, the North Carolina Presbyterian for whom Emily had left her people and her state? He was a small, precisely made man, with fine dark features (Harriet looked very like him). A lawyer, but widely read in literature, especially the English nineteenth century. He had a courtly manner, and sometimes a wicked tongue; melancholy eyes, and an odd, sudden, ratchety laugh. He looked ten years younger than Emily; the actual difference was less than two.

"Well," said Margot, settling into a Queen Anne chair—a new antique—on our porch one stifling hot July morning, "I heard some really interesting gossip about your friends."

Margot had met and admired Harriet, and Harriet liked her, too—

Margot made Harriet laugh, and she praised Harriet's fine brown hair. But on some instinct (I am not sure whose) the parents had not met. Very likely, Emily, with her Southern social antennae, had somehow sensed that this meeting would be a mistake.

That morning, Harriet and I were going on a picnic in the woods to the steep rocky side of Laurel Hill, but I forced myself to listen, or half listen, to Margot's story.

"Well, it seems that some years ago Lawrence Farr fell absolutely madly in love with a beautiful young girl—in fact, the orphaned daughter of a friend of his. Terribly romantic. Of course, she loved him, too, but he felt so awful and guilty that they never did anything about it."

I did not like this story much; it made me obscurely uncomfortable, and I think that at some point both Margot and I wondered why she was telling it. Was she pointing out imperfections in my chosen other family? But I asked, in Harriet's indifferent voice, "He never kissed her?"

"Well, maybe. I don't know. But of course everyone in town knew all about it, including Emily Farr. And with her back! Poor woman," Margot added somewhat piously but with real feeling, too.

I forgot the story readily at the time. For one thing, there was something unreal about anyone as old as Lawrence Farr "falling in love." But looking back to Emily's face, Emily looking at Lawrence, I can see that pained watchfulness of a woman who has been hurt, and by a man who could always hurt her again.

In those days, what struck me most about the Farrs was their extreme courtesy to each other—something I had not seen before. Never a harsh word. (Of course, I did not know then about couples who cannot afford a single harsh word.)

Possibly because of the element of danger (very slight—the slope was gentle), the roof over the front porch was one of the places Harriet and I liked to sit on warm summer nights when I was invited to stay over. There was a country silence, invaded at intervals by summer country sounds—the strangled croak of tree frogs from down in the glen; the crazy baying of a distant hound. There, in the heavy scent of roses, on the scratchy shingles, Harriet and I talked about sex.

"A girl I know told me that if you do it a lot your hips get very wide."

"My cousin Duncan says it makes boys strong if they do it."

"It hurts women a lot—especially at first. But I knew this girl from Santa Barbara, and she said that out there they say Filipinos can do it without hurting."

"Colored people do it a lot more than whites."

"Of course, they have all those babies. But in Boston so do Catholics!"

We are seized with hysteria. We laugh and laugh, so that Emily hears and calls up to us, "Girls, why haven't you-all gone to bed?" But her voice is warm and amused—she likes having us laughing up there.

And Emily liked my enthusiasm for lemon cake. She teased me about the amounts of it I could eat, and she continued to keep me supplied. She was not herself much of a cook—their maid, a young black girl named Evelyn, did most of the cooking.

Once, but only once, I saw the genteel and opaque surface of that family shattered—saw those three people suddenly in violent opposition to each other, like shards of splintered glass. (But what I have forgotten is the cause—what brought about that terrible explosion?)

The four of us, as so often, were seated at lunch. Emily was at what seemed to be the head of the table. At her right hand was the small silver bell that summoned Evelyn to clear, or to bring a new course. Harriet and I across from each other. Lawrence across from Emily. (There was always a tentativeness about Lawrence's posture. He could have been an honored guest, or a spoiled and favorite child.) We were talking in an easy way. I have a vivid recollection only of words that began to career and gather momentum, to go out of control. Of voices raised. Then Harriet rushes from the room. Emily's face reddens dangerously, the corners of her mouth twitch downward, and Lawrence, in an exquisitely icy voice, begins to lecture me on the virtues of reading Trollope. I am supposed to help him pretend that nothing has happened, but I can hardly hear what he is saying. I am in shock.

That sudden unleashing of violence, that exposed depth of terrible emotions might have suggested to me that the Farrs were not quite as I had imagined them, not the impeccable family in my mind—but it did not. I was simply and terribly—and selfishly—upset, and hugely relieved when it all seemed to have passed over.

During that summer, the Ouija board spoke only gibberish to Margot, or it answered direct questions with repeated evasions:

"Will I ever see Johnny Kilgore again, in this life?"

"Yes no perhaps."

"Honey, that means you've got no further need of the board, not right now. You've got to think everything out with your own heart and instincts," Dolly said.

Margot seemed to take her advice. She resolutely put the board away, and she wrote to Johnny that she wanted a divorce.

I had begun to notice that these days, on these sultry August nights, Margot and Dolly were frequently joined on their small excursions by a man named Larry—a jolly, red-faced man who was in real estate and who reminded me considerably of my father.

I said as much to Margot, and was surprised at her furious reaction. "They could not be more different, they are altogether opposite. Larry is a Southern gentleman. You just don't pay any attention to anyone but those Farrs."

A word about Margot's quite understandable jealousy of the Farrs. Much later in my life, when I was unreasonably upset at the attachment of one of my own daughters to another family (unreasonable because her chosen group were all talented musicians, as she was), a wise friend told me that we all could use more than one set of parents—our relations with the original set are too intense, and need dissipating. But no one, certainly not silly Dolly, was around to comfort Margot with this wisdom.

The summer raced on. ("Not without dust and heat," Lawrence several times remarked, in his private ironic voice.) The roses wilted on the roof and on the banks next to the road. The creek dwindled, and beside it honeysuckle leaves lay limply on the vines. For weeks, there was no rain, and then, one afternoon, there came a dark torrential thunderstorm. Harriet and I sat on the side porch and watched its violent start—the black clouds seeming to rise from the horizon, the cracking, jagged streaks of lightning, the heavy, welcome rain. And, later, the clean smell of leaves and grass and damp earth.

Knowing that Margot would be frightened, I thought of calling her, and then remembered that she would not talk on the phone during storms. And that night she told me, "The phone rang and rang, but I didn't think it was you, somehow."

"No."

"I had the craziest idea that it was Johnny. Be just like him to pick the middle of a storm for a phone call."

"There might not have been a storm in New Orleans."

But it turned out that Margot was right.

The next day, when I rode up to the Farrs' on my bike, Emily was sitting out in the grass where I had first seen her. I went and squatted beside her there. I thought she looked old and sad, and partly to cheer her I said, "You grow the most beautiful flowers I've ever seen."

She sighed, instead of smiling as she usually did. She said, "I seem to have turned into a gardener. When I was a girl, I imagined that I would grow up to be a writer, a novelist, and that I would have at least four children. Instead, I grow flowers and write book reviews."

I was not interested in children. "You never wrote a novel?"

She smiled unhappily. "No. I think I was afraid that I wouldn't come up to Trollope. I married rather young, you know."

And at that moment Lawrence came out of the house, immaculate in white flannels.

He greeted me, and said to Emily, "My dear, I find that I have some rather late appointments, in Hillsboro. You won't wait dinner if I'm a trifle late?"

(Of course she would; she always did.)

"No. Have a good time," she said, and she gave him the anxious look that I had come to recognize as the way she looked at Lawrence.

Soon after that, a lot happened very fast. Margot wrote to Johnny (again) that she wanted a divorce, that she intended to marry Larry. (I wonder if this was ever true.) Johnny telephoned—not once but several times. He told her that she was crazy, that he had a great job with some shipbuilders near San Francisco—a defense contract. He would come to get us, and we would all move out there. Margot agreed. We would make a new life. (Of course, we never knew what happened to the girl.)

I was not as sad about leaving the Farrs and that house, that town, those woods as I was to be later, looking back. I was excited about San Francisco, and I vaguely imagined that someday I would come back and that we would all see each other again. Like parting lovers, Harriet and I promised to write each other every day.

And for quite a while we did write several times a week. I wrote about San Francisco—how beautiful it was: the hills and pastel houses, the sea. How I wished that she could see it. She wrote about school and friends. She described solitary bike rides to places we had been. She told me what she was reading.

In high school, our correspondence became more generalized. Responding perhaps to the adolescent mores of the early nineteen-forties, we wrote about boys and parties; we even competed in making ourselves sound "popular." The truth (my truth) was that I was sometimes popular, often not. I had, in fact, a stormy adolescence. And at that time I developed what was to be a long-lasting habit. As I reviewed a situation in which I had been ill-advised or impulsive, I would reënact the whole scene in my mind with Harriet in my own role—Harriet, cool and controlled, more intelligent, prettier. Even more than I wanted to see her again, I wanted to *be* Harriet.

Johnny and Margot fought a lot and stayed together, and gradually a sort of comradeship developed between them in our small house on Russian Hill.

I went to Stanford, where I halfheartedly studied history. Harriet was at Radcliffe, studying American literature, writing poetry.

We lost touch with each other.

Margot, however, kept up with her old friend Dolly, by means of Christmas cards and Easter notes, and Margot thus heard a remarkable piece of news about Emily Farr. Emily "up and left Lawrence without so much as a by-your-leave," said Dolly, and went to Washington, D.C., to work in the Folger Library. This news made me smile all day. I was so proud of Emily. And I imagined that Lawrence would amuse himself, that they would both be happier apart.

By accident, I married well—that is to say, a man whom I still like and enjoy. Four daughters came at uncalculated intervals, and each is remarkably unlike her sisters. I named one Harriet, although she seems to have my untidy character.

From time to time, over the years, I would see a poem by Harriet Farr, and I always thought it was marvelous, and I meant to write her. But I distrusted my reaction. I had been (I was) so deeply fond of Harriet

(Emily, Lawrence, that house and land) and besides, what would I say—
"I think your poem is marvellous"? (I have since learned that this is neither
an inadequate nor an unwelcome thing to say to writers.) Of course, the
true reason for not writing was that there was too much to say.

Dolly wrote to Margot that Lawrence was drinking "all over the place."
He was not happier without Emily. Harriet, Dolly said, was travelling
a lot. She married several times and had no children. Lawrence developed
emphysema, and was in such bad shape that Emily quit her job and
came back to take care of him—whether because of feelings of guilt or duty
or possibly affection, I didn't know. He died, lingeringly and miserably,
and Emily, too, died, a few years later—at least partly from exhaustion,
I would imagine.

Then, at last, I did write Harriet, in care of the magazine in which I had
last seen a poem of hers. I wrote a clumsy, gusty letter, much too long,
about shared pasts, landscapes, the creek. All that. And as soon as I had
mailed it I began mentally rewriting, seeking more elegant prose.

When for a long time I didn't hear from Harriet, I felt worse and
worse, cumbersome, misplaced—as too often in life I had felt before.
It did not occur to me that an infrequently staffed magazine could be at
fault.

Months later, her letter came—from Rome, where she was then living.
Alone, I gathered. She said that she was writing it at the moment of
receiving mine. It was a long, emotional, and very moving letter, out of
character for the Harriet that I remembered (or had invented).

She said, in part: "It was really strange, all that time when Lawrence
was dying, and God! so long! and as though 'dying' were all that he was
doing—Emily, too, although we didn't know that—all that time the picture
that moved me most, in my mind, that moved me to tears, was not
of Lawrence and Emily but of you and me. On our bikes at the top of
the hill outside our house. Going somewhere. And I first thought that that
picture simply symbolized something irretrievable, the lost and irrecoverable
past, as Lawrence and Emily would be lost. And I'm sure that was
partly it.

"But they were so extremely fond of you—in fact, you were a rare area
of agreement. They missed you, and they talked about you for years.
It's a wonder that I wasn't jealous, and I think I wasn't only because I
felt included in their affection for you. They liked me best with you.

"Another way to say this would be to say that we were all three a little
less crazy and isolated with you around, and, God knows, happier."

An amazing letter, I thought. It was enough to make me take a long
look at my whole life, and to find some new colors there.

A postscript: I showed Harriet's letter to my husband, and he said, "How
odd. She sounds so much like you."

ALICE ADAMS

473

JANE RULE

(b. 1931) Born in New Jersey, Jane Rule studied at Mills College in California. She has held many jobs, some taken to gain background material for her writing; she has been a teacher of handicapped children and has taught in preparatory school. She now teaches at the University of British Columbia in Vancouver. She also operates her own printing press. Her first novel, *The Desert of the Heart,* appeared in 1964; she has published two other novels and many short stories, which have appeared in both literary and popular periodicals. Her most recent work is a critical survey entitled *Lesbian Images* (1976).

MIDDLE CHILDREN

Clare and I both come from big families, a bossy, loving line of voices stretching away above us to the final authority of our parents, a chorus of squawling, needy voices beneath us coming from crib or play pen or notch in tree. We share, therefore, the middle child syndrome: we are both over earnest, independent, inclined to claustrophobia in crowds. The dreams of our adolescent friends for babies and homes of their own we privately considered nightmares. Boys were irredeemably brothers who took up more physical and psychic space than was ever fair. Clare and I, in cities across the continent from each other, had the same dream: scholarships for college where we would have single rooms, jobs after that with our own apartments. But scholarship students aren't given single rooms; and the matchmakers, following that old cliche that opposites attract, put us, east and west, into the same room.

Without needing to discuss the matter, we immediately arranged the furniture as we had arranged furniture with sisters all our lives, mine along one wall, hers along the other, an invisible line drawn down the center of the room, over which no sock or book or tennis racket should ever stray. Each expected the other to be hopelessly untidy; our sisters were. By the end of the first week, ours was the only room on the corridor that looked like a military barracks. Neither of us really liked it, used to the posters and rotting corsages and dirty clothes of our siblings, but neither of us could bring herself to contribute any clutter of her own. "Maybe a painting?" Clare suggested. I did not know where we could get one. Clare turned out to be a painter. I, a botanist, who could never grow things in my own room before where they might be watered with Coke or broken by a thrown magazine or sweater, brought in a plant stand, the first object to straddle the line because it needed to be under the window. The friends each of us made began to straddle that line, too, since we seemed to be interchangeably good listeners, attracting the same sort of flamboyant, needy first or last or only children.

"Sandra thinks she may be pregnant," I would say about Clare's friend who had told me simply because Clare wasn't around.

"Aren't they all hopeless?" Clare would reply, and we middle children would shake our wise, cautious heads.

We attracted the same brotherly boys as well who took us to football games and fraternity drunks and sexual wrestling matches on the beach. We used the same cool defenses, gleaned not from the advice of our brothers but from observing their behavior.

"Bobby always told me not to take the 'respect' bit too seriously if I wanted to have any fun," Clare said, "but I sometimes wonder why I'd want 'respect' or 'fun.' Doesn't it all seem to you too much trouble? This Saturday there's a marvelous exhibit. Then we could just go out to dinner and come home."

We had moved our desks by then. Shoved together, they could share one set of reference books conveniently and frugally for us both. We asked to have one chest of drawers taken out of the room. Neither of us had many clothes, and, since we wore the same size, we had begun to share our underwear and blouses to keep laundry day to once a week. I can't remember what excuse we had for moving the beds. Perhaps by the time we did, we didn't need an excuse, for ourselves anyway.

I have often felt sorry for people who can't have the experience of falling in love like that, gradually, without knowing it, touching first because pearls have to be fastened or a collar straightened, then more casually because you are standing close together looking at the same assignment sheet or photograph, then more purposefully because you know that there is comfort and reassurance for an exam coming up or trouble in the family. So many people reach out to each other before there is any sympathy or affection. When Clare turned into my arms, or I into hers—neither of us knows just how it was—the surprise was like coming upon the right answer to a question we did not even know we had asked.

Through the years of college, while our friends suffered all the uncertainties of sexual encounter, of falling into and out of love, of being too young and then perhaps too old in a matter of months, of worrying about how to finance graduate school marriages, our only problem was the clutter of theirs. We would have liked to clear all of them out earlier in order to enjoy the brief domestic sweetness of our own sexual life. But we were from large families. We knew how to maintain privacy, a space of our own, so tactfully that no one ever noticed it. Our longing for our own apartment, like the trips we would take to Europe, was an easy game. Nothing important to us had to be put off until then.

Putting off what was unimportant sometimes did take ingenuity. The boys had no objection to being given up, but our corridor friends were continually trying to arrange dates for us. We decided to come back from one Christmas holiday engaged to boys back home. That they didn't exist was never discovered. We gave each other rings and photographs of brothers. Actually I was very fond of Bobby, and Clare got on just as well with my large and boisterous family. Our first trip to Europe, between college and graduate school, taught us harder lessons. It seemed harmless enough to drink and dance with the football team traveling with us on the ship, but, when they turned up, drunken and disorderly at our London hotel, none of our own outrage would convince the night porter that we were not at fault. Only when we got to graduate school did we find the social answer: two young men as in need of protection as we were, who cared about paintings and concerts and growing things and going home to their own bed as much as we did.

When Clare was appointed assistant professor in art history and I got a job with the parks board, we had been living together in dormitories and student digs for eight years. We could finally leave the clutter of other lives behind us for an apartment of our own. Just at a time when we saw other relationships begin to grow stale or burdened with the continual demands of children, we were discovering the new privacy of making love on our own living room carpet at five o'clock in the afternoon, too hungry then to bother with cocktails or dressing for dinner. Soon we got quite out of the habit of wearing clothes except when we went out or invited people in. We woke making love, ate breakfast and made love again before we went to work, spent three or four long evenings a week in the same new delight until I saw in Clare's face that bruised, ripe look of a new, young wife, and she said at the same moment, "You don't look safe to go out."

In guilt we didn't really discuss, we arranged more evenings with friends, but, used to the casual interruptions of college life, we found such entertainment often too formal and contrived. Then for a week or two we would return to our honeymoon, for alone together we could find no reason not to make love. It is simply not true to say such things don't improve with practice.

"It's a good thing we never knew how bad we were at it," Clare said, one particularly marvelous morning.

When we didn't know, however, we had had more sympathy for those around us, accommodating themselves to back seats of cars or gritty blankets on the beach. Now our friends, either newly wed in student digs where quarreling was the only acceptable—that is, unavoidable—noise, or exhausted by babies, made wry jokes about missing the privacy of drive-in movies or about the merits of longer bathtubs. They were even more avid readers of pornography than they had been in college. We were not the good listeners we had been. I heard Clare being positively high minded about what a waste of time all those dirty books were.

"You never used to be a prude," Sandra said in surprise.

That remark, which should have made Clare laugh, kept her weeping half the night instead. I had never heard her so distressed, but then perhaps she hadn't had the freedom to be. "We're too different," she said, and "We're not kind any more."

"Maybe we should offer to baby sit for Sandra and lend them the apartment," I suggested, not meaning it.

We are both very good with babies. It would be odd if we weren't. Any middle child knows as much about colic and croup as there is to know by the time she's eight or nine. The initial squeamishness about changing diapers is conquered at about the same age. Sandra, like all our other friends, had it all to learn at twenty-three. Sometimes we did just as I had suggested, sitting primly across from each other like maiden aunts, Clare marking papers, I thumbing through books that could help me to imagine what was going on in our apartment. Or sometimes Sandra would call late at night, saying, "You're fond of this kid, aren't you? Well, come and get him before we kill him." Then we'd take the baby for a midnight ride over the rough back roads that are better for gas pains than any pacing. I didn't mind that assignment, but I was increasingly restless with the evenings we spent in somebody else's house.

"You know, if we had a house of our own," I said, "we could take the baby for the night, and they could just stay home."

I realize that there is nothing really immoral about lending your apartment to a legally married couple for the evening so that you can spend a kind and moral night out with their baby, but it seemed to me faintly and unpleasantly obscene: our bed . . . perhaps even our living room rug. I was back to the middle child syndrome. I wanted to draw invisible lines.

"They're awfully tidy and considerate," Clare said, "and they always leave us a bottle of scotch."

"Well, we leave them a bottle of scotch as well."

"We drink more of it than they do."

I didn't want to sound mean.

"If we had a house, we could have a garden."

"You'd like that," Clare decided.

Sandra's husband said we could never get a mortgage, but our combined income was simply too impressive to ignore. We didn't really need a large house, just the two of us, though I wanted a studio for Clare, and she wanted a green house and work shop for me. The difficulty was that neither of us could think of a house that was our size. We weren't used to them. The large, old houses that felt like home were really no more expensive than the new, compact and efficient boxes the agent thought suitable to our career centered lives. Once we had wandered through the snarled, old garden and up into the ample rooms of the sort of house we had grown up in, we could not think about anything else.

"Well, why not?" I asked.

"It has five bedrooms."

"We don't have to use them all."

"We might take a student," Clare said.

We weren't surprised at the amount of work involved in owning an old house. Middle children aren't. Our friends, most of whom were still cooped up in apartments, liked to come out in those early days for painting and repair parties, which ended with barbecue suppers on the back lawn, fenced in and safe for toddlers. Our current couple of boys were very good at the heavy work of making drapes and curtains. They even enjoyed helping me dig out old raspberry canes. It was two years before Clare had time to paint in the studio, and my green house turned out to be a very modest affair since I had so many other things to do, cooking mostly.

We have only one room left now for stray children. The rest are filled with students, boys we decided, which is probably a bit prudish, and it's quite true that they take up more physical and psychic space than is ever fair. Still, they're only kids, and, though it takes our saintly cleaning woman half a day a week just to dig out their rooms, they're not bad about the rest of the house.

Harry is a real help to me with the wine making, inclined to be more careful about the chemical details than I am. Pete doesn't leave his room except to eat unless we've got some of the children around; then he's even willing to stay with them in the evening if we have to go out. Carl, who's never slept a night alone in his life since he discovered it wasn't necessary, doesn't change girls so often that we don't get to know them, and he has a knack for finding people who fit in: take a turn at the dishes, walk the dogs, check to see that we have enough cream for breakfast.

Clare and I have drawn one very careful line across the door of our bedroom, and, though it's not as people proof as our brief apartment, it's a good deal better than a dormitory. We even occasionally have what we explain as our cocktail there before dinner when one of Carl's girls is minding the vegetables; and, if we don't get involved in too interesting a political or philosophical discussion, we sometimes go upstairs for what we call the late news. Both of us are still early to wake, and, since Pete will get up with any visiting child, the first of the day is always our own.

"Pete's a middle child," Clare said the other morning, hearing him sing a soft song to Sandra's youngest as he carried her down the stairs to give her an early bottle. "I hope he finds a middle child for himself one day."

"I'd worry about him if he were mine," I said.

"Oh, well, I'd worry about any of them if they were mine. I simply couldn't cope."

"I just wouldn't want to."

"There's a boy in my graduate seminar . . ." Clare began.

I was tempted to say that, if we had a family of our own, we'd always be worrying and talking about them even when we had time to ourselves, but there was still an hour before we had to get up, and I've always felt generous in the early morning, even when I was a kid in a house cluttered with kids from which I dreamed that old dream of escape.

LUCILLE CLIFTON

(b. 1936) Born in New York state, Lucille Clifton attended Howard University and Fredonia State Teachers College. The mother of six children, she has written several children's books. She is best known for her poetry, *Good Times* (1969) and *Good News About the Earth* (1972). Her autobiography, *An Ordinary Woman,* appeared in 1974. Her most recent work is *Amifika* (1977).

MISS ROSIE

When I watch you
wrapped up like garbage
sitting, surrounded by the smell
of too old potato peels
or
when I watch you
in your old man's shoes
with the little toe cut out
sitting, waiting for your mind
like next week's grocery
I say
when I watch you
you wet brown bag of a woman
who used to be the best looking gal in Georgia
used to be called the Georgia Rose
I stand up
through your destruction
I stand up

(b. 1943) Susan Griffin has an A.B. in English and experience in many different jobs usually filled by women: waitress, teacher, and artist's model. A divorcée and single parent, she lives in San Francisco with other women. She has published two collections of poems; a play, *Voices* (1975); and a philosophical essay about women and ecology, *Women and Nature* (1979).

I LIKE TO THINK OF
HARRIET TUBMAN

I like to think of Harriet Tubman.
Harriet Tubman who carried a revolver,
who had a scar on her head from a rock thrown
by a slave-master (because she
talked back), and who
had a ransom on her head
of thousands of dollars and who
was never caught, and who
had no use for the law
when the law was wrong,
who defied the law. I like
to think of her.
I like to think of her especially
when I think of the problem of
feeding children.

The legal answer
to the problem of feeding children
is ten free lunches every month,
being equal, in the child's real life,

to eating lunch every other day.
Monday but not Tuesday.
I like to think of the President
eating lunch Monday, but not
Tuesday.
And when I think of the President
and the law, and the problem of
feeding children, I like to
think of Harriet Tubman
and her revolver.

And then sometimes
I think of the President
and other men,
men who practice the law,
who revere the law,
who make the law,
who enforce the law
who live behind
and operate through
and feed themselves
at the expense of
starving children
because of the law,
men who sit in paneled offices
and think about vacations
and tell women
whose care it is
to feed children
not to be hysterical
not to be hysterical as in the word
hysterikos, the greek for
womb suffering,
not to suffer in their
wombs,
not to care,
not to bother the men
because they want to think
of other things
and do not want
to take the women seriously.
I want them

to take women seriously.
I want them to think about Harriet Tubman,
and remember,
remember she was beat by a white man
and she lived
and she lived to redress her grievances,
and she lived in swamps
and wore the clothes of a man
bringing hundreds of fugitives from
slavery, and was never caught,
and led an army,
and won a battle,
and defied the laws
because the laws were wrong, I want men
to take us seriously.
I am tired wanting them to think
about right and wrong.
I want them to fear.
I want them to feel fear now
as I have felt suffering in the womb, and
I want them
to know
that there is always a time
there is always a time to make right
what is wrong,
there is always a time
for retribution
and that time
is beginning.

DENISE LEVERTOV

(b. 1923) Born in England, Denise Levertov had her first book of poetry published there before coming to the United States with her hubsand in 1948. Since then she has written many volumes of poetry. An antiwar activist during the Vietnam war, she frequently read her poems to raise money for antiwar groups. Recent volumes include *Relearning the Alphabet* (1970), *Footprints: Poems* (1972), *The Poet in the World* (1973), and *The Freeing of the Dust* (1975), all published by New Directions.

STEPPING WESTWARD

What is green in me
darkens, muscadine.

If woman is inconstant,
good, I am faithful to

ebb and flow, I fall
in season and now

is a time of ripening.
If her part

is to be true,
a north star,

good, I hold steady
in the black sky

and vanish by day,
yet burn there

in blue or above
quilts of cloud.

There is no savor
more sweet, more salt

than to be glad to be
what, woman,

and who, myself,
I am, a shadow

that grows longer as the sun
moves, drawn out

on a thread of wonder.
If I bear burdens

they begin to be remembered
as gifts, goods, a basket

of bread that hurts
my shoulders but closes me

in fragrance. I can
eat as I go.

MARTHA COLLINS

(b. 1940) Born in Nebraska, Martha Collins
was raised in Iowa and educated at Stanford
University and the University of Iowa. An
associate professor of English at the University
of Massachusetts, Boston, where she teaches
creative writing, she has published poems in
numerous periodicals and anthologies.

HOMECOMING

So you're home from the wars,
or at least a summer
facsimile of them.
You're welcome, but
please don't rush.
There are some things
to be seen.

First you'll notice
these guests. You'll call
them suitors, and be
mistaken: they've
not cluttered
the hearth or changed
the order of things.

You'll find the bed
in the same quiet place,
neatly spread as before.
But you should know
I've grown accustomed

to sleeping in all
its spaces.

The sun-colored table
sits in the kitchen, prepared
for the usual
feasts, you'll think.
But I'm not quite ready
to serve your dinners,
to pour your wines.

I'd rather sit by the big
bay window, the one we saved
for special times.
There's an extra chair,
but please be still,
for it's here I've come
to reflect.

Perhaps you'll resent
the uncommon manner
in which I've come
to possess our rooms.
But you can't conceive
of the more extreme measures
I've thought of taking,

like pounding stakes
in the floor and stretching
ropes to inform you
this or that is mine,
stamping my name
on favorite walls,
carving initials

on window sills,
or merely breathing
autograph spaces
on panes of glass.
But of course
we're bound
to share, and it's more

than a neat
arrangement
of tables and chairs and beds.
And perhaps it's as
simple as getting familiar,
accepting
the common places again.

But please
understand,
and try to find
your own space
where you can see beyond
these ceilings and floors
and windows and walls.

It shouldn't be hard:
you have been miles
away, after all,
while I have been
making myself at home.

ANN BEATTIE

(b. 1947) Born in Washington, D.C., Ann Beattie studied at American University and the University of Connecticut. She has been a Guggenheim fellow and a lecturer at the University of Virginia and Harvard University. She now lives in Connecticut. She has published a novel and two collections of short stories. She says that she writes about "chaos"; her characters have more questions than answers about life. Her most recent work is the novel *Falling in Place* (1980).

TUESDAY NIGHT

Henry was supposed to bring the child home at six o'clock, but they usually did not arrive until eight or eight-thirty, with Joanna overtired and complaining that she did not want to go to bed the minute she came through the door. Henry had taught her that phrase. "The minute she comes through the door" was something I had said once, and he mocked me with it in defending her. "Let the poor child have a minute before she goes to bed. She *did* just come through the door." The poor child is, of course, crazy about Henry. He allows her to call him that, instead of "Daddy." And now he takes her to dinner at a French restaurant that she adores, which doesn't open until five-thirty. That means that she gets home close to eight. I am a beast if I refuse to let her eat her escargots. And it would be cruel to tell her that her father's support payments fluctuate wildly, while the French dining remains a constant. Forget the money—Henry has been a good father. He visits every Tuesday night, carefully twirls her crayons in the pencil sharpener, and takes her every other weekend. The only bad thing he has done to her—and even Henry agreed about that—was to introduce her to the sleepie he had living with him right after the divorce: an obnoxious woman, who taught Joanna to sing "I'm a Woman." Fortunately, she did not remember many of the words, but I thought I'd lose my mind when she went around the house singing "Doubleyou oh oh em ay en" for two weeks. Sometimes the sleepie tucked a fresh flower in Joanna's hair—like Maria Muldaur, she explained. The child had the good sense to be embarrassed.

The men I know are very friendly with one another. When Henry was at the house last week, he helped Dan, who lives with me, carry a bookcase up the steep, narrow steps to the second floor. Henry and Dan talk about nutrition—Dan's current interest. My brother Bobby, the only person I know who is seriously interested in hallucinogens at the age of twenty-six, gladly makes a fool of himself in front of Henry by bringing out his green yoyo, which glows by the miracle of two internal batteries. Dan tells Bobby that if he's going to take drugs he should try dosing his body with vitamins before and after. The three of them Christmas-shop for me. Last year they had dinner at an Italian restaurant downtown. I asked Dan what they ordered, and he said, "Oh, we all had manicotti."

I have been subsisting on red zinger tea and watermelon, trying to lose weight. Dan and Henry and Bobby are all thin. Joanna takes after her father in her build. She is long and graceful, with chiselled features that would shame Marisa Berenson. She is ten years old. When I was at the laundry to pick up the clothes yesterday, a woman mistook me, from the back, for her cousin Addie.

In Joanna's class at school they are having a discussion of problems with the environment. She wants to take our big avocado plant in to school. I have tried patiently to explain that the plant does not have anything to do with environmental problems. She says that they are discussing nature, too. "What's the harm?" Dan says. So he goes to work and leaves it to me to fit the towering avocado into the Audi. I also get roped into baking cookies, so Joanna can take them to school and pass them around to celebrate her birthday. She tells me that it is the custom to put the cookies in a box wrapped in birthday paper. We select a paper with yellow bears standing in concentric circles. Dan dumps bran into the chocolate-chip-cookie dough. He forbids me to use a dot of red food coloring in the sugar-cookie hearts.

My best friend, Dianne, comes over in the mornings and turns her nose up at my red zinger. Sometimes she takes a shower here, because she loves our shower head. "How come you're not in there all the time?" she says. My brother is sweet on her. He finds her extremely attractive. He asked me if I had noticed the little droplets of water from the shower on her forehead, just at the hairline. Bobby lends her money, because her husband doesn't give her enough. I know for a fact that Dianne is thinking of having an affair with him.

Dan has to work late at his office on Tuesday nights, and a while ago I decided that I wanted that one night to myself each week—a night without any of them. Dianne said, "I know what you mean," but Bobby took great offense and didn't come to visit that night, or any other night, for two weeks. Joanna was delighted that she could be picked up after school by

Dianne, in Dianne's 1966 Mustang convertible, and that the two of them could visit until Henry came by Dianne's to pick her up. Dan, who keeps saying that our relationship is going sour—although it isn't—pursed his lips and nodded when I told him about Tuesday nights, but he said nothing. The first night alone I read a dirty magazine that had been lying around the house for some time. Then I took off all my clothes and looked in the hall mirror and decided to go on a diet, so I skipped dinner. I made a long-distance call to a friend in California who had just had a baby. We talked about the spidery little veins in her thighs, and I swore to her over and over again that they would go away. Then I took one of each kind of vitamin pill we have in the house.

The next week, I had prepared for my spare time better. I had bought whole-wheat flour and clover honey, and I made four loaves of whole-wheat bread, I made a piecrust, putting dough in the sink and rolling it out there, which made a lot of sense but which I would never let anybody see me doing. Then I read *Vogue*. Later on, I took out the yoga book I had bought that afternoon and put it in my plastic cookbook-holder and put that down on the floor and stared at it as I tried to get into the postures. I overcooked the piecrust and it burned. I got depressed and drank a Drambuie. The week after that, I ventured out. I went to a movie and bought myself a chocolate milkshake afterward. I sat at the drugstore counter and drank it. I was going to get my birth-control-pill prescription refilled while I was there, but I decided that would be depressing.

Joanna sleeps at her father's apartment now on Tuesday nights. Since he considers her too old to be read a fairy tale before bed, Henry waltzes with her. She wears a long nightgown and a pair of high-heeled shoes that some woman left there. She says that he usually plays "The Blue Danube" but sometimes he kids around and puts on "Idiot Wind" or "Forever Young" and they dip and twirl to it. She has hinted that she would like to take dancing lessons. Last week, she danced through the living room at our house on her pogo stick. Dan had given it to her, saying that now she had a partner, and it would save him money not having to pay for dancing lessons. He told her that if she had any questions she could ask him. He said she could call him "Mr. Daniel." She was disgusted with him. If she were Dan's child, I am sure he would still be reading her fairy tales.

Another Tuesday night, I went out and bought plants. I used my American Express card and got seventy dollars' worth of plants and some plant-hangers. The woman in the store helped me carry the boxes out to the car. I went home and drove nails into the top of the window frames and hung the plants. They did not need to be watered yet, but I held the plastic plant-waterer up to them, to see what it would be like to water them. I squeezed the plastic bottle, and stared at the curved plastic tube coming out of it. Later, I gave myself a facial with egg whites.

There is a mouse. I first saw it in the kitchen—a small gray mouse, moseying along, taking its time in getting from under the counter to the back of the stove. I had Dan seal off the little mouse hole in the back of the stove. Then I saw the mouse again, under the chest in the living room.

"It's a mouse. It's one little mouse," Dan said. "Let it be."

"Everybody knows that if there's one mouse there are more," I said. "We've got to get rid of them."

Dan, the humanist, was secretly glad the mouse had resurfaced—that he hadn't done any damage in sealing off its home.

"It looked like the same mouse to me," Henry said.

"They all look that way," I said. "That doesn't mean—"

"Poor thing," Dan said.

"Are either of you going to set traps, or do I have to do it?"

You have to do it," Dan said. "I can't stand it. I don't want to kill a mouse."

"I think there's only one mouse," Henry said.

Glaring at them, I went into the kitchen and took the mousetraps out of their cellophane packages. I stared at them with tears in my eyes. I didn't know how to set them. Dan and Henry had made me seem like a cold-blooded killer.

"Maybe it will just leave," Dan said.

"Don't be ridiculous, Dan," I said. "If you aren't going to help, at least don't sit around snickering with Henry."

"We're not snickering," Henry said.

"You two certainly are buddy-buddy."

"What's the matter now? You want us to hate each other?" Henry said.

"I don't know how to set a mousetrap," I said. "I can't do it myself."

"Poor Mommy," Joanna said. She was in the hallway outside the living room, listening. I almost turned on her to tell her not to be sarcastic, when I realized that she was serious. She felt sorry for me. With someone on my side, I felt new courage about going back into the kitchen and tackling the problem of the traps.

Dianne called and said she had asked her husband if he could go out one night a week, so she could go out with friends or stay home by herself. He said no, but agreed to take stained-glass lessons with her.

One Tuesday, it rained. I stayed home and daydreamed, and remembered the past. I thought about the boy I dated my last year in high school, who used to take me out to the country on weekends, to where some cousins of his lived. I wondered why he always went there, because we never got near the house. He would drive partway up their long driveway in the woods and then pull off onto a narrow little road that trucks sometimes used when they were logging the property. We parked on the little road and necked. Sometimes the boy would drive slowly along on the country roads looking for rabbits, and whenever he saw one, which was pretty often—sometimes even two or three rabbits at once—he floored it, trying to run the rabbit down. There was no radio in the car. He had a portable radio that got only two stations (soul music and classical) and I held it on my lap. He liked the volume turned up very loud.

Joanna comes to my bedroom and announces that Uncle Bobby is on the phone.

"I got a dog," he says.

"What kind?"

"Aren't you even surprised?"

"Yes. Where did you get the dog?"

"A guy I knew a little bit in college is going to jail, and he persuaded me to take the dog."

"What is he going to jail for?"

"Burglary."

"Joanna," I say, "don't stand there staring at me when I'm talking on the phone."

"He robbed a house," Bobby says.

"What kind of a dog is it?" I ask.

"Malamute and German shepherd. It's in heat."

"Well," I say, "you always wanted a dog."

"I call you all the time, and you never call me," Bobby says.

"I never have interesting news."

"You could call and tell me what you do on Tuesday nights."

'Nothing very interesting," I say.

"You could go to a bar and have rum drinks and weep," Bobby says. He chuckles.

"Are you stoned?" I ask.

"Sure I am. Been home from work for an hour and a half. Ate a Celeste pizza, had a little smoke."

"Do you really have a dog?" I ask.

"If you were a male dog, you wouldn't have any doubt of it."

"You're always much more clever than I am. It's hard to talk to you on the phone, Bobby."

"It's hard to be me," Bobby says. A silence. "I'm not sure the dog likes me."

"Bring it over. Joanna will love it."

"I'll be around with it Tuesday night," he says.

"Why is it so interesting to you that I have one night a week to myself?"

"Whatever you do," Bobby says, "don't rob a house."

We hang up, and I go tell Joanna the news.

"You yelled at me," she says.

"I did not. I asked you not to stand there staring at me while I was on the phone."

"You raised your voice," she says.
Soon it will be Tuesday night.

Joanna asks me suspiciously what I do on Tuesday nights.
"What does your father say I do?" I ask.
"He says he doesn't know."
"Does he seem curious?"
"It's hard to tell with him," she says.
Having got my answer, I've forgotten about her question.
"So what things do you do?" she says.
"Sometimes you like to play in your tent," I say defensively. "Well, I
like some time to just do what I want to do, too, Joanna."
"That's O.K.," she says. She sounds like an adult placating a child.
I have to face the fact that I don't do much of anything on Tuesdays,
and that one night alone each week isn't making me any less edgy or more
agreeable to live with. I tell Dan this, as if it's his fault.
"I don't think you ever wanted to divorce Henry," Dan says.
"Oh, Dan, I *did*."
"You two seem to get along fine."
"But we fought. We didn't get along."
He looks at me. "Oh," he says. He is being inordinately nice to me,
because of the scene I threw when a mouse got caught in one of the traps.
The trap didn't kill it. It just got it by the paw, and Dan had to beat it to
death with a screwdriver.
"Maybe you'd rather the two of us did something regularly on Tuesday
nights," he says now. "Maybe I could get the night of my meetings
changed."
"Thank you," I say. "Maybe I should give it a little longer."
"That's up to you," he says. "There hasn't been enough time to judge
by, I guess."
Inordinately kind. Deferential. He has been saying for a long time that
our relationship is turning sour, and now it must have turned so sour for
him that he doesn't even want to fight. What does he want?
"Maybe you'd like a night—" I begin.
"The hell with that," he says. "If there has to be so much time alone,
I can't see the point of living together."
I hate fights. The day after this one, I get weepy and go over to Dianne's.
She ends up subtly suggesting that I take stained-glass lessons. We drink
some sherry and I drive home. The last thing I want is to run into her
husband, who calls me "the squirrel" behind my back. Dianne says
that when I call and he answers, he lets her know it's me on the phone by
puffing up his cheeks to make himself look like a squirrel.
Tonight, Dan and I each sit on a side of Joanna's tester bed to say
good night to her. The canopy above the bed is white nylon, with small,

puckered stars. She is ready for sleep. As soon as she goes to sleep, Dan will be ready to talk to me. Dan has clicked off the light next to Joanna's bed. Going out of the bedroom before him, I grope for the hall light. I remember Henry saying to me, as a way of leading up to talking about divorce, that going to work one morning he had driven over a hill and had been astonished when at the top he saw a huge yellow tree, and realized for the first time that it was autumn.

ADRIENNE RICH

(b. 1929) A graduate of Radcliffe College, Adrienne Rich has described her life as one of privilege. Her early poems reflect the anguish of role conflict as wife, mother, and writer. More recently she has written of lesbian experience. In addition to writing many volumes of poetry, including *The Dream of a Common Language* (1978), Rich has become a leader in feminist thought and literary theory. A book on motherhood appeared in 1976 and a collection of essays, *On Lies, Secrets, and Silences,* in 1979.

DIVING INTO THE WRECK

First having read the book of myths,
and loaded the camera,
and checked the edge of the knife-blade,
I put on
the body-armor of black rubber
the absurd flippers
the grave and awkward mask.
I am having to do this
not like Cousteau with his
assiduous team
aboard the sun-flooded schooner
but here alone.

There is a ladder.
The ladder is always there
hanging innocently
close to the side of the schooner.
We know what it is for,
we who have used it.
Otherwise
it's a piece of maritime floss
some sundry equipment.

I go down.
Rung after rung and still
the oxygen immerses me
the blue light
the clear atoms
of our human air.
I go down.
My flippers cripple me,
I crawl like an insect down the ladder
and there is no one
to tell me when the ocean
will begin.

First the air is blue and then
it is bluer and then green and then
black I am blacking out and yet
my mask is powerful
it pumps my blood with power
the sea is another story
the sea is not a question of power
I have to learn alone
to turn my body without force
in the deep element.

And now: it is easy to forget
what I came for
among so many who have always
lived here
swaying their crenellated fans
between the reefs
and besides
you breathe differently down here.

I came to explore the wreck.
The words are purposes.
The words are maps.
I came to see the damage that was done
and the treasures that prevail.
I stroke the beam of my lamp
slowly along the flank
of something more permanent
than fish or weed

ADRIENNE RICH

497

the thing I came for:
the wreck and not the story of the wreck
the thing itself and not the myth
the drowned face always staring
toward the sun
the evidence of damage
worn by salt and sway into this threadbare beauty
the ribs of the disaster
curving their assertion
among the tentative haunters.

This is the place.
And I am here, the mermaid whose dark hair
streams black, the merman in his armored body
We circle silently
about the wreck
we dive into the hold.
I am she: I am he

whose drowned face sleeps with open eyes
whose breasts still bear the stress
whose silver, copper, vermeil cargo lies
obscurely inside barrels
half-wedged and left to rot
we are the half-destroyed instruments
that once held to a course
the water-eaten log
the fouled compass

We are, I am, you are
by cowardice or courage
the one who find our way
back to this scene
carrying a knife, a camera
a book of myths
in which
our names do not appear.

OLGA BROUMAS

(b. 1949) Daughter of an officer in the Greek diplomatic corps, Olga Broumas came to the United States when she was ten. She speaks several languages, has studied linguistics, and earned a M.F.A. from the University of Oregon. She now teaches women's studies at Goddard College in Plainfield, Vermont, and travels widely throughout the country giving poetry readings. In 1980 she was awarded a Guggenheim Fellowship. Broumas's first volume of poetry, *Beginning with O,* won the Yale Younger Poets Award in 1977. Her most recent volume is *Soie Sauvage* (1980).

ARTEMIS

Let's not have tea.   White wine
eases the mind along
the slopes
of the faithful body, helps

any memory once engraved
on the twin
chromosome ribbons, emerge, tentative
from the archaeology of an excised past.

I am a woman
who understands
the necessity of an impulse whose goal or origin
still lie beyond me.   I keep the goat

for more
than the pastoral reasons.   I work
in silver the tongue-like forms
that curve round a throat

an arm-pit, the upper
thigh, whose significance stirs in me
like a curviform alphabet
that defies

decoding, appears
to consist of vowels, beginning with O, the O-
mega, horseshoe, the cave of sound.
What tiny fragments

survive, mangled into our language.
I am a woman committed to
a politics
of transliteration, the methodology

of a mind
stunned at the suddenly
possible shifts of meaning—for which
like amnesiacs

in a ward on fire, we must
find words
or burn.

MAY SARTON

(b. 1912) Born in Belgium, May Sarton came to Cambridge, Massachusetts, in 1916 and was educated there before going to New York to study acting. She left the theater in 1937 to teach creative writing and has since lectured and taught at many colleges. Her first volume of poetry appeared in 1937, her first novel in 1938. She has published several volumes of autobiography since 1959. She has been a prolific writer and has received prestigious awards and grants as well as several honorary doctorates; she is a fellow of the American Academy of Arts and Sciences.

JOY IN PROVENCE

(for Camille Mayran)

I found her, rich loser of all,
Whom two wars have stripped to the bone,
High up on her terrace wall
Over vineyards asleep in the sun—
Her riches, that ample scene
Composed in the barn's round door;
Her riches, rough cliff and pine,
Aromatic air—and no more.
Here, seasoned and sweetened by loss,
She thrives like thyme in the grass.

This woman's feet are so light,
So light the weight of her eyes
When she walks her battlements late
To harvest her thoughts as they rise,
She is never caught, only wise.
She rests on the round earth's turning
And follows the radiant skies,
Then reads Pascal in the morning.

And, walking beside her, I learned
How those dazzling silences burned.

On the longest day of June,
When summer wanes as it flowers
And dusk folds itself into dawn,
We shared the light-drenched hours.
We lay on rough rock in the sun,
Conversing till words were rare,
Conversing till words were done,
High up in the pungent air,
Then silently paced while the moon
Rose to dance her slow pavane.

The wine from a meditation
Was mine to drink deeply that night,
O vintage severe, and elation,
To be pressed out of loss, and from light!

Alive to her thought, yet alone,
As I lay in my bed, close to prayer,
A whisper came and was gone:
"Rejoice" was the word in the air.
But when the silence was broken,
Not by me, not by her, who had spoken?

ANN STANFORD

(b. 1916) Professor of English at California State University at Northridge, Ann Stanford is the author of six books of poetry, a verse translation of *The Bhagavad–Gita* (1970), and an introduction to the poetry of the Puritan Anne Bradstreet. She edited an anthology *The Women Poets in English* (1973). Winner of several prizes, she recently received a grant from the National Endowment for the Arts to write poetry.

THE DESCENT

Let us, therefore, bend all our force and thoughts of soul to this most holy light, that showeth us the way which leadeth to heaven; and after it, putting off the affections we were clad withal at our coming down, let us clime up the stairs which at the lowermost step have the shadow of sensual beauty, to the high mansion-place where the heavenly, amiable, and right beauty dwelleth.
—Baldassare Castiglione

As I descend from ideal to actual touch
As I trade all the golden angel crowns
And rings of light for gross engrossing sense,
As I descend Plotinus' stairs,
Angel, man, beast, but not yet plant and stone,
The sense of that height clings, the earthen hand

Transmutes again to light, is blessed from black
Through alchemy to rise rich red, green, blue,
Fractions of vision broke from ample crowns.

As I from the mind's distance fall on voyages
I test the strength of water where I walk

And lose the air for wings. I am lifted
As I descend past clouds and gusts of air
As I go down with wind to tops of trees
As I walk down from mountain tops and cold.

As I descend to gardens warm with leaves
As I enter the new morning harsh in sun
I count the earth with all its destinies
Come down to prove what idea does not know.

I descended out of nothing into green
I descended out of spaces where the spare
Stepping stones of islands roughed my way.
I descended into solidness, to dense
And mingled shrubberies where the birds
Alone choose wings for crossing my old sky.

Caught in this day within a sound of hours
Walled into shadows, stripped of multitudes,
I try this spring the growing into light.

MEGAN TERRY

(b. 1932) Born and educated in Seattle, Washington, Megan Terry has spent her life in the theater. A prolific playwright, she has also directed and taught drama at many colleges. She has won many awards and fellowships, including a Guggenheim in 1978. Terry's innovative techniques of cooperation between author and actors in developing a play have challenged dramatic conventions. Her constant theme has been that sacrifices accompany change. She is now playwright-in-residence at the University of Nebraska–Omaha. *Approaching Simone* was first produced at Boston University in 1970.

APPROACHING SIMONE

Characters

SIMONE
FATHER
MOTHER
BROTHER
VISITOR
SIMONE, a college friend of Simone's
ALBERT
JEAN-PAUL
CAROLINA
BOARD HEAD I
BOARD HEAD II
SEVERAL FRENCH MILITARY MEN   (all played by the same actor)
THE ENSEMBLE
QUEENS
KINGS

Act I

The stage of the proscenium opening should be raked at a high enough angle so that any floor movement or choreography can be seen from anywhere in the house. Throughout the auditorium should be built at least five small platforms, covering the theater seats, with stairs or ropes or bridges for the actors to reach them. There should be a balcony to stage left and stage right where the opera singers will stand and sing in spotlights when necessary. Coming out from the proscenium opening on both stage right and stage left should be two platforms against the house walls, wide enough to hold ornate chairs and from four to eight actors each. On stage right platform, which should be lower than the height of the main stage but high enough that the audience can see heads and shoulders, should be male actors, dressed in the costumes of kings, emperors, presidents, prelates, etc. They are all very very old. On stage left platform jutting out from the proscenium are female actors dressed in haute couture of the thirties. They are anybody's idea of society and culture leaders. They are very very old.

Draped above the proscenium opening are the intermingled flags of France, Nazi Germany, Russia, England, and the United States. In the center of the flags is a giant ikon, painted in muted, glowing colors and illuminated with gold leaf, of God in a flowing white beard at the top, Jesus below and to the left, a golden glow below and to the right.

In the corners of the proscenium arch where the arch and the walls of the house join, stage right and stage left, are papier-mâché cherubs painted in gold. They stand from floor to ceiling. In their belly buttons are golden rings: to the rings are attached golden cords. The cords are held by the old men and old women and will be pulled at the appropriate time.

On the ceiling is a beautiful head with an open mouth. The COMPANY *enters from back of the auditorium in precession. As they reach the stage, they turn and face the audience. The woman who plays Simone takes up position at extreme stage left and silently stares at the audience. The* COMPANY *sings.*

ALL

THE DARKNESS, THE DARKNESS
I'M NOT AFRAID OF THE NIGHT
THE DARKNESS, THE DARKNESS
WHERE I GROPED INSIDE
I LOVED THE LIGHT ON THE SNOW
I SENT MY SUGAR TO THE WAR
I WATCHED GOOD FRENCHMEN
GO
INTO THE GROUND
BUT I PAID ATTENTION TO THE SOUND
OF THE POUNDING DARK
WITHIN MY HEAD
I FOLLOWED WHERE THE HEARTBEAT LED
AND MY MIND SEEMED TO BLEED

WOMAN BECOMING

BARITONE

IF THE FOOL PERSISTS IN HIS FOLLY
HE WILL BECOME WISE
IF THE FOOL PERSISTS IN HIS FOLLY
HE WILL BECOME WISE
DESIRE! DESIRE! DESIRE! DESIRE!
ECSTASY! MIND ECSTASY! DESIRE!
DESIRE!
ECLIPSE THE FIRE OF THE SEXUAL DRIVE
REACH OUT THROUGH THE MIND
LEAVE THE SPERM BEHIND
LET THE EGG FALL WHERE SHE MAY
DRIVE, DRIVE, DRIVE
TO MIND ECSTASY

(The CHORUS *keeps singing "Attention, Attention.")*

WOMAN

ANYONE CAN BECOME
ANYONE CAN BECOME

MAN

ANYONE CAN KNOW TRUTH
ANYONE CAN KNOW TRUTH

ALL

DESIRE DESIRE!

DUET

ONLY MAKE THE EFFORT OF ATTENTION
ONLY MAKE THE EFFORT OF ATTENTION
STAY IN THE DARK INSIDE YOUR HEAD
(Repeat)
TILL IT LIGHTS YOUR WAY

ALL

ATTENTION, PULL WITH YOUR WILL
GENIUS IS INVISIBLE.

(One by one everyone sings the name "Simone" on a different note, then everyone taking her or his same note sings the name "Simone" five times together.)

ACTOR *(intones from platform)* Simone taught herself the art of perpetual attention. Simone taught herself the art of perpetual attention.
(Exit.)

No matter what age SIMONE *is during a scene, she always behaves and speaks as if she were somewhere near thirty.*

   SIMONE *enters running and flings herself down. Her family follows. They mime carrying luggage.*

MOTHER   Get up, Simone. We have a long way to walk to the lodge.

SIMONE   I have nothing to carry.

MOTHER   You're too little.

FATHER   You don't have to carry anything.

BROTHER   You can't carry anything, you're only five.

SIMONE   I can carry anything.

MOTHER   Get up at once.

SIMONE   I can carry as much as Brother.

FATHER   My dear little girl. Father can carry you and the luggage too climb on my back.

SIMONE   I want to carry my share.

MOTHER   There's no need.

BROTHER   You're melting the snow.

MOTHER   You'll catch pneumonia.

FATHER   T.B.

BROTHER   I'm starving. Come on, Simone.

SIMONE   No.

MOTHER   Simone.

SIMONE   No.

FATHER   Simone.

SIMONE   No.

MOTHER   You'll get bronchitis, you'll get the flu, you'll have a headache, your clothes will be wet. You'll not sleep a wink. I won't sleep a wink. I'll be up all night with you coughing. You're too frail, you were not only ill all this fall, but you were in bed most of the summer. Please, my little darling, come now and take Mama's hand.

SIMONE   No. I can carry as much as he can.

BROTHER   Let's see.

(SIMONE *stands up and* BROTHER *mimes transference of luggage on his back to Simone's back. She wobbles, gets her balance, and slowly trudges ahead.*)

MOTHER What will we do with her, she'll break her bones before she's six.

FATHER Let her have her way. She can't keep it up.

BROTHER *(running off)* I'll eat up all the croissants.

(MOTHER *and* FATHER *freeze.*)
This series of scenes should be played very quickly in different pools of light.
BROTHER *and* SIMONE.

BROTHER Do you know your Racine?

SIMONE Of course.

BROTHER Then whoever dries up first gets slapped by the other.

(*He begins to recite* Phaedra. *He stumbles.* SIMONE *slaps him and continues the passage. She falters and he slaps her.*)

BROTHER Continue.

(SIMONE *continues to recite; she gets slapped twice.*)
Continue. Continue.
VISITOR, MOTHER, BROTHER, SIMONE.
BROTHER I solved all the math problems before the teacher could.

MOTHER He's been first in his class in everything since he started school.

VISITOR He's the genius, and *(pointing to* SIMONE) she's the beauty.

(SIMONE *turns away as if slapped by an invisible hand.*)
SIMONE, BROTHER, *and* MOTHER.

MOTHER My dearest children, where are your stockings?

BROTHER We gave them away.

MOTHER It's raining and freezing out.

SIMONE The worker's children don't wear stockings, and neither do I!

MOTHER I won't permit this. Your father won't permit this. You're not to leave the house till I send out for more stockings for you.

SIMONE I will never wear stockings again.

SIMONE *and* MOTHER: SIMONE *is pouring sugar into an envelope.*

MOTHER My precious baby, my own, my darling, what are you doing with that precious sugar? It was so hard for me to get. I had the maid stand in line for three hours for it.

SIMONE I'm mailing my sugar to the soldiers at the front.

MOTHER But why?

SIMONE They don't have any.

At the beach: FATHER *and* SIMONE. SIMONE *is gazing at the sunset. (The* ENSEMBLE *become waves, gulls, shore birds, etc.)*

FATHER Simone, you've been sitting looking out over the water for hours—go and play with the other children.

SIMONE It's so beautiful. I'd much rather watch the sunset than play.

(She screams a long agonized scream. The ENSEMBLE *rush upstage and turn with their mouths open in mirror agony.)*
Father, I have an impossible headache. I've never never known such pain. It's driving me out of my mind.

FATHER It's probably only connected to your menstrual cycle. This often happens the first few times.

SIMONE It's not like an ordinary pain. I'm going blind. I'm afraid I'll vomit.

FATHER *(feeling her forehead)* You don't have a fever. Where's the pain centered?

SIMONE It started in my left eye and now has traveled to the right. I can't stand the light. I can't stand the noise. The noise in the street is trampling on my brain.

FATHER Sounds like a migraine. I hope not, my precious child. Go and lie down in your room. I'll bring an ice cloth for your head, and make it very dark until you feel better.
(Exit.)

Simone at Fourteen—When and Why She Wants to Kill Herself
SIMONE *is alone in her room with the wet cloth. As her pain and anguish build, aspects of her self-doubt, self-loathing, and pain and anguish appear to torture her. Each one brings a larger and larger piece of white wet cloth until she is all wrapped up except for her head, with a piece left to strangle herself. (or one giant white cloth can be used).*

SIMONE Oh Father, Father, it's unbearable. Surely it's some kind of punishment.

ONE You have no talent, Simone.

TWO You're stupid, Simone.

THREE You're awkward, Simone.

FOUR Not only is your body miserable, but your mind can't move either.

FIVE You're nothing but a girl, Simone.

SIX You'll never amount to anything, Simone.

SEVEN You'll never match your brother, Simone.

EIGHT You're only a girl, Simone.
(Taunts from the auditorium in three languages, equivalent to "You're nothing but a stupid cunt.")
NINE The pain in your head is evidence.

TEN Evidence of your lack of brains, Simone.

ELEVEN You'll never know the truth, Simone.

TWELVE Your mind is too dim to perceive the truth, Simone.

THIRTEEN Put an end to your stupidity, Simone.

FOURTEEN Beauty is useless, Simone; it isn't the path to the truth.

FIFTEEN You're unworthy, Simone.

SIXTEEN You're wretched, Simone.

SEVENTEEN You're unfit for this world, Simone.

EIGHTEEN You're arrogant, Simone.

NINETEEN You'll never create anything, Simone.

TWENTY You have no talent, Simone.

TWENTY-ONE You have no genius, Simone.

TWENTY-TWO You're a girl, Simone.

TWENTY-THREE Your pain is your proof, Simone.

TWENTY-FOUR You're always sick and you'll always be sick, Simone.

TWENTY-FIVE Your head will always ache, Simone.

TWENTY-SIX You can't even draw a straight line, Simone.

TWENTY-SEVEN You have poor circulation, Simone.

TWENTY-EIGHT Your hands are always swollen, Simone.

TWENTY-NINE It takes brains to discover the truth, Simone.

SIMONE If I can't find the way to justice and truth, then I don't want to live! I'm mediocre! Only the truly great can enter that transcendant kingdom where truth lives.

THIRTY Kill yourself, Simone.
(THIRTY unrolls the white sheet. SIMONE rolls tortuously out. As the SINGER sings, SIMONE is drawn back to the will to live. She slowly rises.)

MEGAN TERRY

511

SINGER

ANYONE CAN KNOW TRUTH
DESIRE, DESIRE
ONLY MAKE THE EFFORT OF ATTENTION
FOCUS ON THE DARK INSIDE YOUR HEAD
UNTIL IT LIGHTS YOUR WAY
THE SIMPLEST MAN MAY KNOW TRUTH
IF HE REACHES OUT EVERY DAY.

A nightclub, SIMONE *sits smoking buried behind the menu. Her friends* SIMONE, JEAN-PAUL, ALBERT, *and some others sit around tables. There is a small band playing in the background.*

SIMONE TWO Simone, roll me a cigarette.

JEAN-PAUL She's too clumsy.

ALBERT She's getting better.

SIMONE TWO They burn longer—she packs them tight.

JEAN-PAUL Simone, your lips.

SIMONE Eh?

ALBERT You're reading the script off the menu.

JEAN-PAUL She won't order anything anyway.

ALBERT I'll order for her. Tonight we eat.

JEAN-PAUL Tonight we drink. Whiskey!

SIMONE TWO Whiskey! Whiskey, Simone?

SIMONE No.

SIMONE TWO Here, take my tobacco.

SIMONE Thanks.

JEAN-PAUL *(watching* SIMONE *roll cigarette):* Hey, she's doing it with one hand.

ALBERT American.

SIMONE TWO Twist the end, like yours. Ah.
(SIMONE *rolling cigarettes in each hand, drops them and gets tobacco all over her skirt, the table. She tries to brush it together. Everyone sputters.)*

JEAN-PAUL Get it out of the way. Carolina is almost on.

SIMONE TWO We were lucky to get in.

ALBERT I'm in love with her.

SIMONE How long has she been in France?

ALBERT I hope she never leaves; she's promised never to leave.

SIMONE I'd like to talk with her sometime.
(Her friends laugh. Successfully rolling another cigarette for herself, she lights it with the stub of the one in her mouth.)
They've been so exploited. We do the same in our colonies. How can you sit here drinking and grinning like apes when we are grinding down the blacks in Africa?

JEAN-PAUL We'll change all that tomorrow. Tonight we have fun.

SIMONE TWO Simone is right. Have you written a position paper on the colonies?

JEAN-PAUL I will, I will. I have to form a coalition with the workers first.

ALBERT It won't be hard. The monetary system is cracking. I predict within six months, a year at most, we'll have no trouble recruiting.

JEAN-PAUL The international capitalistic beast has fed on itself so long, it won't find even a kernel of corn left in its shit to keep it going.

SIMONE It's beginning to happen in Germany. I plan to go there to examine the new workers' alliances at first hand.

JEAN-PAUL I'll publish anything you send back.

SIMONE Good, but I won't have much time to write. I intend to work.

ALBERT Work, work. Always work. Whiskey!

SIMONE Everything begins and ends with work. Work is constant. You and I pass through, but the work is always here.

SIMONE TWO One day the machines will do all the work.

SIMONE If we are not careful, we will work for the machines.

JEAN-PAUL Technology will free man from manual labor.

SIMONE I hope not.

ALBERT What is so sacred about working with your hands. I've never worked with my hands and I never intend to—we're freed from that.

SIMONE You are privileged; they are not.

ALBERT I want to think; I want to plan, create.

SIMONE You above all should understand work. Work, in contrast to reflection, to persuasion or to magic, is a sequence of actions that have no direct connection either with the initial emotion, or the end aimed at . . . Colors, sounds, dimensions can change, while the law of work, which is to be endlessly indifferent to what has preceded and what will follow, never changes. Qualities, forms, and distances change, but the law of work remains the constant factor to which qualities, forms, and distances serve only as signs. The law of exterior relations defines space. To *see* space is to grasp that work's raw material is always passive, always outside one's self. . . .

ALBERT Whiskey.

SIMONE TWO Here she comes.

JEAN-PAUL Simone. Attend her closely. Tell me if Carolina is working or creating magic.

SIMONE *(smoking again, she sits back)* Now *you're* working too hard, Jean-Paul.

WAITER Caro—lin—A!!

(CAROLINA, *a black American entertainer, takes the stage. She sings first in a blues style that changes to a Charleston and then back to a shoutin' blues. She's backed by a mixed chorus who dance in the style of 1928–29).*

CAROLINA *(singing and dancing, blues, Charleston, tap, stomp)*
THE BLUES WAS A PASS TIME
THE BLUES WAS A PASS TIME
FOR THAT TIME
I DIDN'T HAVE NO TIME
FOR NOTHIN BUT THE BLUES

I COULD SPEND THE DAY
I COULD LAY THERE ALL THE DAY
PASSIN TIME WITH MY BLUES

THE BLUES WAS MY PASS TIME
THAT WAS THE LAST TIME THAT I
LET THE BLUES GET ME THAT WAY

MY LATEST OLD MAN LEFT ME IN MY BED
HE WALKED ON DOWN TO THE STORE
HE'D WATCHED MY RED HEART
TURN TO LEAD
HE SAID "CHILE, CHILE, CHILE,
I JES CAIN'T SLEEP WITH YOU NO MORE."

IT'S PAST TIME FOR THE BLUES
THEY DON'T GONNA GRAB ME NO MORE
I AIN'T LAYIN' WITH THE BLUES
I'M SICK OF THE HEARTSICK
I DONE LICKED THE BLUES

IT'S LONG PAST TIME FOR THE BLUES
MY RED HEART DONE TURNED TO BLUE
BUT ALONG CAME A PRETTY MAN
WHO MADE ME KNOW MY EYES WAS BLACK
HE TOLE ME, BABY, YOU IS MINE NOW AND
YORE OLD MAN AIN'T NEVER COMIN BACK

AND I'M GLAD HE'S GONE
OH YES, I'M GLAD HE'S GONE
I GOT A NEW MAN, NOT A BLUE MAN

HE GIVES ME SUGAR AT NIGHT
HE GIVES ME SUGAR AT NIGHT
HE BAKES MY BREAD
HE HOLDS ME TIGHT

HE CALLS ME HIS PEACHES
I CALLS HIM MY CREAM
HE CREAMS
MY PEACHES
HE CREAMS MY PEACHES,
AND BABY LET ME TELL YOU,
BABY LET ME TELL YOU,
THIS AIN'T NO DREAM!!

(They applaud wildly, bang the table; ALBERT *jumps up and invites her to the table. She comes over and he introduces her around. She shakes hands.* SIMONE *crunches down in her chair. She is very shy, lights two cigarettes at once, and starts to pick up the menu again. The band begins a mild Charleston.* CAROLINA *bends over* SIMONE.)

CAROLINA Hello baby, give me some sugar. Hey baby, give me some sugar.

(As SIMONE *turns red,* CAROLINA *kisses her on the neck, and then pulls her to her feet.)*

Come on and Charleston, Charleston with me.

SIMONE I beg your pardon?

CAROLINA Dance, baby.

SIMONE I don't know how.

CAROLINA Follow me.

(SIMONE *hands notebook to* ALBERT.)

SIMONE I'm afraid I . . .

CAROLINA Don't work so hard . . . like this, nice and easy does it. . .
(SIMONE, *awkward, makes some attempt. Her friends are delighted.)*

SIMONE I can't get my hands right.

CAROLINA You'll get it, you'll get it. Let it come up through the floor. Let it creep right up ya spine. Yeah, yeah, you gettin' it. Who's buyin'?

ALBERT *(yelling)* Whiskey.

JEAN-PAUL Work or magic, Simone?

SIMONE It's divine, Jean-Paul.
(They all laugh.)

ALBERT So are you. What do you drink, Carolina?

CAROLINA Old Forrester, neat.
(As they exit:)

ALBERT Say you will never leave France. Say you will never leave me.

CAROLINA Anything you say, baby—it's really true what they said about Paree.

(SIMONE remains alone onstage. The ENSEMBLE appears in grotesque gray bags. They move slowly to smother her. She remains in one place.)

SIMONE *(a litany)* What I am, I endure. What I am, I endure. I suffer, I desire, I doubt, I'm stupid. I'm ignorant, I'm not well put together. What I am does not satisfy me. I have become me without my consent. Tomorrow is an I that now I cannot change. What I am, I endure, I suffer.

(The ENSEMBLE covers her for an instant. Then break and dissolve upstage. Alone:)

I desire, I am stupid! What I am, I endure!

SIMONE *and her* MOTHER *arrive in a truck made of the* ENSEMBLE *at the rooms where Simone's first teaching post is to be.* SIMONE *is chainsmoking and reading newspapers and magazines throughout the scene. The truck is loaded with all sorts of furniture, etc. The* MOTHER *directs* TWO WORKMEN *who mime unloading and placing the articles.* SIMONE *sits, smokes, reads, and makes rapid notes.*

MOTHER A delightful cottage. Looks tight. I shall check for drafts. Bring in the furniture.

(SIMONE takes a fast glance and goes back to her reading; the minute a chair is placed she sits and continues.)

The bed there, the photos there, the commode there, the bureau there, the table there, the chairs here, the sofa there, the rug here, no the bed here out of the draft, now the rug back here, the bureau there, the desk here.
(She pays MOVERS. They exit.)

Simone, see the view from your desk. You'll be able to correct your papers while you watch the sun set. Be sure not to open the window when you work; it gives you pain in your neck. We'll all miss you and write every week. Take possession of your pupils; they're lucky to have you.

I've furnished your room. It's beautiful. See how well everything fits. Be well and happy and write every week. Do you like what I've done?

SIMONE *(taking cigarette out of her mouth)* It's beautiful, darling.

MOTHER You must keep well and let me know the minute anything happens. Don't catch cold, and try to remember to eat. Promise me you'll remember to eat.

SIMONE I promise, my darling mother, and I promise I'll write you both every week.

(MOTHER kisses SIMONE, then exits. SIMONE starts to speak but lights another cigarette and methodically rounds up all the furniture except desk, chair, and bed and pushes them over into the orchestra pit. Then she goes to sleep on the floor.)

Lights dim a moment—then come up bright morning. Her first class of girls is entering, chattering, and wondering about their new teacher.

ALL *Bonjour,* etc.

(SIMONE rises and waves her hand at them without looking; she's deep in thought.)

PUPIL Does that mean we're supposed to sit down?

(They push one another into the classroom, trying to suppress laughter and excitement. The men in the ENSEMBLE have assumed the position of desks—the girls each choose one and sit on his back.)

SIMONE *(pacing)* To teach or not to teach, that is the way to earn my bread. To teach or not to teach. That is the way to earn my soul. I hate to eat. What is feeding?

(During all this the GIRLS are secretly looking at her, making fun of her, sizing her up, passing notes and making gestures.)

Bonjour mes chers enfants. Bon. It's a good day. Did you see the sunrise?

(CLASS giggles.)

It's good to get up in time to see the sunrise. You all do it. You have to get to school on time.

CLASS *(bored)* *Bonjour, Mademoiselle.*

(They turn off and look out at the audience and stay very stiff while shuffling their feet and picking their ears, or secretly scratching their crotches.)

SIMONE I have some new ideas.

(Many groans from CLASS.)

They will stimulate your minds.

(Many more groans and stamping of feet. SIMONE walks around in agitation. STUDENTS watch her.)

Listen to me. If you won't bend a little, I'll have to smoke.

(CLASS *laughs and claps.*)
I'm fighting off lighting up a cigarette, because I'm trying to teach you.

CLASS *(sighs, mocking)* Ohhh!

SIMONE I've been educated in Paris.

CLASS *(sighs)* Oooo!

SIMONE I've been educated by your bourgeoisie to teach you to be like me, and if that is what you want, that is what you'll get.

STUDENT We knew that before we came. That's why we're here. How else will we get good jobs?

SIMONE At the same time that I teach you to be like what your parents expect, because I too love and respect my parents and wish to live up to what they respect, I do wish to make some innovations.

CLASS Not another innovation.

SIMONE What I as a teacher would like to do with my life is to try to work out with you as I'm working out with myself some of the things important to all of us. Since this class is concerned with the philosophy syllabus, what I'd like to do is to demonstrate to you how philosophy came into being as a name, as a way of thinking; I want you to know the history and the definition of it and not just the name "philosophy" that will be found one day written in your exercise books. I care to speak to you about how to live.

STUDENT *(laughs)* But we're already alive.

SIMONE Everywhere?

STUDENT Where's that.

SIMONE That is what we'll discover. Class dismissed for today.
(GIRLS *rise and exit—talking bewilderedly—then return. As they enter the classroom again, they push their desks closer to* SIMONE.)
SIMONE *Bonjour.*

CLASS *Bonjour (Hi—Hello, etc.)*

SIMONE Who wishes to hike this weekend?
(ALL *raise hands, with exclamations.*)
We're taking a difficult trail.
(*Still* ALL *raise hands, make sounds of assurance.*)
I think we'll have good weather, and I don't want to miss it before it gets too cold. I want you to begin to take yourselves more seriously as writers. It seems to me a good way to do this would be for you to see your work in print. Therefore, I've procured a printing press, and from now on all

compositions in philosophy will be printed. This will mean extra hours because you'll have to learn to run the printing press, but that will be a good lesson in physics and mathematics as it relates to work.

(GIRLS *run out while* MEN *become a printing press.* GIRLS *slide down a ramp, into the press—*MEN *stamp them as* GIRLS *triumphantly laugh and then run out to audience to read to them their bits of poems or philosophy. The actors should write or choose these things themselves. Each* GIRL *finds several audience members to speak to.*

After GIRLS *have reached as many audience members as possible, they gather at back of auditorium and begin their hike—over and through the audience.*)

SIMONE *on a hike with her pupils. They carry packs. They climb and struggle forward toward the stage.*

SIMONE   Let me carry that.

ONE   I can manage.

SIMONE   No, I'll carry your pack. The way is steep *(To another)* Give me yours, too.

TWO   Thank you, *Mademoiselle.* I don't see how you do it—you don't look that strong. *(To audience member)* Would you pass my pack across to her? Thank you.

SIMONE   This is how one becomes strong.

THREE   How does one become in love?

SIMONE   Love?

FOUR   We understand what you teach us about physics. Could you tell us about love.

SIMONE   Love?

ALL *(on stage now)*   Falling in love. Loving. Being in love. Is it good or bad?

THREE   I want to know love.

SIMONE   Love?

ALL   Love!

SIMONE   I have no advice to give you about love.

ALL   Yes. Yes.

SIMONE   I have no advice to give you about love.

ALL   But you must—you know all about calculus.

SIMONE   Love? No, I have no advice to give you but I must warn you: love is a very serious thing.

ALL *(expectant)* Yes, *Mademoiselle.*

SIMONE Love often means pledging one's own life and that of another human being forever. It always means that, unless one of the two treats the other as a plaything. In that case, a love is something odious. The essential point in love is this: one human being feels a vital need of another human being. The problem then arises of reconciling this need with freedom. A problem men have struggled with from time immemorial.

THREE But if one is in love and pledged forever, why would you want to be free?

SIMONE When I was your age, I was tempted to try to get to know love. I decided not to. I didn't want to commit my life in a direction impossible to foresee until I was sufficiently mature to know what I wish from life and what I expect from it.

FOUR But I want to know now.

SIMONE I'm not offering myself as an example; every life evolves by its own laws. But you might think about it. Love seems to me to involve an even more terrifying risk than blindly pledging one's own existence. I mean the risk, if one is the object of a profound love, of having absolute power over another human being. It's not that one should avoid love, but while you're very young, don't seek it, let it come and find you. Let's say hello to the mountains. There's new snow up there.
(They climb higher as SIMONE *walks back down mountain to her classroom. She finds several* SCHOOL BOARD MEMBERS *waiting for her.)*
HEAD OF BOARD *(holding four other* MEMBERS *in donkey reins)* Mademoiselle!
*(*SIMONE *walks in front of them reading a newspaper and puffing cigarette smoke like crazy.)*
SIMONE M-m-m-m-m-m-m-m. . .

BOARD *Mademoiselle* Instructor!

SIMONE M-m-m-m-m-m-m-m. . . *(continues to read and smoke).*

BOARD The board finds that you are not paying attention to the board.

MEN The board.

SIMONE M-m-m-m-m-m-m-m. . .

BOARD The board finds that you are not paying attention to the board.

MEN Attention!

SIMONE There is not enough time to pay attention to the students.

BOARD You smoke.

MEN Smoke!

SIMONE   Yes. . . *(starts making note and takes out a cigarette)*.

BOARD   You had the effrontery to print the students' work.

MEN   Work?

SIMONE   M-m-m-m-m-m-m-m. . . ?

BOARD   This is nothing but the work of students.
(They shake printed papers in front of her.)
MEN   Students!

SIMONE   It is the printed word.

BOARD   You were not authorized to print the work of nobodys.

MEN   Nobodys!

SIMONE   That is how they become somebodys.

BOARD   You are fired.

SIMONE   That is a fact I accepted in advance.
(The SCHOOL BOARD *exits in a chaos of entangled reins. Blackout.)*

SIMONE *at a new school. It is a tougher school than before—the* GIRLS *pretend to be blasé—no desks. They enter and stand around in what they think are tough, sophisticated poses.*
SIMONE   *Bonjour, Mesdemoiselles.*

CLASS   We don't want *Bonjour*. We want life.

SIMONE   First you must learn to think.

CLASS   We want to live.

SIMONE   What is living?

CLASS   Enjoyment of the now.

SIMONE   If you cannot think, you will be robbed of the riches of the past and the future. To live in the now is pleasurable, but to think in the past and future is necessary to the development of your person and your family; therefore your roots and your country.

CLASS   Teach us to think.

SIMONE   It is hard, but if you pay attention, hard things can bring you good. Who would like to hike with me this weekend?
(Some hands up.)
I have reports that there will be a break up of the ice, and possibly a flood. Who is strong enough to swim through the ice floes?
(Rest of hands up.)

Bon, meet me at the river bank at three in the morning, with a little food for the two days, and matches wrapped carefully so that we can dry ourselves out, if we have to swim or rescue anyone. How many again wish to go on the hike?

(All hands up.)

Bon. Girls are getting stronger. It's important. It's only through hard work that one understands one's intelligence.

GIRL *(delayed reaction)* Yeah.

(After much reluctance and teasing, they pull off their clothes and one by one dive into an ice river. One GIRL almost doesn't make it, but she's saved by another. They swim to high ground and put their clothes back on again. SIMONE *dresses and walks back to the classroom area.)*

SIMONE *walking and smoking in front of the* SCHOOL BOARD.

BOARD *Mademoiselle!*

SIMONE M-m-m-m-m-m-m-m. . .

BOARD *Mademoiselle,* You took the students on an unauthorized hike.

SIMONE A swim. . .

BOARD On an unauthorized swim under the most dangerous of conditions in the middle of winter.

SIMONE The sun was out.

BOARD There had been no permission granted by the school board or by the parents, and in fact you are to be considered under arrest for kidnapping.

SIMONE *(reading and walking and smoking)* M-m-m-m-m-m-m. . .

BOARD Three people caught pneumonia.

SIMONE Five were saved from drowning.

BOARD Your students saved by other students.

SIMONE An excellent experience in learning.

BOARD You have been noticed to smoke and read and not pay attention at teachers' meetings.

SIMONE M-m-m-m-m-m-m-m. . .

BOARD You are hereby fired for insubordination, and endangering the lives and the moral attitudes of your pupils. You are hereby separated from us, uh fired, uh terminated.

SIMONE *(walking and smoking)* M-m-m-m-m-m-m-m. . . It is the condition of my teaching.

BOARD MEMBER *(on way out)* And remove your coffee cup from the teachers' room.
(Exit.)

SIMONE *meets with her old teacher and master* ALAIN.
ALAIN I've been following your articles closely.

SIMONE They're only beginnings—I'm so awkward and confused.

ALAIN No, I've never had a pupil like you. Your power of thought is rare.

SIMONE All I have so far are hazy outlines and overweening ambitions.

ALAIN Simone, on the contrary, it's like a game for you. I want to see you turn from playing games with abstract subtleties and train yourself in direct analysis.

SIMONE I intend to. I'm going into the fields, I'm going into the factories, I'm going to study the relationship of the worker to his work. Modern science has lost its soul because it reasons only about conventional symbols—objects, they become objects by the fact that they are black marks on white paper, but which are universal by virtue of their definition. There should be a new way of conceiving mathematics—a way that its theoretical and practical value would no longer be distinct, but would reside in analogies. In man's struggle with the universe, symbols would thus be relegated back to their rank as mere instruments, and their real function would be revealed, which is not to assist the understanding but the imagination. Scientific work would thus be seen to be in fact artistic work—namely, the training of the imagination. It would be necessary to foster and develop to the maximum the faculty of conceiving analogies without making use of algebraic symbols.

ALAIN It sounds like an excellent project, but please, Simone, when you write about it, try to make your language more penetrable to the ordinary mind.

SIMONE I hope you'll excuse the confusion and disorder and also the audacity of my embryo ideas. If there is any value in them, it's clear that they could only be developed in silence. *(Hurriedly)* Also, I want to do a series of studies of the various existing forms of property, related to the idea that property consists, in reality, of the power to dispose of goods.
(Fade on ALAIN *as* SIMONE *walks into her room.)*

1934. Several ex-pupils come to visit SIMONE *in the factory town where she works.*
SIMONE How good to see you again.

ONE You didn't answer our letters.

TWO   We were worried.

THREE   Have you been ill?

SIMONE   Work in a factory isn't conducive to letter writing. How did you know where I was?

FOUR   The Derieu sisters.

SIMONE   Please don't tell anyone else. Promise me. This is the "contact with real life" we often talked about together.

ONE   But you're so frail.

SIMONE   Clumsy too, and slow, and not very robust.

TWO   How did they hire you?

ONE   There's no work these days.

SIMONE   One of my best friends knows the managing director of the company.

THREE   What's it like?

SIMONE   I'm glad to be working in a factory, but I'm equally glad not to be compulsorily committed to it. It's simply a year's leave for "private study."

(As the speech continues, the ENSEMBLE *enters and builds and becomes the factory and machines.* SIMONE *works at her machine, and the speed of her speech builds with the speed of her work.)*

If a man is very skilled, very intelligent, and very tough, there is just a chance, in the present conditions of French industry, for him to attain a factory job, which offers interesting and humanly satisfying work; even

Her visitors become machine parts.

so, these opportunities are becoming fewer every day, thanks to technical progress. But the women! The women are restricted to purely mechanical labor—Nothing is required of them but speed. . .

The machines begin to work in earnest.

When I say mechanical labor, don't imagine that it allows for daydreaming, much less reflection or thought. No. No. The tragedy is that, although the work is too mechanical to engage the mind, it prevents one from thinking of anything else. If you think, you work more slowly:

The machines slow down and are silent.

BARITONE *(sings)*
   SPEED, SPEED, SPEED
   SPEED, SPEED, SPEED
   SPEED, OR THE SACK
   SPEED, DON'T TALK BACK

SPEED, SPEED, SPEED
IF YOU WISH TO FEED.

(speaks) Hurry up, Simone, you made only six hundred yesterday. If you make eight hundred today, maybe I won't fire you.

The machines abruptly speed again.

SIMONE I still can't achieve the required speeds. I'm not familiar with the work, I'm innately awkward. I'm naturally slow moving, my head aches, and then I have a peculiar inveterate habit of thinking, which I can't shake off. Believe me, they would throw me out if I wasn't protected by influence. Theoretically, with the eight-hour day, one should have leisure, but really one's leisure hours are swallowed up by a fatigue which often amounts to a dazed stupor. Also, life in the factory involves a perpetual humiliating subordination, forever at the orders of foremen.

THREE How can you stand the suffering?

SIMONE I do suffer from it, but I'm more glad than I can say to be where I am. I've wanted it for I-don't-know-how-many years.

The ENSEMBLE *slowly breaks up the giant machine and exits, but* SIMONE *continues to work as she speaks.*

But I'm not sorry I didn't do it sooner, because it's only at my age now that I can extract all the profit there is in the experience. Above all, I feel I've escaped from a world of abstractions, to find myself among real men— some good and some bad, but with *real* goodness or badness. Goodness especially, when it exists in a factory, is something real. The least act of kindness, from a mere smile to some little service, calls for victory over fatigue and the obsession with pay—all the overwhelming influences which drive a man in on himself. Thought then calls for an almost miraculous effort of rising above the conditions of one's life. Because it's not like at a university, where one is paid to think, or pretend to think. In a factory one is paid not to think. So, if you ever recognize a gleam of intelligence, you can be sure it is genuine. Besides, I really find the machines themselves highly attractive and interesting.

As members of ENSEMBLE *arrive very slowly with real machines which they carry or manipulate,* SIMONE *exits, as if in a trance. The* ENSEMBLE *members stare and work their machines as if the machines were controlling them. Slow fade.*

The OLD LADIES *pull the cord attached to one cherub. The belly opens and jewels made of jello and candy tumble out, showering the audience.*

Act II

SIMONE *enters with materials for letter. As she speaks the* ENSEMBLE *work out math forms (i.e. equations or symbols) with their bodies.*

SIMONE I need a physicist. I really need a physicist. Dearest Brother, please ask a physicist in America the following question: Planck justifies the introduction of quanta of energy by the assimilation of entropy to a probability (strictly, the logarithm of a probability): because, in order to calculate the probability of a macroscopic state of a system, it is necessary to postulate a finite number of corresponding microscopic states (discrete states). So the justification is that the calculus of probabilities is numerical. But why was it not possible to use a continuous calculus of probabilities, with generalized number instead of discrete numbers (considering that there are games of chance in which probability is continuous)? There would then have been no need of quanta. Why couldn't this have been tried? Planck says nothing about it. T. does not know of any physicist here who could enlighten me. What do you think about this?

The ENSEMBLE *recites theories, goes into the audience to lecture them. Each actor should make up his own, outrageous theories or speculations. The* ENSEMBLE *says to each other and the audience: "What do you think about this?" as they exit.*

SIMONE Your reply about Planck did not satisfy me. Have you read St. John of the Cross?

Blackout. ENSEMBLE *stays in auditorium aisles walking back and forth resolutely with eyes closed whispering: "You don't interest me."*

SOPRANO You don't interest me.

BARITONE You don't interest me.

SOPRANO I can't see you.

BARITONE You can't see me.

SOPRANO I look right through you. I look right through you because when I look, there is nothing there to see.

BARITONE You don't interest me.
You don't interest me.
A Pharisee interests me more than how
Definitely
You don't interest me.

(SIMONE *on stage. This is her inside now: it slowly comes out as the* SINGERS *sing, she passes people; as she passes them, she "fixes" on them. They feel it, and begin to reach out to her as if in a trance. They stop short of touching, but their eyes stay locked.*)

CHORUS

YOU HAVE NOTHING FOR ME.
I WALK RIGHT THROUGH YOU
YOU DON'T EVEN BORE ME
I'VE NEVER HEARD YOU.

SIMONE *(into mike)* No one can say you don't interest me, without showing grave cruelty and profound injustice to the uniqueness of the individual soul.

(The ENSEMBLE *actors move up onto the stage and form moving human structures two and three people high.)*

SIMONE There is something sacred in every person.

CHORUS There is something sacred in every person.

SIMONE But it is not his person.

CHORUS But it is not his person. Not his person? Not his person? But if not his person, then what is sacred in every person, if it is not his person?

SIMONE It isn't his personality.

CHORUS How can we sell him.

SIMONE It isn't his personality, the personality he carries in his person.

CHORUS But that's the package.

SIMONE So much baggage.

CHORUS Give me a good personality any day, and I can come with him in every way.

SIMONE So much baggage.

SOPRANO I agree with the chorus.

SIMONE So much baggage.

BARITONE I wouldn't mind for a while to carry the chorus for an extra mile.

SIMONE Not his person, nor his thoughts that I don't know.
Not his person, nor the way his arms grow.
Not his person, nor the way his eye is lit.
Not his person, but his total sacredness of it.
His presence. His presence that hurts us
when we must do without it.

CHORUS His presence when we must do without it. King, Queen, father, father, mother, mother, sister, brother, friend, friend, friend, when you are gone and we have to live without your other.

SIMONE Personality: Human personality means nothing to me. Personality isn't what's sacred to me. If it did, I could easily put out the eyes of anyone as Oedipus did his own. He still had exactly the same personality as before. I wouldn't have touched the person in him, I would only have destroyed his eyes. What is it? What is it that prevents me from putting out that man's eyes if I'm allowed to do it and if I feel like doing it?

CHORUS Put out his eyes. Burn his thighs. Put out his tongue, put it in Washington where it belongs on the heaps of the other rotting dungs of tongues.

(SIMONE *addresses audience, while human pyramids made by the actors begin slowly to revolve:*)

The whole of your being is sacred to me, each one of you. But you are not sacred in all respects nor from every point of view. You are not sacred because of your long bright hair, or your thick wrists, or your strong long arms, or your kind heart, or the twinkle in your knowing eye, or even because your thoughts don't interfere with mine—none of these facts could keep me from hurting you without the knowledge that if I were to put out your eyes, your soul would be lacerated by knowing the pain, and the fact that *harm* was being done to you

CHORUS

AT THE BOTTOM OF YOUR HEART
FROM THE TIME YOU'RE A BABE
THOUGH YOU GROW MILES APART
FROM THE PEOPLE THROUGH WHICH
YOU WERE MADE

DUET

YOU EXPECT. YOU EXPECT. YOU EXPECT.

SOPRANO

WITH THE CERTAINTY AND THE LIGHT
WHEN THE SPERM ENTERED THE EGG.

BARITONE

YOU EXPECT TO GO ON BEING REMADE
   AS THE FIRST
ECSTASY OF THE TRINITY WHEN
YOU WERE MADE.

(*Pyramids disassemble and* ENSEMBLE *goes into Dance formations.*)

CHORUS

YOU WERE MADE
YOU WERE MADE

SOPRANO

YOU WERE MADE IN ECSTASY

BARITONE

LYING DOWN OR STANDING UP,

SOPRANO

CROSSED HORIZONS OR AGAINST THE G.E.

BARITONE

YOU WERE LAID AS YOU WERE MADE.

CHORUS

ECSTASY. ECSTASY. ECSTASY.

SIMONE (*tough and strong*) There is something in all of us that goes on indomitably *expecting,* in the teeth of all experience of crimes committed, suffered, and witnessed, that good.

CHORUS (*softly*)
GOOD. GOOD.

SIMONE That good and not evil will be done to you. It is this faith above all that is sacred in every human being.

ALL woo!
(*Begin to dance.*)

CHORUS (*like a thirties musical*)
THIS ABOVE ALL,
THIS ABOVE ALL,
THIS ABOVE ALL,
LEARN TO WALK IN HIGHER HEELS
THIS ABOVE ALL, BABY
THIS ABOVE ALL
LEARN TO WALK LIKE YOU OWN
   THE WORLD
(*Simone exits.*)

LEARN HOW TO KICK AND FLY
LEARN HOW TO FLY
   WITHOUT GETTING SICK
LEARN HOW TO THROW AWAY THE STICK
WHAT YOU DO IS SHOVE IT UP THEIR ASS
IT'S ESPECIALLY GOOD
   WHEN THEY RUN OUT OF GAS
AND YOU WANT NERVE
TO CARRY THE VERVE
AND SHOW THOSE NIPPLES
LET THEM RIPPLE
THIS ABOVE ALL
GET AS TALL AS YOU CAN BEFORE
THE GEESE BEGIN
   TO STEP ALL OVER YOU AND
WHEN YOU FALL
WHEN YOU FALL BABY
PRACTICE HOW TO DO IT WITH A SMILE.

MEGAN TERRY

I'D WALK A MILLION MILES
FOR ONE OF YOUR LUCKIES
MY BUCKY LITTLE RAG-TIME
   SON-OF-A-BITCH
YOU WITCH
THIS WAS THE DAYS BEFORE GARY
LEARNED TO SWITCH HIS HORSE
AND COCAINE WAS RUNNING A CLOSE
SECOND TO ANYONE'S OPIUM DREAM,
   IT'S A SCREAM
BUT THIS ABOVE ALL,
THIS ABOVE ALL, LEARN HOW
TO LOOK LIKE YOU'RE TALL.
THE FALL IS FUNNIER.
THE FALL IS FUNNIER WHEN YOU FALL
   RIGHT OFF THAT WALL.
OH BE TALL.
THERE MIGHT BE A LIGHT
   OUTSIDE THE GATE,
DON'T YOU SEE IT.
THERE MIGHT BE A LIGHT
   OUTSIDE THE GATE,
DON'T YOU SEE IT.
LET'S BURN GIN TO THAT.
WE NEED A LIGHT TO SHOW
WE'RE RIGHT,
WE'RE RIGHT
BECAUSE WE KNOW IN THE
BOTTOMS OF YOUR CUPS
THAT MIGHT CAN'T CONQUER RIGHT,
THAT MIGHT CAN'T CONQUER RIGHT, ETC.
(softer under next two lines)

BARITONE
THERE IS NO WAR ON.
THERE IS NO WAR ON.
(Blackout.)

Series of rapid scenes:
Out of work MEN *of the town are pounding huge stones with sledge*
hammers.

SIMONE Why are you cracking the rocks?

ONE We have to.

SIMONE Are you going to build a wall or a garden.

TWO We're out of work.

SIMONE What do you mean you're out of work, you're working harder than I do.

THREE We have to do this or they won't give us our unemployment checks.

SIMONE Give me one of those and I'll help you.
(She stands beside the MEN *and though she's slower, she still works. Then* ALL *run to the next scene.)*

In the factory. The WORKERS *are having a sit-in. They sit on the floor, arms linked and swaying, singing the end of "The International."* SIMONE *is there too, arms linked with the* WORKERS, *between two men,* TWO MEN *in charge of running the factory are conferring with one another as the song ends. They turn and shout at the* WORKERS.

MANAGER ONE Seven percent increase.

WORKERS Fifteen.

MANAGER TWO Seven percent.

WORKERS *Fifteen.*
(They yell this back and forth in mounting crescendo. Moment of silence.)
WORKERS Fifteen and a joint committee of workers and management.

MANAGER ONE I'll hire and fire whom I choose.

WORKERS Joint committee or no work done. Joint committee or no work done.

MANAGER TWO We'll close down the factory.

MANAGER ONE We'll close down the factory—that will put some sense into you.

WORKERS Good, good, good. Close down the factory and we'll take it over and run it ourselves. We run this factory ourselves anyway.

MANAGER ONE This is a gross infringement of liberty.

WORKERS We want fifteen percent more.

MANAGER TWO You make me sick.

WORKERS Fifteen! Fifteen! Fifteen! Fifteen! We'll make you sick, all right.
(Go for the managers' throats—then immediately transform into COMRADES *at a meeting.)*

A political meeting of leftist coalition parties.
SIMONE *(addressing the crowd)* Friends and fellow workers. Some of us have been greatly troubled and alarmed by news of the continuing purge

in Russia. I'm afraid that in this struggle that begins to look like the classic struggle between the conservatives and the innovators the value of life is being forgotten. The conservatives do not know what to conserve, and the innovators do not know what to innovate—

VOICE   Revisionists! Traitorous revisionists!

SIMONE   Please, I ask you to pay one more minute of attention. It's true so far as we know it that Stalin's lieutenant S. M. Kirov was murdered. But Stalin is using this crime as a tool against many comrades who fought and sacrificed many long years to bring Marxist-Leninist concepts into being. If he is allowed to continue unchecked in this "purge," there will be no chance for the dictatorship of the proletariat, because all his brothers will have been eliminated resulting in the dictatorship of one man, Joseph Stalin. We must show him that there is a world of opinion, considered and humane opinion by his brothers in other countries that condemn his actions, that he must cease and desist in this cruel persecution—

ONE   Traitor! She's a Trotskyite.
(Some people walk out.)
TWO   The purge is just and moral. Those men were working with the Germans to overthrow Stalin and so are you. I denounce Simone as a Trotskyite!

THREE   Get her.

FOUR   Beat her up.
(They move slowly toward her.)
FIVE   Smash her mouth.

SIX   Don't let her open it again.

SEVEN   Kill her.

SIMONE   I'm not a Trotskyite, I belong to no party. I am against totalitarianism in all its forms. If this "purge" continues in Russia, Stalin will succeed in creating a monolithic totalitarian unity and it will be an end to Lenin's ideals and an end to people's democracy.

EIGHT   Get her. Trotskyite!
(They grab her. NINE and a small group of friends holding two guns surround SIMONE to protect her.)
TEN   I support Stalin.

ELEVEN   Shut that Trotskyite's trap.

SIMONE   I'm not a Trotskyite, I'm a Frenchman.

NINE   Simone, comrade, stay in the middle of us. We'll get you out safely.

TWELVE   You're a Trotskyite and you're a Jew!

(With some brief scuffling, they get her out of the meeting.)
Outside the meeting, SIMONE *is talking with* MAN *who rescued her.*

SIMONE   Thank you, Pierre. I'll never forget your kindness and your bravery.

PIERRE   Those Communist fanatics want to drive us into war. You know that during the general strike they were working on the side of management to *prevent our* strike!

SIMONE   I know, because they want all the armaments built as soon as possible to speed up the prospect of war. Well, I'm going off to fight in a war, a just war. I've decided to go to Spain. At least *there,* my one more pair of hands might be useful.

PIERRE   Be careful your rifle doesn't backfire on you, you're not so clever with your hands.

SIMONE   Don't worry. I'm a pacifist. I'll never carry a rifle, there's other work to do.

(Blackout.)

SIMONE *in Spain: on the banks of the Ebro River. The Anarchist forces she has joined are on one side and Fascist forces are on the other. Sound of airplane overhead.*

CAPTAIN   Get that plane!

(The SQUADRON, *including* SIMONE, *who does have a rifle in hand, begin to shoot.* SIMONE *lies on her back and shoots straight up into the air.)*

The pisser's flying too high.

(Sound of small bomb exploding.)

At least their bombs are getting smaller. That means we're winning.

(A small squad of MEN *come in dragging* TWO PRIESTS.)*

ONE   Captain! Captain! Look what we found hiding in the rushes on the river bank.

CAPTAIN   This will make forty priests we've shot. *(He points at one of them)* Kneel with your head in prayer.

(The other MEN *laugh;* SIMONE *lowers her rifle. The* CAPTAIN *shoots the* PRIEST. *He falls forward and dies, crying out "Jesus" in Spanish.)*

CAPTAIN *(to the* SECOND PRIEST)   We're going to let you go, so you can tell the rest of your brothers to get the hell out of our country. Get going, on the double.

(As the PRIEST *turns, he shoots him too. The* MEN *laugh again.* SIMONE *throws down her rifle.)*

MEGAN TERRY

Squadron. Attention! We're going out on patrol. The Fascists are just across the river, and at dawn we're going to start picking them off. Simone?

SIMONE I'll stay in camp and cook.

TWO *(sotto voce, to a comrade)* Thank God, she's so awkward with a gun, she'll kill one of us one day.

CAPTAIN Good, you stay and deep-fry me some of those chickens we commandeered. I haven't had fresh meat in two months.

(They march off stealthily. SIMONE *puts a pot of oil on the fire. Another* WOMAN *helps her peel vegetables to throw into the oil. They pluck chickens.)*

SIMONE Atrocities. On both sides.

WOMAN *(laughing)* Did you see how the other thought God had saved his life?

SIMONE How can you laugh at a thing like that?

WOMAN It was funny. Did you see the look on his face after the bullet hit his head?

SIMONE This isn't our war. This is nothing but a war fought by Germany against Russia. We're fools and pawns.

(She's so angry she hits the pot of oil so hard that it spills over onto her leg. She screams and falls.)

WOMAN Oh, my God, your leg is burning.

(She runs out screaming for help.)

SIMONE *alone in a field hospital reciting math formulas to avoid the pain. Her* FATHER *and* MOTHER *rush on.*

FATHER Simone, my precious.

MOTHER Simone, my own.

FATHER It's taken us a month to find you.

MOTHER *(not daring to look)* How bad?

FATHER What butcher has been tending you? This dressing hasn't been changed in a week, half the flesh is exposed. *(He brings things out of his bag, gives her a sedative.)* Here, this will still the pain.

SIMONE I'm getting used to it.

MOTHER We'll take her home to recover.

SIMONE No, no, father, I have to rejoin my unit.

FATHER I'm your father and your doctor and you'll do as I say. Let's get a stretcher.

(MOTHER *and* FATHER *exit.*)

SIMONE *is alone in her room.*
Visitation.

SIMONE My spirit is sick. Do I have a spirit. Pains in the throat, double pains. I can't swallow but I feel constantly that I'll vomit. My spine. My spine is sick. I can't work and that makes me sicker. Not to be able to work. No work. Work beating in my head, but my hands refuse to close around a pencil, my mind won't work for me, but something in me is working, and I'm so sick and weak. The struggle against this stupid body is getting too much to bear. I've got to think my way out of it but I can't think. My God, my God, I can't think. I can't move, out of this bed, my God I can't stand. I can't walk. I can't think, I can't think, this stupid pain. My God. My God, I need something. I need something. I need my work. I need to work. Any work. I'd cry for joy to be able to bend in the dirt and pick up potatoes till my back ached from work. Honest work, not the work of fighting this endless headache. I'll try to vomit. I'll get it out, I'll vomit out the illness. Oh my God, can't I get any light into my head? My God! My God! My God!

(*The* ENTIRE CAST *comes on stage and lifts* SIMONE *up, giving her a total caress. They hum. They take her pain into their bodies, until all but five who lift her up to God are feeling the pain that she had.*

As they lift SIMONE, *they take her clothes off, and as the clothes fall, other actors put them on, continuing a pain centered at a point in the body the garment covers. They lift her straight up if they can, her arms outstretched, smiling with her eyes closed.*

They put her down and exit.)

LOVE III.
The Poem of George Herbert

SIMONE (*transfixed, warmed, and filled with divine love, sings*)
LOVE BADE ME WELCOME
    YET MY SOUL DREW BACK,
    GUILTY OF DUST AND SINNE.
BUT QUICK-EY'D LOVE,
    OBSERVING ME GROW SLACK
    FROM MY FIRST ENTRANCE IN,
DREW NEARER TO ME,
    SWEETLY QUESTIONING,
    IF I LACK'D ANY THING

A GUEST, I ANSWER'D,
    WORTHY TO BE HERE:
    LOVE SAID, YOU SHALL BE HE.
I THE UNKINDE, UNGRATEFULL?
    AH MY DEARE,
    I CANNOT LOOK ON THEE.
LOVE TOOK MY HAND,
    AND SMILING DID REPLY,
    WHO MADE THE EYES BUT I?

TRUTH LORD, BUT I HAVE MARR'D THEM:
    LET MY SHAME GO WHERE
    IT DOTH DESERVE.
AND KNOW YOU NOT, SAYES LOVE,
    WHO BORE THE BLAME?
    MY DEARE, THEN I WILL SERVE.
YOU MUST SIT DOWN, SAYES LOVE,
    AND TASTE MY MEAT:
    SO I DID SIT AND EAT.

(ENSEMBLE *dancers enter and dance with* SIMONE, *while the* CHORUS *sings:*)
Song for SIMONE, OPERA SINGERS, CHORUS *and* DANCERS.

I BELIEVE GOD CREATED
SO HE COULD BE LOVED
GOD CREATED TO BE LOVED
GOD CREATED AROUND AND ABOVE
SO THAT HE, GOD COULD BE LOVED.

BUT GOD CAN'T CREATE GOD
GOD CAN'T CREATE ANYTHING TO BE GOD

BUT GOD CANNOT BE LOVED BY ANYTHING
WHICH ISN'T GOD, GOD NEEDS
GOD TO SING
GOD NEEDS GOD TO SING TO HIM OF HIS LOVE
    OF GOD FOR GOD
GOD NEEDS GOD TO LOVE HIM INTO GOD.

THIS IS A CONTRADICTION!
NOT A FICTION BUT A PERFECT
A PERFECT, AN EXACT CONTRADICTION.
I HAVE THE CONVICTION.
THAT THIS CONTRADICTION
CONTAINS IN ITSELF NECESSITY ITSELF.
THIS IS NOT PERVERSITY

THIS IS NOT MIND PLAY
OR PLAY OF MIND
BUT THIS IS A PERFECT CONTRADICTION
CONTRADICTION CREATES ACTION
THIS IS A CONTRADICTION THAT DEFINES
NECESSITY. NECESSITY. *NECESSITY!*

BUT EVERY CONTRADICTION
HAS THE CONDITION OF RESOLVING
ITSELF THROUGH THE PROCESS
THROUGH THE PROCESS
THROUGH THE PROCESS OF
BECOMING, BECOMING, BECOMING,
BECOMING, *BECOMING!*

GOD CREATED ME TO SEE THE SEA
AND TO LOVE HIM
AND TO LOVE HIM
"I"—"I"—"I" THIS FINITE BEING
I THIS THIS "I"
"I"AND "I," THIS LITTLE "I"
I CAN'T LOVE GOD
UNTIL
UNTIL, THROUGH THE ACTION OF GRACE
THAT TAKES OVER THE EMPTY SPACE
OF MY TOTAL SOUL—
THE GRACE THAT FILLS MY SOUL
THE GRACE TO MAKE ME WHOLE WITH GOD.

AND AS THE LITTLE "I" DISAPPEARS
GOD LOVES HIMSELF
GOD LOVES HIMSELF

BY MY GIVING UP MY "I"
AS I BECOME NOT "I"
AS I CANNOT SEE THE SKY, NOR BE THE SKY
GOD LOVES ME AS I DISAPPEAR
I GIVE GOD TO GOD AND
AND GOD LOVES HIMSELF
AS THE PROCESS GOES ON FOREVER
THEREFORE GOD
HAS CREATED TIME
TIME IS INDIFFERENT TO ME,
THERE IS ALL THE TIME
IN MY SHORT WORLD

MEGAN TERRY

537

FOR ME TO BECOME NOT ME
SO THAT GOD
SO THAT GOD CAN LOVE HIMSELF
THIS
THIS
THIS
THIS
THIS
THIS IS THE NECESSITY, THE NECESSITY,
THE NECESSITY.
  NECESSITY!

A police station, three POLICEMEN *and a* SECRETARY.

ONE   It's been reported that you are a Gaulliste.

TWO   You were seen distributing *Témoignage chrétien.*

THREE   An illegal paper.

SIMONE   It has a higher literary style than the government censors.

TWO   So you admit to this underground activity.

SIMONE   I admit that I read everything I can get my hands on.

ONE   If you don't tell us who the rest of your comrades are . . .

TWO   You'll go to prison.

THREE   And I'll personally see that you, a teacher of philosophy, will be put into the same cells as the prostitutes.

ONE   As the prostitutes.

SIMONE   Why I've always wanted to know about such circles of women. It will be a very good opportunity to get to know them. Yes, please do send me to jail.

TWO   She's crazy.

THREE   She's crazy, no professor of philosophy would want to associate with filthy prostitutes.

SIMONE   But I would. It's a subject I haven't had time to study yet.

ONE   Release the prisoner. She's crazy.
(Blackout.)

SIMONE *arrives in Marseilles and goes to the Dominican monastery where she can ask a* PRIEST *who is helping people to get out of the country for work while she waits to get out too. There are several* PEOPLE *before her, one is in his office and is just leaving.*

MAN   Thank you for getting me the passport, Father, it's saved my life.

FATHER *(a warm man with natural charm)*   Safe journey and God bless, my son.

SIMONE *(enters shyly)*   Excuse me, Father. I hate to take away from your valuable time, but I need some sort of work, preferably manual labor, where I can fade into a group. Is there any farm work about, perhaps the grape harvest?

FATHER   My child, you look so frail, I hardly. . .

SIMONE   I'm not as frail as I look—I've worked in factories.

FATHER   You don't speak like a factory worker.

SIMONE   You know about the laws: we're not allowed to work. My family and I are bound for Morocco on our way to the States. I want to work to occupy my time.

FATHER   Are you sure you can manage. The sun's hot.

SIMONE   Good.

FATHER   I have a friend, just outside of town who might take you on. . .

SIMONE   Thank you Father . . . Father . . . may I come to speak with you sometime again. . .

FATHER   I'm taken up with many duties besides my clerical ones—so many people are being hounded down by the police, so many people need help · and advice.

SIMONE   I'd like to speak to you about Christ.

(They freeze, walk in a circle. She hesitantly approaches him again.)

SIMONE   After working in the factories, I finally understood affliction. I began to see myself as a slave and I was often able to rise above the physical affliction of my headaches. Then in a Chapel in Solesmes where I'd gone to hear the Gregorian music at Easter I was able to listen to the music in spite of pain. By an extreme effort of attention I was able to get outside this miserable flesh, leaving it to suffer by itself, and I found a pure and perfect joy in the unspeakable beauty of the chanting and the words. During the time I was there I also met a young man, a messenger I think of him now, who introduced me to George Herbert's poem "Love." From then on whenever my headache would reach a painful crisis, I would recite this poem fixing all my attention on it, clinging with all my soul to the tenderness it enshrines. One day, while saying this poem with all my attention, Christ Himself came down and He took possession of me.

FATHER   Did you see Him?

SIMONE No, it was the presence of love, of infinite love, a certainty of love, a love which I have never sought and which I'd never thought existed.

FATHER My child, are you seeking Catholic instruction?

SIMONE I don't wish Baptism.

FATHER But that is complete union.

SIMONE I prefer to stand at the door of the church.

FATHER Then you're still a long way from Christianity.
(Again they freeze, walk in a small circle, relax, and she approaches him again.)

SIMONE Every day before I go out to harvest I say the "Our Father" in Greek. I try to do this with the utmost attention and if I do, Christ comes nearer to me now than He did that first time.

FATHER It gives me joy to see the light growing within you.
(They freeze, she kneels and says the Pater Noster in Greek, or any language the actress would like. Then she stands. They approach each other again.)

FATHER My child, you suffer too much from your former intellectual life. You're confusing reality with distortions of it. I feel you're hardest and most severe in your judgments on that which could touch you the most.

SIMONE I have to beware of you. Friendship and the power of suggestion is what I'm most susceptible to.

FATHER But Baptism is—

SIMONE I don't want to belong to any groups. I want to be invisible, so that I can move among all groups. I'm suspicious of structures, and especially the structure of the Catholic Church, it has been totalitarian since the time of the Roman Empire.

FATHER You're still locked into the narrow philosophy of Spinoza.

SIMONE I'd never read any of the mystics till my love of Christ, but now I see that Dionysus and Osiris are an early form of Christ. The *Bhagavad-Gita* when read aloud is a marvelous Christian sound. Yes, even Plato was a mystic. I see the *Iliad* now as bathed in Christian light.

FATHER Your early intellectual training and culture are keeping you from contemplating the true mysteries of the Church dogma. Baptism is a complete union.

SIMONE I want to thank you for bearing with me for so long. I'd never really considered the problem of Baptism as a practical one before. I'm sorry to withhold from you what would give you the greatest joy, but God has other uses for me. If I felt His command to be baptized, I would come running at once. For now I think God doesn't want me in the Church, perhaps at the moment of death. . .

FATHER It's my only concern that you stay in readiness. . .

SIMONE I could only say all this to you because I'm leaving tomorrow. Goodbye, you've been a father and a brother to me . . . It's impossible to think of you without thinking of God.
(*Exit.*)

Outside a Harlem church. Sounds of Gospel music.

CLAIRE We're the only white people here. Are you sure we won't offend?

SIMONE I've been to a different church in Harlem every Sunday since I arrived in New York.

CLAIRE I'm a bit uneasy.

SIMONE Are you my friend?

CLAIRE Yes, you know it; we've talked for days and nights together.

SIMONE Will you be my friend?

CLAIRE We're going to get back to France together; we're going to sabotage the Nazis together.

SIMONE Come, let's enter this church of God.

(CLAIRE *presses Simone's hand and they enter the church together. A song is ending and they sit in first row of auditorium.*)

PREACHER Brothers and Sisters, let us pray for our President. Let us pray for our great President Franklin Delano Roosevelt. He faces trying times in this terrible war. The people on the East is attacking us, and the people in the West is attacking us. Brothers and Sisters, let us pray to Jesus to help our President in these terrible times so that with the help of You, oh Lord, and Your chosen Son, Jesus, our President Roosevelt can make peace all over God's great, green and beautiful garden.
Give yourself up to the power of Our Lord,
Give yourself up to the power of Our Lord,
If you ever gonna find yourself
You got to give yourself up,
Give yourself up to the power of Our Lord.

PREACHER (*sings*)
BROTHERS AND SISTERS
BROTHERS AND SISTERS
WHAT SEX IS JESUS?
WHAT SEX IS GOD?

CHORUS (*repeats and claps*)
WHAT SEX IS JESUS:

WHAT SEX IS GOD?

PREACHER

WHAT SEX WAS MARY?
WHAT SEX WAS SAUL
   AFTER HE CHANGED HIS NAME TO PAUL?
JESUS LETS US INTO HIM
BOTH MEN AND WOMEN
JESUS LETS US INTO HIM
BOTH SAINTS AND SINNIN'

MALE SINGER Simone, Simone, Simone. Your body is women and your head talks to God. *(Brings* SIMONE *on stage.)*

CHORUS

JESUS HAD A PRICK
HE DIDN'T USE TO FUCK WITH
BUT PENETRATING THE WATERS
HE MADE ENOUGH FISHES TO
   FEED THE MULTITUDE
WITHOUT LICKING ESSENTIAL OILS, JESUS
MADE BREAD WITHOUT AN OVEN
HE FED A THOUSAND DOZENS

CLAIRE Simone, I feel I have to leave. I'm overcome with emotion. I feel I might dissolve. Let's go before I can't control myself any longer.

SIMONE Get up with the congregation. Let's go with them to Jesus.

CLAIRE I'm afraid.

SIMONE You're ready to face the Nazis, but you're still not ready to approach God?

(They rise and join the congregation, who are singing and jitterbugging and throwing themselves into a trance with their closeness to the Lord.)
(A woman leaps up from the congregation. She is possessed and sings. The CHORUS *echoes her.)*

WOMAN

OH LORD, OH LORD, OH LORD
I'M OPENING UP FOR YOU
OH LORD, OH LORD,
I'M READY TO RECEIVE
MY JESUS,
OH JESUS, SON OF GOD,
I'LL DO YOU RIGHT
OH JESUS, SON OF GOD,
I'LL DO RIGHT TO YOU

MY ARMS ARE OPEN
MY ARMS ARE OPEN
OH LORD, OH JESUS,
I'LL GIVE IT ALL BACK TO YOU.
TAKE MY HANDS
TAKE MY FEET

(Repeat all the parts of the body till end of scene.)

CHORUS

SHE'S A JESUS LADY
SHE'S A JESUS LADY
WHAT SEX IS JESUS?
JESUS DONE ENTERED HER
JESUS DONE ENTERED HER
JESUS DONE ENTERED HER

PREACHER

SHE'S A JESUS LADY
SHE'S A JESUS LADY
SHE'S A JESUS LADY
RIGHT NOW AND FOREVERMORE.

(Exit.)

French headquarters in England.
As this scene progresses it should be as if SIMONE *is visiting a series of offices.*
Each official, and, if possible, his secretary too, gets taller and fatter,
until the final one is a giant figure somewhat like De Gaulle.
     On screens and slides, on scrolls, that come down, from projections,
etc., we should see films and stills of people in their death agonies.

SIMONE *Bonjour, mon cher ami,* It's good to see you again. I had no idea
how long it would take me to get to London.

MAN Did you go to America?

SIMONE Only because I thought it would be a faster way to get here, so
that I can be of service to France. It took much longer than I'd hoped.

MAN Your parents?

SIMONE They wanted to escape from the anti-Semitism without being
separated from me. I've come to offer you my services to work for France.
I distributed one of the most important clandestine publications in the
free zone, *Les Cahiers du témoignage chrétien.* But when I was there, I
was consoled by sharing the suffering of my country. I've come back to
offer myself, because France's misfortunes hurt me much more at a distance
than when I was there. Leaving was like tearing up my roots. But I only
left in the hope that I could take a bigger and more effective part in the
efforts, dangers and sufferings of this great struggle. I have an idea.

MAN Perhaps you'd like to explain it to the Captain?

CAPTAIN *(enters and bows)* *Mademoiselle.*

SIMONE I have an idea.

CAPTAIN *Bon,* they are needed.

SIMONE This idea will save the lives of many soldiers.

CAPTAIN *Bon.*

SIMONE Many needless deaths happen on the battlefield due to the lack of immediate care, cases of shock, exposure, loss of blood.

CAPTAIN Correct.

SIMONE Please consider it seriously, I want to work in secret operations, preferably dangerous.

CAPTAIN Perhaps you should speak to the major. *(Exits.)*

MAJOR *(enters)* *Mademoiselle.*

SIMONE I really believe I can be useful. I appeal to you as a comrade to get me out of this painful moral situation. A lot of people don't understand why it's a painful moral situation, but you certainly do. We had a great deal in common when we were students together. It gave me a real joy to learn that you have such an important position in London. I'm relying on you.

MAJOR We can certainly use your brilliant mind. You were first in your class.

SIMONE I want action. Here's the idea: create a special body of front-line nurses.

MAJOR Of women?

SIMONE *(nods and hurries on)* It would be a very mobile organization and should always be at the points of greatest danger.

MAJOR But the horrors of war at the front—

SIMONE —are so distinct today in everyone's imagination that one can regard any woman who is capable of volunteering for such work as being very probably capable of performing it.

MAJOR But they risk certain death.

SIMONE They would need to have a good deal of courage. They would need to offer their lives as a sacrifice.

MAJOR But we have never put our women in such danger. That's why we men leave for the front to defend our homes and families.

SIMONE   There is no reason to regard the life of a woman, especially if she has passed her first youth without marrying or having children, as more valuable than a man's life. All the less so if she has accepted the risk of death.

MAJOR   But how to regulate . . .

SIMONE   Simply make mothers, wives and girls below a certain age ineligible.

MAJOR   I'm considering the idea.

SIMONE   The moral support would be inestimable. They would comfort the men's last moments, they would mitigate by their presence and their words the agony of waiting for the arrival of the stretcher-bearers. You must understand the essential role played in the present war by moral factors. They count for very much more than in past wars. It's one of the main reasons for Hitler's successes that he was the first to see this.

MAJOR   I believe you should explain this to the General. *(Exits.)*
(General enters, only nods.)

SIMONE   *(Exhorting)* Hitler has never lost sight of the essential need to strike everybody's imagination; his own people's, his enemies', and the innumerable spectators'. One of his most effective instruments has been the SS. These men are unmoved by suffering and death, either for themselves or for all the rest of humanity. Their heroism originates from an extreme brutality that corresponds perfectly to the spirit of the regime and the designs of their leader. We cannot copy these methods of Hitler's. First, because we fight in a different spirit and with different motives. But when it is a question of striking the imagination, copies never succeed. Only the new is striking. We give a lot of thought to propaganda for the rear, yet it is just as important at the front. At the rear, propaganda is carried on by words. At the front, verbal propaganda must be replaced by the propaganda of action.

GENERAL   What do you propose?

SIMONE   A simple corps of women performing a few humane services in the very center of the battle—the climax of inhumanity—would be a signal defiance of the inhumanity which the enemy has chosen for himself and which he also compels us to practice. A small group of women exerting day after day a courage of this kind with a maternal solicitude would be a spectacle so new, so much more striking than Hitler's young SS fanatics. The contrast between these women and the SS would make a more telling argument than any propaganda slogan. I would illustrate with supreme clarity the two roads between which humanity today is forced to choose.

GENERAL   *Merci.* A very good idea. We will think about it. In the meantime we have some essential work for you to do.

(Typewriter and mounds of papers are wheeled out.)

Four copies of each as soon as possible. There's a war on.

(Blackout. The OLD MEN *pull the cord attached to their cherub and ashes, bones and plastic baby dolls shower the audience.)*

SIMONE, *with a mike on a high platform, addresses a crowd. As she speaks, lights begin to go off and on. Strange noises—gunshot. Bit by bit the* PEOPLE *leave and take up sides to fight the war.*

SIMONE We're in a conflict with no definable objective. When there is no objective, there is no common measure of proportion. Compromise is inconceivable. The only way the importance of such a battle can be measured is by the sacrifices it demands. From this it follows that the sacrifices already made are a perpetual argument for new sacrifices. There would never be any reason to stop killing and dying, except that there is fortunately a limit to human endurance.

(Silence.)

This paradox is so extreme as to defy analysis. And yet the most perfect example of it is known to every so-called educated man, but, by a sort of taboo, we read it without understanding. The Greeks and Trojans massacred one another for ten years on account of Helen. Not one of them except the dilettante warrior Paris cared two straws about her. All of them wished she'd never been born. Its importance was simply imagined as corresponding to the deaths incurred and the further massacres expected.

(Lights flicker and go out. PEOPLE *crawl in aisles and over audience. Lights— flashing; crying, running.)*

This implied an importance beyond all reckoning. Hector foresaw that his city would be destroyed, his father and brothers massacred, his wife degraded to a slavery worse than death. Achilles knew that he was condemning his father to the miseries and humiliations of a defenseless old age. All of them were aware that their long absence at the war would bring ruin on their homes; yet no one felt the cost too great, because they were all in pursuit of a literal non-entity whose only value was in the *price paid for it!*

(Silence—then the war begins again.)

For the clear-sighted, there is no more distressing symptom of this truth than the unreal character of most of the conflicts that are taking place today. They have even less reality than the war between Greeks and Trojans. At the heart of the Trojan War there was at least a woman, and what is more, a woman of perfect beauty. For our contemporaries the role of Helen is played by words with capital letters. If we grasp one of these words, all swollen with blood and tears, and squeeze it, we find it is empty.

(Silence—then just breathing. Then war begins again.)

Words with content and meaning are not murderous. When empty words are given capital letters, then men on the slightest pretext will begin shedding blood. In these conditions the only definition of success is to crush a rival group of men who have a hostile word on their banners. When a word is properly defined, it loses its capital letter and can no longer serve either as a banner or as a hostile slogan.

(Screams. Someone is shot while pleading not to be. Silence.)

It becomes simply a sign, helping us to grasp some concrete reality, concrete objective or method of activity. To clarify thought, to discredit the intrinsically meaningless words and to define the use of others by precise analysis—to do this, strange though it may appear, might be a way of saving human lives.

BARITONE   How like a woman to reduce war to semantics.

SOPRANO   How like a man to reduce war to mathematics.

(All the MEN *are lying on stage or in aisles. The* WOMEN *drag their bodies to a pile on stage as* SIMONE *speaks.)*

SIMONE   My dearest brothers, lying twenty years in your hospital beds, you are privileged men. The present state of the world is reality for you. You are experiencing more reality in your constant affliction than those who are dying in the war, at this moment killing and dying, wounded and being wounded. Because they are taken unaware. They don't know where they are. They don't know what is happening to them. People not in the middle of the war don't know what's real. But you men have been repeating in thought, for twenty years, that act which took and then released so many men. But you were seized permanently. And now the war is here again to kill millions of men. You are ready to think. Or if you are still not quite ready—as I feel you are not—you only have the thinnest shell to break before emerging from the darkness inside the egg into the light of truth. It is a very ancient image. The egg is this world we see. The bird in it is Love, the Love which is God Himself and which lives in the depths of every man, though at first as an invisible seed.

MAN   Will you help me kill myself.

SIMONE   Break your shell and you will no longer be inside. Space is opened and torn apart.

(Silence for a moment. In pain and twitching like the men, Simone's voice at first mirrors migraine pain, but then rises above the pain through the speech.)

The spirit throws the miserable body in some corner and is transported to a point outside space. Space has become an infinity. The moment stands still.

WOMEN *(singing, facing audience from stage or in position in aisles)*

THE MOMENT STANDS STILL!

THE MOMENT STANDS STILL!

THE MOMENT STANDS STILL!

THE MOMENT STANDS STILL!

MEGAN TERRY

547

THE SILENCE IS DENSE
SOUNDS
SOUNDS
SILENCE IS
THE WHOLE OF SPACE IS FILLED
NOT AN ABSENCE OF SOUND
BUT THE MOMENT IS FILLED
WITH THE SECRET WORD
ONCE YOU BREAK OUT OF YOUR SHELL
YOU WILL KNOW WHAT IS REAL
ABOUT WAR
YOU WILL KNOW THE SECRET WORD
YOU NEVER KNEW BEFORE
NOT THE ABSENCE OF SOUND
BUT LOVE, LOVE, LOVE, LOVE, LOVE.

SIMONE *(speaking)* It is not an absence of sound, but a positive object of sensation.
Singing
YOU, WHEN YOU'VE EMERGED
FROM THE SHELL,
WILL KNOW THE REALITY OF WAR.
THE MOST PRECIOUS REALITY TO KNOW
IS THAT, WAR IS UNREALITY ITSELF.
(Speaking) You are infinitely privileged. War has permanently lodged in your body.

WOMEN *(singing)*
WAR IS AFFLICTION,
FORTUNATE ARE YOU TO KNOW.

SIMONE War is affliction. It isn't easy to direct one's thought toward affliction voluntarily. To think affliction, it's necessary to bear it in one's flesh, driven very far in like a nail, and for a long time, so that thought may have time to grow strong enough to regard it.

WOMEN *(singing)*
WAR IS AFFLICTION,
    FORTUNATE ARE WE TO KNOW.
FORTUNATE ARE WE.
WAR IS AFFLICTION.
FORTUNATELY WE CANNOT SEE IT.
WAR IS AFFLICTION.

SIMONE You have the opportunity and the function of knowing the truth of the world's affliction. Contemplate its reality!
(MEN *rise and take their places facing the audience.* SIMONE *begins to move through them, climbing ever higher on the platforms.*)

MAN ONE Eat, Simone.

(She shakes her head and moves up ramp.)

MAN TWO Eat, Simone.

(She shakes head and climbs to highest platform. She's weak and must hold onto the bars to stand up.

An ACTRESS *mounts an auditorium platform and mechanically intones.)*

WOMAN DOCTOR *(at an inquest, British accent)* I tried to persuade Simone to take some food, and she said she would try. She did not eat, however, and gave as a reason the thought of her people in France starving.

*(*ENSEMBLE *whispers "Strange suicide" over and over.)*

She died on the twenty-fourth of August, and death was due to cardiac failure due to degeneration through starvation.

BARITONE *(singing, as a judge)* Simone, aged thirty-four, committed suicide by starvation while the balance of her mind was disturbed.

CHORUS *speaks.*

WOMEN Strange suicide. Strange suicide.

MEN Refused to eat.

WOMEN Strange suicide. Strange suicide.

MEN Refused to eat.

MEN AND WOMEN *(as lights begin to dim on* ENSEMBLE*)* She refused. She refused. She refused.

WOMAN ONE She wouldn't eat. She wouldn't eat the bombs of the Germans, she wouldn't eat the furnaces of the Nazis. She swallowed the pride of France, but it didn't stick to her ribs.

CHORUS Strange, strange, strange, strange, strange—Simone wouldn't eat. Simone wouldn't eat.

WOMAN TWO Her soul was full, she didn't have to eat. There's no such thing as a personality. There's no such thing as a mind when the body dies. The mind can die before the body dies.

WOMAN THREE She wouldn't eat. She wouldn't eat. She couldn't eat when others starved. She wouldn't eat while Hitler carved the meat of her countryside.

WOMAN FOUR While everyone else lived on spoiled cabbage leaves and boiled rainwater, Simone ate nothing.

(Blackout on ENSEMBLE*.)*

WOMAN FIVE How thin she must have been. What a tiny coffin they must have buried her in.

(Pin spot on SIMONE*, dimming slowly, slowly, slowly, slowly to black.)*

MEGAN TERRY

ALICE WALKER

(b. 1944) Born in Georgia, Alice Walker was educated at Spelman College and Sarah Lawrence College. She spent many years in Mississippi but currently lives in San Francisco. She has been a fellow of the Radcliffe Institute and has taught and read her poetry in many colleges. She has published two novels, a collection of short stories *In Love and Trouble: Stories of Black Women* (1973), and two volumes of poetry; an influential essay, "In Our Mother's Gardens" (*Ms.* magazine, 1972), explores the problems of women as artists.

BEYOND WHAT

We reach for destinies beyond
what we have come to know
and in the romantic hush
of promises
perceive each
the other's life
as known mystery.
Shared. But inviolate.
No melting. No squeezing
into One.
We swing our eyes around
as well as side to side
to see the world.

To choose, renounce,
this, or that—
call it a council between equals
call it love.

SUGGESTIONS FOR
FURTHER READING

The proliferation of works relevant to the study of images of women in literature has been so great that no one reader can begin to keep up. Fortunately, bibliographical aids have appeared for women's studies as an interdisciplinary field and for literary topics. Books that serve as guides to bibliographies are listed below; periodicals that regularly include bibliographies are listed separately. From these sources a student can find referrals to material on every aspect of images of women: special topics, author bibliographies, genre bibliographies, and references to specific countries and historical periods.

Bibliographies

Alternate Press Index, P. O. Box 7229, Baltimore, MD 21218.
Keeps list of current small presses; more complete and up to date than Williamson (below).

Bergman, Len V., and Marie B. Rosenberg, eds. *Women and Society: A Critical Review of the Literature with a Selected Bibliography.* Beverly Hills, Calif.: Sage Publications, 1975; 2d ed., 1978.
Although it does not aim at completeness, this impressive 3-volume bibliography is very thorough. It is listed in Williamson as items 44 and 45, but the annotation does not adequately indicate its usefulness for literary studies. Two categories are important: Women in Literature and the Arts and Women in Biographies, Autobiographies, and Memoirs.

Myers, Carol Fairbanks, ed. *Women in Literature: Criticism of the Seventies* (1976) and *More Women in Literature: Criticism of the Seventies* (1979). Metuchen, N.J.: Scarecrow Press.
List, by author, books and articles about women writers and about images of women by men and women; include general bibliographies of literary criticism.

Reardon, Joan, and Kristine A. Thorsen, eds., *Poetry by American Women, 1900–1975: A Bibliography.* Metuchen, N.J.: Scarecrow Press, 1979.
Both a primary bibliography of works by poets and a secondary one of works about poets. It aims at completeness and is important for researchers seeking to identify women's style and interests.

Williamson, Jane, ed. *New Feminist Scholarship: A Guide to Bibliographies.* Old Westbury, N.Y.: The Feminist Press Clearinghouse on Women's Studies, 1979.
Lists 391 bibliographies published before 1979 in books or periodicals in English. Fifty-two percent of the entries are annotated. Items 192–210 (pp. 62–67) are under the category Literature; bibliographies of individual women writers are *not* included. A detailed index of titles augments the 30 subject categories. A useful list of publishers with addresses includes small feminist presses.

Periodicals

Only periodicals that frequently or regularly include bibliographies, bibliographical essays, and/or book reviews are listed here. Often they have complete
issues on special topics; some of these published too late for inclusion in
Williamson are noted below. For more complete lists of issues of general
periodicals on specific women's studies topics, see items 42 and 43 in Williamson;
two bibliographies on special periodical issues list the tables of contents of
those issues. In the list below, date in parentheses is that of the first issue.

Chrysalis: A Magazine of Womens' Culture (1977). Nos. 8 and 9 have a
catalogue of feminist publishers; nos. 10 and 11 contain annotated lists of
feminist plays, published and unpublished.

Concerns (1974). A quarterly newsletter published by the Women's Caucus for
the Modern Languages of the Modern Language Association of America. It
lists works in progress on feminist criticism and literary theory.

Conditions (1977). This magazine emphasizes lesbian writing. Issue no. 5
was a special issue on black women.

Feminist Studies (1972). This quarterly, interdisciplinary in scope, has frequent
literary articles.

Frontiers: A Journal of Women Studies (1975). Frequent articles and reviews
on literary topics; the spring 1979 issue contains a review of feminist poetry
for the last 10 years and an article on using literary criticism in the classroom. Beginning with the spring 1980 issue, this journal publishes abstracts
of the proceedings of the National Women's Studies Association's annual
convention.

Resources for Feminist Research (1979). Appearing since 1972 as *Canadian
Newsletter of Research on Women,* this quarterly is a major source of
bibliography; it publishes abstracts of articles in most other feminist periodicals as well as complete thematic bibliographies, including one on literature
and the arts. It is international in scope.

Signs: Journal of Women in Culture and Society (1975). Frequently surveys
publication in special fields; a review article on literature is scheduled for
early 1981.

Sinister Wisdom (1976). This journal appears three times a year and focuses on
lesbian concerns.

Women and Literature: An Annual (1980). Beginning in 1974 with the
subtitle *A Quarterly Journal of Women Writers and the Literary Treatment
of Writers,* this journal focuses on literature.

Women's Studies: An Interdisciplinary Journal (1972). This long-established
journal is broad in scope and has had many distinguished articles and reviews
of literary importance. Vol. V (1977) and vol. VII (1980) had special issues
on women's poetry; vol. VI, no. 2 (1979) focuses on mothers and daughters
in literature.

Women's Studies International Quarterly (1978). This journal, published in
England, aims at the "rapid publication" of research findings and
review articles.

Women's Studies Newsletter (1972). This quarterly, published by the Feminist Press, is now the official organ of the National Women's Studies Association.

Literary Criticism

Included here are a list of books about literary images of and by women and a list of recent anthologies of articles of literary criticism and theory.

During the last 10 years, two major activities have linked feminist literary criticism and interdisciplinary studies on women. Feminist literary critics have explored the past, amply documenting male domination both of literature and of literary criticism. They have analyzed the effects of this domination for literary periods and genres as well as for individual authors, both male and female. They have resurrected forgotten works and reassessed underrated ones. They have even suggested avenues for contemporary women writers to follow in order to decrease these effects. At the same time, women interested in literature have followed research in other fields, which establishes the unsound basis for many literary images and myths. Works on literature make use of new research in many fields, from anthropology, biology, psychology, and sociology to linguistics.

Separate Works This list is a sampling of the works the editor has found most useful; it can be viewed as a basic reading list for understanding where feminist criticism is today and how it got here. Some of the works listed, especially those by Mary Ellman, Elizabeth Janeway, and Nancy Reeves, influenced the basic concepts upon which this anthology is based; others corroborate and expand ideas apparent in this and earlier editions.

Adams, Margaret. *Single Blessedness*. New York: Basic Books, 1976.

Allen, Mary. *The Necessary Blankness: Women in Major American Fiction of the Sixties*. Bloomington: University of Illinois Press, 1976.

Barker-Benfield, G. J. *The Horrors of the Half-Known Life: Male Attitudes Toward Women and Sexuality in Nineteenth-Century America*. New York: Harper & Row, 1975.

Baym, Nina. *Woman's Fiction: A Guide to Novels by and About Women in America, 1820–1870*. Ithaca, N.Y.: Cornell University Press, 1978.

Bernard, Jessie. *The Future of Motherhood*. New York: Penguin, 1975.

Broner, E. M., and Cathy N. Davidson, eds. *Mothers and Daughters*. New York: Frederick Ungar, 1979.

Chodorov, Nancy. *The Reproduction of Mothering: Psychoanalysis and the Sociology of Gender*. Berkeley: University of California Press, 1978.

Christ, Carol P. *Diving Deep and Surfacing: Women Writers on Spiritual Quest*. Boston: Beacon Press, 1980.

de Beauvoir, Simone. *The Second Sex*. New York: Knopf, 1953.

Deegan, Dorothy. *The Stereotype of the Single Woman in the American Novel*. 1905. Reprint. New York: Octagon Books, 1969.

de Rougemont, Denis. *Love in the Western World*. New York: Pantheon, 1956.

Dinnerstein, Dorothy. *The Mermaid and the Minotaur: Sexual Arrangements and Human Malaise*. New York: Harper & Row, 1976.

Ellman, Mary. *Thinking About Women.* New York: Harcourt Brace Jovanovich, 1968.

Ferrante, Joan M. *Woman as Image in Medieval Literature, From the Twelfth Century to Dante.* New York: Columbia University Press, 1975.

Fiedler, Leslie A. *Love and Death in the American Novel.* Rev. ed. New York: Stein and Day, 1966.

Foster, Jeanette. *Sex Variant Women in Literature.* 1956. Reprint. Baltimore: Diana Press, 1975.

Friedan, Betty. *The Feminine Mystique.* New York: Norton, 1963.

———. "Second Stage," *Redbook,* January 1980.

Fryer, Judith. *The Faces of Eve: Women in the Nineteenth Century American Novel.* New York: Oxford University Press, 1976..

Gilbert, Sandra M., and Susan Gubar. *The Madwoman in the Attic: The Woman Writer and the Nineteenth-Century Literary Imagination.* New Haven: Yale University Press, 1979.

Hardwick, Elizabeth, ed. *Rediscovered Fiction by American Women: A Personal Selection.* 18 vols. New York: Arno Press, 1977.

Hays, H. Q. *The Dangerous Sex: The Myth of Feminine Evil.* New York: Putnam, 1964.

Heilbrun, Carolyn. *Toward a Recognition of Androgyny.* New York: Knopf, 1973.

———. *Reinventing Womanhood.* New York: Norton, 1979.

Hiatt, Mary. *The Way Women Write.* New York: Teachers College, 1977.

Janeway, Elizabeth. *Between Myth and Morning: Women Awakening.* New York: Morrow, 1974.

Juhasz, Susan. *Naked and Fiery Forms: Modern American Poetry by Women, A New Tradition.* New York: Harper & Row, 1976.

Kolbenschlag, Madonna. *Kiss Sleeping Beauty Good-Bye.* New York: Doubleday, 1979.

Kolodny, Annette. *The Lay of the Land: Metaphor as Experience and History in American Life and Letters.* Chapel Hill: University of North Carolina Press, 1976.

Maccoby, Eleanor E., and Caroline N. Jacklin. *The Psychology of Sex Differences.* Stanford, Calif.: Stanford University Press, 1974.

Mainiero, Lina, ed. *American Women Writers: A Critical Reference Guide from Colonial Times to the Present.* New York: Ungar, 1979 (vol. 1), 1980 (vol. 2).

Miller, Jean Baker. *Toward a New Psychology of Women.* Boston: Beacon Press, 1976.

Millett, Kate. *Sexual Politics.* New York: Doubleday, 1970.

Moers, Ellen. *Literary Women: The Great Writers.* New York: Doubleday, 1976.

Notable American Women, 1607–1950. 3 vols. Cambridge, Mass.: Harvard University Press, 1974, 1980.

Olsen, Tillie. *Silences: Why Writers Don't Write.* New York: Delacorte, 1978.

Pomeroy, Sarah B. *Goddesses, Whores, Wives, and Slaves: Women in Classical Antiquity*. New York: Schocken, 1975.

Reeves, Nancy. *Womankind: Beyond the Stereotypes*. Chicago: Aldine-Atherton, 1971.

Rich, Adrienne. *Of Woman Born: Motherhood as Experience and Institution*. New York: Norton, 1976.

Rivers, Caryl, Rosalind Barnett, and Grace Baruch. *Beyond Sugar and Spice: How Women Grow, Learn, and Thrive*. New York: Putnam, 1979.

Rogers, Katharine M. *The Troublesome Helpmate: A History of Misogyny in Literature*. Seattle: University of Washington Press, 1966.

Rule, Jane. *Lesbian Images*. New York: Doubleday, 1975.

Sherfey, Mary Jane. *The Nature and Evolution of Female Sexuality*. New York: Random House, 1972.

Showalter, Elaine. *A Literature of Their Own: British Women Novelists from Brontë to Lessing*. Princeton, N.J.: Princeton University Press, 1977.

Spacks, Patricia. *The Female Imagination*. New York: Knopf, 1975.

Walsh, Mary Roth. *Doctors Wanted, No Women Need Apply: Sexual Barriers in the Medical Profession, 1835–1975*. New Haven: Yale University Press, 1977.

Watts, Emily Stipes. *The Poetry of American Women from 1632 to 1945*. Austin: University of Texas Press, 1977.

Anthologies of Literary Criticism and Theory

Listed here are collections of essays, most of them especially written for their volumes but some reprinted from periodicals. Although some of these are listed in the bibliographies above, they are listed here as a convenience to users of this anthology.

Brown, Cheryl and Karen Olson, eds. *Feminist Criticism: Essays on Theory, Poetry, and Prose*. Metuchen, N.J.: Scarecrow Press, 1978.
Most of the 26 essays have been previously published; some are papers presented at academic conventions. Four are theoretical essays on the relationship between feminism and literary criticism; 12 are theoretical/historical essays on prose writers, including Doris Lessing, Anaïs Nin, and Jean Rhys; 10 are practical criticism of women poets, including Emily Dickinson, H.D., Sylvia Plath, Anne Sexton, and Adrienne Rich.

Butturff, Douglas and Edmund L. Epstein, eds. *Women's Language and Style*. Studies in Contemporary Language, No. 1. New York: E. L. Epstein, 1978.
Contains revised versions of 13 papers delivered at a conference at the CUNY Graduate Center in April 1977. Articles vary from statistical analysis of ordinary speech and surveys of written language in a variety of contexts to analyses of specific authors and works, including Katherine Mansfield, Djuna Barnes, Virginia Woolf. Linguists included are Peggy Rosenthal, M. Waltman Frank, and Robin Lakoff.

Cornillon, Susan Koppelman, ed. *Images of Women in Literature: Feminist Perspectives*. Bowling Green, Ohio: Bowling Green University Popular Press, 1972.
Contains 23 critical essays organized thematically: Woman as Heroine—Joanna Russ's essay on conventional myths and their use in literature and 4 essays on the female stereotypes in individual authors or genres; The Invisible Woman—5 essays, including Tillie Olsen's "Silences"; most examine women characters as background or foil for male protagonists; Woman as Hero—5 analyses of women in fiction as self-determining persons; Feminist Aesthetics—6 essays on the limitations of traditional criticism and suggestions for feminist alternatives. Includes lists of works considered feminist, works by black women, and works portraying lesbian relationships.

Diamond, Arlyn, and Lee R. Edwards, eds. *The Authority of Experience: Essays in Feminist Criticism*. Amherst: University of Massachusetts Press, 1977.
Three theoretical essays of feminist criticism and 13 applications of it to works of English and American literature, most of which are considered classics. No attempt is made to define the term *feminist criticism*, but all the essays operate on the assumption that art is a part of a larger social context which it embodies and/or challenges. Works examined include *Troilus and Criseyde, The Taming of the Shrew, Moll Flanders, Jane Eyre, Mrs. Dalloway, The Golden Notebook, The Awakening,* and *A Farewell to Arms.*

Donovan, Josephine, ed. *Feminist Literary Criticism: Explorations in Theory.* Lexington: University of Kentucky Press, 1975.
Five essays and a conclusion by the editor that identify male-dominated literary criticism with patriarchal ideology. Together the essays move toward a definition of feminist criticism as explicit rejection of male norms and a conscious attempt to apply a feminist perspective, with Virginia Woolf as a model.

Edwards, Lee R., Mary Heath, and Lisa Baskin. *Woman: An Issue.* Boston: Little, Brown, 1972.
This work (which was first published as vol. 13 of *The Massachusetts Review*) includes essays, poems, fiction, documents, pictures. Three important essays of feminist criticism appear: one on stereotypes by Cynthia Wolff; one on feminist theater by Joan Goulianos; and one on the feminist ideas in George Eliot's *Middlemarch.*

Farrer, Claire R., ed. *Women and Folklore.* Austin: University of Texas Press, 1976.
This reprint of an issue of the *Journal of American Folklore* contains 8 essays that show parallels between literary and folk images of women.

Gilbert, Sandra M., and Susan Gubar, eds. *Shakespeare's Sisters: Feminist Essays on Women Poets.* Bloomington: University of Indiana Press, 1979.
Twenty-one scholarly and critical essays written especially for this volume consider British and American women poets in the context of the male-dominated environment of their personal life and/or of the literary world of their time. Includes 2 important theoretical essays about gender and creativity and about stages of development for women poets, a survey of Afro-American women poets, and essays on individual authors (Jane Lead, Anne Bradstreet, Anne Finch, Emily Brontë, Elizabeth Barrett Browning,

Christina Rossetti, Emily Dickinson, Marianne Moore, H.D., Edna St. Vincent Millay, May Swenson, Gwendolyn Brooks, Sylvia Plath, Anne Sexton, and others). Also has a 14-page bibliography of feminist criticism.

Hoch-Smith, Judith, and Anita Spring, eds. *Women in Ritual and Symbolic Roles*. New York: Plenum Press, 1978.
Although not literary criticism, the 13 essays in this volume show the origin of many literary images of women, such as those of nurturer, healer, prostitute, witch; dualistic images (both negative and positive) are shown to be not only held by men but internalized by women.

Jelinek, Estelle C., ed. *Women's Autobiography: Essays in Criticism*. Bloomington: Indiana University Press, 1980.
Critical essays about the theory and practice of women's autobiography and its difference from men's autobiography. Includes essays on Lillian Hellman, Gertrude Stein, Maya Angelou, Anaïs Nin, and Kate Millett among others.

Anthologies of Literature

Listed here are collections of works by and/or about women; some, like this anthology, are broad in scope, but recently collections sharply focused on a single image of women have appeared. Some of the collections are textbooks, many are regular "trade" books available at bookstores, and a few are small-press products. All listed here are now in print and can be obtained from the publishers.

Baker, Denys Val, ed. *Women Writing*. New York: St. Martin's Press, 1978.
Contains 12 short stories by the best-known British women writers. The stories are varied, with no thematic organization; they represent, according to the editor, women's ability to master "that most difficult of art forms, the short story."

Bankier, Joanna, et al., eds. *Twentieth Century Women's Poetry*. New York: Norton, 1976.
Poems from 31 languages in English translation. Organized thematically into 5 sections, the poems support the contention of Adrienne Rich in the Foreword that there is a worldwide female culture.

Bell, Roseann P., et al., eds. *Visions of Black Women in Literature*. New York: Anchor Press, 1979.
By juxtaposing stereotypes of black women with the varied reality presented by black women and men writers, this collection undercuts the stereotypes of black women. It includes works by critics as well as selections by such writers as Paule Marshall, Mari Evans, Margaret Walker, Sonia Sanchez, and Audre Lorde.

Blicksilver, Edith, ed. *The Ethnic American Woman: Problems, Protests, Lifestyle*. Dubuque, Iowa: Kendall Hunt, 1979.
A collection of writings by and about 23 American ethnic groups, organized thematically around the chronology of women's lives, education, work, religion, and search for identity and love. Works of several genres, including historical and critical essays. There are tables of contents by ethnic group and by genre.

Cahill, Susan, ed. *Women and Fiction 2*. New York: New American Library, 1978.
A sequel to *Women and Fiction 1* (1975), this book contains 26 stories by internationally known women writers from 12 countries, including Jean Rhys, Isak Dinesen, Selma Lägerlof, Ruth Prawer Jhabvala, and Elizabeth Bowen.

Cosman, Carol, Joan Keefe, and Kathleen Weaver, eds. *The Penguin Book of Women Poets*. New York: Penguin, 1979.
Aimed at showing the timelessness and universality of women's concerns and talent, this collection spans 3,500 years and 40 literary traditions. It is organized chronologically and includes many 20th century works.

Edwards, Lee R., and Arlyn Diamond, eds. *American Voices, American Women*. New York: Avon, 1973.
Contains works by 8 American women writers born in the 1800s who made important contributions to American literature, but had been forgotten: Harriet Spofford, Elizabeth Stuart Phelps, Mary Wilkins Freeman, Kate Chopin, Mary Austin, Dorothy Canfield Fisher, Susan Glaspell, and Jessie Fauset.

Fairbairns, Zoe, et al., eds. *Tales I Tell My Mother: A Collection of Feminist Short Stories*. West Nyack, N.Y., and London: Journeyman Press, 1978.
Fifteen short stories and 5 essays by 5 British women writers with a Socialist perspective appear in 3 categories: Feminist Fiction and Language, Feminist Fiction and Politics, and Feminist Fiction and Aesthetics.

Fannin, Alice, Rebecca Lukens, and Catherine Hoyser Mann, eds. *Woman: An Affirmation*. Lexington, Mass.: Heath, 1979.
Contains works from many genres (autobiography, short story, folk tale, poetry, drama) to illustrate such themes as reawakening, self-definition, tensions caused by societal expectations, autonomy, women's life experience. Two male authors and many women authors, mostly contemporary.

Fisher, Dexter, ed. *The Third Woman: Minority Women Writers of the United States*. Boston: Houghton Mifflin, 1980.
Contains essays on and writings by third-world women: American Indian, black, Chicana, and Asian American writers. Many of the selections are recent and most have not been previously anthologized.

France, Rachel, ed. *A Century of Plays by American Women*. New York: Richard Rosen Press, 1979.
Includes 23 short plays by Rachel Crothers, Susan Glaspell, Djuna Barnes, Gertrude Stein, Megan Terry, and others.

Grahn, Judy, ed. *True to Life Adventure Stories*. Oakland, Calif.: Diana Press, 1978.
Contains 18 stories and 2 poems by less-known contemporary American women writers; the focus is on working-class women's views on making a living, dealing with poverty, trouble with the law, and women's love for themselves, each other, their families, their friends.

Hamalian, Linda, and Leo Hamalian, eds. *Solo: Woman on Woman Alone*.
Contains 30 short stories by contemporary women writers with a focus on the dilemma faced by most women: "how to conquer that self-destructive longing for dependency without denying the deep satisfactions of emotional sharing

and security." Among the authors represented are Penelope Gilliatt, Edna O'Brien, Jean Stafford, Wakaka Yamauchko, Rebecca Morris, Jean Rhys.

Hedges, Elaine, and Ingrid Wendt, eds. *In Her Own Image: Women Working in the Arts*. Old Westbury, N.Y.: The Feminist Press, 1980.
Essays, poetry, fiction, autobiographical excerpts, letters, as well as visual and other arts are presented in 4 sections: Household Work and Women's Art; Obstacles and Challenges; Definitions and Discoveries; Women's Art and Social Change.

Holliday, Laurel, ed. *Heart Songs: The Intimate Diaries of Young Girls*. San Francisco: Bluestocking Books, 1978.
Includes material from 9 women writers from several countries, focusing on the authors' experiences from age 12 to 18; themes illustrated include self-definition, autonomy, loneliness, and love.

Howe, Florence, and Ellen Bass, eds. *No More Masks: An Anthology of Poems by Women*. New York: Doubleday, 1973.
Poems by 20th-century women poets focus on themes of the divided woman and the search for wholeness; positive views of usually negative images, such as that of the witch, appear. Includes both well-established and comparatively unknown writers.

Kleinberg, Seymour, ed. *The Other Persuasion*. New York: Random House, 1977.
Half of this collection of contemporary works about homosexual love focuses on lesbians. Stories and excerpts from novels by such writers as Gertrude Stein, Radclyffe Hall, Doris Betts, and Jane Rule are included.

Konek, Carol, and Dorothy Walters, eds. *I Hear My Sisters Saying: Poems by Twentieth Century Women*. New York: Crowell, 1976.
Organized both thematically and chronologically, this collection includes many major 20th-century poets; the poems selected focus on women's discovery of self and self-affirmation.

Kriegel, Harriet, ed., *Women in Drama*. New York: Mentor, 1975.
Plays focus on images of women, mostly by male playwrights from Euripides to Shaw. The only 2 plays by women are Megan Terry's *Approaching Simone* and Susan Glaspell's *Trifles*.

Lerner, Gerder, ed. *Black Women in White America: A Documentary History*. New York: Random House, 1972.
Organized in ten sections from slavery times to the present under categories such as "Slavery," "The Struggle for Education," and "Race Pride," this collection brings together many works, most of which have never before been published.

Lifshin, Lyn, ed. *Tangled Vines: A Collection of Mother and Daughter Poems*. Boston: Beacon Press, 1978.
Poems by Anne Sexton, Shirley Kaufman, Diane Wakoski, Erica Jong, Marge Piercy, Sandra Hochman, Adrienne Rich, and others express the complicated emotional relationships between mothers and daughters and daughters and mothers.

Macarthur, Mary, Jonis Agree, and Mary Mackey, eds. *These Women*. Washington, D.C.: Gaillimaufry Press, 1978.

Contains short works—poems, stories, experimental forms—by 21 women writers, some well known (Kay Boyle, Marge Piercy) and others published here for the first time.

Mahl, Mary R., and Helene Koon, eds. *The Female Spectator: English Women Writers Before 1800*. Old Westbury, N.Y.: The Feminist Press, 1977.
This volume includes selections from *The Female Spectator* (a journal) as well as from British women writers who lived and wrote before 1800, including Julian of Norwich, Margery Kemp, Queen Catharine Parr, Queen Elizabeth, Katherine Philips, Aphra Behn, and Eliza Haywood.

Mason, Mary Grimley, and Carol Hurd Green, eds. *Journeys: Autobiographical Writings by Women*. Boston: G. K. Hall, 1979.
Stories of personal liberation through involvement with a person or cause, from Anne Bradstreet to Susan Sontag.

Mazow, Julia Wolf, ed. *The Woman Who Lost Her Names: Selected Writings of American Jewish Women*. San Francisco: Harper & Row, 1979.
Short stories, memoirs, and excerpts from novels that counter the stereotypes of the Jewish mother and the Jewish "princess."

Moore, Honor, ed. *The New Women's Theater: Ten Plays by Contemporary American Women*. New York: Random House, 1977.
Recent plays that explore women's experience and focus on 4 recurring themes: mother-daughter relationships, rites of autonomy, conflicts with men, and the need for self-definition. Authors include Myrna Lamb, Eve Merriam, Joanna Russ, Ursula Molinaro, Corrinne Jacher, Tina Howe, Honor Moore, Ruth Wolff, Joanna Krauss.

Murray, Michele, ed. *A House of Good Proportion: Images of Women in Literature*. New York: Simon & Schuster, 1973.
Poems, stories, and excerpts from novels by women and men, organized thematically to show the stages of women's lives, the important events (love, marriage, motherhood, search for self), and above all the sense of self as human.

Newman, Felice, ed. *Cameos: 12 Small Press Women Poets*. New York: The Crossing Press, 1978.
Includes short autobiographical introductions and poems by 13 women poets who have not yet received serious critical consideration. Included are Kate Ellen Braverman, Jan Clausen, Miriam Dyak, Virginia Gilbert, Alexandra Grilikhes, Elizabeth Keeler, Rachel Maines, Dona Stein, Beverly Tanenhaus, Mary Winfrey.

Norris, Joan, ed. *Banquet*. Lincoln, Mass.: Penmaen Press, 1979.
Five stories about women by Joyce Carol Oates, Maxine Kumin, Rosellen Brown, Jean McGarry, and Lynne Sharon Schwartz are handprinted, and illustrated with wood engravings.

Parker, Jeri, ed. *Uneasy Survivors: Five Women Writers*. Santa Barbara, Calif.: Peregrine Smith, 1975.
Includes stories by women authors influential in moving American literature "in the direction that was to become its mainstream—realism." Authors are Sarah Orne Jewett, Mary Wilkins Freeman, Willa Cather, Ellen Glasgow, and Edith Wharton.

Rogers, Katharine M., ed. *Before Their Time: Six Women Writers of the Eighteenth Century*. New York: Ungar, 1979.
Includes writings of British authors Anne Finch, Mary Astell, Mary Wortley Montagu, Charlotte Smith, Fanny Burney, and Mary Wollstonecraft.

Sargent, Pamela, ed. *Women of Wonder; More Women of Wonder; The New Women of Wonder*. New York: Random House, 1974, 1976, 1978.
Three collections of science fiction by women on such themes as all-women societies, genderless childbearing, and Amazonian visions of the future world; authors include Sonia Dorman, Carol Emswiler, and Joanna Russ.

Spinner, Stephanie, ed. *Motherlove: Stories by Women about Motherhood*. New York: Dell, 1978.
Sixteen major contemporary American and British women writers break through old myths about motherhood and present varied, complex, and interesting characters who are mothers.

Stanley, Julia Penelope, and Susan Wolfe, eds. *The Coming Out Stories*. Watertown, Mass.: Persephone Press, 1980.
Contains 41 autobiographical accounts of their coming out process by lesbians of different ages, habits, lifestyles, and beliefs. Well-known authors like Alix Dobkin and Joanna Russ appear along with previously unpublished writers; introduction by Adrienne Rich.

Sullivan, Victoria, and James Hatch, eds. *Plays by and About Women*. New York: Random House, 1973.
Includes short plays by Alice Gerstenberg, Megan Terry, and Alice Childress, as well as longer ones by Lillian Hellman, Doris Lessing, Natalia Ginzburg, and Maureen Duffy.

Swansea, Charleen, and Barbara Campbell, eds. *Love Stories by New Women*. New York: Avon Books, 1979; Charlotte, N.C.: Red Clay Books, 1978.
Eighteen stories focus on heterosexual and homosexual love relationships. The stories were selected from over 300 sent in by women from all over the United States in response to a request from Red Clay Books, a publishing house in Charlotte, N.C., run by women.

Solomon, Barbara, ed. *The Experience of the American Woman*. New York: New American Library, 1978.
Contains 18 stories by women focused on the experience of American women in the 19th and 20th centuries. Themes touched on in many of the stories are female/male encounters, courtship, women with children, and women among other women.

Tanenhaus, Beverly, ed. *To Know Each Other and to Be Known: Women's Writing Workshops*. Brooklyn, N.Y.: Out & Out Books, 1978.
Contains comments by the editor and samples of the work of women who since 1975 have participated in a summer workshop of intensive work and mutual criticism by novices and established writers such as Adrienne Rich, Audre Lorde, Alice Walker, and Grace Paley.

Washington, Mary Helen, ed. *Black-Eyed Susans: Classic Stories by and About Black Women*. New York: Doubleday, 1975.
Contains 10 stories by 6 black women writers with a critical and historical introduction by the editor. Authors included are Gwendolyn Brooks, Toni

Morrison, Toni Cade Bambara, Alice Walker, Louise Meriwether, Jean Wheeler Smith.

Washington, Mary Helen, ed. *Midnight Birds: Stories of Contemporary Black Women Writers*. New York: Anchor Press, 1980.
Contains 12 stories by 9 authors, organized thematically, with critical comments for each category and a critical introduction by the editor. Authors represented are Paulette Childress White, Alexis DeVeaux, Alice Walker, Ntozake Shange, Frenchy Hodges, Gayl Jones, Toni Morrison, Toni Cade Bambara, and Sherley Anne Williams. All of the images combat the stereotype of the castrating black matriarch.

Wetherby, Teny, ed. *New Poets: Women*. Millbraie, Calif.: Les Femmes, 1976.
Contains poems by 41 poets, mainly young and all new voices, who speak from a variety of experiences, lifestyles, and educational backgrounds.

Wolff, Cynthia Griffin, ed. *Classic American Women Writers*. New York: Harper & Row, 1979.
Short stories by Sarah Orne Jewett, Kate Chopin, Edith Wharton, and Willa Cather chosen to show the quality that makes them classics.

ACKNOWLEDGMENTS

ALICE ADAMS "Roses, Rhododendron," copyright © 1975 by Alice Adams. Reprinted from *Beautiful Girl*, by Alice Adams, by permission of Alfred A. Knopf, Inc. Originally appeared in *The New Yorker*.

SHERWOOD ANDERSON "Death in the Woods," reprinted from *The American Mercury*, September 1926 by permission of Harold Ober Associates Incorporated. Copyright 1926 by The American Mercury, Inc. Renewed 1953 by Eleanor Copenhaver Anderson.

MARGARET ATWOOD "This story was told to me by another traveller" from *You Are Happy* by Margaret Atwood. Copyright © 1974 by Margaret Atwood. Reprinted by permission of Harper & Row, Publishers, Inc., and Phoebe Larmore.

W. H. AUDEN "Let me tell you a little story" ("Miss Gee"), copyright 1960 and renewed 1968 by W. H. Auden. Reprinted from *Collected Shorter Poems, 1927–1957*, by W. H. Auden, by permission of Random House, Inc., and Faber and Faber Ltd.

ANN BEATTIE "Tuesday Night," copyright © 1977 by Ann Beattie. Reprinted from *Secrets and Surprises*, by Ann Beattie, by permission of Random House, Inc. Originally appeared in *The New Yorker*.

SALLY BENSON "Little Woman," reprinted by permission; © 1938, 1966 The New Yorker Magazine, Inc.

DORIS BETTS "Still Life with Fruit," (p. 70) in *Beasts of the Southern Wild and Other Stories* by Doris Betts. Copyright © 1970 by Doris Betts. Reprinted by permission of Harper & Row, Publishers, Inc.

HAROLD BRODKEY "Verona: A Young Woman Speaks," © 1977 by Harold Brodkey. First published in *Esquire* Magazine, July 1977.

GWENDOLYN BROOKS "The Mother," (p. 85) from *The World of Gwendolyn Brooks* by Gwendolyn Brooks. Copyright 1945 by Gwendolyn Brooks Blakely. Reprinted by permission of Harper & Row, Publishers, Inc.

OLGA BROUMAS "Artemis," from "Twelve Aspects of God," reprinted by permission of Yale University Press from *Beginning With O*. Copyright © 1977 by Olga Broumas.

KATE CHOPIN "The Story of an Hour," first published in *Vogue*, IV (December 1894), 360.

LUCILLE CLIFTON "Miss Rosie," from *Good Times*, by Lucille Clifton. Copyright © 1969 by Lucille Clifton. Reprinted by permission of Random House, Inc.

FLORENCE COHEN "Mrs. Poe," copyright © Florence Cohen, 1979, reprinted from *The Monkey Puzzle Tree and Other Stories*, Story Press, (1979), Chicago, Il. 60091.

COLETTE "The Other Wife," from *The Other Woman* by Colette, translated by Margaret Crosland, copyright © 1972 by the Bobbs-Merrill Company. Reprinted by permission of the publisher. Published by Peter Owen, London but available in Canada through General Publishing, Toronto.

MARTHA COLLINS "Homecoming," reprinted by permission of the author. Copyright © 1972 by Martha Collins. This poem originally appeared in the *Southern Review*.

ADELAIDE CRAPSEY "Susanna and the Elders," reprinted from *Complete Poems & Collected Letters of Adelaide Crapsey* by permission of the State University of New York Press and of the editor, Susan Sutton Smith. © 1977 State University of New York; all rights reserved.

CATHERINE DAVIS "She," reprinted by permission of the author. © Catherine B. Davis.

HELENE DAVIS "Affair," copyright © 1973 by Helene Davis.

EMILY DICKINSON "A Prison gets to be a friend," reprinted by permission of the publishers and the Trustees of Amherst College from *The Poems of Emily Dickinson*, edited by Thomas H. Johnson, Cambridge, Mass.: The Belknap Press of Harvard University Press, Copyright © 1951, 1955, 1979 by the President and Fellows of Harvard College. Copyright 1929 by Martha Dickinson Bianchi. Copyright © 1957 by Mary L. Hampson. By permission of Little, Brown and Company.

MARY E. WILKINS FREEMAN "A New England Nun," from *A New England Nun and Other Stories, 1891*.

ERNEST J. GAINES "The Sky is Gray," excerpted from the book *Bloodline* by Ernest J. Gaines. Copyright © 1963, 1964, 1968 by Ernest J. Gaines. Reprinted by permission of *The Dial Press*.

ISABELLA GARDNER "At a Summer Hotel," reprinted from *The Looking Glass* by Isabella Gardner by permission of The University of Chicago Press. *The Looking Glass,* copyright © 1961, University of Chicago Press.

SUSAN GLASPELL "Trifles," reprinted by permission of Dodd, Mead & Company, Inc. from *Plays* by Susan Glaspell. Copyright 1920 by Dodd, Mead & Company, Inc. Copyright renewed 1948 by Susan Glaspell.

MYRA GOLDBERG "Gifts," copyright © 1979 by Myra Goldberg. First published in *A Shout in the Street.* Reprinted by permission of the author.

MAXIM GORKY "Twenty-Six Men and a Girl," from *Twenty-Six Men and a Girl and Other Stories,* translated by Emily Jakowleff and Dora B. Montefiore. Freeport, N.Y.: Books for Libraries, copyright 1902, reprinted 1969.

SUSAN GRIFFIN "I Like to Think of Harriet Tubman," from *Like the Iris of an Eye* by Susan Griffin. Copyright © 1976 by Susan Griffin. Reprinted by permission of Harper & Row, Publishers, Inc.

HEINRICH HEINE "The Loreley," from *Heinrich Heine: Paradox and Poet—The Poems* by Louis Untermeyer, copyright 1937 by Harcourt Brace Jovanovich, Inc.; copyright 1965 by Louis Untermeyer. Reprinted by permission of the publisher.

ERNEST HEMINGWAY "The Short Happy Life of Francis Macomber," from *The Short Stories of Ernest Hemingway* is reprinted by permission of Charles Scribner's Sons. Copyright 1936 Ernest Hemingway; copyright renewal © 1964 Mary Hemingway.

WILLIAM DEAN HOWELLS *"Editha,"* from *Harper's Monthly,* January 1905, 214–224.

RONA JAFFE "Rima the Bird Girl," copyright © 1960, 1962, 1963, 1964, 1965 by Rona Jaffe. Reprinted by permission of London & Buttenwieser.

JOHN KEATS "La Belle Dame sans Merci," first published in *The Indicator,* May 10, 1920.

DORIS LESSING "One Off the Short List," from *A Man and Two Women.* Copyright © 1958, 1962, 1963 by Doris Lessing. Reprinted by permission of Simon and Schuster, a Division of Gulf & Western Corporation, and Curtis Brown Ltd.

DENISE LEVERTOV "Relearning the Alphabet–Section U," from Denise Levertov, *Relearning the Alphabet.* Copyright © 1970 by Denise Levertov Goodman. "Stepping Westward" from Denise Levertov, *The Sorrow Dance.* Copyright © 1966 by Denise Levertov Goodman. Both selections reprinted by permission of New Directions.

NORMAN MAILER "The Time of Her Time," reprinted by permission of the author and the author's agents, Scott Meredith Literary Agency, Inc., 845 Third Avenue, New York, New York 10022.

ALBERTO MORAVIA "The Chase," from *Command, and I Will Obey You* by Alberto Moravia. Translated from the Italian by Angus Davidson. English translation © 1969 by Martin Secker and Warburg Limited. Reprinted by permission of Farrar, Straus and Giroux, Inc. and Martin Secker and Warburg Limited.

ALICE MUNRO "Royal Beatings," Copyight © 1977, 1978 by Alice Munro. Reprinted from *The Beggar Maid,* by Alice Munro, by permission of Alfred A. Knopf, Inc. In Canada from *Who Do You Think You Are* (Macmillan/Canada). All rights reserved. This story originally appeared in *The New Yorker.*

MICHELE MURRAY "Coming to Self," from *The Great Mother and Other Poems.* Reprinted by permission of James M. Murray, trustee under the will of Judith Michele Murray. © 1974 by Sheed & Ward, Inc.

JOYCE CAROL OATES "The Girl," reprinted from *The Goddess and Other Women* by Joyce Carol Oates by permission of the publisher, Vanguard Press, Inc. Copyright © 1974, 1973, 1972, 1971, 1970, 1968, 1967, 1966 by Joyce Carol Oates.

EDNA O'BRIEN "The Call," copyright © 1979 by The New Yorker Magazine, Inc. Reprinted by permission of The Lescher Agency.

TILLIE OLSEN "Tell Me a Riddle," excerpted from the book *Tell Me a Riddle* by Tillie Olsen. Copyright © 1960, 1961 by Tillie Olsen. Reprinted by permission of Delacorte Press/Seymour Lawrence.

EUGENE O'NEILL "Before Breakfast," from *The Plays of Eugene O'Neill,* by Eugene O'Neill. Copyright 1924 by Boni and Liveright, Inc. Reprinted by permission of Random House, Inc.

MARGE PIERCY "Unlearning to not speak" first appeared in KPFA Folio, October 1971, from

To Be of Use by Marge Piercy. Copyright © 1969, 1971, 1973 by Marge Piercy. Reprinted by permission of Doubleday & Company, Inc.

JAYNE ANNE PHILLIPS "Souvenir," excerpted from the book *Black Tickets* by Jayne Anne Phillips. Copyright © 1975, 1976, 1977, 1978, 1979 by Jayne Anne Phillips. Originally published in *Weekend* Magazine. Reprinted by permission of Delacorte Press/Seymour Lawrence.

SYLVIA PLATH "The Jailor," (p. 62) from the forthcoming book *Complete Poems* by Sylvia Plath. Copyright © 1963 by Ted Hughes. Reprinted by permission of Harper & Row, Publishers, Inc.

ADRIENNE RICH "Diving into the Wreck" is reprinted from *Diving into the Wreck, Poems 1971–1972*, by Adrienne Rich, with the permission of W. W. Norton Company, Inc. Copyright © 1973 by W. W. Norton & Company, Inc.

JANE RULE "Middle Children," from *Theme for Diverse Instruments.* Reprinted by permission of the author. Copyright © 1975 by Jane Rule.

MAY SARTON "Joy in Provence," from *A Private Mythology* by May Sarton, is reprinted by permission of W. W. Norton & Company, Inc. Copyright © 1966 by May Sarton.

ELIZABETH SCHULTZ "Bone." This story was first printed in *Cimarron Review* No. 17 (October, 1971). Copyright © 1971 by Board of Regents for Oklahoma State University. Reprinted by permission.

NTOZAKE SHANGE "With no immediate cause," from *Nappy Edges,* St. Martin's Press, Inc. Reprinted by permission.

IRWIN SHAW "The Girls in Their Summer Dresses," copyright 1939 and renewed 1967 by Irwin Shaw. Reprinted from *Selected Short Stories of Irwin Shaw,* by Irwin Shaw, by permission of the author and his agent, Irving Lazar.

TESS SLESINGER "On Being Told that Her Second Husband Has Taken His First Lover," copyright © 1971 by Quadrangle/The New York Times Book Co. Reprinted by permission of Times Books, a division of Quadrangle/The New York Times Book Co., Inc., from *On Being Told That Her Second Husband Has Taken His First Lover.*

ANN STANFORD "The Descent," from *The Descent* by Ann Stanford. Copyright © 1970 by Ann Stanford. Reprinted by permission of Viking Penguin Inc.

MAY SWENSON "Women," from *New & Selected Things Taking Place* by May Swenson, by permission of Little, Brown and Co. in association with the Atlantic Monthly Press. Copyright © 1968 by May Swenson.

MEGAN TERRY "Approaching Simone," © 1970 by Megan Terry. For stock and amateur rights apply to Samuel French, Inc. For all other rights to Elisabeth Marton, 96 Fifth Avenue, New York, N.Y. 10010.

JAMES TIPTREE, JR. "The Women Men Don't See," copyright 1973, 1978 by James Tiptree, Jr.

JEAN TOOMER "Fern" is reprinted from *Cane* by Jean Toomer, with permission of Liveright Publishing Corporation. Copyright 1923 by Boni & Liveright. Copyright renewed 1951 by Jean Toomer.

ALICE WALKER "Beyond What," from *Revolutionary Petunias and Other Poems,* copyright © 1973 by Alice Walker. Reprinted by permission of Harcourt Brace Jovanovich, Inc.

RUTH WHITMAN "Cutting the Jewish Bride's Hair," from *The Marriage Wig and Other Poems,* copyright © 1968 by Ruth Whitman. Reprinted by permission of Harcourt Brace Jovanovich, Inc.

KATE WILHELM "Baby, You Were Great," from *Orbit 2,* reprinted by permission of the author. Copyright © 1969 by Damon Knight.

WILLIAM CARLOS WILLIAMS "The Widow's Lament in Springtime," from *The Collected Earlier Poems* of William Carlos Williams. Copyright 1938 by New Directions Publishing Corporation. Reprinted by permission of New Directions.